THE
MACMILLAN
READER

THIRD EDITION

THE
MACMILLAN
READER

Judith Nadell
Rowan College of New Jersey

John Langan
Atlantic Community College

Linda McMeniman
Rowan College of New Jersey

Macmillan Publishing Company
New York

Editor: Eben W. Ludlow
Development Editor: Nancy Perry
Production Supervisor: Katherine Mara Evancie
Production Manager: Nicholas Sklitsis
Text and Cover Designer: Patricia Smythe
Cover Illustration: © Charles Mouzy 1991/AllStock

This book was set in Galliard by Digitype, Inc., and was printed and bound by R.R. Donnelley & Sons Company. The cover was printed by New England Book Components.

Macmillan Publishing Company
866 Third Avenue, New York, New York 10022

Macmillan Publishing Company is part of
the Maxwell Communication Group of Companies.

Maxwell Macmillan Canada, Inc.
1200 Eglinton Avenue East, Suite 200
Don Mills, Ontario M3C 3N1

Library of Congress Cataloging-in-Publication Data

Nadell, Judith.
    The Macmillan Reader / Judith Nadell, John Langan,
Linda McMeniman.
        p. cm.
    Includes index.
    ISBN 0-02-385882-6 (pbk.)
    1. College readers.   2. English language—Rhetoric.
    I. Langan, John.   II. McMeniman, Linda.   III. Title.
PE1417.N33   1993
808'.0427—dc20   92-5193
                        CIP

Copyright acknowledgments begin on page 755, which constitutes an extension of the copyright page.

Printing: 4 5 6 7   Year: 3 4 5 6 7 8 9

PREFACE

Our bookshelves, and perhaps yours, sag under the weight of all the readers published over the years. Semester after semester, we used to switch texts until we finally realized that we wanted more than was offered. For one thing, we found that many of the readers contained an all-too-predictable blend of selections, with the same pieces cropping up from one book to the next. We also discovered that the books provided students with little guidance on ways to read, think, and write about the selections. And so, when we first began working on *The Macmillan Reader*, we aimed for a different kind of text — one that would offer fresh examples of professional prose, one that would take a more active role in helping students become stronger readers, thinkers, and writers.

As in the first two editions, our primary goal in the third edition has been to enliven the mix of selections commonly appearing in readers. Although *The Macmillan Reader* includes widely read and classic essays, a number of our selections have not yet appeared in other anthologies. Among these are Susan

Jacoby's "Common Decency," Gordon Parks's "Flavio's Home," and Deborah Tannen's "Sex, Lies, and Conversation." We've been careful to choose selections that range widely in subject matter and approach, from the humorous to the informative, from personal meditation to polemic. We've also made sure that each selection captures students' interest and clearly illustrates a specific pattern of development or combination of patterns.

Our second concern has remained the quality of instruction in the book. As before, our objective has been to help students bridge the gap between the product and process approaches to reading and writing. Throughout, we describe possible sequences and structures but emphasize that such steps and formats are not meant to be viewed as rigid prescriptions; rather they are strategies for helping students discover what works best in a particular situation. Buoyed by compliments about the previous editions' teachability, we haven't tinkered with the book's underlying format. Such a structure, we've been told, does indeed help students read more critically, think more logically, and write more skillfully. The book's basic format thus remains as follows:

- **Chapter 1, "The Reading Process,"** provides guided practice in a three-part process for reading with close attention and a high level of interpretive skill. This step-by-step process sharpens students' understanding of the book's selections and promotes the rigorous thinking needed to write effective essays. An activity at the end of the chapter gives students a chance to use the three-step process. First, they read an essay by journalist Phyllis Theroux. Then we show them how to apply the suggested sequence to the selection. Last, they respond to sample questions and writing assignments, all similar to those accompanying each of the book's selections. The chapter thus does more than just tell students how to sharpen their reading abilities; it guides them through a clearly sequenced plan for developing critical reading skills.
- **Chapter 2, "The Writing Process,"** introduces students to essay writing. To make the composing process easier for students to grasp, we provide a separate section for each of the following stages: prewriting, identifying a thesis, supporting the thesis with evidence, organizing the evidence,

writing the first draft, and revising. From the start, we point out that the stages are fluid. Indeed, the case history of an evolving student paper illustrates just how recursive and individualized the writing process can be. Guided activities at the end of each section give students practice taking their essays through successive stages in the composing process.

To illustrate the link between reading and writing, the writing chapter presents the progressive stages of a student paper written in response to Phyllis Theroux's "The Worry Factor," the selection presented in the reading chapter. Commentary following the student paper highlights the essay's strengths and points out spots that could use additional work. In short, by the end of the second chapter, the entire reading-writing process has been illustrated, from reading a selection to writing about it.

- **Chapters 3–11** of *The Macmillan Reader* contain selections grouped according to **nine patterns of development**: description, narration, exemplification, division-classification, process analysis, comparison-contrast, cause-effect, definition, and argumentation-persuasion. The sequence progresses from the more personal and expressive patterns to the more public and analytic. However, because each chapter is self-contained, the patterns may be covered in any order. Instructors preferring a thematic approach will find the alternative thematic table of contents helpful.

The Macmillan Reader treats the patterns separately because such an approach helps students grasp the distinctive characteristics of each pattern. At the same time, the book continually shows the way writers usually combine patterns in their work. We also encourage students to view the patterns as strategies for generating and organizing ideas. Writers, we explain, rarely set out to compose an essay in a specific pattern. Rather, they choose a pattern or combination of patterns because it suits their purpose, audience, and subject.

Each of the nine pattern-of-development chapters follows this format:

1. **A detailed explanation of the pattern** begins the chapter. The explanation includes (1) a definition of the pattern, (2) a description of the way the pattern helps a writer accommodate his or her purpose and audience, and (3) step-by-step guidelines for using the pattern.

2. Next, we present **an annotated student essay** using the pattern. Written in response to one of the professional selections in the chapter, each essay illustrates the characteristic features of the pattern discussed in the chapter.

3. **Commentary** after each student essay points out the blend of patterns in the piece, identifies the paper's strengths, and locates areas needing improvement. "First draft" and "revised" versions of one section of the essay reveal how the student writer went about revising, thus illustrating the relationship between the final draft and the steps taken to produce it.

4. The **professional selections** in the pattern-of-development chapters are accompanied by these items:

   - *A biographical note and preview* give students a perspective on the author and create interest in the piece.
   - *Questions for Close Reading* help students dig into and interpret the selection. The first question asks them to identify the selection's thesis; the last provides work on vocabulary development.
   - *Questions About the Writer's Craft* deal with such matters as purpose, audience, tone, organization, sentence structure, diction, and figures of speech. The first question in the series (labeled "The Pattern") focuses on the distinctive features of the pattern used in the selection. And often there's another question (labeled "Other Patterns") that asks students to analyze the writer's use of additional patterns in the piece.
   - *Questions for Further Thought* inspire lively classroom discussion and help students refine their thoughts before beginning to write.
   - *Writing Assignments*, four in all, follow each selection. Packed with suggestions on how to proceed, the assignments use the selection as a springboard. The first two assignments ask students to write an essay using the same pattern as the one in the selection;

the last two encourage students to discover for themselves which combination of patterns would be most appropriate for an essay. Frequently, the assignments are preceded by the symbol ∞, indicating a cross-reference to at least one other professional selection in the book. By encouraging students to make connections among readings, such assignments broaden students' perspective and give them additional material to draw on when they write. These "paired assignments" will be especially welcome to instructors stressing recurring ideas and themes.

5. At the end of each pattern-of-development chapter are two sets of **Additional Writing Assignments**: "General Assignments" and "Assignments with a Specific Purpose and Audience." The first set provides open-ended topics that prompt students to discover the best way to use a specific pattern; the second set develops their sensitivity to rhetorical context by asking them to apply the pattern in a real-world situation.

The Macmillan Reader also includes a glossary that lists all the key terms presented in the text. In addition, a comprehensive *Instructor's Manual* contains the following: in-depth answers to the "Questions for Close Reading" and "Questions About the Writer's Craft"; suggested activities; pointers about using the book; a detailed syllabus; and a list of the book's "paired" writing assignments.

WHAT'S NEW IN THE THIRD EDITION

In preparing the third edition of *The Macmillan Reader*, we looked closely at scores of questionnaires completed by instructors using the book. Their comments helped us identify additional directions the book might take. Here, then, are the most important new features of this edition of *The Macmillan Reader*:

- *There are more selections than in previous editions. The Macmillan Reader* now includes 58 selections, 20 of which are new to this edition. Many of these new readings were suggested by instructors across the country; others were chosen after a lengthy search through magazines, nonfiction collections, newspapers, autobiographies, and the like. Whether written by a recognized pro like William Raspberry ("The Handicap of Definition") or a relative newcomer like Diane Cole ("Don't Just Stand There"), the new selections are bound to stimulate strong writing on a variety of topics—free speech, family life, date rape, poverty, friendship, prejudice, and the mass media, to name just a few. When selecting new readings, we took special care to include pieces dealing with international themes as well as with gender, ethnic, and class issues.

- *Chapter 1, "The Reading Process," has been revised to reflect more fully current theories about the way reading, thinking, and writing interact.* Specifically, a professional selection is annotated to show students how such written comments can help a reader analyze a piece of writing. The annotations also illustrate how close, critical reading of a selection can point the way to possible writing topics.

- *Chapter 2, "The Writing Process," provides more practical advice to help students progress through the various composing stages.* The chapter now explains how to (1) translate a journal entry into a writing topic, (2) move from prewriting to thesis, (3) turn an outline into a first draft, (4) approach revision as a multi-stage process, and (5) use a word processor in different phases of the writing sequence.

- *Guided writing activities have also been added to "The Writing Process" chapter.* These nuts-and-bolts activities show students how to move their papers through successive steps in the composing sequence.

- *A full first draft of a student essay is now presented in "The Writing Process" chapter.* When compared with its earlier and later versions, the first draft demonstrates how a paper is continuously reshaped as it moves from prewriting through revision.

- *The value of collaborative learning is underscored.* Activities in "The Writing Process" chapter and many assignments elsewhere provide opportunities for group brainstorming and peer review.

- *Annotations are included on all student essays.* The annotations make it possible to identify an essay's key features at a glance.

- *There's increased emphasis on the patterns of development as strategies for generating and organizing ideas.* Textual explanations, illustrative material, activities, and assignments reinforce students' understanding that the patterns enlarge options in every phase of the writing process.

- *More attention is given to the way writers blend patterns of development.* The commentary following each student essay highlights the way the paper mixes patterns. Also, the majority of selections have one Craft question (labeled "Other Patterns") that asks students to analyze the combination of patterns in the piece. Moreover, the selections in Chapter 12, "For Further Reading," illustrate with special clarity how patterns blend; this chapter also provides specific guidelines to help students analyze the fusing of patterns within the selections.

- *Chapter 11, "Argumentation-Persuasion," is more comprehensive than ever.* It now offers fuller coverage of logical fallacies and discusses objectivity, bias, and common ground. Also, to encourage students to consider opposing viewpoints, six of the chapter's eleven selections are grouped thematically into three pro-con pairs on controversial issues: date rape, capital punishment, and the legalization of drugs.

- *Chapter 12, "For Further Reading," has been expanded* to include six selections: two apiece by Martin Luther King, Jr., Joan Didion, and Virginia Woolf.

- *Chapter 13, "A Concise Guide to Documentation," and an argumentation essay with MLA citations* illustrate the use of outside sources in a paper.

- *An enlarged glossary, including an entry on gender-biased language,* provides a convenient guide to the book's key terms and concepts.

The third edition of *The Macmillan Reader* has one other new feature: Linda McMeniman joins the book's original team of authors. A free-lance writer, educational consultant, and co-author of *The Macmillan Writer*, Linda is a member of the faculty at Rowan College of New Jersey, where she teaches a variety of writing courses for the past fifteen years. Linda's wide-ranging experience and considerable talents have helped strengthen this new edition. Her presence is indeed welcome.

ACKNOWLEDGMENTS

At Macmillan our thanks go to Nancy Perry, Senior Development Editor, for her enthusiastic support, unfailing efficiency, and insightful editorial guidance. Executive Editor Eben Ludlow, who played a key role in helping to shape the book's two previous editions, kept a watchful eye on the development of this edition and offered perceptive suggestions throughout. We're also indebted to Wendy Polhemus-Annibel for her scrupulous copyediting and to Pat Smythe for giving the book such a clear, crisp design. And Katherine Evancie, Production Supervisor, deserves our thanks for her skillful handling of the never-ending complexities of the production process.

Over the years, many writing instructors have reviewed *The Macmillan Reader* and responded to detailed questionnaires about its selections and pedagogy. Their comments have guided our work every step of the way. To the following reviewers we are indeed grateful: James C. Addison, Jr., Western Carolina University; Ken Anania, Massasoit Community College; Chris Anson, University of Minnesota; Bruce Coad, Mountain View College; David Cole, Quinnipiac College; F. Marino D'Amato, Manchester Community College; Benjamin Fiester, Wilkes College; Sister Pauline Fox, Mt. Mercy College; Margaret Franson, Valparaiso University; Lois Friesen, Butler County Community College; Loris Galford, McNeese State University; Gary Griswold, California State University, Long Beach; Betty Boyd Heard, Averett College; Patricia Hummel, Albright College; Eleanor D. James, Montgomery County Community College; Shakuntala Jayswal, University of New Haven; Kellie Jones, University of Tennessee at Martin; Robert Lesman, Northern Virginia Community College; Barry Maid, University of Arkansas at Little Rock; Catherine Mau, Leeward Community College; Brian McRea, University of Florida; Elizabeth Metzger, University of South Florida; Kathy Mincey, Morehead State University; R. H. Moody, Madison Area Tech College; Steve Odden, University of Wisconsin at Stevens

Point; Michael G. O'Hara, Muscatine Community College; Marie Secor, Pennsylvania State University; Carl Singleton, Fort Hays State University; Carolyn Smith, University of Florida; Eric R. Smith, SUNY College at Cortland; James Gregory Smith, Lamar University; Cynthia Somin, Long Beach City College; Charles Staats, Broward Community College–North; Judith Stanford, Merrimack College; Jacqueline Stark, Los Angeles Valley College; Virginia Stein, Community College of Allegheny County; George Stoll, Broward Community College–North; Ralph Sturm, Edinboro University of Pennsylvania; Vivian Tortorici, Hudson Valley Community College; Larry K. Uffelman, Mansfield University; Anna Villegas, San Joaquin Delta College; David Wickham, Mountain View College; and Dorena Allen Wright, Loyola Marymount University.

For help in preparing the third edition of *The Macmillan Reader*, we owe thanks to the insightful comments of these reviewers: Donald W. Adams, Chipola Junior College; Rebecca L. Allen, Louisburg College; Bruce J. Ardinger, Columbus State Community College; Constantina Rhodes Bailly, Hillsborough Community College; A. M. Belmont, Southern Arkansas University; Wilson C. Boynton, Holyoke Community College; John S. Capps, Virginia Western Community College; Barbara Carr, Stephen F. Austin State University; Howard J. Coughlin, Jr., Eastern Connecticut University; Michael Cross, Tulsa Junior College; Betty Keating Dietz, Ohlone College; Benjamin B. Edwards, Tulsa Junior College; Mary Faraci, Florida Atlantic University; Raymond W. Foster, Scottsdale Community College; Loris D. Galford, McNeese State University; Anita Gandolfo, West Virginia University; Michael G. Gessner, Central Arizona College; Mary M. Hatcher, Burlington County College; Ginger A. Hurajt, Northern Essex Community College; Eleanor D. James, Montgomery County Community College; Wanda L. Jared, Tennessee Technological University; Sue V. Lape, Columbus State Community College; Stephen Larson, Wake Technical Community College; Paul Marx, University of New Haven; M. Cathleen Raymond, Florida Atlantic University; Marcia Bundy Seabury, University of Hartford; Margo Smith, Rogers State College; John W. Taylor, South Dakota State University; Robert Thompson, Macomb County Community College; Cyrilla M. Vessey, Northern Virginia Community College; Cheryl L. Ware, McNeese State

University; Samuel W. Whyte, Montgomery County Community College; and Wei-hsiung Kitty Wu, Bowie State University. We are also grateful to Patricia Graves, Georgia State University, and Teresa Miller, Rogers State College, for their suggestions on fine-tuning the argumentation and documentation chapters. Our work on this edition was influenced too by the many students who took advantage of the questionnaire at the back of the second edition to tell us which selections they preferred.

Special thanks go to Dorothy Carroll in our at-home office. Over the past ten years, we've come to depend increasingly on her friendship as well as on her research skills, word-processing abilities, and organizational talents. Finally, we're thankful to our students. Their reaction to various drafts of material sharpened our thinking and helped focus our work. And we are especially indebted to the ten students whose essays are included in the book. Their thoughtful, carefully revised papers dramatize the potential of student writing and the power of the composing process.

Judith Nadell
John Langan
Linda McMeniman

CONTENTS

3 DESCRIPTION   81

Gordon Parks FLAVIO'S HOME   96

Having battled poverty and prejudice himself, writer-
photographer Gordon Parks visits a Brazilian slum and
finds, among the wretched thousands forgotten by the
outside world, a dying yet smiling boy.

Russell Baker IN MY DAY   106

The author visits his elderly mother in the hospital and
muses on the entwining of lives within a family.

Annie Dillard IN THE JUNGLE   115

White egrets and piranhas, deer and tarantulas are all part
of the eternal beauty of the Ecuadorian jungle.

E. B. White ONCE MORE TO THE LAKE   122

Past, present, and future merge when White returns to a
beloved boyhood spot.

Jeanne Wakatsuki Houston and James D. Houston
MANZANAR   132

Jitterbug dancing and armed guards, cheerleading squads
and barbed wire—all were found at an internment camp for
Japanese-Americans, a place that was part all-American
fantasy, part prison.

Additional Writing Topics   141

6 DIVISION-CLASSIFICATION   271

11 ARGUMENTATION-PERSUASION   571

Jean Marzollo   MY PISTOL-PACKING KIDS   605

Parents are sometimes appalled by the violent fantasy games
their kids play, but such games, Marzollo contends, may be
good for children.

Migdia Chinea-Varela   MY LIFE AS A "TWOFER"   613

The author wonders whether she should acept a professional
opportunity offered to her because she is a "minority
writer" or whether she should insist on being treated simply
as a "writer."

Mark Twain   THE DAMNED HUMAN RACE   619

With scathing irony, this celebrated writer exposes the
violent nature of the lowest creature on earth.

Jonathan Swift   A MODEST PROPOSAL   628

One of the world's great satirists proposes an outrageous
solution to his country's economic problems.

Nat Hentoff   FREE SPEECH ON CAMPUS   640

Are America's campuses still havens for political debate, or
has the prevailing mood silenced all views except those that
are "politically correct"?

Pro-Con Pair: Date Rape

Camille Paglia   RAPE: A BIGGER DANGER THAN
                    FEMINISTS KNOW   650

The widespread prevalence of date rape, says the author, is
evidence that feminism has failed young women.

12 FOR FURTHER READING   695

If neither acquiescence nor violence is the proper response
to an unjust system, what is?

Tired of being considered a hypochondriac, a migraine
sufferer argues convincingly that her pain is real and not
imagined.

When Didion's faith in the power of clean hair, good
manners, and a high IQ is shaken, she's encouraged to
ponder the notion that inner peace has to do with
something more substantial and deeply rooted.

Watching the death-throes of a moth leads Woolf to
wonder at the mystery of life and at the force that opposes it.

A celebrated writer describes whom she had to kill in order
to succeed in her chosen work.

THEMATIC
CONTENTS

COMMUNICATION AND LANGUAGE

FAMILY AND CHILDREN

GOVERNMENT AND LAW

HEALTH AND MEDICINE

HUMAN GROUPS AND SOCIETY

HUMOR AND SATIRE

MEANING IN LIFE

MEMORIES AND AUTOBIOGRAPHY

MEN AND WOMEN

NATURE AND SCIENCE

THE
MACMILLAN
READER

1

THE READING PROCESS

More than two hundred years ago, essayist Joseph Addison commented, "Of all the diversions of life, there is none so proper to fill up its empty spaces as the reading of useful and entertaining authors." Addison might have added that reading also challenges our beliefs, deepens our awareness, and stimulates our imagination.

Why, then, don't more people delight in reading? After all, most children feel great pleasure and pride when they first learn to read. As children grow older, though, the initially magical world of books is more and more associated with homework, tests, and grades. Reading turns into an anxiety-producing chore. Also, as demands on a person's time accumulate throughout adolescence and adulthood, reading often gets pushed aside in favor of something that takes less effort. It's easier simply to switch on the television and passively view the ready-made images that flash across the screen. In contrast, it's almost impossible to remain passive while reading. Even a slick best-seller requires that the reader decode, visualize, and interpret what's on the page.

The more challenging the material, the more actively involved the reader must be.

The essays we selected for this book call for active reading. Representing a broad mix of styles and subjects, the essays range from the classic to the contemporary. They contain language that will move you, images that will enlarge your understanding of other people, ideas that will transform your views on complex issues.

The selections serve other purposes as well. For one thing, they'll help you develop a repertoire of reading skills — abilities that will benefit you throughout life. Second, as you become a better reader, your own writing style will become more insightful and polished. Increasingly, you'll be able to draw on the ideas presented in the selections and employ the techniques that professional writers use to express such ideas. As novelist Saul Bellow has observed, "A writer is a reader moved to emulation."

In the pages ahead, we outline a three-step approach for getting the most out of this book's selections. Our suggestions will enhance your understanding of the book's essays, as well as help you read other material with greater ease and assurance.

STEP 1: GET AN OVERVIEW OF THE SELECTION

Ideally, you should get settled in a quiet place that encourages concentration. If you can focus your attention while sprawled on a bed or curled up in a chair, that's fine. But if you find that being very comfortable is more conducive to daydreaming and dozing off than it is to studying, avoid getting too relaxed.

Once you're settled, it's time to read the selection. To ensure a good first reading, try the following hints:

- Get an overview of the essay and its author. Start by reading the biographical note and preview that precede the selection. By providing background information about the author, the biographical note helps you evaluate the writer's credibility as well as his or her slant on the subject. For example, if you know that George Gallup, Jr., is president of a well-known research firm that measures public opinion, you can better assess whether he is a credible source for the analysis he presents in his essay "The Faltering Family" (page 479). The preview introduces you to the essay's subject and often raises questions to consider as you read.

- Consider the selection's title. A good title often expresses the essay's main idea, giving you insight into the selection even before you read it. For example, the title of Marie Winn's essay, "TV Addiction" (page 558), suggests that the piece will focus on television's negative effects. A title may also hint at a selection's tone. Paul Roberts's "How to Say Nothing in 500 Words" (page 378) points to an essay that's light in spirit, whereas George Orwell's "Shooting an Elephant" (page 166) suggests a piece with a serious mood.

- Read the selection straight through purely for pleasure. Allow yourself to be drawn into the world the author has created. Just as you first see a painting from the doorway of a room and form an overall impression without perceiving the details, you can have a preliminary, subjective feeling about a reading selection. Moreover, because you bring your own experiences and viewpoints to the piece, your reading will be unique. As Emerson said, "Take the book, my friend, and read your eyes out; you will never find there what I find."

- After this initial reading of the selection, focus your first impressions by asking yourself whether you like the selection. In your own words, briefly describe the piece and your reaction to it.

STEP 2: DEEPEN YOUR SENSE OF THE SELECTION

At this point, you're ready to move further into the selection. A second reading will help you identify the specific features that triggered your initial reaction. Here are some suggestions on how to proceed:

- Mark off the selection's main idea, or thesis, often found near the beginning or end. If the thesis isn't stated explicity, write down your own version of the selection's main idea.

- Locate the main supporting evidence used to develop the thesis. You may even want to number in the margin each key supporting point.

- Take a minute to write "Yes" or "No" beside points with which you strongly agree or disagree. Your reaction to these points often explains your feelings about the aptness of the selection's ideas.

- Return to any unclear passages you encountered during the first reading. The feeling you now have for the piece as a whole will probably help you make sense of initially confusing spots. However, this second reading may also reveal that, in places, the writer's thinking isn't as clear as it could be.

- Use your dictionary to check the meanings of any unfamiliar words.

- Ask yourself if your initial impression of the selection has changed in any way as a result of this second reading. If your feelings *have* changed, try to determine why you reacted differently on this reading.

STEP 3: EVALUATE THE SELECTION

Now that you have a good grasp of the selection, you may want to read it a third time, especially if the piece is long or complex. This time, your goal is to make judgments about the essay's effectiveness. Keep in mind, though, that you shouldn't evaluate the selection until after you have a strong hold on it. A negative, even a positive reaction is valid only if it's based on an accurate reading.

At first, you may feel uncomfortable about evaluating the work of a professional writer. But remember: Written material set in type only *seems* perfect; all writing can be finetuned. By identifying what does and doesn't work in others' writing, you're taking an important first step toward developing your own power as a writer. You might find it helpful at this point to get together with other students to discuss the selection. Comparing viewpoints often opens up a piece, enabling you to gain a clearer perspective on the selection and the author's approach.

To evaluate the essay, ask yourself the following questions:

1. *Where does support for the selection's thesis seem logical and sufficient? Where does support seem weak?* Which of the author's supporting facts, arguments, and examples seem pertinent and convincing? Which don't?
2. *Is the selection unified? If not, why not?* Where does something in the selection not seem relevant? Where are there any unnecessary digressions or detours?
3. *How does the writer make the selection move smoothly from beginning to end?* How does the writer create an easy flow between ideas? Are any parts of the essay abrupt and jarring? Which ones?
4. *Which stylistic devices are used to good effect in the selection?* Which pattern of development or combination of patterns does the writer use to develop the piece? Why do you think those patterns were selected? How do paragraph development, sentence structure, and word choice contribute to the piece's overall effect? What tone does the writer adopt? Where does the writer use figures of speech effectively? (The next chapter and the glossary explain these terms.)
5. *How does the selection encourage further thought?* What new perspective on an issue does the writer provide? What ideas has the selection prompted you to explore in an essay of your own?

It takes some work to follow the three-step approach just described, but the selections in *The Macmillan Reader* are worth the effort. Bear in mind that none of the selections sprang full-blown from the pen of its author. Rather, each essay is the result of hours of work — hours of thinking, writing, rethinking, and revising. As a reader, you should show the same willingness to work with the selections, to read them carefully and thoughtfully. Henry David Thoreau, an avid reader and prolific writer, emphasized the importance of this kind of attentive reading when he advised that "books must be read as deliberately and unreservedly as they were written."

To illustrate the multi-stage reading process just described, we've annotated the professional essay that follows: "The Worry Factor" by Phyllis Theroux. Note that annotations are provided in the margin of the essay as well as at the end of the essay. As you read Theroux's essay, try applying the three-step sequence. You can measure your ability to dig into the selection by making your own annotations on Theroux's essay and then comparing them to ours. You can also see how well you evaluated the piece by answering the preceding five questions and then comparing your responses to ours on pages 11–12.

Phyllis Theroux

A frequent contributor to the *Washington Post, McCall's,* and *Reader's Digest*, Phyllis Theroux (1939–   ) won special recognition for a series of pieces she wrote for the *New York Times'* "Hers" column. Theroux's essays, often about the complex relationship between child and parent, combine wry humor with keen insight. Theroux has collected her work in three books: *California and Other States of Grace: A Memoir* (1980), *Peripheral Visions* (1982), and *Night Lights* (1987), from which the following selection is taken.

The Worry Factor

Worrying kills joy and saps energy. Yet the tendency to obsess about real and imagined problems is something most of us cling to—almost as though it were a precious, life-affirming right. As Phyllis Theroux points out in the following essay, rarely is the destructive nature of worrying more apparent than when the worrier is a much-loved child.

Marginal annotations

Relevant?

Drops this idea.

Means "ineffective"

Awkward transition (like "And" in ¶1)

Theroux also a worrier

1   It is commonly acknowledged that the organ that gives us the most pain in life is our brain—or somebody else's in close proximity. And, according to the "EST" training[1] I have so far managed to avoid, a great many heads are badly "wired" and can electrocute us with worries that the human being is not rubberized to withstand.

2   Why we like to worry is another question, as is the difference between feckless and fertile worrying, which can produce ulcers or symphonies. But once, while moving half-witted with worry around the kitchen, I stopped, mentally pushed everything that I couldn't do anything about at

[1]A self-help program, especially popular during the 1970s.

that moment out of my head, and then, re-grounded, looked around to see who was sharing that moment with me. My eyes fell upon my eleven-year-old daughter. Her eyes were full of tears.

Narrative to support thesis starts here.

She needed to talk. We went into the living room and sat down. She felt terrible, she said. It became clear, as she explained herself, that she had a lot of worries on her mind.

Smoother transitions

Paragraph gives examples of the daughter's worries.

For one thing, she was not very pretty. For another, she was not very smart. She was not rich, didn't have clothes as nice as everyone else's, her brother was oftentimes mean to her, and her best friend, to quote her exactly, "totally hates my guts."

Sounds like a child talking; essay has chatty tone.

There were other deprivations, deeper and therefore deserving of a curtain of privacy that I will now draw across the rods. But it was a fairly devastating list of liabilities, many of them not of her own making, and I let her spread them all out in their full horror without jumping in like some kind of Red Cross worker to tell her that her worries were only in her mind. Of course, that's where they were!

Figure of speech shows that Theroux realizes her efforts are probably futile. (See ¶s 7, 10, 11.)

Without necessarily agreeing with her on every point, I talked about people who had more than she did, and people who had less. Some rich girls are ugly. Some pretty girls are poor. I felt compelled to add that, inexplicably, some rich girls are also pretty, which is a mystery and nothing we can truly understand. But it seemed to me, I said, that one could look at the world in a couple of ways: as an imperfect place that makes us miserable or as a place that is imperfect and gives us something positive to do.

Advice doesn't help.

"You know," I explained, "like when you see a little boy crying in the playground. You can either say, 'How awful, he is so sad,' or go up and ask him what's the matter and try to fix it up."

3

4

5

6

7

Touching image

Like "Red Cross worker" in ¶5

My daughter of the heart-shaped face didn't   8
quite understand this friendly-carpenter approach to existence. In her mind, at that moment, she was the kid crying on the playground
and her chief worry was who (or Who) would *fix
her up*.

"I used to ask God to please, please give me   9
a nice day. But it never worked, so I stopped
asking."

Feels daughter's pain

"Maybe," I suggested (telling my heart to   10
stop twitching), "you could turn the question
around and ask God to please let you give the day
something nice."

Again, advice doesn't work.

"As" shows time passing.

Maybe yes, but maybe no. Maybe I hadn't   11
heard her the first time when she listed her problems, and as we walked upstairs to her bedroom
she repeated them for me again. As I watched her
climb into bed I observed, "You know, if all you
were were your worries, you wouldn't even exist.
You'd be a minus."

Hiding under the quilt that all too soon she   12
would be forced to throw off the next morning,
my daughter tried to understand this.

Part of implied thesis

"You can wreck the day you're still in," I   13
continued, "worrying about the day that hasn't
even arrived."

What many people think!

"But you *have* to worry!" she exclaimed, and   14
the look on her face poking over the quilt was
incredulous that someone my age did not know
that this was one of the first facts and obligations
of life.

Part of implied thesis

"You do?" I answered. "But doesn't worry-   15
ing just make you more tense by the time tomorrow finally comes?"

A small but hopeful expression flickered   16
across her features. Perhaps, she conceded, there
was something to this line of thinking. She
smiled, nodded her head and yawned.

"Why don't you take all your worries," I   17

said, bending down to kiss her goodnight, "and shove them right out the window where they belong."

Then, in a final bit of dialogue that reminded me that two heads in close proximity can produce something a great deal more significant than pain, she changed the subject.   18

Dialogue here and earlier conveys mother–daughter relationship.

"This doesn't have anything to do with what we're talking about," she said, "but why is it that when I cry my nose gets stuffy?"   19

"I don't know," I answered. "Maybe there are just too many tears to fit in your eyes."   20

"My tears are salty."   21

"That's because you have salt in your body."   22

"Mom," she asked, "can you taste my forehead and tell me if it's salty?"   23

I gave it a taste and said, "No, actually it isn't."   24

Surprise ending — the girl has been worrying about this, too.

"Oh, good!" she exclaimed, her face breaking into a wide, relieved smile. "That means I don't have cystic fibrosis."   25

Annotations at end of selection

Thesis (implied): We know that worrying is a waste of time, but that doesn't keep us from worrying.

First reading: Humorous and fun to read but also touching. Easy to relate to. Nicely captures what worry warts we can be.

Second and third readings:
1. Uses narration and examples of the daughter's worries to show the negative effect of worrying (thesis).
2. Not everything works (awkward transitions and reference to EST), but overall the essay succeeds.
3. Unexpected ending holds up even after additional readings. Shows how endless and groundless our worries can be. Creates sympathy for the young girl but also pokes gentle fun at her.
4. Possible essay topics: A humorous paper on how to avoid worrying about something (school, social life) or a serious paper on the positive aspects of worrying (it encourages action, we can anticipate and avoid problems, and so on).

The following answers to the questions on page 5 will help crystallize your reactions to Theroux's essay.

1. *Where does support for the selection's thesis seem logical and sufficient? Where does support seem weak?*

   The most explicit statement of Theroux's thesis lies in her comments to her daughter: "You can wreck the day you're still in worrying about the day that hasn't even arrived" (paragraph 13), and "But doesn't worrying just make you more tense by the time tomorrow finally comes?" (paragraph 15). But these two remarks are not the most complete statement of Theroux's main idea: They do not mention the essay's central paradox — that although Theroux tries to allay her daughter's anxieties, she herself is also a worrier. Stating the thesis in your own words may be best: Worrying is a painful waste of energy, yet knowing this does not necessarily help us resist it.

   Theroux dramatizes her thesis with a single, strong example — a conversation in which she attempts to allay her daughter's numerous worries. The author provides several examples of what a parent might say to reduce a child's anxiety. Although these reassurances don't entirely console her daughter, they do offer some relief.

2. *Is the selection unified? If not, why not?*

   The introductory paragraph contains a somewhat distracting reference to "EST" training, and the second paragraph raises an issue — "Why we like to worry" — that is then dropped. From the end of the second paragraph on, however, the essay focuses tightly on a single conversation between Theroux and her daughter. While some of Theroux's suggestions fail to help her daughter (for example, the suggestion in paragraph 10 that her daughter do something positive), these unsuccessful efforts belong in the essay because they illustrate how hard it is to make someone else's worries go away. The concluding bit of conversation turns out to be anything but a change of subject: It reveals that the daughter has been worrying about cystic fibrosis, as well as about her looks, her clothes, her popularity, and almost everything else.

3. *How does the writer make the selection move smoothly from beginning to end?*

   Theroux's first two paragraphs are not as smooth as one might like. The second sentence begins with the word "And" even though the point Theroux makes in the sentence is not a continuation of the first sentence. Similarly, in the second paragraph, the phrase "But once" that she uses to lead into the conversation doesn't contrast (as the "But" implies) with the idea expressed in the preceding paragraph. From this point on, however, Theroux writes sharply focused paragraphs and provides clear signals that guide the reader through the conversation with her daughter. For example, she signals her daughter's worries using "For one thing" and "For another" (paragraph 4). She also supplies cues indicating the passage of time: "*as* we walked," "*As* I watched" (paragraph 11), and "*Then*" (paragraph 18).

4. *Which stylistic devices are used to good effect in the selection?*

Theroux uses several patterns of development in her essay. The selection as a whole shows the *effect* of useless worry; paragraphs 2 and 7–25 are developed through *narration*; paragraphs 4, 6, and 7 use *examples*. *Short dramatic sentences* highlight her daughter's strong emotions ("She needed to talk") and punctuate Theroux's own ideas ("Some rich girls are ugly," "Some pretty girls are poor"). The first-person point of view contributes to Theroux's *informal tone* ("I talked about," "I explained," "I felt compelled"). Lively dialogue, including colloquial language ("totally hates my guts," "You'd be a minus"), as well as a fragment ("Maybe yes, but maybe no") add to the essay's conversational feeling. *Figurative language* in paragraphs 1 ("a great many heads are badly 'wired'"), 5 ("some kind of Red Cross worker"), and 8 ("friendly-carpenter approach to existence") further enliven the essay. Finally, although Theroux is concerned about the corrosive effect of worrying, she leavens her essay with dashes of humor. Certainly, her decision to include the final bit of conversation ("That means I don't have cystic fibrosis") shows how laughable our self-imposed anxieties can be.

5. *How does the selection encourage further thought?*

Theroux's essay treats a broad issue that affects everyone — the tendency to worry and thus cause ourselves pain. Her specific concern is the difficulties that parents face trying to divert children from needless fretting. Although Theroux offers no solutions, her personal account sharpens our awareness and prompts us to reexamine what is and is not worth worrying about.

If, for each essay you read in this book, you consider the preceding questions, you'll be able to respond thoughtfully to the *Questions for Close Reading, Questions About the Writer's Craft,* and *Questions for Further Thought* presented after each selection. Your responses will, in turn, prepare you for the writing assignments that follow the questions. Interesting and varied, the assignments invite you to examine issues raised by the selections and encourage you to experiment with various writing styles and organizational patterns.

Following are some sample questions and writing assignments based on the Theroux essay; all are similar to the sort that appear later in this book. Note that the final writing assignment paves the way for a student essay, the stages of which are illustrated in Chapter 2.

Questions for Close Reading

1. How do you know that Theroux is herself a worrier? How does she handle her anxieties?
2. Why do you suppose Theroux's daughter restates her problems as she goes up to bed? What kind of response does she most likely want from her mother?

Questions About the Writer's Craft

1. The last sentence in paragraph 4 tumbles along in a somewhat rambling fashion. Why might Theroux have decided to write the sentence this way?
2. Why do you think Theroux ends the essay with her daughter's comment, rather than with her own response to that comment?

Questions for Further Thought

1. What specifically can parents do to minimize the everyday anxieties that children feel?
2. Do you think that television contributes in any way to children's anxieties? Discuss the kinds of shows that you think might disturb or confuse children.

Writing Assignments

1. Theroux has difficulty allaying her daughter's worries. Write an essay explaining the steps that you think parents and/or schools should take to minimize children's anxieties about a specific present-day danger—perhaps AIDS, sexual abuse, or divorce.
2. Because the contemporary world is a difficult, even dangerous place, parents understandably worry about their children. Write an essay supporting the idea that today's world is, in many ways, hostile—particularly to children.

The benefits of active reading are many. Books in general and the selections in *The Macmillan Reader* in particular will bring you face to face with issues that concern all of us. If you study the selections and the questions that follow them, you'll be on the way to discovering ideas for your own papers. Chapter 2, "The Writing Process," offers practical suggestions for turning those ideas into well-organized, thoughtful essays.

2

THE WRITING PROCESS

Not many people retire at age thirty-eight. But Michel Montaigne, a sixteenth-century French attorney, did exactly that. Montaigne retired at a young age because he wanted to read, think, and write about all the subjects that interested him. After spending years getting his ideas down on paper, Montaigne finally published his short prose pieces. He called them *essais* — French for "trials" or "attempts."

In fact, all writing is an attempt to transform ideas into words, thus giving order and meaning to life. By using the term *essais*, Montaigne acknowledged that a written piece is never really finished. Of course, writers have to stop at some point, especially if they have deadlines to meet. But, as all experienced writers know, even after they dot the final *i*, cross the final *t*, and say "That's it," there's always something that could have been explored further or expressed a little better.

Because writing is a process, shaky starts and changes in direction aren't uncommon. Although there's no way to eliminate the work needed to write effectively, certain approaches can make the process more manageable and rewarding. This chapter describes a sequence of steps for writing essays. Familiarity with a specific sequence develops your awareness of strategies and choices, making you feel more confident when it comes time to write. You're less likely to look at a blank piece of paper and think, "Help! Now what do I do?" During the sequence, you do the following:

1. Prewrite
2. Identify the thesis
3. Support the thesis with evidence
4. Organize the evidence
5. Write the first draft
6. Revise the essay

We present the sequence as a series of steps, but we urge you not to view it as a rigid formula that must be followed step by unchanging step. Most people develop personalized approaches to the writing process. Some writers mull over a topic in their heads, then move quickly into a promising first draft; others outline their essays in detail before beginning to write. Between these two extremes are any number of effective approaches. The sequence here can be streamlined, juggled around, or otherwise altered to fit individual writing styles as well as the requirements of specific assignments.

STAGE 1: PREWRITE

Prewriting refers to strategies you can use to generate ideas *before* starting the first draft of a paper. Prewriting techniques are like the warm-ups you do before going out to jog — they loosen you up, get you moving, and help you to develop a sense of well-being and confidence. Since prewriting techniques encourage imaginative exploration, they also help you discover what interests you most about your subject. Having such a focus early in the writing process keeps you from plunging into your initial draft without first giving some thought to what you want to say.

Prewriting can help in other ways, too. When we write, we often sabotage our ability to generate material because we continually critique what we put down on paper. During prewriting, you deliberately ignore your internal critic. Your purpose is simply to get ideas down on paper *without evaluating* their effectiveness. Writing without immediately judging what you produce can be liberating. Once you feel less pressure, you'll probably find that you can generate a good deal of material. And that can make your confidence soar.

Keep a Journal

Of all the prewriting techniques, keeping a journal (daily or almost daily) is the one most likely to make writing a part of your life. Some journal entries focus on a single theme; others wander from topic to topic. Your starting point may be a dream, a snippet of overheard conversation, a video on MTV, a political cartoon, an issue raised in class or in your reading — anything that surprises, interests, angers, depresses, confuses, or amuses you. You may also use a journal to experiment with your writing style — say, to vary your sentence structure if you tend to use predictable patterns.

Here is a fairly focused excerpt from a student's journal:

Today I had to show Paul around school. He and Mom got here by 9. I didn't let on that this was the earliest I've gotten up all semester! He got out of the car looking kind of nervous. Maybe he thought his big brother would be different after a couple of months of college. I walked him around part of the campus and then he went with me to Am. Civ. and then to lunch. He met Greg and some other guys. Everyone seemed to like him. He's got a nice, quiet sense of humor. When I went to Bio., I told him that he could walk around on his own since he wasn't crazy about sitting in on a science class. But he said "I'd rather stick with you." Was he flattering me or was he just scared? Anyway it made me feel good. Later when he was leaving, he told me he's definitely going to apply. I guess that'd be kind of nice, having him here. Mom thinks it's great and she's pushing it. I don't know. I feel kind of like it would invade my privacy. I found this school and have made a life for myself here. Let him find his own school! But it could be great having my kid brother here. I guess this is a classic case of what my psych teacher calls ambivalence. Part of me wants him to come, and part of me doesn't! (November 10)

Although some instructors collect students' journals, you needn't be overly concerned with spelling, grammar, sentence structure, or organization. While journal writing is typically more structured than freewriting (see page 26), you don't have to strive for entries that read like mini-essays. The important thing is to let your journal writing prompt reflection and new insights, providing you with material to draw upon in your writing. It is, then, a good idea to reread each week's entries to identify recurring themes and concerns. Keep a list of these issues at the back of your journal, under a heading like "Possible Essay Subjects." Here, for instance, are a few topics suggested by the preceding journal entry: deciding which college to attend, leaving home, sibling rivalry. Each of these topics could be developed in a full-length essay.

Journal writing stimulates thinking in a loose, unstructured way. But when you have a specific piece to write, you should approach prewriting in a purposeful, focused manner. You need to:

- Understand the boundaries of the assignment.
- Determine your purpose, audience, and tone.
- Discover your essay's limited subject.
- Generate raw material about your limited subject.
- Organize the raw material.

We'll discuss each of these steps in turn. But first, here's a practical tip: If you don't use a word processor during the prewriting stage, try using a pencil and scrap paper. They're less intimidating than pen, typewriter, and "official" paper; they also reinforce the notion that prewriting is tentative and exploratory. If you *do* use a word processor, you'll probably find that the computer's speed helps you capture the often helter-skelter thoughts that emerge during prewriting. Indeed, after a while, writing in longhand (or even on a typewriter) may seem too slow or confining. A word of warning, though: When using a computer, save your work as you go; that is, store your writing on the disk. Otherwise, you risk losing a hefty chunk of text through a keystroke error, power failure, or system glitch. And always keep a backup disk of work in progress.

Understand the Boundaries of the Assignment

You shouldn't start writing a paper until you know what's expected. First, clarify the *kind of paper* the instructor has in mind. Assume the instructor asks you to discuss the key ideas in an assigned reading. What does the instructor want you to do? Should you include a brief summary of the selection? Should you compare the author's ideas with your own view of the subject? Should you determine if the author's view is supported by valid evidence?

If you're not sure about an assignment, ask your instructor —not the student behind you, who may be as confused as you— to make the requirements clear. Most instructors are more than willing to provide an explanation. They would rather take a few minutes of class time to explain the assignment than spend hours reading dozens of student essays that miss the mark.

Second, find out *how long* the paper is expected to be. Many instructors will indicate the approximate length of the papers they assign. If no length requirements are provided, discuss with the instructor what you plan to cover and indicate how long you think your paper will be. The instructor will either give you the go-ahead or help you refine the direction and scope of your work.

Determine Your Purpose, Audience, and Tone

Once you understand the requirements for a writing assignment, you're ready to begin thinking about the essay. What is its *purpose*? For what *audience* will it be written? What *tone* will you use? Later on, you may modify your decisions about these issues. That's fine. But you need to understand the way these considerations influence your work in the early phases of the writing process.

Purpose.   The papers you write in college are usually meant to *inform* or *explain*, to *convince* or *persuade*, and sometimes to *entertain*. In practice, writing often combines purposes. You might, for example, write an essay trying to *convince* people to support a new trash recycling program in your community. But before you win readers over, you most likely would have to *explain* something about current waste-disposal technology.

When purposes blend this way, the predominant one determines the essay's content, organization, emphasis, and choice of words. Assume you're writing about a political campaign. If your primary goal is to *entertain,* to take a gentle poke at two candidates, you might start with several accounts of one candidate's "foot-in-mouth" disease and then describe the attempts of the other candidate, a multi-millionaire, to portray himself as an average Joe. Your language, full of exaggeration, would reflect your objective. But if your primary purpose is to *persuade* readers that the candidates are incompetent and shouldn't be elected, you might adopt a serious, straightforward style. Rather than poke fun at one candidate's gaffes, you would use them to illustrate her insensitivity to important issues. Similarly, the other candidate's posturing would be presented, not as a foolish pretension, but as evidence of his lack of judgment.

Audience.   To write effectively, you need to identify who your readers are and to take their expectations and needs into account. An essay about the artificial preservatives in the food served by the campus cafeteria would take one form if submitted to your chemistry professor and a very different one if written for the college newspaper. The chemistry paper would probably be formal and technical, complete with chemical formulations and scientific data: "Distillation revealed sodium benzoate particles suspended in a gelatinous medium." But such technical material would be inappropriate in a newspaper column intended for general readers. In this case, you might provide specific examples of cafeteria foods loaded with additives — "Those deliciously smoky cold cuts are loaded with nitrates and nitrites, both known to cause cancer in laboratory animals" — and suggest ways to eat more healthfully — "Pass by the deli counter and fill up instead on vegetarian pizza and fruit juices."

Ask yourself the following questions when analyzing your audience:

- What are my readers' age, sex, and educational level?
- What are their political, religious, and other beliefs?

- What interests and needs motivate my audience?
- How much do my readers already know about my subject? Do they have any misconceptions?
- What biases do they have about me, my subject, my opinion?
- How do my readers expect me to relate to them?
- What values do I share with my readers that will help me communicate with them?

Tone.   Just as your voice may project a range of feelings, your writing can convey one or more *tones*, or emotional states: enthusiasm, anger, resignation, and so on. Tone is integral to meaning; it permeates writing and reflects your attitude toward yourself, your purpose, your subject, and your readers. How do you project tone? You pay close attention to sentence structure and word choice.

Sentence structure refers to the way sentences are shaped. Although the two paragraphs that follow deal with exactly the same subject, note how differences in sentence structure create sharply dissimilar tones:

> During the 1960s, many inner-city minorities considered the police an occupying force and an oppressive agent of control. As a result, violence against police grew in poorer neighborhoods, as did the number of residents killed by police.

> An occupying force. An agent of control. An oppressor. That's how many inner-city minorities in the '60s viewed the police. Violence against police soared. Police killings of residents mounted.

Informative in its approach, the first paragraph projects a neutral, almost dispassionate tone. The sentences are fairly long, and clear transitions ("During the 1960s"; "As a result") mark the progression of thought. But the second paragraph, with its dramatic, almost alarmist tone, seems intended to elicit a strong emotional response; its short sentences, fragments, and abrupt transitions reflect the turbulence of earlier times.

Word choice also plays a role in establishing the tone of an essay. Words have *denotations,* neutral dictionary meanings, as well as *connotations,* emotional associations that go beyond the literal meaning. The word *beach,* for instance, is defined in the dictionary as "a nearly level stretch of pebbles and sand beside a body of water." This definition, however, doesn't capture individual responses to the word. For some, *beach* suggests warmth and relaxation; for others, it calls up images of hospital waste and sewage.

Since tone and meaning are tightly bound, you must be sensitive to the emotional nuances of words. In a respectful essay about police officers, you wouldn't refer to *cops, narcs,* or *flatfoots*; such terms convey a contempt inconsistent with the tone intended. Your words must also convey tone clearly. Suppose you're writing a satirical piece criticizing a local beauty pageant. Dubbing the participants "livestock on view" leaves no question about your tone. But if you simply referred to the participants as "attractive young women," readers might be unsure of your attitude. Remember, readers can't read your mind, only your paper.

Discover Your Essay's Limited Subject

Once you have a firm grasp of the assignment's boundaries and have determined your purpose, audience, and tone, you're ready to focus on a limited aspect of the general assignment. Because too broad a subject can result in a diffuse, rambling essay, be sure to restrict your general subject before starting to write.

The following examples show the difference between general subjects that are too broad for an essay and limited subjects that are appropriate and workable. The examples, of course, represent only a few among many possibilities.

General Subject	Less General	Limited
Education	Computers in education	Computers in elementary school arithmetic classes
	High school education	High school electives

General Subject	Less General	Limited
Transportation	Low-cost travel	Hitchhiking
	Getting around a metropolitan area	The transit system in a nearby city
Work	Planning for a career	College internships
	Women in the work force	Women's success as managers

How do you move from a general to a narrow subject? Imagine that you're asked to prepare a straightforward, informative essay for your writing class. The assignment, prompted by Phyllis Theroux's essay "The Worry Factor" (page 7), is as follows:

> Because the contemporary world is a difficult, even dangerous place, parents understandably worry about their children. Write an essay supporting the idea that today's world is, in many ways, hostile—particularly to children.

You might feel unsure about how to proceed. But two techniques can help you limit such a general assignment. Keeping your purpose, audience, and tone in mind, you may *question* or *brainstorm* the general subject. These two techniques have a paradoxical effect. Although they encourage you to roam freely over a subject, they also help restrict the discussion by revealing which aspects of the subject interest you most.

1. Question the general subject.   One way to narrow a subject is to ask a series of *who, how, why, where, when,* and *what* questions. The following example shows how one student, Harriet Davids, used this technique to limit the Theroux assignment. A thirty-eight-year-old college student and mother of two teenagers, Harriet was understandably intrigued by the assignment. She started by asking a number of pointed questions about the general topic. As she proceeded, she was aware that the same questions could have led to different limited subjects—just as other questions would have.

General Subject: We live in a world that is difficult, even dangerous for children.

Question	Limited Subject
<u>Who</u> is to blame for the difficult conditions under which children grow up?	Parent's casual attitude toward childrearing
<u>How</u> have schools contributed to the problems children face?	Not enough counseling programs for kids in distress
<u>Why</u> do children feel frightened?	Divorce
<u>Where</u> do kids go to escape?	Television, which makes the world seem even more dangerous
<u>When</u> are children most vulnerable?	The special problems of adolescents
<u>What</u> dangers or fears should parents discuss with their children?	AIDS, drugs, alcohol, war, terrorism

2. Brainstorm the general subject.   Another way to focus on a limited subject is to list quickly everything about the general topic that pops into your mind. Working vertically down the page, jot down brief words, phrases, and abbreviations to capture your free-floating thoughts. Writing in complete sentences will slow you down. Don't try to organize or censor your ideas. Even the most fleeting, random, or seemingly outrageous thoughts can be productive.

Here's an example of the brainstorming that Harriet Davids decided to do in an effort to gather even more material on the Theroux assignment:

General Subject: We live in a world that is difficult, even dangerous for children.

- Too many divorces
- Parents squabbling over material goods in settlements
- Kids feel unimportant
- Families move a lot

- I moved in fourth grade--hated it
- Nobody graduates from high school in the same district they went to kindergarten in
- Drug abuse all over, in little kids' schools
- Pop music glorifies drugs
- Kids not innocent--know too much
- TV shows depict corrupt politicians, sex, pollution, violence
- Kids babysat by TV
- Kids raise selves
- Single-parent homes
- Day-care problems
- TV coverage of day-care abuse frightens kids
- Perfect families on TV make kids feel inadequate

As you can see, questioning and brainstorming suggest many possible limited subjects. To identify especially promising ones, reread your material. What arouses your interest, anger, or curiosity? What themes seem to dominate and cut to the heart of the matter? Star or circle ideas with potential.

After marking the material, write several phrases or sentences summarizing the most promising limited subjects. These, for example, are just a few that emerged from Harriet Davids's questioning and brainstorming the Theroux assignment:

- TV partly to blame for children having such a hard time
- Relocation stressful to children
- Schools also at fault
- The special problems that parents face raising children today

Harriet decided to write on the last of these limited subjects — the special problems that parents face raising children today. This topic, in turn, is the focus of our discussion in the pages ahead.

Generate Raw Material About Your Limited Subject

When a limited subject strikes you as having possibilities, your next step is to see if you have enough interesting and insightful things to say about the subject to write an effective essay.

To find out if you do, you may use any or all of the following techniques:

1. Freewrite on your limited subject.   *Freewriting* means jotting down in rough sentences or phrases everything that comes to mind. To capture this continuous stream of thought, write nonstop for ten minutes or more. Don't censor anything; put down whatever pops into your head. Don't reread, edit, or pay attention to organization, spelling, or grammar. If your mind goes blank, repeat words until another thought emerges.

Here is part of the freewriting that Harriet Davids generated about her limited subject, "The special problems that parents face raising children today":

> Parents today have tough problems to face. Lots of dangers. Drugs and alcohol for one thing. Also crimes of violence against kids. Parents also have to keep up with cost of living, everything costs more, kids want and expect more. Television? Another thing is Playboy, Penthouse. Sexy ads on TV, movies deal with sex. Kids grow up too fast, too fast. Drugs. Little kids can't handle knowing too much at an early age. Both parents at work much of the day. Finding good day care a real problem. Lots of latchkey kids. Another problem is getting kids to do homework, lots of other things to do. Especially like going to the mall! When I was young, we did homework after dinner, no excuses accepted by my parents.

2. Brainstorm your limited subject.   Let your mind wander freely, as you did when using brainstorming to narrow your subject. This time, though, list every idea, fact, and example that occurs to you about your limited subject. Use brief words and phrases, so you don't get bogged down writing full sentences. For now, don't worry whether ideas fit together or whether the points listed make sense.

To gather additional material on her limited subject for the Theroux assignment ("The special problems that parents face raising children today"), Harriet Davids brainstormed the following list:

- Trying to raise kids when both parents work
- Day care not always the answer--cases of abuse
- Day care very expensive
- Prices of everything outrageous

- Commercials make kids want <u>more</u> of everything
- Clothes so important
- Sexy clothes on little kids. Absurd!
- Sex everywhere--TV, movies, magazines
- Sexual abuse of kids
- Violence against kids when parents abuse drugs
- Cocaine, crack, AIDS
- Schools have to teach kids about these things
- Schools doing too much--not as good as they used to be
- Not enough homework assigned--kids unprepared
- Distractions from homework--malls, TV, phones, stereos, MTV

3. Use group brainstorming.   Brainstorming can also be conducted as a group activity. Thrashing out ideas with other people stretches the imagination, revealing possibilities you may not have considered on your own. Group brainstorming doesn't have to be conducted in a formal classroom situation. You can bounce ideas around with friends and family anywhere—over lunch, at the student center, and so on.

4. Map out the limited subject.   If you're the kind of person who doodles while thinking, you may want to try *mapping*, sometimes called *diagramming* or *clustering*. Like other prewriting techniques, mapping proceeds rapidly and encourages the free flow of ideas. Begin by expressing your limited subject in a crisp phrase and placing it in the center of a blank sheet of paper. As ideas come to you, put them along lines or in boxes or circles around the limited subject. Draw arrows and lines to show the relationships among ideas. Don't stop there, however. Focus on each idea; as subpoints and details come to you, connect them to their source idea, again using boxes, lines, circles, or arrows to clarify how everything relates.

5. Use the patterns of development.   Throughout this book, we show how writers use various patterns of development (narration, process analysis, definition, and so on), singly or in combination, to develop and organize their ideas. Because each pattern has its own distinctive logic, the patterns encourage you, when you prewrite, to think about a subject in different ways, causing insights to surface that might otherwise remain submerged.

The various patterns of development are discussed in detail in Chapters 3–11. At this point, though, you should find the following chart helpful. It not only summarizes the broad purpose of each pattern but also shows the way each pattern can generate different raw material for the limited subject of Harriet Davids's essay:

Limited Subject: The special problems that parents face raising children today.

Pattern	Purpose	Raw Material
Description	To detail what a person, place or object is like	Detail the sights and sounds of a glitzy mall that attracts kids
Narration	To relate an event	Recount what happened when neighbors tried to forbid their kids from going to a rock concert
Illustration	To provide specific instances or examples	Offer examples of family arguments. Can a friend known to use drugs visit? Can a child go to a party where alcohol will be served? Can parents outlaw MTV?
Division-classification	To divide something into parts or to group related things in categories	Identify components of a TV commercial that distorts kids' values
		Classify the kinds of commercials that make it difficult to teach kids values

Pattern	Purpose	Raw Material
Process analysis	To explain how something happens or how something is done	Explain step by step how family life can disintegrate when parents have to work all the time to make ends meet
Comparison-contrast	To point out similarities and/or dissimilarities	Contrast families today with those of a generation ago
Cause-effect	To analyze reasons and consequences	Explain why parents are not around to be with their kids: Industry's failure to provide day care and inflexibility about granting time off for parents with sick kids
		Explain the consequences of absentee parents: Kids feel unloved; they're undisciplined; they take on adult responsibility too early
Definition	To explain the meaning of a term or concept	What is meant by "tough love"
Argumentation-persuasion	To win people over to a point of view	Convince parents to work with schools to develop programs that make kids feel more safe and secure

(For more on ways to use the patterns of development in different phases of the writing process, see pages 40–41, 46–47, and 57.)

6. Conduct research.   Depending on your topic, you may find it helpful to visit the library and look for books and articles about your limited subject in the card catalog, the *Readers' Guide to Periodical Literature*, or a computerized reference system. At this point, you don't need to read closely the material you find. Just skim and perhaps take a few brief notes on ideas and points that could be useful.

If researching the Theroux assignment, for instance, Harriet Davids could look under headings and subheadings like the following:

> Day care
> Drug abuse
> Family
> Parent–child relationship
>   Child abuse
>   Children of divorced parents
>   Children of working mothers
> School and home

Organize the Raw Material

Once you generate the raw material for your limited subject, you're ready to shape your rough, preliminary ideas. Preparing a *scratch outline* or list is an effective strategy. On pages 50–51, we talk about the more formal outline you may need later on in the writing process. Here we show how a rough outline or scratch list can impose order on the tentative ideas generated during prewriting.

Reread your exploratory thoughts about the limited subject. Cross out anything not appropriate for your purpose, audience, and tone; add points that didn't originally occur to you. Star or circle compelling items that warrant further development. Then draw arrows between related items, your goal being to group such material under a common heading. Finally, determine what seems to be the best order for those headings. If you use a word processor, you may find the "split screen" or "window function" helpful. Such a feature (common in many software packages) makes it possible to display simultaneously your prewriting and scratch outline. With the two documents in view, you can — with just a few keystrokes — jump from document to document, refining either or both.

By giving you a sense of the way your free-form material might fit together, a scratch outline makes the writing process more manageable. You're less likely to feel overwhelmed once you actually start writing because you'll already have some idea about how to shape your material into a meaningful statement. Remember, though, the scratch outline can, and most likely will, be modified along the way.

The following scratch outline shows how Harriet Davids began to shape her brainstorming (pages 26–27) into a more organized format. (If you'd like to see Harriet's first draft, turn to pages 66–67.)

Limited Subject: The special problems that parents face raising children today.

1. Day care for two-career families
   • Expensive
   • Cases of abuse

2. Distractions from homework
   • Stereos, televisions in room at home
   • Places to go--malls, video arcades, fast-food restaurants, rock concerts

3. Sexually explicit materials
   • Magazines and books
   • Television shows
   • MTV
   • Movies
   • Rock posters

4. Life-threatening dangers
   • AIDS
   • Drugs
   • Drinking
   • Violence against children

The prewriting strategies just described provide a solid foundation for the next stages of your work. But invention and imaginative exploration don't end when prewriting is completed. As you'll see, remaining open to new ideas is crucial during all phases of the writing process.

Activities: Prewrite

1. Number the items in each set from 1 (*broadest subject*) to 5 (*most limited subject*):

Set A	Set B
3 Abortion	4 Business majors
2 Controversial social issue	3 Students' majors
5 Cutting state abortion funds	1 College students
4 Federal funding of abortions	2 Kinds of students on campus
1 Social issues	5 Why many students major in business

2. Which of the following topics are too broad for an essay of two to five typewritten pages: soap operas' appeal to college students; day care; trying to "kick" the junk-food habit; male and female relationships; international terrorism?

3. Use the techniques indicated in parentheses to limit each general topic listed below. Then, identify a specific purpose, audience, and tone for the one limited subject you consider most interesting. Next, with the help of the patterns of development, generate raw material about that limited subject. (You may find it helpful to work with others when developing this material.) Finally, shape your raw material into a scratch outline—crossing out, combining, and adding ideas as needed. (Save your scratch outline so you can work with it further after reading about the next stage in the writing process.)

   Friendship (*journal writing*)
   Malls (*mapping*)
   Leisure (*freewriting*)
   Television (*brainstorming*)
   Required courses (*group brainstorming*)
   Manners (*questioning*)

STAGE 2: IDENTIFY THE THESIS

[handwritten: Main idea / your view]

The process of prewriting—discovering a limited subject and generating ideas about it—prepares you for the next stage in writing an essay: identifying the paper's *thesis*, or controlling idea. Presenting your stand on a subject, the thesis should focus on an interesting and significant issue, one that engages your energies and merits your consideration. You may think of the thesis as the essay's hub—the central point around which all the other material revolves. Your thesis determines what does and does not belong in the essay. The thesis, especially when it occurs early in an essay, also helps focus the reader on the piece's central point.

Sometimes the thesis emerges early in the prewriting stage, particularly if a special angle on your limited topic sparks your interest or becomes readily apparent. Often, though, you'll need to do some work to determine your thesis. To identify a promising thesis, look through your prewriting and ask yourself questions like these: "What statement does all this prewriting support? What aspect of the limited subject is covered in most detail? What is the focus of the most provocative material?" If you use a computer when you write, you can play out hunches about your thesis by keying in several tentative thesis statements. If you decide that none is on the right track, key in other possibilities. Then you can juggle alternatives, comparing them side by side.

For a look at the process of finding the thesis within prewriting material, glance back at the scratch outline (page 31) that Harriet Davids prepared for the limited subject "The special problems that parents face raising children today." One thesis that captures the focus of this prewriting is "Being a parent today is much more difficult than it was a generation ago."

Writing an Effective Thesis

What makes a thesis effective? Generally expressed in one or two sentences, a thesis statement often has two parts. One part presents your paper's *limited subject*; the other presents your *point of view*, or *attitude*, about that subject. Here are some examples of the way you might move from general subject to limited subject to thesis statement. In each thesis statement, the limited subject is underlined once and the attitude twice.

General Subject	Limited Subject	Thesis
Education	Computers in elementary school arithmetic classes	Computer programs in arithmetic can individualize instruction more effectively than the average elementary school teacher can.
Transportation	A metropolitan transit system	Although the city's transit system still has problems, it has become safer and more efficient in the last two years.
Work	College internships	College internships provide valuable opportunities to students uncertain about what to do after graduation.
Our anti-child world	Special problems that parents face raising children today	Being a parent today is much more difficult than it was a generation ago.

(*Note:* The last of these thesis statements is the one that Harriet Davids devised for the essay she planned to write in response to the assignment on page 23. Harriet's prewriting appears on page 31. You can find her first draft on pages 66–67.)

Because identifying your thesis statement is an important step in writing a sharply focused essay, you need to avoid three common problems that lead to an ineffective thesis.

Don't make an announcement.   Some writers use the thesis statement merely to announce the limited subject of their paper and forget to indicate their attitude toward the subject. Such statements are announcements of intent, not thesis statements.

Compare the following three announcements with the thesis statements beside them.

Announcements	Thesis Statements
My essay will discuss whether a student pub should exist on campus.	This college should not allow a student pub on campus.
Handgun legislation is the subject of this paper.	Banning handguns is the first step toward controlling crime in America.
I want to discuss cable television.	Cable television has not delivered on its promise to provide an alternative to network programming.

Don't make a factual statement.   Your thesis and thus your essay should focus on an issue capable of being developed. If a fact is used as a thesis, you have no place to go; a fact generally doesn't invite much discussion.

Notice the difference between these factual statements and thesis statements:

Factual Statements	Thesis Statements
Many businesses pollute the environment.	Tax penalties should be levied against businesses that pollute the environment.
Many movies today are violent.	Movie violence provides a healthy outlet for aggression.

Factual Statements	Thesis Statements
America's population is growing older.	The aging of the American population will eventually create a crisis in the delivery of health-care services.

Don't make a broad statement.   Avoid stating your thesis in vague, general, or sweeping terms. Broad statements make it difficult for readers to grasp your essay's point. Moreover, if you start with a broad thesis, you're saddled with the impossible task of trying to develop a book-length idea with an essay that runs only several pages.

The following examples contrast statements that are too broad with thesis statements that are focused effectively:

Broad Statement	Thesis Statement
Nowadays, high school education is often meaningless.	High school diplomas have been devalued by grade inflation.
Newspapers cater to the taste of the American public.	The success of *USA Today* indicates that people want newspapers that are easy to read and entertaining.
The computer revolution is not all that we have been led to believe it is.	Home computers are still an impractical purchase for many people.

You have considerable freedom regarding the placement of the thesis in an essay. The thesis is often stated near the beginning, but it may be delayed, especially if you need to provide background information before it can be understood. Sometimes the thesis is reiterated—using fresh words—in the essay's conclusion or elsewhere. You may even leave the thesis unstated, relying on strong evidence to convey the essay's central idea.

One final point: Once you start writing your first draft, some feelings, thoughts, and examples may emerge that qualify, even contradict your initial thesis. Don't resist these new ideas; they frequently move you toward a clearer statement of your main point. Remember, though, your essay must have a thesis. Without this central concept, you have no reason for writing.

Activities: Identify the Thesis

1. For each of the following limited subjects, four possible thesis statements are given. Indicate whether each is an announcement (*A*), a factual statement (*FS*), too broad a statement (*TB*), or an acceptable thesis (*OK*). Then, for each acceptable thesis, identify a possible purpose, audience, and tone.

   Limited Subject: The ethics of treating severely handicapped infants

   Some babies born with severe handicaps have been allowed to die. *FS*

   There are many serious issues involved in the treatment of handicapped newborns. *TB*

   The government should pass legislation requiring medical treatment for handicapped newborns. *OK*

   This essay will analyze the controversy surrounding the treatment of severely handicapped babies who would die without medical care. *A*

   Limited Subject: Privacy and computerized records

   Computers raise some significant and crucial questions for all of us. *TB*

   Computerized records keep track of consumer spending habits, credit records, travel patterns, and other personal information. *FS*

   Computerized records have turned our private lives into public property. *OK*

   In this paper, the relationship between computerized records and the right to privacy will be discussed. *A*

2. Following are four pairs of general and limited subjects. Generate an appropriate thesis statement for each pair.

General Subject	Limited Subject
Psychology	The power struggles in a classroom
Health	Doctors' attitudes toward patients

General Subject	Limited Subject
American politics	Television's coverage of presidential campaigns
Work	Minimum-wage jobs for young people

3. Each of the following sets lists the key points in an essay. Based on the information provided, prepare a possible thesis for each essay.

Set A

- One evidence of this growing conservatism is the reemerging popularity of fraternities and sororities.
- Beauty contests, ROTC training, and corporate recruiting—once rejected by students on many campuses—are again popular.
- Most important, many students no longer choose risky careers that enable them to contribute to society but select, instead, safe fields with money-making potential.

Set B

- We do not know how engineering new forms of life might affect the earth's delicate ecological balance.
- Another danger of genetic research is its potential for unleashing new forms of disease.
- Even beneficial attempts to eliminate genetic defects could contribute to the dangerous idea that only perfect individuals are entitled to live.

4. Return to the scratch outline you prepared for activity 3 on page 32. After examining the outline, identify a thesis that conveys the central idea behind most of the raw material. Then, ask others to evaluate your thesis in light of the material in the outline. Finally, keeping the thesis—as well as your purpose, audience, and tone—in mind, refine the scratch outline by deleting inappropriate items, adding relevant ones, and indicating where more material is needed. (Save your refined scratch outline and thesis so you can work with them further after reading about the next stage in the writing process.)

STAGE 3: SUPPORT THE THESIS WITH EVIDENCE

After identifying a preliminary thesis, you should develop the evidence needed to support the central idea. Such supporting material grounds your essay, showing readers you have good reason for feeling as you do about your subject. Your evidence also adds interest and color to your writing. In college essays of 500 to 1,500 words, you usually need at least three major points of evidence to develop your thesis. These major points —each focusing on related but separate aspects of the thesis— eventually become the supporting paragraphs in the body of the essay.

By *evidence*, we mean a number of different kinds of support. *Examples* are just one option. To develop your thesis, you might also include *reasons, facts, details, statistics, anecdotes*, and *quotations from experts*. Imagine you're writing an essay with the thesis, "People normally unconcerned about the environment can be galvanized to constructive action if they feel personally affected by an environmental problem." You could support this thesis with any combination of the following types of evidence:

- *Examples* of successful recycling efforts in several neighborhoods.
- *Reasons* why people got involved in a neighborhood recycling effort.
- *Facts* about other residents' efforts to preserve the quality of their well water.
- *Details* about the steps that people can take to get involved in environmental issues.
- *Statistics* showing the number of Americans concerned about the environment.
- An *anecdote* about your involvement in environmental efforts.
- A *quotation* from a well-known scientist about the impact that citizens can have on environmental legislation.

Where do you find these examples, anecdotes, and details to support your thesis? A good deal of evidence is generated during the prewriting stage. The library is another rich source of supporting evidence. In addition, the patterns of development are a valuable source of evidence.

How the Patterns of Development Help Generate Evidence

On page 28, we discussed the way patterns of development help generate material about a limited subject. The same patterns also help develop support for a thesis. Consider the way they generate evidence for this thesis: "To those who haven't done it, babysitting looks easy. In practice, though, babysitting can be difficult, frightening, even dangerous."

Pattern	Evidence Generated
Description	Details about a child who, while being babysat, was badly hurt.
Narration	Story about the time a friend babysat an ill child whose condition was worsened by the babysitter's actions.
Illustration	Examples of potential babysitting problems: an infant rolls off a changing table; a toddler sticks objects in an electric outlet; a school-age child is bitten by a neighborhood dog.
Division-classification	A typical babysitting evening divided into stages: playing with the kids; putting them to bed; dealing with their nighttime fears once they're in bed.
	Classify kids' nighttime fears: of monsters under their beds; of bad dreams; of being abandoned by their parents.
Process analysis	Step-by-step account of what a babysitter should do if a child becomes ill or injured.
Comparison-contrast	Contrast between two

Pattern	Evidence Generated
	babysitters: one well-prepared, the other unprepared.
Cause-effect	Why children have temper tantrums; the effect of such tantrums on an unskilled babysitter.
Definition	What is meant by a *skilled* babysitter?
Argumentation-persuasion	A proposal for a babysitting training program.

(For more on ways to use the patterns of development in different phases of the writing process, see pages 28, 46–47, and 57.)

No matter how it is generated, all types of supporting evidence share the following characteristics.

The evidence is relevant and unified.   All the evidence in an essay must clearly support the thesis. It makes no difference how riveting material might be; if the evidence doesn't *relate directly* to the essay's central point, it should be eliminated. Irrelevant material can weaken your position by implying that no relevant support exists. It also distracts readers from your controlling idea, thus disrupting the paper's overall unity.

The following paragraph, taken from an essay illustrating recent changes in Americans' television-viewing habits, demonstrates the importance of unified evidence. The paragraph focuses on people's reasons for switching from network to cable television. As you'll see, the paragraph lacks unity because it contains points (underlined) unrelated to its main idea. Specifically, the comments about cable's foul language should be deleted. Although these observations bring up interesting points, they shift the paragraph's focus. If the writer wants to present a balanced view of the pros and cons of cable and network television, these points *should* be covered, but *in another paragraph*.

Nonunified Support

Many people consider cable TV an improvement over network television. For one thing, viewers usually prefer the movies on cable.

Unlike network films, cable movies are often only months old, they have not been edited by censors, and they are not interrupted by commercials. Growing numbers of people also feel that cable specials are superior to the ones the networks grind out. Cable viewers may enjoy such pop stars as Bruce Springsteen, Tina Turner, or Eddie Murphy in concert, whereas the networks continue to broadcast tired Bob Hope variety shows and boring awards ceremonies. There is, however, one problem with cable comedians. The foul language many of them use makes it hard to watch these cable specials with children. The networks, in contrast, generally present "clean" shows that parents and children can watch together. Then, too, cable TV offers viewers more flexibility since it schedules shows at various times over the month. People working night shifts or attending evening classes can see movies in the afternoon, and viewers missing the first twenty minutes of a show can always catch them later. It's not surprising that cable viewership is growing while network ratings have taken a plunge.

The evidence is specific.   When evidence is vague and general, readers lose interest in what you're saying, become skeptical of your ideas' validity, and feel puzzled about your meaning. In contrast, *specific, concrete evidence* provides sharp *word pictures* that engage your readers, persuade them that your thinking is sound, and clarify meaning.

Following are two versions of a paragraph from an essay about trends in the business community. Although both paragraphs focus on one such trend — flexible working hours — note how the first version's vague generalities leave meaning unclear. *What*, for example, is meant by "flex-time scheduling"? *Which* companies have tried it? *Where*, specifically, are these companies located? *How*, exactly, does flex-time increase productivity, lessen conflict, and reduce accidents? The second paragraph answers these questions with specifics and, as a result, is more informative and interesting.

Nonspecific Support

More and more companies have begun to realize that flex-time scheduling offers advantages. Several companies outside Boston have tried flex-time scheduling and are pleased with the way the system reduces the difficulties their employees face getting to work. Studies show that flex-time scheduling also increases productivity, reduces on-the-job conflict, and minimizes work-related accidents.

Specific Support

More and more companies have begun to realize that flex-time scheduling offers advantages over a rigid 9-to-5 routine. Along suburban Boston's Route 128, such companies as Compugraphics and Consolidated Paper now permit employees to come to work any time between 6 a.m. and 11 a.m. The corporations report that rush-hour jams and accidents have been dramatically reduced, so that employees arrive at work free from traffic-induced stress. Studies sponsored by the journal <u>Business Quarterly</u> show that this relaxed state of mind benefits corporations. Stress-free employees increase productivity by working harder and taking fewer days off. Also, the more relaxed the employee, the more quickly conflicts with co-workers and customers are resolved. Perhaps most importantly, employees arriving at work relatively free of tension are less susceptible to on-the-job accidents, such as injuries resulting from a fall or improper handling of dangerous equipment. Flex-time improves employee well-being, and as well-being rises, so do company profits.

The evidence is adequate.   Readers won't automatically accept your thesis; you need to provide *enough specific evidence* to support your viewpoint. On occasion, a single extended example will suffice. Generally, though, you'll need a variety of evidence: facts, examples, reasons, personal observations, expert opinion, and so on.

Following are two versions of a paragraph from a paper showing how difficult it is to get personal, attentive service nowadays at gas stations, supermarkets, and department stores. Both paragraphs focus on the problem at gas stations, but one paragraph is much more effective. As you'll see, the first paragraph starts with good specific support, yet fails to provide enough of it. The second paragraph offers additional examples, descriptive details, and dialogue—all of which make the writing stronger and more convincing.

Inadequate Support

Gas stations are a good example of this impersonal attitude. At many stations, attendants have even stopped pumping gas. Motorists pull up to a combination convenience store and gas island where an attendant is enclosed in a glass booth with a tray for taking money. The driver must get out of the car, pump the gas, and walk over to the booth to pay. That's a real inconvenience, especially when compared with the way service stations used to be run.

Adequate Support

Gas stations are a good example of this impersonal attitude. At many stations, attendants have even stopped pumping gas. Motorists pull up to a combination convenience store and gas island where an attendant is enclosed in a glass booth with a tray for taking money. The driver must get out of the car, pump the gas, and walk over to the booth to pay. Even at stations that still have "pump jockeys," employees seldom ask, "Check your oil?" or wash windshields, although they may grudgingly point out the location of the bucket and squeegee. And customers with a balky engine or a nonfunctioning heater are usually out of luck. Why? Many gas stations have eliminated on-duty mechanics. The skillful mechanic who could replace a belt or fix a tire in a few minutes has been replaced by a teenager in a jumpsuit who doesn't know a carburetor from a charge card and couldn't care less.

The evidence is accurate.   When you have a strong belief and want readers to see things your way, you may be tempted to overstate or downplay facts, disregard information, misquote, or make up details. Suppose you plan to write an essay making the point that dormitory security is lax. You begin supporting your thesis by narrating the time you were nearly mugged in your dorm hallway. Realizing the essay would be more persuasive if you also mentioned other episodes, you decide to invent some material. Perhaps you describe several supposed burglaries on your dorm floor or exaggerate the amount of time it took campus security to respond to an emergency call from a residence hall. Yes, you've supported your point—but at the expense of truth.

The evidence is representative.   Using representative evidence means that you rely on the typical, the usual, to show that your point is valid. Contrary to the maxim, exceptions don't prove the rule. Perhaps you plan to write an essay contending that the value of seat belts has been exaggerated. To support your position, you mention a friend who survived a head-on collision without wearing a seat belt. Such an example isn't representative because the facts and figures on accidents suggest your friend's survival was a fluke.

Borrowed evidence is documented.   If you include evidence from outside sources (books, articles, interviews), you need to acknowledge where that information comes from. If you don't, readers may consider your evidence nothing more than your point of view, or they may regard as dishonest your failure to cite your indebtedness to others for ideas that obviously aren't your own.

For help in documenting sources in brief, informal papers, turn to page 580. For information on acknowledging sources in longer, more formal papers, refer to Chapter 13.

Strong supporting evidence is at the heart of effective writing. Without it, essays lack energy and fail to convey the writer's perspective. Such lifeless writing is more apt to put readers to sleep than to engage their interest and convince them that the points being made are valid. Taking the time to accumulate solid supporting material is, then, a critical step in the writing process.

Activities: Support the Thesis with Evidence

1. Each of the following sets includes a thesis statement and four points of support. In each set, identify the one point that is off target.

Set A

Thesis: Colleges should put less emphasis on sports.

Encourages grade fixing
Creates a strong following among former graduates
Distracts from real goals of education
Causes extensive and expensive injuries

Set B

Thesis: America is becoming a homogenized country.

Regional accents vanishing
Chain stores blanket country
Americans proud of their ethnic identities
Metropolitan areas almost indistinguishable from one another

2. For each of the following thesis statements, develop three points of relevant support. Then use the patterns of development to generate evidence for each point of support.

Thesis: The trend toward disposable, throw-away products has gone too far.

Thesis: The local (or college) library fails to meet the needs of those it is supposed to serve.

Thesis: Television portrays men as incompetent creatures.

3. Look at the thesis and refined scratch outline you prepared in response to activity 4 on page 38. Where do you see gaps in the support for your thesis? By brainstorming with others, generate material to fill these gaps. If some of the new points generated suggest that you should modify your thesis, make the appropriate changes now. (Save this material so you can work with it further after reading about the next stage in the writing process.)

STAGE 4: ORGANIZE THE EVIDENCE

After you've generated supporting evidence, you're ready to *organize* that material. Even highly compelling evidence won't illustrate the validity of your thesis or achieve your purpose if readers have to plow through a maze of chaotic evidence. Some writers can move quickly from generating support to writing a clearly structured first draft. (They usually say they have sequenced their ideas in their heads). Most, however, need to spend some time sorting out their thoughts on paper before starting the first draft; otherwise, they tend to lose their way in a tangle of ideas.

Use the Patterns of Development

As you saw on pages 28, 40–41, 46–47, and 57, the patterns of development (definition, narration, process analysis, and others) can help you develop prewriting material and generate evidence for a thesis. In the organizing stage, the patterns provide frameworks for presenting evidence in an orderly, accessible way. Here's how.

Each pattern of development has its own internal logic that makes it appropriate for some writing purposes but not others. (You may find it helpful at this point to turn to pages 28–29 so you can review the broad purpose of each pattern.) Once you see which pattern (or combination of patterns) is implied by your purpose, you can block out your paper's general structure. Imagine that you're writing an essay *explaining why* some students drop out of college during the first semester. You might organize the essay around a three-part discussion of the key *causes* contributing to the difficulty that students have adjusting to college: (1) they miss friends and family, (2) they take inappropriate courses, and (3) they experience conflicts with roommates. As you can see, your choice of pattern of development significantly influences your essay's content and organization.

Some essays follow a single pattern, but most blend them, with a predominant pattern providing the piece's organizational framework. In our example essay, you might include a brief *description* of an overwhelmed first-year college student; you might *define* the psychological term "separation anxiety"; you might end the paper by briefly explaining a *process* for making students' adjustment to college easier. Still, the essay's overall organizational pattern would be *cause-effect* since the paper's primary purpose is to explain why students drop out of college.

Although writers often combine the patterns of development, your composition instructor may ask you to write an essay organized according to a single pattern. Such an assignment helps you understand a particular pattern's unique demands. Keep in mind, though, that most writing begins not with a specific pattern but with a specific *purpose*. The pattern or combination of patterns used to develop and organize an essay evolves out of that purpose.

Use Four Basic Organizational Approaches

No matter which pattern(s) of development you select, you need to know four general approaches for organizing supporting evidence. These are explained below.

Chronological approach.   When an essay is organized *chronologically*, supporting material is arranged in a clear time sequence, usually starting with what happened first and ending with what happened last. Occasionally, chronological sequences can be rearranged to create flashback or flashforward effects, two techniques discussed in Chapter 4 on narration. Essays using narration (for example, an experience with prejudice) or process analysis (for instance, how to deliver an effective speech) are most likely to be organized chronologically. The paper on public speaking might use a time sequence to present its points: how to prepare a few days before the presentation is due; what to do right before the speech; what to concentrate on during the speech itself. (For examples of chronologically arranged student essays, turn to pages 153 and 351.)

Spatial approach.   When you arrange supporting evidence spatially, you discuss details as they occur in space, or from certain locations. This strategy is particularly appropriate for description. Imagine that you plan to write an essay describing the joyous times you spent as a child playing by a towering old oak tree in the neighborhood park. Using spatial organization, you start by describing the rich animal life (the plump earthworms, swarming anthills, and numerous animal tracks) you observed while hunkered down *at the base* of the tree. Next, you re-create the contented feeling you experienced sitting on a branch *in the middle* of the tree. Finally, you end by describing the glorious view of the world you had *from the top* of the tree.

Although spatial arrangement is flexible (you could, for instance, start with a description from the top of the tree), you should always proceed systematically. And once you select a particular spatial order, you should usually maintain that sequence throughout the essay; otherwise, readers may get lost along the way. (A spatially arranged student essay appears on page 89.)

Emphatic approach.   In *emphatic* order, the most compelling evidence is saved for last. This arrangement is based on the psychological principle that people remember best what they experience last. Emphatic order has built-in momentum because it starts with the least important point and builds to the most significant. This method is especially effective in argumentation-persuasion essays, in papers developed through examples, and in pieces involving comparison-contrast, division-classification, or causal analysis.

Consider an essay analyzing the negative effect that workaholic parents can have on their children. The paper might start with a brief discussion of relatively minor effects like the family's eating mostly frozen or take-out foods. Paragraphs on more serious effects might follow: children get no parental help with homework; they try to resolve personal problems without parental advice. Finally, the essay might close with a detailed discussion of the most significant effect — children's lack of self-esteem because they feel unimportant in their parents' lives. (The student essays on pages 212, 414, and 533 all use an emphatic arrangement.)

Simple-to-complex approach.   A final way to organize an essay is to proceed from relatively *simple* concepts to more *complex* ones. By starting with easy-to-grasp, generally accepted evidence, you establish rapport with your readers and assure them that the essay is firmly grounded in shared experience. In contrast, if you open with difficult or highly technical material, you risk confusing and alienating your audience.

Assume you plan to write a paper arguing that your college has endangered students' health by not making an all-out effort to remove asbestos from dormitories and classroom buildings. It probably wouldn't be a good idea to begin with a medically sophisticated explanation of precisely how asbestos damages lung tissue. Instead, you might start with an observation that is likely to be familiar to your readers — one that is part of their everyday experience. You could, for example, open with a description of asbestos — as readers might see it — wrapped around air ducts and furnaces or used as electrical insulation and fireproofing material. Having provided a basic, easy-to-visualize description, you could then go on to explain the complicated process by which asbestos can cause chronic lung inflammation. (See page 471 for an example of a student essay using the simple-to-complex arrangement.)

Depending on your purpose, any one of these four organizational approaches might be appropriate. For example, assume that you want to develop this thesis: "Being a parent today is much more difficult than it was a generation ago." To emphasize that the various stages in children's lives present parents with different difficulties, you'd probably select a *chronological* sequence. To show that the challenges that parents face vary depending on whether children are at home, at school, or in the world at large, you'd probably choose a *spatial* sequence. To stress the range of problems that parents face (from less to more serious), you'd probably use an *emphatic* sequence. To illustrate today's confusing array of theories for raising children, you might take a *simple-to-complex* approach, moving from the basic to the most sophisticated theories.

Prepare an Outline

Do you, if asked to submit an outline, prepare it *after* you've written the essay? If you do, we hope to convince you that having an outline — a skeletal version of your paper — *before* you begin the first draft makes the writing process much more manageable. The outline helps you organize your thoughts beforehand, and it guides your writing as you work on the draft. Even though ideas continue to evolve during the draft, an outline clarifies how ideas fit together, which points are major, which should come first, and so on. An outline may also reveal places where evidence is weak, underscoring the need, perhaps, for more prewriting.

Like previous stages in the writing process, outlining is individualized. Some people prepare highly structured outlines; others make only a few informal jottings. Sometimes outlining will go quickly, with points falling easily into place; at other times you'll have to work hard to figure out how points are related. Also, the amount of detail in an outline will vary according to the paper's length and the instructor's requirements. A scratch outline (like the one on page 31) is often sufficient, but for longer papers, you'll probably need a more detailed and formal outline. In such cases, the suggestions in the accompanying checklist will help you develop a sound plan. Feel free to modify these guidelines to suit your needs.

Outlining Checklist

- Keeping your purpose, audience, and tone in mind, write your thesis at the top of the outlining page.
- Reevaluate your supporting material. Delete anything that doesn't develop the thesis or that isn't appropriate for your purpose, audience, and tone.
- Add any new points or material.
- Sort the evidence by grouping related items. Give each group a heading that represents a main topic in support of your thesis.
- Label these main topics with roman numerals (I, II, III,

and so on). Let the order of the numerals indicate the best sequence.

- Identify subtopics and group them under the appropriate main topics. Indent and label these subtopics with capital letters (A, B, C, and so on). Let the order of the letters indicate the best sequence.

- Identify supporting points (often reasons and examples) and group them under the appropriate subtopics. Indent and label these supporting points with arabic numbers (1, 2, 3, and so on). Let the numbers indicate the best sequence.

- Identify specific details (secondary examples, facts, statistics, expert opinions, quotations) and group them under the appropriate supporting points. Indent and label these specific details with lower-case letters (a, b, c, and so on). Let the letters indicate the best sequence.

- Examine your outline, looking for places where evidence is weak. Where appropriate, add new evidence.

- Doublecheck that all main topics, subtopics, supporting points, and specific details develop some aspect of the thesis. Also confirm that all items are arranged in the most logical order.

(Note: If you use a word processor, you might want to use a program that provides a ready-to-fill-in skeleton outline. Such a feature can be helpful.)

The following sample outline develops the thesis "Being a parent today is much more difficult than it was a generation ago." (You may remember that this is the thesis that Harriet Davids devised for the essay she planned to write in response to the assignment on page 23. Harriet's prewriting appears on pages 26–27 and 31.) The plan shown on page 52 is called a *topic outline* because it uses phrases, or topics, for each entry. For a lengthier or more complex paper, a *sentence outline* would be more appropriate.

Purpose: To inform

Audience: Instructor as well as class members, most of whom are 18–20 years old

Tone: Serious and straightforward

Thesis: Being a parent today is much more difficult than it was a generation ago.

I. Distractions from homework
   A. At home
      1. Stereos, radios, tapes
      2. Television
   B. Outside home
      1. Malls
      2. Video arcades
      3. Fast-food restaurants

II. Sexually explicit materials
   A. In print
      1. Sex magazines
         a. Hustler
         b. Penthouse
      2. Pornographic books
   B. In movies
      1. Seduction scenes
      2. Casual sex
   C. On television
      1. Soap operas
      2. R-rated comedians
      3. R-rated movies on cable

III. Increased dangers
   A. Drugs
   B. Alcohol
   C. Violent crimes against children

(If you'd like to see the first draft that resulted from Harriet's outline, turn to pages 66–67. Hints for moving from an outline to a first draft appear on page 54.)

Before starting to write your first draft, show your outline to several people (your instructor, friends, classmates). Their reactions will indicate whether your proposed organization is appropriate for your thesis, purpose, audience, and tone. Their comments can also highlight areas needing additional work. After making whatever changes are needed, you're in a good position to go ahead and write the first draft of your essay.

Activities: Organize the Evidence

1. The thesis statement below is followed by a scrambled list of supporting points. Prepare an outline for a potential essay, being sure to distinguish between major and secondary points.

   Thesis: Our schools, now in crisis, could be improved in several ways.

   Certification requirements for teachers
   Schedules
   Teachers
   Longer school year
   Merit pay for outstanding teachers
   Curriculum
   Better textbooks for classroom use
   Longer school days
   More challenging content in courses

2. Assume you plan to write an essay based on the following brief outline, which consists of a thesis and several points of support. Determine which pattern of development (pages 46–47) you would probably use for the essay's overall framework. Also identify which organizational approach (pages 47–49) you would most likely adopt to sequence the points of support listed. Then, use one or more patterns of development to generate material to support those points. Having done that, review the material generated, deleting, adding, combining, and arranging ideas in logical order. Finally, make an outline for the body of the essay.

   Thesis: Friends of the opposite sex fall into one of several categories: the pal, the confidante, or the pest.

   • Frequently, an opposite-sex friend is simple a "pal."
   • Sometimes, though, a pal turns, step by step, into a confidante.
   • If a confidante begins to have romantic thoughts, he or she may become a pest, thus disrupting the friendship.

3. Look again at the thesis and scratch outline you refined and elaborated in response to activity 3 on page 46. Reevaluate this material by deleting, adding, combining, and rearranging ideas as needed. Then, in preparation for writing an essay, outline your ideas. Next, keeping your purpose, audience, and tone in mind, consider whether an emphatic, chronological, spatial, or simple-to-complex approach

will be most appropriate. Finally, ask at least one person to evaluate your organizational plan. (Save your outline. After reading about the next stage in the writing process, you can use it to write the essay's first draft.)

STAGE 5: WRITE THE FIRST DRAFT

After prewriting, deciding on a thesis, and developing and organizing evidence, you're ready to write a *first draft*—a rough, provisional version of your essay. Because of your work in the preceding stages, the first draft may flow quite smoothly. But don't be discouraged if it doesn't. You may find that your thesis has to be reshaped, that a point no longer fits, that you need to return to a prewriting activity to generate additional material. Such stopping and starting is to be expected. Writing the first draft is a process of discovery, involving the continual clarification and refining of ideas.

How to Proceed

There's no single right way to prepare a first draft. Some writers rely on their scratch lists or outlines heavily; others glance at them only occasionally. Some people write the first draft in longhand; others use a typewriter or key the draft into a computer. However you choose to proceed, consider the following suggestions when moving from an outline or scratch list to a first draft:

- Make the outline's *main topics* (I, II, III) the *topic sentences* of the essay's supporting paragraphs. (Topic sentences are discussed later on pages 56–57.)
- Make the outline's *subtopics* (A, B, C) the *subpoints* in each paragraph.
- Make the outline's *supporting points* (1, 2, 3) the key *examples* and *reasons* in each paragraph.
- Make the outline's *specific details* (a, b, c) the *secondary examples, facts, statistics, expert opinion,* and *quotations* in each paragraph.

(To see how one student, Harriet Davids, moved from outline to first draft, turn to pages 66–67.)

Although outlines and lists are valuable for guiding your work, don't be so dependent on them that you shy away from new ideas that surface during your writing of the first draft. If promising new thoughts pop up, jot them down in the margin. Then, at the appropriate point, go back and evaluate them: Do they support your thesis? Are they appropriate for your essay's purpose, audience, and tone? If so, go ahead and include the material in your draft.

It's easy to get bogged down while preparing the first draft if you try to edit as you write. Remember: A draft isn't intended to be perfect. For the time being, adopt a relaxed, noncritical attitude. Working as quickly as you can, don't stop to check spelling, correct grammar, or refine sentence structure. Save these tasks for later. One good way to help remind you that the first draft is tentative is to use scrap paper and pencil. Writing on alternate lines also underscores your intention to revise later on, when the extra space will make it easier to add and delete material. If you prepare your first draft on a word processor, you may want to zap out several possible versions of a sentence or paragraph, saving them to evaluate later on.

What should you do if you get stuck while writing your first draft? Stay calm and try to write something—no matter how awkward or imprecise it may seem. Just jot a reminder to yourself in the margin ("Fix this," "Redo," or "Ugh!") to finetune the section later. Or leave a blank space to hold a spot for the right words when they finally break loose. It may also help to reread— out loud is best—what you've already written. Regaining a sense of the larger context is often enough to get you moving again. You might also try talking your way through a troublesome section. By speaking aloud, you tap your natural oral fluency and put it to work in your writing.

If a section of the essay strikes you as particularly difficult, don't spend time struggling with it. Move on to an easier section, write that, and then return to the challenging part. If you're still getting nowhere, take a break. Watch television, listen to music, talk with friends. While you're relaxing, your thoughts may loosen up and untangle the knotty section.

Because you read essays from beginning to end, you may assume that writers work the same way, starting with the introduction and going straight through to the conclusion. Often, however, this isn't the case. In fact, since an introduction depends so heavily on everything that follows, it's usually best to write the introduction *after* the essay's body.

When preparing your first draft, you may find it helpful to follow this sequence:

1. Write the essay's supporting paragraphs.
2. Connect ideas in the supporting paragraphs.
3. Write the introduction.
4. Write the conclusion.
5. Write a title.

Write the Supporting Paragraphs

Drawn from the main sections in your outline or scratch list, each *supporting paragraph* should develop an aspect of your essay's thesis. Besides containing relevant, concrete, and sufficient evidence (see pages 41–44), a strong supporting paragraph is (1) often focused by topic sentences and (2) organized around one or more patterns of development. We'll focus on both features in the pages ahead. As you read our discussion, though, keep in mind that you shouldn't expect your draft paragraphs to be perfect; you'll have a chance to revise them later on.

Use topic sentences. Frequently, each supporting paragraph in an essay is focused by a *topic sentence* that functions as a kind of mini-thesis for the paragraph. Generally one or two sentences in length, the topic sentence usually appears at or near the beginning of the paragraph. However, it may also appear at the end, in the middle, or — with varied wording — several times within the paragraph.

Regardless of its length or location, the topic sentence states the paragraph's main idea. The other sentences in the paragraph provide support for this central point in the form of examples, facts, expert opinion, and so on. Like a thesis statement, the topic sentence *signals the paragraph's subject* and frequently *indicates the writer's attitude* toward that subject. In the topic sentences that follow, the subject of the paragraph is underlined once and the attitude toward that subject is underlined twice:

Some students select a particular field of study <u>for the wrong reasons</u>.

The <u>ocean dumping of radioactive waste</u> <u>is a ticking time bomb</u>.

Several <u>contemporary rock groups</u> <u>show unexpected sensitivity to social issues</u>.

<u>Political candidates</u> <u>are sold like slickly packaged products</u>.

As you work on the first draft, you may find yourself writing paragraphs without paying too much attention to topic sentences. That's fine, as long as you evaluate the paragraphs later on. When revising, you can provide a topic sentence for a paragraph that needs a sharper focus, recast a topic sentence for a paragraph that ended up taking an unexpected turn, even eliminate a topic sentence altogether if a paragraph's content is sufficiently unified to imply its point.

Use the patterns of development.   As you saw on pages 46–47, an entire essay can be organized around one or more patterns of development (narration, process analysis, definition, and so forth.) These patterns can also provide the organizational framework for an essay's supporting paragraphs. Assume you're writing an article for your town newspaper with the thesis "Year-round residents of an ocean community must take an active role in safeguarding the seashore environment." Your supporting paragraphs could develop this thesis through a variety of patterns, with each paragraph's topic sentence suggesting a specific pattern or combination of patterns. For example, one paragraph might start with the topic sentence "In a nearby ocean community, signs of environmental danger are everywhere" and go on to *describe* a seaside town with polluted waters, blighted trees, and diseased marine life. The next paragraph might have the topic sentence "Fortunately, not all seaside towns are plagued by such environmental problems" and continue by *contrasting* the troubled community with another, more ecologically sound shore town. A later paragraph, focused by the topic sentence "Residents can get involved in a variety of pro-environment activities," might use *division-classification* to elaborate on activities at the neighborhood, town, and municipal levels.

Connect Ideas in the Supporting Paragraphs

While writing the supporting paragraphs, you can try to smooth out the progression of ideas within and between paragraphs. In a *coherent* essay, the relationship between points is clear; readers can easily follow the development of your thoughts. (Sometimes, working on coherence causes a first draft to get bogged down; if this happens, move on, and wait until the revision stage to focus on such matters.)

Using a clear chronological, spatial, emphatic, or simple-to-complex sequence is one way to make writing coherent (see pages 47–49). Another way is to include *signaling* or *connecting devices* that tell readers where you have been and where you are going.

Aim to include some signals—however awkward or temporary—in your first draft. If you find you *can't*, that's probably a warning that your ideas may not be arranged logically. A light touch should be your goal with such signals. Too many call attention to themselves, making the essay mechanical and plodding. In any case, here are some signaling devices to consider:

1. Transitions.   Words and phrases that ease readers from one idea to another are called *transitions*. Among such signals are the following:

Time	Space	Addition	Examples
first	above	moreover	for instance
next	below	also	for example
now	next to	furthermore	to illustrate
finally	behind	in addition	specifically

Contrast	Comparison	Summary
but	similarly	therefore
however	also	thus
otherwise	likewise	in short
on the one/other hand	too	in conclusion

Here's an earlier paragraph from this chapter. Note how the italicized transitions show readers how ideas fit together.

> *After* you've generated supporting evidence, you're ready to organize that material. Even highly compelling evidence won't illustrate the validity of your thesis or achieve your purpose if the readers have to plow through a maze of chaotic evidence. Some writers can move quickly from generating support to writing a clearly structured first draft. (They usually say they have sequenced their ideas in their heads.) Most, *however*, need to spend some time sorting out their thoughts on paper before starting the first draft; *otherwise*, they tend to lose their way in a tangle of ideas.

2. Bridging sentences.   Although bridging sentences may be used within a paragraph, they are more often used to move readers from one paragraph to the next. Look again at the first sentence in the preceding paragraph. Note that the sentence consists of two parts: The first part reminds readers that the previous discussion focused on techniques for generating evidence; the second part tells readers that the focus will now be the organization of such evidence.

3. Repeated words, synonyms, and pronouns.   The repetition of important words maintains continuity, reassures readers that they are on the right track, and highlights key ideas. Synonyms — words similar in meaning to key words or phrases — also provide coherence, while making it possible to avoid unimaginative and tedious repetitions. Finally, pronouns (*he, she, it, they, this, that*) enhance coherence by causing readers to think back to the original word (antecedent) the pronoun replaces. When using pronouns, however, be sure there is no ambiguity about antecedents.

Reprinted here is another paragraph from this chapter. Repeated words have been underlined once, synonyms underlined twice, and pronouns printed in italic type to illustrate how these techniques were used to integrate the paragraph's ideas.

> The process of prewriting — discovering a limited subject and generating ideas about *it* — prepares you for

the next stage in writing an essay: identifying the paper's thesis, or controlling idea. Presenting your stand on a subject, the thesis should focus on an interesting and significant issue, *one* that engages your energies and merits your consideration. You may think of the thesis as the essay's hub — the central point around which all the other material revolves. Your thesis determines what does and does not belong in the essay. The thesis, especially when *it* occurs early in an essay, also helps focus the reader on the piece's central point.

Write the Introduction

Many writers don't prepare an introduction until they have started to revise, but others feel more comfortable if their first draft includes in basic form all parts of the final essay. If that's how you feel, you'll probably write the introduction as you complete your first draft. No matter when you prepare it, keep in mind how crucial the introduction is to your essay's success. Specifically, the introduction serves three distinct functions: It arouses readers' interest, introduces your subject, and presents your thesis.

The length of your introduction will vary according to your paper's scope and purpose. Most essays you write, however, will be served best by a one- or two-paragraph beginning. To write an effective introduction, use any of the following methods, singly or in combination. The thesis statement in each sample introduction is underlined.

Broad Statement Narrowing to a Limited Subject

For generations, morality has been molded primarily by parents, religion, and schools. Children traditionally acquired their ideas about what is right and wrong, which goals are important in life, and how other people should be treated from these three sources. But now there is another powerful force influencing youngsters. Television is implanting in children negative values about sex, work, and family life.

Brief Anecdote

At a local high school recently, students in a psychology course were given a hint of what it is like to be the parents of a newborn.

Each "parent" had to carry a raw egg around at all times to symbol-ize the responsibilities of parenthood. The egg could not be left alone; it limited the "parents'" activities; it placed a full-time emo-tional burden on "Mom" and "Dad." This class exercise illustrates a common problem facing the majority of new mothers and fathers. Most people receive little preparation for the job of being parents.

Ideas That Are the Opposite of the One Developed

We hear a great deal about divorce's disastrous impact on children. We are deluged with advice on ways to make divorce as painless as possible for youngsters; we listen to heartbreaking stories about the confused, grieving children of divorced parents. Little attention has been paid, however, to a different kind of effect that divorce may have on children. Children from divorced families may become skilled manipulators, playing off one parent against the other, worsening an already painful situation.

Series of Short Questions

What happens if a child is caught vandalizing school property? What happens if a child goes for a joyride in a stolen car and accidentally hits a pedestrian? Should parents be liable for their children's mistakes? Should parents have to pay what might be hundreds of thousands of dollars in damages? Adults have begun to think seriously about such questions because the laws concerning the limits of parental responsibility are changing rapidly. With un-fortunate frequency, courts have begun to hold parents legally and financially accountable for their children's misdeeds.

Quotation

The comic W. C. Fields is reputed to have said, "Anyone who hates children and dogs can't be all bad." Most people do not share Fields's cynicism. Viewing childhood as a time of purity, they are alarmed at the way television exposes children to the seamy side of life, stripping youngsters of their innocence and giving them a glib sophistication that is a poor substitute for wisdom.

Refutation of a Common Belief

Adolescents care only about material things; their lives revolve around brand-name sneakers, designer jeans, the latest fad in stereo equipment. They resist education, don't read, barely know who is president, mainline rock 'n' roll, experiment with drugs, and exist on a steady diet of Ring-Dings, nachos, and beer. This is what many adults, including parents, seem to believe about the young. <u>The reality is, however, that young people today show more maturity and common sense than most adults give them credit for</u>.

Dramatic Fact or Statistic

Seventy percent of the respondents in a poll conducted by columnist Ann Landers stated that, if they could live their lives over, they would choose not to have children. This startling statistic makes one wonder what these people believed parenthood would be like. <u>Most parents, it seems, have unrealistic expectations about their children</u>. Parents want their children to accept their values, follow their paths, and succeed where they failed.

Introductory paragraphs sometimes end with a *plan of development*: a quick preview of the essay's major points in the order in which those points will be discussed. The plan of development may be part of the thesis (as in the first sample introduction) or it may immediately follow the thesis (as in the last sample introduction). Because the plan of development outlines the essay's organizational structure, it helps prepare the reader for the essay's progression of ideas. In a brief essay, readers can often keep track of the ideas without this extra help. In a longer paper, though, a plan of development can be an effective unifying device since it highlights the main ideas the essay will develop.

Write the Conclusion

You may have come across essays that ended with jarring abruptness because they had no conclusions at all. Other papers may have had conclusions, but they sputtered to a weak close, a sure sign that the writers had run out of steam and wanted to finish as quickly as possible. Just as satisfying closes are an important part of everyday life (we feel cheated if dinner doesn't end with dessert or if a friend leaves without saying goodbye), a strong conclusion is an important part of an effective essay. Generally one or two paragraphs in length, the conclusion should give the reader a feeling of completeness and finality. One way to achieve this sense of "rounding off" is to return to an image, idea, or anecdote from the introduction. Because people tend to remember most clearly the points they read last, the conclusion is also a good place to remind readers of your thesis. You may also use the conclusion to make a final point about your subject. Be careful, though, not to open an entirely new line of thought at the essay's close.

Illustrated briefly here are several strategies for writing sound conclusions. These techniques may be used singly or in combination. The first strategy, the summary conclusion, can be especially helpful in long, complex essays since readers may appreciate a review of your points. Tacked onto a short essay, though, a summary conclusion often seems boring and mechanical.

Summary

Contrary to what many adults think, most adolescents are not only aware of the important issues of the times but also deeply concerned about them. They are sensitive to the plight of the homeless, the destruction of the environment, and the pitfalls of rampant materialism. Indeed, today's young people are not less mature and sensible than their parents were. If anything, they are more so.

Prediction

The growing tendency on the part of the judicial system to hold parents responsible for the reactions of their wayward children can have a disturbing impact on all of us. Parents will feel bitter toward their own children and cynical about a system that allows such an injustice. Children, continuing to escape the consequences of their actions, will become even more lawless and destructive. Society cannot afford two such possibilities.

Quotation

The comic W. C. Fields is reputed to have said, "Anyone who hates children and dogs can't be all bad." Most people do not share Fields's cynicism. Viewing childhood as a time of purity, they are alarmed at the way television exposes children to the seamy side of life, stripping youngsters of their innocence and giving them a glib sophistication that is a poor substitute for wisdom.

Statistic

Granted, divorce may, in some cases, be the best thing for families torn apart by parents who battle one another. However, in longitudinal studies of children from divorced families, psychologist Judith Wallerstein found that only 10 percent of the youngsters felt relief at their parents' divorce; the remaining 90 percent felt devastated. Such statistics surely call into question parents' claims that they are divorcing for their children's sake.

Recommendation or Call for Action

It is a mistake to leave parenting to instinct. Instead, we should make parenting skills a required course in schools. In addition, a nationwide hotline should be established to help parents deal with crises. Such training and continuing support would help adults deal more effectively with many of the problems they face as parents.

Write the Title

Some writers say that they began a certain piece with only a title in mind. But for most people, writing a title is a finishing touch. Although creating a title for your paper is usually one of the last steps in writing an essay, it shouldn't be done haphazardly. It may take time to write an effective title — one that hints at the essay's thesis and snares the reader's interest.

Good titles may make use of the following techniques: repetition of sounds ("Why I Want a Wife"); questions ("Are the Homeless Crazy?"), and humor ("How to Say Nothing in 500 Words"). More often, though, titles are straightforward phrases derived from the essay's subject or thesis: "Shooting an Elephant" and "TV Addiction," for example.

Pulling It All Together

Now that you know how to prepare a first draft, you might find it helpful to examine the accompanying illustration to see how the different parts of a draft can fit together. Keep in mind that not every essay you write will take this shape. As your purpose, audience, and tone change, so will your essay's structure. An introduction or conclusion, for instance, may be developed in more than one paragraph; the thesis statement may be implied or delayed until the essay's middle or end; not all paragraphs may have topic sentences; and several supporting paragraphs may be needed to develop a single topic sentence. Even so, the basic format presented here offers a strategy for organizing a variety of writing assignments — from term papers to lab reports. Once you feel comfortable with the structure, you have a foundation on which to base your variations. (This book's student and professional essays illustrate some possibilities.) Even when using a specific format, you always have room to give your spirit and imagination free play. The language you use, the details you select, the perspective you offer are uniquely yours. They are what make your essay different from everyone else's.

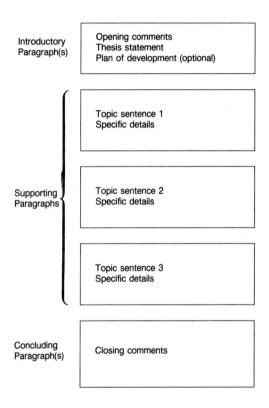

Introductory Paragraph(s)	Opening comments Thesis statement Plan of development (optional)
Supporting Paragraphs	Topic sentence 1 Specific details
	Topic sentence 2 Specific details
	Topic sentence 3 Specific details
Concluding Paragraph(s)	Closing comments

Sample First Draft

Here is the first draft of Harriet Davids's essay. (The assignment and prewriting for the essay appear on pages 23, 26–27, and 31.) Harriet wrote the draft in one sitting. Working at a computer, she started by typing her thesis at the top of the first page. Then, following the guidelines on page 54, she moved the material in her outline (page 52) to her draft. Harriet worked rapidly; she started with the first body paragraph and wrote straight through to the last supporting paragraph.

By moving quickly, Harriet got down her essay's basic text rather easily. Once she felt she had captured in rough form what she wanted to say, she reread her draft to get a sense of how she might open and close the essay. Then she drafted her introduction and conclusion; both appear here, together with the body of the essay. The commentary following the draft will give you a clearer sense of how Harriet proceeded.

Challenges for Today's Parents
by Harriet Davids

Thesis: Being a parent today is much more difficult than it was a generation ago.

Raising children used to be much simpler in the 50s and 60s. I remember TV images from that era showing that parenting involved simply teaching kids to clean their rooms, do their homework, and _____ (ADD SPECIFICS). But being a parent today is much more difficult because nowadays parents have to shield/protect kids from lots of things, like distractions from schoolwork, from sexual material, from dangerous situations.

Parents have to control all the new distractions/temptations that turn kids away from schoolwork. These days many kids have stereos and televisions in their rooms. Certainly, my girls can't resist the urge to listen to MTV, especially if it's time to do homework. Unfortunately, though, kids aren't assigned much homework and what is assigned too often is busywork. And there are even more distractions outside the home. Teens no longer hang out/congregate on the corner where Dad and Mom can yell to them to come home and do homework. Instead they hang out at the mall, in video arcades, and fast-food restaurants. Obviously, parents and school can't compete with all this.

Also (WEAK TRANS.) parents have to help kids develop responsible sexual values even though sex is everywhere. Kids see sex magazines and dirty paperbacks in the corner store where they used to get candy and comic books. And instead of the artsy nude shots of the past, kids see ronchey (SP?), explicit shots in <u>Playboy</u> and

Hustler. And movies have sexy stuff in them today. Teachers seduce students and people treat sex casually/as a sport. Not exactly traditional values. Even worse is what's on TV. Kids see soap-opera characters in bed and cable shows full of nudity by just flipping the dial (FIX). The situation has gotten so out of hand that maybe the government should establish guidelines on what's permissible.

Worst of all are the life-threatening dangers that parents must help children fend off over the years. With older kids, drugs fall into place as a main concern (AWK). Peer pressure to try drugs is bigger (WRONG WORD) to kids than their parents' warnings. Other kinds of warnings are common when children are small. Then parents fear violence since news shows constantly report stories of little children being abused (ADD SPECIFICS). And when kids aren't much older, they have to resist the pressure to drink. Alcohol has always attracted kids, but nowadays they are drinking more and this can be deadly, especially when drinking is combined with driving (REDO).

Most adults love their children and want to be good parents. But it's difficult because the world seems stacked against young people. Even Holden Caufield (SP?) had trouble dealing with society's confusing pressures. Parents must give their children some freedom but not so much that the kids lose sight of what's important.

Commentary

As you can see, Harriet's draft is rough. Because she knew she would revise later on (page 68), she "zapped out" the draft in an informal, colloquial style. For example, she occasionally expressed her thoughts in fragments ("Not exactly traditional values"), relied heavily on "and" as a transition, and used slangy expressions like "kids," "dirty paperbacks," and "lots of things." Similarly, rather than finetuning, Harriet simply used capital letters to type parenthetic notes to herself: "REDO" or "FIX" to signal awkward sentences; "ADD SPECIFICS" to mark overly general statements; "WRONG WORD" after an imprecise word; "SP" to remind herself to check spelling in the dictionary; "WEAK TRANS." to indicate where a stronger signaling device was needed. Note, too, that she used slashes between alternative word choices and left a blank space when wording just wouldn't come. (Harriet's final draft appears on page 73.)

Writing a first draft may seem like quite a challenge, but the tips offered in these pages should help you proceed with confidence. Indeed, as you work on the draft, you may be surprised how much you enjoy writing. After all, this is your chance to get down on paper something you want to say.

Activity: Write the First Draft

Referring to the outline you prepared in response to activity 3 on page 53, draft the body of your essay, making your evidence as strong as possible. As you work, keep your purpose, audience, and tone in mind. After reading what you've prepared, go ahead and draft a rough introduction, conclusion, and title. Finally, ask at least one other person to react to your draft by listing its strengths and weaknesses.

STAGE 6: REVISE THE ESSAY

By now, you've probably abandoned any preconceptions you might have had about good writers sitting down and creating a finished product in one easy step. Alexander Pope's comment that "true ease in writing comes from art, not chance" is as true today as it was more than two hundred years ago. Writing that seems effortlessly clear is often the result of sustained work, not of good luck or even inborn talent. And much of this work takes place during the final stage of the writing process when ideas, paragraphs, sentences, and words are refined and reshaped.

Professional writers — novelists, journalists, textbook authors — seldom submit a piece of writing that hasn't been revised. They recognize that rough, unpolished work doesn't do them justice. What's more, they often look forward to revising. Columnist Ellen Goodman puts it this way: "What makes me happy is rewriting. . . . It's like cleaning house, getting rid of all the junk, getting things in the right order, tightening up."

In a sense, revision occurs throughout the writing process: At some earlier stage, you may have dropped an idea, overhauled your thesis, or shifted paragraph order. What, then, is different about the rewriting that occurs in the revision stage? The answer has to do with the literal meaning of the word *revision* — to resee, or to see again. Genuine revision involves casting clear eyes on your work, viewing it as though you're a reader rather than the writer. Revision means that you go through your paper looking for trouble, ready to pick a fight with your own writing. And then you must be willing to sit down and make the changes needed for your writing to be as effective as possible.

Revision is not, as some believe, simply touch-up work—changing a sentence here or a word there, eliminating spelling errors, typing a neat final copy. Revision means cutting deadwood, rearranging paragraphs, substituting new words for old ones, recasting sentences, improving coherence, even generating new material when appropriate. Because such work is challenging, you may resist revision or feel shaky about how to proceed. The following pointers should help get you going if you balk at or feel overwhelmed by revising.

- *Set your writing aside for a while* before revising. When you pick up your paper again, you'll have a fresh, more objective point of view.
- *Work from typed material* whenever possible. Having your essay in neutral typed letters instead of in your own familiar writing helps you see the paper impartially, as if someone else had written it. Each time you make major changes, try to retype that section so that you can see it anew.

  Using a word processor speeds up the process considerably. It takes only a few keystrokes to move, add, or delete words, sentences, or whole segments of text. At some point, you should print out your draft, including any changes you've made, so you can get a better look at it. Having the printout allows you to jot down marginal notes, cross out portions of text, or handwrite additions between lines. Or, if you prefer revising exclusively at the computer, scroll through the entire first draft for an overview and jot down any notes you may need to guide your on-screen editing. If you feel more comfortable working from handwritten drafts, don't boldly strike out or erase as you revise. Instead, lightly cross out material, in case you want to retrieve it later on.
- *Read your draft aloud* as often as you can. Hearing how your writing sounds helps you pick up problems that passed you by before: places where sentences are awkward, meaning is ambiguous, words are imprecise. Even better, have another person read aloud to you what you have

written. If the reader slows to a crawl over a murky paragraph or trips over a convoluted sentence, you know where you have to do some rewriting.

- *Ask for feedback.* Many instructors include feedback sessions as a regular part of a composition course. If your instructor does not, you can set up feedback sessions on your own, adapting the suggestions here to fit your needs. Start by selecting readers who are critical (not a love-struck admirer or doting grandparent) and who are skilled enough to provide useful commentary. To ensure that you leave feedback sessions with specific observations about what does and doesn't work in your writing, give your readers a clear sense of what you want from them. If you simply ask, "How's this?" you may receive a vague comment like "It's not very effective." What you want are concrete observations and suggestions: "I'm confused because what you say in the fifth sentence contradicts what you say in the second."

    To promote such specific responses, ask your readers targeted questions like "I'm having trouble moving from my second to my third point. How can I make the transition smoother?" Such questions require more than "yes" or "no" responses; they encourage readers to dig into your writing where you sense it needs work. You may develop your own questions or adapt the revision checklist on pages 71–72.

- *Listen with an open mind* to those giving you feedback. Take notes on their observations, and when everyone is finished commenting, reread your notes. Which remarks seem valid? Which don't? Try using a *feedback chart* or a system of *marginal annotations* to help you evaluate and remedy any perceived weaknesses in your draft.

    Here's how to use a three-column feedback chart. In the first column, list the major problems you and your readers see in the draft. Next, rank the problems, designating the most critical as 1. Then, in the second column, jot down possible solutions — your own as well as your readers'. Finally, in the third column, briefly describe what action you'll take to correct each problem.

    If you don't use a feedback chart, be sure to enter

marginal annotations on your draft before revising it. In the margins, jot down any major problems, numbered in order of importance, along with possible remedies. Marking your draft this way, much as an instructor might, helps you view your paper as though it were written by someone else. Then, keeping the draft's problems in mind, start revising. You may make changes directly above the appropriate line, or, when necessary, rework sections on a separate sheet of paper.

- *View revision as a series of steps.* Don't try to tackle all of a draft's problems at once; instead, proceed step by step. (The feedback chart and annotation system just described will help you do just that.) Whenever possible, read your draft several times, each time focusing on different issues and asking yourself different questions. Move from a broad view of the draft to an up-close look at its mechanics.

The following checklist describes a number of questions you and your readers can ask when moving through the various steps in the revising process. (To see how one student, Harriet Davids, used the checklist when revising, turn to pages 77–78.) Keep in mind, though, that there are no hard-and-fast rules about the revision steps outlined here. Everyone approaches revision differently, so feel free to adapt our suggestions to your individual needs.

Revision Checklist

First Step: Revise Overall Meaning and Structure

- Considering the essay's purpose, audience, and tone (pages 19–22), in what ways does or doesn't the paper accomplish what was intended?
- What is the essay's thesis (pages 33–37)? Is it stated explicitly, or is it implied? If the perceived thesis isn't what was intended, what changes need to be made?
- What are the essay's main points of support (pages 38–39)? If any of these stray from or contradict the thesis (pages 41–42), what changes need to be made?
- Are the main points arranged in a spatial, chronological, emphatic, or simple-to-complex sequence (pages 47–49)? How does this organizational format reinforce the thesis?

- Which patterns of development (pages 46–47) provide the essay's organizational framework? How do these patterns reinforce the thesis?

Second Step: Revise Paragraph Development

- Where in each paragraph does support seem irrelevant, vague, insufficient, inaccurate, or nonrepresentative (pages 41–44)? What could be done to remedy these problems?
- What signal devices (pages 58–60) are used to connect ideas within and between paragraphs? Where are there too few signals or too many?
- What strategies are used to open (pages 60–62) and close (pages 63–64) the essay? How could the introduction and conclusion be made more effective?

Third Step: Revise Sentences and Words

- Which sentences seem inconsistent with the essay's intended tone (pages 21–22)? How could the problem be corrected?
- Where does sentence structure become monotonous and predictable (pages 88 and 150–151)? How could a different sentence pattern add variety?
- Which words are vague and overly general (pages 87–88 and 151)? How could the language be made more vigorous and concrete?
- Where does gender-biased language (pages 744–45) appear? How could the problem be eliminated?

Fourth Step: Proofread for Grammar, Punctuation, and Typing Errors

- A note about proofreading: although proofing seems to involve relatively minor matters, an accumulation of small errors — misspellings, typos, misplaced commas — can distract readers and sabotage an otherwise strong essay. So before handing in the final draft of your essay, proofread it closely, keeping a dictionary and English handbook nearby. When proofing, people tend to see what they think is on the page rather than what really is there. Reading the essay out loud and backwards, starting with the last word first, can highlight errors that otherwise might slip by.

STUDENT ESSAY

In this chapter, we've taken you through the various stages in the writing process. You've seen how Harriet Davids used prewriting (pages 26–27 and 31) and outlining (page 52) to arrive at her first draft (pages 66–67). In the following pages, you'll look at Harriet's final draft—the paper she submitted to her instructor.

Harriet, a thirty-eight-year-old college student and mother of two teenagers, wanted to write an informative paper with a straightforward, serious tone. While preparing her essay, she kept in mind that her audience would include her course instructor as well as her classmates, most of them considerably younger than she. This is the assignment that prompted Harriet's essay:

> Because the world these days is a difficult, even danger-ous place, parents understandably worry about their children. Write an essay supporting the idea that today's world is, in many ways, hostile—particularly to children.

Harriet's essay is annotated so you can see how it illustrates the essay format described on page 65. As you read her essay, try to determine how well it reflects the principles of effective writing. The commentary following the paper will help you look at the essay more closely and give you some sense of the way Harriet went about revising her first draft.

Challenges for Today's Parents

Introduction

Reruns of situation comedies from the 1950s 1 and early 1960s dramatize the kinds of problems that parents used to have with their children. The Cleavers scold Beaver for not washing his hands before dinner; the Andersons ground Bud for not doing his homework; the Nelsons dock little Ricky's allowance because he keeps forgetting to clean his room. But times have changed dramati-

Thesis —————

Plan of —————
development

First
supporting
paragraph

Topic sentence —

Second
supporting
paragraph

Topic sentence
with link to
previous
paragraph

Third
supporting
paragraph

Topic sentence
with emphasis —
signal

cally. Being a parent today is much more difficult than it was a generation ago. Parents nowadays must protect their children from a growing number of distractions, from sexually explicit material, and from life-threatening situations.

Today's parents must try, first of all, to control all the new distractions that tempt children away from schoolwork. At home, a child may have a room furnished with a stereo and television. Not many young people can resist the urge to listen to an album or watch MTV--especially if it is time to do schoolwork. Outside the home, the distractions are even more alluring. Children no longer "hang out" on a neighborhood corner within earshot of Mom or Dad's reminder to come in and do homework. Instead, they congregate in vast shopping malls, buzzing video arcades, and gleaming fast-food restaurants. Parents and school assignments have obvious difficulty competing with such enticing alternatives.

Besides dealing with these distractions, parents have to shield their children from a flood of sexually explicit materials. Today, children can find sex magazines and pornographic paperbacks in the same corner store that once offered only comics and candy. Children will not see the fuzzily photographed nudes that a previous generation did but will encounter the hard-core raunchiness of Hustler or Penthouse. Moreover, the movies young people attend often focus on highly sexual situations. It is difficult to teach children traditional values when films show teachers seducing students and young people treating sex as a casual sport. An even more difficult matter for parents is the heavily sexual content of programs on television. With just a flick of the dial, children can see soap-opera stars cavorting in bed or watch cable programs where nudity is common.

Most disturbing to parents today, however, is the increase in life-threatening dangers that face young people. When children are small, parents fear that their youngsters may be victims of violence. Every news program seems to carry a report

2

3

4

about a mass murderer who preys on young girls, a deviant who has buried six boys in his cellar, or an organized child pornography ring that molests preschoolers. When children are older, parents begin to worry about their kids' use of drugs. Peer pressure to experiment with drugs is often stronger than parents' warnings. This pressure to experiment can be fatal. Finally, even if young people escape the hazards associated with drugs, they must still resist the pressure to drink. Although alcohol has always held an attraction for teenagers, reports indicate that they are drinking more than ever before. As many parents know, the consequences of this attraction can be deadly--especially when drinking is combined with driving.

Conclusion

References to TV shows recall introduction

Within one generation, the world as a place to raise children has changed dramatically. One wonders how yesterday's parents would have dealt with today's problems. Could the Andersons have kept Bud away from MTV? Could the Nelsons have shielded little Ricky from sexually explicit material? Could the Cleavers have protected Beaver from drugs and alcohol? Parents must be aware of all these distractions and dangers yet be willing to give their children the freedom they need to become responsible adults. It is not an easy task.

5

COMMENTARY

Introduction and thesis. The opening paragraph attracts readers' interest by recalling several vintage television shows that have almost become part of our cultural heritage. Harriet begins with these examples from the past because they offer such a sharp contrast to the present, thus underscoring the idea expressed in her *thesis*: "Being a parent today is much more difficult than it was a generation ago." Opening in this way, with material that serves as a striking contrast to what follows, is a common and effective strategy. Note, too, that Harriet's thesis states the paper's subject (being a parent) as well as her attitude toward the subject (the job is more demanding than it was years ago).

Plan of development.   Harriet follows her thesis with a *plan of development* that anticipates the three major points to be covered in the essay's supporting paragraphs. Unfortunately, this particular plan of development is somewhat mechanical, with the major points being trotted past the reader in one long, awkward sentence. To deal with the problem, Harriet could have rewritten the sentence or eliminated the plan of development altogether, ending the introduction with her thesis.

Patterns of development.   Although Harriet develops her thesis primarily through *examples*, she also draws on two other patterns of development. The whole paper implies a *contrast* between the way life is now and the way it used to be. The essay also contains an element of *causal analysis* since all the factors that Harriet cites affect children and the way they are raised.

Purpose, audience, and tone.   Given the essay's *purpose* and *audience*, Harriet adopts a serious *tone*, providing no-nonsense evidence to support her thesis. But assume she had been asked by her daughters' school newspaper to write a humorous column about the trials and tribulations that parents face raising children. Aiming for a different tone, purpose, and audience, Harriet would have taken another approach. Drawing on her experience as a mother of two teenage daughters, she might have confessed how she survives MTV's flash and dazzle, as well as the din of stereos blasting rock music at all hours: she stuffs her ears with cotton, hides her daughters' tapes, and cuts off the electricity. This material — with its personalized perspective, exaggeration, and light tone — would be appropriate.

Organization.   Structuring the essay around a series of *relevant* and *specific examples*, Harriet uses *emphatic order* to sequence the paper's three main points: that a growing number of distractions, sexually explicit materials, and life-threatening situations make parenting difficult nowadays. The third supporting paragraph begins with the words "Most disturbing to parents today . . . ," signaling that Harriet feels particular concern about the physical dangers children face. Moreover, she uses basic organizational strategies to sequence the supporting examples within each paragraph. The details in the first supporting paragraph are organized *spatially*, starting with distractions at home and moving to those outside the home. The second supporting paragraph arranges examples *emphatically*. Harriet starts with sexually explicit publications and ends with the "even more difficult matter" of sexuality on television. The third and final supporting paragraph is organized *chronologically*; it begins by discussing dangers to small children and concludes by talking about teenagers.

The essay also displays Harriet's familiarity with other kinds of organizational strategies. Each supporting paragraph opens with a *topic sentence*. Further, *signal devices* are used throughout the paper to show the relationship among ideas: *transitions* ("Instead, they congregate in vast shopping malls"; "Moreover, the movies young people attend often focus on highly sexual situations"); *repetition* ("sexual situations" and "sexual content"); *synonyms* ("distractions . . . enticing alternatives" and "life-threatening . . . fatal"); *pronouns* ("young people . . . they"); and *bridging sentences* ("Besides dealing with these distractions, parents also have to shield their children from a flood of sexually explicit material").

A minor problem. Harriet's efforts to write a well-organized essay result in a somewhat predictable structure. It might have been better had she rewritten one of the paragraphs, perhaps embedding the topic sentence in the middle of the paragraph or saving it for the end. Similarly, Harriet's signal devices are a little heavy-handed. Even so, an essay with a sharp focus and clear signals is preferable to one with a confusing or inaccessible structure. As she gains more experience, Harriet can work on making the structure of her essays more subtle.

Conclusion. Harriet brings the essay to a satisfying *close* by reminding readers of the paper's central idea and three main points. The final paragraph also extends the essay's scope by introducing a new but related issue: that parents have to strike a balance between their need to provide limitations and their children's need for freedom.

Revising the first draft. With the help of several classmates, Harriet reworked her essay a number of times. Using the checklist on pages 71–72 to focus their feedback, Harriet's revising team offered various suggestions to strengthen the paper. To get a sense of Harriet's revising process, compare the final version of her conclusion (page 75) with the original version reprinted here.

Original Version of Conclusion

Most adults love their children and want to be good parents. But it's difficult because the world seems stacked against young people. Even Holden Caulfield had trouble dealing with society's pressures. Parents must give their children some freedom but not so much that kids lose sight of what's important.

As soon as Harriet heard her paper read aloud during a group session, she realized the conclusion didn't work at all, but she wisely waited to rework the conclusion until after she had fine-tuned the rest of the essay. At that point, she made marginal annotations summarizing the problems that she and her editing group detected in the conclusion. Together, they identified three problems, numbered in order of importance. First, the conclusion seemed tacked on, rather like a tired afterthought. Second, the allusion to *The Catcher in the Rye* misrepresented the essay's focus since Harriet discusses children of all ages, not just teens. Third, the first sentence in the conclusion was bland and boring.

Keeping these points in mind, Harriet decided to scrap her original conclusion. Working at a word processor, she prepared a much stronger concluding paragraph. Besides eliminating the distracting reference to Holden Caulfield, she replaced the shop-worn opening sentence ("Most people love their children") with three interesting and rhythmical questions ("Could the Andersons . . . Could the Nelsons . . . Could the Cleavers . . . ?"). Because these questions recall the essay's main points and echo the introduction's reference to vintage television shows, they help unify Harriet's paper and bring it to a satisfying close.

These are just a few of the changes Harriet made when reworking her essay. Realizing that writing is a process, she left herself enough time to revise. She was gratified by her classmates' responses to what she had written and pleased by the lively discussion her essay provoked. Early in her composition course, Harriet learned that attention to the various stages in the writing process yields satisfying results, for writer and reader alike.

Activity: Revise the Essay

Return to the draft you wrote in response to the activity on page 68. Also look at the written feedback you received on the draft. To identify any further problems in the draft, get together with several people (classmates, friends, or family members) and request that one of them read the draft aloud to you. Then ask your audience focused questions about the areas you sense need work, or use the checklist on pages 71–72 to focus the feedback. In either case, summarize and rank the comments on a feedback chart or in marginal annotations. Then, using the comments as a guide, go ahead and revise the draft. Either type a new version or do your revising by hand, perhaps on a photocopy of the draft. Don't forget to proofread closely before submitting the paper to your instructor.

3

DESCRIPTION

WHAT IS DESCRIPTION?

All of us respond in a strong way to sensory stimulation. The sweet perfume of a candy shop takes us back to childhood; the blank white walls of the campus infirmary remind us of long vigils at a hospital where a grandmother lay dying; the screech of a subway car sets our nerves on edge.

Without any sensory stimulation, we sink into a less-than-human state. Neglected babies, left alone with no human touch, no colors, no lullabies, become withdrawn and unresponsive. And prisoners dread solitary confinement, knowing that the sensory deprivation can be unbearable, even to the point of madness.

Because sensory impressions are so potent, descriptive writing has a unique power and appeal. *Description* can be defined as the expression, in vivid language, of what the five senses experience. A richly rendered description freezes a subject in time, evoking sights, smells, sounds, textures, and tastes in such a way that readers become one with the writer's world.

HOW DESCRIPTION FITS YOUR PURPOSE AND AUDIENCE

Description can be a supportive technique that develops part of an essay, or it can be the dominant technique used throughout an essay. Here are some examples of the way description can help you meet the objective of an essay developed chiefly through another pattern of development:

- In a *causal analysis* showing the *consequences* of pet overpopulation, you might describe the desperate appearance of a pack of starving stray dogs.
- In an *argumentation-persuasion* essay urging more rigorous handgun control, you might start with a description of a violent family confrontation that ended in murder.
- In a *process analysis* explaining the pleasure of making ice cream at home, you might describe the beauty of an old-fashioned, hand-cranked ice cream maker.
- In a *narrative essay* recounting a day in the life of a street musician, you might describe the musician's energy and the joyous appreciation of passersby.

In each case, the essay's overall purpose would affect the amount of description needed.

Your readers also influence how much description to include. As you write, ask yourself, "What do my particular readers need to know to understand and experience keenly what I'm describing? What descriptive details will they enjoy most?" Your answers to these and similar questions will help you tailor your description to specific readers. Consider an article intended for professional horticulturists; its purpose is to explain a new technique for controlling spider mites. Because of readers' expertise, there would be little need for a lengthy description of the insects. Written for a college newspaper, however, the article would probably provide a detailed description of the mites so student gardeners could distinguish between the pesky parasites and flecks of dust.

While your purpose and audience define *how much* to describe, you have great freedom deciding *what* to describe. Description is especially suited to objects (your car or desk, for example), but you can also describe a person, an animal, a place, a time, and a phenomenon or concept. You might write an effective description about a friend who runs marathons (person), a pair of ducks who return each year to a neighbor's pond (animals), the kitchen of a fast-food restaurant (place), a period when you were unemployed (time), the "fight or flight" response to danger (phenomenon or concept).

Description can be divided into two types: *objective* and *subjective*. In an objective description, you describe the subject in a straightforward and literal way, without revealing your attitude or feelings. Reporters, as well as technical and scientific writers, specialize in objective description; their jobs depend on their ability to detail experiences without emotional bias. For example, a reporter may write an unemotional account of a township meeting that ended in a fistfight. Or a marine biologist may write a factual report describing the way sea mammals are killed by the plastic refuse (sandwich wrappings, straws, fishing lines) that humans throw into the ocean.

In contrast, when writing a subjective description, you convey a highly personal view of your subject and seek to elicit a strong emotional response from your readers. Such subjective descriptions often take the form of reflective pieces or character studies. For example, in an essay describing the rich plant life in an inner-city garden, you might reflect on people's longing to connect with the soil and express admiration for the gardeners' hard work — an admiration you'd like readers to share. Or, in a character study of your grandfather, you might describe his stern appearance and gentle behavior, hoping that the contradiction will move readers as much as it moves you.

The *tone* of a subjective description is determined by your purpose, your attitude toward the subject, and the reader response you wish to evoke. Consider an essay about a dynamic woman who runs a center for disturbed children. If your goal is to make readers admire the woman, your tone will be serious and appreciative. But if you want to criticize the woman's high-pressure tactics and create distaste for her management style, your tone will be disapproving and severe.

The language of a descriptive piece also depends, to great extent, on whether your purpose is primarily objective or subjective. If the description is objective, the language is straightforward, precise, and factual. Such *denotative* language consists of neutral dictionary meanings. If you want to describe as dispassionately as possible fans' violent behavior at a football game, you might write about the "large crowd" and its "mass movement onto the field." But if you are shocked by the fans' behavior and want to write a subjective piece that inspires similar outrage in readers, then you might write about the "swelling mob" and its "rowdy stampede onto the field." In the latter case, the language used would be *connotative* and emotionally charged so that readers would share your feelings.

Subjective and objective descriptions often overlap. Sometimes a single sentence contains both objective and subjective elements: "Although his hands were large and misshapen by arthritis, they were gentle to the touch, inspiring confidence and trust." Other times, part of an essay may provide a factual description (the physical appearance of a summer cabin your family rented), while another part of the essay may be highly subjective (how you felt in the cabin, sitting in front of a fire on a rainy day).

SUGGESTIONS FOR USING DESCRIPTION IN AN ESSAY

The following suggestions will be helpful whether you use description as a dominant or supportive pattern of development.

1. Focus a descriptive essay around a dominant impression.   Like other kinds of writing, a descriptive essay must have a thesis, or main point. In a descriptive essay with a subjective slant, the thesis usually centers on the *dominant impression* you have about your subject. Suppose you decide to write an essay on your ninth-grade history teacher, Ms. Hazzard. You want the paper to convey how unconventional and flamboyant she was. The essay could, of course, focus on a different dominant impression — how insensitive she could be to students, for example. What's important is that you establish — early in the paper — the dominant impression you intend to convey. Although descriptive essays often imply, rather than explicitly state, the dominant impression, that impression should be unmistakable.

2. Select the details to include. The power of description hinges on your ability to select from all possible details only those that support the dominant impression. All others, no matter how vivid or interesting, must be left out. If you're describing how flamboyant Ms. Hazzard could be, the details in the following paragraph would be appropriate.

> A large-boned woman, Ms. Hazzard wore her bright red hair piled on top of her head, where it perched precariously. By the end of class, wayward strands of hair tumbled down and fell into eyes fringed by spiky false eyelashes. Ms. Hazzard's nails, filed into crisp points, were painted either bloody burgundy or neon pink. Plastic bangle bracelets, also either burgundy or pink, clattered up and down her ample arms as she scrawled on the board the historical dates that had, she claimed, "changed the world."

Such details—the heavy eye makeup, stiletto nails, gaudy bracelets—contribute to the impression of a flamboyant, unusual person. Even if you remembered times that Ms. Hazzard seemed perfectly conventional and understated, most likely you wouldn't describe those times since they contradict the dominant impression.

You must also be selective in the *number of details* you include. Having a dominant impression helps you eliminate many details gathered during prewriting, but there still will be choices to make. For example, it would be inappropriate to describe in exhaustive detail everything in a messy room:

> The brown desk, made of a grained plastic laminate, is directly under a small window covered by a torn yellow-and-gold plaid curtain. In the left corner of the desk are four crumbled balls of blue-lined yellow paper, three red markers, two fine-point blue pens, an ink eraser, and four letters, two bearing special wildlife stamps. A green down-filled vest and a red cable knit sweater are thrown over the back of the bright blue metal bridge chair pushed under the desk. Under the chair is an oval braided rug, its once brilliant blues and greens spotted by old coffee stains.

Readers will be reluctant to wade through such undifferentiated specifics. Even more important, such excessive detailing dilutes the focus of the essay. You end up with a seemingly endless list of specifics, rather than with a carefully crafted picture in words. In this regard, sculptors and writers are similar — what they take away is as important as what they leave in.

Perhaps you're wondering how to generate the details that support your dominant impression. As you can imagine, you have to develop heightened powers of observation and recall. To sharpen these key faculties, it can be helpful to make up a chart with separate columns for each of the five senses. If you can observe your subject directly, enter in the appropriate columns what you see, hear, taste, and so on. If you're attempting to remember something from the past, try to recollect details under each of these sense headings. Ask yourself questions ("How did it smell? What did I hear?") and list each memory recaptured. You'll be surprised how this simple technique can tune you in to your experiences and help uncover the specific details needed to develop your dominant impression.

3. Organize the descriptive details. Select the organizational pattern (or combination of patterns) that best supports your dominant impression. The paragraphs in a descriptive essay are usually sequenced *spatially* (from top to bottom, interior to exterior, near to far) or *chronologically* (as the subject is experienced in time). But the paragraphs can also be ordered *emphatically* (ending with your subject's most striking elements) or by *sensory impression* (first smell, then taste, then touch, and so on).

You might, for instance, use a *spatial* pattern to organize a description of a large city as you viewed it from the air, a taxi, and a subway car. A description of your first day on a new job might move *chronologically*, starting with how you felt when you woke up that morning and proceeding through the day's events. In a paper describing a bout with the flu, you might arrange details *emphatically*, beginning with a description of your low-level aches and pains and concluding with an account of your raging fever. An essay about a neighborhood garbage dump, euphemistically called an "ecology landfill" by its owners, could be organized by *sensory impressions*: the sights of the dump, its smells, its sounds. Regardless of the organizational pattern you use, provide enough *signal devices* (for example, *about, next, worst of all*) so that readers can follow the description easily.

Finally, although descriptive essays don't always have conventional topic sentences, each descriptive paragraph should have a clear focus. Often this focus is indicated by a sentence early in the paragraph that names the scene, object, or individual to be described. Such a sentence functions as a kind of *informal topic sentence*; the paragraph's descriptive details then develop that topic sentence.

4. Use vivid sensory language and varied sentence structure. The connotative language typical of subjective description should be richly evocative. The words you select must etch in readers' minds the same picture that you have in yours. For this reason, rather than relying on vague generalities, you must use language that involves readers' senses. Consider the difference between the following paired descriptions:

Vague	Vivid
The food was unappetizing.	The stew congealed into an oval pool of milky-brown fat.
The toothpaste was refreshing.	The toothpaste, tasting minty sweet, felt good against slippery teeth, free finally from braces.
Filled with passengers and baggage, the car moved slowly down the road.	Burdened with its load of clamoring children and well-worn suitcases, the car labored down the interstate on bald tires and worn shocks, emitting puffs of blue exhaust and an occasional backfire.

Unlike the *concrete, sensory-packed* sentences on the right, the sentences on the left fail to create vivid word pictures that engage readers. While all good writing blends abstract and concrete language, descriptive writing demands an abundance of specific sensory language.

Keep in mind, too, that *verbs pack more of a wallop* than adverbs. The following sentence has to rely on adverbs (italicized) because its verbs are so weak: "She walked *casually* into the room

and *deliberately* tried not to pay much attention to their stares."
Rewritten, so that verbs (italicized), not adverbs, do the bulk of
the work, the sentence becomes more powerful: "She *strolled* into
the room and *ignored* their stares."

Figures of speech — nonliteral, imaginative comparisons between two basically dissimilar things — are another way to enliven descriptive writing. *Similes* use the words *like* or *as* when
comparing; *metaphors* state or imply that two things being compared are alike; and *personification* attributes human characteristics to inanimate things.

The examples that follow show how effective figurative language can be in descriptive writing.

> Moving as jerkily as a marionette on strings, the old man
> picked himself up off the sidewalk and staggered down
> the street. (*simile*)

> Stalking their prey, the hall monitors remained hidden
> in the corridors, motionless and ready to spring on any
> unsuspecting student who dared to sneak into class late.
> (*metaphor*)

> The scoop of vanilla ice cream, plain and unadorned,
> cried out for hot fudge sauce and a sprinkling of sliced
> pecans. (*personification*)

Finally, when writing descriptive passages, you need to *vary
sentence structure*. Don't use the same subject-verb pattern in all
sentences. The second example above, for instance, could have
been written as follows: "The hall monitors stalked their prey.
They hid in the corridors. They remained motionless and ready to
spring on any unsuspecting student who tried to sneak into class
late." But the sentence is richer and more interesting when the
descriptive elements are embedded, eliminating what would
otherwise have been a clipped and predictable subject-verb
pattern.

———————

Henry James, American novelist and master of description,
gave this advice to beginning writers: "Try to be one of the people

on whom nothing is lost." If you work to become the kind of writer "on whom nothing is lost," you will find you have a rich mine of sensory impressions to explore and transmute into written form. To develop your descriptive powers, you must be alert to your inner and outer worlds. And you must develop sensitivity to the nuances of language, finding just the right words to convey the essence of your experiences. It is no wonder that descriptive writing can be a source of such pleasure for writer and reader alike.

STUDENT ESSAY

The following student essay was written by Marie Martinez in response to this assignment:

> The essay "Once More to the Lake" is an evocative piece about a spot that had special meaning in E. B. White's life. Write an essay about a place that holds rich significance for you, centering the description on a dominant impression.

While reading Marie's paper, try to determine how well it applies the principles of description. The annotations on Marie's paper and the commentary following it will help you look at the essay more closely.

Salt Marsh

by Marie Martinez

Introduction
          In one of his journals, Thoreau told of the difficulty he had escaping the obligations and cares of society: "It sometimes happens that I cannot easily shake off the village. The thought of some work will run in my head and I am not where my body is--I am out of my senses. In my walks I . . . return to my senses." All of us feel out of our senses at times. Overwhelmed by problems or everyday annoyances, we lose touch with sensory pleasures as we spend our days in noisy cities and stuffy classrooms. Just as Thoreau walked in the woods

Dominant
impression
(thesis)

to return to his senses, I have a special place where I return to mine: the salt marsh behind my grandparents' house.

Informal topic sentence: Definition paragraph

My grandparents live on the East Coast, a mile or so inland from the sea. Between the ocean and the mainland is a wide fringe of salt marsh. A salt marsh is not a swamp, but an expanse of dark, spongy soil threaded with saltwater creeks and clothed in a kind of grass called salt meadow hay. All the water in the marsh rises and falls daily with the ocean tides, an endless cycle that changes the look of the marsh--partly flooded or mostly dry--as the day progresses.

Informal topic sentence: First paragraph in a four-part spatial sequence

Heading out to the marsh from my grandparents' house, I follow a short path through the woods. As I walk along, a sharp smell of salt mixed with the rich aroma of peaty soil fills my nostrils. I am always amazed by the way the path changes with the seasons. Sometimes I walk in the brilliant green of spring, sometimes in the tawny gold of autumn, sometimes in the grayish-tan of winter.

Simile

No matter the season, the grass flanking the trail is often flattened into swirls, like thick Van Gogh brush strokes that curve and recurve in circular patterns. No people come here. The peacefulness heals me like a soothing drug.

Informal topic sentence: Second paragraph in the spatial sequence

After a few minutes, the trail suddenly opens up to a view that calms me no matter how upset or discouraged I might be: a line of tall waving reeds bordering and nearly hiding the salt marsh creek. To get to the creek, I part the reeds.

Informal topic sentence: Third paragraph in the spatial sequence

The creek is a narrow body of water no more than fifteen feet wide, and it ebbs and flows as the ocean currents sweep toward the land or rush back toward the sea. The creek winds in a sinuous pattern so that I cannot see its beginning or end, the places where it trickles into the marsh or spills into the open ocean. Little brown birds dip in and out of the reeds on the far shore of the creek, making a special "tweep-tweep" sound peculiar to the marsh. When I stand at low tide on the shore of the creek, I am on a miniature cliff, for the bank of the creek falls abruptly and steeply into the water.

Informal topic
sentence: Last
paragraph in
the spatial
sequence

Simile

Below me, green grasses wave and shimmer under the water while tiny minnows flash their silvery sides as they dart through the underwater tangles. The creek water is often much warmer than the ocean, so I can swim there in three seasons. Sitting on the edge of the creek, I scoop some water into my hand, rub my face and neck, then ease into the water. Where the creek is shallow, my feet sink into a foot of muck that feels like mashed potatoes mixed with motor oil. But once I become accustomed to it, I enjoy squishing the slimy mud through my toes. Sometimes I feel brushing past my legs the blue crabs that live in the creek. Other times, I hear the splash of a turtle or otter as it slips from the shore into the water. Otherwise, it is silent. The salty water is buoyant and lifts my spirits as I stroke through it to reach the middle of the creek. There in the center, I float weightlessly, surrounded by tall reeds that reduce the world to water and sky. I am at peace.

6

Conclusion

Echo of idea in
introduction

The salt marsh is not the kind of dramatic landscape found on picture postcards. There are no soaring mountains, sandy beaches, or lush valleys. The marsh is a flat world that some consider dull and uninviting. I am glad most people do not respond to the marsh's subtle beauty because that means I can be alone there. Just as the rising tide sweeps over the marsh, floating debris out to the ocean, the marsh washes away my concerns and restores me to my senses.

7

COMMENTARY

The dominant impression.   Marie responded to the assignment by writing a moving tribute to a place having special meaning for her — the salt marsh near her grandparents' home. Like most descriptive pieces, Marie's essay is organized around a *dominant impression*: the marsh's peaceful solitude and gentle, natural beauty. The essay's introduction provides a context for the dominant impression by comparing the pleasure Marie experiences in the marsh to the happiness Thoreau felt in his walks around Walden Pond.

Other patterns of development.   Before developing the essay's dominant impression, Marie uses the second paragraph to *define* a salt marsh. An *objective description*, the definition clarifies that a salt marsh — with its spongy soil, haylike grass, and ebbing tides — is not to be confused with a swamp. Because Marie offers such a factual definition, readers have the background needed to enjoy the personalized view that follows.

Besides the definition paragraph and the comparison in the opening paragraph, the essay contains a strong element of *causal analysis*: Throughout, Marie describes the marsh's effect on her.

Sensory language.   At times, Marie develops the essay's dominant impression explicitly, as when she writes "No people come here" (paragraph 3) and "I am at peace" (6). But Marie generally uses the more subtle techniques characteristic of *subjective description* to convey the dominant impression. First of all, she fills the essay with strong *connotative language*, rich with *sensory images*. The third paragraph describes what she smells (the "sharp smell of salt mixed with the rich aroma of peaty soil") and what she sees ("brilliant green," "tawny gold," and "grayish-tan"). In the fifth paragraph, she tells us that she hears the chirping sounds of small birds. And the sixth paragraph includes vigorous descriptions of how the marsh feels to Marie's touch. She splashes water on her face and neck; she digs her toes into the mud at the bottom of the creek; she delights in the delicate brushing of crabs against her legs.

Figurative language, vigorous verbs, and varied sentence structure.   You might also have noted that *figurative language*, *energetic verbs* and *varied sentence patterns* contribute to the essay's descriptive power. Marie develops a *simile* in the third paragraph when she compares the flattened swirls of swamp grass to the brush strokes in a painting by Van Gogh. Later she uses another simile when she writes that the creek's thick mud feels "like mashed potatoes mixed with motor oil." Moreover, throughout the essay, she uses lively verbs ("shimmer," "flash") to capture the marsh's magical quality. Similarly, Marie enhances descriptive passages by varying the length of her sentences. Long, fairly elaborate sentences are interspersed with short, dramatic statements. In the third paragraph, for example, the long sentence describing the circular swirls of swamp grass is followed by the brief statement "No people come here." And the sixth paragraph uses two short sentences ("Otherwise, it is silent" and "I am at peace") to punctuate the paragraph's longer sentences.

Organization.   We can follow Marie's journey through the marsh because she uses an easy-to-follow combination of *spatial*, *chronological*, and *emphatic* patterns to sequence her experience. The essay relies primarily on a spatial arrangement since the four body paragraphs focus on the different spots that Marie reaches: first, the path behind her grandparents' house (paragraph 3); then the area bordering the creek (4); next, her view of the creek (5); last, the creek itself (6). Each stage of her walk is signaled by an *informal topic sentence* near the start of each paragraph. Further-more, *signal devices* (marked by italics here) indicate not only her location but also the chronological passage of time: "*As* I walk along, a sharp smell . . . fills my nostrils" (3); "*After* a few minutes, the trail suddenly opens up . . ." (4); "*Below* me, green grasses wave . . ." (5). And to call attention to the creek's serene beauty, Marie saves for last the description of the peace she feels while floating in the creek.

An inappropriate figure of speech.   Although the four body paragraphs focus on the distinctive qualities of each location, Marie runs into a minor problem in the third paragraph. Take a moment to reread that paragraph's last sentence. Comparing the peace of the marsh to the effect of a "soothing drug" is jarring. The effectiveness of Marie's essay hinges on her ability to create a picture of a pure, natural world. A reference to drugs is inappro-priate. Now, reread the paragraph aloud, stopping after "No people come here." Note how much more in keeping with the essay's dominant impression the paragraph is when the reference to drugs is omitted.

Conclusion.   The concluding paragraph brings the essay to a graceful close. The powerful *simile* found in the last sentence contains an implied reference to Thoreau and to Marie's earlier statement about the joy to be found in special places having restorative powers. Such an allusion echoes, with good effect, the paper's opening comments.

Revising the first draft. When Marie met with some class-mates during a group feedback session, the students agreed that Marie's first draft was strong and moving. But they also said that they had difficulty following her route through the marsh; they found her third paragraph especially confusing. Marie kept track of her classmates' comments on a separate piece of paper and then entered them, numbered in order of importance, in the margin of her first draft. Reprinted here is the original version of Marie's third paragraph.

Original Version of the Third Paragraph

As I head out to the marsh from the house, I follow a short trail through the woods. A smell of salt mixed with the aroma of soil fills my nostrils. The end of the trail suddenly opens up to a view that calms me no matter how upset or discouraged I might be: a line of tall waving reeds bordering the salt marsh creek. Civilization seems far away as I walk the path of flattened grass and finally reach my goal, the salt marsh creek hidden behind the tall waving reeds. The path changes with the seasons; sometimes I walk in the brilliant green of spring, sometimes in the tawny gold of autumn, sometimes in the quiet grayish-tan of winter. In some areas, the grass is flat-tened into swirls that make the marsh resemble one of those paint-ings by Van Gogh. No people come here. The peacefulness heals me like a soothing drug. The path stops at the line of tall waving reeds, standing upright at the border of the creek. I part the reeds to get to the creek.

When Marie looked more carefully at the paragraph, she agreed it was confusing. For one thing, the paragraph's third and fourth sentences indicated that she had come to the path's end and had reached the reeds bordering the creek. In the following sentences, however, she was on the path again. Then, at the end, she was back at the creek, as if she had just arrived there. Marie resolved this confusion by breaking the single paragraph into two separate ones — the first describing the walk along the path, the second describing her arrival at the creek. This restructuring, especially when combined with clearer transitions, eliminated the confusion.

While revising her essay, Marie also intensified the sensory images in her original paragraph. She changed the "smell of salt and soil" to the "sharp smell of salt mixed with the rich aroma of peaty soil." And when she added the phrase "thick Van Gogh brush strokes that curve and recurve in circular patterns," she made the comparison between the marsh grass and a Van Gogh painting more vivid.

These are just some of the changes Marie made while rewriting her paper. Her skillful revisions provided the polish needed to make an already strong essay even more evocative.

All the selections ahead use description to make their subjects come alive and to provide supporting evidence for a controlling idea or impression. Gordon Parks's "Flavio's Home" assaults the reader with the sights, sounds, and smells of the Brazilian slum that is home to one sickly boy. Russell Baker's "In My Day" is a wistful memoir of the author's aging mother. Annie Dillard's "In the Jungle" depicts the timeless quality of primeval places. In "Once More to the Lake," E. B. White recalls his youth when visiting a childhood vacation spot with his son. Finally, in "Manzanar," Jeanne Wakatsuki Houston and James D. Houston describe an ordinary, middle-class town — except that it happens to be a prison for its Japanese-American residents.

Gordon Parks

The son of deeply religious tenant farmers, Gordon Parks
(1912–) grew up in Kansas knowing both the comforts of
familial love and the torments of poverty and racism. Sent as a
teenager to live with his sister in Minnesota after his mother's
death, Parks was thrown out on his own in a frigid winter by
his brother-in-law. To support himself, Parks worked as a jani-
tor in a flophouse and as a piano player in a bordello. These
and other odd jobs gave Parks the means to buy his first
camera. Fascinated by photographic images, Parks studied the
masters and eventually developed his own powers as a photographer. So evocative were his photographic studies that both
Life and *Vogue* brought him on staff, the first black photographer to be hired by the two magazines. Parks's prodigious
creativity has found expression in filmmaking (*Shaft*), musical
composition (both classical and jazz), fiction, nonfiction, and
poetry (titles include *The Learning Tree, A Choice of Weapons*,
and *To Smile in Autumn*, published, respectively, in 1986,
1987, and 1988). But it is Parks's photographic essays, covering five decades of American life, that have brought him the
most acclaim. In the following essay, taken from his 1990
autobiography, *Voices in the Mirror*, Parks tells the story behind
one of his most memorable photographic works.

Flavio's Home

On the outskirts of Rio de Janeiro, Brazil, seven hundred
thousand people live in the slums known as *favelas*. Sent to
one *favela* by *Life* magazine, photographer Gordon Parks
found a twelve-year-old boy, Flavio da Silva, whose story spoke
volumes about the horrors of poverty. Parks's photo-essay on
Flavio generated an unprecedented response from *Life* readers.
Indeed, they sent so much money to the da Silvas that the
family was able to leave the *favela* for better living conditions.
Parks brought Flavio to the United States for medical treatment, and the boy's health was restored. However, Flavio's
story didn't have an unqualifiedly happy ending. Although he
overcame his illness and later married and had a family, Flavio

continuously fantasized about returning to the United States, convinced that only by returning to America could he improve his life. His obsession eventually eroded the promise of his life in Brazil.

I've never lost my fierce grudge against poverty. It is the   1
most savage of all human afflictions, claiming victims who can't mobilize their efforts against it, who often lack strength to digest what little food they scrounge up to survive. It keeps growing, multiplying, spreading like a cancer. In my wanderings I attack it wherever I can — in barrios, slums and favelas.

Catacumba was the name of the favela where I found Flavio   2
da Silva. It was wickedly hot. The noon sun baked the mud-rot of the wet mountainside. Garbage and human excrement clogged the open sewers snaking down the slopes. José Gallo, a *Life* reporter, and I rested in the shade of a jacaranda tree halfway up Rio de Janeiro's most infamous deathtrap. Below and above us were a maze of shacks, but in the distance alongside the beach stood the gleaming white homes of the rich.

Breathing hard, balancing a tin of water on his head, a small   3
boy climbed toward us. He was miserably thin, naked but for filthy denim shorts. His legs resembled sticks covered with skin and screwed into his feet. Death was all over him, in his sunken eyes, cheeks and jaundiced coloring. He stopped for breath, coughing, his chest heaving as water slopped over his bony shoulders. Then jerking sideways like a mechanical toy, he smiled a smile I will never forget. Turning, he went on up the mountainside.

The detailed *Life* assignment in my back pocket was to find   4
an impoverished father with a family, to examine his earnings, political leanings, religion, friends, dreams and frustrations. I had been sent to do an essay on poverty. This frail boy bent under his load said more to me about poverty than a dozen poor fathers. I touched Gallo, and we got up and followed the boy to where he entered a shack near the top of the mountainside. It was a leaning crumpled place of old plankings with a rusted tin roof. From inside we heard the babblings of several children. José knocked. The door opened and the boy stood smiling with a bawling naked baby in his arms.

Still smiling, he whacked the baby's rump, invited us in and   5
offered us a box to sit on. The only other recognizable furniture
was a sagging bed and a broken baby's crib. Flavio was twelve,
and with Gallo acting as interpreter, he introduced his younger
brothers and sisters: "Mario, the bad one; Baptista, the good one;
Albia, Isabel and the baby Zacarias." Two other girls burst into
the shack, screaming and pounding on one another. Flavio
jumped in and parted them. "Shut up, you two." He pointed at
the older girl. "That's Maria, the nasty one." She spit in his face.
He smacked her and pointed to the smaller sister. "That's Luzia.
She thinks she's pretty."

Having finished the introductions, he went to build a fire   6
under the stove—a rusted, bent top of an old gas range resting
on several bricks. Beneath it was a piece of tin that caught the hot
coals. The shack was about six by ten feet. Its grimy walls were a
patchwork of misshapen boards with large gaps between them,
revealing other shacks below stilted against the slopes. The floor,
rotting under layers of grease and dirt, caught shafts of light
slanting down through spaces in the roof. A large hole in the far
corner served as a toilet. Beneath that hole was the sloping
mountainside. Pockets of poverty in New York's Harlem, on
Chicago's south side, in Puerto Rico's infamous El Fungito
seemed pale by comparison. None of them had prepared me for
this one in the favela of Catacumba.

Flavio washed rice in a large dishpan, then washed Zacarias's   7
feet in the same water. But even that dirty water wasn't to be
wasted. He tossed in a chunk of lye soap and ordered each child
to wash up. When they were finished he splashed the water over
the dirty floor, and, dropping to his knees, he scrubbed the planks
until the black suds sank in. Just before sundown he put beans on
the stove to warm, then left, saying he would be back shortly.
"Don't let them burn," he cautioned Maria. "If they do and
Poppa beats me, you'll get it later." Maria, happy to get at the
licking spoon, switched over and began to stir the beans. Then
slyly she dipped out a spoonful and swallowed them. Luzia eyed
her. "I see you. I'm going to tell on you for stealing our supper."

Maria's eyes flashed anger. "You do and I'll beat you, you   8
little bitch." Luzia threw a stick at Maria and fled out the door.
Zacarias dropped off to sleep. Mario, the bad one, slouched in a
corner and sucked his thumb. Isabel and Albia sat on the floor

clinging to each other with a strange tenderness. Isabel held onto Albia's hair and Albia clutched at Isabel's neck. They appeared frozen in an act of quiet violence.

Flavio returned with wood, dumped it beside the stove and   9
sat down to rest for a few minutes, then went down the mountain for more water. It was dark when he finally came back, his body sagging from exhaustion. No longer smiling, he suddenly had the look of an old man and by now we could see that he kept the family going. In the closed torment of that pitiful shack, he was waging a hopeless battle against starvation. The da Silva children were living in a coffin.

When at last the parents came in, Gallo and I seemed to be   10
part of the family. Flavio had already told them we were there. "Gordunn Americano!" Luzia said, pointing at me. José, the father, viewed us with skepticism. Nair, his pregnant wife, seemed tired beyond speaking. Hardly acknowledging our presence, she picked up Zacarias, placed him on her shoulder and gently patted his behind. Flavio scurried about like a frightened rat, his silence plainly expressing the fear he held of his father. Impatiently, José da Silva waited for Flavio to serve dinner. He sat in the center of the bed with his legs crossed beneath him, frowning, waiting. There were only three tin plates. Flavio filled them with black beans and rice, then placed them before his father. José da Silva tasted them, chewed for several moments, then nodded his approval for the others to start. Only he and Nair had spoons; the children ate with their fingers. Flavio ate off the top of a coffee can. Afraid to offer us food, he edged his rice and beans toward us, gesturing for us to take some. We refused. He smiled, knowing we understood.

Later, when we got down to the difficult business of obtain-   11
ing permission from José da Silva to photograph his family, he hemmed and hawed, wallowing in the pleasant authority of the decision maker. He finally gave in, but his manner told us that he expected something in return. As we were saying good night Flavio began to cough violently. For a few moments his lungs seemed to be tearing apart. I wanted to get away as quickly as possible. It was cowardly of me, but the bluish cast of his skin beneath the sweat, the choking and spitting were suddenly unbearable.

Gallo and I moved cautiously down through the darkness   12 trying not to appear as strangers. The Catacumba was no place for strangers after sundown. Desperate criminals hid out there. To hunt them out, the police came in packs, but only in daylight. Gallo cautioned me. "If you get caught up here after dark it's best to stay at the da Silvas' until morning." As we drove toward the city the large white buildings of the rich loomed up. The world behind us seemed like a bad dream. I had already decided to get the boy Flavio to a doctor, and as quickly as possible.

The plush lobby of my hotel on the Copacabana waterfront   13
was crammed with people in formal attire. With the stink of the favela in my clothes, I hurried to the elevator hoping no passengers would be aboard. But as the door was closing a beautiful girl in a white lace gown stepped in. I moved as far away as possible. Her escort entered behind her, swept her into his arms and they indulged in a kiss that lasted until they exited on the next floor. Neither of them seemed to realize that I was there. The room I returned to seemed to be oversized; the da Silva shack would have fitted into one corner of it. The steak dinner I had would have fed the da Silvas for three days.

Billowing clouds blanketed Mount Corcovado as we ap-   14
proached the favela the following morning. Suddenly the sun burst through, silhouetting Cristo Redentor, the towering sculpture of Christ with arms extended, its back turned against the slopes of Catacumba. The square at the entrance to the favela bustled with hundreds of favelados. Long lines waited at the sole water spigot. Others waited at the only toilet on the entire mountainside. Women, unable to pay for soap, beat dirt from their wash at laundry tubs. Men, burdened with lumber, picks and shovels and tools important to their existence threaded their way through the noisy throngs. Dogs snarled, barked and fought. Woodsmoke mixed with the stench of rotting things. In the mist curling over the higher paths, columns of favelados climbed like ants with wood and water cans on their heads.

We came upon Nair bent over her tub of wash. She wiped   15
away sweat with her apron and managed a smile. We asked for her husband and she pointed to a tiny shack off to her right. This was José's store, where he sold kerosene and bleach. He was sitting on a box, dozing. Sensing our presence, he awoke and commenced complaining about his back. "It kills me. The doctors don't help

because I have no money. Always talk and a little pink pill that does no good. Ah, what is to become of me?" A woman came to buy bleach. He filled her bottle. She dropped a few coins and as she walked away his eyes stayed on her backside until she was out of sight. Then he was complaining about his back again.

"How much do you earn a day?" Gallo asked.   16

"Seventy-five cents. On a good day maybe a dollar."   17

"Why aren't the kids in school?"   18

"I don't have money for the clothes they need to go to   19
school."

"Has Flavio seen a doctor?"   20

He pointed to a one-story wooden building. "That's the   21
clinic right there. They're mad because I built my store in front of their place. I won't tear it down so they won't help my kids. Talk, talk, talk and pink pills." We bid him good-bye and started climbing, following mud trails, jutting rock, slime-filled holes and shack after shack propped against the slopes on shaky pilings. We sidestepped a dead cat covered with maggots. I held my breath for an instant, only to inhale the stench of human excrement and garbage. Bare feet and legs with open sores climbed above us — evils of the terrible soil they trod every day, and there were seven hundred thousand or more afflicted people in favelas around Rio alone. Touching me, Gallo pointed to Flavio climbing ahead of us carrying firewood. He stopped to glance at a man descending with a small coffin on his shoulder. A woman and a small child followed him. When I lifted my camera, grumbling erupted from a group of men sharing beer beneath a tree.

"They're threatening," Gallo said. "Keep moving. They fear   22
cameras. Think they're evil eyes bringing bad luck." Turning to watch the funeral procession, Flavio caught sight of us and waited. When we took the wood from him he protested, saying he was used to carrying it. He gave in when I hung my camera around his neck. Then, beaming, he climbed on ahead of us.

The fog had lifted and in the crisp morning light the shack   23
looked more squalid. Inside the kids seemed even noisier. Flavio smiled and spoke above their racket. "Someday I want to live in a real house on a real street with good pots and pans and a bed with sheets." He lit the fire to warm leftovers from the night before. Stale rice and beans — for breakfast and supper. No lunch; mid-day eating was out of the question. Smoke rose and curled up

through the ceiling's cracks. An air current forced it back, filling the place and Flavio's lungs with fumes. A coughing spasm doubled him up, turned his skin blue under viscous sweat. I handed him a cup of water, but he waved it away. His stomach tightened as he dropped to his knees. His veins throbbed as if they would burst. Frustrated, we could only watch; there was nothing we could do to help. Strangely, none of his brothers or sisters appeared to notice. None of them stopped doing whatever they were doing. Perhaps they had seen it too often. After five interminable minutes it was over, and he got to his feet, smiling as though it had all been a joke. "Maria, it's time for Zacarias to be washed!"

"But there's rice in the pan!"   24

"Dump it in another pan — and don't spill water!"   25

Maria picked up Zacarias, who screamed, not wanting to be   26
washed. Irritated, Maria gave him a solid smack on his bare bottom. Flavio stepped over and gave her the same, then a free-for-all started with Flavio, Maria and Mario slinging fists at one another. Mario got one in the eye and fled the shack calling Flavio a dirty son-of-a-bitch. Zacarias wound up on the floor sucking his thumb and escaping his washing. The black bean and rice breakfast helped to get things back to normal. Now it was time to get Flavio to the doctor.

The clinic was crowded with patients — mothers and chil-   27
dren covered with open sores, a paralytic teenager, a man with an ear in a state of decay, an aged blind couple holding hands in doubled darkness. Throughout the place came wailings of hunger and hurt. Flavio sat nervously between Gallo and me. "What will the doctor do to me?" he kept asking.

"We'll see. We'll wait and see."   28

In all, there were over fifty people. Finally, after two hours, it   29
was Flavio's turn and he broke out in a sweat, though he smiled at the nurse as he passed through the door to the doctor's office. The nurse ignored it; in this place of misery, smiles were unexpected.

The doctor, a large, beady-eyed man with a crew cut, had an   30
air of impatience. Hardly acknowledging our presence, he began to examine the frightened Flavio. "Open your mouth. Say 'Ah.' Jump up and down. Breathe out. Take off those pants. Bend over. Stand up. Cough. Cough louder. Louder." He did it all with such

cold efficiency. Then he spoke to us in English so Flavio wouldn't understand. "This little chap has just about had it." My heart sank. Flavio was smiling, happy to be over with the examination. He was handed a bottle of cough medicine and a small box of pink pills, then asked to step outside and wait.

"This the da Silva kid?"   31

"Yes."   32

"What's your interest in him?"   33

"We want to help in some way."   34

"I'm afraid you're too late. He's wasted with bronchial   35
asthma, malnutrition and, I suspect, tuberculosis. His heart,
lungs and teeth are all bad." He paused and wearily rubbed his
forehead. "All that at the ripe old age of twelve. And these hills
are packed with other kids just as bad off. Last year ten thousand
died from dysentery alone. But what can we do? You saw what's
waiting outside. It's like this every day. There's hardly enough
money to buy aspirin. A few wealthy people who care help keep us
going." He was quiet for a moment. "Maybe the right climate,
the right diet, and constant medical care might. . . ." He
stopped and shook his head. "Naw. That poor lad's finished. He
might last another year — maybe not." We thanked him and left.

"What did he say?" Flavio asked as we scaled the hill.   36

"Everything's going to be all right, Flav. There's nothing to   37
worry about."

It had clouded over again by the time we reached the top.   38
The rain swept in, clearing the mountain of Corcovado. The huge
Christ figure loomed up again with clouds swirling around it.
And to it I said a quick prayer for the boy walking beside us. He
smiled as if he had read my thoughts. "Papa says 'El Cristo' has
turned his back on the favela."

"You're going to be all right, Flavio."   39

"I'm not scared of death. It's my brothers and sisters I worry   40
about. What would they do?"

"You'll be all right, Flavio."   41

Questions for Close Reading

1. What is the selection's thesis (or dominant impression)? Locate the sentence(s) in which Parks states his main idea. If he doesn't state the thesis explicitly, express it in your own words.

2. What is Flavio's family like? Why does Flavio have so much responsibility in the household?
3. What are some of the distinctive characteristics of Flavio's neighborhood and home?
4. What seems to be the basis of Flavio's fear of giving food to Parks and Gallo? What did Parks and Gallo understand that led them to refuse?
5. Refer to your dictionary as needed to define the following words used in the selection: *barrios* (paragraph 1), *jacaranda* (2), *jaundiced* (3), and *spigot* (14).

Questions About the Writer's Craft

1. **The Pattern.** Without stating it explicitly, Parks conveys a dominant impression about Flavio. What is that impression? What details create it?
2. **Other Patterns.** When relating how Flavio performs numerous household tasks, Parks describes several processes. How do these step-by-step explanations reinforce Parks's dominant impression of Flavio?
3. Parks provides numerous sensory specifics to depict Flavio's home. Look closely, for example, at the description in paragraph 6. Which words and phrases convey strong sensory images? How does Parks use transitions to help the reader move from one sensory image to another?
4. Paragraph 13 includes a scene that occurs in Parks's hotel. What's the effect of this scene? What does it contribute to the essay that the most detailed description of the *favela* could not?

Questions for Further Thought

1. Examine the scene in which Flavio's parents return to the shack (paragraph 10). Why do you think the da Silva parents treat their children as they do? How do you feel about the way the parents interact with their children?
2. Parks feels it was cowardly of him to want "to get away as quickly as possible" when Flavio was seized by a coughing spell. Do you agree with Parks's self-assessment? Why or why not?
3. The *favela*, which isn't far from the "gleaming white homes of the rich," is on the outskirts of a major city, Rio de Janeiro. Do you think there's something about large cities that desensitizes affluent people to the plight of the poverty-stricken? Would people in small towns be more sensitive? Why or why not?
4. Flavio's family, already suffering terrible deprivation, can hardly afford another child, yet Flavio's mother is once again pregnant. Some

people argue that one way to help break the poverty cycle is to pay financial incentives to poor women to use birth control. Why do you think such a policy is controversial? What are your views on this approach to the problem of poverty?

Writing Assignments Using Description as a Pattern of Development

∞ 1. Parks paints a wrenching portrait of a person who remains vibrant and hopeful even though he is suffering greatly—from physical illness, poverty, overwork, and worry. Write a description about someone you know who has shown courage or other positive qualities during a time of personal trouble. Include, as Parks does, plentiful details about the person's appearance and behavior so that you don't have to state directly what you admire about the person. Maya Angelou's "Grandmother's Victory" (page 158) shows how one writer conveys the special quality of an admirable individual.

2. Parks presents an unforgettable description of the *favela* and the living conditions there. Write an essay about a region, city, neighborhood, or building that also projects an overwhelming negative feeling. Include only those details that convey your dominant impression, and provide—as Parks does—vivid sensory language to convey your attitude toward your subject.

Writing Assignments Using Other Patterns of Development

∞ 3. The doctor reports that a few wealthy people contribute to the clinic, but the reader can tell from the scene in Parks's hotel that most people are insensitive to those less fortunate. Write an essay describing a specific situation that you feel reflects people's tendency to ignore the difficulties of others. Analyze why people distance themselves from the problem; then present specific steps that could be taken to sensitize them to the situation. Jonathan Kozol's "Are the Homeless Crazy?" (page 515) and Mark Twain's "The Damned Human Race" (page 619) will provide some perspective on the way people harden themselves to the pain of others.

4. Although Parks celebrates Flavio's generosity of spirit, the writer also illustrates the brutalizing effect of an impoverished environment. Prepare an essay in which you also show that setting, architecture, even furnishings can influence mood and behavior. You may, as Parks does, focus on the corrosive effect of a negative environment, or you may write about the nurturing effect of a positive environment. Possible subjects include a park in the middle of a city, a bus terminal, and a college library.

Russell Baker

In his regular column "The Observer" for the *New York Times*, Russell Baker applies his unique brand of humor to social commentary. Born in Virginia in 1925, Baker received his B.A. from Johns Hopkins University and spent several years working as a reporter for the *Baltimore Sun* before joining the *Times* in the mid-1950s. In 1979, Baker won a Pulitzer Prize, journalism's highest honor. Baker's columns have been collected in several books, including *No Cause for Panic* (1969), *Poor Russell's Almanac* (1972), and *So This Is Depravity* (1980). Baker has written a widely read and critically acclaimed two-volume autobiography, *Growing Up* (1982), which was awarded a Pulitzer Prize, and *The Good Times* (1989). The following selection is taken from *Growing Up*.

In My Day

We often expect the most from — and are most intolerant of — the people we depended on when we were young. In the following selection, Russell Baker describes his aging mother and the tangled feelings she arouses in him as she takes refuge in her memories. Her mental deterioration leads Baker to ponder the weaving of past and present that flows through all families.

At the age of eighty my mother had her last bad fall, and after that her mind wandered free through time. Some days she went to weddings and funerals that had taken place half a century earlier. On others she presided over family dinners cooked on Sunday afternoons for children who were now gray with age. Through all this she lay in bed but moved across time, traveling among the dead decades with a speed and ease beyond the gift of physical science.

"Where's Russell?" she asked one day when I came to visit at the nursing home.

"I'm Russell," I said.

She gazed at this improbably overgrown figure out of an 4
inconceivable future and promptly dismissed it.

"Russell's only this big," she said, holding her hand, palm 5
down, two feet from the floor. That day she was a young country
wife with chickens in the backyard and a view of hazy blue Virginia mountains behind the apple orchard, and I was a stranger
old enough to be her father.

Early one morning she phoned me in New York. "Are you 6
coming to my funeral today?" she asked.

It was an awkward question with which to be awakened. 7
"What are you talking about, for God's sake?" was the best reply I
could manage.

"I'm being buried today," she declared briskly, as though 8
announcing an important social event.

"I'll phone you back," I said and hung up, and when I did 9
phone back she was all right, although she wasn't all right, of
course, and we all knew she wasn't.

She had always been a small woman — short, light-boned, 10
delicately structured — but now, under the white hospital sheet,
she was becoming tiny. I thought of a doll with huge, fierce eyes.
There had always been a fierceness in her. It showed in that angry,
challenging thrust of the chin when she issued an opinion, and a
great one she had always been for issuing opinions.

"I tell people exactly what's on my mind," she had been fond 11
of boasting. "I tell them what I think, whether they like it or
not." Often they had not liked it. She could be sarcastic to people
in whom she detected evidence of the ignoramus or the fool.

"It's not always good policy to tell people exactly what's on 12
your mind," I used to caution her.

"If they don't like it, that's too bad," was her customary 13
reply, "because that's the way I am."

And so she was. A formidable woman. Determined to speak 14
her mind, determined to have her way, determined to bend those
who opposed her. In that time when I had known her best, my
mother had hurled herself at life with chin thrust forward, eyes
blazing, and an energy that made her seem always on the run.

She ran after squawking chickens, an axe in her hand, deter- 15
mined on a beheading that would put dinner in the pot. She ran
when she made the beds, ran when she set the table. One Thanks-
giving she burned herself badly when, running up from the cellar

oven with the ceremonial turkey, she tripped on the stairs and tumbled back down, ending at the bottom in the debris of giblets, hot gravy, and battered turkey. Life was combat, and victory was not to the lazy, the timid, the slugabed, the drugstore cowboy, the libertine, the mushmouth afraid to tell people exactly what was on his mind whether people liked it or not. She ran.

But now the running was over. For a time I could not accept   16
the inevitable. As I sat by her bed, my impulse was to argue her back to reality. On my first visit to the hospital in Baltimore, she asked who I was.

"Russell," I said.   17

"Russell's way out west," she advised me.   18

"No, I'm right here."   19

"Guess where I came from today?" was her response.   20

"Where?"   21

"All the way from New Jersey."   22

"When?"   23

"Tonight."   24

"No. You've been in the hospital for three days," I insisted.   25

"I suggest the thing to do is calm down a little bit," she   26
replied. "Go over to the house and shut the door."

Now she was years deep into the past, living in the neighbor-   27
hood where she had settled forty years earlier, and she had just been talking with Mrs. Hoffman, a neighbor across the street.

"It's like Mrs. Hoffman said today: The children always   28
wander back to where they come from," she remarked.

"Mrs. Hoffman has been dead for fifteen years."   29

"Russ got married today," she replied.   30

"I got married in 1950," I said, which was the fact.   31

"The house is unlocked," she said.   32

So it went until a doctor came by to give one of those oral   33
quizzes that medical men apply in such cases. She failed cata-strophically, giving wrong answers or none at all to "What day is this?" "Do you know where you are?" "How old are you?" and so on. Then, a surprise.

"When is your birthday?" he asked.   34

"November 5, 1897," she said. Correct. Absolutely correct.   35

"How do you remember that?" the doctor asked.   36

"Because I was born on Guy Fawkes Day," she said.   37

"Guy Fawkes?" asked the doctor. "Who is Guy Fawkes?"   38

She replied with a rhyme I had heard her recite time and   39
again over the years when the subject of her birth date arose:

> "*Please to remember the Fifth of November,*
> *Gunpowder treason and plot.*
> *I see no reason why gunpowder treason*
> *Should ever be forgot.*"

Then she glared at this young doctor so ill informed about Guy
Fawkes' failed scheme to blow King James off his throne with
barrels of gunpowder in 1605. She had been a schoolteacher, after
all, and knew how to glare at a dolt. "You may know a lot about
medicine, but you obviously don't know any history," she said.
Having told him exactly what was on her mind, she left us again.

The doctors diagnosed a hopeless senility. Not unusual, they   40
said. "Hardening of the arteries" was the explanation for laymen.
I thought it was more complicated than that. For ten years or
more the ferocity with which she had once attacked life had been
turning to a rage against the weakness, the boredom, and the
absence of love that too much age had brought her. Now, after
the last bad fall, she seemed to have broken chains that imprisoned her in a life she had come to hate and to return to a time
inhabited by people who loved her, a time in which she was
needed. Gradually I understood. It was the first time in years I
had seen her happy.

She had written a letter three years earlier which explained   41
more than "hardening of the arteries." I had gone down from
New York to Baltimore, where she lived, for one of my infrequent
visits and, afterwards, had written her with some banal advice to
look for the silver lining, to count her blessings instead of bur-
dening others with her miseries. I suppose what it really
amounted to was a threat that if she was not more cheerful during
my visits I would not come to see her very often. Sons are capable
of such letters. This one was written out of a childish faith in the
eternal strength of parents, a naive belief that age and wear could
be overcome by an effort of will, that all she needed was a good
pep talk to recharge a flagging spirit. It was such a foolish,
innocent idea, but one thinks of parents differently from other
people. Other people can become frail and break, but not parents.

She wrote back in an unusually cheery vein intended to   42

demonstrate, I suppose, that she was mending her ways. She was never a woman to apologize, but for one moment with the pen in her hand she came very close. Referring to my visit, she wrote: "If I seemed unhappy to you at times — " Here she drew back, reconsidered, and said something quite different:

"If I seemed unhappy to you at times, I am, but there's really   43
nothing anyone can do about it, because I'm just so very tired and lonely that I'll just go to sleep and forget it." She was then seventy-eight.

Now, three years later, after the last bad fall, she had man-   44
aged to forget the fatigue and loneliness and, in these free-wheeling excursions back through time, to recapture happiness. I soon stopped trying to wrest her back to what I considered the real world and tried to travel along with her on those fantastic swoops into the past. One day when I arrived at her bedside she was radiant.

"Feeling good today," I said.   45

"Why shouldn't I feel good?" she asked. "Papa's going to   46
take me up to Baltimore on the boat today."

At that moment she was a young girl standing on a wharf at   47
Merry Point, Virginia, waiting for the Chesapeake Bay steamer with her father, who had been dead sixty-one years. William Howard Taft was in the White House, Europe still drowsed in the dusk of the great century of peace, America was a young country, and the future stretched before it in beams of crystal sunlight. "The greatest country on God's green earth," her father might have said, if I had been able to step into my mother's time machine and join him on the wharf with the satchels packed for Baltimore.

I could imagine her there quite clearly. She was wearing a   48
blue dress with big puffy sleeves and long black stockings. There was a ribbon in her hair and a big bow tied on the side of her head. There had been a childhood photograph in her bedroom which showed all this, although the colors of course had been added years later by a restorer who tinted the picture.

About her father, my grandfather, I could only guess, and   49
indeed, about the girl on the wharf with the bow in her hair, I was merely sentimentalizing. Of my mother's childhood and her people, of their time and place, I knew very little. A world had lived and died, and though it was part of my blood and bone I knew

little more about it than I knew of the world of the pharaohs. It was useless now to ask for help from my mother. The orbits of her mind rarely touched present interrogators for more than a moment.

Sitting at her bedside, forever out of touch with her, I wondered about my own children, and their children, and children in general, and about the disconnections between children and parents that prevent them from knowing each other. Children rarely want to know who their parents were before they were parents, and when age finally stirs their curiosity there is no parent left to tell them. If a parent does lift the curtain a bit, it is often only to stun the young with some exemplary tale of how much harder life was in the old days. 50

I had been guilty of this when my children were small in the early 1960s and living the affluent life. It galled me that their childhoods should be, as I thought, so easy when my own had been, as I thought, so hard. I had developed the habit, when they complained about the steak being overcooked or the television being cut off, of lecturing them on the harshness of life in my day. 51

"In my day all we got for dinner was macaroni and cheese, and we were glad to get it." 52

"In my day we didn't have any television." 53

"In my day . . ." 54

"In my day . . ." 55

At dinner one evening a son had offended me with an inadequate report card, and as I leaned back and cleared my throat to lecture, he gazed at me with an expression of unutterable resignation and said, "Tell me how it was in your days, Dad." 56

I was angry with him for that, but angrier with myself for having become one of those ancient bores whose highly selective memories of the past become transparently dishonest even to small children. I tried to break the habit, but must have failed. A few years later my son was referring to me when I was out of earshot as "the old-timer." Between us there was a dispute about time. He looked upon the time that had been my future in a disturbing way. My future was his past, and being young, he was indifferent to the past. 57

As I hovered over my mother's bed listening for muffled signals from her childhood, I realized that this same dispute had existed between her and me. When she was young, with life ahead 58 of her, I had been her future and resented it. Instinctively, I wanted to break free, cease being a creature defined by her time, consign her future to the past, and create my own. Well, I had finally done that, and then with my own children I had seen my exciting future become their boring past.

These hopeless end-of-the-line visits with my mother made   59 me wish I had not thrown off my own past so carelessly. We all come from the past, and children ought to know what it was that went into their making, to know that life is a braided cord of humanity stretching up from time long gone, and that it cannot be defined by the span of a single journey from diaper to shroud.

Questions for Close Reading

1. What is the selection's thesis (or dominant impression)? Locate the sentence(s) in which Baker states his main idea. If he doesn't state the thesis explicitly, express it in your own words.
2. What was Mrs. Baker's philosophy of life? How did it change in her old age?
3. Why does Baker feel "forever out of touch" with his mother? Does he feel equally out of touch with his children?
4. Why does Baker stop trying to get his eighty-year-old mother to return to the real world? Is he being kind or unkind?
5. Refer to your dictionary as needed to define the following words used in the selection: *inconceivable* (paragraph 4), *libertine* (15), *banal* (41), *wrest* (44), *exemplary* (50), *galled* (51), and *consign* (58).

Questions About the Writer's Craft

1. **The pattern.** How does the series of scenes in "In My Day" develop the essay's dominant impression?
2. Baker describes his mother by using details about her actions and her appearance, as well as by quoting things she said. Both are typical techniques for revealing character in a descriptive piece. Which technique is more effective in conveying Mrs. Baker's personality?
3. In paragraph 15, Baker repeats the word *ran* when describing his mother's energy. He also speaks several times of her *falls*. What do you think might have been Baker's purpose for repeating these words? What do they suggest about the pattern of his mother's life?
4. If something is *ironic*, there is a discrepancy between what is said and what is known. In paragraph 28, Mrs. Baker says, "The children always wander back to where they come from." How is this comment

by Baker's mother ironic? Find some other examples of irony in the essay.

Questions for Further Thought

1. Baker writes, "Other people can become frail and break, but not parents" (41). What does he mean? What illusions do we have about our parents?
2. On the whole, would you say Russell Baker has been a good son? A good father? What do you think he would do differently if he had another chance? Will reading this essay affect your behavior toward your parents or children?
3. Baker feels that there is no way for parents and children truly to know each other. Do you agree or not — and why?
4. Is it inevitable that children will reject their parents' values and their parents' lives? What forms might this rejection take?

Writing Assignments Using Description as a Pattern of Development

∞ 1. Write a description of a parent or relative at a certain age, for example, "My Brother at Fourteen" or "My Mother at Fifty-five." Your description should create a dominant impression by conveying the person's characteristic approach to life. Be sure to select lively details that support this dominant impression. Before planning your paper, you might want to read Maya Angelou's "My Grandmother's Victory" (page 158), an essay that pays loving tribute to an indomitable figure.
2. Describe one or more active, vital older people who have not retreated into the past to find happiness. Your examples could be people you know, people you have heard about, or people in the public eye. Choose vivid details that show how such people's actions and attitudes keep them "young." Draw some conclusions about what older people can do to stay involved with life.

Writing Assignments Using Other Patterns of Development

3. Russell Baker's essay concerns a crisis in his family. Write an essay about a crisis situation in a family — your own or someone else's. The crisis might be a divorce, serious or chronic illness, loss of a job, financial difficulties, or some other serious problem. Your essay might explore the causes and/or effects of the crisis; it might outline

the steps the family has taken to deal with the crisis; it might be a narrative that points to some conclusion about how people deal with crises.

4. In the past, most elderly parents lived in an extended family—children, grandchildren, and other relatives were all part of a single household. Today, though, many old people are isolated from families. In addition, our society—unlike some others—doesn't seem to revere older people; indeed, we often disregard their experience, wisdom, and traditions. Write an essay showing how society's attitude toward older people affects the lives of both the old and the young.

Annie Dillard

Pilgrim at Tinker Creek (1974) is probably Annie Dillard's best-known work. A collection of lyrical observations and reflections about the natural world, *Pilgrim* was awarded a Pulitzer Prize for general nonfiction. Born in 1945, Dillard is currently Adjunct Professor at Wesleyan University in Connecticut and a contributing editor at *Harper's*. Over the years, she has published a variety of books: *Tickets for a Prayer Wheel* (1974), a book of poetry; *Holy the Firm* (1978) and *Teaching a Stone to Talk* (1982), both collections of essays; *Living by Fiction* (1982), literary criticism; *Encounters With Chinese Writers* (1984), narrative nonfiction; *An American Childhood* (1987), an autobiography; and *The Writing Life* (1989), miscellaneous reflections on writing. "In the Jungle" is taken from *Teaching a Stone to Talk*.

In the Jungle

In the world inhabited by most North Americans, the quality of life is often defined in terms of possessions: cars, stereos, apartments. But in the Ecuadorian jungle, Annie Dillard discovers that such items have no meaning. Indeed, the richness of the rain forest underscores how impoverished contemporary life may be.

Like any out-of-the-way place, the Napo River in the Ecua- 1 dorian jungle seems real enough when you are there, even central. Out of the way of *what*? I was sitting on a stump at the edge of a bankside palm-thatch village, in the middle of the night, on the headwaters of the Amazon. Out of the way of human life, tenderness, or the glance of heaven?

A nightjar in a deep-leaved shadow called three long notes, 2 and hushed. The men with me talked softly in clumps: three North Americans, four Ecuadorians who were showing us the jungle. We were holding cool drinks and idly watching a hand-sized tarantula seize moths that came to the lone bulb on the generator shed beside us.

It was February, the middle of summer. Green fireflies spat- 3 tered lights across the air and illumined for seconds, now here, now there, the pale trunks of enormous, solitary trees. Beneath us the brown Napo River was rising, in all silence; it coiled up the sandy bank and tangled its foam in vines that trailed from the forest and roots that looped the shore.

Each breath of night smelled sweet, more moistened and 4 sweet than any kitchen, or garden, or cradle. Each star in Orion seemed to tremble and stir with my breath. All at once, in the thatch house across the clearing behind us, one of the village's Jesuit priests began playing an alto recorder, playing a wordless song, lyric, in a minor key, that twined over the village clearing, that caught in the big trees' canopies, muted our talk on the bankside, and wandered over the river, dissolving downstream.

This will do, I thought. This will do, for a weekend, or a 5 season, or a home.

Later that night I loosed my hair from its braids and combed 6 it smooth—not for myself, but so the village girls could play with it in the morning.

We had disembarked at the village that afternoon, and I had 7 slumped on some shaded steps, wishing I knew some Spanish or some Quechua so I could speak with the ring of little girls who were alternately staring at me and smiling at their toes. I spoke anyway, and fooled with my hair, which they were obviously dying to get their hands on, and laughed, and soon they were all braiding my hair, all five of them, all fifty fingers, all my hair, even my bangs. And then they took it apart and did it again, laughing, and teaching me Spanish nouns, and meeting my eyes and each other's with open delight, while their small brothers in blue jeans climbed down from the trees and began kicking a volleyball around with one of the North American men.

Now, as I combed my hair in the little tent, another of the 8 men, a free-lance writer from Manhattan, was talking quietly. He was telling us the tale of his life, describing his work in Holly-wood, his apartment in Manhattan, his house in Paris. . . . "It makes me wonder," he said, "what I'm doing in a tent under a tree in the village of Pompeya, on the Napo River, in the jungle of

Ecuador." After a pause he added, "It makes me wonder why I'm going *back*."

The point of going somewhere like the Napo River in Ecua-   9
dor is not to see the most spectacular anything. It is simply to see
what is there. We are here on the planet only once, and might as
well get a feel for the place. We might as well get a feel for the
fringes and hollows in which life is lived, for the Amazon basin,
which covers half a continent, and for the life that—there, like
anywhere else—is always and necessarily lived in detail: on the
tributaries, in the riverside villages, sucking this particular white-
fleshed guava in this particular pattern of shade.

What is there is interesting. The Napo River itself is wide (I   10
mean wider than the Mississippi at Davenport) and brown,
opaque, and smeared with floating foam and logs and branches
from the jungle. White egrets hunch on shoreline deadfalls and
parrots in flocks dart in and out of the light. Under the water in
the river, unseen, are anacondas—which are reputed to take a
few village toddlers every year—and water boas, stingrays, croco-
diles, manatees, and sweet-meated fish.

Low water bares gray strips of sandbar on which the natives   11
build tiny palm-thatch shelters, arched, the size of pup tents, for
overnight fishing trips. You see these extraordinarily clean people
(who bathe twice a day in the river, and whose straight black hair
is always freshly washed) paddling down the river in dugout
canoes, hugging the banks.

Some of the Indians of this region, earlier in the century,   12
used to sleep naked in hammocks. The nights are cold. Gordon
MacCreach, an American explorer in these Amazon tributaries,
reported that he was startled to hear the Indians get up at three in
the morning. He was even more startled, night after night, to
hear them walk down to the river slowly, half asleep, and bathe in
the water. Only later did he learn what they were doing: they were
getting warm. The cold woke them; they warmed their skins in
the river, which was always ninety degrees; then they returned to
their hammocks and slept through the rest of the night.

The riverbanks are low, and from the river you see an unbro-   13
ken wall of dark forest in every direction, from the Andes to the
Atlantic. You get a taste for looking at trees: trees hung with the
swinging nests of yellow troupials, trees from which ant nests
the size of grain sacks hang like black goiters, trees from which

seven-colored tanagers flutter, coral trees, teak, balsa and bread-
fruit, enormous emergent silk-cotton trees, and the pale-barked
samona palms.

When you are inside the jungle, away from the river, the trees   14
vault out of sight. It is hard to remember to look up the long
trunks and see the fans, strips, fronds, and sprays of glossy leaves.
Inside the jungle you are more likely to notice the snarl of
climbers and creepers round the trees' boles, the flowering bro-
meliads and epiphytes in every bough's crook, and the fantastic
silk-cotton tree trunks thirty or forty feet across, trunks buttressed
in flanges of wood whose curves can make three high walls of a
room — a shady, loamy-aired room where you would gladly live,
or die. Butterflies, iridescent blue, striped, or clear-winged, thread
the jungle paths at eye level. And at your feet is a swath of ants
bearing triangular bits of green leaf. The ants with their leaves
look like a wide fleet of sailing dinghies — but they don't quit. In
either direction they wobble over the jungle floor as far as the eye
can see. I followed them off the path as far as I dared, and never
saw an end to ants or to those luffing chips of green they bore.

Unseen in the jungle, but present, are tapirs, jaguars, many   15
species of snake and lizard, ocelots, armadillos, marmosets,
howler monkeys, toucans and macaws and a hundred other birds,
deer, bats, peccaries, capybaras, agoutis, and sloths. Also present
in this jungle, but variously distant, are Texaco derricks and
pipelines, and some of the wildest Indians in the world, blow-
gun-using Indians, who killed missionaries in 1956 and ate them.

Long lakes shine in the jungle. We traveled one of these in   16
dugout canoes, canoes with two inches of freeboard, canoes pad-
dled with machete-hewn oars chopped from buttresses of silk-cotton trees, or poled in the shallows with peeled cane or bamboo.
Our part-Indian guide had cleared the path to the lake the day
before; when we walked the path we saw where he had impaled
the lopped head of a boa, open-mouthed, on a pointed stick by
the canoes, for decoration.

The lake was wonderful. Herons, egrets, and ibises plodded   17
the sawgrass shores, kingfishers and cuckoos clattered from sunlight to shade, great turkeylike birds fussed in dead branches, and
hawks lolled overhead. There was all the time in the world. A
turtle slid into the water. The boy in the bow of my canoe slapped
stones at birds with a simple sling, a rubber throng and leather

pad. He aimed brilliantly at moving targets, always, and always missed; the birds were out of range. He stuffed his sling back in his shirt. I looked around.

The lake and river waters are as opaque as rain-forest leaves; they are veils, blinds, painted screens. You see things only by their effects. I saw the shoreline water roil and the sawgrass heave above a thrashing *paichi*, an enormous black fish of these waters; one had been caught the previous week weighing 430 pounds. Piranha fish live in the lakes, and electric eels. I dangled my fingers in the water, figuring it would be worth it.   18

We would eat chicken that night in the village, and rice, yucca, onions, beets, and heaps of fruit. The sun would ring down, pulling darkness after it like a curtain. Twilight is short, and the unseen birds of twilight wistful, uncanny, catching the heart. The two nuns in their dazzling white habits — the beautiful-boned young nun and the warm-faced old — would glide to the open cane-and-thatch schoolroom in darkness, and start the children singing. The children would sing in piping Spanish, highpitched and pure; they would sing "Nearer My God to Thee" in Quechua, very fast. (To reciprocate, we sang for them "Old MacDonald Had a Farm"; I thought they might recognize the animal sounds. Of course they thought we were out of our minds.) As the children became excited by their own singing, they left their log benches and swarmed around the nuns, hopping, smiling at us, everyone smiling, the nuns' faces bursting in their cowls, and the clear-voiced children still singing, and the palm-leafed roofing stirred.   19

The Napo River: it is not out of the way. It is *in* the way, catching sunlight the way a cup catches poured water; it is a bowl of sweet air, a basin of greenness, and of grace, and, it would seem, of peace.   20

Questions for Close Reading

1. What is the selection's thesis (or dominant impression)? Locate the sentence(s) in which Dillard states her main idea. If she doesn't state the thesis explicitly, express it in your own words.
2. To what extent do the non-natives of the Ecuadorian jungle — the North Americans, priests, and nuns — harmonize with the place and its Indian inhabitants? Are there any times the non-natives seem out of place or ludicrous? When?

3. What can we infer about Dillard's attitude toward the natives who display severed snake heads, sling stones at birds, and eat other human beings?

4. Although Dillard writes that the Napo River is a place "of peace" (paragraph 20), an undercurrent of menace runs throughout her essay. Where does she mention threatening possibilities? What do these dangers suggest about the jungle? About life?

5. Refer to your dictionary as needed to define the following words used in the selection: *tributary* (paragraphs 9 and 12), *opaque* (10, 18), *bole* (14), *buttressed* (14), *derrick* (15), and *impaled* (16).

Questions About the Writer's Craft

1. **The pattern.** In descriptive essays, writers often use a fairly straight-forward organizational structure. Why doesn't Dillard use strict chronological, sensory, spatial, or emphatic order to structure her essay? Why, for example, does she delay the account of her arrival until paragraph 7?

2. Dillard is a master of rich sensory detail. For instance, she writes that the Napo River "coiled up the sandy bank and tangled its foam in vines" (paragraph 3). Find additional examples of words and phrases that appeal powerfully to the senses. How do these word choices support Dillard's thesis?

3. **Other patterns.** Dillard contrasts descriptions of the sweet and peaceful directly with descriptions of the sinister and violent. In one sentence, for example, she matter-of-factly mentions refreshing drinks and a tarantula attacking its prey. Find other instances of such startling juxtapositions. What do they suggest about the jungle? About life?

4. Although Dillard relies heavily on visual details, she also refers repeatedly to the invisibly present (paragraphs 10, 14, 15, 18). What is her purpose in reminding readers of what is unseen?

Questions for Further Thought

1. Dillard seems to accept all creatures and behaviors as a natural part of life. Do you have the same attitude, or are you more judgmental? What are the dangers of being either too judgmental or too accepting?

2. What effect does Dillard's not understanding Spanish or Quechua have on her experience with the natives? Were you ever in a region where you didn't understand the language? What effect did this have on your impression of the place?

3. Were you disturbed when you read about the moths being eaten by

the tarantula? Were you more disturbed when you read about the boy attempting to pelt the birds with stones? Or perhaps only the references to cannibalism and human-eating animals upset you. What might your reactions reveal about your attitude toward living things?

4. Dillard depicts a continuous cycle of life and death in which chronological time is of little importance. Do you feel society is too conscious of schedules and deadlines? If you think it is, what do we lose by such regimentation? What do we gain?

Writing Assignments Using Description as a Pattern of Development

∞ 1. Dillard suggests that many of us feel frazzled by our everyday lives. Where do you go when you want to get away from it all? Do you shut yourself in your room and turn on the music? Do you go to a gym? Write an essay describing where you feel most at peace. Like Dillard, use vivid sensory details and figurative language to convey your paper's dominant impression. Before writing the essay, you might want to read Anne Morrow Lindbergh's "Channelled Whelk" (page 219), an essay filled with rich descriptive details of a peaceful place.

∞ 2. Write a description of a place that seems ugly, harmful, or otherwise offensive—cigarette stubs and debris on the beach, tipped-over trash cans and cracked sidewalks in a nearby neighborhood. Organized around a clear dominant impression, your description should capture the look, smell, sound, and feel of this unpleasant place. Use the description to make a point about humans' interaction with their environment. Gordon Parks's "Flavio's Home" (page 96) might give you some good ideas for your essay.

Writing Assignments Using Other Patterns of Development

3. Write an essay arguing that living in what Dillard calls "out of the way places" is superior to city living. Or take the opposing stance and argue that urban living is preferable. Support your contention through vivid examples of the inconvenience, danger, and unhappiness experienced by those dwelling in the area you find unpleasant. The essay's tone may be serious or playful. One part of the paper, perhaps the introduction, should recognize the opposing viewpoint.

4. Dillard seems to suffer little or no culture shock in the Ecuadorian jungle. Narrate a time you felt out of place—in a new school, foreign country, another region of the country, a stranger's home. To show what happened, focus on the experience's humorous, embarrassing, or threatening elements. What did the experience teach you about yourself and your ability to adapt?

E. B. White

Elwyn Brooks White (1899–1985) is considered one of America's finest essayists. For many years, White was a member of the *New Yorker* magazine staff and wrote the magazine's popular column, "The Talk of the Town." He also wrote children's books, including the classic *Charlotte's Web* (1952), and was the coauthor with William Strunk, Jr., of the renowned guide for writers, *The Elements of Style* (1959). But most memorable are the essays White produced during his life — gems of clarity, wit, and heartfelt expression. White's contribution to literature earned him many awards, including the Presidential Medal of Freedom and the National Medal for Literature. The classic essay reprinted here is taken from *The Essays of E. B. White* (1977).

Once More to the Lake

In this celebrated essay, E. B. White describes his return to a vacation spot he had known intimately in his childhood, a cabin on a lake in Maine. This time White is accompanied by his son. In many ways the lake, the cabin, and the surrounding fields and woods are the same, but in other respects they are different. With great skill, White describes his past and present experiences at the lake, exploring the nature of life cycles and of change itself.

One summer, along about 1904, my father rented a camp on 1
a lake in Maine and took us all there for the month of August. We all got ringworm from some kittens and had to rub Pond's Extract on our arms and legs night and morning, and my father rolled over in a canoe with all his clothes on; but outside of that the vacation was a success and from then on none of us ever thought there was any place in the world like that lake in Maine. We returned summer after summer — always on August 1 for one month. I have since become a salt-water man, but sometimes in

summer there are days when the restlessness of the tides and the
fearful cold of the sea water and the incessant wind that blows
across the afternoon and into the evening make me wish for the
placidity of a lake in the woods. A few weeks ago this feeling got
so strong I bought myself a couple of bass hooks and a spinner
and returned to the lake where we used to go, for a week's fishing
and to revisit old haunts. *"the boy" could be him*

I took along my son, who had never had any fresh water up   2
his nose and who had seen lily pads only from train windows. On
the journey over to the lake I began to wonder what it would be
like. I wondered how time would have marred this unique, this
holy spot — the coves and streams, the hills that the sun set
behind, the camps and the paths behind the camps. I was sure that
the tarred road would have found it out, and I wondered in what
other ways it would be desolated. It is strange how much you can
remember about places like that once you allow your mind to
return into the grooves that lead back. You remember one thing,
and that suddenly reminds you of another thing. I guess I remembered clearest of all the early mornings, when the lake was
cool and motionless, remembered how the bedroom smelled of
the lumber it was made of and of the wet woods whose scent
entered through the screen. The partitions in the camp were thin
and did not extend clear to the top of the rooms, and as I was
always the first up I would dress softly so as not to wake the
others, and sneak out into the sweet outdoors and start out in the
canoe, keeping close along the shore in the long shadows of
the pines. I remembered being very careful never to rub my
paddle against the gunwale for fear of disturbing the stillness of
the cathedral.

The lake had never been what you would call a wild lake.   3
There were cottages sprinkled around the shores, and it was in
farming country although the shores of the lake were quite heavily wooded. Some of the cottages were owned by nearby farmers,
and you would live at the shore and eat your meals at the farmhouse. That's what our family did. But although it wasn't wild, it
was a fairly large and undisturbed lake and there were places in it
that, to a child at least, seemed infinitely remote and primeval.

I was right about the tar: it led to within half a mile of the   4
shore. But when I got back there, with my boy, and we settled
into a camp near a farmhouse and into the kind of summertime I

had known, I could tell that it was going to be pretty much the same as it had been before—I knew it, lying in bed the first morning, smelling the bedroom and hearing the boy sneak quietly out and go off along the shore in a boat. I began to sustain the illusion that he was I, and therefore, by simple transposition, that I was my father. This sensation persisted, kept cropping up all the time we were there. It was not an entirely new feeling, but in this setting it grew much stronger. I seemed to be living a dual existence. I would be in the middle of some simple act, I would be picking up a bait box or laying down a table fork, or I would be saying something, and suddenly it would be not I but my father who was saying the words or making the gesture. It gave me a creepy sensation.

We went fishing the first morning. I felt the same damp moss covering the worms in the bait can, and saw the dragonfly alight on the tip of my rod as it hovered a few inches from the surface of the water. It was the arrival of this fly that convinced me beyond any doubt that everything was as it always had been, that the years were a mirage and that there had been no years. The small waves were the same, chucking the rowboat under the chin as we fished at anchor, and the boat was the same boat, the same color green and the ribs broken in the same places, and under the floorboards the same fresh-water leavings and débris—the dead helgramite, the wisps of moss, the rusty discarded fishhook, the dried blood from yesterday's catch. We stared silently at the tips of our rods, at the dragonflies that came and went. I lowered the tip of mine into the water, tentatively, pensively dislodging the fly, which darted two feet away, poised, darted two feet back, and came to rest again a little farther up the rod. There had been no years between the ducking of this dragonfly and the other one—the one that was part of memory. I looked at the boy, who was silently watching his fly, and it was my hands that held his rod, my eyes watching. I felt dizzy and didn't know which rod I was at the end of.

We caught two bass, hauling them in briskly as though they were mackerel, pulling them over the side of the boat in a businesslike manner without any landing net, and stunning them with a blow on the back of the head. When we got back for a swim before lunch, the lake was exactly where we had left it, the same number of inches from the dock, and there was only the merest suggestion of a breeze. This seemed an utterly enchanted sea, this lake you could leave to its own devices for a few hours and come back to, and find that it had not stirred, this constant and trustworthy body of water. In the shallows, the dark, water-soaked sticks and twigs, smooth and old, were undulating in clusters on the bottom against the clean ribbed sand, and the track of the mussel was plain. A school of minnows swam by, each minnow with its small individual shadow, doubling the attendance, so clear and sharp in the sunlight. Some of the other campers were in swimming, along the shore, one of them with a cake of soap, and the water felt thin and clear and unsubstantial. Over the years there had been this person with the cake of soap, this cultist, and here he was. There had been no years.

Up to the farmhouse to dinner through the teeming, dusty   7
field, the road under our sneakers was only a two-track road. The middle track was missing, the one with the marks of the hooves and the splotches of dried, flaky manure. There had always been three tracks to choose from in choosing which track to walk in; now the choice was narrowed down to two. For a moment I missed terribly the middle alternative. But the way led past the tennis court, and something about the way it lay there in the sun reassured me; the tape had loosened along the backline, the alleys were green with plantains and other weeds, and the net (installed in June and removed in September) sagged in the dry noon, and the whole place steamed with midday heat and hunger and emptiness. There was a choice of pie for dessert, and one was blueberry and one was apple, and the waitresses were the same country girls, there having been no passage of time, only the illusion of it as in a dropped curtain — the waitresses were still fifteen; their hair had been washed, that was the only difference — they had been to the movies and seen the pretty girls with the clean hair.

Summertime, oh, summertime, pattern of life indelible, the   8
fade-proof lake, the woods unshatterable, the pasture with the sweetfern and the juniper forever and ever, summer without end; this was the background, and the life along the shore was the design, the cottagers with their innocent and tranquil design, their tiny docks with the flagpole and the American flag floating against the white clouds in the blue sky, the little paths over the roots of the trees leading from camp to camp and the paths leading back to the outhouses and the can of lime for sprinkling,

and at the souvenir counters at the store the miniature birch-bark canoes and the postcards that showed things looking a little better than they looked. This was the American family at play, escaping the city heat, wondering whether the newcomers in the camp at the head of the cove were "common" or "nice," wondering whether it was true that the people who drove up for Sunday dinner at the farmhouse were turned away because there wasn't enough chicken.

It seemed to me, as I kept remembering all this, that those 9 times and those summers had been infinitely precious and worth saving. There had been jollity and peace and goodness. The arriving (at the beginning of August) had been so big a business in itself, at the railway station the farm wagon drawn up, the first smell of the pine-laden air, the first glimpse of the smiling farmer, and the great importance of the trunks and your father's enormous authority in such matters, and the feel of the wagon under you for the long ten-mile haul, and at the top of the last long hill catching the first view of the lake after eleven months of not seeing this cherished body of water. The shouts and cries of the other campers when they saw you, and the trunks to be unpacked, to give up their rich burden. (Arriving was less exciting nowadays, when you sneaked up in your car and parked it under a tree near the camp and took out the bags and in five minutes it was all over, no fuss, no loud wonderful fuss about trunks.)

Peace and goodness and jollity. The only thing that was 10 wrong now, really, was the sound of the place, an unfamiliar nervous sound of the outboard motors. This was the note that jarred, the one thing that would sometimes break the illusion and set the years moving. In those other summertimes all motors were inboard; and when they were at a little distance, the noise they made was a sedative, an ingredient of summer sleep. They were one-cylinder and two-cylinder engines, and some were make-and-break and some were jump-spark, but they all made a sleepy sound across the lake. The one-lungers throbbed and fluttered, and the twin-cylinder ones purred and purred, and that was a quiet sound, too. But now the campers all had outboards. In the daytime, in the hot mornings, these motors made a petulant, irritable sound; at night, in the still evening when the afterglow lit the water, they whined about one's ears like mosquitoes. My boy loved our rented outboard, and his great desire was to achieve single-handed mastery over it, and authority, and he soon learned the trick of choking it a little (but not too much), and the adjustment of the needle valve. Watching him I would remember the things you could do with the old one-cylinder engine with the heavy flywheel, how you could have it eating out of your hand if you got really close to it spiritually. Motorboats in those days didn't have clutches, and you would make a landing by shutting off the motor at the proper time and coasting in with a dead rudder. But there was a way of reversing them, if you learned the trick, by cutting the switch and putting it on again exactly on the final dying revolution of the flywheel, so that it would kick back against compression and begin reversing. Approaching a dock in a strong following breeze, it was difficult to slow up sufficiently by the ordinary coasting method, and if a boy felt he had complete mastery over his motor, he was tempted to keep it running beyond its time and then reverse it a few feet from the dock. It took a cool nerve, because if you threw the switch a twentieth of a second too soon you would catch the flywheel when it still had speed enough to go up past center, and the boat would leap ahead, charging bullfashion at the dock.

We had a good week at the camp. The bass were biting well   11 and the sun shone endlessly, day after day. We would be tired at night and lie down in the accumulated heat of the little bedrooms after the long hot day and the breeze would stir almost imperceptibly outside and the smell of the swamp drift in through the rusty screens. Sleep would come easily and in the morning the red squirrel would be on the roof, tapping out his gay routine. I kept remembering everything, lying in bed in the mornings — the small steamboat that had a long rounded stern like the lip of a Ubangi, and how quietly she ran on the moonlight sails, when the older boys played their mandolins and the girls sang and we ate doughnuts dipped in sugar, and how sweet the music was on the water in the shining night, and what it had felt like to think about girls then. After breakfast we would go up to the store and the things were in the same place — the minnows in a bottle, the plugs and spinners disarranged and pawed over by the youngsters from the boys' camp, the Fig Newtons and the Beeman's gum. Outside, the road was tarred and cars stood in front of the store.

Inside, all was just as it had always been, except there was more Coca-Cola and not so much Moxie and root beer and birch beer and sarsaparilla. We would walk out with the bottle of pop apiece and sometimes the pop would backfire up our noses and hurt. We explored the streams, quietly, where the turtles slid off the sunny logs and dug their way into the soft bottom; and we lay on the town wharf and fed worms to the tame bass. Everywhere we went I had trouble making out which was I, the one walking at my side, the one walking in my pants.

One afternoon while we were there at the lake a thunder-storm came up. It was like the revival of an old melodrama that I had seen long ago with childish awe. The second-act climax of the drama of the electrical disturbance over a lake in America had not changed in any important respect. This was the big scene, still the big scene. The whole thing was so familiar, the first feeling of oppression and heat and a general air around camp of not want-ing to go very far away. In midafternoon (it was all the same) a curious darkening of the sky, and a lull in everything that had made life tick; and then the way the boats suddenly swung the other way at their moorings with the coming of a breeze out of the new quarter, and premonitory rumble. Then the kettle drum, then the snare, then the bass drum and cymbals, then cackling light against the dark, and the gods grinning and licking their chops in the hills. Afterward the calm, the rain steadily rustling in the calm lake, the return of light and hope and spirits, and the campers running out in joy and relief to go swimming in the rain, their bright cries perpetuating the deathless joke about how they were getting simply drenched, and the children screaming with delight at the new sensation of bathing in the rain, and the joke about getting drenched linking the generations in a strong inde-structible chain. And the comedian who waded in carrying an umbrella.

When the others went swimming, my son said he was going in, too. He pulled his dripping trunks from the line where they had hung all through the shower and wrung them out. Languidly, and with no thought of going in, I watched him, his hard little body, skinny and bare, saw him wince slightly as he pulled up around his vitals the small, soggy, icy garment. As he buckled the swollen belt, suddenly my groin felt the chill of death.

Questions for Close Reading

1. What is the selection's thesis (or dominant impression)? Locate the sentence(s) in which White states his main idea. If he doesn't state the thesis explicitly, express it in your own words.
2. Why does White return to the lake in Maine he had visited as a child? Why do you think he has waited to revisit it until he has a young son to bring along?
3. Several times in the essay, White notes that he felt as if he were his own father—and that his son became his childhood self. What event first prompts this sensation? What actions and thoughts cause it to recur?
4. How is the latest visit to the lake similar to White's childhood summers? What differences does White notice? What effects do the differences have on him?
5. Refer to your dictionary as needed to define the following words used in the selection: *incessant* (paragraph 1), *placidity* (1), *primeval* (3), *transposition* (4), *undulating* (6), *indelible* (8), *petulant* (10), and *languidly* (13).

Questions About the Writer's Craft

1. **The pattern.** Through vivid language, descriptive writing evokes sensory experiences. In "Once More to the Lake," White overlays two sets of sensory details: those of the present-day lake and those of the lake as it was in his boyhood. Which set of details is more objective? Which seems sharper and more powerful? Why?
2. To describe the lake, White chooses many words and phrases with religious connotations. Give some examples. What might have been his purpose in using such language?
3. **Other patterns.** In paragraph 12, White uses a metaphor to describe a thunderstorm. To what does he compare a thunderstorm? Why does he make this comparison?
4. White refers to "the chill of death" in the final paragraph. What brings on this feeling? Why does he feel it "in his groin"? Where has this idea been hinted at previously in the essay?

Questions for Further Thought

1. In paragraph 9, White says about his boyhood visits to the lake that "those times and those summers had been infinitely precious and worth saving." From your own perspective, what makes an experience worth savoring and storing in the memory?

2. When White refers to his son, he never uses the boy's first name (he calls him "the boy" or "my boy"); only in the last scene does he call him "my son." Why do you think White uses this impersonal form of reference? Would this essay have been different if the author's child had been a girl?

3. In your opinion, was the visit to the lake a good experience for White — or a bad one? In general, is it or is it not a good idea to try to relive the past?

4. This essay touches on a universal human feeling — the sensation that time is slipping by, that our lives are spinning out their allotted spans. When do people first become aware of their own mortality? What events or phases of life heighten this feeling?

Writing Assignments Using Description as a Pattern of Development

1. Write an essay describing a special place in your life. The place need not be a natural setting like White's lake; it could be a city or building that has meant a great deal to you. Use sensory details and figurative language, as White does, to enliven your description and convey the place's significance for you.

∞ 2. White was fortunate that his lake had remained virtually unchanged. But many other special spots have been destroyed or are threatened with destruction. Write an essay describing a place (a park, a school, an old-fashioned ice cream parlor) that is "infinitely precious and worth saving." For your dominant theme, show which aspects of your subject make it worthy of being preserved for future generations. Before writing your essay, you might want to read Rachel Carson's "A Fable for Tomorrow" (page 421), an essay that laments the loss of a special place.

Writing Assignments Using Other Patterns of Development

3. Sometimes, we, like White, are suddenly reminded of the nearness of death: a crushed animal lies in the road, a politician is assassinated, a classmate is killed in a car crash. Write an essay about a time you were forced to think about mortality. Explain what happened and describe your thoughts and feelings afterwards.

4. Have your older relatives attempted to share with you some special experiences of their younger years? Have you done the same thing

with your own children, nephews, or nieces? You may have taken loved ones to a special place, as White did, or listened to stories or looked at photographs. Write an essay recounting such an experience. Explain the motivations of the older generation and the effects on the younger one.

Jeanne Wakatsuki Houston and James D. Houston

Jeanne Wakatsuki Houston was born in California in 1934. During the Second World War, she and her family, along with 120,000 other Japanese-Americans, were confined to government-run internment camps. She graduated from San Jose State University and later attended the Sorbonne in Paris. James D. Houston, born in 1933, graduated from San Jose State University and Stanford University. Primarily a novelist, he has taught writing at several universities. The couple married in 1956 and later coauthored *Farewell to Manzanar: A True Story of Japanese American Experience During and After the World War II Internment* (1973). The book and the screenplay based on it have received several honors, including the Humanities Prize, the Christopher Award, and the National Women's Political Caucus Award. The following selection is a chapter from *Farewell to Manzanar*.

Manzanar

Although there was no evidence of subversion, soon after the bombing of Pearl Harbor, President Franklin D. Roosevelt authorized the expulsion of West Coast Japanese-Americans —many of them born in this country—from their homes and businesses. Much has been written about the subsequent imprisonment of the Japanese-Americans in compounds surrounded by barbed wire and armed guards. But there's a special power to the reminiscences of an adult who, as a child, was forced to call such an internment center "home." Jeanne Wakatsuki Houston and James D. Houston provide us with a child's-eye view of the camp, its residents, and their dogged attempts to live normal lives in an abnormal setting.

132

In Spanish, Manzanar means "apple orchard." Great 1
stretches of Owens Valley were once green with orchards and
alfalfa fields. It has been a desert ever since its water started
flowing south into Los Angeles, sometime during the twenties.
But a few rows of untended pear and apple trees were still growing there when the camp opened, where a shallow water table had
kept them alive. In the spring of 1943 we moved to Block 28,
right up next to one of the old pear orchards. That's where we
stayed until the end of the war, and those trees stand in my
memory for the turning of our life in camp, from the outrageous
to the tolerable.

Papa pruned and cared for the nearest trees. Late that sum- 2
mer we picked the fruit green and stored it in a root cellar he had
dug under our new barracks. At night the wind through the leaves
would sound like the surf had sounded in Ocean Park, and while
drifting off to sleep I could almost imagine we were still living by
the beach.

Mama had set up this move. Block 28 was also close to the 3
camp hospital. For the most part, people lived there who had to
have easy access to it. Mama's connection was her job as dietician.
A whole half of one barracks had fallen empty when another
family relocated. Mama hustled us in there almost before they'd
snapped their suitcases shut.

For all the pain it caused, the loyalty oath[1] finally did speed 4
up the relocation program. One result was a gradual easing of the
congestion in the barracks. A shrewd househunter like Mama
could set things up fairly comfortably — by Manzanar standards
—if she kept her eyes open. But you had to move fast. As soon as
the word got around that so-and-so had been cleared to leave,
there would be a kind of tribal restlessness, a nervous rise in the
level of neighborhood gossip as wives jockeyed for position to see
who would get the empty cubicles.

---

[1]The U.S. government required Japanese-Americans to sign an oath pledging
unqualified allegiance to the United States. Outraged by the implication of possible disloyalty, many Japanese-Americans refused to sign the oath, creating a
painful rift within the Japanese-American community. Some internees who *did*
sign the loyalty oath were permitted to leave the camps — if they had a job away
from the West Coast and were fortunate enough to secure an inland sponsor.

In Block 28 we doubled our living space—four rooms for   5
the twelve of us. Ray and Woody[2] walled them with sheetrock.
We had ceilings this time, and linoleum floors of solid maroon.
You had three colors to choose from—maroon, black, and forest
green—and there was plenty of it around by this time. Some
families would vie with one another for the most elegant floor
designs, obtaining a roll of each color from the supply shed,
cutting it into diamonds, squares, or triangles, shining it with
heating oil, then leaving their doors open so that passers-by could
admire the handiwork.

Papa brought his still with him when we moved. He set it up   6
behind the door, where he continued to brew his own sake and
brandy. He wasn't drinking as much now, though. He spent a lot
of time outdoors. Like many of the older Issei men, he didn't take
a regular job in camp. He puttered. He had been working hard for
thirty years and, bad as it was for him in some ways, camp did
allow him time to dabble with hobbies he would never had found
time for otherwise.

Once the first year's turmoil cooled down, the authorities   7
started letting us outside the wire for recreation. Papa used to
hike along the creeks that channeled down from the base of the
Sierras. He brought back chunks of driftwood, and he would pass
long hours sitting on the steps carving myrtle limbs into benches,
table legs, and lamps, filling our rooms with bits of gnarled,
polished furniture.

He hauled stones in off the desert and built a small rock   8
garden outside our doorway, with succulents and a patch of
moss. Near it he laid flat steppingstones leading to the stairs.

He also painted watercolors. Until this time I had not known   9
he could paint. He loved to sketch the mountains. If anything
made that country habitable it was the mountains themselves,
purple when the sun dropped and so sharply etched in the morning light the granite dazzled almost more than the bright snow
lacing it. The nearest peaks rose ten thousand feet higher than the
valley floor, with Whitney, the highest, just off to the south. They
were important for all of us, but especially for the Issei. Whitney
reminded Papa of Fujiyama, that is, it gave him the same kind of
spiritual sustenance. The tremendous beauty of those peaks was

[2]Jeanne Wakatsuki Houston's brothers.

inspirational, as so many natural forms are to the Japanese (the rocks outside our doorway could be those mountains in miniature). They also represented those forces in nature, those powerful and inevitable forces that cannot be resisted, reminding a man that sometimes he must simply endure that which cannot be changed.

Subdued, resigned, Papa's life — all our lives — took on a   10
pattern that would hold for the duration of the war. Public shows of resentment pretty much spent themselves over the loyalty oath crises. *Shikata ga nai*[3] again became the motto, but under altered circumstances. What had to be endured was the climate, the confinement, the steady crumbling away of family life. But the camp itself had been made livable. The government provided for our physical needs. My parents and older brothers and sisters, like most of the internees, accepted their lot and did what they could to make the best of a bad situation. "We're here," Woody would say. "We're here, and there's no use moaning about it forever."

Gardens had sprung up everywhere, in the firebreaks, be   11
tween the rows of barracks — rock gardens, vegetable gardens, cactus and flower gardens. People who lived in Owens Valley during the war still remember the flowers and lush greenery they could see from the highway as they drove past the main gate. The soil around Manzanar is alluvial and very rich. With water siphoned off from the Los Angeles-bound aqueduct, a large farm was under cultivation just outside the camp, providing the mess halls with lettuce, corn, tomatoes, eggplant, string beans, horseradish, and cucumbers. Near Block 28 some of the men who had been professional gardeners built a small park, with mossy nooks, ponds, waterfalls, and curved wooden bridges. Sometimes in the evenings we could walk down the raked gravel paths. You could face away from the barracks, look past a tiny rapids toward the darkening mountains, and for a while not be a prisoner at all. You could hang suspended in some odd, almost lovely land you could not escape from yet almost didn't want to leave.

As the months at Manzanar turned to years, it became a   12
world unto itself, with its own logic and familiar ways. In time, staying there seemed far simpler than moving once again to another, unknown place. It was as if the war were forgotten, our

---

[3]A Japanese phrase meaning "it can't be helped."

reason for being there forgotten. The present, the little bit of busywork you had right in front of you, became the most urgent thing. In such a narrowed world, in order to survive, you learn to contain your rage and your despair, and you try to re-create, as well as you can, your normality, some sense of things continuing. The fact that America had accused us, or excluded us, or imprisoned us, or whatever it might be called, did not change the kind of world we wanted. Most of us were born in this country; we had no other models. Those parks and gardens lent it an oriental character, but in most ways it was a totally equipped American small town, complete with schools, churches, Boy Scouts, beauty parlors, neighborhood gossip, fire and police departments, glee clubs, softball leagues, Abbott and Costello movies, tennis courts, and traveling shows. (I still remember an Indian who turned up one Saturday billing himself as a Sioux chief, wearing bear claws and head feathers. In the firebreak he sang songs and danced his tribal dances while hundreds of us watched.)

In our family, while Papa puttered, Mama made daily rounds   13
to the mess halls, helping young mothers with their feeding, planning diets for the various ailments people suffered from. She wore a bright yellow, longbilled sun hat she had made herself and always kept stiffly starched. Afternoons I would see her coming from blocks away, heading home, her tiny figure warped by heat waves and that bonnet a yellow flower wavering in the glare.

In their disagreement over serving the country, Woody and   14
Papa had struck a kind of compromise. Papa talked him out of volunteering; Woody waited for the army to induct him. Meanwhile he clerked in the co-op general store. Kiyo, nearly thirteen by this time, looked forward to the heavy winds. They moved the sand around and uncovered obsidian arrowheads he could sell to old men in camp for fifty cents apiece. Ray, a few years older, played in the six-man touch football league, sometimes against Caucasian teams who would come in from Lone Pine or Independence. My sister Lillian was in high school and singing with a hillbilly band called the Sierra Stars — jeans, cowboy hats, two guitars, and a tub bass. And my oldest brother, Bill, led a dance band called the Jive Bombers — brass and rhythm, with cardboard fold-out music stands lettered J. B. Dances were held every weekend in one of the recreation halls. Bill played trumpet and took vocals on Glenn Miller arrangements of such tunes as *In the*

Mood, String of Pearls, and *Don't Fence Me In*. He didn't sing *Don't Fence Me In* out of protest, as if trying quietly to mock the authorities. It just happened to be a hit song one year, and they all wanted to be an up-to-date American swing band. They would blast it out into recreation barracks full of bobbysoxed, jitterbugging couples:

> *Oh, give me land, lots of land*
> *Under starry skies above,*
> *Don't fence me in.*
> *Let me ride through the wide*
> *Open country that I love . . .*

Pictures of the band, in their bow ties and jackets, appeared   15
in the high school yearbook for 1943–1944, along with pictures of just about everything else in camp that year. It was called *Our World*. In its pages you see school kids with armloads of books, wearing cardigan sweaters and walking past rows of tarpapered shacks. You see chubby girl yell leaders, pompons flying as they leap with glee. You read about the school play, called *Growing Pains* ". . . the story of a typical American home, in this case that of the McIntyres. They see their boy and girl tossed into the normal awkward growing up stage, but can offer little assistance or direction in their turbulent course . . ." with Shoji Katayama as George McIntyre, Takudo Ando as Terry McIntyre, and Mrs. McIntyre played by Kazuko Nagai.

All the class pictures are in there, from the seventh grade   16
through twelfth, with individual head shots of seniors, their names followed by the names of the high schools they would have graduated from on the outside: Theodore Roosevelt, Thomas Jefferson, Herbert Hoover, Sacred Heart. You see pretty girls on bicycles, chicken yards full of fat pullets, patients back-tilted in dental chairs, lines of laundry, and finally, two large blowups, the first of a high tower with a searchlight, against a Sierra backdrop, the next a two-page endsheet showing a wide path that curves among rows of elm trees. White stones border the path. Two dogs are following an old woman in gardening clothes as she strolls along. She is in the middle distance, small beneath the trees, beneath the snowy peaks. It is winter. All the elms are bare. The scene is both stark and comforting. This path leads toward

one edge of camp, but the wire is out of sight, or out of focus. The tiny woman seems very much at ease. She and her tiny dogs seem almost swallowed by the landscape, or floating in it.

Questions for Close Reading

1. What is the selection's thesis (or dominant impression)? Locate the sentence(s) in which the Houstons state their main idea. If they don't state the thesis explicitly, express it in your own words.
2. How do Jeanne Wakatsuki Houston's parents pass the time at Manzanar? What details of their personalities are revealed by their choices of activities?
3. The authors write that "Papa's life — all our lives — took on a pattern that would hold for the duration of the war" (paragraph 10). What was this pattern? To what extent did it reflect the Japanese origins of those interned?
4. What nature-oriented activities did the Japanese-Americans enjoy at Manzanar? What do these activities say about their attitude toward being confined at the camp?
5. Refer to your dictionary as needed to define the following words used in the selection: *sheetrock* (paragraph 5), *still* (6), *sake* (6), *Issei* (6), *sustenance* (9), *internees* (10), *firebreak* (11), *alluvial* (11), *obsidian* (14), and *pullets* (16).

Questions About the Writers' Craft

1. **The pattern.** Descriptive writing uses imagery that appeals to the senses, especially the sense of sight. The Houstons point out that Papa is a talented painter with watercolors. Locate places where the authors, like Papa, "paint" pictures that linger in the reader's mind. What imagery do the authors use to create these word pictures?
2. **Other patterns.** The Houstons don't focus on the political and moral issues surrounding the internment. Instead, they emphasize the effect that the imprisonment has on the Japanese-Americans. How does this focus on effects help illustrate the *ironies* of life at Manzanar? Which passages help dramatize these ironies? (If you're unsure of the meaning of the word *ironies*, consult the glossary at the back of the book.)
3. Although the authors focus on everyday life at the camp, they also refer a number of times to the mountains outside the camp (paragraphs 9, 11, and 16). What might be the Houstons' purpose for mentioning the mountains? What significance do the mountains have for those interned at Manzanar?

4. The selection ends with a sustained description of the two blow-ups contained in the high school yearbook for 1943–44. What two aspects of detention do these two pictures seem to symbolize? Why might the Houstons have chosen to end the piece with the image of the tiny woman?

Questions for Further Thought

1. Do you think the U.S. government had valid reasons for imprisoning families like Jeanne Wakatsuki Houston's? Why or why not?

2. In 1988, Congress passed a law promising financial reparations ($20,000) to each Japanese-American internment survivor and his or her descendants. Do you think the government should provide such compensation? Explain.

3. Are any people in the world today in a situation parallel to that of Jeanne Wakatsuki Houston and her family? Who are these people? In what way is their situation similar to the wartime experience of the Japanese-Americans? How is it different?

4. The Houstons point out that in order to survive the ordeal of imprisonment, "You learn how to contain your rage and your despair, and you try to re-create . . . your normality, some sense of things continuing." If you and your family were imprisoned simply because of your ancestry, what reactions do you think you would have? What would you need to maintain your emotional stability and a sense of continuity?

Writing Assignments Using Description as a Pattern of Development

1. The Houstons use words to paint sketches and "watercolors" of the residents and the environment of Manzanar. Think about a place whose setting and people inspire strong emotion in you, and use connotative words and specific sensory details to create a "watercolor in words" of this place and its people.

2. Jeanne Wakatsuki's father became a "putterer" during the internment, while her mother worked industriously to serve the community. Write an essay describing either someone who's a "putterer" or someone who's committed to serving others. Like the Houstons, avoid using adjectives that explicitly state the person's distinctive attributes; instead, present telling scenes and significant behaviors to reveal the individual.

Writing Assignments Using Other Patterns of Development

∞ 3. The Houstons describe the drastic effects of anti-Japanese prejudice during the Second World War. Focusing on discriminatory behavior that you have experienced, witnessed, or heard about, write an essay in which you examine the effects of such prejudice on those concerned. Peter Farb's "In Other Words" (page 491), William Raspberry's "The Handicap of Definition" (page 563), and Migdia Chinea-Varela's "My Life as a 'Twofer'" (page 613) should provide some interesting perspectives on the issue.

∞ 4. The Wakatsuki family show strength and industry in the face of a difficult and an unjust situation. You probably know or have heard about individuals who have also responded with courage to adverse circumstances. Write an essay recounting a significant event in the life of a person who persevered despite having to struggle against powerful forces. You may want to read Gordon Parks's "Flavio's Home" (page 96) and Maya Angelou's "Grandmother's Victory" (page 158) to see how other writers have depicted the resilience of the human spirit.

Additional Writing Topics

DESCRIPTION

General Assignments

Write an essay using description to develop any of the following topics. Remember that an effective description focuses on a dominant impression and arranges details in a way that best supports that impression. Your details — vivid and appealing to the senses — should be carefully chosen so that the essay isn't overburdened with material of secondary importance. When writing, keep in mind that varied sentence structure and imaginative figures of speech are ways to make a descriptive piece compelling.

1. A favorite item of clothing
2. The world as a certain kind of animal might see it
3. An athletic shoe or high-heeled shoes
4. An individualist's appearance
5. A coffee shop, bus shelter, newsstand, or some other small place
6. A parade or victory celebration
7. A banana, squash, or other fruit or vegetable
8. A particular drawer in a desk or bureau
9. A houseplant
10. A "media event"
11. A dorm room
12. An elderly person
13. An attractive man or woman
14. A prosthetic device or wheelchair
15. A TV, film, or music celebrity
16. A student lounge
17. A once-in-a-lifetime event
18. The inside of something, such as a cave, boat, shed, or machine
19. A friend, roommate, or other person you know well
20. An essential gadget or a useless gadget

Assignments with a Specific Purpose and Audience

1. For an audience of incoming first-year students, prepare a speech describing registration day at your college. Use specific details to help prepare students for the actual event. Choose an adjective that represents your dominant impression of the experience, and keep that word in mind as you write.

2. As a subscriber to a dating service, you've been asked to submit a description of the kind of person you'd like to meet. Describe your ideal date. Focus on specifics about physical appearance, personal habits, character traits, and interests.

3. Your college has decided to replace an old campus structure (for example, a dorm or dining hall) with a new version. Write a letter of protest to the administration, describing the place so vividly and appealingly that its value and need for preservation are unquestionable.

4. As a staff member of the campus newspaper, you have been asked to write a weekly column of social news and gossip. For your first column, you plan to describe a recent campus event—a dance, party, concert, or other social activity. With a straightforward or tongue-in-cheek tone, describe where the event was held, the appearance of the people who attended, and so on.

5. Students at your college have complained that the course catalog is inaccurate. Its course descriptions are often brief, misleading, or just plain incorrect. You're part of a student-faculty group responsible for revising the catalog. Write a full and accurate description of a course with which you're familiar. Tell exactly what the course is about, who teaches it, and how it is run.

6. As a resident of a particular town, you're angered by the appearance of a certain spot and by the activities that take place there. Write a letter to the town council, describing in detail the undesirable nature of this place (a video arcade, an adult bookstore, a bar, a bus station, a neglected park or beach). End with some suggestions about ways to improve the situation.

4

NARRATION

WHAT IS NARRATION?

Human beings are instinctively storytellers. In prehistoric times, our ancestors huddled around campfires to hear tales of hunting and magic. In ancient times, warriors gathered in halls to listen to bards praise in song the exploits of epic heroes. Things are no different today. Boisterous children invariably settle down to listen when their parents read to them; millions of people tune in day after day to the ongoing drama of their favorite soap operas; vacationers sit motionless on the beach, caught up in the latest best-sellers; and all of us enjoy saying, "Just listen to what happened to me today." Our hunger for storytelling is a basic part of us.

Narration means telling a single story or several related stories. The story can be a means to an end, a way to support a main idea or thesis. For instance, to demonstrate that television has become the constant companion of many children, you might narrate a typical child's day in front of the television—starting with frantic cartoons in the morning and ending with dizzy situation comedies at night. Or to support the point that the college registration process should be reformed, you could tell the tale of a chaotic morning spent trying to enroll in classes.

Narration is powerful. Every public speaker, from politician to classroom teacher, knows that stories capture the attention of listeners as nothing else can. Narration speaks to us strongly because it is about us; we want to know what happened to others, not simply because we're curious, but because their experiences shed light on the nature of our own lives. Narration lends force to opinions, triggers the flow of memory, and evokes places and times in ways that are compelling and affecting.

HOW NARRATION FITS YOUR PURPOSE AND AUDIENCE

Since narratives tell a story, you may think they are found only in novels or short stories. But narration can also appear in essays, sometimes as a supplemental pattern of development. For example, if your purpose in a paper is to *persuade* apathetic readers that airport security regulations must be followed strictly, you might lead off with a brief account of an armed terrorist who easily boarded a plane. In a paper *defining* good teaching, you might keep readers engaged by including satirical anecdotes about one hapless instructor, the antithesis of an effective teacher. An essay on the *effects* of an overburdened judicial system might provide —in an attempt to involve readers—a dramatic account of the way one clearly guilty murderer plea-bargained his way to freedom.

In addition to providing effective support in one section of your paper, narration can also serve as an essay's dominant pattern of development. In fact, most of this chapter shows you how to use a single extended narrative to convey a central point and share with readers you view of what happened. You might choose to narrate the events of a day spent with your three-year-old nephew as a way of revealing how you rediscovered the importance of family life. Or you might relate the story of your roommate's mugging, evoking the powerlessness and terror of being a victim. Any story can form the basis for a narrative essay as long as you convey the essence of the experience and evoke its meaning.

SUGGESTIONS FOR USING NARRATION IN AN ESSAY

The following suggestions will be helpful whether you use narration as a dominant or supportive pattern of development.

1. Identify the conflict in the event. The power of many narratives is rooted in a special kind of tension that "hooks" readers and makes them want to follow the story to its end. This narrative tension is often a by-product of some form of *conflict* within the story. Many narratives revolve around an internal dilemma experienced by a key person in the story. Or the conflict may be between people in the story or between a pivotal character and some social institution or natural phenomenon.

2. Identify the point of the narrative. In *The Adventures of Huckleberry Finn*, Mark Twain warned: "Persons attempting to find a motive in this narrative will be prosecuted; persons attempting to find a moral in it will be banished; persons attempting to find a plot in it will be shot." Twain was, of course, being ironic; his novel's richness lies in its "motives" and "morals." Similarly, when you recount a narrative, it's your responsibility to convey the event's *significance* or *meaning*. In other words, be sure readers are clear about your *narrative point*, or thesis.

Suppose you decide to write about the time you got locked in a mall late at night. Your narrative might focus on the way the mall looked after hours and the way you struggled with mounting terror. But you would also use the narrative to make a point. Perhaps you want to emphasize that fear can be instructive. Or your point might be that malls have a disturbing, surreal underside. You could state this thesis explicitly. ("After hours, the mall shed its cheerful daytime demeanor for a more sinister quality.") Or you could refrain from stating the thesis directly, relying on your details and language to convey the point of the narrative: "The mannequins stared at me with glazed eyes and frozen smiles" and "The steel grates pulled over each store glinted in the cold light, making each shop look like a prison cell."

3. Develop only those details that advance the narrative point. You know from experience that nothing is more boring than a storyteller who gets sidetracked and drags out a story with nonessential details. If a friend started to tell about the time his car broke down in the middle of an expressway — but interrupted his story to complain at length about the slipshod work done by his auto repair shop — you might clench your teeth in annoyance, wishing your friend would hurry up and get back to the interesting part of the story.

Brainstorming ("What happened? When? Where? Who was involved? Why did it happen?") can be valuable for helping you amass narrative details. Then, after generating the specifics, you cull out the nonessential and devote your energies to the key specifics needed to advance your narrative point. When telling a story, you maintain an effective narrative pace by focusing on that point and eliminating details that don't support it. A good narrative depends not only on what is included, but also on what has been left out.

But how do you determine which specifics to omit, which to treat briefly, and which to emphasize? Having a clear sense of your narrative point and knowing your audience are crucial. Assume you're writing a narrative about a disastrous get-acquainted dance sponsored by your college the first week of the academic year. In addition to telling what happened, you want to make a point; perhaps you want to emphasize that, despite the college's good intentions, such "official" events actually make it difficult to meet people. With this purpose in mind, you might write about how stiff and unnatural students seemed, all dressed up in their best clothes; you might narrate snatches of strained conversation you overheard; you might describe the way males gathered on one side of the room, females on the other — reverting to behaviors supposedly abandoned in fifth grade. All these details would support your narrative point.

Because you don't want to get waylaid by detours that lead away from that point, you would leave out details about the topnotch band and the appetizing refreshments at the dance. The music and food may have been surprisingly good, but since these details don't advance the point you want to make, they should be omitted.

You also need to keep your audience in mind when selecting

narrative details. If the audience consists of your instructor and other students — all of them familiar with the new student center where the dance was held — specific details about the center probably wouldn't have to be provided. But imagine that the essay is going to appear in the quarterly magazine published by the college's community relations office. Many of the magazine's readers are former graduates who haven't been on campus for several years. They may need some additional specifics about the student center: its location, how many people it holds, how it is furnished.

As you write, keep asking yourself, "Is this detail or character or snippet of conversation essential? Does my audience need this detail to understand the conflict in the situation? Does this detail advance or intensify the narrative action?" Summarize details that have some importance but do not deserve lengthy treatment ("Two hours went by . . ."). And try to limit *narrative commentary* — statements that tell rather than show what happened — since such remarks interrupt the narrative flow. Focus instead on the specifics that propel action forward in a vigorous way.

Sometimes, especially if the narrative re-creates an event from the past, you won't be able to remember what happened detail for detail. In such a case, you should take advantage of what is called *dramatic license*. Using as a guide your powers of recall as well as the perspective you now have of that particular time, feel free to reshape events to suit your narrative point.

4. Organize the narrative sequence.   All of us know the traditional beginning of fairy tales: "Once upon a time. . . ." Every narrative begins somewhere, presents a span of time, and ends at a certain point. Frequently, you'll want to use a straightforward time order, following the event *chronologically* from beginning to end: first this happened, next this happened, finally this happened.

But sometimes a strict chronological recounting may not be effective — especially if the high point of the narrative gets lost somewhere in the middle of the time sequence. To avoid that possibility, you may want to disrupt chronology, plunge the reader into the middle of the story, and then return in a *flashback* to the beginning of the tale. You're probably familiar with the way flashback is used on television and in film. You see someone appealing to the main character for financial help, then return to an earlier time when both were students in the same class, before learning how the rest of the story unfolds. Narratives can also use *flashforward*. You give readers a glimpse of the future (the main character being jailed) before the story continues in the present (the events leading to the arrest). These techniques shift the story onto several planes and keep it from becoming a step-by-step, predictable account. Reserve flashforwards and flashbacks, however, for crucial incidents only, since breaking out of chronological order acts as emphasis. Here are examples of how flashback and flashforward can be used in narrative writing:

Flashback

Standing behind the wooden counter, Greg wielded his knife expertly as he shucked clams--one every ten seconds--with practiced ease. The scene contrasted sharply with his first day on the job, when his hands broke out in blisters and when splitting each shell was like prying open a safe.

Flashforward

Rushing to move my car from the no-parking zone, I waved a quick good-bye to Karen as she climbed the steps to the bus. I didn't know then that by the time I picked her up at the bus station later that day, she had made a decision that would affect both our lives.

Whether or not you choose to include flashbacks or flashforwards in an essay, remember to limit the time span covered by the narrative. Otherwise, you will have trouble generating the details needed to give the story depth and meaning. Also, regardless of the time sequence you select, organize the tale so it drives toward a strong finish. Be careful that your story doesn't trail off into minor, anticlimactic details.

5. Make the narrative easy to follow.   Describing each distinct action in a separate paragraph helps readers grasp the flow of events. Although narrative essays don't always have conventional topic sentences, each narrative paragraph should have a clear focus. Often this focus is indicated by a sentence early in the paragraph that directs attention to the action taking place. Such a sentence functions as a kind of *informal topic sentence*; the rest of the paragraph then develops that topic sentence. You should also be sure to use time signals when narrating a story. Words like *now, then, next, after*, and *later* ensure that your reader won't get lost as the story progresses.

6. Make the narrative vigorous and immediate. A compelling narrative provides an abundance of specific details, making readers feel as if they're experiencing the story being told. Readers must be able to see, hear, touch, smell, and taste the event you're narrating. *Vivid sensory description* is, therefore, an essential part of an effective narrative. Not only do specific sensory details make writing a pleasure to read—we all enjoy learning the particulars about people, places, and things—but they also give the narrative the stamp of reality. The specifics convince the reader that the event being described actually did, or could, occur.

Compare the following excerpts from a narrative essay. The first version is lifeless and dull; the revised version, packed with sensory images, grabs readers with its sense of foreboding:

That eventful day started out like every other summer day. My sister Tricia and I made several elaborate mudpies, which we decorated with care. A little later on, as we were spraying each other with the garden hose, we heard my father walk up the path.

That sad summer day started out uneventfully enough. My sister Tricia and I spent a few hours mixing and decorating mudpies. Our hands caked with dry mud, we sprinkled each lopsided pie with alternating rows of dandelion and clover petals. Later when the sun got hotter, we tossed our white T-shirts over the red picket fence--forgetting my grandmother's frequent warnings to be more ladylike. Our sweaty backs bared to the sun, we doused each other with icy sprays from the garden hose. Caught up in the primitive pleasure of it all, we barely heard my father as he walked up the garden path, the gravel crunching under his heavy work boots.

A caution: Sensory language enlivens narration, but it also slows the pace. Be sure that the slower pace suits your purpose. For example, a lengthy description fits an account of a leisurely summer vacation but is inappropriate in a tale about a frantic search for a misplaced wallet.

Another way to create an aura of narrative immediacy is to use *dialogue* while telling a story. Our sense of other people comes, in part, from what they say and from the way they sound. Conversational exchanges allow the reader to experience characters directly. Compare the following fragments of a narrative, one with dialogue and one without, noting how much more energetic the second version is.

When I finally found my way back to the campsite, the trail guide commented on my disheveled appearance.

When I finally found my way back to the campsite, the trail guide took one look at me and drawled, "What on earth happened to you, Daniel Boone? You look as though you've been dragged through a haystack backwards."

"I'd look a lot worse if I hadn't run back here. When a bullet whizzes by me, I don't stick around to see who's doing the shooting."

Note that, when using dialogue, you generally begin a new paragraph to indicate a shift from one person's speech to another's (as in the second example above).

Using *varied sentence structure* is another strategy for making narratives lively and vigorous. Sentences that plod along predictably (subject – verb, subject – verb) put readers to sleep. Experiment with your sentences by juggling length and sentence type; mix long and short sentences, simple and complex. Compare the following original and revised versions to get an idea of how effective varied sentence rhythm can be in narrative writing.

Original

The store manager went to the walk-in refrigerator every day. The heavy metal door clanged shut behind her. I had visions of her freezing to death among the hanging carcasses. The shiny door finally swung open. She waddled out.

Revised

Each time the store manager went to the walk-in refrigerator, the heavy metal door clanged shut behind her. Visions of her freezing to death among the hanging carcasses crept into my mind until the shiny door finally swung open and she waddled out.

Original

The yellow-and-blue-striped fish struggled on the line. Its scales shimmered in the sunlight. Its tail waved frantically. I saw its desire to live. I decided to let it go.

Revised

Scales shimmering in the sunlight, tail waving frantically, the yellow-and-blue-striped fish struggled on the line. Seeing its desire to live, I let it go.

Finally, *vigorous verbs* lend energy to narratives. Use active verb forms ("The boss *yelled at* him") rather than passive ones ("He *was yelled at* by the boss"), and try to replace anemic *to be* verbs ("She *was* a good basketball player") with more dynamic constructions ("She *played* basketball well").

7. Keep your point of view and verb tense consistent. All stories have a *narrator*, the person who tells the story. If you, as narrator, tell a story as you experienced it, the story is written in the *first-person point of view* ("*I* saw the dog pull loose"). But if you observed the event (or heard about it from others) and want to tell how someone else experienced the incident, you would use the *third person point of view* ("*Anne* saw the dog pull loose"). Each point of view has advantages and limitations. First person allows you to express ordinarily private thoughts and to re-create an event as you actually experienced it. This point of view is limited, though, in its ability to depict the inner thoughts of other people involved in the event. By way of contrast, third person makes it easier to provide insight into the thoughts of all the participants. However, its objective, broad perspective may undercut some of the subjective immediacy typical of the "I was there" point of view.

Knowing whether to use the *past* or *present tense* ("I *strolled* into the room" as opposed to "I *stroll* into the room") is important. In most narrations, the past tense predominates, enabling the writer to span a considerable period of time. Although more rarely used, the present tense can be powerful for events of short duration—a wrestling match or a medical emergency, for instance. A narrative in the present tense prolongs each moment, intensifying the reader's sense of participation. Be careful, though; unless the event is intense and fast-paced, the present tense can seem contrived. Whichever tense you choose, avoid shifting midstream — starting, let's say, in the past tense ("she skated") and switching to present ("she runs").

Effective narratives may be exciting or charming or moving; writing them can be great fun and devilishly difficult at the same time. It's no mean feat to re-create an event, drawing on your powers of recall as well as your skill with language to make the narrative action come alive.

Although some narratives relate unusual experiences, most tread familiar ground, telling tales of joy, love, loss, frustration, fear — all common emotions experienced during a life. Don't think, however, that writing about the familiar makes your story predictable. On the contrary. All of us feel an energizing shock of recognition whenever the human condition is written about with grace and power. Narratives can take the ordinary and transmute it into something significant, even extraordinary. As Willa Cather, the American novelist, wrote: "There are only two or three human stories and they go on repeating themselves as fiercely as if they had never happened before." The challenge lies in applying your own vision to a tale, thereby making it unique.

STUDENT ESSAY

The following student essay was written by Paul Monahan in response to this assignment.

> In "Shooting an Elephant," George Orwell tells about an incident that forced him to act in a manner that ran counter to his better instincts. Write a narrative about a time when you faced a disturbing conflict and ended up doing something you later regretted.

While reading Paul's paper, try to determine how well it applies the principles of narration. The annotations on Paul's paper and the commentary following it will help you look at the essay more closely.

If Only

by Paul Monahan

Introduction

Having worked at a 7-Eleven store for two 1
years, I thought I had become successful at what
our manager calls "customer relations." I firmly
believed that a friendly smile and an automatic
"sir," "ma'am," and "thank you" would see me
through any situation that might arise, from soothing impatient or unpleasant people to apologizing

Narrative point
(thesis)

for giving out the wrong change. But the other
night an old woman shattered my belief that a glib
response could smooth over the rough spots of
dealing with other human beings.

Informal topic
sentence

The moment she entered, the woman pre- 2
sented a sharp contrast to our shiny store with its
bright lighting and neatly arranged shelves. Walking as if each step were painful, she slowly pushed
open the glass door and hobbled down the nearest

Sensory details

aisle. She coughed dryly, wheezing with each
breath. On a forty-degree night, she was wearing
only a faded print dress, a thin, light-beige sweater
too small to button, and black vinyl slippers with
the backs cut out to expose calloused heels. There
were no stockings or socks on her splotchy, blue-
veined legs.

After strolling around the store for several 3
minutes, the old woman stopped in front of the
rows of canned vegetables. She picked up some
corn niblets and stared with a strange intensity at

Informal topic
sentence

the label. At that point, I decided to be a good,
courteous employee and asked her if she needed
help. As I stood close to her, my smile became

Sensory details

harder to maintain; her red-rimmed eyes were partially closed by yellowish crusts; her hands were
covered with layer upon layer of grime, and the
stale smell of sweat rose in a thick vaporous cloud
from her clothes.

Start of
dialogue

"I need some food," she muttered in reply to 4
my bright "Can I help you?"

"Are you looking for corn, ma'am?" 5

"I need some food," she repeated. "Any kind." 6

"Well, the corn is ninety-five cents," I said in 7

my most helpful voice. "Or, if you like, we have a special on bologna today."

"I can't pay," she said.   8

Conflict established → For a second, I was tempted to say, "Take the   9
corn." But the employee rules flooded into my mind: Remain polite, but do not let customers get the best of you. Let them know that you are in control. For a moment, I even entertained the idea that this was some sort of test, and that this woman was someone from the head office, testing my loyalty. I responded dutifully, "I'm sorry, ma'am, but I can't give away anything free."

Informal topic sentence → The old woman's face collapsed a bit more, if   10
that were possible, and her hands trembled as she put the can back on the shelf. She shuffled past me toward the door, her torn and dirty clothing barely covering her bent back.

Conclusion   Moments after she left, I rushed out the door   11
with the can of corn, but she was nowhere in sight. For the rest of my shift, the image of the woman haunted me. I had been young, healthy, and smug.

Echoing of narrative point in the introduction — She had been old, sick, and desperate. Wishing with all my heart that I had acted like a human being rather than a robot, I was saddened to realize how fragile a hold we have on our better instincts.

COMMENTARY

Point of view, tense, and conflict.   Paul chose to write "If Only" from the *first person point of view*, a logical choice because he appears as a main character in his own story. Using the *past tense*, Paul recounts an incident filled with *conflicts*—between him and the woman and between his fear of breaking the rules and his human instinct to help someone in need.

Narrative point.   It isn't always necessary to state the *narrative point* of an essay; it can be implied. But Paul decided to express the controlling idea of his narrative in two places—in the introduction ("But the other night an old woman shattered my belief that a glib response could smooth over the rough spots of dealing with other human beings") and again in the conclusion, where he expands his idea about rote responses overriding impulses of independent judgment and compassion. All of the essay's *narrative details* contribute to the point of the piece; Paul does not include any extraneous information that would detract from the central idea he wants to convey.

Organization and other patterns of development.   The narrative is *organized chronologically*, from the moment the woman enters the store to Paul's reaction after she leaves. Paul limits the narrative's time span. The entire incident probably occurs in under ten minutes, yet the introduction serves as a kind of *flashback* by providing some necessary background about Paul's past experiences. To help the reader follow the course of the narrative, Paul uses *time signals*: "*The moment* she entered, the woman presented a sharp contrast" (paragraph 2); "*At that point*, I decided to be a good, courteous employee" (3); "*For the rest of my shift*, the image of the woman haunted me" (11).

The paragraphs (except for those consisting solely of dialogue) also contain *informal topic sentences* that direct attention to the specific stage of action being narrated. Indeed, each paragraph focuses on a distinct event: the elderly woman's actions when she first enters the store, the encounter between Paul and the woman, Paul's resulting inner conflict, the woman's subsequent response, and Paul's delayed reaction.

This chain of events, with one action leading to another, illustrates that the *cause-effect* pattern underlies the essay's basic structure. And another pattern — *description* — gives dramatic immediacy to the events being recounted. Throughout, rich sensory details engage the reader's interest. For instance, the sentence "her red-rimmed eyes were partially closed by yellowish crusts" (3) vividly re-creates the woman's appearance while also suggesting Paul's inner reaction to the woman.

Dialogue and sentence structure.   Paul uses other techniques to add energy and interest to his narrative. For one thing, he dramatizes his conflict with the woman through *dialogue* that crackles with tension. And he achieves a vigorous narrative pace by *varying the length and structure of his sentences*. In the second paragraph, a short sentence ("There were no stockings or socks on her splotchy, blue-veined legs") alternates with a longer one ("On a forty-degree night, she was wearing only a faded print dress, a thin, light-beige sweater too small to button, and black vinyl slippers with the backs cut out to expose calloused heels"). Some sentences in the essay open with a subject and verb ("She coughed dryly"), while others start with dependent clauses or participial phrases ("As I stood close to her, my smile became harder to maintain"; "Walking as if each step were painful, she slowly pushed open the glass door") or with a prepositional phrase ("For a second, I was tempted").

Revising the first draft.   Comparing the final version of the essay's third paragraph, shown above, with the preliminary version reprinted below reveals some of the changes Paul made while revising the essay.

Original Version of the Third Paragraph

After sneezing and hacking her way around the store, the old woman stopped in front of the vegetable shelves. She picked up a can of corn and stared at the label. She stayed like this for several minutes. Then I walked over to her and asked if I could be of help.

After putting the original draft aside for a while, Paul reread his paper aloud and realized the third paragraph especially lacked power. So he decided to add compelling descriptive details about the woman ("the stale smell of sweat," for example). When revising, he also worked to reduce the paragraph's choppiness. By expanding and combining sentences, he gave the paragraph an easier, more graceful rhythm. Much of the time, revision involves paring down excess material. In this case, though, Paul made the right decision to elaborate his sentences. Furthermore, he added the following comment to the third paragraph: "I decided to be a good, courteous employee." These few words introduce an appropriate note of irony and serve to echo the essay's controlling idea.

Finally, Paul decided to omit the words "sneezing and hacking" because he realized they were too comic or light for his subject. Still, the first sentence in the revised paragraph is somewhat jarring. The word *strolling* isn't quite appropriate since it implies a leisurely grace inconsistent with the impression he wants to convey. Replacing *strolling* with, say, *shuffling* would bring the image more into line with the essay's overall mood.

Despite this slight problem, Paul's revisions are right on the mark. The changes he made strengthened his essay, turning it into a more evocative, more polished piece of narrative writing.

The following selections are examples of skillfully written narratives, each with vivid characters, compelling scenes, dramatic conflicts, and vigorous language. In "Grandmother's Victory," Maya Angelou recalls the day neighborhood girls did their best to humiliate her beloved grandmother. George Orwell's classic "Shooting an Elephant" recounts a man's encounter with an unruly crowd, a rampaging animal, and his own conscience. In "Little Deaths," T. H. Watkins joins a professional trapper on his rounds and learns something important about the complexity of life. Langston Hughes in "Salvation" narrates the wrenching loss of his innocence. Last, in "By Any Other Name," Santha Rama Rau re-creates her painful first day in a British-run school.

Maya Angelou

Born Marguerita Johnson in 1928, Maya Angelou spent her childhood in Stamps, Arkansas, with her brother, Bailey, and her grandmother, "Momma." Although her youth was difficult—she was raped at age eight and a mother at sixteen—Angelou somehow managed to thrive. Multi-talented, she later worked as a professional dancer, starred in an off-Broadway play, appeared in the television miniseries *Roots*, served as a coordinator for the Southern Christian Leadership Conference, and wrote several well-received volumes of poetry—among them *Oh Pray My Wings Are Gonna Fit Me Well* (1975) and *And Still I Rise* (1978). The recipient of numerous honorary doctorates, Angelou is best known for her series of five autobiographical books, starting with *I Know Why the Caged Bird Sings* (1970) and concluding with *All God's Children Need Traveling Shoes* (1986). The following essay is taken from *I Know Why the Caged Bird Sings*.

Grandmother's Victory

Maya Angelou's proper, deeply religious grandmother created a loving yet strictly ordered environment for her grandchildren. But that orderly world was surrounded by a larger and far more chaotic world, one in which hatred and racism reigned supreme. In this account from her childhood, Angelou tells about her grandmother's reaction to a painful encounter with that other reality.

"Thou shalt not be dirty" and "Thou shall not be impudent" 1 were the two commandments of Grandmother Henderson upon which hung our total salvation.

Each night in the bitterest winter we were forced to wash 2 faces, arms, necks, legs and feet before going to bed. She used to add, with a smirk that unprofane people can't control when venturing into profanity, "and wash as far as possible, then wash possible."

We would go to the well and wash in the ice-cold, clear   3
water, grease our legs with the equally cold stiff Vaseline, then
tiptoe into the house. We wiped the dust from our toes and
settled down for schoolwork, cornbread, clabbered milk, prayers
and bed, always in that order. Momma was famous for pulling
the quilts off after we had fallen asleep to examine our feet. If they
weren't clean enough for her, she took the switch (she kept one
behind the bedroom door for emergencies) and woke up the
offender with a few aptly placed burning reminders.

The area around the well at night was dark and slick, and   4
boys told about how snakes love water, so that anyone who had
to draw water at night and then stand there alone and wash knew
that moccasins and rattlers, puff adders and boa constrictors were
winding their way to the well and would arrive just as the person
washing got soap in her eyes. But Momma convinced us that not
only was cleanliness next to Godliness, dirtiness was the inventor
of misery.

The impudent child was detested by God and a shame to its   5
parents and could bring destruction to its house and line. All
adults had to be addressed as Mister, Missus, Miss, Auntie,
Cousin, Unk, Uncle, Buhbah, Sister, Brother and a thousand
other appellations indicating familial relationship and the lowli-
ness of the addressor.

Everyone I knew respected these customary laws, except for   6
the powhitetrash children.

Some families of powhitetrash lived on Momma's farm land   7
behind the school. Sometimes a gaggle of them came to the Store,
filling the whole room, chasing out the air and even changing the
well-known scents. The children crawled over the shelves and
into the potato and onion bins, twanging all the time in their
sharp voices like cigar-box guitars. They took liberties in my Store
that I would never dare. Since Momma told us that the less you
say to white-folks (or even powhitetrash) the better, Bailey and I
would stand, solemn, quiet, in the displaced air. But if one of the
playful apparitions got close to us, I pinched it. Partly out of
angry frustration and partly because I didn't believe in its flesh
reality.

They called my uncle by his first name and ordered him   8
around the Store. He, to my crying shame, obeyed them in his
limping dip-straight-dip fashion.

My grandmother, too, followed their orders, except that she 9
didn't seem to be servile because she anticipated their needs.

"Here's sugar, Miz Potter, and here's baking powder. You 10
didn't buy soda last month, you'll probably be needing some."

Momma always directed her statements to the adults, but 11
sometimes, Oh painful sometimes, the grimy, snotty-nosed girls
would answer her.

"Naw, Annie . . ." — to Momma? Who owned the land 12
they lived on? Who forgot more than they would ever learn? If
there was any justice in the world, God should strike them dumb
at once! — "Just give us some extra sody crackers, and some more
mackerel."

At least they never looked in her face, or I never caught them 13
doing so. Nobody with a smidgen of training, not even the worst
roustabout, would look right in a grown person's face. It meant
the person was trying to take the words out before they were
formed. The dirty little children didn't do that, but they threw
their orders around the Store like lashes from a cat-o'-nine-tails.

When I was around ten years old, those scruffy children 14
caused me the most painful and confusing experience I had ever
had with my grandmother.

One summer morning, after I had swept the dirt yard of 15
leaves, spearmint-gum wrappers and Vienna-sausage labels, I
raked the yellow-red dirt, and made half-moons carefully, so that
the design stood out clearly and mask-like. I put the rake behind
the Store and came through the back of the house to find Grandmother on the front porch in her big, wide white apron. The
apron was so stiff by virtue of the starch that it could have stood
alone. Momma was admiring the yard, so I joined her. It truly
looked like a flat redhead that had been raked with a big-toothed
comb. Momma didn't say anything but I knew she liked it. She
looked over toward the school principal's house and to the
right at Mr. McElroy's. She was hoping one of those community
pillars would see the design before the day's business wiped it out.
Then she looked upward to the school. My head had swung with
hers, so at just about the same time we saw a troop of the
powhitetrash kids marching over the hill and down by the side of
the school.

I looked to Momma for direction. She did an excellent job of 16
sagging from her waist down, but from the waist up she seemed

to be pulling for the top of the oak tree across the road. Then she began to moan a hymn. Maybe not to moan, but the tune was so slow and the meter so strange that she could have been moaning. She didn't look at me again. When the children reached halfway down the hill, halfway to the Store, she said without turning, "Sister, go on inside."

I wanted to beg her, "Momma, don't wait for them. Come   17
on inside with me. If they come in the Store, you go to the bedroom and let me wait on them. They only frighten me if you're around. Alone I know how to handle them." But of course I couldn't say anything, so I went in and stood behind the screen door.

Before the girls got to the porch I heard their laughter crack-   18
ling and popping like pine logs in a cooking stove. I suppose my lifelong paranoia was born in those cold, molasses-slow minutes. They came finally to stand on the ground in front of Momma. At first they pretended seriousness. Then one of them wrapped her right arm in the crook of her left, pushed out her mouth and started to hum. I realized that she was aping my grandmother. Another said, "Naw, Helen, you ain't standing like her. This here's it." Then she lifted her chest, folded her arms and mocked that strange carriage that was Annie Henderson. Another laughed, "Naw, you can't do it. Your mouth ain't pooched out enough. It's like this."

I thought about the rifle behind the door, but I knew I'd   19
never be able to hold it straight, and the .410, our sawed-off shotgun, which stayed loaded and was fired every New Year's night, was locked in the trunk and Uncle Willie had the key on his chain. Through the fly-specked screen-door, I could see that the arms of Momma's apron jiggled from the vibrations of her hum-ming. But her knees seemed to have locked as if they would never bend again.

She sang on. No louder than before, but no softer either. No   20
slower or faster.

The dirt of the girls' cotton dresses continued on their legs,   21
feet, arms and faces to make them all of a piece. Their greasy uncolored hair hung down, uncombed, with a grim finality. I knelt to see them better, to remember them for all time. The tears that had slipped down my dress left unsurprising dark spots, and made the front yard blurry and even more unreal. The world had

taken a deep breath and was having doubts about continuing to revolve.

The girls had tired of mocking Momma and turned to other   22
means of agitation. One crossed her eyes, stuck her thumbs in both sides of her mouth and said, "Look here, Annie." Grandmother hummed on and the apron strings trembled. I wanted to throw a handful of black pepper in their faces, to throw lye on them, to scream that they were dirty, scummy peckerwoods, but I knew I was as clearly imprisoned behind the scene as the actors outside were confined to their roles.

One of the smaller girls did a kind of puppet dance while her   23
fellow clowns laughed at her. But the tall one, who was almost a woman, said something very quietly, which I couldn't hear. They all moved backward from the porch, still watching Momma. For an awful second I thought they were going to throw a rock at Momma, who seemed (except for the apron strings) to have turned into stone herself. But the big girl turned her back, bent down and put her hands flat on the ground — she didn't pick up anything. She simply shifted her weight and did a hand stand.

Her dirty bare feet and long legs went straight for the sky.   24
Her dress fell down around her shoulders, and she had on no drawers. The slick pubic hair made a brown triangle where her legs came together. She hung in the vacuum of that lifeless morning for only a few seconds, then wavered and tumbled. The other girls clapped her on the back and slapped their hands.

Momma changed her song to "Bread of Heaven, bread of   25
Heaven, feed me till I want no more."

I found that I was praying too. How long could Momma   26
hold out? What new indignity would they think of to subject her to? Would I be able to stay out of it? What would Momma really like me to do?

Then they were moving out of the yard, on their way to   27
town. They bobbed their heads and shook their slack behinds and turned, one at a time:

"'Bye, Annie."   28
"'Bye, Annie."   29
"'Bye, Annie."   30

Momma never turned her head or unfolded her arms, but she   31
stopped singing and said, "'Bye, Miz Helen, 'bye, Miz Ruth, 'bye, Miz Eloise."

I burst. A firecracker July-the-Fourth burst. How could 32
Momma call them Miz? The mean nasty things. Why couldn't
she have come inside the sweet, cool store when we saw them
breasting the hill? What did she prove? And then if they were
dirty, mean and impudent, why did Momma have to call them
Miz?

She stood another whole song through and then opened the 33
screen door to look down on me crying in rage. She looked until I
looked up. Her face was a brown moon that shone on me. She
was beautiful. Something had happened out there, which I
couldn't completely understand, but I could see that she was
happy. Then she bent down and touched me as mothers of the
church "lay hands on the sick and afflicted" and I quieted.

"Go wash your face, Sister." And she went behind the candy 34
counter and hummed, "Glory, glory, hallelujah, when I lay my
burden down."

I threw the well water on my face and used the weekday 35
handkerchief to blow my nose. Whatever the contest had been
out front, I knew Momma had won.

I took the rake back to the front yard. The smudged foot- 36
prints were easy to erase. I worked for a long time on my new
design and laid the rake behind the wash pot. When I came back
in the Store, I took Momma's hand and we both walked outside
to look at the pattern.

It was a large heart with lots of hearts growing smaller inside, 37
and piercing from the outside rim to the smallest heart was an
arrow. Momma said, "Sister, that's right pretty." Then she turned
back to the Store and resumed, "Glory, glory, hallelujah, when I
lay my burden down."

Questions for Close Reading

1. What is the selection's thesis (or narrative point)? Locate the sen-
   tence(s) in which Angelou states her main idea. If she doesn't state
   the thesis explicitly, express it in your own words.
2. What standing does Grandmother Henderson have in the community? What are her values and standards?
3. Who are the "powhitetrash" children? In what ways do the "powhitetrash" children violate Grandmother Henderson's standards? What
   might have been some of the reasons for the children's impudence
   and mockery?

4. How does Mrs. Henderson behave during the girls' mockery of her? Why is Grandmother Henderson's behavior a "victory"?
5. Refer to your dictionary as needed to define the following words used in the selection: *appellations* (paragraph 5), *familial* (5), *gaggle* (7), *twanging* (7), *apparitions* (7), *smidgen* (13), *roustabout* (13), *paranoia* (18), *finality* (21), *agitation* (22), and *indignity* (26).

Questions About the Writer's Craft

1. **The pattern.** The main conflict in the narrative occurs between Momma and the "powhitetrash" children. What additional conflicts make the story suspenseful?
2. **Other patterns.** Angelou's introductory paragraphs about Momma's philosophy of child-rearing serve to contrast the children in Momma's care with the "powhitetrash" children. How does this contrast prepare the reader for the selection's narrative point?
3. Angelou uses the slang term "powhitetrash" even though it isn't in the dictionary. Why do you think she uses this term instead of a more standard or "official" expression? What effect might she hope the term will have on readers?
4. Angelou provides an explicit description of Momma—her values, her philosophy of child-rearing, her appearance, her behavior—all of which helps the reader understand Grandmother Henderson. Angelou doesn't offer a comparably explicit description of herself, yet the reader learns a good deal about her. How does Angelou go about creating a portrait of herself as a young girl?

Questions for Further Thought

1. How good a child-rearer do you think Momma was? Do you agree with her two "commandments"? Or do you believe there are other more important values that should be stressed when raising children? What would these values be?
2. "Nobody with a smidgen of training . . . would look right in a grown person's face," Angelou writes. What types of behaviors were considered impudent by the adults who raised you? Are these still considered disrespectful today? Why or why not?
3. Momma advises that "the less you say to white-folks . . . the better." Do you agree that distancing yourself from those who treat you disrespectfully is the best policy? Explain.
4. The term "powhitetrash" is a label with numerous negative connotations. What other stereotyped terms have you heard to describe people? Consider, for example, language that describes women, college

athletes, people having specific religious, ethnic, or racial backgrounds. What's the effect of these labels?

Writing Assignments Using Narration as a Pattern of Development

∞ 1. Angelou's narrative explains a mystery—the fact that her all-powerful grandmother accepted ill-treatment and impudence. Children often are mystified by the responses of the adults around them. Write a narrative about an incident in which a respected adult behaved in a manner that confused you or that caused you to change your views of the adult, the situation, or life. Before planning your paper, you might read Langston Hughes's "Salvation" (page 186), another narrative about the different ways that adults and children view the world.

2. Angelou writes that she was "mad enough to kill" during the incident at her grandmother's store. Write a narrative about a time when a strong emotion overwhelmed you or another person, creating conflict about whether to act on the emotion or to suppress it. Tell how the conflict was resolved, and indicate whether the resolution was satisfying to the person involved. The emotion you focus on may be negative, like rage and envy, or positive, like pride and affection.

Writing Assignments Using Other Patterns of Development

3. The "powhitetrash" children attempt to irritate Grandmother Henderson in a variety of ways. In truth, most children have a repertoire of tricks they can draw upon to irritate adults or otherwise get attention. Write an essay classifying the various techniques that children (including yourself when younger) deliberately use to annoy parents, teachers, or each other. Your essay may be serious or light in tone.

∞ 4. Momma's power to resist insult seems based partly on her ability to stand still as stone and partly on her value system, in which politeness and forbearance rank high. Determine what you believe is the best way to respond when confronted by hostility. Then explain the process that you would recommend to someone being attacked. Santha Rama Rau's "By Any Other Name" (page 191), Barbara Ehrenreich's "What I've Learned From Men" (page 261), and Diane Cole's "Don't Just Stand There" (page 394) will help you think about strategies for dealing with insulting behavior.

George Orwell

Born Eric Blair in the British colony of India, George Orwell (1903–50) is probably best known for his two novels, *Animal Farm* (1946) and *1984* (1949), both searing depictions of totalitarian societies. Orwell was also the author of numerous books and essays, many based on his diverse life experiences. He served with the Indian imperial police in Burma, worked at various jobs in London and Paris, and fought in the Spanish Civil War. His experiences in Burma provide the basis for the following essay, which is taken from his collection, *Shooting an Elephant and Other Essays* (1950).

Shooting an Elephant

At one time or another, most of us have done something just so people wouldn't laugh at or think badly of us. In this essay, George Orwell describes how he felt pressured into taking an action against his better judgment — killing an elephant that had strayed into the center of a town in Burma. Beside offering powerful insights into human behavior, Orwell's essay presents a vivid and horrifying picture of an animal's death.

In Moulmein, in Lower Burma, I was hated by large numbers   1
of people — the only time in my life that I have been important enough for this to happen to me. I was sub-divisional police officer of the town, and in an aimless, petty kind of way anti-European feeling was very bitter. No one had the guts to raise a riot, but if a European woman went through the bazaars alone somebody would probably spit betel juice over her dress. As a police officer I was an obvious target and was baited whenever it seemed safe to do so. When a nimble Burman tripped me up on the football field and the referee (another Burman) looked the other way, the crowd yelled with hideous laughter. This happened more than once. In the end the sneering yellow faces of young men that

met me everywhere, the insults hooted after me when I was at a safe distance, got badly on my nerves. The young Buddhist priests were the worst of all. There were several thousand of them in the town and none of them seemed to have anything to do except stand on street corners and jeer at Europeans.

All this was perplexing and upsetting. For at that time I had   2
already made up my mind that imperialism was an evil thing and the sooner I chucked up my job and got out of it the better. Theoretically — and secretly, of course — I was all for the Burmese and all against their oppressors, the British. As for the job I was doing, I hated it more bitterly than I can perhaps make clear. In a job like that you see the dirty work of Empire at close quarters. The wretched prisoners huddling in the stinking cages of the lock-ups, the grey, cowed faces of the long-term convicts, the scarred buttocks of the men who had been flogged with bamboos — all these oppressed me with an intolerable sense of guilt. But I could get nothing into perspective. I was young and ill-educated and I had had to think out my problems in the utter silence that is imposed on every Englishman in the East. I did not even know that the British Empire is dying, still less did I know that it is a great deal better than the younger empires that are going to supplant it. All I knew was that I was stuck between my hatred of the empire I served and my rage against the evil-spirited little beasts who tried to make my job impossible. With one part of my mind I thought of the British Raj as an unbreakable tyranny, as something clamped down, in *saecula saeculorum*,[1] upon the will of prostrate peoples; with another part I thought that the greatest joy in the world would be to drive a bayonet into a Buddhist priest's guts. Feelings like these are the normal by-products of imperialism; ask any Anglo-Indian official, if you can catch him off duty.

One day something happened which in a roundabout way   3
was enlightening. It was a tiny incident in itself, but it gave me a better glimpse than I had had before of the real nature of imperialism — the real motives for which despotic governments act. Early one morning the sub-inspector at a police station the other end of the town rang me up on the 'phone and said that an elephant was ravaging the bazaar. Would I please come and do

[1]For ever and ever.

something about it? I did not know what I could do, but I wanted to see what was happening and I got on to a pony and started out. I took my rifle, an old .44 Winchester and much too small to kill an elephant, but I thought the noise might be useful *in terrorem*.[2] Various Burmans stopped me on the way and told me about the elephant's doings. It was not, of course, a wild elephant, but a tame one which had gone "must." It had been chained up, as tame elephants always are when their attack of "must" is due, but on the previous night it had broken its chain and escaped. Its mahout, the only person who could manage it when it was in that state, had set out in pursuit, but had taken the wrong direction and was now twelve hours' journey away, and in the morning the elephant had suddenly reappeared in the town. The Burmese population had no weapons and were quite helpless against it. It had already destroyed somebody's bamboo hut, killed a cow and raided some fruit-stalls and devoured the stock; also it had met the municipal rubbish van and, when the driver jumped out and took to his heels, had turned the van over and inflicted violence upon it.

The Burmese sub-inspector and some Indian constables were   4 waiting for me in the quarter where the elephant had been seen. It was a very poor quarter, a labyrinth of squalid bamboo huts, thatched with palm-leaf, winding all over a steep hillside. I re-member that it was a cloudy, stuffy morning at the beginning of the rains. We began questioning the people as to where the elephant had gone and, as usual, failed to get any definite infor-mation. That is invariably the case in the East; a story always sounds clear enough at a distance, but the nearer you get to the scene of events the vaguer it becomes. Some of the people said that the elephant had gone in one direction, some said that he had gone in another, some professed not even to have heard of any elephant. I had almost made up my mind that the whole story was a pack of lies, when we heard yells a little distance away. There was a loud, scandalized cry of "Go away, child! Go away this instant!" and an old woman with a switch in her hand came round the corner of a hut, violently shooing away a crowd of naked children. Some more women followed, clicking their tongues and exclaiming; evidently there was something that the

[2]As a warning.

children ought not to have seen. I rounded the hut and saw a man's dead body sprawling in the mud. He was an Indian, a black Dravidian coolie, almost naked, and he could not have been dead many minutes. The people said that the elephant had come suddenly upon him round the corner of the hut, caught him with its trunk, put its foot on his back and ground him into the earth. This was the rainy season and the ground was soft, and his face had scored a trench a foot deep and a couple of yards long. He was lying on his belly with arms crucified and head sharply twisted to one side. His face was coated with mud, the eyes wide open, the teeth bared and grinning with an expression of unendurable agony. (Never tell me, by the way, that the dead look peaceful. Most of the corpses I have seen looked devilish.) The friction of the great beast's foot had stripped the skin from his back as neatly as one skins a rabbit. As soon as I saw the dead man I sent an orderly to a friend's house nearby to borrow an elephant rifle. I had already sent back the pony, not wanting it to go mad with fright and throw me if it smelt the elephant.

The orderly came back in a few minutes with a rifle and five   5
cartridges, and meanwhile some Burmans had arrived and told us that the elephant was in the paddy fields below, only a few hundred yards away. As I started forward practically the whole population of the quarter flocked out of the houses and followed me. They had seen the rifle and were all shouting excitedly that I was going to shoot the elephant. They had not shown much interest in the elephant when he was merely ravaging their homes, but it was different now that he was going to be shot. It was a bit of fun to them, as it would be to an English crowd; besides they wanted the meat. It made me vaguely uneasy. I had no intention of shooting the elephant — I had merely sent for the rifle to defend myself if necessary — and it is always unnerving to have a crowd following you. I marched down the hill, looking and feeling a fool, with the rifle over my shoulder and an ever-growing army of people jostling at my heels. At the bottom, when you got away from the huts, there was a metalled road and beyond that a miry waste of paddy fields a thousand yards across, not yet ploughed but soggy from the first rains and dotted with coarse grass. The elephant was standing eight yards from the road, his left side towards us. He took not the slightest notice of the crowd's approach. He was tearing up bunches of grass, beating

them against his knees to clean them and stuffing them into his mouth.

I had halted on the road. As soon as I saw the elephant I knew with perfect certainty that I ought not to shoot him. It is a serious matter to shoot a working elephant — it is comparable to destroying a huge and costly piece of machinery — and obviously one ought not to do it if it can possibly be avoided. And at that distance, peacefully eating, the elephant looked no more danger-ous than a cow. I thought then and I think now that his attack of "must" was already passing off; in which case he would merely wander harmlessly about until the mahout came back and caught him. Moreover, I did not in the least want to shoot him. I decided that I would watch him for a little while to make sure that he did not turn savage again, and then go home.   6

But at that moment I glanced round at the crowd that had followed me. It was an immense crowd, two thousand at the least and growing every minute. It blocked the road for a long distance on either side. I looked at the sea of yellow faces above the garish clothes — faces all happy and excited over this bit of fun, all certain that the elephant was going to be shot. They were watch-ing me as they would watch a conjurer about to perform a trick. They did not like me, but with the magical rifle in my hands I was momentarily worth watching. And suddenly I realized that I should have to shoot the elephant after all. The people expected it of me and I had got to do it; I could feel their two thousand wills pressing me forward, irresistibly. And it was at this moment, as I stood there with the rifle in my hands, that I first grasped the hollowness, the futility of the white man's dominion in the East. Here was I, the white man with his gun, standing in front of the unarmed native crowd — seemingly the leading actor of the piece; but in reality I was only an absurd puppet pushed to and fro by the will of those yellow faces behind. I perceived in this moment that when the white man turns tyrant it is his own freedom that he destroys. He becomes a sort of hollow, posing dummy, the conventionalized figure of a sahib. For it is the condition of his rule that he shall spend his life in trying to impress the "natives," and so in every crisis he has got to do what the "natives" expect of him. He wears a mask, and his face grows to fit it. I had got to shoot the elephant. I had committed myself to doing it when I sent for the rifle. A sahib has got to act like a sahib; he has got to   7 appear resolute, to know his own mind and do definite things. To come all that way, rifle in hand, with two thousand people marching at my heels, and then to trail feebly away, having done nothing—no, that was impossible. The crowd would laugh at me. And my whole life, every white man's life in the East, was one long struggle not be laughed at.

But I did not want to shoot the elephant. I watched him 8 beating his bunch of grass against his knees, with that preoccupied grandmotherly air that elephants have. It seemed to me that it would be murder to shoot him. At that age I was not squeamish about killing animals, but I had never shot an elephant and never wanted to. (Somehow it always seems worse to kill a *large* animal.) Besides, there was the beast's owner to be considered. Alive, the elephant was worth at least a hundred pounds; dead, he would only be worth the value of his tusks, five pounds, possibly. But I had got to act quickly. I turned to some experienced-looking Burmans who had been there when we arrived, and asked them how the elephant had been behaving. They all said the same thing: he took no notice of you if you left him alone, but he might charge if you went too close to him.

It was perfectly clear to me what I ought to do. I ought to 9 walk up to within, say, twenty-five yards of the elephant and test his behavior. If he charged, I could shoot; if he took no notice of me, it would be safe to leave him until the mahout came back. But also I knew that I was going to do no such thing. I was a poor shot with a rifle and the ground was soft mud into which one would sink at every step. If the elephant charged and I missed him, I should have about as much chance as a toad under a steam-roller. But even then I was not thinking particularly of my own skin, only of the watchful yellow faces behind. For at that moment, with the crowd watching me, I was not afraid in the ordinary sense, as I would have been if I had been alone. A white man mustn't be frightened in front of "natives"; and so, in general, he isn't frightened. The sole thought in my mind was that if anything went wrong those two thousand Burmans would see me pursued, caught, trampled on and reduced to a grinning corpse like that Indian up the hill. And if that happened it was quite probable that some of them would laugh. That would never do. There was only one alternative. I shoved the cartridges into the magazine and lay down on the road to get a better aim.

The crowd grew very still, and a deep, low, happy sigh, as of   10
people who see the theatre curtain go up at last, breathed from
innumerable throats. They were going to have their bit of fun
after all. The rifle was a beautiful German thing with cross-hair
sights. I did not then know that in shooting an elephant one
would shoot to cut an imaginary bar running from ear-hole to
ear-hole. I ought, therefore, as the elephant was sideway on, to
have aimed straight at his ear-hole; actually I aimed several inches
in front of this, thinking the brain would be further forward.

When I pulled the trigger I did not hear the bang or feel the   11
kick — one never does when a shot goes home — but I heard the
devilish roar of glee that went up from the crowd. In that instant,
in too short a time, one would have thought, even for the bullet
to get there, a mysterious, terrible change had come over the
elephant. He neither stirred nor fell, but every line of his body
had altered. He looked suddenly stricken, shrunken, immensely
old, as though the frightful impact of the bullet had paralyzed
him without knocking him down. At last, after what seemed a
long time — it might have been five seconds, I dare say — he
sagged flabbily to his knees. His mouth slobbered. An enormous
senility seemed to have settled upon him. One could have imagined him thousands of years old. I fired again into the same spot.
At the second shot he did not collapse but climbed with desperate
slowness to his feet and stood weakly upright, with legs sagging
and head drooping. I fired a third time. That was the shot that did
for him. You could see the agony of it jolt his whole body and
knock the last remnant of strength from his legs. But in falling he
seemed for a moment to rise, for as his hind legs collapsed
beneath him he seemed to tower upward like a huge rock top-
pling, his trunk reaching skywards like a tree. He trumpeted, for
the first and only time. And then down he came, his belly towards
me, with a crash that seemed to shake the ground even where I
lay.

I got up. The Burmans were already racing past me across the   12
mud. It was obvious that the elephant would never rise again, but
he was not dead. He was breathing very rhythmically with long
rattling gasps, his great mound of a side painfully rising and
falling. His mouth was wide open — I could see far down into
caverns of pale pink throat. I waited a long time for him to die,
but his breathing did not weaken. Finally I fired my two remain-

ing shots into the spot where I thought his heart must be. The thick blood welled out of him like red velvet, but still he did not die. His body did not even jerk when the shots hit him, the tortured breathing continued without a pause. He was dying, very slowly and in great agony, but in some world remote from me where not even a bullet could damage him further. I felt that I had got to put an end to that dreadful noise. It seemed dreadful to see the great beast lying there, powerless to move and yet powerless to die, and not even to be able to finish him. I sent back for my small rifle and poured shot after shot into his heart and down his throat. They seemed to make no impression. The tortured gasps continued as steadily as the ticking of a clock.

In the end I could not stand it any longer and went away. I 13 heard later that it took him half an hour to die. Burmans were bringing dahs and baskets even before I left, and I was told they had stripped the body almost to the bones by the afternoon.

Afterwards, of course, there were endless discussions about 14 the shooting of the elephant. The owner was furious, but he was only an Indian and could do nothing. Besides, legally I had done the right thing, for a mad elephant has to be killed, like a mad dog, if its owner fails to control it. Among the Europeans opinion was divided. The older men said I was right, the younger men said it was a damn shame to shoot an elephant for killing a coolie, because an elephant was worth more than any damn Coringhee coolie. And afterwards I was very glad that the coolie had been killed; it put me legally in the right and it gave me a sufficient pretext for shooting the elephant. I often wondered whether any of the others grasped that I had done it solely to avoid looking a fool.

Questions for Close Reading

1. What is the selection's thesis (or narrative point)? Locate the sentence(s) in which Orwell states his main idea. If he doesn't state the thesis explicitly, express it in your own words.
2. How does Orwell feel about the Burmans? What words does he use to describe them?
3. What reasons does Orwell give for shooting the elephant?
4. In paragraph 3, Orwell says that the elephant incident gave him a better understanding of "the real motives for which despotic govern-

ments act." What do you think he means? Before you answer, reread paragraph 7 carefully.
5. Refer to your dictionary as needed to define the following words used in the selection: *imperialism* (paragraph 2), *prostrate* (2), *despotic* (3), *mahout* (3), *miry* (5), *conjurer* (7), *futility* (7), and *sahib* (7).

Questions About the Writer's Craft

1. **The pattern.** Most effective narratives encompass a restricted time span. How much time elapses from the moment Orwell gets his gun to the death of the elephant? What time signals does Orwell provide to help the reader follow the sequence of events in this limited time span?
2. Orwell doesn't actually begin his narrative until the third paragraph. What purposes do the first two paragraphs serve?
3. **Other patterns.** In paragraph 6, Orwell says that shooting a working elephant "is comparable to destroying a huge and costly piece of machinery." This kind of comparison is called an *analogy* — describing something unfamiliar, often abstract, in terms of something more familiar and concrete. Find at least three additional analogies in Orwell's essay. What effect do they have?
4. **Other patterns.** Much of the power of Orwell's narrative comes from his ability to convey sensory impressions — what he saw, heard, smelled. Orwell's description becomes most vivid when he writes about the death of the elephant in paragraphs 11 and 12. Find some evocative words and phrases that give the description its power.

Questions for Further Thought

1. In the first paragraph of "Shooting an Elephant," Orwell tells us he was "hated by large numbers of people — the only time in my life that I have been important enough for this to happen to me." What is Orwell implying about people's attitudes toward authority? Do you think Orwell has a valid point? To decide, think about the people who have power over you and how you feel about their authority.
2. The Burmese population was eager to see Orwell shoot the elephant. Why do you believe this incident held such significance for them?
3. In paragraph 7, Orwell comments that "when the white man turns tyrant it is his own freedom that he destroys." This is a *paradox* — a statement that seems to contradict itself. Explain the meaning of this paradox.
4. At the end of his essay, Orwell says he is glad the elephant had killed someone because it put him "legally in the right" for shooting the

animal. What actions today are considered legally right that you, or others, feel are morally wrong?

Writing Assignments Using Narration as a Pattern of Development

∞ 1. Orwell recounts a time he acted under great pressure. Write a narrative about an action you once took simply because you felt pressured. Perhaps you were attempting to avoid ridicule or to fulfill someone else's expectations. Like Orwell, use vivid details to bring the incident to life and to convey its effect on you. Langston Hughes's "Salvation" (page 186) may lead you to some insights about the way stress influences behavior.

2. Write a narrative essay about an experience that gave you, like Orwell, a deeper insight into your own nature. You may have discovered, for instance, that you can be surprisingly naive, compassionate, petty, brave, rebellious, or good at something.

Writing Assignments Using Other Patterns of Development

3. Was Orwell justified in shooting the elephant? Write an essay arguing that Orwell was either justified *or* not justified. To develop your thesis, cite several specific reasons, each supported by details drawn from the essay. Here are some points you might consider: The legality of Orwell's act, the elephant's temperament, the crowd's presence, the aftermath of the elephant's death, the death itself.

∞ 4. Orwell's essay concerns, in part, the tendency to conceal indecision and confusion with a facade of authority. Focusing on one or two groups of people (parents, teachers, doctors, politicians, and so on), write an essay about the way people in authority sometimes *pretend* to know what they are doing so that subordinates won't suspect their insecurity or incompetence. Part of your essay should focus on the consequences of such behaviors. Before planning your paper, you'll find it helpful to read "Making Medical Mistakes" (page 309), in which physician David Hilfiker talks openly about his professional fallibility.

T. H. Watkins

Historian and environmentalist T. H. Watkins has written more than ten books, including *American Landscape* (1987), *On the Shore of the Sundown Sea* (1990), and *Righteous Pilgrim: The Life and Times of Harold Ickes* (1990). One of his books, *California: An Illustrated History* (1973), was nominated for a Pulitzer Prize. Watkins's numerous articles have appeared in a wide range of publications, including *American Heritage*, *American West*, and the *Sierra Club Bulletin*, in which the following selection was published in 1974.

Little Deaths

We Americans coddle our pets; yet every year, thousands of cats and dogs are abandoned by their owners. We take our children to zoos to see the beauty of wild animals, but we wear furs fashioned from the pelts of nearly extinct species. In this selection, T. H. Watkins describes an expedition he took with his cousin, a professional trapper whose job is to "clear the varmints" from the land. As Watkins accompanies his cousin, he experiences some conflicting emotions.

It has been more than ten years since the day my cousin let me walk his traplines with him. We never see each other now. Our worlds, never very close, have grown even farther apart. He left California several years ago to become a trapping supervisor somewhere in Nevada, while I have joined the ranks of those who would cheerfully eliminate his way of life. He would, rightly enough, consider me one of his natural enemies, and it is not likely that we would have much to say if we did meet. Still, I am grateful to him for giving me a glimpse into the reality of a world normally hidden from us, a dark little world where death is the only commonplace.

At the time, my cousin was a lowly field trapper at the beck

and call of any rancher or farmer who made an official complaint
to the trapping service about varmint troubles—coyotes or wild-
cats getting after newborn lambs, foxes sneaking into chicken
coops, that sort of thing. His current assignment was to trap out
the varmint population of some ranchland high in the Diablo
Hills southeast of Oakland, a country of rolling grassland, scrub
oak, and chaparral dominated by the 3,000-foot upthrust of
Mount Diablo. His base was a house trailer planted on the edge
of one of the ranches he was servicing near Livermore, although
he got into Oakland quite a lot for weekend visits to a lady of his
acquaintance. I lived in Oakland at the time, and he usually made
a point of stopping by to see my children, of whom he was
particularly fond.

I was then a practicing student of western history and thor-   3
oughly intrigued by the glittering adventure that pervaded my
reading—especially in the stories of the mountain men, those
grizzled, anarchic beings with a lust for far places and far things,
stubborn individualists who had lived freer than any Indian and
had followed their quest for beaver pelts into nearly all the mysterious blanks of the American West, from Taos, New Mexico, to
Puget Sound, from the Marys River of the northern Rockies to
the Colorado River of the Southwest; hopelessly romantic creatures with a predilection for Indian women, a talent for profanity,
and a thirst for liquor profound enough to melt rivets. And here
was my cousin, the literary—if not lineal—descendant of the
mountain man. True, he was neither grizzled nor given much to
profanity, nor had he, so far as I knew, ever offered his blanket to
an Indian woman. Still, he was a *trapper*, by God, and when on
one of his visits he invited me to accompany him on his rounds, I
was entranced with the notion.

Late one spring afternoon I bundled wife and children into   4
the car and drove down to Livermore and out to the ranch where
he was staying. After a dinner cooked in the trailer's tiny kitchen,
my wife and the children bedded down in the trailer's two little
bunks. "When we get back tomorrow afternoon," my cousin told
the children, "I'll take you out and show you some spring lambs.
You'd like that, right?" he added, giving them a pinch and tickle
that set them to giggling in delight. He and I bundled up in
sleeping bags on the ground outside.

It was pitch black when he woke me that next morning at five   5 o'clock. After shocking ourselves out of sleep by bathing our faces in water from the outside faucet, we got into his pickup and drove off for breakfast at an all-night diner on the road. Dawn was insinuating itself over the dark hills by the time we finished breakfast, and had laid a neon streak across the sky when we finally turned off the highway and began climbing a rutted dirt road that led to the first trapline (we would be walking two traplines, my cousin explained, one on the western side of the hills, one on the eastern; these were two of the six he had scattered over the whole range, each of them containing between 15 and 20 traps and each checked out and reset or moved to a new location every ten days or so). As we bumped and rattled up the road, daylight slowly illuminated the hills. For two or three months in the spring, before the summer sun turns them warm and brown, these hills look as if they had been transplanted whole from Ireland or Wales. They are a celebration of green, all shades of green, from the black-green of manzanita leaves to the bright, pool-table green of the grasses. Isolated bunches of cows and sheep stood almost motionless, like ornaments added for the effect of contrast, and morning mist crept around the base of trees and shrouded dark hollows with the ghost of its presence. Through all this, the exposed earth of the road cut like a red scar, and the sounds of the pickup's engine and the country-western music yammering out of its radio intruded themselves on the earth's silence gracelessly.

We talked of my cousin's father, whom he worshipped and   6
emulated. My cousin was, in fact, almost literally following in his father's footsteps, for "the old man" had been a state trapper himself and was now a trapping supervisor. Before that, back in the deep of the Depression, he had been a lion hunter for the state, when a mountain lion's ears were good as money, and before that he had "cowboyed some," as he put it; at one time, according to family tradition, his grandfather's ranch had encompassed much of what became the town of San Bernardino in Southern California. At one point in his life, he had led jaguar-hunting trips to the jungles of northwestern Mexico, and he was still a noteworthy hunter, though now he confined himself principally to an occasional deer, antelope, or bear. My cousin had grown up in a house where skins of various types served as rugs and couchthrows, where stuffed heads glared unblinkingly from

the walls, where sleek hounds were always in-and-out, where hunting magazines dominated the tables, hunting talk dominated the conversations, and everywhere was the peculiarly masculine smell of newly oiled guns, all kinds of guns — pistols (including an old Colt once used by my cousin's great-grandfather, legend had it, to kill a man), rifles, shotguns. It was a family that had been killing things for a long time, sometimes for meat, sometimes for a living, sometimes for what was called the sport of it, and one of my cousin's consuming ambitions was to bag a bighorn sheep, something his father had never managed to do.

I had never killed anything in my life except fish, and since fish neither scream, grunt, squeal, nor moan when done in, it had never seemed like killing at all. In any case, I was by no means prepared for the first sight of what my cousin did to earn his bread. I don't know what I had expected with my romantic notions of the trapper's life, but surely it was something other than what I learned when we crawled up the road through increasingly heavy underbrush and stopped to check out the first of my cousin's traps.   7

We got out of the truck and beat our way through the brush   8 to a spot perhaps 30 feet from the road. I did not see the animal until we were nearly on top of it. It was a raccoon, the first raccoon I had ever seen in person, and at that moment I wished that I never had seen one. It was dead, had been dead for several days, my cousin informed me. "Hunger, thirst, and shock is what kills them, mostly," he said in response to my question. "That, and exhaustion, I reckon." The animal seemed ridiculously tiny in death. It lay on its side, its small mouth, crawling with ants, open in a bared-tooth grin, and its right rear leg in the clutch of the steel trap. It was easy to see how the animal had exhausted itself; it had been at its leg. A strip of flesh perhaps three inches in width had been gnawed away, leaving the white bone and a length of tendon exposed. Tiny flies sang about the ragged wound and over the pool of dried blood beneath the leg. There was a stink in the air, and it suddenly seemed very, very warm to me there in the morning shadows of the brush.

"Once in a while," my cousin said, prying open the curved   9 jaws of the trap, "one of them will chew his way loose, and if he doesn't lose too much blood he can live. I caught a three-legged coyote once. Too stupid to learn, I guess."

"Do you ever find one of them still alive?" I asked.   10
"Sometimes."   11
"What do you do with them?"   12
He looked up at me. "Do with them? I shoot them," he said,   13
patting the holstered pistol at his waist. He lifted the freed raccoon by the hind legs and swung it off into the brush. "Buzzard
meat," he said. He then grabbed the steel stake to which the trap
was attached by a chain and worked it out of the ground. "I've
had this line going for over a month, now. The area's just about
trapped out." He carried the trap back to the road, threw it in the
back of the pickup, and we drove up the increasingly rough road
to the next trap. It was empty, as was the one after it. I was
beginning to hope they would all be empty, but the fourth one
contained a small skunk, a black-and-white pussycat of a creature
that had managed to get three of its feet in the trap at once and
lay huddled in death like a child's stuffed toy. It, too, was disen-
gaged and tossed into the brush. A little further up the ridge, and
we found a fox, to my cousin's visible relief. "Great," he said.
"That has to be the mate to the one I got a couple of weeks ago.
Pregnant, too. There won't be any little foxes running around
this year." Into the brush the animal went.

By the time we reached the top of the long ridge on which my   14
cousin had set his traps, the morning had slipped toward noon
and our count had risen to seven animals: three raccoons, three
skunks, and the pregnant fox. There was only one trap left now,
but it was occupied by the prize of the morning, a bobcat. "I'll be
damned," my cousin said, "I've been after that bugger all month.
Just about give up hope." The bobcat had not died well, but in
anger. The marks of its rage and anguish were laid out in a torn
circle of earth described by the length of the chain that had linked
the animal to its death. Even the brush had been ripped and
clawed at, leaves and twigs stripped from branches, leaving
sweeping scars. Yellow tufts of the animal's fur lay scattered on
the ground, as if the bobcat had torn at its own body for betraying
it, and its death-mask was a silent howl of outrage. My cousin
took it out of the trap and heaved it down the side of the hill.
Buzzard meat.

We had to go back down the hills and around the range in   15
order to come up the eastern slopes and check out the second
trapline, and on the way we stopped at a small roadhouse in

Clayton for a hamburger and a beer. I found I could eat, which surprised me a little, and I certainly had a thirst for the beer. We sat side-by-side at the bar, not saying much. Something Wallace Stegner had once written kept flashing through my mind. "Like most of my contemporaries," he had said, "I grew up careless. I grew up killing things." I wondered if my cousin would know what Stegner had been talking about, and decided it would be best not to bring it up. I could have cancelled out right there, I suppose, asking him to take me back to his camp, explaining that I had seen enough, too much, of the trapper's life. I could always plead exhaustion. After all, the day's hiking had been more real exercise than I had had in months, and I was, in fact, tired. A stubborn kernel of pride would not let me do it. I would see the day through to the end.

So the ritual continued. We climbed back up into the hills on the east side of the range in the oven-heat of a strong spring sun. The day's count rose even more as the pickup bounced its way up the ragged weedgrown road: two more skunks, another fox, two more raccoons. The work went more slowly than the morning's run, for this was a new line, and each trap had to be reset. My cousin performed this task with an efficient swiftness and the kind of quiet pride any craftsman takes in his skill, snapping and locking the jaws of the traps, covering them with a thin scattering of earth and twigs, sprinkling the ground about with dog urine from a plastic squeeze bottle to cover up the man-smell. By the time we were ready to approach the last three traps of the line, it was well after three o'clock. We were very high by then, well up on the slopes of Mount Diablo itself, and we had to abandon the pickup to hike the rest of the way on foot. We broke out of the brush and walked along a spur of the hills. About 1,500 feet below us and some miles to the east, we could see the towns of Pittsburgh and Martinez sending an urban haze into the air. Ahead of me, my cousin suddenly stopped.

"Wait a minute. Listen," he said. 17

A distant thrashing and rattling sound came from the slope 18 below us. "That's where the trap is," he said. "Might be a bobcat, but I didn't expect to get him so soon. Come on."

The slope was very steep, and we slid much of the way down 19 to the trap on our bottoms, slapped at and tangled by brush. The animal was not a bobcat. It was a dog, a large, dirty-white mongrel whose foreleg was gripped in the trap. The dog snarled at us as we approached it. Saliva had gathered at its lips and there was a wildness in its eyes.

"*Dammit,*" my cousin said. He had owned dogs all his life. 20 "A wild dog. Probably abandoned by somebody. They do it all the time. Dogs turn wild and start running in packs. Some people ought to be shot."

I didn't know what he wanted to do. He hadn't pulled out 21 his gun. "Can we turn him loose? Maybe he isn't wild. Maybe he just wandered up here on his own."

My cousin looked at me. "Maybe. There's a noose-pole in the 22 back of the truck—a kind of a long stick with a loop of rope at the end. Why don't you get it?"

I scrambled back up the slope and made my way back to the 23 pickup, where I found the noose-pole. As thick as a broomhandle and about five feet in length, it looked like a primitive fishing pole. When I got back down to the trap, the dog was still snarling viciously. My cousin took the pole from me, opened the loop at the end, and extended it toward the dog. "If I can hook him," he said, "I'll hold his head down while you open the trap. You've seen how I do it."

It was useless. The dog fought at the loop frantically in a 24 madness of pain and fear. After perhaps 15 minutes, my cousin laid the pole down. "He just isn't going to take it."

"What'll we do?" I asked, though I'm sure I knew. 25

He shrugged. "Can't just leave him here to die." He uns- 26 napped his holster and pulled out the gun. He duck-walked to within a couple of feet of the animal, which watched him suspiciously. "I'll try to do it with one shot," he said. The gun's discharge slammed into the silence of the mountain. The dog howled once, a long, penetrating song of despair that ran in echoes down the hill. My cousin nudged the animal with his boot. It was dead. He opened the trap, freed the leg, and heaved the body down the slope. The crashing of its fall seemed to go on for a long time. My cousin reset the trap. "Come on," he said. "It's getting late."

The last trap of the day held a dead raccoon. 27

My cousin was pleased with the day's work. "If it keeps up 28 like this," he said as we rattled down the highway toward his trailer, "I could be out of here in a month."

"What's the hurry?"   29

He indicated a small housing development by the side of the   30
road. "Too much civilization around here for me. Too many
people. I need to get back up into the mountains."

There was plenty of light left when we got back, and true to   31
his promise, my cousin took the children out into the fields to see
a newborn lamb. While its mother bleated in protest, he ran one
down and brought it to my children so they could pet it. I
watched his face as he held the little creature. There was no hint in
it of all the death we had harvested that day, no hint of the
half-eaten legs we had seen, no hint of the fearful thrashing agony
the animals had endured before dying. No hint, even, of the
death-howl of the dirty white dog that may or may not have been
wild. There was neither irony nor cynicism in him. He held the
lamb with open, honest delight at the wonder my children found
in touching this small, warm, live thing.

My cousin is not an evil man. We are none of us evil men.   32

Questions for Close Reading

1. What is the selection's thesis (or narrative point)? Locate the sentence(s) in which Watkins states his main idea. If he does not state the thesis explicitly, express it in your own words.
2. Watkins explains that even ten years ago, he and his cousin weren't close or much alike. Why, then, was Watkins so eager to accompany his cousin on a trapping expedition? What fascination did trapping hold for Watkins?
3. Although Watkins doesn't approve of what his cousin does for a living, he is fair to him. Find places in the essay where Watkins points out (a) his cousin's good qualities and (b) his cousin's reasons for trapping.
4. What is the difference between the incident of the trapped dog and the other trapping incidents described in the essay? Why do you think Watkins described the episode with the dog at such length?
5. Refer to your dictionary as needed to define the following words used in the selection: *chaparral* (paragraph 2), *anarchic* (3), *predilection* (3), *lineal* (3), *emulated* (6), and *encompassed* (6).

Questions About the Writer's Craft

1. **The pattern.** Narratives rely on vivid description for much of their impact. As a narrator, Watkins is a master of sensory detail, particu-

larly when he wants us to see the death agonies of the trapped animals. Locate two paragraphs in which his descriptions of death are especially vivid. Which words and phrases make you understand the pain and horror of the animals' deaths?

2. What are some of the time signals that Watkins uses to indicate the sequence of events in his essay?

3. Watkins skillfully employs *simile*, a technique that uses the word *like* or *as* to highlight the similarities between two seemingly unlike objects. One example of simile can be found in paragraph 13, where Watkins describes the dead skunk as looking "like a child's stuffed toy." Find two more examples of similes in "Little Deaths."

4. How does Watkins use dialogue to reveal his cousin's attitudes toward animals? How do these comments help us understand Watkins's thesis?

Questions for Further Thought

1. In what ways are the animals' deaths "little" deaths? In what ways are they significant deaths? What else might have "died" during Watkins's experience?

2. The last paragraph of the selection reads, "My cousin is not an evil man. We are none of us evil men." Do you think Watkins is correct about his cousin? About humanity in general?

3. How might Watkins's cousin, so gentle with young children and a newborn lamb, justify to himself what he does for a living? Is there necessarily a conflict between the two sides of his character?

4. The essay raises the question of justifiable killing. Was the trapper justified in killing the animals because they were "varmints"? Should human needs and desires take precedence over an animal's right to live?

Writing Assignments Using Narration as a Pattern of Development

∞ 1. As Watkins has done, write a narrative about a moment of harsh discovery in your life. Describe how someone or something you had idealized turned out to be sharply different from what you had expected. Be sure you describe briefly, perhaps in the introduction, your original expectations. Langston Hughes's "Salvation" (page 186) may spark some insight into the all-too-common discrepancy between expectation and reality.

2. Undoubtedly, Watkins feels that his cousin treats life too casually. Write a narrative about a time when you treated life too lightly. The

life could be an animal's, another person's, even your own. Use specific details to tell what happened.

Writing Assignments Using Other Patterns of Development

3. Write an essay on either the pros or the cons of hunting. To identify helpful articles, look up "Hunting" or "Wildlife Management" in the *Readers' Guide to Periodical Literature*. In addition, you might talk to people you know about their attitudes toward hunting. Then take a position. Direct your essay to a confirmed nonhunter and show that hunting is beneficial. Or, conversely, direct the essay to an enthusiastic hunter and support the nonhunting position.

4. The philosopher Hannah Arendt refers in her writings to "the banality of evil." Evil may sometimes be part of the most ordinary, most normal people or activities. Write an essay about one commonly accepted activity that you believe is evil — or at least immoral. Offer detailed support showing how or why this activity is wrong. You might consider one of the following: killing animals for fur or food; our treatment of old people or children; our neglect or abuse of our environment. The scathing indictment of human nature that Mark Twain presents in "The Damned Human Race" (page 619) may give you some ideas for your essay.

Langston Hughes

One of the foremost members of the 1920s literary movement known as the Harlem Renaissance, Langston Hughes (1902–67) committed himself to portraying the richness of black life in America. A poet and a writer of short stories, Hughes was greatly influenced by the rhythms of blues and jazz. In his later years, he published two autobiographical works, *The Big Sea* (1940) and *I Wonder as I Wander* (1956), and he wrote a history of the National Association for the Advancement of Colored People (NAACP). The following selection is from *The Big Sea*.

Salvation

Disillusionment is part of growing up. As children, we start out expecting the best from people and from life. But as we grow older, experiences tend to chip away our cherished beliefs and trusting expectations. In "Salvation," Langston Hughes uses humor and poignancy to recount a time in his own childhood when he faced such a moment of disillusionment.

I was saved from sin when I was going on thirteen. But not really saved. It happened like this. There was a big revival at my Auntie Reed's church. Every night for weeks there had been much preaching, singing, praying, and shouting, and some very hardened sinners had been brought to Christ, and the membership of the church had grown by leaps and bounds. Then just before the revival ended, they held a special meeting for children, "to bring the young lambs to the fold." My aunt spoke of it for days ahead. That night I was escorted to the front row and placed on the mourners' bench with all the other young sinners, who had not yet been brought to Jesus.

My aunt told me that when you were saved you saw a light, and something happened to you inside! And Jesus came into your life! And God was with you from then on! She said you could see and hear and feel Jesus in your soul. I believed her. I had heard a great many old people say the same thing and it seemed to me they ought to know. So I sat there calmly in the hot, crowded church, waiting for Jesus to come to me.

The preacher preached a wonderful rhythmical sermon, all 3 moans and shouts and lonely cries and dire pictures of hell, and then he sang a song about the ninety and nine safe in the fold, but one little lamb was left out in the cold. Then he said: "Won't you come? Won't you come to Jesus? Young lambs, won't you come?" And he held out his arms to all us young sinners there on the mourners' bench. And the little girls cried. And some of them jumped up and went to Jesus right away. But most of us just sat there.

A great many older people came and knelt around us and 4 prayed, old women with jet-black faces and braided hair, old men with work-gnarled hands. And the church sang a song about the lower lights are burning, some poor sinners to be saved. And the whole building rocked with prayer and song.

Still I kept waiting to *see* Jesus. 5

Finally all the young people had gone to the altar and were 6 saved, but one boy and me. He was a rounder's son named Westley. Westley and I were surrounded by sisters and deacons praying. It was very hot in the church, and getting late now. Finally Westley said to me in a whisper: "God damn! I'm tired o' sitting here. Let's get up and be saved." So he got up and was saved.

Then I was left all alone on the mourners' bench. My aunt 7 came and knelt at my knees and cried, while prayers and songs swirled all around me in the little church. The whole congregation prayed for me alone, in a mighty wail of moans and voices. And I kept waiting serenely for Jesus, waiting, waiting—but he didn't come. I wanted to see him, but nothing happened to me. Nothing! I wanted something to happen to me, but nothing happened.

I heard the songs and the minister saying: "Why don't you 8 come? My dear child, why don't you come to Jesus? Jesus is waiting for you. He wants you. Why don't you come? Sister Reed, what is this child's name?"

"Langston," my aunt sobbed.   9

"Langston, why don't you come? Why don't you come and   10
be saved? Oh, Lamb of God! Why don't you come?"

Now it was really getting late. I began to be ashamed of   11
myself, holding everything up so long. I began to wonder what
God thought about Westley, who certainly hadn't seen Jesus
either, but who was now sitting proudly on the platform, swinging his knickerbockered legs and grinning down at me, surrounded by deacons and old women on their knees praying. God
had not struck Westley dead for taking his name in vain or for
lying in the temple. So I decided that maybe to save further
trouble, I'd better lie, too, and say that Jesus had come, and get
up and be saved.

So I got up.   12

Suddenly the whole room broke into a sea of shouting, as   13
they saw me rise. Waves of rejoicing swept the place. Women
leaped in the air. My aunt threw her arms around me. The minister took me by the hand and led me to the platform.

When things quieted down, in a hushed silence, punctuated   14
by a few ecstatic "Amens," all the new young lambs were blessed
in the name of God. Then joyous singing filled the room.

That night, for the last time in my life but one — for I was a   15
big boy twelve years old — I cried. I cried, in bed alone, and
couldn't stop. I buried my head under the quilts, but my aunt
heard me. She woke up and told my uncle I was crying because
the Holy Ghost had come into my life, and because I had seen
Jesus. But I was really crying because I couldn't bear to tell her
that I had lied, that I had deceived everybody in the church, and I
hadn't seen Jesus, and that now I didn't believe there was a Jesus
any more, since he didn't come to help me.

Questions for Close Reading

1. What is the selection's thesis (or narrative point)? Locate the sen-
   tence(s) in which Hughes states his main idea. If Hughes doesn't state
   the thesis explicitly, express it in your own words.
2. During the revival meeting, what pressures are put on the young
   Langston to get up and be saved?
3. How does Westley's attitude differ from Hughes's?
4. Does the narrator's Auntie Reed really understand him? Why can't he
   tell her the truth about his experience in the church?

5. Refer to your dictionary as needed to define the following words used in the selection: *revival* (paragraph 1), *knickerbockered* (11), *punctuated* (14), and *ecstatic* (14).

Questions About the Writer's Craft

1. **The pattern.** A narrative's power can often be traced to a conflict within the event being recounted. What conflict does the narrator of "Salvation" experience? How does Hughes create tension about this conflict?
2. What key role does Westley serve in the resolution of the narrator's dilemma? How does Hughes's inclusion of Westley in the story help us to understand the narrator better?
3. The thirteenth paragraph presents a metaphor of the church as an ocean. What images develop this metaphor? What does the metaphor tell us about Hughes's feelings and those of the church people?
4. The singing of hymns is a major part of this religious service. Why do you think Hughes has the narrator reveal the subjects and even the lyrics of some of the hymns?

Questions for Further Thought

1. What did Hughes expect to happen when he was "saved"? Was he led to have unrealistic expectations about this religious moment? Do you think children understand religious ideas differently from the way adults do? Explain.
2. Given the circumstances, do you think young Langston Hughes did the right thing? Why or why not?
3. Young people often feel pressured by family and community to adopt certain values, beliefs, or traditions. What are some of the pressures that you've experienced? Should young people presume that the older generation knows more about what to believe and do?
4. Is disillusionment with adults and with society's institutions an inevitable part of growing up? Why or why not?

Writing Assignments Using Narration as a Pattern of Development

1. Like Hughes, we sometimes believe that deception is our best alternative. Write a narrative about a time you felt deception was the best way either to protect those you care about or to maintain the respect of those important to you.
2. Write a narrative essay about a chain of events that caused you to become disillusioned about a person or institution you had pre-

viously regarded highly. Begin as Hughes does by presenting your initial beliefs. Relate the sequence of events that changed your evaluation of the person or organization. In the conclusion, explain the short- and long-term effects of the incident.

Writing Assignments Using Other Patterns of Development

3. Hughes writes, "My aunt told me that when you were saved, you saw a light, and something happened to you inside! And Jesus came into your life!" What causes people to change their beliefs? Do such changes come from waiting calmly, as Hughes tried to do in church, or must they come from a more active process? Write an essay explaining your viewpoint. You may use process analysis, causal analysis, or some other organizational pattern to develop your thesis. Be sure to include specific examples to support your understanding of the way beliefs change.

4. Write a persuasive essay arguing either that lying is sometimes right or that lying is always wrong. Apply your thesis to particular situations and show how lying is or is not the right course of action. Remember to acknowledge the opposing viewpoint. Lewis Thomas's "The Lie Detector" (page 510) may help you define your position. You might even mention Thomas's perspective in your essay.

Santha Rama Rau

Born in Madras, India, in 1923, Santha Rama Rau was educated in England and in the United States. While a senior at Wellesley College outside of Boston, she began writing an account of her return from the West at age sixteen to her upper-class Indian family. Her story turned into the popular, widely read memoir *Home to India*, published in 1945. *East of Home*, the tale of a trip through the Far East, followed in 1950, and *This Is India* in 1954. Her other novels and collected essays include *Remember the House* (1955), *Gifts of Passage* (1961), and *The Adventuress* (1970). The selection that follows, from *Gifts of Passage*, illustrates the gentle humor and depth of feeling that suffuse Rau's work, enabling Western readers to gain a surer understanding of Eastern culture.

By Any Other Name[1]

It can be painful to grow up in a country where a conquering power imposes its traditions and values on the native culture. In such a country, there's a constant tension between clinging to one's native identity and learning to cope with the dominant culture. In this selection, Santha Rama Rau recalls her experience as an Indian child in a British-run school, where the price of admission was her sense of self.

At the Anglo-Indian day school in Zorinabad to which my sister and I were sent when she was eight and I was five and a half, they changed our names. On the first day of school, a hot, windless morning of a north Indian September, we stood in the head-

1

---

[1]Rau's title is a reference to a line from Shakespeare's *Romeo and Juliet*. In the play, the Capulet and Montague families are engaged in a bitter feud, yet Juliet, a Capulet, and Romeo, a Montague, fall in love. During the famous balcony scene, Juliet cries out to Romeo, "O, be some other name! / What's in a name? That which we call a rose / By any other name would smell as sweet." To Rau, however, being called a name not one's own is anything but sweet.

191

mistress's study and she said, "Now you're the *new* girls. What are your names?"

My sister answered for us. "I am Premila, and she" — nodding in my direction — "is Santha." 2

The headmistress had been in India, I suppose, fifteen years 3 or so, but she still smiled her helpless inability to cope with Indian names. Her rimless half-glasses glittered, and the precarious bun on top of her head trembled as she shook her head. "Oh, my dears, those are much too hard for me. Suppose we give you pretty English names. Wouldn't that be more jolly? Let's see, now — Pamela for you, I think." She shrugged in a baffled way at my sister. "That's as close as I can get. And for *you*," she said to me, "how about Cynthia? Isn't that nice?"

My sister was always less easily intimidated than I was, and 4 while she kept a stubborn silence, I said, "Thank you," in a very tiny voice.

We had been sent to that school because my father, among 5 his responsibilities as an officer of the civil service, had a tour of duty to perform in the villages around that steamy little provincial town, where he had his headquarters at that time. He used to make his shorter inspection tours on horseback, and a week before, in the stale heat of a typically postmonsoon day, we had waved good-by to him and a little procession — an assistant, a secretary, two bearers, and the man to look after the bedding rolls and luggage. They rode away through our large garden, still bright green from the rains, and we turned back into the twilight of the house and the sound of fans whispering in every room.

Up to then, my mother had refused to send Premila to school 6 in the British-run establishments of that time, because, she used to say, "you can bury a dog's tail for seven years and it still comes out curly, and you can take a Britisher away from his home for a lifetime, and he still remains insular." The examinations and degrees from entirely Indian schools were not, in those days, considered valid. In my case, the question had never come up, and probably never would have come up if Mother's extraordinary good health had not broken down. For the first time in my life, she was not able to continue the lessons she had been giving us every morning. So our Hindi books were put away, the stories of the Lord Krishna as a little boy were left in midair, and we were sent to the Anglo-Indian school.

That first day at school is still, when I think of it, a remark-   7
able one. At that age, if one's name is changed, one develops a
curious form of dual personality. I remember having a certain
detached and disbelieving concern in the actions of "Cynthia,"
but certainly no responsibility. Accordingly, I followed the thin,
erect back of the headmistress down the veranda to my classroom
feeling, at most, a passing interest in what was going to happen to
me in this strange, new atmosphere of School.

The building was Indian in design, with wide verandas open-   8
ing onto a central courtyard, but Indian verandas are usually
white-washed, with stone floors. These, in the tradition of British
schools, were painted dark brown and had matting on the floors.
It gave a feeling of extra intensity to the heat.

I suppose there were about a dozen Indian children in the   9
school — which contained perhaps forty children in all — and
four of them were in my class. They were all sitting at the back of
the room, and I went to join them. I sat next to a small, solemn
girl who didn't smile at me. She had long, glossy-black braids and
wore a cotton dress, but she still kept on her Indian jewelry — a
gold chain around her neck, thin gold bracelets, and tiny ruby
studs in her ears. Like most Indian children, she had a rim of
black kohl around her eyes. The cotton dress should have looked
strange, but all I could think of was that I should ask my mother
if I couldn't wear a dress to school, too, instead of my Indian
clothes.

I can't remember too much about the proceedings in class   10
that day, except for the beginning. The teacher pointed to me and
asked me to stand up. "Now, dear, tell the class your name."

I said nothing.   11

"Come along," she said frowning slightly. "What's your   12
name, dear?"

"I don't know," I said, finally.   13

The English children in the front of the class — there were   14
about eight or ten of them — giggled and twisted around in their
chairs to look at me. I sat down quickly and opened my eyes very
wide, hoping in that way to dry them off. The little girl with the
braids put out her hand and very lightly touched my arm. She still
didn't smile.

Most of that morning I was rather bored. I looked briefly at   15
the children's drawings pinned to the wall, and then concentrated

on a lizard clinging to the ledge of the high, barred window behind the teacher's head. Occasionally it would shoot out its long yellow tongue for a fly, and then it would rest, with its eyes closed and its belly palpitating, as though it were swallowing several times quickly. The lessons were mostly concerned with reading and writing and simple numbers — things that my mother had already taught me — and I paid very little attention. The teacher wrote on the easel blackboard words like "bat" and "cat," which seemed babyish to me; only "apple" was new and incomprehensible.

When it was time for the lunch recess, I followed the girl with braids out onto the veranda. There the children from the other classes were assembled. I saw Premila at once and ran over to her, as she had charge of our lunchbox. The children were all opening packages and sitting down to eat sandwiches. Premila and I were the only ones who had Indian food — thin wheat chapatties,[2] some vegetable curry, and a bottle of buttermilk. Premila thrust half of it into my hand and whispered fiercely that I should go and sit with my class, because that was what the others seemed to be doing.   16

The enormous black eyes of the little Indian girl from my class looked at my food longingly, so I offered her some. But she only shook her head and plowed her way solemnly through her sandwiches.   17

I was very sleepy after lunch, because at home we always took a siesta. It was usually a pleasant time of day, with the bedroom darkened against the harsh afternoon sun, the drifting off into sleep with the sound of Mother's voice reading a story in one's mind, and, finally, the shrill, fussy voice of the ayah waking one for tea.   18

At school, we rested for a short time on low, folding cots on the veranda, and then we were expected to play games. During the hot part of the afternoon we played indoors, and after the shadows had begun to lengthen and the slight breeze of the evening had come up we moved outside to the wide courtyard.   19

I had never really grasped the system of competitive games. At home, whenever we played tag or guessing games, I was always allowed to "win" — "because," Mother used to tell Premila, "she   20

---

[2] A flat, cracker-like bread.

is the youngest, and we have to allow for that." I had often heard her say it, and it seemed quite reasonable to me, but the result was that I had no clear idea of what "winning" meant.

When we played twos-and-threes that afternoon at school, in   21
accordance with my training, I let one of the small English boys catch me, but was naturally rather puzzled when the other children did not return the courtesy. I ran about for what seemed like hours without ever catching anyone, until it was time for school to close. Much later I learned that my attitude was called "not being a good sport," and I stopped allowing myself to be caught, but it was not for years that I really learned the spirit of the thing.

When I saw our car come up to the school gate, I broke away   22
from my classmates and rushed toward it yelling, "Ayah! Ayah!" It seemed like an eternity since I had seen her that morning—a wizened, affectionate figure in her white cotton sari, giving me dozens of urgent and useless instructions on how to be a good girl at school. Premila followed more sedately, and she told me on the way home never to do that again in front of the other children.

When we got home we went straight to Mother's high, white   23
room to have tea with her, and I immediately climbed onto the bed and bounced gently up and down on the springs. Mother asked how we had liked our first day in school. I was so pleased to be home and to have left that peculiar Cynthia behind that I had nothing whatever to say about school, except to ask what "apple" meant. But Premila told Mother about the classes, and added that in her class they had weekly tests to see if they learned their lessons well.

I asked, "What's a test?"   24

Premila said, "You're too small to have them. You won't   25
have them in your class for donkey's years." She had learned the expression that day and was using it for the first time. We all laughed enormously at her wit. She also told Mother, in an aside, that we should take sandwiches to school the next day. Not, she said, that *she* minded. But they would be simpler for me to handle.

That whole lovely evening I didn't think about school at all.   26
I sprinted barefoot across the lawns with my favorite playmate, the cook's son, to the stream at the end of the garden. We quarreled in our usual way, waded in the tepid water under the

lime trees, and waited for the night to bring out the smell of the jasmine. I listened with fascination to his stories of ghosts and demons, until I was too frightened to cross the garden alone in the semidarkness. The ayah found me, shouted at the cook's son, scolded me, hurried me into supper—it was an entirely usual, wonderful evening.

It was a week later, the day of Premila's first test, that our lives changed rather abruptly. I was sitting at the back of my class, in my usual inattentive way, only half listening to the teacher. I had started a rather guarded friendship with the girl with the braids, whose name turned out to be Nalini (Nancy, in school). The three other Indian children were already fast friends. Even at that age it was apparent to all of us that friendship with the English or Anglo-Indian children was out of the question. Occasionally, during the class, my new friend and I would draw pictures and show them to each other secretly.   27

The door opened sharply and Premila marched in. At first, the teacher smiled at her in a kindly and encouraging way and said, "Now, you're little Cynthia's sister?"   28

Premila didn't even look at her. She stood with her feet planted firmly apart and her shoulders rigid, and addressed herself directly to me. "Get up," she said. "We're going home."   29

I didn't know what had happened, but I was aware that it was a crisis of some sort. I rose obediently and started to walk toward my sister.   30

"Bring your pencils and your notebook," she said.   31

I went back for them, and together we left the room. The teacher started to say something just as Premila closed the door, but we didn't wait to hear what it was.   32

In complete silence we left the school grounds and started to walk home. Then I asked Premila what the matter was. All she would say was "We're going home for good."   33

It was a very tiring walk for a child of five and a half, and I dragged along behind Premila with my pencils growing sticky in my hand. I can still remember looking at the dusty hedges, and the tangles of thorns in the ditches by the side of the road, smelling the faint fragrance from the eucalyptus trees and wondering whether we would ever reach home. Occasionally a horse-drawn tonga[3] passed us, and the women, in their pink or green   34

[3]A carriage.

silks, stared at Premila and me trudging along on the side of the road. A few coolies and a line of women carrying baskets of vegetables on their heads smiled at us. But it was nearing the hottest time of day, and the road was almost deserted. I walked more and more slowly, and shouted to Premila, from time to time, "Wait for me!" with increasing peevishness. She spoke to me only once, and that was to tell me to carry my notebook on my head, because of the sun.

When we got to our house the ayah was just taking a tray of   35
lunch into Mother's room. She immediately started a long, worried questioning about what are you children doing back here at this hour of the day.

Mother looked very startled and very concerned, and asked   36
Premila what had happened.

Premila said, "We had our test today, and she made me and   37
the other Indians sit at the back of the room, with a desk between each one."

Mother said, "Why was that, darling?"   38

"She said it was because Indians cheat," Premila added. "So I   39
don't think we should go back to that school."

Mother looked very distant, and was silent a long time. At   40
last she said, "Of course not, darling." She sounded displeased.

We all shared the curry she was having for lunch, and after-   41
ward I was sent off to the beautifully familiar bedroom for my siesta. I could hear Mother and Premila talking through the open door.

Mother said, "Do you suppose she understood all that?"   42
Premila said, "I shouldn't think so. She's a baby."   43
Mother said, "Well, I hope it won't bother her."   44
Of course, they were both wrong. I understood it perfectly,   45
and I remember it all very clearly. But I put it happily away, because it had all happened to a girl called Cynthia, and I never was really particularly interested in her.

Questions for Close Reading

1. What is the selection's thesis (or narrative point)? Locate the sentence(s) in which Rau states her main idea. If she doesn't state the thesis explicitly, express it in your own words.
2. What does Rau's mother mean when she says that "you can bury a dog's tail for seven years and it still comes out curly, and you can take a Britisher away from his home for a lifetime, and he can still remain

insular" (paragraph 6)? How does Rau's narrative verify the validity of this statement?

3. What confusions does Rau experience at school? What new ideas and behaviors does she encounter?

4. Why do the two sisters leave school? What does their decision suggest about the relationship between the British and Indian cultures?

5. Refer to your dictionary as needed to define the following words used in the selection: *precarious* (paragraph 3), *intimidated* (4), *insular* (6), *veranda* (7), *palpitating* (15), *ayah* (18), *jasmine* (26), and *eucalyptus* (34).

Questions About the Writer's Craft

1. **The pattern.** Find places in the narrative where Rau uses dialogue to tell her story. Why might she have included dialogue at these points and not at others?

2. **Other patterns.** Where in the selection does Rau use contrasts? How do these contrasts help dramatize the essay's narrative point?

3. **Other patterns.** In several places, Rau uses vivid descriptive detail. Locate these descriptive passages. How do they help convey the overall meaning of Rau's experiences in the British-run school?

4. Look closely at the selection's first sentence. Pay special attention to the way meaning unfolds and to the placement of the main subject and verb. Why might Rau have chosen to open her narrative with such a sentence? What effect might she have hoped the sentence would have on readers?

Questions for Further Thought

1. Have you, like the young Rau, ever been a newcomer in a situation where everyone else was familiar with the situation's ongoing routines? How long did it take you to fit in and feel as though you belonged? How difficult was the transition?

2. Rau felt that the English name forced upon her didn't represent her true self. Do you agree that your name *is* you or is a part of you? Could you change your name, or have it changed, without feeling some violation of your sense of identity? Or is there something else about you that you feel is as basic a part of your identity as Rau's name was to her? If so, what?

3. Rau's eight-year-old sister took charge and made an adult-like decision not to endure insult. Do you agree that she handled the situation in the best way—by walking out? What would you have done if you were (a) Premila, (b) her mother, or (c) the other Indians in the school?

4. When we find ourselves in a hostile, unfriendly environment, most of us gravitate toward those who remind us of ourselves. That's why the five-year-old Rau instinctively seeks out the small Indian girl with unsmiling eyes. What are the advantages of this tendency to band together with those who are like us? What are its disadvantages?

Writing Assignments Using Narration as a Pattern of Development

∞ 1. Rau's mother describes the British as being "insular." Convinced that their ways are right, they remain insensitive to those they perceive as "different." In an essay, tell about a specific time that you had trouble recognizing another person's individuality and worth because you tended to view the person from a limited perspective. Perhaps you dismissed the person because his or her appearance, family background, or circle of friends was different from yours. Conversely, you may write about a time when someone was unable to see the real you. In either case, explain what you learned from the event, and include only those details and conversational exchanges that dramatize your narrative point. Peter Farb's "In Other Words" (page 491) and Migdia Chinea-Varela's "My Life as a 'Twofer'" (page 613) may provide some ideas to explore in your own essay.

∞ 2. Premila exerts pressure on her little sister to conform to the unspoken rules of the school — for example, not to second-guess a teacher and not to eat lunch with younger children. Such pressure, whether from a sibling, friend, or family, is a powerful force in the lives of most people. Write an essay narrating a time when pressure was exerted on you to change in some way. Tell how you handled the pressure, and indicate whether you did indeed change. If you did change, what did you change and how did you feel about it? Make sure that you focus on specific moments, individual scenes, and conversations. Also, take time to characterize the people who pressured you or helped you resist. Langston Hughes's "Salvation" (page 186) should spark some interesting thoughts about the way external pressures influence behavior and self-concept.

Writing Assignments Using Other Patterns of Development

∞ 3. As Indians, Rau and her sister are made to feel like outsiders in the British-run school. But cultural differences aren't the only factors that cause children to feel uncomfortable in school. For example, they may have trouble fitting in because they have a learning disability, are shy, or need more (or less) structure than the school provides. Select one such problem, and write an essay arguing that students with this problem must cope with teachers' indifference and insensitivity. Alternatively, you may write a paper arguing that such students are treated with sensitivity and respect. No matter which position you take, acknowledge the opposing viewpoint and provide numerous examples to support your viewpoint. You may want to brainstorm with others to gather material for your essay. Peter Farb's "In Other Words" (page 491) should also spark some ideas worth considering.

4. As Rau shows, a new experience often brings about significant and unexpected change. Select a major event (the birth of a baby, a divorce, going away to school) in your life or in the life of someone you know well. Then write an essay comparing and contrasting what life was like before and after the change.

Additional Writing Topics

NARRATION

General Assignments

Prepare an essay on any of the following topics, using narration as the paper's dominant method of development. Be sure to select details that advance the essay's narrative purpose; you may even want to experiment with flashback or flashforward. In any case, keep the sequence of events clear by using transitional cues. Within the limited time span covered, use vigorous details and varied sentence structure to enliven the narrative. Tell the story from a consistent point of view.

1. An emergency that brought out the best or worst in you
2. The hazards of taking children out to eat
3. An incident that made you believe in fate
4. Your best or worst day at school or work
5. A major decision
6. An encounter with a machine
7. An important learning experience
8. A narrow escape
9. Your first date, first day on the job, or first anything
10. A memorable childhood experience
11. A fairy tale the way you would like to hear it told
12. A painful moment
13. An incredible but true story
14. A significant family event
15. An experience in which a certain emotion (pride, anger, regret, or some other) was dominant

Assignments with a Specific Purpose and Audience

1. As the fund-raiser for a particular organization (for example, Red Cross, SPCA, Big Brothers/Big Sisters), you're sending a newsletter to contributors. Support your cause by telling the story of a time when your organization made all the difference—the blood donation that saved a life, the animal that was rescued from abuse, and so on.

2. A friend of yours has seen someone cheat on a test, shoplift, or violate an employer's trust. In a letter, convince this friend to inform the instructor, store owner, or employer by narrating an incident in

which a witness did (or did not) speak up in such a situation. Tell what happened as a result.

3. You have had a disturbing encounter with one of the people who seem to have "fallen through the cracks" of society—a street person, an unwanted child, or anyone else who is alone and abandoned. Write a letter to the local newspaper describing this encounter. Your purpose is to arouse people's indignation and compassion and to get help for such unfortunates.

4. Write an article for your old high school newspaper. The article will be read primarily by seniors who are planning to go away to college next year. In the article, narrate a story that points to some truth about the "breaking away" stage of life.

5. A close friend has written a letter to you telling about a bad experience that he or she had with a teacher, employer, doctor, repairperson, or some other professional. Based on that single experience, your friend now negatively stereotypes the entire profession. Write a letter to your friend balancing his or her cynical picture by narrating a story that shows the "flip side" of this profession—someone who made every effort to help.

6. Your younger brother, sister, relative, or neighborhood friend can't wait to be your age. By narrating an appropriate story, show the young person that your age isn't as wonderful as he or she thinks. Be sure to select a story that the person can understand and appreciate.

5

EXEMPLIFICATION

WHAT IS EXEMPLIFICATION?

If someone asked you, "Have you been to any good restaurants lately?" you probably wouldn't answer "Yes" and then immediately change the subject. Most likely, you would go on to illustrate with *examples*. Perhaps you'd give the names of restaurants you've enjoyed and talk briefly about the specific things you liked: the attractive prices, the tasty main courses, the pleasant service, the tempting desserts. Such examples and details are needed to convince others that your opinion—in this or any matter—is valid. Similarly, when you talk about larger and more important issues, people won't pay much attention to your opinion if all you do is string together vague generalizations: "We have to do something about acid rain. It's had disastrous consequences for the environment. Its negative effects increase every year. Action must be taken to control the problem." To be taken seriously and convince others that your point is well-founded, you must provide specific supporting examples: "the forests in the Adirondacks are dying"; "yesterday's rainfall was fifty times more acidic than normal"; "Pine Lake, in the northern part of the state, was once a great fishing spot but now has no fish population."

Examples are equally important when you write an essay. It's not fuzzy generalities and highfaluting abstractions that make writing impressive. Just the opposite is true. Facts, anecdotes, statistics, details, opinions, and observations are at the heart of effective writing, giving your work substance and solidity.

HOW EXEMPLIFICATION FITS YOUR PURPOSE AND AUDIENCE

The wording of assignments and essay exam questions may signal the need for specific examples:

> Soap operas, whether shown during the day or in the evening, are among the most popular television programs. Why do you think this is so? Provide specific examples to support your position.

> Some observers claim that college students are less interested in learning than in getting ahead in their careers. Cite evidence to support or refute this claim.

> A growing number of people feel that parents should not allow young children to participate in highly competitive team sports. Basing your conclusion on your own experiences and observations, indicate whether you think this point of view is reasonable.

Such phrases as "Provide specific examples," "Cite evidence," and "Basing your conclusion on your own experiences and observations" signal that each essay would be developed through examples.

Usually, though, you won't be told so explicitly to provide examples. Instead, as you think about the best way to achieve your essay's purpose, you'll see the need for illustrative details — no matter which patterns of development you use. For instance, to *persuade* skeptical readers that the country needs a national health system, you might mention specific cases to dramatize the inadequacy of our current health-care system: a family bank-rupted by medical bills; an uninsured accident victim turned away by a hospital; a chronically ill person rapidly deteriorating be-cause he didn't have enough money to visit a doctor. Or imagine a lightly satiric piece that pokes fun at cat lovers. Insisting that "cat people" are pretty strange creatures, you might make your point — and make readers chuckle — with a series of examples *contrasting* cat lovers and dog lovers: the qualities admired by each group (loyalty in dogs versus independence in cats) and the different expectations each group has for its pets (dog lovers want Fido to be obedient and lovable, whereas cat lovers are satisfied with Felix's occasional spurts of docility and affection). Similarly, you would supply examples in a *causal analysis* speculating on the likely impact of a proposed tuition hike at your college. To convince the college administration of the probable negative ef-fects of such a hike, you might cite the following examples: articles reporting a nationwide upswing in student transfers to less expensive schools; statistics indicating a significant drop in grades among already employed students forced to work more hours to pay increased tuition costs; interviews with students too financially strapped to continue their college education.

Whether you use examples as the primary or supplemental method of development, they serve a number of important pur-poses. For one thing, examples make writing *interesting*. Assume you're writing an essay about sexism in television commercials. Your essay would be lifeless and boring if all it did was repeat, in a general way, that commercials present stereotyped views of men and women:

Sexism is rampant in television commercials. It is very much alive, yet most viewers seem to take it all in stride. Few people protest the obviously sexist characters and statements on such com-mercials. Surely, these commercials misrepresent the way most of us live.

Without interesting particulars, readers may respond, "Who cares?" But if you provide specific examples, you'll attract your readers' attention:

Sexism is rampant in television commercials. Although millions of women hold responsible jobs outside the home, commercials continue to portray women as simple creatures who spend most of their time thinking about wax buildup, cottony-soft bathroom tissue, and static-free clothes. Men, apparently, have better things to do than fret over such mundane household matters. How many commercials can you recall that depict men proclaiming the virtues of squeaky-clean dishes or sparkling bathrooms? Not many.

Examples also make writing *persuasive*. Most writing conveys a point, but many readers are reluctant to accept someone else's point of view unless evidence demonstrates its validity. Imagine you're writing an essay showing that latchkey children are more self-sufficient and emotionally secure than children who return from school to a home where a parent awaits them. Your thesis is obviously controversial. Without specific examples — from your own experience, personal observations, or research studies — your readers would undoubtedly question your position's validity.

Further, examples *help explain* difficult, abstract, or unusual ideas. Suppose you're assigned an essay on a complex subject such as inflation, zero population growth, or radiation exposure. As a writer, you have a responsibility to your readers to make these difficult concepts concrete and understandable. If writing an essay on radiation exposure in everyday life, you might start by providing specific examples of home appliances that emit radiation — color televisions, computers, and microwave ovens — and tell exactly how much radiation we absorb in a typical day from such equipment. To illustrate further the extent of our radiation exposure, you could also provide specifics about unavoidable sources of natural radiation (the sun, for instance) and details about the widespread use of radiation in medicine (X-rays, radiation therapy). These examples would ground your discussion, making it immediate and concrete, preventing it from flying off into the vague and theoretical.

Finally, examples *help prevent unintended ambiguity*. All of us have experienced the frustration of having someone misinterpret what we say. In face-to-face communication, we can provide on-the-spot clarification. In writing, however, instantaneous feedback isn't available, so it's crucial that meaning be as unambiguous as possible. Examples will help.

Assume you're writing an essay asserting that ineffective teaching is on the rise in today's high schools. To clarify what you mean by "ineffective," you provide examples: the instructor who spends so much time disciplining unruly students that he never gets around to teaching; the moonlighting teacher who is so tired in class that she regularly takes naps during tests; the teacher who accepts obviously plagiarized reports because he's grateful that students hand in something. Without such concrete examples, your readers will supply their own ideas — and these may not be what you had in mind. Readers might imagine "ineffective" to mean harsh and punitive, whereas your concrete examples would show that you intend it to mean out of control and irresponsible. Such specifics help prevent misunderstanding.

SUGGESTIONS FOR USING EXEMPLIFICATION IN AN ESSAY

The following suggestions will be helpful whether you use examples as a dominant or supportive pattern of development.

1. Generate examples.   Where do you get the examples to develop your essay? The first batch of examples is generated during the prewriting stage. With your purpose and thesis in mind, you make a broad sweep for examples, using brainstorming, freewriting, the mapping technique — whichever prewriting technique you prefer. During this preliminary search for examples, you may also read through your journal for relevant specifics, interview other people, or conduct library research.

Examples can take several forms, including specific names (of people, places, products, and so on), anecdotes, personal observations, expert opinion, as well as facts, statistics, and case studies gathered through research. While prewriting, try to generate more examples than you think you'll need. Starting with abundance — and then picking out the strongest examples — will give you a firm base on which to build the essay. If you have a great deal of trouble finding examples to support your thesis, you may need to revise the thesis; you may be trying to support an idea that has little validity. On the other hand, while prewriting, you may unearth numerous examples but find that many of them contradict the point you started out to support. If that happens, don't hesitate to recast your central point, always remembering that your thesis and examples must fit.

2. Select the examples to include.   Once you've used prewriting to generate as many examples as possible, you're ready to limit your examples to the strongest. Keeping your purpose, thesis, and audience in mind, ask yourself several key questions: "Which examples support my thesis? Which do not? Which are most convincing? Which are most likely to interest readers and clarify meaning?"

You may include several brief examples within a single sentence:

> The French people's fascination with some American literary figures, such as Poe and Hawthorne, is understandable, but their great respect for "artists" like comedian Jerry Lewis is a mystery.

Or you may develop a paragraph with a number of "for instances":

> A uniquely American style of movie-acting reached its peak in the 1950s. Certain charismatic actors completely abandoned the stage techniques and tradition that had been the foundation of acting up to that time. Instead of articulating their lines clearly, the actors mumbled; instead of making firm eye contact with their colleagues, they hung their heads, shifted their eyes, even talked with their eyes closed. Marlon Brando, Montgomery Cliff, and then James Dean, were three actors who exemplified this new trend.

As the preceding paragraph shows, *several examples* are usually needed to make a point. An essay with the thesis "Rock videos are dangerously violent" wouldn't be convincing if you gave only one example of a violent rock video. Several strong examples would be needed for readers to feel you had illustrated your point sufficiently. Occasionally, *one extended example,* fully developed with many details, can support an essay. It might be possible, for instance, to support the thesis "Federal legislation should raise the legal drinking age to twenty-one" with a single compelling, highly detailed example of the effects of one teenager's drunken-driving spree.

The examples you choose must also be *relevant*; that is, they must have direct bearing on the point you want to make. You would have a hard time convincing readers that Americans have callous attitudes toward the elderly if you described the wide range of new programs, all staffed by volunteers, at a well-financed center for senior citizens. Because these examples *contradict*, rather than support, your thesis, readers are apt to dismiss what you have to say.

Make certain, too, that your examples are *accurate*. Exercise special caution when using statistics. An old saying warns that there are lies, damned lies, and statistics — meaning that statistics can be misleading. A commercial may claim, "In a taste test, 80 percent of those questioned indicated that they preferred Fizzy Cola." Impressed? Don't be — at least, not until you find out how the test was conducted. Perhaps the subjects had to choose between Fizzy Cola and battery acid, or perhaps there were only five subjects, all Fizzy Cola vice presidents.

Finally, select *representative* examples. Picking the oddball, one-in-a-million example to support a point — and passing it off as typical — is dishonest. Consider an essay with the thesis "Part-time jobs contribute to academic success." Citing only one example of a student who works at a job twenty-five hours a week while earning straight A's isn't playing fair. Why not? You've made a *sweeping generalization* based on only one case. To be convincing, you need to show how holding down a job affects *most* students' academic performance. (For more on sweeping generalizations, see pages 585–588.)

3. Develop your examples sufficiently.   To ensure that you get your ideas across, your examples must be *specific*. An essay on the types of heroes in American movies wouldn't succeed if you simply strung together a series of undeveloped examples in paragraphs like this one:

> Heroes in American movies usually fall into types. One kind of hero is the tight-lipped loner, men like Clint Eastwood and Humphrey Bogart. Another movie hero is the quiet, shy, or fumbling type who has appeared in movies since the beginning. The main characteristic of this hero is lovableness, as seen in actors like Jimmy Stewart. Perhaps the most one-dimensional and predictable hero is the superman who battles tough odds. This kind of hero is best illustrated by Sylvester Stallone as Rocky and Rambo.

If you developed the essay in this way — if you moved from one undeveloped example to another — you would be doing little more than making a list. To be effective, key examples must be expanded in sufficient detail. The examples in the preceding paragraph could be developed in paragraphs of their own. You could, for instance, develop the first example this way:

> Heroes can be tight-lipped loners who appear out of nowhere, form no permanent attachments, and walk, drive, or ride off into the sunset. In many of his Westerns, from the low-budget "spaghetti Westerns" of the 1960s to <u>Pale Rider</u> in 1985, Clint Eastwood personifies this kind of hero. He is remote, mysterious, and untalkative. Yet he guns down an evil sheriff, runs other villains out of town, and helps a handicapped girl--acts that cement his heroic status. The loner might also be Sam Spade as played by Humphrey Bogart. Spade solves the crime and sends the guilty off to jail, yet he holds his emotions in check and has no permanent ties beyond his faithful secretary and shabby office. One gets the feeling that he could walk away from these, too, if necessary. Even in <u>The Right Stuff</u>, an account of America's early astronauts, the scriptwriters mold Chuck Yeager, the man who broke the sound barrier, into a classic loner. Yeager, portrayed by the aloof Sam Shepard, has a wife, but he is nevertheless insular. Taking mute pride in his ability to distance himself from politicians, bureaucrats, even colleagues, he soars into space, dignified and detached. (For hints on ways to make writing specific, see pages 42–43.)

4. Organize the examples.   If, as is usually the case, several examples support your point, be sure to present the examples in an *organized* manner. Often you'll find that other patterns of development (cause-effect, comparison-contrast, definition, and so on) suggest ways to sequence examples. Let's say you're writing an essay showing that stay-at-home vacations offer numerous opportunities to relax. You might begin the essay with examples that *contrast* stay-at-home and get-away vacations. Then you might move to a *process analysis* that illustrates different techniques for unwinding at home. The essay might end with examples showing the *effect* of such leisurely at-home breaks.

Finally, you need to select an *organizational approach consistent* with your *purpose* and *thesis*. Imagine you're writing an essay about students' adjustment during the first months of college. The supporting examples could be arranged *chronologically*. You might start by illustrating the ambivalence many students feel the first day of college when their parents leave for home; you might then offer an anecdote or two about students' frequent calls to Mom and Dad during the opening weeks of the semester; the essay might close with an account of students' reluctance to leave campus at the midyear break.

Similarly, an essay demonstrating that a room often reflects the character of its occupant might be organized *spatially*: from the empty soda cans on the floor to the spitballs on the ceiling. In an essay illustrating the kinds of skills taught in a composition course, you might move from *simple* to *complex* examples: starting with relatively matter-of-fact skills like spelling and punctuation and ending with more conceptually difficult skills like formulating a thesis and organizing an essay. Last, the *emphatic sequence* —in which you lead from your first example to your final, most significant one—is another effective way to organize an essay with many examples. A paper about Americans' characteristic impatience might progress from minor examples (dependence on fast food, obsession with ever-faster mail delivery) to more disturbing manifestations of impatience (using drugs as quick solutions to problems, advocating simple answers to complex international problems: "Bomb them!").

Without appropriate and dynamic examples, an essay is a dry, bloodless thing. Even provocative and intriguing ideas lose their power—or may be misunderstood—if writers don't provide the specific details needed to explain and develop their central points. Remember that most readers will not take seriously a writer who has been too lazy to do anything but spout a series of vague generalities. If you examine a stirring speech, a riveting newspaper article, an informative book, you're sure to find clear, well-developed examples. These specifics engage the reader and provide the writing with its distinctive energy.

STUDENT ESSAY

The following student essay was written by Michael Pagano in response to this assignment:

Anne Morrow Lindbergh states in "Channelled Whelk" that Americans impose unnecessary complications on their lives. Observe closely the way you and others conduct your daily lives. Use your observations to generate evidence for an essay that supports or refutes Lindbergh's point of view.

While reading Michael's paper, try to determine how effectively it applies the principles of exemplification. The annotations on Michael's paper and the commentary following it will help you look at the essay more closely.

Pursuit of Possessions
by Michael Pagano

Introduction

In the essay "Channelled Whelk," Anne Morrow Lindbergh states that Americans "who could choose simplicity, choose complication." Lindbergh herself is a prime example of the phenomenon she discusses. A wife and a mother, as well as a writer, Lindbergh has many obligations that make for a complicated life. Even so, Lindbergh attempts to simplify her life by escaping to a beach cottage that is bare except for driftwood and shells for decoration; there she is happy. But very few of us would be willing to simplify our lives as Lindbergh does. Instead, we choose to clutter our lives with a stream of material possessions. And what is the result of this mania for possessions? Much of our time goes to buying new things, dealing with the complications they create, and working madly to buy more things or pay for the things we already have.   1

Thesis

Plan of development

Topic sentence

The first of three paragraphs in a chronological sequence

We devote a great deal of our lives to acquiring the material goods we imagine are essential to our well-being. Hours are spent planning and thinking about our future purchases. We window-shop for designer jogging shoes; we leaf through magazines looking at ads for elaborate stereo equipment; we research back issues of Consumer Reports to find out about recent developments in exercise equipment. Moreover, once we find what we are looking for, more time is taken up when we decide to actually buy the items. How do we find   2 this time? That's easy. We turn evenings, weekends, and holidays--time that used to be set aside for family and friends--into shopping expeditions. No wonder family life is deteriorating and children spend so much time in front of television sets. Their parents are seldom around.

Topic sentence ⟶

The second paragraph in the chronological sequence

A paragraph with many specific examples

As soon as we take our new purchases home, they begin to complicate our lives. A sleek new sports car has to be washed, waxed, and vacuumed. A fashionable pair of skintight jeans can't be thrown in the washing machine but has to be taken to the dry cleaner. New stereo equipment has to be connected with a tangled network of cables to the TV, radio, and cassette deck. Eventually, of course, the inevitable happens. Our indispensable possessions break down and need to be repaired. The home computer starts to lose data, the microwave has to have its temperature controls adjusted, and the videotape recorder has to be serviced when a cassette becomes jammed in the machine.

Topic sentence ⟶

The third paragraph in the chronological sequence

After more time has gone by, we sometimes discover that our purchases don't suit us anymore, and so we decide to replace them. Before making our replacement purchases, though, we have to find ways to get rid of the old items. If we want to replace our black-and-white 19-inch television set with a 25-inch color set, we have to find time to put an ad in the classified section of the paper. Then we have to handle phone calls and set up times people can come to look at the TV. We could store the set in the basement--if we are lucky enough to find a spot that isn't already filled with other discarded purchases.

Topic sentence with emphasis signal

Worst of all, this mania for possessions often influences our approach to work. It is not unusual for people to take a second or even a third job to pay off the debt they fall into because they have overbought. After paying for food, clothing, and shelter, many people see the rest of their paycheck go to Visa, MasterCard, department store charge accounts, and time payments. Panic sets in when they realize there simply is not enough money to cover all their expenses. Just to stay afloat, people

3

4

5

Conclusion

may have to work overtime or take on additional jobs.

It is clear that many of us have allowed the   6
pursuit of possessions to dominate our lives. We are so busy buying, maintaining, and paying for our worldly goods that we do not have much time to think about what is really important. We should try to step back from our compulsive need for more of everything and get in touch with the basic values that are the real point of our lives.

COMMENTARY

Thesis, other patterns of development, and plan of development.   In "Pursuit of Possessions," Michael analyzes the American mania for acquiring material goods. He begins with a quotation from Anne Morrow Lindbergh's "Channelled Whelk" and briefly explains Lindbergh's strategy for simplifying her life. The reference to Lindbergh gives Michael a chance to *contrast* the way she tries to lead her life with the acquisitive and frenzied way many Americans lead theirs. This contrast leads logically to the essay's *thesis*: "We choose to clutter our lives with a stream of material possessions."

Besides introducing the basic contrast at the heart of the essay, Michael's opening paragraph helps readers see that the essay contains an element of *causal analysis*. Michael asks, "What is the result of this mania for possessions?" and then answers that question in the next sentence. This sentence also serves as the essay's *plan of development* and reveals that Michael feels the pursuit of possessions negatively affects our lives in three key ways.

Essays of this length often don't need a plan of development. But since Michael's paper is filled with many *examples*, the plan of development helps readers see how all the details relate to the essay's central point.

Evidence.   Support for the thesis consists of examples organized around the three major points signaled by the plan of development. Michael uses one paragraph to develop his first and third points and two paragraphs to develop his second point. Each of the four supporting paragraphs is focused by a *topic sentence* that appears at the start of the paragraph. The transitional phrase "Worst of all" (paragraph 5) signals that Michael has sequenced his major points *emphatically,* saving for last the issue he considers most significant: how the "mania for possessions . . . influences our approach to work."

Organizational strategies. Emphatic order isn't Michael's only organizational technique. When reading the paper, you probably felt that there was an easy flow from one supporting paragraph to the next. How does Michael achieve such *coherence between paragraphs*? For one thing, he sequences paragraphs 2–4 *chronologically*: what happens before a purchase is made; what happens afterward. Secondly, topic sentences in paragraphs 3 and 4 include *signal devices* that indicate this passage of time. The topic sentences also strengthen coherence by *linking back* to the preceding paragraph: "*As soon as we take our new purchases home,* they . . . complicate our lives" and "*After more time has gone by,* we . . . discover that our purchases don't suit us anymore."

The same organizing strategies are used *within paragraphs* to make the essay coherent. Details in paragraphs 2–4 are sequenced *chronologically,* and to help readers follow the chronology, Michael uses *signal devices*: "*Moreover, once* we find what we are looking for, more time is taken up . . ." (2); "*Eventually*, of course, the inevitable happens" (3); "*Then* we have to handle phone calls . . ." (4).

Problems with paragraph development.   You probably recall that an essay developed primarily through exemplification must include examples that are *relevant, interesting, convincing, representative, accurate,* and *specific.* On the whole, Michael's examples meet these requirements. The third and fourth paragraphs, especially, include vigorous details that show how our mania for buying things can govern our lives. We may even laugh with self-recognition when reading about "skintight jeans that can't be thrown in the washing machine" or a basement "filled . . . with discarded purchases."

The fifth paragraph, however, is underdeveloped. We know that this paragraph presents what Michael considers his most significant point, but the paragraph's examples are rather *flat* and *unconvincing*. To make this final section more compelling, Michael could mention specific people who overspend, revealing how much they are in debt and how much they have to work to become solvent again. Or he could cite a television documentary or magazine article dealing with the issue of consumer debt. Such specifics would give the paragraph the solidity it now lacks.

Shift in tone.   The fifth paragraph has a second, more subtle problem; a *shift in tone*. Although Michael has, up to this point, been critical of our possession-mad culture, he has poked fun at our obsession and kept his tone conversational and gently satiric. In this paragraph, though, he adopts a serious tone and, in the next paragraph, his tone becomes even weightier, almost preachy. It is, of course, legitimate to have a serious message in a lightly satiric piece. In fact, most satiric writing has such an additional layer of meaning. But because Michael has trouble blending these two moods, there's a jarring shift in the essay.

Shift in focus.   The second paragraph shows another kind of shift — in *focus*. The paragraph's controlling idea is that too much time is spent acquiring possessions. However, starting with "No wonder family life is deteriorating," Michael includes two sentences that introduce a complex issue beyond the scope of the essay. Since these last two sentences disrupt the paragraph's unity, they should be deleted.

Revising the first draft.   Although the final version of the essay needs work in spots, it's much stronger than Michael's first draft. To see how Michael went about revising the draft, compare his paper's second and third supporting paragraphs with his draft version reprinted here.

Original Version of the Second Paragraph

Our lives are spent not only buying things but in dealing with the inevitable complications that are created by our newly acquired possessions. First, we have to find places to put all the objects we bring home. More clothes demand more closets; a second car demands more garage space; a home entertainment center requires elaborate shelving. We shouldn't be surprised that the average American family moves once every three years. A good many families move simply because they need more space to store all the things they buy. In addition, our possessions demand maintenance time. A person who gets a new car will spend hours washing it, waxing it, and vacuuming it. A new pair of jeans has to go to the dry cleaners. New stereo systems have to be connected to already existing equipment. Eventually, of course, the inevitable happens. Our new items need to be repaired. Or we get sick of them and decide to replace them. Before making our replacement purchases, though, we have to get rid of the old items. That can be a real inconvenience.

When Michael looked more closely at this paragraph, he realized it rambled and lacked energy. He started to revise the paragraph by tightening the first sentence, making it more focused and less awkward. Certainly, the revised sentence ("As soon as we take our new purchases home, they begin to complicate our lives") is crisper than the original. Next, he decided to omit the discussion about finding places to put new possessions; these sentences about inadequate closet, garage, and shelf space were so exaggerated that they undercut the valid point he wanted to make. He also chose to eliminate the sentences about the mobility of American families. This was, he felt, an interesting point, but it introduced an issue too complex to be included in the paragraph.

Michael strengthened the rest of the paragraph by making his examples more specific. A "new car" became a "sleek new sports car," and a "pair of jeans" became a "fashionable pair of skintight jeans." Michael also realized he had to do more than merely write, "Eventually, . . . our new items need to be repaired." This point had to be dramatized by sharp, convincing details. Therefore, Michael added lively examples to describe how high-tech possessions — microwaves, home computers, VCRs — break down. Similarly, Michael realized it wasn't enough simply to say, as he had in the original, that we run into problems when we try to replace out-of-favor purchases. Vigorous details were again needed to illustrate the point. Michael thus used a typical "replaceable" (an old black-and-white TV) as his key example and showed the annoyance involved in handling phone calls and setting up appointments so people could see the TV.

After adding these specifics, Michael realized he had enough material to devote a separate paragraph to the problems associated with replacing old purchases. By dividing his original paragraph, Michael ended up with two well-focused paragraphs, neither of which has the rambling quality found in the original.

In short, Michael strengthened his essay through substantial revision. Another round of rewriting would have made the essay stronger still. Even without this additional work, Michael's essay provides an interesting perspective on an American preoccupation.

The selections that follow use abundant examples to make their points. In "Channelled Whelk," Anne Morrow Lindbergh provides examples of two lives, one busy and chaotic, the other stripped to essentials. "Sexism and Language," by Alleen Pace Nilsen, presents numerous instances of the way our language discriminates against women. Hilarious examples of college misadventures make James Thurber's "University Days" a longstanding favorite. Neil Postman cites evidence from numerous sources to make his point that America is eagerly embracing a culture of "Future Shlock." Finally, in "What I've Learned From Men," Barbara Ehrenreich uses an event from her own life to discuss the conditioning that women receive to be pleasant and ladylike—no matter the cost to their personal well-being.

Anne Morrow Lindbergh

Anne Morrow Lindbergh (1906–   ) has had a successful career as a novelist, diarist, essayist, and poet. In 1962, she published her first novel, *Dearly Beloved,* a book about the Apollo moon mission, to be followed in 1969 by *Earth Shine.* She is also the author of several well-received volumes of collected letters and diaries. The following selection first appeared in *Gift From the Sea* (1955).

Channelled Whelk

"The world is too much with us, late and soon / Getting and spending, we lay waste our powers." Poet William Wordsworth wrote these lines in the early nineteenth century, but they still characterize our lives today. Like human pinballs, many of us bounce from one set of responsibilities to another —from career to family life to school and community service. In this essay, Anne Morrow Lindbergh reflects on the longed-for goal of simplicity and explains why it often eludes us.

The shell in my hand is deserted. It once housed a whelk, a 1 snail-like creature, and then temporarily, after the death of the first occupant, a little hermit crab, who has run away, leaving his tracks behind him like a delicate vine on the sand. He ran away, and left me his shell. It was once a protection to him. I turn the shell in my hand, gazing into the wide open door from which he made his exit. Had it become an encumbrance? Why did he run away? Did he hope to find a better home, a better mode of living? I too have run away, I realize, I have shed the shell of my life, for these few weeks of vacation.

But his shell — it is simple; it is bare, it is beautiful. Small, 2 only the size of my thumb, its architecture is perfect, down to the finest detail. Its shape, swelling like a pear in the center, winds in a gentle spiral to the pointed apex. Its color, dull gold, is whitened by a wash of salt from the sea. Each whorl, each faint knob, each criss-cross vein in its egg-shell texture, is as clearly defined as on the day of creation. My eye follows with delight the outer circumference of that diminutive winding staircase up which this tenant used to travel.

My shell is not like this, I think. How untidy it has become! 3 Blurred with moss, knobby with barnacles, its shape is hardly recognizable any more. Surely, it had a shape once. It has a shape still in my mind. What is the shape of my life?

The shape of my life today starts with a family. I have a 4 husband, five children and a home just beyond the suburbs of New York. I have also a craft, writing, and therefore work I want to pursue. The shape of my life is, of course, determined by many other things; my background and childhood, my mind and its education, my conscience and its pressures, my heart and its desires. I want to give to and take from my children and husband, to share with friends and community, to carry out my obligations to man and to the world as a woman, as an artist, as a citizen.

But I want first of all—in fact, as an end to these other 5 desires—to be at peace with myself. I want a singleness of eye, a purity of intention, a central core to my life that will enable me to carry out these obligations and activities as well as I can. I want, in fact—to borrow from the language of the saints—to live "in grace" as much of the time as possible. I am not using this term in a strictly theological sense. By grace I mean an inner harmony, essentially spiritual, which can be translated into outward harmony. I am seeking perhaps what Socrates asked for in the prayer from the *Phaedrus* when he said, "May the outward and inward man be at one." I would like to achieve a state of inner spiritual grace from which I could function and give as I was meant to in the eye of God.

Vague as this definition may be, I believe most people are 6 aware of periods in their lives when they seem to be "in grace" and other periods in their lives when they feel "out of grace," even though they may use different words to describe these states. In the first happy condition, one seems to carry all one's tasks before one lightly, as if borne along on a great tide; and in the opposite state one can hardly tie a shoe-string. It is true that a large part of life consists in learning a technique of tying the shoe-string, whether one is in grace or not. But there are techniques of living too; there are even techniques in the search for grace. And techniques can be cultivated. I have learned by some experience, by many examples, and by the writings of countless others before me, also occupied in the search, that certain environments, certain modes of life, certain rules of conduct are more conducive to inner and outer harmony than others. There are, in fact, certain roads that one may follow. Simplification of life is one of them.

I mean to lead a simple life, to choose a simple shell I can carry easily—like a hermit crab. But I do not. I find that my frame of life does not foster simplicity. My husband and five children must make their way in the world. The life I have chosen as wife and mother entrains a whole caravan of complications. It involves a house in the suburbs and either household drudgery or household help which wavers between scarcity and non-existence for most of us. It involves food and shelter; meals, planning, marketing, bills, and making the ends meet in a thousand ways. It involves not only the butcher, the baker, the candlestickmaker but countless other experts to keep my modern house with its modern "simplifications" (electricity, plumbing, refrigerator, gas-stove, oil-burner, dish-washer, radios, car, and numerous other labor-saving devices) functioning properly. It involves health; doctors, dentists, appointments, medicine, cod-liver oil, vitamins, trips to the drugstore. It involves education, spiritual, intellectual, physical; schools, school conferences, carpools, extra trips for basket-ball or orchestra practice; tutoring; camps, camp equipment and transportation. It involves clothes, shopping, laundry, cleaning, mending, letting skirts down and sewing buttons on, or finding someone else to do it. It involves friends, my husband's, my children's, my own, and endless arrangements to get together; letters, invitations, telephone calls and transportation hither and yon.

For life today in America is based on the premise of ever-widening circles of contact and communication. It involves not only family demands, but community demands, national demands, international demands on the good citizen, through social and cultural pressures, through newspapers, magazines, radio programs, political drives, charitable appeals, and so on. My mind reels with it. What a circus act we women perform every day of our lives. It puts the trapeze artist to shame. Look at us. We run a tight rope daily, balancing a pile of books on the head. Baby-carriage, parasol, kitchen chair, still under control. Steady now!

This is not the life of simplicity but the life of multiplicity   9

7

8

that the wise men warn us of. It leads not to unification but to fragmentation. It does not bring grace; it destroys the soul. And this is not only true of my life, I am forced to conclude; it is the life of millions of women in America. I stress America, because today, the American woman more than any other has the privilege of choosing such a life. Woman in large parts of the civilized world has been forced back by war, by poverty, by collapse, by the sheer struggle to survive, into a smaller circle of immediate time and space, immediate family life, immediate problems of existence. The American woman is still relatively free to choose the wider life. How long she will hold this enviable and precarious position no one knows. But her particular situation has a significance far above its apparent economic, national or even sex limitations.

For the problem of the multiplicity of life not only confronts   10
the American woman, but also the American man. And it is not merely the concern of the American as such, but of our whole modern civilization, since life in America today is held up as the ideal of a large part of the rest of the world. And finally, it is not limited to our present civilization, though we are faced with it now in an exaggerated form. It has always been one of the pitfalls of mankind. Plotinus was preaching the dangers of multiplicity of the world back in the third century. Yet, the problem is particularly and essentially woman's. Distraction is, always has been, and probably always will be, inherent in woman's life.

For to be a woman is to have interests and duties, raying out   11
in all directions from the central mother-core, like spokes from the hub of a wheel. The pattern of our lives is essentially circular. We must be open to all points of the compass; husband, children, friends, home, community; stretched out, exposed, sensitive like a spider's web to each breeze that blows, to each call that comes. How difficult for us, then, to achieve a balance in the midst of these contradictory tensions, and yet how necessary for the proper functioning of our lives. How much we need, and how arduous of attainment is that steadiness preached in all rules for holy living. How desirable and distant is the ideal of the contemplative, artist, or saint — the inner inviolable core, the single eye.

With a new awareness, both painful and humorous, I begin   12
to understand why the saints were rarely married women. I am convinced it has nothing inherently to do, as I once supposed,

with chastity or children. It has to do primarily with distractions. The bearing, rearing, feeding and educating of children; the running of a house with its thousand details; human relationships with their myriad pulls — woman's normal occupations in general run counter to creative life, or contemplative life, or saintly life. The problem is not merely one of *Woman and Career, Woman and the Home, Woman and Independence.* It is more basically: how to remain whole in the midst of the distractions of life; how to remain balanced, no matter what centrifugal forces tend to pull one off center; how to remain strong, no matter what shocks come in at the periphery and tend to crack the hub of the wheel.

What is the answer? There is no easy answer, no complete answer. I have only clues, shells from the sea. The bare beauty of the channelled whelk tells me that one answer, and perhaps a first step, is in simplification of life, in cutting out some of the distractions. But how? Total retirement is not possible. I cannot shed my responsibilities. I cannot permanently inhabit a desert island. I cannot be a nun in the midst of family life. I would not want to be. The solution for me, surely, is neither in total renunciation of the world, nor in total acceptance of it. I must find a balance somewhere, or an alternating rhythm between these two extremes; a swinging of the pendulum between solitude and communion, between retreat and return. In my periods of retreat, perhaps I can learn something to carry back into my worldly life. I can at least practice for these two weeks the simplification of outward life, as a beginning. I can follow this superficial clue, and see where it leads. Here, in beach living, I can try. 13

One learns first of all in beach living the art of shedding; how little one can get along with, not how much. Physical shedding to begin with, which then mysteriously spreads into other fields. Clothes, first. Of course, one needs less in the sun. But one needs less anyway, one finds suddenly. One does not need a closet-full, only a small suitcase-full. And what a relief it is! Less taking up and down of hems, less mending, and — best of all — less worry about what to wear. One finds one is shedding not only clothes — but vanity. 14

Next, shelter. One does not need the airtight shelter one has in winter in the North. Here I live in a bare sea-shell of a cottage. No heat, no telephone, no plumbing to speak of, no hot water, a 15 two-burner oil stove, no gadgets to go wrong. No rugs. There were some, but I rolled them up the first day; it is easier to sweep the sand off a bare floor. But I find I don't bustle about with unnecessary sweeping and cleaning here. I am no longer aware of the dust. I have shed my Puritan conscience about absolute tidiness and cleanliness. Is it possible that, too, is a material burden? No curtains. I do not need them for privacy; the pines around my house are enough protection. I want the windows open all the time, and I don't want to worry about rain. I begin to shed my Martha-like anxiety about many things. Washable slipcovers, faded and old—I hardly see them; I don't worry about the impression they make on other people. I am shedding pride. As little furniture as possible; I shall not need much. I shall ask into my shell only those friends with whom I can be completely honest. I find I am shedding hypocrisy in human relationships. What a result that will be! The most exhausting thing in life, I have discovered, is being insincere. That is why so much of social life is exhausting; one is wearing a mask. I have shed my mask.

I find I live quite happily without those things I think neces- 16
sary in winter in the North. And as I write these words, I remember, with some shock at the disparity in our lives, a similar statement made by a friend of mine in France who spent three years in a German prison camp. Of course, he said, qualifying his remark, they did not get enough to eat, they were sometimes atrociously treated, they had little physical freedom. And yet, prison life taught him how little one can get along with, and what extraordinary spiritual freedom and peace such simplification can bring. I remember again, ironically, that today more of us in America than anywhere else in the world have the luxury of choice between simplicity and complication of life. And for the most part, we, who could choose simplicity, choose complication. War, prison, survival periods, enforce a form of simplicity on man. The monk and the nun choose it of their own free will. But if one accidentally finds it, as I have for a few days, one finds also the serenity it brings.

Is it not rather ugly, one may ask? One collects material 17
possessions not only for security, comfort or vanity, but for beauty as well. Is your sea-shell house not ugly and bare? No, it is beautiful, my house. It is bare, of course, but the wind, the sun, the smell of the pines blow through its bareness. The unfinished

beams in the roof are veiled by cobwebs. They are lovely, I think, gazing up at them with new eyes; they soften the hard lines of the rafters as grey hairs soften the lines on a middle-aged face. I no longer pull out grey hairs or sweep down cobwebs. As for the walls, it is true they looked forbidding at first. I felt cramped and enclosed by their blank faces. I wanted to knock holes in them, to give them another dimension with pictures or windows. So I dragged home from the beach grey arms of driftwood, worn satin-smooth by wind and sand. I gathered trailing green vines with floppy red-tipped leaves. I picked up the whitened skeletons of conchshells, their curious hollowed-out shapes faintly reminiscent of abstract sculpture. With these tacked to walls and propped up in corners, I am satisfied. I have a periscope out to the world. I have a window, a view, a point of flight from my sedentary base.

I am content. I sit down at my desk, a bare kitchen table with   18
a blotter, a bottle of ink, a sand dollar to weight down one corner, a clam shell for a pen tray, the broken tip of a conch, pink-tinged, to finger, and a row of shells to set my thoughts spinning.

I love my sea-shell of a house. I wish I could live in it always.   19
I wish I could transport it home. But I cannot. It will not hold a husband, five children and the necessities and trappings of daily life. I can only carry back my little channelled whelk. It will sit on my desk in Connecticut, to remind me of the ideal of a simplified life, to encourage me in the game I played on the beach. To ask how little, not how much, can I get along with. To say — is it necessary? — when I am tempted to add one more accumulation to my life, when I am pulled toward one more centrifugal activity.

Simplification of outward life is not enough. It is merely the   20
outside. But I am starting with the outside. I am looking at the outside of a shell, the outside of my life — the shell. The complete answer is not to be found on the outside, in an outward mode of living. This is only a technique, a road to grace. The final answer, I know, is always inside. But the outside can give a clue, can help one to find the inside answer. One is free, like the hermit crab, to change one's shell.

Channelled whelk, I put you down again, but you have set   21
my mind on a journey, up an inwardly winding spiral staircase of thought.

Questions for Close Reading

1. What is the selection's thesis? Locate the sentence(s) in which Lindbergh states her main idea. If she doesn't state the thesis explicitly, express it in your own words.
2. What does Lindbergh find appealing about the shell of the channelled whelk?
3. Why, according to Lindbergh, are distraction and "multiplicity" so much a problem for women? Why are they less of a problem for men?
4. Since Lindbergh prefers the life at the beach house, why doesn't she remain there? Why does she take the shell away with her?
5. Refer to your dictionary as needed to define the following words used in the selection: *apex* (paragraph 2), *conducive* (6), *myriad* (12), *periphery* (12), and *sedentary* (17).

Questions About the Writer's Craft

1. **The pattern.** Exemplification essays often develop key points through extended illustrations. In what paragraphs does Lindbergh use extended illustrations to clarify what she means by "simplification"? What's the effect of these extended illustrations?
2. Why do you suppose Lindbergh begins her essay with a few paragraphs about a whelk shell? Where does she return to the shell? What does the shell come to represent?
3. In paragraph 6, the author uses the image of "tying a shoestring." To what aspects of life is she referring? At what point do you recognize that "tying a shoestring" serves as a metaphor for a larger part of life?
4. Why do you think Lindbergh ends the essay with a short "speech" or address to the whelk shell? How does this last paragraph extend an idea suggested in the preceding paragraph?

Questions for Further Thought

1. Lindbergh writes, "I want first of all . . . to be at peace with myself." Besides her method of simplification, how else could she achieve this inner peace?
2. Could we ever eliminate all the distractions from our lives? Do you think this would be desirable?
3. Lindbergh says the problem she has with distractions is particularly a woman's problem. Do you agree? Have women's lives — and men's — changed much since she wrote this essay?
4. How would *you* simplify your life, if you were given the opportunity? What would you shed? What would you be unable to shed? What might you be able to shed . . . but only after agonizing over it or getting help?

Writing Assignments Using Exemplification as a Pattern of Development

1. Write an essay about the excess possessions in people's lives today. Give examples of people you know or have heard about who are obsessed with possessions. Part of your essay should discuss the effect these possessions have on people's lives.

∞ 2. Lindbergh writes that she often feels fragmented into a series of selves because of the numerous demands—family, community, and political—made on her. Analyze your own life to identify the different roles you play. Write an essay detailing the "balancing act" you perform in your life. When describing each of your roles, be sure to provide specific examples of the demands claiming your attention. In the conclusion, point briefly to some things you could do to make your life less fragmented and more harmonious. Virginia Woolf's "Professions for Women" (page 721) may provide additional insight into the effect of the everyday roles we assume.

Writing Assignments Using Other Patterns of Development

∞ 3. Imagine simplifying your own life to achieve greater inner harmony. How would you go about it? Before planning the paper, you might want to read Janet Mendell Goldstein's "The Quick Fix Society" (page 332), an essay that focuses on the value of leading a more easy-paced life. Then write an essay describing such a process. For each step, include specific examples of activities, objects, relationships, and the like that you would eliminate.

4. Taking a position opposed to Lindbergh's, contend that we benefit from the multiplicity of our lives. Argue that material possessions and numerous "circles of contact" are necessary and advantageous. Your tone can be either serious or humorous. In either case, be sure to acknowledge the dissenting viewpoint.

Alleen Pace Nilsen

A specialist in sexist language and children's literature, Alleen
Pace Nilsen (1936–   ) teaches at Arizona State University.
Nilsen's doctoral dissertation concerned linguistic sexism in
books written for children. She has written several books on
language, including *Language Play: An Introduction to Language* (1983) and *The Language of Humor/The Humor of Language* (1985). The following selection is from *Sexism and
Language* (1977), a collection of essays published by the National Council of Teachers of English.

Sexism and Language

Is there anything wrong in calling a woman a "fox" or a
"chick"? Why is it embarrassing for a man to perform a job
labeled "women's work," while it's a compliment for a woman
to do "a man's job"? Would you rather be a female named
"Sam" or a male called "Carroll"? Your response to these
questions most likely results from the attitudes you've acquired as a speaker of American English. In the following
selection, Alleen Pace Nilsen will help you look more closely at
the language you use, showing how seemingly innocent words
and phrases reflect society's attitudes toward the roles — and
worth — of men and women.[1]

Over the last hundred years, American anthropologists have   1
travelled to the corners of the earth to study primitive cultures.
They either became linguists themselves or they took linguists
with them to help in learning and analyzing languages. Even if
the culture was one that no longer existed, they were interested in
learning its language because besides being tools of communica-

---

[1]*Note*: If you'd like some advice on ways to avoid sexist language in your
writing, turn to the entry "gender-biased language" in the Glossary.

tion, the vocabulary and structure of a language tell much about the values held by its speakers.

However, the culture need not be primitive, nor do the people making observations need to be anthropologists and linguists. Anyone living in the United States who listens with a keen ear or reads with a perceptive eye can come up with startling new insights about the way American English reflects our values. 2

Animal Terms for People — Mirrors of the Double Standard

If we look at just one semantic area of English, that of animal terms in relation to people, we can uncover some interesting insights into how our culture views males and females. References to identical animals can have negative connotations when related to a female, but positive or neutral connotations when related to a male. For example, a *shrew* has come to mean "a scolding, nagging, evil-tempered woman," while *shrewd* means "keen-witted, clever, or sharp in practical affairs; astute . . . businessman, etc." (*Webster's New World Dictionary of the American Language,* 1964). 3

A *lucky dog* or a *gay dog* may be a very interesting fellow, but when a woman is a *dog,* she is unattractive, and when she's a *bitch* she's the personification of whatever is undesirable in the mind of the speaker. When a man is self-confident, he may be described as *cocksure* or even *cocky,* but in a woman this same self-confidence is likely to result in her being called a *cocky bitch,* which is not only a mixed metaphor, but also probably the most insulting animal metaphor we have. *Bitch* has taken on such negative connotations — children are taught it is a swear word — that in everyday American English, speakers are hesitant to call a female dog a *bitch*. Most of us feel that we would be insulting the dog. When we want to insult a man by comparing him to a dog, we call him a *son of a bitch,* which quite literally is an insult to his mother rather than to him. 4

If the female is called a *vixen* (a female fox), the dictionary says this means she is "an ill-tempered, shrewish, or malicious woman." The female seems both to attract and to hold on longer to animal metaphors with negative connotations. A *vampire* was originally a corpse that came alive to suck the blood of living 5 persons. The word acquired the general meaning of an unscrupulous person such as a blackmailer and then, the specialized meaning of "a beautiful but unscrupulous woman who seduces men and leads them to their ruin." From this latter meaning we get the word *vamp*. The popularity of this term and of the name *vampire bat* may contribute to the idea that a female being is referred to in a phrase such as *the old bat*.

Other animal metaphors do not have definitely derogatory 6 connotations for the female, but they do seem to indicate frivolity or unimportance, as in *social butterfly* and *flapper*. Look at the differences between the connotations of participating in a *hen party* and in a *bull session*. Male metaphors, even when they are negative in connotation, still relate to strength and conquest. Metaphors related to aggressive sex roles, for example, *buck, stag, wolf,* and *stud,* will undoubtedly remain attached to males. Perhaps one of the reasons that in the late sixties it was so shocking to hear policemen called *pigs* was that the connotations of *pig* are very different from the other animal metaphors we usually apply to males.

When I was living in Afghanistan, I was surprised at the 7 cruelty and unfairness of a proverb that said, "When you see an old man, sit down and take a lesson; when you see an old woman, throw a stone." In looking at Afghan folk literature. I found that young girls were pictured as delightful and enticing, middle-aged women were sometimes interesting but more often just tolerable, while old women were always grotesque and villainous. Probably the reason for the negative connotation of old age in women is that women are valued for their bodies while men are valued for their accomplishments and their wisdom. Bodies deteriorate with age but wisdom and accomplishments grow greater.

When we returned home from Afghanistan, I was shocked to 8 discover that we have remnants of this same attitude in America. We see it in our animal metaphors. If both the animal and the woman are young, the connotation is positive, but if the animal and the woman are old, the connotation is negative. Hugh Hefner might never have made it to the big time if he had called his girls *rabbits* instead of *bunnies*. He probably chose *bunny* because he wanted something close to, but not quite so obvious as *kitten* or *cat* — the all-time winners for connoting female sexuality. Also *bunny*, as in the skiers' *snow bunny*, already had some of the connotations Hefner wanted. Compare the connotations of *filly* to *old nag*; *bird* to *old crow* or *old bat*; and *lamb* to *crone* (apparently related to the early modern Dutch *kronje, old ewe* but now *withered old woman*).

Probably the most striking examples of the contrast between 9 young and old women are animal metaphors relating to cats and chickens. A young girl is encouraged to be *kittenish,* but not *catty.* And though most of us wouldn't mind living next door to a *sex kitten,* we wouldn't want to live next door to a *cat house.* Parents might name their daughter *Kitty* but not *Puss* or *Pussy,* which used to be a fairly common nickname for girls. It has now developed such sexual connotations that it is used mostly for humor, as in the James Bond movie featuring Pussy Galore and her flying felines.

In the chicken metaphors, a young girl is a *chick.* When she 10 gets old enough she marries and soon begins feeling *cooped up.* To relieve the boredom she goes to *hen parties* and *cackles* with her friends. Eventually she has her *brood,* begins to *henpeck* her husband, and finally turns into an *old biddy.*

How English Glorifies Maleness

Throughout the ages physical strength has been very impor- 11 tant, and because men are physically stronger than women, they have been valued more. Only now in the machine age, when the difference in strength between males and females pales into insignificance in comparison to the strength of earth-moving machinery, airplanes, and guns, males no longer have such an inherent advantage. Today a man of intellect is more valued than a physical laborer, and since women can compete intellectually with men, their value is on the rise. But language lags far behind cultural changes, so the language still reflects this emphasis on the importance of being male. For example, when we want to compliment a male, all we need to do is stress the fact that he is male by saying he is a *he-man,* or he is *manly,* or he is *virile.* Both *virile* and *virtuous* come from the Latin *vir,* meaning *man.*

The command or encouragement that males receive in sen- 12 tences like "Be a man!" implies that *to be a man* is to be honorable, strong, righteous, and whatever else the speaker thinks desirable. But in contrast to this, a girl is never told to be a *woman.*

And when she is told to be a *lady,* she is simply being encouraged to "act feminine," which means sitting with her knees together, walking gracefully, and talking softly.

The armed forces, particularly the Marines, use the positive   13 masculine connotation as part of their recruitment psychology. They promote the idea that to join the Marines (or the Army, Navy, or Air Force) guarantees that you will become a man. But this brings up a problem, because much of the work that is necessary to keep a large organization running is what is traditionally thought of as *women's work.* Now, how can the Marines ask someone who has signed up for a *man-sized job* to do *women's work?* Since they can't, they euphemize and give the jobs titles that either are more prestigious or, at least, don't make people think of females. Waitresses are called *orderlies,* secretaries are called *clerk-typists,* nurses are called *medics,* assistants are called *adjutants,* and cleaning up an area is called *policing* the area. The same kind of word glorification is used in civilian life to bolster a man's ego when he is doing such tasks as cooking and sewing. For example, a *chef* has higher prestige than a *cook* and a *tailor* has higher prestige than a *seamstress.*

Little girls learn early in life that the boy's role is one to be   14 envied and emulated. Child psychologists have pointed out that experimenting with the role of the opposite sex is much more acceptable for little girls than it is for little boys. For example, girls are free to dress in boys' clothes, but certainly not the other way around. Most parents are amused if they have a daughter who is a *tomboy,* but they are genuinely distressed if they have a son who is a *sissy.* The names we give to young children reflect this same attitude. It is all right for girls to have boys' names, but pity the boy who has a girl's name! Because parents keep giving boys' names to girls, the number of acceptable boys' names keeps shrinking. Currently popular names for girls include *Jo, Kelly, Teri, Chris, Pat, Shawn, Toni,* and *Sam* (short for *Samantha*). *Evelyn, Carroll, Gayle, Hazel, Lynn, Beverley, Marion, Francis,* and *Shirley* once were acceptable names for males. But as they were given to females, they became less and less acceptable. Today, men who are stuck with them self-consciously go by their initials or by abbreviated forms such as *Haze, Shirl, Frank,* or *Ev.* And they seldom pass these names on to their sons.

Many common words have come into the language from   15

people's names. These lexical items again show the importance of maleness compared to the triviality of the feminine activities being described. Words derived from the names of women include *Melba toast,* named for the Australian singer Dame Nellie Melba; *Sally Lunn cakes,* named after an eighteenth-century woman who first made them; *pompadour,* a hair style named after Madame Pompadour; and the word *maudlin,* as in *maudlin sentiment,* from Mary Magdalene, who was often portrayed by artists as displaying exaggerated sorrow.

There are trivial items named after men — *teddy bear* after   16
Theodore Roosevelt and *sideburns* after General Burnside — but most words that come from men's names relate to significant inventions or developments. These include *pasteurization* after Louis Pasteur, *sousaphone* after John Philip Sousa, *mason jar* after John L. Mason, *boysenberry* after Rudolph Boysen, *pullman car* after George M. Pullman, *braille* after Louis Braille, *franklin stove* after Benjamin Franklin, *diesel engine* after Rudolf Diesel, *ferris wheel* after George W. G. Ferris, and the verb *to lynch* after William Lynch, who was a vigilante captain in Virginia in 1780.

The latter is an example of a whole set of English words   17
dealing with violence. These words have strongly negative connotations. From research using free association and semantic differentials, with university students as subjects, James Ney concluded that English reflects both an anti-male and an anti-female bias because these biases exist in the culture (*Etc.: A Review of General Semantics,* March 1976, pp. 67 – 76). The students consistently marked as masculine such words as *killer, murderer, robber, attacker, fighter, stabber, rapist, assassin, gang, hood, arsonist, criminal, hijacker, villain,* and *bully,* even though most of these words contain nothing to specify that they are masculine. An example of bias against males, Ney observed, is the absence in English of a pejorative term for women equivalent to *rapist.* Outcomes of his free association test indicated that if "English speakers want to call a man something bad, there seems to be a large vocabulary available to them but if they want to use a term which is good to describe a male, there is a small vocabulary available. The reverse is true for women."

Certainly we do not always think positively about males;   18
witness such words as *jerk, creep, crumb, slob, fink,* and *jackass.* But much of what determines our positive and negative feelings re-

lates to the roles people play. We have very negative feelings toward someone who is hurting us or threatening us or in some way making our lives miserable. To be able to do this, the person has to have power over us and this power usually belongs to males.

On the other hand, when someone helps us or makes our life   19 more pleasant, we have positive feelings toward that person or that role. *Mother* is one of the positive female terms in English, and we see such extensions of it as *Mother Nature, Mother Earth, mother lode, mother superior,* etc. But even though a word like *mother* is positive it is still not a word of power. In the minds of English speakers being female and being powerless or passive are so closely related that we use the terms *feminine* and *lady* either to mean female or to describe a certain kind of quiet and unobtrusive behavior.

Words Labelling Women as Things

Because of our expectations of passivity, we like to compare   20 females to items that people acquire for their pleasure. For example, in a recent commercial for the television show "Happy Days," one of the characters announced that in the coming season they were going to have not only "cars, motorcycles, and girls," but also a band. Another example of this kind of thinking is the comparison of females to food since food is something we all enjoy, even though it is extremely passive. We describe females as such delectable morsels as a *dish,* a *cookie,* a *tart, cheesecake, sugar and spice,* a *cute tomato, honey,* a *sharp cookie,* and *sweetie pie.* We say a particular girl has a *peaches and cream complexion* or "she looks good enough to eat." And parents give their daughters such names as *Candy* and *Cherry.*

Other pleasurable items that we compare females to are toys.   21 Young girls are called *little dolls* or *China dolls,* while older girls —if they are attractive—are simply called *dolls.* We might say about a woman, "She's pretty as a picture," or "She's a fashion plate." And we might compare a girl to a plant by saying she is a *clinging vine,* a *shrinking violet,* or a *wallflower.* And we might name our daughters after plants such as *Rose, Lily, Ivy, Daisy, Iris,* and *Petunia.* Compare these names to boys' names such as *Martin* which means warlike, *Ernest* which means resolute fighter, *Nicholas* which means victory, *Val* which means strong or valiant, and *Leo* which means lion. We would be very hesitant to give a boy the name of something as passive as a flower although we might say about a man that he is a *late-bloomer*. This is making a comparison between a man and the most active thing a plant can do, which is to bloom. The only other familiar plant metaphor used for a man is the insulting *pansy*, implying that he is like a woman.

Questions for Close Reading

1. What is the selection's thesis? Locate the sentence(s) in which Nilsen states her main idea. If she doesn't state the thesis explicitly, express it in your own words.
2. According to Nilsen, what do animal metaphors usually imply when used to describe women? What do male animal metaphors imply?
3. Why, according to Nilsen, do some professions have different names depending on whether the job is performed by a male or female? What is suggested by the existence of two different terms for the same occupation?
4. When positive terms are used for women, what personality characteristics do such terms suggest? Why are words connoting violence most often applied to men?
5. Refer to your dictionary as needed to define the following words used in the selection: *unscrupulous* (paragraph 5), *enticing* (7), *connotation* (8), *virile* (11), *lexical* (15), *maudlin* (15), and *vigilante* (16).

Questions About the Writer's Craft

1. **The pattern.** Why does Nilsen use so many examples to illustrate each type of sexism in the English language? What point of view is she trying to anticipate and counteract?
2. What three main sexist motifs in English does Nilsen examine? How does she signal her movement from one to the next?
3. Why do you think Nilsen begins by discussing animal terms for humans? What effect does placing this section first have on the reader?
4. What is Nilsen's tone? What terms and expressions reveal her personal viewpoint on sexism in our language?

Questions for Further Thought

∞ 1. Do you think most users of English are aware of the sexism in many everyday expressions? Were you surprised by any of Nilsen's examples? Why or why not?

2. Nilsen writes that "American English reflects our values." Do you agree that phrases like "man-sized jobs," "women's work," and "old biddy" indicate that Americans are sexist? Should we guard against gender-biased terms, or is such watchfulness being overly sensitive?

3. The names for many professions and occupations are gender-identified: Consider, for example, *policeman, chairman, actor/actress, foreman,* and *journeyman*. Should these terms be changed to gender-neutral ones, such as *police officer, chairperson, actor, supervisor,* and so on? Do gender-identified terms affect our thinking about people's worth? Do they influence the decisions young people make about their futures? Explain.

4. Can our language ever be made completely nonsexist? Should it be? Why or why not?

Writing Assignments Using Exemplification as a Pattern of Development

1. Nilsen claims that our language glorifies maleness and denigrates femaleness. Are there other areas of our lives where typical male behavior and attitudes are valued more than typical female roles or characteristics? Consider such areas as dating, marriage, sports, clothing, and occupations. Focusing on a single area, write an essay showing that our culture glorifies one sex over the other. Try to include in your paper points made in one of the following essays: Barbara Ehrenreich's "What I've Learned From Men" (page 261), Deborah Tannen's "Sex, Lies, and Conversation" (page 440), Judy Brady's "Why I Want a Wife" (page 546), or Virginia Woolf's "Professions for Women" (page 721).

∞ 2. The English language embodies many prejudices besides sexism. Many words and expressions, for example, reflect prejudice against skin color, old age, youth, left-handedness, shortness, fatness, and so on. Focusing on *one* such area, write an essay using specific examples of prejudicial language to show how the words we use reflect our stereotypes and biases. William Raspberry's "The Handicap of Definition" (page 563) will develop further your understanding of the way language influences attitudes.

Writing Assignments Using Other Patterns of Development

∞ 3. Would your life have been different if you had been born the opposite sex? Would you have been treated differently by your parents, teachers, and friends? Are there any specific experiences or events that would have turned out differently had you been a different sex? Write an essay persuading readers that your life would have been essentially the same *or* very different had you been born exactly as you were except for your sex. Virginia Woolf's "Professions for Women" (page 721) should spark some interesting ideas worth exploring in your paper.

∞ 4. Gender-based stereotyping exists in many areas of our culture besides language. Imagine you're a visitor to the United States and know nothing about the culture — perhaps you're a visitor from Mars. You observe people, watch television for a week, and study several issues of a popular general interest magazine, like *People, Time*, or *Newsweek*. Then you write a report back to your home about the differences between males and females in the United States. Providing numerous examples to explain the dissimilarities, cover one or two of the following in your analysis: occupations, recreational activities, friendships, and so forth. Barbara Ehrenreich's "What I've Learned From Men" (page 261), Deborah Tannen's "Sex, Lies, and Conversation" (page 440), and Judy Brady's "Why I Want a Wife" (page 546) highlight some issues to consider.

James Thurber

American humorist James Thurber (1894–1961) is perhaps best known as the author of "The Secret Life of Walter Mitty." Thurber often wrote about people's longings, using his skill as a satirist to portray the humor and poignancy of the human condition. He was able to give his wit — which often bordered on the acerbic — full play during his long career at the *New Yorker*, where he wrote satiric essays and drew cartoons. He also wrote several humorous books, including *Is Sex Necessary?* (1929), which he coauthored with E. B. White; *Fables for Our Time* (1940); *My World and Welcome to It* (1942); and *Thurber Country* (1953). The following selection first appeared in *My Life and Hard Times* (1933).

University Days

College and university catalogs depict higher education as one of life's loftier experiences, with confident undergrads strolling eagerly toward ivy-covered lecture halls. But in this hilarious essay, James Thurber takes the pomp and circumstance out of higher education. He reveals the bumbling, the incompetence, and the embarrassment that frequently beset him and his fellow students at Ohio State University. He shows professors with gritted teeth trying to educate the ineducable and coach the uncoachable. Even back in the early days of the twentieth century, college life was far from the idealized image depicted in the catalogs.

I passed all the other courses that I took at my university, but 1 I could never pass botany. This was because all botany students had to spend several hours a week in a laboratory looking through a microscope at plant cells, and I could never see through a microscope. I never once saw a cell through a microscope. This used to enrage my instructor. He would wander around the laboratory pleased with the progress all the students were making in drawing the involved and, so I am told, interesting structure of flower cells, until he came to me. I would just be standing there. "I can't see anything," I would say. He would begin patiently enough, explaining how anybody can see through a microscope, but he would always end up in a fury, claiming that I could *too* see through a microscope but just pretended that I couldn't. "It takes away from the beauty of flowers anyway," I used to tell him. "We are not concerned with beauty in this course," he would say. "We are concerned solely with what I may call the *mechanics* of flars." "Well," I'd say, "I can't see anything." "Try it just once again," he'd say, and I would put my eye to the microscope and see nothing at all, except now and again a nebulous milky substance —a phenomenon of maladjustment. You were supposed to see a vivid, restless clockwork of sharply defined plant cells. "I see what looks like a lot of milk," I would tell him. This, he claimed, was the result of my not having adjusted the microscope properly, so he would readjust it for me, or rather, for himself. And I would look again and see milk.

I finally took a deferred pass, as they called it, and waited a   2
year and tried again. (You had to pass one of the biological sciences or you couldn't graduate.) The professor had come back from vacation brown as a berry, bright-eyed, and eager to explain cell-structure again to his classes. "Well," he said to me, cheerily, when we met in the first laboratory hour of the semester, "we're going to see cells this time, aren't we?" "Yes, sir," I said. Students to right of me and to left of me and in front of me were seeing cells; what's more, they were quietly drawing pictures of them in their notebooks. Of course, I didn't see anything.

"We'll try it," the professor said to me, grimly, "with every   3
adjustment of the microscope known to man. As God is my witness, I'll arrange this glass so that you see cells through it or I'll give up teaching. In twenty-two years of botany, I — " He cut off abruptly for he was beginning to quiver all over, like Lionel Barrymore, and he genuinely wished to hold onto his temper; his scenes with me had taken a great deal out of him.

So we tried it with every adjustment of the microscope   4
known to man. With only one of them did I see anything but blackness or the familiar lacteal opacity, and that time I saw, to my pleasure and amazement, a variegated constellation of flecks, specks, and dots. These I hastily drew. The instructor, noting my

activity, came back from an adjoining desk, a smile on his lips and his eyebrows high in hope. He looked at my cell drawing. "What's that?" he demanded, with a hint of a squeal in his voice. "That's what I saw," I said. "You didn't, you didn't, you *didn't*!" he screamed, losing control of his temper instantly, and he bent over and squinted into the microscope. His head snapped up. "That's your eye!" he shouted. "You've fixed the lens so that it reflects! You've drawn your eye!"

Another course that I didn't like, but somehow managed to   5
pass, was economics. I went to that class straight from the botany class, which didn't help me any in understanding either subject. I used to get them mixed up. But not as mixed up as another student in my economics class who came there direct from a physics laboratory. He was a tackle on the football team, named Bolenciecwcz. At that time Ohio State University had one of the best football teams in the country, and Bolenciecwcz was one of its outstanding stars. In order to be eligible to play it was necessary for him to keep up in his studies, a very difficult matter, for while he was not dumber than an ox he was not any smarter. Most of his professors were lenient and helped him along. None gave him more hints in answering questions or asked him simpler ones than the economics professor, a thin, timid man named Bassum. One day when we were on the subject of transportation and distribution, it came Bolenciecwcz's turn to answer a question. "Name one means of transportation," the professor said to him. No light came into the big tackle's eyes. "Just any means of transportation," said the professor. Bolenciecwcz sat staring at him. "That is," pursued the professor, "any medium, agency, or method of going from one place to another." Bolenciecwcz had the look of a man who is being led into a trap. "You may choose among steam, horse-drawn, or electrically propelled vehicles," said the instructor. "I might suggest the one which we commonly take in making long journeys across land." There was a profound silence in which everybody stirred uneasily, including Bolenciecwcz and Mr. Bassum. Mr. Bassum abruptly broke this silence in an amazing manner. "Choo-choo-choo," he said, in a low voice, and turned instantly scarlet. He glanced appealingly around the room. All of us, of course, shared Mr. Bassum's desire that Bolenciecwcz should stay abreast of the class in economics, for the Illinois game, one of the hardest and most important of

the season, was only a week off. "Toot, toot, too-toooooot!" some student with a deep voice moaned, and we all looked encouragingly at Bolenciecwcz. Somebody else gave a fine imitation of a locomotive letting off steam. Mr. Bassum himself rounded off the little show. "Ding, dong, ding, dong," he said, hopefully. Bolenciecwcz was staring at the floor now, trying to think, his great brow furrowed, his huge hands rubbing together, his face red.

"How did you come to college this year, Mr. Bolenciecwcz?"   6 asked the professor. "*Chuffa* chuffa, *chuffa* chuffa."

"M'father sent me," said the football player.   7

"What on?" asked Bassum.   8

"I git an 'lowance," said the tackle, in a low, husky voice,   9 obviously embarrassed.

"No, no," said Bassum. "Name a means of transportation.   10 What did you *ride* here on?"

"Train," said Bolenciecwcz.   11

"Quite right," said the professor. "Now, Mr. Nugent, will   12 you tell us —"

If I went through anguish in botany and economics — for   13 different reasons — gymnasium work was even worse. I don't even like to think about it. They wouldn't let you play games or join in the exercises with your glasses on and I couldn't see with mine off. I bumped into professors, horizontal bars, agricultural students, and swinging iron rings. Not being able to see, I could take it but I couldn't dish it out. Also, in order to pass gymnasium (and you had to pass it to graduate) you had to learn to swim if you didn't know how. I didn't like the swimming pool, I didn't like swimming, and I didn't like the swimming instructor, and after all these years I still don't. I never swam but I passed my gym work anyway, by having another student give my gymnasium number (978) and swim across the pool in my place. He was a quiet, amiable blond youth, number 473, and he would have seen through a microscope for me if we could have got away with it, but we couldn't get away with it. Another thing I didn't like about gymnasium work was that they made you strip the day you registered. It is impossible for me to be happy when I am stripped and being asked a lot of questions. Still, I did better than a lanky agricultural student who was cross-examined just before I was. They asked each student what college he was in — that is, whether

Arts, Engineering, Commerce, or Agriculture. "What college are you in?" the instructor snapped at the youth in front of me. "Ohio State University," he said promptly.

It wasn't that agricultural student but it was another a whole lot like him who decided to take up journalism, possibly on the ground that when farming went to hell he could fall back on newspaper work. He didn't realize, of course, that that would be very much like falling back full-length on a kit of carpenter's tools. Haskins didn't seem cut out for journalism, being too embarrassed to talk to anybody and unable to use a typewriter, but the editor of the college paper assigned him to the cow barns, the sheep house, the horse pavilion, and the animal husbandry department generally. This was a genuinely big "beat," for it took up five times as much ground and got ten times as great a legislative appropriation as the College of Liberal Arts. The agricultural student knew animals, but nevertheless his stories were dull and colorlessly written. He took all afternoon on each of them, on account of having to hunt for each letter on the typewriter. Once in a while he had to ask somebody to help him hunt. "C" and "L," in particular, were hard letters for him to find. His editor finally got pretty much annoyed at the farmer-journalist because his pieces were so uninteresting. "See here, Haskins," he snapped at him one day, "why is it we never have anything hot from you on the horse pavilion? Here we have two hundred head of horses on this campus — more than any other university in the Western Conference except Purdue — and yet you never get any real lowdown on them. Now shoot over to the horse barns and dig up something lively." Haskins shambled out and came back in about an hour; he said he had something. "Well, start it off snappily," said the editor. "Something people will read." Haskins set to work and in a couple of hours brought a sheet of typewritten paper to the desk; it was a two-hundred-word story about some disease that had broken out among the horses. Its opening sentence was simple but arresting. It read: "Who has noticed the sores on the tops of the horses in the animal husbandry building?"

Ohio State was a land grant university and therefore two years of military drill was compulsory. We drilled with old Springfield rifles and studied the tactics of the Civil War even though the World War was going on at the time. At 11 o'clock

14

15

each morning thousands of freshmen and sophomores used to deploy over the campus, moodily creeping up on the old chemistry building. It was good training for the kind of warfare that was waged at Shiloh but it had no connection with what was going on in Europe. Some people used to think there was German money behind it, but they didn't dare say so or they would have been thrown in jail as German spies. It was a period of muddy thought and marked, I believe, the decline of higher education in the Middle West.

As a soldier I was never any good at all. Most of the cadets were glumly indifferent soldiers, but I was no good at all. Once General Littlefield, who was commandant of the cadet corps, popped up in front of me during regimental drill and snapped, "You are the main trouble with this university!" I think he meant that my type was the main trouble with the university but he may have meant me individually. I was mediocre at drill, certainly — that is, until my senior year. By that time I had drilled longer than anybody else in the Western Conference, having failed at military at the end of each preceding year so that I had to do it all over again. I was the only senior still in uniform. The uniform which, when new, had made me look like an interurban railway conductor, now that it had become faded and too tight made me look like Bert Williams in his bellboy act. This had a definitely bad effect on my morale. Even so, I had become by sheer practice little short of wonderful at squad maneuvers.

One day General Littlefield picked our company out of the whole regiment and tried to get it mixed up by putting it through one movement after another as fast as we could execute them: squads right, squads left, squads on right into line, squads right about, squads left front into line, etc. In about three minutes one hundred and nine men were marching in one direction and I was marching away from them at an angle of forty degrees, all alone. "Company, halt!" shouted General Littlefield. "That man is the only man who has it right!" I was made a corporal for my achievement.

The next day General Littlefield summoned me to his office. He was swatting flies when I went in. I was silent and he was silent too, for a long time. I don't think he remembered me or why he had sent for me, but he didn't want to admit it. He swatted some more flies, keeping his eyes on them narrowly

16

17

18

before he let go with the swatter. "Button up your coat!" he snapped. Looking back on it now I can see that he meant me although he was looking at a fly, but I just stood there. Another fly came to rest on a paper in front of the general and began rubbing its hind legs together. The general lifted the swatter cautiously. I moved restlessly and the fly flew away. "You startled him!" barked General Littlefield, looking at me severely. I said I was sorry. "That won't help the situation!" snapped the General, with cold military logic. I didn't see what I could do except offer to chase some more flies toward his desk, but I didn't say anything. He stared out the window at the faraway figures of co-eds crossing the campus toward the library. Finally, he told me I could go. So I went. He either didn't know which cadet I was or else he forgot what he wanted to see me about. It may have been that he wished to apologize for having called me the main trouble with the university; or maybe he had decided to compliment me on my brilliant drilling of the day before and then at the last minute decided not to. I don't know. I don't think about it much any more.

Questions for Close Reading

1. What is the selection's thesis? Locate the sentence(s) in which Thurber states his main idea. If he doesn't state the thesis explicitly, express it in your own words.
2. In his writings and cartoons, Thurber reveals a distaste for authority. Find evidence of such an attitude in this selection.
3. Thurber passes gym class by having another student assume his identification number. What does this fact indicate about his gym class in particular and about his university in general?
4. Thurber sets up a comparison between himself and the fly in General Littlefield's office. How is this comparison related to Thurber's thesis?
5. Refer to your dictionary as needed to define the following words used in the selection: *nebulous* (paragraph 1), *lacteal* (4), *opacity* (4), *variegated* (4), *husbandry* (14), and *appropriation* (14).

Questions About the Writer's Craft

1. **The pattern.** Thurber develops his piece through a series of examples, each in the form of a brief anecdote. Which two anecdotes does Thurber develop in most detail? What might have been his reason for proceeding in this way?

2. *Satire* uses humor to criticize a situation and create awareness of the need for change. One satiric technique is *caricature:* an oversimplified description in which one quality of an individual is exaggerated, resulting in a distorted stereotype. Where in "University Days" does Thurber employ caricature? What is he satirizing?

3. Thurber often uses dialogue rather than commentary to convey humor. Find several places in the essay where dialogue is especially effective in enhancing the essay's humor.

4. The inability to see is a recurrent theme in Thurber's essay. Locate instances of such difficulty. What might this inability symbolize?

Questions for Further Thought

1. Thurber shows an entire class struggling to help a slow-witted athlete. Do you think colleges and universities should make special concessions to athletes who may not be doing well academically? Why or why not?

2. Did Thurber act dishonorably in having another student pass his swimming test for him? Do you view this as cheating or as a way of getting around an unreasonable school requirement?

3. Thurber shows teachers having difficulty explaining concepts to students. Who is at fault when learning grinds to a halt? Teachers? Students? Both? What should teachers and students realistically expect from each other?

4. With great wit, Thurber looks under the surface to disclose some of the inadequacies of the education he received at Ohio State University. What shortcomings do you perceive with the education you received in the past? What were its merits?

Writing Assignments Using Exemplification as a Pattern of Development

1. Read William Zinsser's "College Pressures" (page 298). Zinsser sees college students as overly ambitious, driven to achieve credentials that will lead to financial success. But Thurber shows students too dull or apathetic to make much effort to move in any direction. Which view of students is more accurate? Using concrete examples of students you know or have observed, write an essay developing the point that college students are either too competitive or too lackadaisical. Save for last your most convincing example.

2. With great relish, Thurber illustrates ineptitude, showing people unable to master even the simplest of tasks. Write an essay illustrating excellence. Give several vivid examples of skill, even virtuosity, by depicting individuals engaged in tasks they have fully mastered. You

might recall a rock musician you heard in concert, an Olympic gymnast you saw on television, a mechanic you watched repair a car. The people cited, though at first glance possibly quite dissimilar, should share one common trait: their basic excellence.

Writing Assignments Using Other Patterns of Development

3. Thurber and his instructors have different views about what's important. Write an essay recounting one or more occasions when your sense of what was important clashed with someone else's. How was the disagreement resolved? You might want to conclude with some generalization about the type of individual with whom you tend to come into conflict.

4. Thurber's instructors show varying degrees of patience, empathy, and success in dealing with their recalcitrant students. In a serious or playful essay, contrast a teacher you consider excellent with one you consider inferior. Address the same aspects of each teacher's style — for example, patience, command of subject matter, ability to create and maintain interest. No matter which tone you select, the essay should make clear those traits you consider most essential to excellent teaching.

Neil Postman

Born in Brooklyn in 1931, Neil Postman became known as a leading advocate of educational reform with the publication of the books *Teaching as a Subversive Activity* (1969) and *The Soft Revolution* (1971), both coauthored with Charles Weingartner. Postman continues to write extensively about education, publishing articles in major periodicals such as the *Atlantic* and the *Nation*. He has also written and lectured widely on the effect of mass media on American culture and politics. Postman's more recent books include *The Disappearance of Childhood* (1982) and *Amusing Ourselves to Death: Public Discourse in the Age of Show Business* (1985). A professor of media ecology at New York University, Postman numbers among the teaching and writing awards he has received the George Orwell Award for Clarity in Language. "Future Shlock" is taken from Postman's 1988 book *Conscientious Objections: Stirring Up Trouble About Language, Technology, and Education*.

Future Shlock

Politicians conduct their campaigns in thirty-second "sound bites"; television commentaries on political upheavals abroad are punctuated by jingles for fast-food restaurants; televangelists, using the talk-show format, gaze soulfully into the camera and pretend to wrestle with weighty moral issues. We are becoming a trivial people, says Neil Postman, unwilling to think about complex subject matter unless it's packaged as entertainment.

Human intelligence is among the most fragile things in nature. It doesn't take much to distract it, suppress it, or even annihilate it. In this century, we have had some lethal examples of how easily and quickly intelligence can be defeated by any one of its several nemeses: ignorance, superstition, moral fervor, cruelty, cowardice, neglect. In the late 1920s, for example, Germany was, 1 by any measure, the most literate, cultured nation in the world. Its legendary seats of learning attracted scholars from every corner. Its philosophers, social critics, and scientists were of the first rank; its humane traditions an inspiration to less favored nations. But by the mid-1930s — that is, in less than ten years — this cathedral of human reason had been transformed into a cesspool of barbaric irrationality. Many of the most intelligent products of German culture were forced to flee — for example, Einstein, Freud, Karl Jaspers, Thomas Mann, and Stefan Zweig. Even worse, those who remained were either forced to submit their minds to the sovereignty of primitive superstition, or — worse still — willingly did so: Konrad Lorenz, Werner Heisenberg, Martin Heidegger, Gerhardt Hauptmann. On May 10, 1933, a huge bonfire was kindled in Berlin and the books of Marcel Proust, André Gide, Emile Zola, Jack London, Upton Sinclair, and a hundred others were committed to the flames, amid shouts of idiot delight. By 1936, Joseph Paul Goebbels, Germany's Minister of Propaganda, was issuing a proclamation which began with the following words: "Because this year has not brought an improvement in art criticism, I forbid once and for all the continuance of art criticism in its past form, effective as of today." By 1936, there was no one left in Germany who had the brains or courage to object.

Exactly why the Germans banished intelligence is a vast and   2
largely unanswered question. I have never been persuaded that the desperate economic depression that afflicted Germany in the 1920s adequately explains what happened. To quote Aristotle: Men do not become tyrants in order to keep warm. Neither do they become stupid — at least not *that* stupid. But the matter need not trouble us here. I offer the German case only as the most striking example of the fragility of human intelligence. My focus here is the United States in our own time, and I wish to worry you about the rapid erosion of our own intelligence. If you are confident that such a thing cannot happen, your confidence is misplaced, I believe, but it is understandable.

After all, the United States is one of the few countries in the   3
world founded by intellectuals — men of wide learning, of extraordinary rhetorical powers, of deep faith in reason. And although we have had our moods of anti-intellectualism, few people have been more generous in support of intelligence and

learning than Americans. It was the United States that initiated the experiment in mass education that is, even today, the envy of the world. It was America's churches that laid the foundation of our admirable system of higher education; it was the Land-Grant Act of 1862 that made possible our great state universities; and it is to America that scholars and writers have fled when freedom of the intellect became impossible in their own nations. This is why the great historian of American civilization Henry Steele Commager called America "the Empire of Reason." But Commager was referring to the United States of the eighteenth and nineteenth centuries. What term he would use for America today, I cannot say. Yet he has observed, as others have, a change, a precipitous decline in our valuation of intelligence, in our uses of language, in the disciplines of logic and reason, in our capacity to attend to complexity. Perhaps he would agree with me that the Empire of Reason is, in fact, gone, and that the most apt term for America today is the Empire of Shlock.

In any case, this is what I wish to call to your notice: the   4
frightening displacement of serious, intelligent public discourse in American culture by the imagery and triviality of what may be called show business. I do not see the decline of intelligent discourse in America leading to the barbarisms that flourished in Germany, of course. No scholars, I believe, will ever need to flee America. There will be no bonfires to burn books. And I cannot imagine any proclamations forbidding once and for all art criticism, or any other kind of criticism. But this is not a cause for complacency, let alone celebration. A culture does not have to force scholars to flee to render them impotent. A culture does not have to burn books to assure that they will not be read. And a culture does not need a Minister of Propaganda issuing proclamations to silence criticism. There are other ways to achieve stupidity, and it appears that, as in so many other things, there is a distinctly American way.

To explain what I am getting at, I find it helpful to refer to   5
two films, which taken together embody the main lines of my argument. The first film is of recent vintage and is called *The Gods Must Be Crazy*. It is about a tribal people who live in the Kalahari Desert plains of southern Africa, and what happens to their culture when it is invaded by an empty Coca-Cola bottle tossed from the window of a small plane passing overhead. The bottle lands in

the middle of the village and is construed by these gentle people to be a gift from the gods, for they not only have never seen a bottle before but have never seen glass either. The people are almost immediately charmed by the gift, and not only because of its novelty. The bottle, it turns out, has multiple uses, chief among them the intriguing music it makes when one blows into it.

But gradually a change takes place in the tribe. The bottle 6 becomes an irresistible preoccupation. Looking at it, holding it, thinking of things to do with it displace other activities once thought essential. But more than this, the Coke bottle is the only thing these people have ever seen of which there is only one of its kind. And so those who do not have it try to get it from the one who does. And the one who does refuses to give it up. Jealousy, greed, and even violence enter the scene, and come very close to destroying the harmony that has characterized their culture for a thousand years. The people begin to love their bottle more than they love themselves, and are saved only when the leader of the tribe, convinced that the gods must be crazy, returns the bottle to the gods by throwing it off the top of a mountain.

The film is great fun and it is also wise, mainly because it is 7 about a subject as relevant to people in Chicago or Los Angeles or New York as it is to those of the Kalahari Desert. It raises two questions of extreme importance to our situation: How does a culture change when new technologies are introduced to it? And is it always desirable for a culture to accommodate itself to the demands of new technologies? The leader of the Kalahari tribe is forced to confront these questions in a way that Americans have refused to do. And because his vision is not obstructed by a belief in what Americans call "technological progress," he is able with minimal discomfort to decide that the songs of the Coke bottle are not so alluring that they are worth admitting envy, egotism, and greed to a serene culture.

The second film relevant to my argument was made in 1967. 8 It is Mel Brooks's first film, *The Producers*. *The Producers* is a rather raucous comedy that has at its center a painful joke: An unscrupulous theatrical producer has figured out that it is relatively easy to turn a buck by producing a play that fails. All one has to do is induce dozens of backers to invest in the play by promising them exorbitant percentages of its profits. When the play fails, there being no profits to disperse, the producer walks away with thousands of dollars that can never be claimed. Of course, the central problem he must solve is to make sure that his play is a disastrous failure. And so he hits upon an excellent idea: he will take the most tragic and grotesque story of our century — the rise of Adolf Hitler — and make it into a musical.

Because the producer is only a crook and not a fool, he 9 assumes that the stupidity of making a musical on this theme will be immediately grasped by audiences and that they will leave the theater in dumbfounded rage. So he calls his play *Springtime for Hitler*, which is also the name of its most important song. The song begins with the words:

> *Springtime for Hitler and Germany;*
> *Winter for Poland and France.*

The melody is catchy, and when the song is sung it is accom- 10 panied by a happy chorus line. (One must understand, of course, that *Springtime for Hitler* is no spoof of Hitler, as was, for example, Charlie Chaplin's *The Great Dictator*. The play is instead a kind of denial of Hitler in song and dance; as if to say, it was all in fun.)

The ending of the movie is predictable. The audience loves 11 the play and leaves the theater humming *Springtime for Hitler*. The musical becomes a great hit. The producer ends up in jail, his joke having turned back on him. But Brooks's point is that the joke is on us. Although the film was made years before a movie actor became President of the United States, Brooks was making a kind of prophecy about that — namely, that the producers of American culture will increasingly turn our history, politics, religion, commerce, and education into forms of entertainment, and that we will become as a result a trivial people, incapable of coping with complexity, ambiguity, uncertainty, perhaps even reality. We will become, in a phrase, a people amused into stupidity.

For those readers who are not inclined to take Mel Brooks as 12 seriously as I do, let me remind you that the prophecy I attribute here to Brooks was, in fact, made many years before by a more formidable social critic than he. I refer to Aldous Huxley, who wrote *Brave New World*[1] at the time that the modern monuments to intellectual stupidity were taking shape: Nazism in Germany, fascism in Italy, communism in Russia. But Huxley was not concerned in his book with such naked and crude forms of intellectual suicide. He saw beyond them, and mostly, I must add, he saw America. To be more specific, he foresaw that the greatest threat to the intelligence and humane creativity of our culture would not come from Big Brother and Ministries of Propaganda, or gulags and concentration camps. He prophesied, if I may put it this way, that there is tyranny lurking in a Coca-Cola bottle; that we could be ruined not by what we fear and hate but by what we welcome and love, by what we construe to be a gift from the gods.

And in case anyone missed his point in 1932, Huxley wrote   13
Brave New World Revisited twenty years later. By then, George Orwell's *1984* had been published, and it was inevitable that Huxley would compare Orwell's book with his own. The difference, he said, is that in Orwell's book people are controlled by inflicting pain. In *Brave New World*, they are controlled by inflicting pleasure.

The Coke bottle that has fallen in our midst is a corporation   14
of dazzling technologies whose forms turn all serious public business into a kind of *Springtime for Hitler* musical. Television is the principal instrument of this disaster, in part because it is the medium Americans most dearly love, and in part because it has become the command center of our culture. Americans turn to television not only for their light entertainment but for their news, their weather, their politics, their religion, their history— all of which may be said to be their serious entertainment. The light entertainment is not the problem. The least dangerous things on television are its junk. What I am talking about is television's preemption of our culture's most serious business. It would be merely banal to say that television presents us with entertaining subject matter. It is quite another thing to say that

[1]In *Brave New World* (1932), British novelist Aldous Huxley depicts a frightening futuristic world—one that conditions people to relinquish, happily and without reservation, their individual freedom to an all-controlling central government.

on television all subject matter is presented as entertaining. And that is how television brings ruin to any intelligent understanding of public affairs.

Political campaigns, for example, are now conducted largely   15 in the form of television commercials. Candidates forgo precision, complexity, substance — in some cases, language itself — for the arts of show business: music, imagery, celebrities, theatrics. Indeed, political figures have become so good at this, and so accustomed to it, that they do television commercials even when they are not campaigning, as, for example, Geraldine Ferraro for Diet Pepsi and former Vice-Presidential candidate William Miller and the late Senator Sam Ervin for American Express. Even worse, political figures appear on variety shows, soap operas, and sitcoms. George McGovern, Ralph Nader, Ed Koch, and Jesse Jackson have all hosted "Saturday Night Live." Henry Kissinger and former President Gerald Ford have done cameo roles on "Dynasty." Tip O'Neill and Governor Michael Dukakis have appeared on "Cheers." Richard Nixon did a short stint on "Laugh-In." The late Senator from Illinois, Everett Dirksen,[2] was on "What's My Line?" a prophetic question if ever there was one. What *is* the line of these people? Or, more precisely, *where* is the line that one ought to be able to draw between politics and entertainment? I would suggest that television has annihilated it.

It is significant, I think, that although our current President,[3]   16 a former Hollywood movie actor, rarely speaks accurately and never precisely, he is known as the Great Communicator; his telegenic charm appears to be his major asset, and that seems to

[2]Geraldine Ferraro was the Democrats' choice in 1984 for vice president, the first woman to be nominated for that office; William Miller was the Republican candidate for vice president in 1984; Sam Ervin, a U.S. Senator for many years, chaired the Senate Watergate Investigation Committee; George McGovern was the Democratic presidential nominee in 1972 at the height of the protest against the Vietnam War; Ralph Nader is a prominent consumer advocate; Ed Koch served as mayor of New York City for twelve years; Jesse Jackson, a minister and civil rights activist, ran for the presidency in 1988; Henry Kissinger was Secretary of State during the Nixon years; Gerald Ford was president from 1974 to 1977; Tip O'Neill served as Speaker of the House between 1977 and 1987; Michael Dukakis, a Democrat, ran for the presidency in 1988; Richard Nixon was president from 1969 to 1974, when he was forced to resign; and Everett Dirksen served in the Senate for many years.

[3]Postman is referring to Ronald Reagan here.

be quite good enough in an entertainment-oriented politics. But lest you think his election to two terms is a mere aberration, I must remind you that, as I write [1988], Charlton Heston is being mentioned as a possible candidate for the Republican nomination in 1988. Should this happen, what alternative would the Democrats have but to nominate Gregory Peck? Two idols of the silver screen going one on one. Could even the fertile imagination of Mel Brooks have foreseen this? Heston giving us intimations of Moses as he accepts the nomination; Peck re-creating the courage of his biblical David as he accepts the challenge of running against a modern Goliath. Heston going on the stump as Michelangelo; Peck countering with Douglas MacArthur. Heston accusing Peck of insanity because of *The Boys From Brazil*. Peck replying with the charge that Heston blew the world up in *Return to Planet of the Apes*. *Springtime for Hitler* could be closer than you think.

But politics is only one arena in which serious language has   17
been displaced by the arts of show business. We have all seen how religion is packaged on television, as a kind of Las Vegas stage show, devoid of ritual, sacrality, and tradition. Today's electronic preachers are in no way like America's evangelicals of the past. Men like Jonathan Edwards, Charles Finney, and George Whitefield were preachers of theological depth, authentic learning, and great expository power. Electronic preachers such as Jimmy Swaggart, Jim Bakker, and Jerry Falwell[4] are merely performers who exploit television's visual power and their own charisma for the greater glory of themselves.

We have also seen "Sesame Street" and other educational   18
shows in which the demands of entertainment take precedence over the rigors of learning. And we well know how American businessmen, working under the assumption that potential customers require amusement rather than facts, use music, dance, comedy, cartoons, and celebrities to sell their products.

Even our daily news, which for most Americans means televi-   19
sion news, is packaged as a kind of show, featuring handsome

---

[4]Jonathan Edwards, Charles Finney, and George Whitefield were respected members of the American clergy in the eighteenth century, whereas today's television evangelists Jimmy Swaggart, Jim Bakker, and Jerry Falwell have tended to invite controversy, even scandal.

news readers, exciting music, and dynamic film footage. Most especially, film footage. When there is no film footage, there is no story. Stranger still, commercials may appear anywhere in a news story—before, after, or in the middle. This reduces all events to trivialities, sources of public entertainment and little more. After all, how serious can a bombing in Lebanon be if it is shown to us prefaced by a happy United Airlines commercial and summarized by a Calvin Klein jeans commercial? Indeed, television newscasters have added to our grammar a new part of speech—what may be called the "Now . . . this" conjunction, a conjunction that does not connect two things, but disconnects them. When newscasters say, "Now . . . this," they mean to indicate that what you have just heard or seen has no relevance to what you are about to hear or see. There is no murder so brutal, no political blunder so costly, no bombing so devastating that it cannot be erased from our minds by a newscaster saying, "Now . . . this." He means that you have thought long enough on the matter (let us say, for forty seconds) and you must now give your attention to a commercial. Such a situation is not "the news." It is merely a daily version of *Springtime for Hitler*, and in my opinion accounts for the fact that Americans are among the most ill-informed people in the world. To be sure, we know *of* many things; but we know *about* very little.

To provide some verification of this, I conducted a survey a few years back on the subject of the Iranian hostage crisis. I chose this subject because it was alluded to on television *every day for more than a year*. I did not ask my subjects for their opinions about the hostage situation. I am not interested in opinion polls; I am interested in knowledge polls. The questions I asked were simple and did not require deep knowledge. For example, Where is Iran? What language do the Iranians speak? Where did the Shah come from? What religion do the Iranians practice, and what are its basic tenets? What does "Ayatollah" mean? I found that almost everybody knew practically nothing about Iran. And those who did know something said they had learned it from *Newsweek* or *Time* or the *New York Times*. Television, in other words, is not the great information machine. It is the great disinformation machine. A most nerve-wracking confirmation of this came some time ago during an interview with the producer and the writer of the TV mini-series *Peter the Great*. Defending the historical inac-

20

curacies in the drama—which included a fabricated meeting between Peter and Sir Isaac Newton[5]—the producer said that no
one would watch a dry, historically faithful biography. The writer
added that it is better for audiences to learn something that is
untrue, if it is entertaining, than not to learn anything at all. And
just to put some icing on the cake, the actor who played Peter,
Maximilian Schell, remarked that he does not believe in historical
truth and therefore sees no reason to pursue it.

I do not mean to say that the trivialization of American   21
public discourse is all accomplished on television. Rather, television is the paradigm for all our attempts at public communication. It conditions our minds to apprehend the world through
fragmented pictures and forces other media to orient themselves
in that direction. You know the standard question we put to
people who have difficulty understanding even simple language:
we ask them impatiently, "Do I have to draw a picture for you?"
Well, it appears that, like it or not, our culture will draw pictures
for us, will explain the world to us in pictures. As a medium for
conducting public business, language has receded in importance;
it has been moved to the periphery of culture and has been
replaced at the center by the entertaining visual image.

Please understand that I am making no criticism of the visual   22
arts in general. That criticism is made by God, not by me. You
will remember that in His Second Commandment, God explicitly
states that "Thou shalt not make unto thee any graven image, nor
any likeness of anything that is in Heaven above, or that is in the
earth beneath, or the waters beneath the earth." I have always felt
that God was taking a rather extreme position on this, as is His
way. As for myself, I am arguing from the standpoint of a symbolic relativist. Forms of communication are neither good nor
bad in themselves. They become good or bad depending on their
relationship to other symbols and on the functions they are made
to serve within a social order. When a culture becomes over-
loaded with pictures; when logic and rhetoric lose their binding
authority; when historical truth becomes irrelevant; when the
spoken or written word is distrusted or makes demands on our

[5]Peter the Great was the despotic czar of Russia from 1682 to 1725. English
mathematician and philosopher Sir Issac Newton (1642–1727) formulated the
laws of gravity and motion.

attention that we are incapable of giving; when our politics, history, education, religion, public information, and commerce are expressed largely in visual imagery rather than words, then a culture is in serious jeopardy.

Neither do I make a complaint against entertainment. As an   23
old song has it, life is not a highway strewn with flowers. The sight of a few blossoms here and there may make our journey a trifle more endurable. But in America, the least amusing people are our professional entertainers. In our present situation, our preachers, entrepreneurs, politicians, teachers, and journalists are committed to entertaining us through media that do not lend themselves to serious, complex discourse. But these producers of our culture are not to be blamed. They, like the rest of us, believe in the supremacy of technological progress. It has never occurred to us that the gods might be crazy. And even if it did, there is no mountaintop from which we can return what is dangerous to us.

We would do well to keep in mind that there are two ways in   24
which the spirit of a culture may be degraded. In the first — the Orwellian — culture becomes a prison. This was the way of the Nazis, and it appears to be the way of the Russians. In the second — the Huxleyan — culture becomes a burlesque. This appears to be the way of the Americans. What Huxley teaches is that in the Age of Advanced Technology, spiritual devastation is more likely to come from an enemy with a smiling countenance than from one whose face exudes suspicion and hate. In the Huxleyan prophecy, Big Brother does not watch us, by his choice; we watch him, by ours. When a culture becomes distracted by trivia; when political and social life are redefined as a perpetual round of entertainments; when public conversation becomes a form of baby talk; when a people become, in short, an audience and their public business a vaudeville act, then — Huxley argued — a nation finds itself at risk and culture-death is a clear possibility. I agree.

Questions for Close Reading

1. What is the selection's thesis? Locate the sentence(s) in which Postman states his main idea. If he doesn't state the thesis explicitly, express it in your own words.
2. In paragraphs 11 and 12, Postman says that Mel Brooks, director of

The Producers, made "a kind of prophecy" about America. What did Brooks predict? To what extent did his prediction come true?

3. Why does Postman blame television for the trivialization of American culture? According to the author, which aspects of contemporary life have been affected by television?

4. What does Postman find so telling about the newscasters' phrase "Now . . . this"? What does the phrase say about television's attitude toward the events it depicts? How, according to Postman, does this attitude contribute to the decline of serious thought?

5. Refer to your dictionary as needed to define the following words used in the selection: *schlock* (title and paragraph 3), *lethal* (1), *nemeses* (1), *fervor* (1), *rhetorical* (3), *precipitous* (3), *apt* (3), *ambiguity* (11), *Nazism* (12), *fascism* (12), *gulags* (12), *preemption* (14), *banal* (14), *forgo* (15), *cameo* (15), *telegenic* (16), *sacrality* (17), *expository* (17), *conjunction* (19), *paradigm* (21), *periphery* (21), *relativist* (22), *rhetoric* (22), *burlesque* (24), *countenance* (24), and *exudes* (24).

Questions About the Writer's Craft

1. **The pattern.** Look again at the extended examples of the two movies that Postman provides in paragraphs 5 – 7 and 8 – 11. How do these examples help the author clarify what he believes is wrong with American culture?

2. **Other patterns.** Postman compares and contrasts the cultural situation in the United States with that in Germany (paragraphs 1 – 4) and Russia (24). Why might he have chosen these comparison-contrasts to begin and end the essay? What other contrasting examples does Postman supply?

3. Examine the sentences in paragraph 4 and at the end of paragraphs 22 and 24. What technique does Postman use to make these sentences striking? Why might he have put special effort into the style of these paragraphs?

4. Locate places where Postman uses the personal pronouns *I*, *we*, *us*, *our*, and *you*. What effect do these references have on the essay's tone? What do they suggest about Postman's assumptions about his audience?

Questions for Further Thought

1. According to Postman, television's emphasis on "show business" hinders our ability to deal with serious and complex issues. Do you find this to be so in your own life? Do you, for example, expect television news to be entertaining? Are there other areas of your life

that you expect to be entertaining? Consider your classes, the newspapers you read, and so forth.

2. In your opinion, is the United States becoming — as Postman claims in paragraph 11 — a nation of "trivial people, incapable of coping with complexity, ambiguity, uncertainty, perhaps even reality"? What signs do you notice in our society that support or disprove his statement?

3. In paragraph 14, Postman writes that "the least dangerous things on television are its junk." Do you agree that the light entertainment on television is harmless? Can you think of some light entertainment that might contribute to our becoming — as Postman states in paragraph 11 — "a people amused into stupidity"?

4. Reflecting on the situation depicted in *The Gods Must Be Crazy*, Postman asks whether it's always desirable for cultures to accommodate to new technologies. Do you think there are new technologies or inventions that we as a society should reject? If so, what are they? Why should we reject them?

Writing Assignments Using Exemplification as a Pattern of Development

∞ 1. Postman suggests that the line between entertainment and politics has been blurred, citing among other things the fact that the American public elected a Hollywood actor, Ronald Reagan, as president. Would you agree that our leaders are fairly "schlocky"? Express your opinion in an essay by examining the quality of leadership in one or two areas of American life (for example, education; religion; business; campus, local, state, or national politics). Provide numerous specific examples to support your thesis. Before planning the paper, you may want to read H. L. Mencken's "The Politician" (page 551) for its cynical insights into American leadership.

2. Postman feels that *The Gods Must Be Crazy* and *The Producers* are two films that reveal much about our lives. What film or films have you seen that reflect a belief or attitude held by society today? Supplying examples of scenes or incidents from two or more films, write an essay showing that such a belief or attitude does indeed prevail in our contemporary culture.

Writing Assignments Using Other Patterns of Development

∞ 3. According to Postman, television has had a destructive effect on contemporary society. Another writer, Marie Winn, argues a similar point in "TV Addiction" (page 558). Is television-viewing (and the mindset it creates) a major problem in our society? Write an essay arguing either that television *is* at the root of most of our social ills or that some other force is weakening society. Before writing your essay, take some time to brainstorm with friends about possible contributing factors. Then select the one factor you feel creates the most problems, and defend your position by illustrating its negative effects. If you focus on television, you may cite some of Postman's points, but be sure to provide your own examples as well.

4. While Postman explores the effects of television on modern life, other innovations — computers, car phones, answering machines, video games, VCRs — also influence the way we live today. Write an essay showing the effects — positive, negative, or neutral — that you see flowing from one or more of these new inventions. You may write a serious analysis or use a comic tone to explore the pitfalls caused by the new product.

Barbara Ehrenreich

Barbara Ehrenreich (1941–) has been a college professor, investigative reporter, magazine editor, and social activist. A graduate of Reed College, Ehrenreich received her Ph.D. in biology from Rockefeller University. She has cowritten several books, including *For Her Own Good: 150 Years of the Experts' Advice to Women* (1978) and *Remaking Love: The Feminization of Sex* (1986). Her more recent books include *Fear of Falling: The Inner Life of the Middle Class* (1989) and *The Worst Years of Our Lives* (1990). A regular columnist for *Ms.* and *Mother Jones*, Ehrenreich has published articles in many other magazines, such as *Esquire, Time, Vogue,* and the *New Republic.* "What I've Learned From Men" first appeared in *Ms.* in 1985.

What I've Learned From Men

"Smile. Be perky. Keep the conversation going. Ask him questions about himself. But don't ask him anything that might threaten his masculinity." From their earliest days on, Barbara Ehrenreich contends, advice like this is drummed into young girls. And what, according to Ehrenreich, is the effect of such advice? Women end up acting like wimps and ninnies.

For many years I believed that women had only one thing to   1
learn from men: how to get the attention of a waiter by some means short of kicking over the table and shrieking. Never in my life have I gotten the attention of a waiter, unless it was an off-duty waiter whose car I'd accidentally scraped in a parking lot somewhere. Men, however, can summon a maître d' just by thinking the word "coffee," and this is a power women would be well-advised to study. What else would we possibly want to learn from them? How to interrupt someone in mid-sentence as if you were performing an act of conversational euthanasia? How to

261

drop a pair of socks three feet from an open hamper and keep right on walking? How to make those weird guttural gargling sounds in the bathroom?

But now, at mid-life, I am willing to admit that there are   2
some real and useful things to learn from men. Not from all men — in fact, we may have the most to learn from some of the men we like the least. This realization does not mean that my feminist principles have gone soft with age: what I think women could learn from men is how to get *tough*. After more than a decade of consciousness-raising, assertiveness training, and hand-to-hand combat in the battle of the sexes, we're still too ladylike. Let me try that again — we're just too *damn* ladylike.

Here is an example from my own experience, a story that I   3
blush to recount. A few years ago, at an international conference held in an exotic and luxurious setting, a prestigious professor invited me to his room for what he said would be an intellectual discussion on matters of theoretical importance. So far, so good. I showed up promptly. But only minutes into the conversation —held in all-too-adjacent chairs — it emerged that he was inter-ested in something more substantial than a meeting of minds. I was disgusted, but not enough to overcome 30-odd years of programming in ladylikeness. Every time his comments took a lecherous turn, I chattered distractingly; every time his hand found its way to my knee, I returned it as if it were something he had misplaced. This went on for an unconscionable period (as much as 20 minutes); then there was a minor scuffle, a dash for the door, and I was out — with nothing violated but my self-esteem. I, a full-grown feminist, conversant with such matters as rape crisis counseling and sexual harassment at the workplace, had behaved like a ninny — or, as I now understand it, like a lady.

The essence of ladylikeness is a persistent servility masked as   4
"niceness." For example, we (women) tend to assume that it is our responsibility to keep everything "nice" even when the per-son we are with is rude, aggressive, or emotionally AWOL. (In the above example, I was so busy taking responsibility for pre-serving the veneer of "niceness" that I almost forgot to take responsibility for myself.) In conversations with men, we do almost all the work: sociologists have observed that in male-female social interactions it's the woman who throws out leading questions and verbal encouragements ("So how did you *feel*

about that?" and so on) while the man, typically, says "Hmmmm." Wherever we go, we're perpetually smiling—the on-cue smile, like the now-outmoded curtsy, being one of our culture's little rituals of submission. We're trained to feel embarrassed if we're praised, but if we see a criticism coming at us from miles down the road, we rush to acknowledge it. And when we're feeling aggressive or angry or resentful, we just tighten up our smiles or turn them into rueful little moues. In short, we spend a great deal of time acting like wimps.

For contrast, think of the macho stars we love to watch.   5 Think, for example, of Mel Gibson facing down punk marauders in "The Road Warrior" . . . John Travolta swaggering his way through the early scenes of "Saturday Night Fever" . . . or Marlon Brando shrugging off the local law in "The Wild One." Would they simper their way through tight spots? Chatter aimlessly to keep the conversation going? Get all clutched up whenever they think they might—just might—have hurt someone's feelings? No, of course not, and therein, I think, lies their fascination for us.

The attraction of the "tough guy" is that he has—or at least   6 seems to have—what most of us lack, and that is an aura of power and control. In an article, feminist psychiatrist Jean Baker Miller writes that "a woman's using self-determined power for herself is equivalent to selfishness [and] destructiveness"—an equation that makes us want to avoid even the appearance of power. Miller cites cases of women who get depressed just when they're on the verge of success—and of women who do succeed and then bury their achievement in self-deprecation. As an example, she describes one company's periodic meetings to recognize outstanding salespeople: when a woman is asked to say a few words about her achievement, she tends to say something like, "Well, I really don't know how it happened. I guess I was just lucky this time." In contrast, the men will cheerfully own up to the hard work, intelligence, and so on, to which they owe their success. By putting herself down, a woman avoids feeling brazenly powerful and potentially "selfish"; she also does the traditional lady's work of trying to make everyone else feel better ("She's not really so smart, after all, just lucky").

So we might as well get a little tougher. And a good place to   7 start is by cutting back on the small acts of deference that we've been programmed to perform since girlhood. Like unnecessary smiling. For many women—waitresses, flight attendants, receptionists—smiling is an occupational requirement, but there's no reason for anyone to go around grinning when she's not being paid for it. I'd suggest that we save our off-duty smiles for when we truly feel like sharing them, and if you're not sure what to do with your face in the meantime, study Clint Eastwood's expressions—both of them.

Along the same lines, I think women should stop taking responsibility for every human interaction we engage in. In a social encounter with a woman, the average man can go 25 minutes saying nothing more than "You don't say?" "Izzat so?" and, of course, "Hmmmm." Why should we do all the work? By taking so much responsibility for making conversations go well, we act as if we had much more at stake in the encounter than the other party—and that gives him (or her) the power advantage. Every now and then, we deserve to get more out of a conversation than we put into it: I'd suggest not offering information you'd rather not share ("I'm really terrified that my sales plan won't work") and not, out of sheer politeness, soliciting information you don't really want ("Wherever did you get that lovely tie?"). There will be pauses, but they don't have to be awkward for *you*.   8

It is true that some, perhaps most, men will interpret any decrease in female deference as a deliberate act of hostility. Omit the free smiles and perky conversation-boosters and someone is bound to ask, "Well, what's come over *you* today?" For most of us, the first impulse is to stare at our feet and make vague references to a terminally ill aunt in Atlanta, but we should have as much right to be taciturn as the average (male) taxi driver. If you're taking a vacation from smiles and small talk and some fellow is moved to inquire about what's "bothering" you, just stare back levelly and say, the international debt crisis, the arms race, or the death of God.   9

There are all kinds of ways to toughen up—and potentially move up—at work, and I leave the details to the purveyors of assertiveness training. But Jean Baker Miller's study underscores a fundamental principle that anyone can master on her own. We can stop acting less capable than we actually are. For example, in the matter of taking credit when credit is due, there's a key difference between saying "I was just lucky" and saying "I had a   10 plan and it worked." If you take the credit you deserve, you're letting people know that you were confident you'd succeed all along, and that you fully intend to do so again.

Finally, we may be able to learn something from men about   11
what to do with anger. As a general rule, women get irritated: men get *mad*. We make tight little smiles of ladylike exasperation; they pound on desks and roar. I wouldn't recommend emulating the full basso profundo male tantrum, but women do need ways of expressing justified anger clearly, colorfully, and, when necessary, crudely. If you're not just irritated, but *pissed off*, it might help to say so.

I, for example, have rerun the scene with the prestigious   12
professor many times in my mind. And in my mind, I play it like Bogart. I start by moving my chair over to where I can look the professor full in the face. I let him do the chattering, and when it becomes evident that he has nothing serious to say, I lean back and cross my arms, just to let him know that he's wasting my time. I do not smile, neither do I nod encouragement. Nor, of course, do I respond to his blandishments with apologetic shrugs and blushes. Then, at the first flicker of lechery, I stand up and announce coolly, "All right, I've had enough of this crap." Then I walk out—slowly, deliberately, confidently. Just like a man.

Or—now that I think of it—just like a woman.   13

Questions for Close Reading

1. What is the selection's thesis? Locate the sentence(s) in which Ehrenreich states her main idea. If she doesn't state the thesis explicitly, express it in your own words.
2. Why did Ehrenreich handle the lecherous professor as she did? In retrospect, how does she wish she had dealt with the situation? How does her current perspective of the way she should have behaved reinforce her thesis in the essay?
3. What does "behaving like a lady" mean, according to Ehrenreich? What is her opinion of "ladylike" behavior?
4. Why, in Ehrenreich's view, do we like "macho stars" (paragraph 5)? What can we learn from them?
5. Refer to your dictionary as needed to define the following words used in the selection: *euthanasia* (paragraph 1), *gutteral* (1), *lecherous* (3), *distractingly* (3), *unconscionable* (3), *ninny* (3), *servility* (4), *veneer* (4), *moues* (4), *marauders* (5), *aura* (6), *brazenly* (6), *deference* (9), *taciturn*

(9), *purveyors* (10), *emulating* (11), *basso profundo* (11), and *blandishments* (12).

Questions About the Writer's Craft

1. **The pattern.** In paragraphs 3 and 12, Ehrenreich uses her own personal experience as a key example. Why do you think she chooses to include this example? Why do you suppose she presents it so early in the essay and then returns to it at the end?
2. **Other patterns.** Locate places in the essay where Ehrenreich uses examples to contrast the different responses and behaviors of males and females. How do these contrasts help the writer develop her main idea?
3. Do you think that Ehrenreich is speaking primarily to a male or to a female audience? What in the essay makes you feel this way? Do you think that the author expects her audience to be positive, hostile, or neutral toward her ideas? What in the essay leads you to this conclusion?
4. In her attack on "ladylikeness," Ehrenreich deliberately avoids using a "ladylike" or "nice" tone. Which of her phrases or expressions seem to defy stereotypes about the way "ladies" should express themselves?

Questions for Further Thought

1. In paragraph 10, Ehrenreich says she'll leave to others the details of how women should "toughen up." Do you agree that women need to "toughen up"? Why or why not? If they do, in what ways do you think women should be tougher? How do you think others might respond to this toughness?
2. Ehrenreich states that women — much more than men — are conditioned to disregard praise but almost welcome criticism. Do you agree that this is a basic difference between the sexes? Explain.
3. In paragraphs 4 and 8, Ehrenreich states that women usually "do all the work" in male-female relationships. Do you feel that Ehrenreich's observation is valid? Why or why not?
4. Psychiatrist Jean Baker Miller claims that women who use their power for themselves are considered selfish and destructive, "an equation," Ehrenreich says, "that makes . . . [women] want to avoid even the appearance of power." Do you agree that having "an aura of power and control" has been a negative for women, but a positive for men? If so, how could women change the way their power is perceived?

Writing Assignments Using Exemplification as a Pattern of Development

∞ 1. If, as Ehrenreich suggests, women have much to learn from men, is it also true that men could learn from women? Write an essay illustrating your belief that men would indeed be better off if they acquired some attitudes and behaviors traditionally associated with women. Be sure to provide numerous examples from your own experience and observations. You may take a humorous or serious approach when showing that men should — in some respects — become more like women. Deborah Tannen's "Sex, Lies, and Conversation" (page 440) may spark some insight into characteristically male and female behavioral patterns.

2. Ehrenreich points to the popularity of several "macho stars": Mel Gibson in *The Road Warrior*, John Travolta in *Saturday Night Fever*, Marlon Brando in *The Wild One*, and Clint Eastwood in anything. Choose several female characters from film or television who you feel provide positive role models for both males and females. Write an essay in which you use these characters as examples of the way that men and women should conduct their lives.

Writing Assignments Using Other Patterns of Development

∞ 3. Ehrenreich suggests that some of the problems women experience in relationships and careers are of their own making — they smile too much, are too deferential, and fail to claim their own achievements. Pick one or two areas in which women tend to experience difficulty and write an essay arguing either that women sabotage themselves or that they are sabotaged by society's attitudes and expectations. Brainstorm with others to gather ideas for your paper. For other perspectives, you may want to read one or more of the following essays: Alleen Pace Nilsen's "Sexism and Language" (page 228), Deborah Tannen's "Sex, Lies, and Conversation" (page 440), Judy Brady's "Why I Want a Wife" (page 546), Camille Paglia's "Rape: A Bigger Danger Than Feminists Know" (page 650), Susan Jacoby's "Common Decency" (page 658), and Virginia Woolf's "Professions for Women" (page 721).

4. Like Ehrenreich, most of us have been subjected at one time or another to the inappropriate or unpleasant behavior of others: slurs on our abilities, interests, or appearance; derision about our sex or sexual preference; taunts about our race, religion, or ethnic back-

ground. Focus on *one* kind of insult, and brainstorm with others to identify ways for dealing with such an affront. Then write an essay describing different strategies for coping with the offensive behavior. Reach some conclusions about which approach is most effective. Maya Angelou's "Grandmother's Victory" (page 158), Santha Rama Rau's "By Any Other Name" (page 191), and Diane Cole's "Don't Just Stand There" (page 394) may spark some ideas worth exploring.

Additional Writing Topics

EXEMPLIFICATION

General Assignments

Use examples to develop any one of the following topics into a well-organized essay. When writing the paper, choose enough relevant examples to support your thesis. Organize the material into a sequence that most effectively illustrates the thesis, keeping in mind that emphatic order is often the most compelling way to present specifics.

1. Many of today's drivers have dangerous habits.
2. Drug and alcohol abuse is (or is not) a serious problem among many young people.
3. One rule of restaurant dining is, "Management often seems oblivious to problems that are perfectly obvious to customers."
4. Children today are not encouraged to use their imaginations.
5. The worst kind of hypocrite is a religious hypocrite.
6. The best things in life are definitely not free.
7. A part-time job is an important experience that every college student should have.
8. Many TV and magazine ads use sexual allusions to sell their products.
9. _____ (name someone you know well) is a _____ (use a quality: open-minded, dishonest, compulsive, reliable, gentle, and so on) person.
10. Television commercials stereotype the elderly (or another minority group).
11. Today, salespeople act as if they're doing you a favor by taking your money.
12. Most people behave decently in their daily interactions with each other.
13. Pettiness, jealousy, and selfishness abound in our daily interactions with each other.
14. You can tell a lot about people by observing what they wear and eat.
15. Too many Americans are overly concerned with being physically fit.
16. There are several study techniques that will help a student learn more efficiently.
17. Some teachers seem to enjoy turning tests into ordeals.
18. "How to avoid bad eating habits" is one course all college students should take.

19. More needs to be done to eliminate obstacles faced by the physically handicapped.
20. Some of the best presents are those that cost the least.

Assignments with a Specific Purpose and Audience

1. A friend of yours has taken a job in a big city or moved to a small town. To prepare your friend for this new environment, write a letter giving examples of what life in a big city or small town is like. You might focus on the benefits or dangers with which your friend is unlikely to be familiar.
2. Shopping for a new car, you become annoyed at how many safety features are available only as expensive options. Write a letter of complaint to the auto manufacturer, citing at least three examples of such options. Avoid sounding hostile.
3. Lately, many people at your college or workplace have been experiencing stress. As a member of the Campus (or Company) Committee on Morale, you've been asked to prepare a pamphlet illustrating different strategies for reducing stress. Decide what strategies you'll discuss and explain them with helpful examples.
4. Assume that you're an elementary school principal planning to give a speech in which you'll try to convince parents that television distorts children's perceptions of reality. Write the speech, illustrating your point with vivid examples.
5. A pet food company is having an annual contest to choose a new animal to feature in its advertising. To win the contest, you must convince the company that your pet is personable, playful, unique. Write an essay giving examples of your pet's special qualities.
6. For your college humor magazine, write an article on what you consider to be the "three best consumer products of the past twenty-five years." Support your opinion with lively, engaging specifics that are consistent with the magazine's offbeat and slightly ironic tone.

6

DIVISION-
CLASSIFICATION

WHAT IS
DIVISION-CLASSIFICATION?

Imagine what life would be like if this is how an average day unfolded:

> You plan to stop at the supermarket for only five items, but your marketing takes over an hour because all the items in the store are jumbled together. Clerks put new shipments anywhere they please; the milk might be with the vegetables on Monday but with laundry detergent on Thursday. Next, you go to the drugstore to pick up some photos you left to be developed. You don't have time, though, to wait while the cashier roots through the large carton into which all the pickup envelopes have been thrown. You return to your car and decide to stop at the town hall to pay a parking ticket. But the town hall baffles you. The offices are unmarked,

and there's not even a directory to tell you on which floor the Violations Bureau can be found. Annoyed, you get back into your car and, minutes later, end up colliding with another car, which is driving toward you in your lane. When you wake up in the hospital, you find there are three other patients in your room: a middle-aged man with a heart problem, a young boy ready to have his tonsils removed, and a woman about to go into labor.

Such a muddled world, lacking the most basic forms of organization, would make daily life chaotic. All of us instinctively look for ways to order our environment. Without systems, categories, or sorting mechanisms, we'd be overwhelmed by life's complexity. An organization like a college or university, for example, is made manageable by being divided into various schools (Liberal Arts, Performing Arts, Engineering, and so on). The schools are then separated into departments (English, History, Political Science), and each department's offerings are grouped into distinct categories—English, for instance, into Literature and Composition—before being further divided into specific courses.

The kind of ordering system we've been discussing is called *division-classification*, a logical way of thinking that allows us to make sense of a complex world. Division and classification, though separate processes, are often used together as complementary techniques. *Division* involves taking a single unit or concept, breaking the unit down into its parts, and then analyzing the connection among the parts and between the parts and the whole. For instance, if we wanted to organize the chaotic hospital described at the start of the chapter, we might think about how the single concept "a hospital" could be broken down into its components. We might come up with the following breakdown: pediatric wing, cardiac wing, maternity wing, and so on.

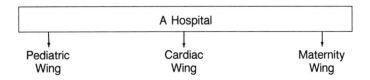

What we have just done involves division: We've taken a single entity (a hospital) and divided it into some of its component parts (wings), each with its own facilities and patients.

In contrast, *classification* brings two or more related items together and categorizes them according to type or kind. If the disorganized supermarket described earlier were to be restructured, the clerks would have to classify the separate items arriving at the loading dock. Cartons of lettuce, tomatoes, cucumbers, butter, yogurt, milk, shampoo, conditioner, and setting lotion would be assigned to the appropriate categories:

Lettuce	Butter	Shampoo
Tomatoes	Yogurt	Conditioner
Cucumbers	Milk	Setting Lotion
↓	↓	↓
Produce	Dairy	Hair Products

HOW DIVISION-CLASSIFICATION
FITS YOUR PURPOSE AND AUDIENCE

The reorganized hospital and supermarket show the way division and classification work in everyday life. But division and classification also come into play during the writing process. Because division involves breaking a subject into parts, it can be a helpful strategy during prewriting, especially if you're analyzing a broad, complex subject: the structure of a film; the motivation of a character in a novel; the problem your community has with vandalism; the controversy surrounding school prayer. An editorial examining a recent hostage crisis, for example, might divide the crisis into three areas: how the hostages were treated by (1) their captors, (2) the governments negotiating their release, and (3) the media. The purpose of the editorial might be to show readers that the governments' treatment of the hostages was particularly exploitative.

Classification can be useful for imposing order on the hodgepodge of ideas generated during prewriting. You examine that material to see which of your rough ideas are alike and which are dissimilar, so that you can cluster related items in the same category. Classification would, then, be a helpful strategy when analyzing topics like these: techniques for impressing teachers;

comic styles of talk-show hosts; views on abortion; reasons for the current rise in volunteerism. You might, for instance, use classification in a paper showing that Americans are undermining their health through their obsessive pursuit of various diets. Perhaps you begin by brainstorming all the diets that have gained popularity in recent years (Weight Watchers', Slim-Fast, Jenny Craig, whatever). Then you categorize the diets according to type: high fiber, low protein, high carbohydrate, and so on. Once the diets are grouped, you can discuss the problems within each category, demonstrating to readers that none of the diets is safe or effective.

Division-classification can be crucial when responding to college assignments like the following:

> Based on your observations, what kinds of appeals do television advertisers use when selling automobiles? In your view, are any of these appeals morally irresponsible?

> Analyze the components that go into being an effective parent. Indicate those you consider most vital for raising confident, well-adjusted children.

> Describe the hierarchy of the typical high school clique, identifying the various parts of the hierarchy. Use your analysis to support or refute the view that adolescence is a period of rigid conformity.

> Many social commentators have observed that discourtesy is on the rise. Indicate whether you think this is a valid observation by characterizing the types of everyday encounters you have with people.

These assignments suggest division-classification through the use of such words as *kinds, components, parts*, and *types*. Generally, though, you won't receive such clear signals to use division-classification. Instead, the broad purpose of the essay—and the point you want to make—will lead you to the analytical thinking characteristic of division-classification.

Sometimes division-classification will be the dominant technique for structuring an essay; other times it will be used as a supplemental pattern in an essay organized primarily according to another pattern of development. Let's look at some examples. Say you want to write a paper *explaining a process* (surviving divorce; creating a hit record; shepherding a bill through Congress; using the Heimlich maneuver on people who are choking). You could *divide* the process into parts or stages, showing, for instance, that the Heimlich maneuver is an easily mastered skill that readers should acquire. Or perhaps you plan to write a light-spirited essay analyzing the *effect* that increased awareness of sexual stereotypes has had on college students' social lives. In such a case, you might use *classification*. To show readers that shifting gender roles make young men and women comically self-conscious, you could categorize the places where students scout each other out: in class, at the library, at parties, in dorms. You could then show how students — not wishing to be macho or coyly feminine — approach each other with laughable tentativeness in these four environments.

Now imagine that you're writing an *argumentation-persuasion* essay urging that the federal government prohibit the feeding of antibiotics to livestock to stimulate their growth. The paper could begin by *dividing* the antibiotics cycle into stages: the effects of antibiotics on animals; the short-term effects on humans who consume the animals; the possible long-term effects of consuming antibiotic-tainted meat. To increase readers' understanding of the problem, you might also discuss the antibiotics controversy in terms of an even larger issue: the dangerous ways food is treated before being consumed. In this case, you would consider the various procedures (use of additives, preservatives, artificial colors, and so on), *classifying* these treatments into several types —from least harmful (some additives or artificial colors, perhaps) to most harmful (you might slot the antibiotics here). Such an essay would be developed using both division *and* classification: first, the division of the antibiotics cycle and then the classification of the various food treatments. Frequently, this interdependence will be reversed, and classification will precede rather than follow division.

SUGGESTIONS FOR USING DIVISION-CLASSIFICATION IN AN ESSAY

The following suggestions will be helpful whether you use division-classification as a dominant or supportive pattern of development.

1. Select a principle of division-classification consistent with your purpose. Most subjects can be divided or classified according to a *number of different principles*. For example, when writing about an ideal vacation, you could divide your subject according to any of these principles: location, cost, recreation available. Similarly, when analyzing students at your college, you could base your classification on a variety of principles: students' majors, their racial or ethnic background, whether they belong to a fraternity or sorority. In all cases, though, the principle of division-classification you select must meet one stringent requirement: it must help you meet your overall purpose and reinforce your central point. Sometimes a principle of division-classification seems so attractive that you latch on to it without examining whether it's consistent with your purpose. Suppose you want to write a paper asserting that several episodes of a new television comedy are destined to become classics. Here's how you might go wrong.

You begin by doing some brainstorming about the episodes. Then, as you start to organize the prewriting material, you hit upon a possible principle of classification: grouping the characters in the show according to the frequency with which they appear (main characters appearing in every show, supporting characters appearing in most shows, and guest characters appearing once or twice). You name the characters and explain which characters fit where. But is this principle of classification significant? Has it anything to do with why the shows will become classics? No, it hasn't. Such an essay would be little more than a meaningless exercise in classifying things just to classify them.

In contrast, a significant principle of classification might involve categorizing a number of shows according to the easily recognized human types portrayed: the Pompous Know-It-All, the Boss Who's Out of Control, the Lovable Grouch, the Surpris-

ingly Savvy Innocent. You might illustrate the way certain episodes offer delightful twists on these stock figures, making such
shows models of comic plotting and humor.

When you write an essay that uses division-classification as
its primary method of development, a *single principle* of division-
classification provides the foundation for each major section of
the paper. Imagine you're writing an essay showing that the
success of contemporary music groups has less to do with musical
talent than with the groups' ability to market themselves to a
distinct segment of the listening audience. To develop your
point, you might categorize several performers according to the
age groups they appeal to (preteens, adolescents, people in their
late twenties) and then analyze the marketing strategies the musicians use to gain their fans' support. The essay's logic would be
undermined if you switched, in the middle of your analysis, to
another principle of classification — say, the influence of earlier
groups on today's music scene.

Don't, however, take this caution to mean that essays can
never use more than one principle of division-classification as
they unfold. They can — as long as the *shift from one principle to
another* occurs in *different parts* of the paper. Imagine you want to
write about widespread disillusionment with student government
leaders at your college. You could develop this point by breaking
down the dissatisfaction into the following: disappointment with
the students' qualifications for office; disenchantment with their
campaign tactics; frustration with their performance once
elected. That section of the essay completed, you might move to a
second principle of division — how students can get involved in
campus government. Perhaps you break the proposed involvement into the following possibilities: serving on nominating
committees; helping to run candidates' campaigns; attending
open sessions of the student government.

2. Apply the principle of division-classification logically.
In an essay using division-classification, you need to demonstrate
to readers that your analysis is the result of careful thought. First
of all, your division-classification should be as *complete* as possible. Your analysis should include — within reason — all the parts
into which you can divide your subject, or all the types into which
you can categorize your subjects. Let's say you're writing an

essay showing that where college students live is an important factor in determining how satisfied they are with college life. Keeping your purpose in mind, you classify students according to where they live: with parents, in dorms, in fraternity and sorority houses. But what about all the students who live in rented apartments, houses, or rooms off campus? If these places of residence are ignored, your classification won't be complete; you will lose credibility with your readers because they'll probably realize that you have overlooked several important considerations.

Your division-classification should also be *consistent*: the parts into which you break your subject or the groups into which you place your subjects should be as mutually exclusive as possible. The parts or categories should not be mixed, nor should they overlap. Assume you're writing an essay describing the animals at the zoo in a nearby city. You decide to describe the zoo's mammals, reptiles, birds, and endangered species. But such a classification is inconsistent. You begin by categorizing the animals according to scientific class (mammals, birds, reptiles), then switch to another principle when you classify some animals according to whether they are endangered. Because you drift over to a different principle of classification, your categories are no longer mutually exclusive: endangered species could overlap with any of the other categories. In which section of the paper, for instance, would you describe an exotic parrot that is obviously a bird but is also nearly extinct? And how would you categorize the zoo's rare mountain gorilla? This impressive creature is a mammal, but it is also an endangered species. Such overlapping categories undercut the logic that gives an essay its integrity.

A helpful tip: a solid outline is invaluable when you use division-classification. The outline encourages you to do the rigorous thinking needed to arrive at divisions and classifications that are logical, complete, and consistent.

3. Prepare an effective thesis. If your essay uses division-classification as its dominant method of development, it might be helpful to prepare a thesis that does more than signal the paper's subject and suggest your attitude toward that general subject. You might also want the thesis to state the principle of division-classification at the heart of the essay. Furthermore, you might want the thesis to reveal which part or category you regard as most important.

Consider the two thesis statements that follow:

As the observant beachcomber moves from the tidal area to the upper beach to the sandy dunes, rich variations in marine life become apparent.

Although most people focus on the dangers associated with the disposal of toxic waste in the land and ocean, the incineration of toxic matter may pose an even more serious threat to human life.

The first thesis statement makes clear that the writer will organize the paper by classifying forms of marine life according to location. Since the purpose of the essay is to inform as objectively as possible, the thesis doesn't suggest the writer's opinion about which category is most significant.

The second thesis signals that the essay will evolve by dividing the issue of toxic waste according to methods of disposal. Moreover, because the paper takes a stance on a controversial subject, the thesis is worded to reveal which aspect of the topic the writer considers most important. Such a clear statement of the writer's position is an effective strategy in an essay of this kind.

You may have noted that each thesis statement also signals the paper's plan of development. The first essay, for example, will use specific facts, examples, and details to describe the kinds of marine life found in the tidal area, upper beach, and dunes. However, thesis statements in papers developed primarily through division-classification don't have to be so structured. If a paper is well written, your principle of division-classification, your opinion about which part or category is most important, and the essay's plan of development will become apparent as the essay unfolds.

4. Organize the paper logically.   Whether your paper is developed wholly or in part by division-classification, it should have a logical structure. As much as possible, you should try to discuss *comparable points* in each section of the paper. In the essay on seashore life, for example, you might describe life in the tidal area by discussing the mollusks, crustaceans, birds, and amphibians that live or feed there. You would then follow through, as much as you could, with this arrangement in the paper's other sections (upper beach and dune). Forgetting to describe the birdlife thriving in the dunes, especially when you had discussed birdlife in the tidal and upper-beach areas, would compromise the paper's structure. Of course, perfect parallelism is not always possible — there are no mollusks in the dunes, for instance. You should also use *signal devices* to connect various parts of the paper: "*Another* characteristic of marine life battered by the tides"; "A *final* important trait of both tidal and upper-beach crustaceans"; "*Unlike* the creatures of the tidal area and the upper beach." Such signals clarify the connections among the essay's ideas.

5. State any conclusions or recommendations in the paper's final section.   The analytic thinking that occurs during division-classification often leads to surprising insights. Such insights may be introduced early on, or they may be reserved for the end, where they are stated as conclusions or recommendations. A paper might categorize different kinds of coaches — from inspiring to incompetent — and make the point that athletes learn a great deal about human relations simply by having to get along with their coaches, regardless of the coaches' skills. Such a paper might conclude that participation in a team sport teaches more about human nature than several courses in psychology. Or the essay might end with a proposal: Rookies and seasoned team members should be paired, so that novice players can get advice on dealing with coaching eccentricities.

As products of Western culture, we consider order and exactness virtues, finding satisfaction in the process of dividing and classifying. Does our urge to divide and classify make us intolerant of that which can't be pigeonholed? Do we lose sight of the whole by focusing on types and parts? Some cultures and philosophers believe we do and criticize our mania for dissecting and segregating. Yet dividing and classifying can be a way to understand the whole. Our achievements in science and technology are based on such analytic thinking. We use division-classification to understand everything from plants to animals, from the geologic history of earth to the mysteries of human evolution. Division-classification can, in short, be a powerful strategy for making sense of the complexities around us.

STUDENT ESSAY

The following student essay was written by Gail Oremland in response to this assignment:

> In "Propaganda Techniques in Today's Advertising," Ann McClintock describes the flaws in many of the persuasive strategies used by advertisers. Choose another group of people whose job is also to communicate — for example, parents, bosses, teachers. Then, in an essay of your own, divide the group into types according to the flaws they make when communicating.

While reading Gail's paper, try to determine how effectively it applies the principles of division-classification. The annotations on Gail's paper and the commentary following it will help you look at the essay more closely.

The Truth About College Teachers
by Gail Oremland

Introduction
A recent TV news story told about a group of college professors from a nearby university who were hired by a local school system to help upgrade the teaching in the community's public schools. The professors were to visit classrooms, analyze teachers' skills, and then conduct workshops to help the teachers become more effective at their jobs. But after the first round of workshops, the superintendent of schools decided to cancel the whole project. He fired the learned professors and sent them back to their ivory tower. Why did the project fall apart? There was a simple reason. The college professors, who were supposedly going to show the public school teachers how to be more effective, were themselves poor teachers. Many

Thesis ——————

college students could have predicted such a disastrous outcome. They know, firsthand, that college teachers are strange. They know that professors often exhibit bizarre behaviors, relating to students in ways that make it difficult for students to stay awake, or--if awake--to learn.

Topic sentence ——————

The first of three paragraphs on the first category of teacher

The first paragraph in a three-part chronological sequence: What happens *before* class

One type of professor assumes, legitimately enough, that her function is to pass on to students the vast store of knowledge she has acquired. But because the "Knowledgeable One" regards herself as an expert and her students as the ignorant masses, she adopts an elitist approach that sabotages learning. The Knowledgeable One enters a lecture hall with a self-important air, walks to the podium, places her yellowed-with-age notes on the stand, and begins her lecture at the exact second the class is officially scheduled to begin. There can be a blizzard or hurricane raging outside the lecture hall; students can be running through freezing sleet and howling winds to get to class on time. Will the Knowledgeable One wait for them to arrive before beginning her lecture? Probably not. The Knowledgeable One's time is precious. She's there, set to begin, and that's what matters.

Topic sentence ——————

The second paragraph on the first category of teacher

The second paragraph in the chronological sequence: What happens *during* class

Once the monologue begins, the Knowledgeable One drones on and on. The Knowledgeable One is a fact person. She may be the history prof who knows the death toll of every Civil War battle, the biology prof who can diagram all the common biological molecules, the accounting prof who enumerates every clause of the federal tax form. Oblivious to students' glazed eyes and stifled yawns, the Knowledgeable One delivers her monologue, dispensing one dry fact after another. The only advantage to being on the receiving end of this boring monologue is that students do not have to worry about being called on to question a point or provide an opinion; the Knowledgeable One is not willing to relinquish one minute of her time by giving students a voice. Assume for one improbable moment that a student actually manages to stay awake during the monologue and is brave enough to ask a question. In such a case, the Knowledgeable One will address the questioning student as

2

3

"Mr." or "Miss." This formality does not, as some students mistakenly suppose, indicate respect for the student as a fledgling member of the academic community. Not at all. This impersonality represents the Knowledgeable One's desire to keep as wide a distance as possible between her and her students.

Topic sentence ——→ The Knowledgeable One's monologue always 4 comes to a close at the precise second the class is

The third paragraph on the first category of teacher

The final paragraph in the chrono-logical sequence: What happens *after* class

scheduled to end. No sooner has she delivered her last forgettable word than the Knowledgeable One packs up her notes and shoots out the door, heading back to the privacy of her office, where she can pursue her specialized academic interests--free of any possible interruption from students. The Knowledgeable One's hasty departure from the lecture hall makes it clear she has no desire to talk with students. In her eyes, she has met her obligations; she has taken time away from her research to transmit to students what she knows. Any closer contact might mean she would risk contagion from students, that great unwashed mass. Such a danger is to be avoided at all costs.

Unlike the Knowledgeable One, the "Leader 5 of Intellectual Discussion" seems to respect students. Emphasizing class discussion, the Leader encourages students to confront ideas ("What is Twain's view of morality?" "Was our intervention in Vietnam justified?" "Should big business be given tax breaks?") and discover their own truths.

Topic sentence —→ Then, about three weeks into the semester, it becomes clear that the Leader wants students to dis-

Paragraph on the second category of teacher

cover his version of the truth. Behind the Leader's democratic guise lurks a dictator. When a student voices an opinion that the Leader accepts, the student is rewarded by hearty nods of approval and "Good point, good point." But if a student is rash enough to advance a conflicting viewpoint, the Leader responds with killing politeness: "Well, yes, that's an interesting perspective. But don't you think that . . . ?" Grade-conscious students soon learn not to chime in with their viewpoint. They know that when the Leader, with seeming honesty, says, "I'd be interested in hearing what you think. Let's open this up for discussion," they had better figure out what the Leader wants to hear before advancing their own theories. "Me-tooism" rather than independent thinking, they discover, guarantees good grades in the Leader's class.

Topic sentence ──────▶ Then there is the professor who comes across 6 as the students' "Buddy." This kind of professor

Paragraph on the third category of teacher

does not see himself as an imparter of knowledge or a leader of discussion but as a pal, just one in a community of equals. The Buddy may start his course this way. "All of us know that this college stuff--grades, degrees, exams, required reading--is a game. So let's not play it, okay?" Dressed in jeans, sweatshirt, and scuffed sneakers, the Buddy projects a relaxed, casual attitude. He arranges the class seats in a circle (he would never take a position in front of the room) and insists that students call him by his first name. He uses no syllabus and gives few tests, believing that such constraints keep students from directing their own learning. A free spirit, the Buddy often teaches courses like "The Psychology of Interpersonal Relations" or "The Social Dynamics of the Family." If students choose to use class time to discuss the course material, that's fine. If they want to discuss something else, that's fine, too. It's the self-expression, the honest dialogue, that counts. In fact, the Buddy seems especially fond of digressions from academic subjects. By talking about his political views, his marital problems, his tendency to drink one too many beers, the Buddy lets students see that he is a regular guy--just like them. At first, students look forward to classes with the Buddy. They enjoy the informality, the chitchat, the lack of pressure. But after a while, they wonder why they are paying for a course where they learn nothing. They might as well stay home and watch the soaps.

Conclusion

Echoes opening anecdote

Obviously, some college professors are excel- 7 lent. They are learned, hardworking, and imaginative; they enjoy their work and like being with students. On the whole, though, college professors are a strange lot. Despite their advanced degrees and their own exposure to many different kinds of teachers, they do not seem to understand how to relate to students. Rather than being hired as consultants to help others upgrade their teaching skills, college professors should themselves hire consultants to tell them what they are doing wrong and how they can improve. Who should these consultants be? That's easy: the people who know them best--their students.

COMMENTARY

Introduction and thesis. After years of being graded by teachers, Gail took special pleasure in writing an essay that gave her a chance to evaluate her teachers — in this case, her college professors. Even the essay's title, "The Truth About College Professors," implies that Gail is going to have fun knocking profs down from their ivory towers. To introduce her subject, she uses a timely news story. This brief anecdote leads directly to the essay's *thesis*: "Professors often exhibit bizarre behaviors, relating to students in ways that make it difficult for students to stay awake, or — if awake — to learn." Note that Gail's thesis isn't highly structured; it doesn't, for example, name the specific categories to be discussed. Still, her thesis suggests that the essay is going to *categorize* a range of teaching behaviors, using as a *principle of classification* the strange ways that college profs relate to students.

Purpose. As with all good papers developed through division-classification, Gail's essay doesn't use classification as an end in itself. Gail uses classification because it helps her achieve a broader *purpose*. She wants to *convince* readers — without moralizing or abandoning her humorous tone — that such teaching styles inhibit learning. In other words, there's a serious underside to her essay. This additional layer of meaning is characteristic of satiric writing.

Categories and topic sentences. The essay's body, consisting of five paragraphs, presents the three categories that make up Gail's analysis. According to Gail, college teachers can be categorized as the Knowledgeable One (paragraphs 2–4), the Leader of Intellectual Discussion (5), or the Buddy (6). Obviously, there are other ways professors might be classified. But given Gail's purpose, audience, tone, and point of view, her categories are appropriate; they are reasonably *complete, consistent*, and *mutually exclusive*. Note, too, that Gail uses *topic sentences* near the beginning of each category to help readers see which professional type she's discussing.

Overall organization and paragraph structure.   Gail is able to shift smoothly and easily from one category to the next. How does she achieve such graceful transitions? Take a moment to reread the sentences that introduce her second and third categories (paragraphs 5 and 6). Look at the way each sentence's beginning (in italics here) links back to the preceding category or categories: "*Unlike the Knowledgeable One*, the 'Leader of Intellectual Discussion' seems to respect students"; and the "Buddy . . . *does not see himself as an imparter of knowledge or a leader of discussion* but as a pal. . . ."

Gail is equally careful about providing an easy-to-follow structure within each section. She uses a *chronological sequence* to organize her three-paragraph discussion of the Knowledgeable One. The first paragraph deals with the beginning of the Knowledgeable One's lecture; the second, with the lecture itself; the third, with the end of the lecture. And the paragraphs' *topic sentences* clearly indicate this passage of time. Similarly, *transitions* are used in the paragraphs on the Leader of Intellectual Discussion and the Buddy to ensure a logical progression of points: "*Then*, about three weeks into the semester, it becomes clear that the Leader wants students to discover *his* version of the truth" (5) and "*At first*, students look forward to classes with the Buddy. . . . But *after a while*, they wonder why they are paying for a course where they learn nothing" (6).

Tone.   The essay's unity can also be traced to Gail's skill in sustaining her satiric tone. Throughout the essay, Gail selects details that fit her gently mocking attitude. She depicts the Knowledgeable One lecturing from "yellowed-with-age notes . . . , oblivious to students' glazed eyes and stifled yawns," unwilling to wait for students who "run . . . through freezing sleet and howling winds to get to class on time." Then she presents another tongue-in-cheek description, this one focusing on the way the Leader of Intellectual Discussion conducts class: "Good point, good point. . . . Well, yes, that's an interesting perspective. But don't you think that . . . ?" Finally, with similar killing accuracy, Gail portrays the Buddy, democratically garbed in "jeans, sweatshirt, and scuffed sneakers."

Other patterns of development.   Gail's satiric depiction of her three professorial types employs a number of techniques associated with *narrative* and *descriptive writing*: vigorous images, highly connotative language, and dialogue. *Definition, exemplification, causal analysis*, and *comparison-contrast* also come into play. Gail defines the characteristics of each type of professor; she provides numerous examples to support her categories; she explains the effects of the different teaching styles on students; and, in her description of the Leader of Intellectual Discussion, she contrasts the appearance of democracy with the dictatorial reality.

Unequal development of categories.   Although Gail's essay is unified, organized, and well-developed, you may have felt that the first category outweighs the other two. There is, of course, no need to balance the categories exactly. But Gail's extended treatment of the first category sets up an expectation that the others will be treated as fully. One way to remedy this problem would be to delete some material from the discussion of the Knowledgeable One. Gail might, for instance, omit the first five sentences in the third paragraph (about the professor's habit of addressing students as Mr. or Miss). Such a change could be made without taking the bite out of her portrayal. Even better, Gail could simply switch the order of her sections, putting the portrait of the Knowledgeable One at the essay's end. Here, the extended discussion wouldn't seem out of proportion. Instead, the sections would appear in *emphatic order*, with the most detailed category saved for last.

Revising the first draft.   It's apparent that an essay as engaging as Gail's must have undergone a good deal of revising. That was in fact the case. Gail made many changes in the body of the essay, but it's particularly interesting to review what happened to the introduction as she revised the paper. Reprinted here is Gail's original introduction.

Original Version of the Introduction

Despite their high IQs, advanced degrees, and published papers, some college professors just don't know how to teach. Found in almost any department, in tenured and untenured positions, they prompt student apathy. They fail to convey ideas effectively and to challenge or inspire students. Students thus finish their courses having learned very little. Contrary to popular opinion, these professors' ineptitude is not simply a matter of delivering boring lectures or not caring about students. Many of them care a great deal. Their failure actually stems from their unrealistic perceptions of what a teacher should be. Specifically, they adopt teaching styles or roles that alienate students and undermine learning. Three of the most common ones are "The Knowledgeable One," "The Leader of Intellectual Discussion," and "The Buddy."

When Gail showed the first draft of the essay to her composition instructor, he laughed — and occasionally squirmed — as he read what she had prepared. He was enthusiastic about the paper but felt that there was a problem with the introduction's tone; it was too serious when compared to the playful, lightly satiric mood of the rest of the essay. When Gail reread the paragraph, she agreed, but she was uncertain about the best way to remedy the problem. After revising other sections of the essay, she decided to let the paper sit for a while before going back to rewrite the introduction.

In the meantime, Gail switched on the TV. The timing couldn't have been better; she tuned into a news story about several supposedly learned professors who had been fired from a consulting job because they had turned out to know so little about teaching. This was exactly the kind of item Gail needed to start her essay. Now she was able to prepare a completely new introduction, making it consistent in spirit with the rest of the paper.

With this stronger introduction and the rest of the essay well in hand, Gail was ready to write a conclusion. Now, as she worked on the concluding paragraph, she deliberately shaped it to recall the story about the fired consultants. By echoing the opening anecdote in her conclusion, Gail was able to end the paper with another poke at professors — a perfect way to close her clever and insightful essay.

The selections in this chapter show how division and classification can be used to explore a variety of subjects. Judith Viorst divides acquaintances into categories that include "Friends, Good Friends — and Such Good Friends." William Zinsser describes the sorts of "College Pressures" that students typically encounter, while David Hilfiker, in "Making Medical Mistakes," confesses to the types of errors he has made as a doctor. Classifying "Propaganda Techniques in Today's Advertising" is the method Ann McClintock uses to demonstrate how pervasive and effective such techniques can be. Finally, in "The Quick Fix Society," Janet Mendell Goldstein examines three different kinds of instant gratification and shows us the harm each causes.

Judith Viorst

A contributing editor at *Redbook*, Judith Viorst (1936–) is perhaps best known for her column in that magazine. She has also written several children's books, including *Alexander and the Terrible, Horrible, No Good, Very Bad Day* (1982); a number of volumes of light verse, including *It's Hard to Be Hip Over Thirty and Other Tragedies of Modern Life* (1970) and *How Did I Get to Be Forty and Other Atrocities* (1984); and *Necessary Losses* (1986), a serious look at the process by which adults deal with change. Viorst's writing style, which often combines deeply felt emotion and wry humor, has made her works popular and widely read. The following selection first appeared in *Redbook* in 1977.

Friends, Good Friends — and Such Good Friends

There are people to whom we bare our souls; there are individuals we enjoy talking to whenever we see them in class or at work; there are those we look forward to seeing every few years when we visit our old high schools or hometowns. The degree of intimacy we share with these people varies greatly; yet all of them, says Judith Viorst, deserve to be called friends.

Women are friends, I once would have said, when they to- 1
tally love and support and trust each other, and bare to each other the secrets of their souls, and run — no questions asked — to help each other, and tell harsh truths to each other (no, you can't wear that dress unless you lose ten pounds first) when harsh truths must be told.

Women are friends, I once would have said, when they share 2
the same affection for Ingmar Bergman, plus train rides, cats,

warm rain, charades, Camus, and hate with equal ardor Newark and Brussels sprouts and Lawrence Welk[1] and camping.

In other words, I once would have said that a friend is a friend all the way, but now I believe that's a narrow point of view. For the friendships I have and the friendships I see are conducted at many levels of intensity, serve many different functions, meet different needs and range from those as all-the-way as the friendship of the soul sisters mentioned above to that of the most nonchalant and casual playmates. 3

Consider these varieties of friendship: 4

1. Convenience friends.   These are women with whom, if our paths weren't crossing all the time, we'd have no particular reason to be friends: a next-door neighbor, a woman in our car pool, the mother of one of our children's closest friends or maybe some mommy with whom we serve juice and cookies each week at the Glenwood Co-op Nursery. 5

Convenience friends are convenient indeed. They'll lend us their cups and silverware for a party. They'll drive our kids to soccer when we're sick. They'll take us to pick up our car when we need a lift to the garage. They'll even take our cats when we go on vacation. As we will for them. 6

But we don't, with convenience friends, ever come too close or tell too much; we maintain our public face and emotional distance. "Which means," says Elaine, "that I'll talk about being overweight but not about being depressed. Which means I'll admit being mad but not blind with rage. Which means that I might say that we're pinched this month but never that I'm worried sick over money." 7

But which doesn't mean that there isn't sufficient value to be found in these friendships of mutual aid, in convenience friends. 8

2. Special-interest friends.   These friendships aren't intimate, and they needn't involve kids or silverware or cats. Their value lies in some interest jointly shared. And so we may have an 9

---

[1]Ingmar Bergman, a Swedish filmmaker noted for his deep probings into the darkness of the human soul; Albert Camus, a French writer whose essays and novels depict the human capacity for moral and responsible action in an otherwise pointless world; Lawrence Welk, a television band leader whose bubbly "champagne" music was often criticized as being bland and homogenized.

office friend or a yoga friend or a tennis friend or a friend from the Women's Democratic Club.

"I've got one woman friend," says Joyce, "who likes, as I do, to take psychology courses. Which makes it nice for me — and nice for her. It's fun to go with someone you know and it's fun to discuss what you've learned, driving back from the classes." And for the most part, she says, that's all they discuss.   10

"I'd say that what we're doing is *doing* together, not being together," Suzanne says of her Tuesday-doubles friends. "It's mainly a tennis relationship, but we play together well. And I guess we all need to have a couple of playmates."   11

I agree.   12

My playmate is a shopping friend, a woman of marvelous taste, a woman who knows exactly *where* to buy *what*, and furthermore is a woman who always knows beyond a doubt what one ought to be buying. I don't have the time to keep up with what's new in eyeshadow, hemlines and shoes and whether the smock look is in or finished already. But since (oh, shame!) I care a lot about eyeshadow, hemlines and shoes, and since I don't *want* to wear smocks if the smock look is finished, I'm very glad to have a shopping friend.   13

3. Historical friends.   We all have a friend who knew us when . . . maybe way back in Miss Meltzer's second grade, when our family lived in that three-room flat in Brooklyn, when our dad was out of work for seven months, when our brother Allie got in that fight where they had to call the police, when our sister married the endodontist from Yonkers and when, the morning after we lost our virginity, she was the first, the only, friend we told.   14

The years have gone by and we've gone separate ways and we've little in common now, but we're still an intimate part of each other's past. And so whenever we go to Detroit we always go to visit this friend of our girlhood. Who knows how we looked before our teeth were straightened. Who knows how we talked before our voice got un-Brooklyned. Who knows what we ate before we learned about artichokes. And who, by her presence, puts us in touch with an earlier part of ourself, a part of ourself it's important never to lose.   15

"What this friend means to me and what I mean to her," says Grace, "is having a sister without sibling rivalry. We know the   16 texture of each other's lives. She remembers my grandmother's cabbage soup. I remember the way her uncle played the piano. There's simply no other friend who remembers those things."

4. Crossroads friends.   Like historical friends, our cross-   17
roads friends are important for *what was* — for the friendship we shared at a crucial, now past, time of life. A time, perhaps, when we roomed in college together; or worked as eager young singles in the Big City together; or went together, as my friend Elizabeth and I did, through pregnancy, birth and that scary first year of new motherhood.

Crossroads friends forge powerful links, links strong enough   18
to endure with not much more contact than once-a-year letters at Christmas. And out of respect for those crossroads years, for those dramas and dreams we once shared, we will always be friends.

5. Cross-generational friends.   Historical friends and cross-   19
roads friends seem to maintain a special kind of intimacy — dormant but always ready to be revived — and though we may rarely meet, whenever we do connect, it's personal and intense. Another kind of intimacy exists in the friendships that form across generations in what one woman calls her daughter-mother and her mother-daughter relationships.

Evelyn's friend is her mother's age — "but I share so much   20
more than I ever could with my mother" — a woman she talks to of music, of books and of life. "What I get from her is the benefit of her experience. What she gets — and enjoys — from me is a youthful perspective. It's a pleasure for both of us."

I have in my own life a precious friend, a woman of 65 who   21
has lived very hard, who is wise, who listens well; who has been where I am and can help me understand it; and who represents not only an ultimate ideal mother to me but also the person I'd like to be when I grow up.

In our daughter role we tend to do more than our share of   22
self-revelation; in our mother role we tend to receive what's revealed. It's another kind of pleasure — playing wise mother to a questing younger person. It's another very lovely kind of friendship.

6. Part-of-a-couple friends.   Some of the women we call our   23
friends we never see alone — we see them as part of a couple at couples' parties. And though we share interests in many things

and respect each other's views, we aren't moved to deepen the relationship. Whatever the reason, a lack of time or — and this is more likely — a lack of chemistry, our friendship remains in the context of a group. But the fact that our feeling on seeing each other is always, "I'm *so* glad she's here" and the fact that we spend half the evening talking together says that this too, in its own way, counts as a friendship.

(Other part-of-a-couple friends are the friends that came with   24
the marriage, and some of these are friends we could live without. But sometimes, alas, she married our husband's best friend; and sometimes, alas, she *is* our husband's best friend. And so we find ourself dealing with her, somewhat against our will, in a spirit of what I'll call *reluctant* friendship.)

7. Men who are friends.   I wanted to write just of women   25
friends, but the women I've talked to won't let me — they say I must mention man-woman friendships too. For these friendships can be just as close and as dear as those that we form with women. Listen to Lucy's description of one such friendship:

"We've found we have things to talk about that are different   26
from what he talks about with my husband and different from what I talk about with his wife. So sometimes we call on the phone or meet for lunch. There are similar intellectual interests — we always pass on to each other the books that we love — but there's also something tender and caring too."

In a couple of crises, Lucy says, "he offered himself for   27
talking and for helping. And when someone died in his family he wanted me there. The sexual, flirty part of our friendship is very small, but *some* — just enough to make it fun and different." She thinks — and I agree — that the sexual part, though small, is always *some*, is always there when a man and a woman are friends.

It's only in the past few years that I've made friends with   28
men, in the sense of a friendship that's *mine*, not just part of two couples. And achieving with them the ease and the trust I've found with women friends has value indeed. Under the dryer at home last week, putting on mascara and rouge, I comfortably sat and talked with a fellow named Peter. Peter, I finally decided, could handle the shock of me minus mascara under the dryer. Because we care for each other. Because we're friends.

8. There are medium friends, and pretty good friends, and   29
very good friends indeed, and these friendships are defined by

their level of intimacy. And what we'll reveal at each of these levels of intimacy is calibrated with care. We might tell a medium friend, for example, that yesterday we had a fight with our husband. And we might tell a pretty good friend that this fight with our husband made us so mad that we slept on the couch. And we might tell a very good friend that the reason we got so mad in that fight that we slept on the couch had something to do with that girl who works in his office. But it's only to our very best friends that we're willing to tell all, to tell what's going on with that girl in his office.

The best of friends, I still believe, totally love and support and trust each other, and bare to each other the secrets of their souls, and run — no questions asked — to help each other, and tell harsh truths to each other when they must be told.   30

But we needn't agree about everything (only 12-year-old girl friends agree about *everything*) to tolerate each other's point of view. To accept without judgment. To give and to take without ever keeping score. And to *be* there, as I am for them and as they are for me, to comfort our sorrows, to celebrate our joys.   31

Questions for Close Reading

1. What is the selection's thesis? Locate the sentence(s) in which Viorst states her main idea. If she doesn't state the thesis explicitly, express it in your own words.
2. Viorst's view of what constitutes a friendship has changed over time. What did she once believe was the essence of friendship? How and why has her definition of friendship changed?
3. According to Viorst, what do historical and crossroad friends have in common? How are they different?
4. What does Viorst mean when she writes that the intimacy level of our relationships is "calibrated with care" (paragraph 29)?
5. Refer to your dictionary as needed to define the following words used in the selection: *ardor* (paragraph 2), *nonchalant* (3), *sibling* (16), *calibrated* (29).

Questions About the Writer's Craft

1. **The pattern.** What principle of division-classification does Viorst use to sequence the "varieties of friendship"?
2. **Other patterns.** What is Viorst's purpose in this essay? What other patterns of development besides division-classification does she use to achieve this purpose?

3. Examine the essay's introduction and conclusion. What idea appears in both sections? What idea appears only in the conclusion? Why do you think Viorst ends with this idea?

4. How would you describe Viorst's tone in this essay? What words and phrases help create this tone? What effect do you think Viorst intends this tone to have on her readers?

Questions for Further Thought

1. Viorst discusses numerous types of friendships. Do you find that your life includes so many types of friends? Which of Viorst's friendship types have you *not* experienced? Do you expect to encounter these other types of friends later in life?

2. Why do some crossroads and historical friendships endure, even though the people no longer live nearby or share similar lives? In your experience, have such friendships survived separation and the passage of time, or have they faded into the past?

3. Viorst writes that women's friendships with men can be "as close and as dear" as women's friendships with women. What is your experience with opposite-sex friendships? Do you agree that they can be as open and trusting as same-sex friendships? Why or why not?

4. In paragraph 31, Viorst says that friends "needn't agree about everything . . . to tolerate each other's point of view." Do you have friends with whom you disagree on some matter of significance, such as music preference, political affiliation, or religious belief? How difficult is it to maintain such friendships?

Writing Assignments Using Division-Classification as a Pattern of Development

∞ 1. Enlarge upon Viorst's analysis by interviewing some males about the types of friendships they typically form. Describe men's friendships in an essay, pointing out in the introduction or conclusion any differences you've discovered in the way males and females approach friendship. Before writing the paper, you may want to read what Deborah Tannen says in "Sex, Lies, and Conversation" (page 440) about the dissimilarities in men's and women's interpersonal styles.

2. Viorst writes about various kinds of friends. Following Viorst's lead, choose another group of people (for example, bosses, salespeople, or parents) and write an essay about the different types of individuals within that broad category. Your tone may be light or serious, but you should, as Viorst does, reach some conclusions about the types of people you describe.

Writing Assignments Using Other Patterns of Development

∞ 3. As Viorst indicates, friends survive disagreements by being tolerant and accepting of each other "without judgment." Sometimes, though, friendships erupt into conflict. Write an essay describing a process by which friends who are having a significant disagreement can restore the harmony of their relationship. Deborah Tannen's "Sex, Lies, and Conversation" (page 440) offers some suggestions for resolving conflict.

4. Viorst suggests that women and men can be friends without there being a distracting sexual element. Think about the opposite-sex friendships you have had, and talk about such friendships with some people you know well. Then decide whether you believe that non-romantic opposite-sex friendship is possible. Write an essay arguing either that all such friendships are tinged with significant sexual overtones or that pure friendship can occur between males and females. Remember to acknowledge the opposing viewpoint, and include plentiful examples from your own and others' experience to support your position.

William Zinsser

Currently executive editor of the Book-of-the-Month Club, William Zinsser has written news journalism, drama criticism, magazine columns, and several books on American culture. Born in 1922 in New York, Zinsser attended Princeton University and worked for the *New York Herald Tribune, Life,* and *Look.* In 1970, Zinsser designed a course in nonfiction writing for Yale University. Based on what he learned at Yale about the way college students approach the writing process, Zinsser wrote the popular guide *On Writing Well* (1976). His other books include *The City Dwellers* (1962), *Pop Goes America* (1966), *The Lunacy Boom* (1970), and *Writing With a Word Processor* (1982). The following essay first appeared in the magazine *Country Journal* in 1979.

College Pressures

Campuses today are flooded with business majors and budding computer scientists. Many students' primary goal is to go where the money is—to transform themselves into marketable commodities who will, by the age of thirty, have luxurious homes, expensive cars, and profitable investment portfolios. William Zinsser sympathizes with the pressures that lead to students' obsession with material success, yet he doubts that such a single-minded concern with a lucrative career is the surest route to happiness.

Dear Carlos: I desperately need a dean's excuse for my chem midterm which will begin in about 1 hour. All I can say is that I totally blew it this week. I've fallen incredibly, inconceivably behind.

Carlos: Help! I'm anxious to hear from you. I'll be in my room and won't leave it until I hear from you. Tomorrow is the last day for . . .

298

Carlos: I left town because I started bugging out again. I stayed up all night to finish a take-home make-up exam & am typing it to hand in on the 10th. It was due on the 5th. P.S. I'm going to the dentist. Pain is pretty bad.

Carlos: Probably by Friday I'll be able to get back to my studies. Right now I'm going to take a long walk. This whole thing has taken a lot out of me.

Carlos: I'm really up the proverbial creek. The problem is I really *bombed* the history final. Since I need that course for my major I . . .

Carlos: Here follows a tale of woe. I went home this weekend, had to help my Mom, & caught a fever so didn't have much time to study. My professor . . .

Carlos: Aargh! Trouble. Nothing original but everything's piling up at once. To be brief, my job interview . . .

Hey Carlos, good news! I've got mononucleosis.

1   Who are these wretched supplicants, scribbling notes so laden with anxiety, seeking such miracles of postponement and balm? They are men and women who belong to Branford College, one of the twelve residential colleges at Yale University, and the messages are just a few of the hundreds that they left for their dean, Carlos Hortas — often slipped under his door at 4 A.M. — last year.

2   But students like the ones who wrote those notes can also be found on campuses from coast to coast — especially in New England and at many other private colleges across the country that have high academic standards and highly motivated students. Nobody could doubt that the notes are real. In their urgency and their gallows humor they are authentic voices of a generation that is panicky to succeed.

3   My own connection with the message writers is that I am master of Branford College. I live in its Gothic quadrangle and know the students well. (We have 485 of them.) I am privy

to their hopes and fears—and also to their stereo music and their piercing cries in the dead of the night ("Does anybody *ca-a-are?*"). If they went to Carlos to ask how to get through tomorrow, they come to me to ask how to get through the rest of their lives.

Mainly I try to remind them that the road ahead is a long one   4
and that it will have more unexpected turns than they think. There will be plenty of time to change jobs, change careers, change whole attitudes and approaches. They don't want to hear such liberating news. They want a map—right now—that they can follow unswervingly to career security, financial security, Social Security and, presumably, a prepaid grave.

What I wish for all students is some release from the clammy   5
grip of the future. I wish them a chance to savor each segment of their education as an experience in itself and not as a grim preparation for the next step. I wish them the right to experiment, to trip and fall, to learn that defeat is as instructive as victory and is not the end of the world.

My wish, of course, is naïve. One of the few rights that   6
America does not proclaim is the right to fail. Achievement is the national god, venerated in our media—the million-dollar athlete, the wealthy executive—and glorified in our praise of possessions. In the presence of such a potent state religion, the young are growing up old.

I see four kinds of pressure working on college students   7
today: economic pressure, parental pressure, peer pressure, and self-induced pressure. It is easy to look around for villains—to blame the colleges for charging too much money, the professors for assigning too much work, the parents for pushing their children too far, the students for driving themselves too hard. But there are no villains; only victims.

"In the late 1960s," one dean told me, "the typical question   8
that I got from students was 'Why is there so much suffering in the world?' or 'How can I make a contribution?' Today it's 'Do you think it would look better for getting into law school if I did a double major in history and political science, or just majored in one of them?'" Many other deans confirmed this pattern. One said: "They're trying to find an edge—the intangible something that will look better on paper if two students are about equal."

Note the emphasis on looking better. The transcript has 9 become a sacred document, the passport to security. How one appears on paper is more important than how one appears in person. *A* is for Admirable and *B* is for Borderline, even though, in Yale's official system of grading, *A* means "excellent" and *B* means "very good." Today, looking very good is no longer good enough, especially for students who hope to go on to law school or medical school. They know that entrance into the better schools will be an entrance into the better law firms and better medical practices where they will make a lot of money. They also know that the odds are harsh. Yale Law School, for instance, matriculates 170 students from an applicant pool of 3,700; Harvard enrolls 550 from a pool of 7,000.

It's all very well for those of us who write letters of recom- 10 mendation for our students to stress the qualities of humanity that will make them good lawyers or doctors. And it's nice to think that admission officers are really reading our letters and looking for the extra dimension of commitment or concern. Still, it would be hard for a student not to visualize these officers shuffling so many transcripts studded with *A*s that they regard a *B* as positively shameful.

The pressure is almost as heavy on students who just want to 11 graduate and get a job. Long gone are the days of the "gentleman's *C*," when students journeyed through college with a certain relaxation, sampling a wide variety of courses — music, art, philosophy, classics, anthropology, poetry, religion — that would send them out as liberally educated men and women. If I were an employer I would rather employ graduates who have this range and curiosity than those who narrowly pursued safe subjects and high grades. I know countless students whose inquiring minds exhilarate me. I like to hear the play of their ideas. I don't know if they are getting *A*s or *C*s, and I don't care. I also like them as people. The country needs them, and they will find satisfying jobs. I tell them to relax. They can't.

Nor can I blame them. They live in a brutal economy. Tui- 12 tion, room, and board at most private colleges now comes to at least $7,000, not counting books and fees. This might seem to suggest that the colleges are getting rich. But they are equally battered by inflation. Tuition covers only 60 percent of what it costs to educate a student, and ordinarily the remainder comes from what colleges receive in endowments, grants, and gifts. Now the remainder keeps being swallowed by the cruel costs — higher every year — of just opening the doors. Heating oil is up. Insurance is up. Postage is up. Health-premium costs are up. Everything is up. Deficits are up. We are witnessing in America the creation of a brotherhood of paupers — colleges, parents, and students, joined by the common bond of debt.

Today it is not unusual for a student, even if he works part time at college and full time during the summer, to accrue $5,000 in loans after four years — loans that he must start to repay within one year after graduation. Exhorted at commencement to go forth into the world, he is already behind as he goes forth. How could he not feel under pressure throughout college to prepare for this day of reckoning? I have used "he," incidentally, only for brevity. Women at Yale are under no less pressure to justify their expensive education to themselves, their parents, and society. In fact, they are probably under more pressure. For although they leave college superbly equipped to bring fresh leadership to traditionally male jobs, society hasn't yet caught up with this fact.   13

Along with economic pressure goes parental pressure. Inevitably, the two are deeply intertwined.   14

I see many students taking pre-medical courses with joyless tenacity. They go off to their labs as if they were going to the dentist. It saddens me because I know them in other corners of their life as cheerful people.   15

"Do you want to go to medical school?" I ask them.   16

"I guess so," they say, without conviction, or "Not really."   17

"Then why are you going?"   18

"Well, my parents want me to be a doctor. They're paying all this money and . . ."   19

Poor students, poor parents. They are caught in one of the oldest webs of love and duty and guilt. The parents mean well; they are trying to steer their sons and daughters toward a secure future. But the sons and daughters want to major in history or classics or philosophy — subjects with no "practical" value. Where's the payoff on the humanities? It's not easy to persuade such loving parents that the humanities do indeed pay off. The intellectual faculties developed by studying subjects like history   20 and classics — an ability to synthesize and relate, to weigh cause and effect, to see events in perspective — are just the faculties that make creative leaders in business or almost any general field. Still, many fathers would rather put their money on courses that point toward a specific profession — courses that are pre-law, pre-medical, pre-business, or, as I sometimes heard it put, "pre-rich."

But the pressure on students is severe. They are truly torn. 21
One part of them feels obligated to fulfill their parents' expectations; after all, their parents are older and presumably wiser. Another part tells them that the expectations that are right for their parents are not right for them.

I know a student who wants to be an artist. She is very 22
obviously an artist and will be a good one — she has already had several modest local exhibits. Meanwhile she is growing as a well-rounded person and taking humanistic subjects that will enrich the inner resources out of which her art will grow. But her father is strongly opposed. He thinks that an artist is a "dumb" thing to be. The student vacillates and tries to please everybody. She keeps up with her art somewhat furtively and takes some of the "dumb" courses her father wants her to take — at least they are dumb courses for her. She is a free spirit on a campus of tense students — no small achievement in itself — and she deserves to follow her muse.

Peer pressure and self-induced pressure are also intertwined, 23
and they begin almost at the beginning of freshman year.

"I had a freshman student I'll call Linda," one dean told me, 24
"who came in and said she was under terrible pressure because her roommate, Barbara, was much brighter and studied all the time. I couldn't tell her that Barbara had come in two hours earlier to say the same thing about Linda."

The story is almost funny — except that it's not. It's symptomatic of all the pressures put together. When every student thinks every other student is working harder and doing better, the only solution is to study harder still. I see students going off to the library every night after dinner and coming back when it closes at midnight. I wish they would sometimes forget about their peers and go to a movie. I hear the clacking of typewriters in the hours before dawn. I see the tension in their eyes when exams are approaching and papers are due: *"Will I get everything done?"*

Probably they won't. They will get sick. They will get 26

"blocked." They will sleep. They will oversleep. They will bug out. *Hey, Carlos, help!*

Part of the problem is that they do more than they are   27
expected to do. A professor will assign five-page papers. Several
students will start writing ten-page papers to impress him. Then
more students will write ten-page papers, and a few will raise the
ante to fifteen. Pity the poor student who is still just doing the
assignment.

"Once you have twenty or thirty percent of the student   28
population deliberately overexerting," one dean points out, "it's
bad for everybody. When a teacher gets more and more effort
from his class, the student who is doing normal work can be
perceived as not doing well. The tactic works, psychologically."

Why can't the professor just cut back and not accept longer   29
papers? He can, and he probably will. But by then the term will be
half over and the damage done. Grade fever is highly contagious
and not easily reversed. Besides, the professor's main concern is
with his course. He knows his students only in relation to the
course and doesn't know that they are also overexerting in their
other courses. Nor is it really his business. He didn't sign up for
dealing with the student as a whole person and with all the
emotional baggage the student brought along from home. That's
what deans, masters, chaplains, and psychiatrists are for.

To some extent this is nothing new: a certain number of   30
professors have always been self-contained islands of scholarship
and shyness, more comfortable with books than with people. But
the new pauperism has widened the gap still further, for professors who actually like to spend time with students don't have as
much time to spend. They are also overexerting. If they are
young, they are busy trying to publish in order not to perish,
hanging by their finger nails onto a shrinking profession. If they
are old and tenured, they are buried under the duties of administering departments — as departmental chairmen or members of
committees — that have been thinned out by the budgetary axe.

Ultimately it will be the students' own business to break the   31
circles in which they are trapped. They are too young to be
prisoners of their parents' dreams and their classmates' fears.
They must be jolted into believing in themselves as unique men
and women who have the power to shape their own future.

"Violence is being done to the undergraduate experience,"   32 says Carlos Hortas. "College should be open-ended: at the end it should open many, many roads. Instead, students are choosing their goal in advance, and their choices narrow as they go along. It's almost as if they think that the country has been codified in the type of jobs that exist — that they've got to fit into certain slots. Therefore, fit into the best-paying slot.

"They ought to take chances. Not taking chances will lead to a life of colorless mediocrity. They'll be comfortable. But something in the spirit will be missing." 33

I have painted too drab a portrait of today's students, making them seem a solemn lot. That is only half of their story; if they were so dreary I wouldn't so thoroughly enjoy their company. The other half is that they are easy to like. They are quick to laugh and to offer friendship. They are not introverts. They are unusually kind and are more considerate of one another than any student generation I have known. 34

Nor are they so obsessed with their studies that they avoid sports and extracurricular activities. On the contrary, they juggle their crowded hours to play on a variety of teams, perform with musical and dramatic groups, and write for campus publications. But this in turn is one more cause of anxiety. There are too many choices. Academically, they have 1,300 courses to select from; outside class they have to decide how much spare time they can spare and how to spend it. 35

This means that they engage in fewer extracurricular pursuits than their predecessors did. If they want to row on the crew and play in the symphony they will eliminate one; in the '60s they would have done both. They also tend to choose activities that are self-limiting. Drama, for instance, is flourishing in all twelve of Yale's residential colleges as it never has before. Students hurl themselves into these productions — as actors, directors, carpenters, and technicians — with a dedication to create the best possible play, knowing that the day will come when the run will end and they can get back to their studies. 36

They also can't afford to be the willing slave of organizations like the *Yale Daily News*. Last spring at the one-hundredth anniversary banquet of that paper — whose past chairmen include such once and future kings as Potter Stewart, Kingman Brewster, and William F. Buckley, Jr. — much was made of the fact that the editorial staff used to be small and totally committed and that 37 "newsies" routinely worked fifty hours a week. In effect they belonged to a club; Newsies is how they defined themselves at Yale. Today's student will write one or two articles a week, when he can, and he defines himself as a student. I've never heard the word Newsie except at the banquet.

If I have described the modern undergraduate primarily as a driven creature who is largely ignoring the blithe spirit inside who keeps trying to come out and play, it's because that's where the crunch is, not only at Yale but throughout American education. It's why I think we should all be worried about the values that are nurturing a generation so fearful of risk and so goal-obsessed at such an early age.   38

I tell students that there is no one "right" way to get ahead —that each of them is a different person, starting from a different point and bound for a different destination. I tell them that change is a tonic and that all the slots are not codified nor the frontiers closed. One of my ways of telling them is to invite men and women who have achieved success outside the academic world to come and talk informally with my students during the year. They are heads of companies or ad agencies, editors of magazines, politicians, public officials, television magnates, labor leaders, business executives, Broadway producers, artists, writers, economists, photographers, scientists, historians — a mixed bag of achievers.   39

I ask them to say a few words about how they got started. The students assume that they started in their present profession and knew all along that it was what they wanted to do. Luckily for me, most of them got into their field by a circuitous route, to their surprise, after many detours. The students are startled. They can hardly conceive of a career that was not pre-planned. They can hardly imagine allowing the hand of God or chance to nudge them down some unforeseen trail.   40

Questions for Close Reading

1. What is the selection's thesis? Locate the sentence(s) in which Zinsser states his main idea. If he doesn't state the thesis explicitly, express it in your own words.
2. According to Zinsser, why are the pressures on college students today so harmful?

3. Zinsser says that some of the pressures are "intertwined." What does he mean? Give examples from the essay.
4. What actions or attitudes on the part of students can help free them from the pressures that Zinsser describes?
5. Refer to your dictionary as needed to define the following words used in the selection: *privy* (paragraph 3), *venerated* (6), *exhorted* (13), *tenacity* (15), *vacillates* (22), *furtively* (22), and *circuitous* (40).

Questions About the Writer's Craft

1. **The pattern.** When analyzing a subject, writers usually try to identify divisions and classifications that are — within reason — mutually exclusive. But Zinsser acknowledges that the four pressures he discusses can be seen as two distinct pairs, with each pair consisting of two "deeply intertwined" pressures. How does this overlapping of categories help Zinsser make his point?
2. **Other patterns.** In addition to using classification in this essay, what other pattern of development does Zinsser use?
3. Why do you suppose Zinsser uses the notes to Carlos as his essay's introduction? What profile of college students does the reader get from these notes?
4. In paragraph 4, the author writes that students want a map "they can follow unswervingly to career security, financial security, Social Security and, presumably, a prepaid grave." What tone is Zinsser using here? Where else does he use this tone?

Questions for Further Thought

1. Zinsser was a college professor at Yale. Do you think he's well qualified to advise students about career choices? Do you think he knows enough about the real world to advise students to "relax" and take a wide range of courses, instead of focusing on a practical "pre-rich" major?
2. Is it possible both to major in something "safe" and practical and to take electives to become liberally educated? Is it desirable? Explain.
3. Zinsser states that today's students "engage in fewer extracurricular pursuits than their predecessors." Do you agree that students are focusing more on their majors? Are extracurricular activities at your college suffering from low membership and lack of interest?
4. What does Zinsser mean by saying that "One of the few rights that America does not proclaim is the right to fail"? Do you agree that students should take more risks? If so, what kinds of risks should they take?

Writing Assignments Using Division-Classification as a Pattern of Development

∞ 1. Zinsser writes as if all students are the same — panicky, overwrought, and materialistic. Take a position counter to his and write an essay explaining that campuses contain many students different from those Zinsser writes about. To support your point, categorize students into types, giving examples of what each type is like. Be sure that the categories you identify refute Zinsser's analysis of the typical student. The tone of your essay may be serious or playful. James Thurber's "University Days" (page 238) may give you some ideas for your essay, especially if you choose to approach your subject from a humorous or satiric perspective.

2. Is economic security the only kind of satisfaction that college students should pursue? Write an essay classifying the various kinds of satisfactions that students could aim for. At the end of the paper, include brief recommendations about ways that students could best spend their time preparing for these different kinds of satisfactions.

Writing Assignments Using Other Patterns of Development

3. Using Zinsser's analysis of the pressures on college students, write an essay explaining how these pressures can be reduced or eliminated. Give practical suggestions showing how students can avoid or get around the pressures. Also, indicate what society, parents, and college staff can do to help ease students' anxieties.

4. Zinsser's essay indicates that today's students are "slotting" themselves into preordained careers and not leaving themselves open to later opportunities. Write an essay arguing that this tendency to specialize early in college is either beneficial or disastrous for students. Consider such issues as individual freedom, career confusion, changing job markets, changes in society, and the like.

David Hilfiker

Dr. David Hilfiker (1945–) spent his childhood years in Buffalo, New York, graduated from Yale University, then earned his medical degree from the University of Minnesota Medical School. He now works in two Washington, D.C., clinics caring for disadvantaged patients. In *Healing Wounds: A Physician Looks at His Work* (1985), Hilfiker reveals the pressures, doubts, and anxieties endured by the ordinary family doctor. The following excerpt is taken from this book.

Making Medical Mistakes

We want our doctors to be human: sympathetic and generous-spirited. We also want them to be godlike: all-knowing and infallible. But physicians do make mistakes, no matter how much we—and they—don't like to recognize this fact. In this selection, Hilfiker confesses that he has made several errors in medical judgment. By breaking the usual code of silence, Hilfiker explores what society can do to ease the burden of perfection imposed on doctors.

A warm July morning. I finish my rounds at our small country hospital around nine o'clock and walk across the parking lot to the clinic. I am a primary-care practitioner, a family doctor; my partners and I work together in a small office building. After greeting the receptionist, I look through the list of my day's appointments and notice that Barb Daily will be in for her first prenatal examination. "Wonderful," I think, recalling the joy of helping her deliver her first child two years ago. Barb and her husband, Russ, had been friends of mine before Heather was born, but we grew much closer with the shared experience of her birth. In a rural family practice such as mine, much of every workday is taken up with disease; I look forward to the prenatal visit with Barb, to the continuing relationship with her over the next months, to the prospect of birth. 1

309

At her appointment that afternoon, Barb seems to be in good   2
health, with all the signs and symptoms of pregnancy: slight
nausea, some soreness in her breasts, a little weight gain. But
when the nurse tests Barb's urine to determine if she is pregnant,
the result is negative. The test measures the level of a hormone
that is produced by a woman and shows up in her urine when she
is pregnant. But occasionally it fails to detect the low levels of the
hormone during early pregnancy. I reassure Barb that she is fine
and schedule another test for the following week.

Barb leaves a urine sample at the clinic a week later, but the   3
test is negative again. I am troubled. Perhaps she isn't pregnant.
Her missed menstrual period and her other symptoms could be a
result of a minor hormonal imbalance. Maybe the embryo has
died within the uterus and a miscarriage is soon to take place. I
could find out by ordering an ultrasound examination. This procedure would give me a "picture" of the uterus and of the embryo. But Barb would have to go to Duluth, 110 miles from our
village in northern Minnesota, for the examination. The procedure is also expensive. I know the Dailys well enough to know
they have a modest income. Besides, by waiting a few weeks, I
should be able to find out for sure without the ultrasound: Either
the urine test will be positive or Barb will have a miscarriage. I call
her and tell her about the negative test result, about the possibility of a miscarriage, and about the necessity of seeing me again if
she misses her next menstrual period.

I work in a summer resort area, and it is, as usual, a hectic   4
summer; I think no more about Barb's troubling state until a
month later, when she returns to my office. Nothing has changed:
still no menstrual period, still no miscarriage. She is confused and
upset. "I feel so pregnant," she tells me. I am bothered, too. Her
uterus, upon examination, is slightly enlarged, as it was on the
previous visit. But it hasn't grown any larger. Her urine test
remains negative. I can think of several possible explanations for
her condition, including a hormonal imbalance or even a tumor.
But the most likely explanation is that she is carrying a dead
embryo. I decide it is time to break the bad news to her.

"I think you have what doctors call a 'missed abortion,'" I   5
tell her. "You were probably pregnant, but the baby appears to
have died some weeks ago, before your first examination. Unfortunately, you didn't have a miscarriage to get rid of the dead

tissue from the baby and the placenta. If a miscarriage doesn't occur within a few weeks, I'd recommend a re-examination, another pregnancy test, and, if nothing shows up, a dilation and curettage procedure to clean out the uterus."

Barb is disappointed; there are tears. She is college educated, 6 and she understands the scientific and technical aspects of her situation; but that doesn't alleviate the sorrow. We talk at some length and make an appointment for two weeks later.

When Barb returns, Russ is with her. Still no menstrual 7 period; still no miscarriage; still another negative pregnancy test, the fourth. I explain to them what has happened. The dead embryo must be removed or there could be serious complications. Barb could become sterile. The conversation is emotionally difficult for all three of us. We schedule the dilation and curettage for later in the week.

Friday morning, Barb is wheeled into the operating room of 8 the sixteen-bed county hospital. Barb, the nurses, and I all know one another — small-town life. The atmosphere is warm and relaxed; we chat before the operation. After Barb is anesthetized, I examine her pelvis again. Her muscles are now completely relaxed, and it is possible to perform a more reliable examination. Her uterus feels bigger than it did two days previously; it is perhaps the size of a small grapefruit. But since all the pregnancy tests were negative and I'm so sure of the diagnosis, I ignore the information from my fingertips and begin the operation.

Dilation and curettage, or D&C, is a relatively simple surgi- 9 cal procedure performed thousands of times each day in this country. First, the cervix is stretched by pushing smooth metal rods of increasing diameter in and out of it. After about five minutes of this, the cervix has expanded enough so that a curette can be inserted through it into the uterus. The curette is another metal rod, at the end of which is an oval ring about an inch at its widest diameter. It is used to scrape the walls of the uterus. The operation is done completely by feel after the cervix has been stretched, since it is still too narrow to see through.

Things do not go easily this morning. There is considerably 10 more blood than usual, and it is only with great difficulty that I am able to extract anything. What should take ten or fifteen minutes stretches out into a half-hour. The body parts I remove are much larger than I expected, considering when the embryo died. They are not bits of decomposing tissue. These are parts of a body that was recently alive!

I do my best to suppress my rising panic and try to complete the procedure. Working blindly, I am unable to evacuate the uterus completely; I can feel more parts inside but cannot remove them. Finally I stop, telling myself that the uterus will expel the rest within a few days. 11

Russ is waiting outside the operating room. I tell him that Barb is fine but that there were some problems with the operation. Since I don't completely understand what happened, I can't be very helpful in answering his questions. I promise to return to the hospital later in the day after Barb has awakened from the anesthesia. 12

In between seeing other patients that morning I place several almost frantic phone calls, trying to piece together what happened. Despite reassurances from a pathologist that it is "impossible" for a pregnant woman to have four consecutive negative pregnancy tests, the realization is growing that I have aborted Barb's living child. I won't know for sure until the pathologist has examined the fetal parts and determined the baby's age and the cause of death. In a daze, I walk over to the hospital and tell Russ and Barb as much as I know for sure without letting them know all I suspect. I tell them that more tissue may be expelled. I can't face my own suspicions. 13

Two days later, on Sunday morning, I receive a tearful call from Barb. She has just passed some recognizable body parts; what is she to do? She tells me that the bleeding has stopped and that she now feels better. The abortion I began on Friday is apparently over. I set up an appointment to meet with her and Russ to review the entire situation. 14

The pathologist's report confirms my worst fears: I aborted a living fetus. It was about eleven weeks old. I can find no one who can explain why Barb had four negative pregnancy tests. My meeting with Barb and Russ later in the week is one of the hardest things I have ever been through. I describe in some detail what I did and what my rationale had been. Nothing can obscure the hard reality: I killed their baby. 15

Politely, almost meekly, Russ asks whether the ultrasound examination would have shown that Barb was carrying a live baby. It almost seems that he is trying to protect my feelings, 16 trying to absolve me of some of the responsibility. "Yes," I answer, "if I had ordered the ultrasound, we would have known the baby was alive." I cannot explain why I didn't recommend it.

Mistakes are an inevitable part of everyone's life. They hap- 17 pen; they hurt — ourselves and others. They demonstrate our fallibility. Shown our mistakes and forgiven them, we can grow, perhaps in some small way become better people. Mistakes, understood this way, are a process, a way we connect with one another and with our deepest selves.

But mistakes seem different for doctors. This has to do with 18 the very nature of our work. A mistake in the intensive care unit, in the emergency room, in the surgery suite, or at the sickbed is different from a mistake on the dock or at the typewriter. A doctor's miscalculation or oversight can prolong an illness, or cause a permanent disability, or kill a patient. Few other mistakes are more costly.

Developments in modern medicine have provided doctors 19 with more knowledge of the human body, more accurate methods of diagnosis, more sophisticated technology to help in examining and monitoring the sick. All of that means more power to intervene in the disease process. But modern medicine —with its invasive tests and potentially lethal drugs — has also given doctors the power to do more harm.

Yet precisely because of its technological wonders and near- 20 miraculous drugs, modern medicine has created for the physician an expectation of perfection. The technology seems so exact that error becomes almost unthinkable. We are not prepared for our mistakes and we don't know how to cope with them when they occur.

Doctors are not alone in harboring expectations of perfec- 21 tion. Patients expect doctors to be perfect, too. Perhaps patients have to consider their doctors less prone to error than other people: How else can a sick or injured person, already afraid, come to trust the doctor? Further, modern medicine has taken much of the treatment of illness out of the realm of common sense; a patient must trust a physician to make decisions that he, the patient, only vaguely understands. But the degree of perfection expected by patients is no doubt also a result of what we doctors have come to believe about ourselves, or, better, have tried to convince ourselves about ourselves.

This perfection is a grand illusion, of course, a game of mirrors that everyone plays. Doctors hide their mistakes from patients, from other doctors, even from themselves. Open discussion of mistakes is banished from the consultation room, from the operating room, from physicians' meetings. Mistakes become gossip, and are spoken of openly only in court.   22

Unable to admit our mistakes, we physicians are cut off from healing. We cannot ask for forgiveness, and we get none. We are thwarted, stunted; we do not grow.   23

During the days, and weeks, and months after I aborted Barb's baby, my guilt and anger grew. I did discuss what had happened with my partners, with the pathologist, with obstetric specialists. Some of my mistakes were obvious: I had relied too heavily on one test; I had not been skillful in determining the size of the uterus by pelvic examination; I should have ordered the ultrasound before proceeding to the D&C. There was no way I could justify what I had done. To make matters worse, there were complications following the D&C, and Barb was unable to become pregnant again for two years.   24

Although I was as honest with the Dailys as I could be, and although I told them everything they wanted to know, I never shared with them my own agony. I felt they had enough sorrow without having to bear my burden as well. I decided it was my responsibility to deal with my guilt alone. I never asked for their forgiveness.   25

When I began at the age of thirty to practice medicine, I was certainly not prepared for the reality of my mistakes or my emotional responses to them. Like many other physicians, I had entered medical school out of a deep desire to serve people and to relieve suffering. I chose to practice in a remote rural area because it desperately needed physicians, because it seemed to offer the opportunity to establish a practice with the kind of personal care I wanted to provide, and because it seemed to be a good place for me and my family to live.   26

Along with three other doctors also committed to personal medical care, I practiced for seven years in that small Minnesota town. Marja and I raised our family, entered into the life of our community, and tried to live out our dreams. Finally, however, I   27 could no longer tolerate the stresses, and I chose to leave. Dealing with my mistakes was among the stresses.

Doctors' mistakes come in a variety of packages and stem   28
from a variety of causes. For primary-care practitioners, who see every kind of problem, from cold sores to cancer, the mistakes are often simply a result of not knowing enough. One evening during my years in Minnesota a local boy was brought into the emergency room after a drunken driver had knocked him off his bicycle. I examined him right away. Aside from swelling and bruising of the left leg and foot, he seemed fine. An X-ray showed what appeared to be a dislocation of the foot from the ankle. I consulted by telephone with an orthopedic specialist in Duluth, and we decided that I could operate on the boy. As was my usual practice, I offered the patient and his mother a choice: I could do the operation or they could travel to Duluth to see the specialist. My pride was hurt when she decided to take her son to Duluth.

My feelings changed considerably when the specialist called   29
the next morning to thank me for the referral. He reported that the boy had actually suffered an unusual muscle injury, a posterior compartment syndrome, which had twisted his foot and caused it to appear to be dislocated. I had never even heard of such a syndrome, much less seen or treated it. The boy had required immediate surgery to save the muscles of his lower leg. Had his mother not decided to take him to Duluth, he would have been permanently disabled.

Sometimes a lack of technical skill leads to a mistake. After I   30
had been in town a few years, the doctor who had done most of the surgery at the clinic left to teach at a medical school. Since the clinic was more than a hundred miles from the nearest surgical center, my partners and I decided that I should get some additional training in order to be able to perform emergency surgery. One of my first cases was a young man with appendicitis. The surgery proceeded smoothly enough, but the patient did not recover as quickly as he should have, and his hemoglobin level (a measure of the amount of blood in the system) dropped slowly. I referred him to a surgeon in Duluth, who, during a second operation, found a significant amount of old blood in his abdomen. Apparently I had left a small blood vessel leaking into the abdominal cavity. Perhaps I hadn't noticed the oozing blood during

surgery; perhaps it had begun to leak only after I had finished. Although the young man was never in serious danger, although the blood vessel would probably have sealed itself without the second surgery, my mistake had caused considerable discomfort and added expense.

Often, I am sure, mistakes are a result of simple carelessness.   31
There was the young girl I treated for what I thought was a minor ankle injury. After looking at her X-rays, I sent her home with what I diagnosed as a sprain. A radiologist did a routine follow-up review of the X-rays and sent me a report. I failed to read it carefully and did not notice that her ankle had been broken. I learned about my mistake five years later when I was summoned to a court hearing. The fracture I had missed had not healed properly, and the patient had required extensive treatment and difficult surgery. By that time I couldn't even remember her original visit and had to piece together what had happened from my records.

Some mistakes are purely technical; most involve a failure of   32
judgment. Perhaps the worst kind involve what another physician has described to me as a "failure of will." She was referring to those situations in which a doctor knows the right thing to do but doesn't do it because he is distracted, or pressured, or exhausted.

Several years ago I was rushing down the hall of the hospital   33
to the delivery room. A young woman stopped me. Her mother had been having chest pains all night. Should she be brought to the emergency room? I knew the mother well, had examined her the previous week, and knew of her recurring bouts of chest pains. She suffered from angina; I presumed she was having another attack.

Some part of me knew that anyone with all-night chest pains   34
should be seen right away. But I was under pressure. The delivery would make me an hour late to the office, and I was frayed from a weekend on call, spent mostly in the emergency room. This new demand would mean additional pressure. "No," I said, "take her over to the office, and I'll see her as soon as I'm done here." About twenty minutes later, as I was finishing the delivery, the clinic nurse rushed into the room. Her face was pale. "Come quick!" she told me. "Mrs. Helgeson just collapsed." I sprinted the hundred yards to the office, where I found Mrs. Helgeson in cardiac arrest. Like many doctors' offices at the time, ours did not

have the advanced life-support equipment that helps keep patients alive long enough to get them to a hospital. Despite everything we did, Mrs. Helgeson died.

Would she have survived if I had agreed to see her in the   35
emergency room, where the requisite staff and equipment were
available? No one will ever know for sure. But I have to live with
the possibility that she might not have died if I had not had a
"failure of will." There was no way to rationalize: I had been
irresponsible, and a patient had died.

Many situations do not lend themselves to a simple determi-   36
nation of whether a mistake has been made. Seriously ill, hospitalized patients, for instance, require of doctors almost continuous
decision-making. Although in most cases no single mistake is
obvious, there always seem to be things that could have been
done differently or better: administering more of this medication,
starting that treatment a little sooner. . . . The fact is that when
a patient dies, the physician is left wondering whether the care he
provided was adequate. There is no way to be certain, for it is
impossible to determine what would have happened if things had
been done differently. In the end, the physician has to suppress
the guilt and move on to the next patient.

Maiya Martinen first came to see me halfway through her   37
pregnancy. I did not know her or her husband well, but I knew
that they were solid, hard-working people. This was to be their
first child. When I examined Maiya, it seemed to me that the fetus
was unusually small, and I was uncertain about her due date. I
sent her to Duluth for an ultrasound examination and an evaluation by an obstetrician. The obstetrician thought the baby would
be small, but he thought it could be safely delivered in the local
hospital.

Maiya's labor was quite uneventful, except it took her longer   38
than usual to push the baby through to delivery. Her baby boy
was born blue and floppy, but he responded well to routine
newborn resuscitation measures. Fifteen minutes after birth, however, he had a short seizure. We checked his blood-sugar level and
found it to be low, a common cause of seizures in small babies
who take longer than usual to emerge from the birth canal. We
immediately administered intravenous glucose, and baby Marko
seemed to improve. He and his mother were discharged from the
hospital several days later.

It was about two months later, a few days after I had given   39
him his first set of immunizations, that Marko began having short
spells. Not long after that he started to have full-blown seizures.
Once again the Martinens made the trip to Duluth, and Marko
was hospitalized for three days of tests. No cause for the seizures
was found, and he was placed on medication. Marko continued
to have seizures, however. When he returned for his second set of
immunizations, it was clear to me that he was not doing well.

The remainder of Marko's short life was a tribute to the faith   40
and courage of his parents. He was severely retarded, and the
seizures became harder and harder to control. Maiya eventually
went east for a few months so Marko could be treated at the
National Institutes of Health. But nothing seemed to help, and
Maiya and her baby returned home. Marko had to be admitted
frequently to the local hospital in order to control his seizures. At
two o'clock one morning I was called to the hospital; the baby
had had a respiratory arrest. Despite our efforts, Marko died,
ending a year and a half struggle with life.

No cause for Marko's condition was ever determined. Did   41
something happen during the birth that briefly cut off oxygen to
his brain? Should Maiya have delivered at the high-risk obstetric
center in Duluth, where sophisticated fetal monitoring is available? Should I have sent Marko to the neonatal intensive care unit
in Duluth immediately after his first seizure in the delivery room?
I subsequently learned that children who have seizures should not
routinely be immunized. Would it have made any difference if I
had never given Marko the shots? There were many such questions in my mind and, I am sure, in the minds of the Martinens.
There was no way to know the answers, no way for me to handle
the guilt I experienced, perhaps irrationally, whenever I saw
Maiya.

The emotional consequences of mistakes are difficult enough   42
to handle. But soon after I started practicing I realized I had to
face another anxiety as well: It is not only in the emergency room,
the operating room, the intensive care unit, or the delivery room
that I can blunder into tragedy. Medicine is not an exact science;
errors are always possible, even in the midst of the humdrum
routine of daily care. Was that baby I just sent home with a
diagnosis of mild viral fever actually in the early stage of serious
meningitis? Will that nine-year-old with stomach cramps whose

mother I just lectured about psychosomatic illness end up in the hospital tomorrow with a ruptured appendix? Did that Vietnamese refugee have a problem I didn't understand because of the language barrier? A doctor has to confront the possibility of a mistake with every patient visit.

My initial response to the mistakes I did make was to question my competence. Perhaps I just didn't have the necessary intelligence, judgment, and discipline to be a physician. But was I really incompetent? My University of Minnesota Medical School class had voted me one of the two "best clinicians." My diploma from the National Board of Medical Examiners showed scores well above average. I knew that the townspeople considered me a good physician; I knew that my partners, with whom I worked daily, and the consultants to whom I referred patients considered me a good physician, too. When I looked at it objectively, my competence was not the issue. I would have to learn to live with my mistakes. 43

A physician is even less prepared to deal with his mistakes than is the average person. Nothing in our training prepares us to respond appropriately to the mistakes we will inevitably make. Medical school is a competitive place, discouraging any sharing of feelings. And resident doctors are typically so overburdened with work that there is literally no time to reflect. An atmosphere of precision pervades the teaching hospital; there is little opportunity to confront the emotional consequences of making mistakes. 44

Physicians in private practice are no more likely to find errors openly acknowledged or discussed, even though they occur regularly. My own mistakes represent only some of those of which I am aware. I know of one physician who administered a potent drug in a dose ten times that recommended; his patient almost died. Another doctor examined a child in an emergency room late one night and told the parents the problem was only a mild viral infection. Only because the parents did not believe the doctor, only because they consulted another doctor the following morning, did the child survive a life-threatening infection. Still another physician killed a patient while administering a routine test: a needle slipped and lacerated a vital artery. Whether the physician is a rural general practitioner with years of experience but only basic training or a recently graduated, highly trained neurosur- 45 geon working in a sophisticated technological environment, the basic problem is the same.

Because doctors do not discuss their mistakes, I do not know   46
how other physicians come to terms with theirs. But I suspect that many cannot bear to face their mistakes directly. We either deny the misfortune altogether or blame the patient, the nurse, the laboratory, other physicians, the System, Fate — anything to avoid our own guilt.

The medical profession seems to have no place for its mis-   47
takes. Indeed, one would almost think that mistakes were sins. If the medical profession has no room for doctors' mistakes, neither does society. The number of malpractice suits filed each year is symptomatic of this. In what other profession are practitioners regularly sued for hundreds of thousands of dollars because of misjudgments? I am sure the Dailys could have successfully sued me for a large amount of money had they chosen to do so.

The drastic consequences of our mistakes, the repeated op-   48
portunities to make them, the uncertainty about our culpability, and the professional denial that mistakes happen all work together to create an intolerable dilemma for the physician. We see the horror of our mistakes, yet we cannot deal with their enormous emotional impact.

Perhaps the only way to face our guilt is through confession,   49
restitution, and absolution. Yet within the structure of modern medicine there is no place for such spiritual healing. Although the emotionally mature physician may be able to give the patient or family a full description of what happened, the technical details are often so difficult for the layperson to understand that the nature of the mistake is hidden. If an error is clearly described, it is frequently presented as "natural," "understandable," or "unavoidable" (which, indeed, it often is). But there is seldom a real confession: "This is the mistake I made; I'm sorry." How can one say that to a grieving parent? To a woman who has lost her mother?

If confession is difficult, what are we to say about restitu-   50
tion? The very nature of a physician's work means that there are things that cannot be restored in any meaningful way.

What can I do to make good the Dailys' loss? . . .   51

Questions for Close Reading

1. What is the selection's thesis? Locate the sentence(s) in which Hilfiker states his main idea. If he doesn't state the thesis explicitly, express it in your own words.
2. What led Hilfiker to believe that Barb Daily was no longer pregnant? Why didn't he order an ultrasound test?
3. What does Hilfiker mean by a mistake caused by a "failure of will"? Why does he believe that this is the worst kind of mistake physicians can make?
4. What is Hilfiker's reaction to his own medical errors? How does the medical profession in general deal with the issue of diagnostic and treatment mistakes?
5. Refer to your dictionary as needed to define the following words used in the selection: *alleviate* (paragraph 6), *rationale* (15), *thwarted* (23), *angina* (33), *rationalize* (35), *culpability* (48), and *absolution* (49).

Questions About the Writer's Craft

1. **The pattern.** How does Hilfiker classify doctors' typical mistakes? What is the principle of classification that he uses to establish these categories?
2. **Other patterns.** Why do you suppose Hilfiker begins his essay with a narrative? What tone does the narrative set for the rest of the essay? What image of Hilfiker emerges from the narrative's tone?
3. **Other patterns.** In addition to division-classification and narration, what other patterns of development does the author use?
4. Locate places where Hilfiker uses questions. What's the effect of these questions? Are they merely rhetorical, or are they questions with possible answers? Explain.

Questions for Further Thought

1. If you were in the Dailys' position, would you have sued Dr. Hilfiker for his mistake? Why or why not? Is legal action a solution to errors in medicine?
2. The author writes that "mistakes seem different for doctors." Is this true? How should doctors deal with their mistakes?
3. Why do you think Hilfiker reveals so many of his own mistakes — and such serious ones? Might this essay serve a personal purpose for him? What might that purpose be?
4. "Mistakes . . . are a process, a way we connect with one another and

with our deepest selves." What do you think Hilfiker means by this statement? How do we in our everyday lives come to terms with the mistakes we make?

Writing Assignments Using Division-Classification as a Pattern of Development

1. Hilfiker writes, "Mistakes are an inevitable part of everyone's life." Using Hilfiker's statement as your point of departure, write a paper that classifies three or four typical kinds of mistakes all of us tend to make. So that you prepare an essay unified by a common theme, make sure your categories are based on the same principle of classification. You might, for instance, use as a principle of classification the kinds of errors you think many parents make relating to their teenage children: parents are overly critical; they are suspicious; they are insensitive. Your essay may be serious or light in tone. In either case, the paper should indicate clearly your attitude toward the mistakes described.

∞ 2. In an essay, classify the types of stress experienced by people in a particular occupation. The occupation should be one you know about through friends, relatives, your reading, or your own experience. For example, an essay on waiting on tables might discuss the stresses of close supervision, physical exertion, and customers' demands. Develop your essay by providing examples of the kinds of factors that cause these stresses. End the essay with some recommendations about ways to ease the stresses identified. William Zinsser's "College Pressures" (page 298) may give you some ideas for ways to approach your paper.

Writing Assignments Using Other Patterns of Development

3. In this country, physicians are high-status professionals. In other countries, such as Russia, this is not so. Write an essay arguing that the high status and pay of physicians in the United States does or does not benefit the American health-care system.
4. Through interviews and/or library research, find out what kind of training medical students receive in the United States. Then write an essay explaining the process involved in becoming a doctor. The concluding section of your paper should evaluate this process and explain why it is or isn't adequate for producing competent, ethical, and responsible physicians.

Ann McClintock

Ann McClintock (1946–   ) was educated at Temple University in Philadelphia and later earned an advanced degree from the University of Pennsylvania. Currently Director of Occupational Therapy at Ancora State Hospital in New Jersey, she has also worked as a free-lance editor and writer. A frequent speaker before community groups, McClintock is especially interested in the effects of advertising on American life. The following selection, revised for this text, is part of a work in progress on the way propaganda techniques are used to sell products and political candidates.

Propaganda Techniques in Today's Advertising

Propaganda is not just the tool of totalitarian governments and dictators. Rather, propaganda is all around us — in the form of commercials and advertisements. The author of this selection shows how Madison Avenue uses many of the techniques typical of political propaganda to convince us that we need certain products and services. After reading the essay, you may regard in a different light the jingles, endorsements, and slogans characteristic of today's commercials.

Americans, adults and children alike, are being seduced. 1
They are being brainwashed. And few of us protest. Why? Because the seducers and the brainwashers are the advertisers we willingly invite into our homes. We are victims, content — even eager — to be victimized. We read advertisers' propaganda messages in newspapers and magazines; we watch their alluring images on television. We absorb their messages and images into our subconscious. We all do it — even those of us who claim to see through advertisers' tricks and therefore feel immune to advertising's charm. Advertisers lean heavily on propaganda to sell their prod-

ucts, whether the "products" are a brand of toothpaste, a candidate for office, or a particular political viewpoint.

Propaganda is a systematic effort to influence people's opinions, to win them over to a certain view or side. Propaganda is not necessarily concerned with what is true or false, good or bad. Propagandists simply want people to believe the messages being sent. Often, propagandists will use outright lies or more subtle deceptions to sway people's opinions. In a propaganda war, any tactic is considered fair.   2

When we hear the word "propaganda," we usually think of a foreign menace: anti-American radio programs broadcast by a totalitarian regime or brainwashing tactics practiced on hostages. Although propaganda may seem relevant only in the political arena, the concept can be applied fruitfully to the way products and ideas are sold in advertising. Indeed, the vast majority of us are targets in advertisers' propaganda war. Every day, we are bombarded with slogans, print ads, commercials, packaging claims, billboards, trademarks, logos, and designer brands — all forms of propaganda. One study reports that each of us, during an average day, is exposed to over *five hundred* advertising claims of various types. This saturation may even increase in the future since current trends include ads on movie screens, shopping carts, videocassettes, even public television.   3

What kind of propaganda techniques do advertisers use? There are seven basic types: 4

1. *Name Calling* Name calling is a propaganda tactic in which negatively charged names are hurled against the opposing side or competitor. By using such names, propagandists try to arouse feelings of mistrust, fear, and hate in their audiences. For example, a political advertisement may label an opposing candidate a "loser," "fence-sitter," or "warmonger." Depending on the advertiser's target market, labels such as "a friend of big business" or "a dues-paying member of the party in power" can be the epithets that damage an opponent. Ads for products may also use name calling. An American manufacturer may refer, for instance, to a "foreign car" in its commercial — not an "imported" one. The label of foreignness will have unpleasant connotations in many people's minds. A childhood rhyme claims that "names can never hurt me," but name calling is an effective   5

way to damage the opposition, whether it is another car maker or a congressional candidate.

2. *Glittering Generalities*   Using glittering generalities is the 6 opposite of name calling. In this case, advertisers surround their products with attractive — and slippery — words and phrases. They use vague terms that are difficult to define and that may have different meanings to different people: *freedom, democratic, all-American, progressive, Christian,* and *justice.* Many such words have strong, affirmative overtones. This kind of language stirs positive feelings in people, feelings that may spill over to the product or idea being pitched. As with name calling, the emotional response may overwhelm logic. Target audiences accept the product without thinking very much about what the glittering generalities mean — or whether they even apply to the product. After all, how can anyone oppose "truth, justice, and the American way"?

The ads for politicians and political causes often use glitter- 7 ing generalities because such "buzz words" can influence votes. Election slogans include high-sounding but basically empty phrases like the following:

"He cares about people." (That's nice, but is he a better candidate than his opponent?)

"Vote for progress." (Progress by *whose* standards?)

"They'll make this country great again." (What does "great" mean? Does "great" mean the same thing to others as it does to me?)

"Vote for the future." (What kind of future?)

"If you love America, vote for Phyllis Smith." (If I don't vote for Smith, does that mean I don't love America?)

Ads for consumer goods are also sprinkled with glittering 8 generalities. Product names, for instance, are supposed to evoke good feelings: *Luvs* diapers, *New Freedom* feminine hygiene products, *Joy* liquid detergent, *Loving Care* hair color, *Almost Home* cookies, *Yankee Doodle* pastries. Product slogans lean heavily on vague but comforting phrases: Kinney is "The Great American Shoe Store," General Electric "brings good things to life," and Dow Chemical "lets you do great things." Chevrolet, we are told, is the "heartbeat of America," and Chrysler boasts cars that are "built by Americans for Americans."

3. *Transfer* In transfer, advertisers try to improve the image of a product by associating it with a symbol most people respect, like the American flag or Uncle Sam. The advertisers hope that the prestige attached to the symbol will carry over to the product. Many companies use transfer devices to identify their products: Lincoln Insurance shows a profile of the president; Continental Insurance portrays a Revolutionary War minuteman; Amtrak's logo is red, white, and blue; Liberty Mutual's corporate symbol is the Statue of Liberty; Allstate's name is cradled by a pair of protective, fatherly hands.   9

Corporations also use the transfer technique when they sponsor prestigious shows on radio and television. These shows function as symbols of dignity and class. Kraft Corporation, for instance, sponsored a "Leonard Bernstein Conducts Beethoven" concert, while Gulf Oil is the sponsor of *National Geographic* specials and Mobil supports public television's *Masterpiece Theater*. In this way, corporations can reach an educated, influential audience and, perhaps, improve their public image by associating themselves with quality programming.   10

Political ads, of course, practically wrap themselves in the flag. Ads for a political candidate often show either the Washington Monument, a Fourth of July parade, the Stars and Stripes, a bald eagle soaring over the mountains, or a white-steepled church on the village green. The national anthem or "America the Beautiful" may play softly in the background. Such appeals to Americans' love of country can surround the candidate with an aura of patriotism and integrity.   11

4. *Testimonial* The testimonial is one of advertisers' most-loved and most-used propaganda techniques. Similar to the transfer device, the testimonial capitalizes on the admiration people have for a celebrity to make the product shine more brightly —even though the celebrity is not an expert on the product being sold.   12

Print and television ads offer a nonstop parade of testimonials: here's Cher for Holiday Spas; here's basketball star Michael Jordan eating Wheaties; Michael Jackson sings about Pepsi;   13

American Express features a slew of well-known people who assure us that they never go anywhere without their American Express card. Testimonials can sell movies, too; newspaper ads for films often feature favorable comments by well-known reviewers. And, in recent years, testimonials have played an important role in pitching books; the backs of paperbacks frequently list complimentary blurbs by celebrities.

Political candidates, as well as their ad agencies, know the 14
value of testimonials. Barbra Streisand lent her star appeal to the presidential campaign of Michael Dukakis, while Arnold Schwarzenegger endorsed George Bush. Even controversial social issues are debated by celebrities. The nuclear freeze, for instance, starred Paul Newman for the pro side and Charlton Heston for the con.

As illogical as testimonials sometimes are (Pepsi's Michael 15
Jackson, for instance, is a health-food adherent who does not drink soft drinks), they are effective propaganda. We like the *person* so much that we like the *product* too.

5. *Plain Folks* The plain folks approach says, in effect, "Buy 16
me or vote for me. I'm just like you." Regular folks will surely like Bob Evans's Down on the Farm Country Sausage or good old-fashioned Countrytime Lemonade. Some ads emphasize the idea that "we're all in the same boat." We see people making long-distance calls for just the reasons we do — to put the baby on the phone to Grandma or to tell Mom we love her. And how do these folksy, warmhearted (usually saccharine) scenes affect us? They're supposed to make us feel that AT&T — the multinational corporate giant — has the same values we do. Similarly, we are introduced to the little people at Ford, the ordinary folks who work on the assembly line, not to bigwigs in their executive offices. What's the purpose of such an approach? To encourage us to buy a car built by these honest, hardworking "everyday Joes" who care about quality as much as we do.

Political advertisements make almost as much use of the 17
"plain folks" appeal as they do of transfer devices. Candidates wear hard hats, farmers' caps, and assembly-line coveralls. They jog around the block and carry their own luggage through the airport. The idea is to convince voters that the candidates are average people, not the elite — not wealthy lawyers or executives but the common citizen.

6. *Card Stacking*   When people say that "the cards were   18
stacked against me," they mean that they were never given a fair
chance. Applied to propaganda, card stacking means that one side
may suppress or distort evidence, tell half-truths, oversimplify the
facts, or set up a "straw man" — a false target — to divert attention from the issue at hand. Card stacking is a difficult form of
propaganda both to detect and to combat. When a candidate
claims that an opponent has "changed his mind five times on this
important issue," we tend to accept the claim without investigating whether the candidate had good reasons for changing his
mind. Many people are simply swayed by the distorted claim that
the candidate is "waffling" on the issue.

Advertisers often stack the cards in favor of the products they   19
are pushing. They may, for instance, use what are called "weasel
words." These are small words that usually slip right past us, but
that make the difference between reality and illusion. The weasel
words are underlined in the following claims:

"<u>Helps control</u> dandruff symptoms." (The audience usually
     interprets this as *stops* dandruff.)
"Most dentists <u>surveyed</u> recommend sugarless gum for their
     patients <u>who chew gum</u>." (We hear the "most dentists"
     and "for their patients," but we don't think about how
     many were surveyed or whether the dentists first recom-
     mended that the patients not chew gum at all.)
"Sticker price $1,000 lower than <u>most comparable</u> cars."
     (How many is "most"? What car does the advertiser
     consider "comparable"?)

Advertisers also use a card stacking trick when they make an   20
unfinished claim. For example, they will say that their product
has "twice as much pain reliever." We are left with a favorable
impression. We don't usually ask, "Twice as much pain reliever as
what?" Or advertisers may make extremely vague claims that
sound alluring but have no substance: Toyota's "Oh, what a
feeling!"; Vantage cigarettes' "The taste of success"; "The spirit
of Marlboro"; Coke's "the real thing." Another way to stack the
cards in favor of a certain product is to use scientific-sounding
claims that are not supported by sound research. When Ford
claimed that its LTD model was "400% quieter," many people
assumed that the LTD must be quieter than all other cars. When

taken to court, however, Ford admitted that the phrase referred to the difference between the noise level inside and outside the LTD. Other scientific-sounding claims use mysterious ingredients that are never explained as selling points: "Retsyn," "special whitening agents," "the ingredient doctors recommend."

7. *Bandwagon* In the bandwagon technique, advertisers 21 pressure, "Everyone's doing it. Why don't you?" This kind of propaganda often succeeds because many people have a deep desire not to be different. Political ads tell us to vote for the "winning candidate." The advertisers know we tend to feel comfortable doing what others do; we want to be on the winning team. Or ads show a series of people proclaiming, "I'm voting for the Senator. I don't know why anyone wouldn't." Again, the audience feels under pressure to conform.

In the marketplace, the bandwagon approach lures buyers. 22 Ads tell us that "nobody doesn't like Sara Lee" (the message is that you must be weird if you don't). They tell us that "most people prefer Brand X two to one over other leading brands" (to be like the majority, we should buy Brand X). If we don't drink Pepsi, we're left out of "the Pepsi generation." To take part in "America's favorite health kick," the National Dairy Council urges us to drink milk. And Honda motorcycle ads, praising the virtues of being a follower, tell us, "Follow the leader. He's on a Honda."

Why do these propaganda techniques work? Why do so many 23 of us buy the products, viewpoints, and candidates urged on us by propaganda messages? They work because they appeal to our emotions, not to our minds. Often, in fact, they capitalize on our prejudices and biases. For example, if we are convinced that environmentalists are radicals who want to destroy America's record of industrial growth and progress, then we will applaud the candidate who refers to them as "treehuggers." Clear thinking requires hard work: analyzing a claim, researching the facts, examining both sides of an issue, using logic to see the flaws in an argument. Many of us would rather let the propagandists do our thinking for us.

Because propaganda is so effective, it is important to detect it 24 and understand how it is used. We may conclude, after close examination, that some propaganda sends a truthful, worthwhile message. Some advertising, for instance, urges us not to drive drunk, to become volunteers, to contribute to charity. Even so, we must be aware that propaganda is being used. Otherwise, we will have consented to handing over to others our independence of thought and action.

Questions for Close Reading

1. What is the selection's thesis? Locate the sentence(s) in which McClintock states her main idea. If she doesn't state the thesis explicitly, express it in your own words.
2. What is *propaganda*? What mistaken associations do people often have with this term?
3. What are "weasel words"? How do they trick listeners?
4. Why does McClintock believe we should be better informed about propaganda techniques?
5. Refer to your dictionary as needed to define the following words used in the selection: *seduced* (paragraph 1), *warmonger* (5), and *elite* (17).

Questions About the Writer's Craft

1. **The pattern and other patterns.** Before explaining the categories into which propaganda techniques can be grouped, McClintock provides a definition of propaganda. Is the definition purely informative, or does it have a larger objective? If you think the latter, what is the definition's broader purpose?
2. In her introduction, McClintock uses loaded words like *seduced* and *brainwashed*. What effect do these words have on the reader?
3. Locate places in the essay where McClintock uses questions. Which are rhetorical and which are genuine queries?
4. What kind of conclusion does McClintock provide for the essay?

Questions for Further Thought

1. Do you agree with McClintock that we are subjected to commercial propaganda every day? Is *propaganda* the right term to use for today's advertising techniques? Explain.
2. Which of the advertising techniques described by McClintock are easiest to identify in an ad? Which are the least obvious? Can you recall examples of ads that make use of these techniques?
3. Do you think that you're relatively immune to advertising's ploys? What factors influence your decision to purchase a particular brand or product?
4. Since propaganda is so effective, is it ethical for advertisers and politi-

cians to use it? Is awareness enough to protect us from the effects of such propaganda — or do we need stronger protection? What other means could we use to protect ourselves?

Writing Assignments Using Division-Classification as a Pattern of Development

1. McClintock cautions us to be sensitive to propaganda in advertising. Young children, however, aren't capable of this kind of awareness. With pen or pencil in hand, watch some commercials aimed at children, such as those for toys, cereals, and fast food. Then analyze the use of propaganda techniques in these commercials. Using division-classification, write an essay describing the main propaganda techniques you observed. Support your analysis with examples drawn from the commercials. Remember to provide a thesis that indicates your opinion of the advertising techniques.

2. Like advertising techniques, television shows can be classified. Avoiding the obvious system of classifying according to game shows, detective shows, and situation comedies, come up with your own original division-classification principle. Possibilities include how family life is depicted, the way work is presented, how male-female relationships are portrayed. Using one such principle, write an essay in which you categorize popular TV shows into three types. Refer to specific shows to support your classification system. Your attitude toward the shows being discussed should be made clear.

Writing Assignments Using Other Patterns of Development

3. McClintock says that card stacking "distort[s] evidence, tell[s] half-truths, oversimplif[ies] the facts" (18). Focusing on an editorial, a political campaign, a print ad, or a television commercial, analyze the extent to which card stacking is used as a persuasive strategy. Neil Postman's "Future Shlock" (page 247) and H. L. Mencken's "The Politician" (page 551) will deepen your understanding of the extent to which the truth can be distorted.

4. To increase further your sensitivity to the moral dimensions of propaganda, write a proposal outlining an ad campaign for a real or imaginary product or elected official. The introduction to your proposal should identify who or what is to be promoted, and the thesis or plan of development should indicate the specific propaganda techniques you suggest. In the paper's supporting paragraphs, explain how these techniques would be used to promote your product or candidate.

Janet Mendell Goldstein

Born in Philadelphia in 1940, Janet Mendell Goldstein did her undergraduate work at Radcliffe College and earned advanced degrees at Harvard University and the University of Pennsylvania. She divides her time between teaching English at Friends Select School in Philadelphia and working as an editorial consultant, free-lance writer, and textbook author. Coauthor of a college reading text, Goldstein is also an essayist and poet. Her work has appeared in a variety of newspapers and magazines, including the *English Journal, Faith and Inspiration,* and the *Philadelphia Inquirer.* The following selection is drawn from a series of pieces Goldstein has written about contemporary life.

The Quick Fix Society

Not so long ago, we were told that if we worked hard and never gave up, we would eventually get what we wanted. These days, however, "eventually" isn't good enough for many people. Janet Mendell Goldstein urges us to consider where we are going in such a rush. And what, she asks, are we missing along the way?

My husband and I just got back from a week's vacation in 1 West Virginia. Of course, we couldn't wait to get there, so we took the Pennsylvania Turnpike and a couple of interstates. "Look at those gorgeous farms!" my husband exclaimed as pastoral scenery slid by us at 55 mph. "Did you see those cows?" But at 55 mph, it's difficult to see anything; the gorgeous farms look like moving green checkerboards, and the herd of cows is reduced to a sprinkling of dots in the rear-view mirror. For four hours, our only real amusement consisted of counting exit signs and wondering what it would feel like to hold still again. Getting there certainly didn't seem like half the fun; in fact, getting there wasn't any fun at all.

So, when it was time to return to our home outside of 2

Philadelphia, I insisted that we take a different route. "Let's explore that countryside," I suggested. The two days it took us to make the return trip were studded with new experiences. We toured a Civil War battlefield and stood on the little hill that fifteen thousand Confederate soldiers had tried to take on another hot July afternoon, one hundred and twenty-five years ago, not knowing that half of them would perish in the vain attempt. We meandered through main streets of sleepy Pennsylvania Dutch towns, slowing to twenty miles an hour so as not to crowd the horses and buggies on their way to market. We admired toy trains and antique cars in county museums and saved 70 percent in factory outlets. We stuffed ourselves with spicy salads and homemade bread pudding in an "all-you-can-eat" farmhouse restaurant, then wandered outside to enjoy the sunshine and the herds of cows — no little dots this time — basking in it. And we returned home refreshed, reeducated, revitalized. This time, getting there had *been* the fun.

Why is it that the featureless turnpikes and interstates are the 3 routes of choice for so many of us? Why doesn't everybody try slowing down and exploring the countryside? But more and more, the fast lane seems to be the only way for us to go. In fact, most Americans are constantly in a hurry — and not just to get from Point A to Point B. Our country has become a nation in search of the quick fix — in more ways than one.

Now instead of later: Once upon a time, Americans under- 4 stood the principle of deferred gratification. We put a little of each paycheck away "for a rainy day." If we wanted a new sofa or a week at a lakeside cabin, we saved up for it, and the banks helped us out by providing special Christmas Club and Vacation Club accounts. If we lived in the right part of the country, we planted corn and beans and waited patiently for the harvest. If we wanted to be thinner, we simply ate less of our favorite foods and waited patiently for the scale to drop, a pound at a time. But today we aren't so patient. We take out loans instead of making deposits, or we use our VISA or Mastercard to get that furniture or vacation trip — relax now, pay later. We buy our food, like our clothing, ready-made and off the rack. And if we're in a hurry to lose weight, we try the latest miracle diet, guaranteed to shed ten pounds in ten days . . . unless we're rich enough to afford liposuction.

Faster instead of slower: Not only do we want it now; we   5
don't even want to be kept waiting for it. This pervasive impatience, the "I-hate-to-wait" syndrome, has infected every level of
our lives. Instead of standing in line at the bank, we withdraw
twenty dollars in as many seconds from an automatic teller machine. Then we take our fast money to a fast convenience store
(why wait in line at the supermarket?), where we buy a frozen
dinner all wrapped up and ready to be popped into the microwave . . . unless we don't care to wait even that long and pick
up some fast food instead. And if our fast meal doesn't agree with
us, we hurry to the medicine cabinet for — you guessed it — some
fast relief. We like fast pictures, so we buy Polaroid cameras. We
like fast entertainment, so we record our favorite TV show on the
VCR so we can "zap" each commercial, and stop watching if
nothing exciting happens in the opening thirty seconds. We like
our information fast, too: messages flashed on a computer screen,
documents FAXed from your telephone to mine, current events
in 90-second bursts on *Eyewitness News*, history reduced to "Bi-
centennial Minutes." Symbolically, the American eagle now flies
for Express Mail. How dare anyone keep America waiting longer
than overnight?

Superficially instead of thoroughly: What's more, we   6
don't even want *all* of it. Once, we lingered over every word of a
classic novel or the latest best-seller. Today, since faster is better,
we read the condensed version or pop an audiocassette of the
book into our car's tape player to listen to on the way to work. Or
we buy the *Cliff's Notes*, especially if we are students, so we don't
have to deal with the book at all. Once, we listened to every note
of Beethoven's Fifth Symphony. Today, we don't have the time;
instead, we can enjoy 26 seconds of that famous "da-da-da-
DUM" theme — and 99 other musical excerpts almost as famous
—on our "Greatest Moments of the Classics" record. After all,
why waste 45 minutes listening to the whole thing when someone
else has saved us the trouble of picking out the best parts? Our
magazine articles come to us pre-digested in *Reader's Digest*. Our
news briefings, thanks to *USA Today*, are more brief than ever.
Even our personal relationships have become compressed. Instead of devoting large segments of our days to our loved ones —
after all, we *are* busy people — we substitute something called

"quality time," which, more often than not, is no time at all. As we rush from book to music to news item to relationship, we do not realize that we are living our lives by the iceberg principle — paying attention only to the top and ignoring the 8/9 that lies just below the surface.

When did it all begin, this urge to do it now, to get it over 7
with, to skim the surface of life? Why are we in such a hurry to save time? And what, pray tell, are we going to do with all the time we save — besides, of course, rushing out to save some more? The sad truth is that we don't know how to use the time we save, because all we're good at is *saving* time . . . not *spending* time.

Don't get me wrong. I'm not saying we should go back to 8
growing our own vegetables or knitting our own sweaters or putting our paychecks into piggy banks. I'm not even advocating a mass movement to cut all our credit cards into little pieces. But I am saying that all of us need to think more seriously about putting the brakes on our "we-want-it-all-and-we-want-it-now" lifestyle before we speed completely out of control. Let's take the time to read every word of that story, hear every note of that music, savor every nuance of that countryside — or that other person. Let's rediscover life in the slow lane.

Questions for Close Reading

1. What is the selection's thesis? Locate the sentence(s) in which Goldstein states her main idea. If she doesn't state the thesis explicitly, express it in your own words.
2. Goldstein and her husband enjoy looking at toy trains and antique cars, eating homemade pudding, and watching cows basking in sunshine. What do all of these pleasures have in common?
3. What evidence does Goldstein give to support her contention that in the past, Americans were willing to defer gratification?
4. In paragraph 6, Goldstein describes "the iceberg principle." What does she mean by this term? How, in Goldstein's view, does this principle apply to the way many people live their lives?
5. Refer to your dictionary as needed to define the following words used in the selection: *pastoral* (paragraph 1), *meander* (2), *bask* (2), *revitalized* (2), *pervasive* (5), *syndrome* (5), and *nuance* (8).

Questions About the Writer's Craft

1. **The pattern.** The body of Goldstein's essay is divided into the three ways Americans seek a quick fix. Are the three subdivisions of the "quick fix" syndrome mutually exclusive? Explain.
2. **Other patterns.** In addition to division-classification, Goldstein uses comparison-contrast to develop her essay. What are some contrasting images in the first and second paragraphs? Where else in the essay do you find similar juxtapositions? What purpose do these contrasts serve?
3. Goldstein often uses *rhetorical questions* — questions she doesn't expect her readers to answer — as when she asks "why wait in line at the supermarket?" (paragraph 5). Where else does she use rhetorical questions? What purposes do such questions serve?
4. Goldstein uses a number of contemporary expressions, abbreviations, and quoted clichés. What is the effect, for example, of "FAXed"? Why does she put "zap" and "quality time" in quotation marks?

Questions for Further Thought

1. According to Goldstein, Americans suffer from the "I-hate-to-wait" syndrome. In which aspects of your life are you willing to defer gratification; in which do you require immediate satisfaction?
2. Goldstein repeats the word *fast* throughout paragraph 5, always with negative implications. Think, however, of some modern convenience (a microwave oven, a word processor, a vacuum cleaner) that speeds up mundane chores. Discuss ways this device has freed you to spend more time in personally meaningful ways.
3. Goldstein's outgoing trip was planned to minimize travel time. The return trip, however, seems to have been more a matter of following impulse and finding surprises. What spontaneous thing have you ever done that led to some discovery or special pleasure? When have you acted on impulse and found the consequences to be disastrous?
4. Most Americans, Goldstein believes, don't know how to spend their time. If you were free of pressures and obligations, how would you spend your time? What would you do differently?

Writing Assignments Using Division-Classification as a Pattern of Development

∞ 1. Goldstein urges readers to slow down and appreciate life more fully. Consider the different activities of your everyday life. Write an essay classifying the activities according to those you like to give time to and those you like to speed through. Reach some conclusions about what is and is not important to you. Anne Morrow Lindbergh's "Channelled Whelk" (page 219) will help you do some serious thinking about your priorities. Indeed, you may want to include some of Lindbergh's ideas in your paper.

2. Goldstein laments the superficiality of many relationships. Consider those people with whom you spend time. Brainstorm and then categorize the characteristics these people do or do not have in common. Use your analysis to identify the qualities you value in others.

Writing Assignments Using Other Patterns of Development

3. Goldstein seems to find the natural and rural more appealing than the technological. Taking the opposite point of view, write a descriptive piece conveying the beauty made possible by modern technology—an aerial view of a bayside city, the lit span of a suspension bridge, the graphics of your favorite computer program. Build your description around a dominant impression, selecting those details that best express your sense of wonder.

4. Although Goldstein writes that Americans like their clothing and food ready-made, many people take pleasure in a more leisurely approach to satisfying their basic needs. Think of something you enjoy cooking, building, or crafting. Or you might consider activities like planting a vegetable garden or going fishing. Write an essay guiding the reader, step by step, through the process you select. Your essay should capture the contentment and pride you experience in the process.

Additional Writing Topics
DIVISION-CLASSIFICATION

General Assignments

Choose one of the following subjects and write an essay developed wholly or in part through division-classification. Start by determining the purpose of the essay. Do you want to inform, compare and contrast, or persuade? Apply a single, significant principle of division or classification to your subject. Don't switch the principle midway through your analysis. Also, be sure that the types or categories you create are as complete and mutually exclusive as possible.

Division

1. A shopping mall
2. A video and/or stereo system
3. A fruit, such as a pineapple, an orange, or a banana
4. A tax dollar
5. A particular kind of team
6. A word-processing system
7. A human hand
8. A meal
9. A meeting
10. A favorite poem, story, or play
11. A favorite restaurant
12. A school library
13. A basement
14. A playground, gym, or other recreational area
15. A church service
16. A wedding or funeral
17. An eventful week in your life
18. A college campus
19. A television show or movie
20. A homecoming or other special weekend

Classification

1. People in a waiting room
2. Holidays
3. Closets
4. Roommates
5. Salad bars

6. Divorces
7. Beds
8. Students in a class
9. Shoes
10. Summer movies
11. Teachers
12. Neighbors
13. College courses
14. Bosses
15. TV watchers
16. Mothers or fathers
17. Commercials
18. Vacations
19. Trash
20. Relatives

Assignments with a Specific Purpose and Audience

1. You are a dorm counselor. During orientation week, you'll be talking to students on your floor about the different kinds of problems they may have with roommates. Write your talk, describing each kind of problem and explaining how to cope.

2. As a driving instructor, you decide to prepare a lecture on the types of drivers that your students are likely to encounter on the road. In your lecture, categorize drivers according to a specific principle and show the behaviors of each type.

3. You have been asked to write a pamphlet for "new recruits" — new workers on your job, new students in your college class, new members of your sports team, or the like. In the pamphlet, identify at least three general qualities needed for the recruits' success.

4. A seasoned camp counselor, you've been asked to prepare, for new counselors, an informational sheet on children's emotional needs. Categorizing those needs into types, explain what counselors can do to nurture youngsters emotionally.

5. As your college newspaper's TV critic, you plan to write a review of the fall shows, most of which — in your opinion — lack originality. To show how stereotypical the programs are, select one type (for example, situation comedies or crime dramas). Then use a specific division-classification principle to illustrate that the same stale formulas are trotted out from show to show.

6. Asked to write an editorial for the campus paper, you decide to do a half-serious piece on taking "mental health" days off from classes. Structure your essay around three kinds of occasions when "playing hooky" is essential for maintaining sanity.

7
PROCESS ANALYSIS

WHAT IS PROCESS ANALYSIS?

Perhaps you've noticed the dogged determination of small children when they learn how to do something new. Whether trying to tie their shoelaces or tell time, little children struggle along, creating knotted tangles, confusing the hour with the minute hand. But they don't give up. Mastering such basic skills makes them feel less dependent on the adults of the world — all of whom seem to know how to do everything. Actually, none of us is born knowing how to do very much. We spend a good deal of our lives learning — everything from speaking our first word to balancing our first bank statement. Indeed, the milestones in our lives are often linked to the processes we have mastered: how to cross the street alone; how to drive a car; how to make a speech without being paralyzed by fear.

Process analysis, a technique that explains the steps or sequence involved in doing something, satisfies our need to learn as well as our curiosity about how the world works. All the self-help books flooding the market today (*Managing Stress, How to Make a Million in Real Estate, Ten Days to a Perfect Body*) are examples of process analysis. The instructions on the federal tax form and the recipes in a cookbook are also process analyses. Several television classics, now seen in reruns, also capitalize on our desire to learn how things happen: *The Wild Kingdom* shows how animals survive in faraway lands, and *Mission: Impossible* has great fun detailing elaborate plans for preventing the triumph of evil. Process analysis can be more than merely interesting or entertaining, though; it can be of critical importance. Consider a waiter hurriedly skimming the "Choking Aid" instructions posted on a restaurant wall or an air-traffic controller following emergency procedures in an effort to prevent a midair collision. In these last examples, the consequences could be fatal if the process analyses were slipshod, inaccurate, or confusing.

Undoubtedly, all of us have experienced less dramatic effects of poorly written process analyses. Perhaps you've tried to assemble a bicycle and spent hours sorting through a stack of parts, only to end up with one or two extra pieces never mentioned in the instructions. Or maybe you were baffled when putting up a set of wall shelves because the instructions used unfamiliar terms like *mitered cleat, wing nut*, and *dowel pin*. No wonder many people stay clear of anything that actually admits "assembly required."

HOW PROCESS ANALYSIS FITS YOUR PURPOSE AND AUDIENCE

You will use process analysis in two types of writing situations: (1) when you want to give step-by-step instructions to readers showing how they can do something, or (2) when you want readers to understand how something happens even though they won't actually follow the steps outlined. The first kind of process analysis is *directional*; the second is *informational*.

When you look at the cooking instructions on a package of frozen vegetables or follow guidelines for completing a job application, you're reading directional process analysis. A serious essay explaining how to select a college and a humorous essay telling readers how to get on the good side of a professor are also examples of directional process analysis. Using a variety of tones, informational process analyses can range over equally diverse subjects; they can describe mechanical, scientific, historical, sociological, artistic, or psychological processes: for example, how the core of a nuclear power plant melts down; how television became so important in political campaigns; how abstract painters use color; how to survive a blind date.

College assignments frequently lead to process analysis essays. Consider these examples:

> Community officials have been accused of mismanaging recent unrest over the public housing ordinance. Describe the steps the officials took, indicating whether you think they acted wisely. If not, how do you think the situation should have been handled?

> Because many colleges and universities have changed the eligibility requirements for financial aid, fewer students can depend on loans or scholarships. How can students cope with the increasing costs of obtaining a higher education?

> Over the years, there have been many reports citing the abuse of small children in day-care centers. What can parents do to guard against the mistreatment of their children?

> *Genius* has been defined as 10 percent inspiration and 90 percent perspiration. Do you consider this an apt description? Support your point by explaining how you or someone you know achieved a goal that required both hard work and imagination.

You may have noted that none of the assignments explicitly requires an essay response using process analysis. However, the wording of the assignments — "*Describe* the steps," "*How* can students *cope*," "*What* can parents *do*," and so on — suggests that process analysis would be an appropriate strategy for developing the responses.

Assignments don't always signal the use of process analysis so clearly. But during the prewriting stage, as you generate material to support your thesis, you'll often realize that you can best achieve your purpose by developing the essay—or part of it—using process analysis.

Sometimes process analysis will be the primary strategy for organizing an essay; other times it will be used to help make a point in an essay organized according to another pattern of development. Let's take a look at process analysis as a supporting strategy.

Assume that you're writing a *causal analysis* examining the impact of television commercials on people's buying behavior. To help readers see that commercials create a need where none existed before, you might describe the various stages in an advertising campaign to pitch a new, completely frivolous product. In an essay *defining* a good boss, you could convey the point that effective managers must be skilled at settling disputes by explaining the steps your boss took to resolve a heated disagreement between two employees. If you write an *argumentation-persuasion* paper urging the funding of programs to ease the plight of the homeless, you would have to dramatize for readers the tragedy of these people's lives. To achieve your purpose, you could devote part of the paper to an explanation of how the typical street person goes about the desperate jobs of finding a place to sleep and getting food to eat.

SUGGESTIONS FOR USING PROCESS ANALYSIS IN AN ESSAY

The suggestions that follow will be helpful whether you use process analysis as a dominant or supportive pattern of development.

1. Identify the desired outcome of the process analysis. Many papers developed primarily through process analysis have a clear-cut purpose—simply to *inform* readers as objectively as possible about a process: "Here's a way of making french fries at home that will surpass the best served in your favorite fast-food restaurant." But a process analysis essay may also have a *persuasive* edge, with the writer advocating a point of view about the process, perhaps even urging a course of action: "If you don't want your arguments to deteriorate into ugly battles, you should follow a series of foolproof steps for having disagreements that leave friendships intact." Before starting to write, you need to decide if the essay is to be purely factual or if it will include this kind of persuasive dimension.

2. Formulate a thesis that clarifies your attitude toward the process. Like the thesis in any other paper, the thesis in a process analysis should do more than announce your subject. ("Here's how the college's work-study program operates.") It should also state or imply your attitude toward the process: "Enrolling in the college's work-study program has become unnecessarily complicated. The procedure could be simplified if the college adopted the helpful guidelines prepared by the Student Senate."

3. Keep your audience in mind. Only when you gauge how much your readers already know (or don't know) about the process can you determine how much explanation you'll have to provide. Suppose you've been asked to write an article informing students of the best way to use the university computer center. The article will be published in a newsletter for computer science majors. You would seriously misjudge your audience — and probably put them to sleep — if you explained in detail how to transfer material from disk to disk or how to delete information from a file. However, an article on the same topic prepared for a general audience — your composition class, for instance — would probably require such detailed instructions.

To determine how much explanation is needed, put yourself in your readers' shoes. Don't assume readers will know something just because you do. Ask questions like these about your audience: "Will my readers need some background about the process before I describe it in depth?" "Are there technical terms I should define?" "If my essay is directional, should I specify near the beginning the ingredients, materials, and equipment needed to perform the process?" (For more help in analyzing your audience, see the checklist on pages 20–21.)

4. Use prewriting to identify the steps in the process. To explain a sequence to your readers, you need to think through the process thoroughly, identifying its major parts and subparts, locating possible missteps or trouble spots. With your purpose, thesis, and audience in mind, use the appropriate prewriting techniques (brainstorming and mapping should be especially helpful) to break down the process into its component parts. When prewriting, it's a good idea to start by generating more material than you expect to use. Then the raw material can be shaped and pruned to fit your purpose and the needs of your audience. The amount of work done during the prewriting stage will have a direct bearing on the clarity of your presentation.

5. Identify the directional and informational aspects of the process analysis.   Directional and informational process analyses are not always distinct. In fact, they may be complementary. Your prewriting may reveal that you'll need to provide background information about a process before outlining its steps. For example, in a paper describing a step-by-step approach for losing weight, you might first need to explain how the body burns calories. Or, in a paper on gardening, you could provide some theory about the way organic fertilizers work before detailing a plan for growing vegetables. Although both approaches may be appropriate in a paper, one generally predominates.

The kind of process analysis chosen has implications for the way you will relate to your reader. When the process analysis is *directional,* the reader is addressed in the *second person*: "You should first rinse the residue from the radiator by . . . ," or "Wrap the injured person in a blanket and then. . . ." (In the second example, the pronoun *you* is implied.)

If the process analysis has an *informational* purpose, you won't address the reader directly but will choose from a number of other options. For example, you might use the *first person*. In a humorous essay explaining how not to prepare for finals, you could cite your own disastrous study habits: "Filled with good intentions, I sit on my bed, pick up a pencil, open my notebook, and promptly fall asleep." The *third person singular or plural* can also be used in informational process essays: "The door-to-door salesperson walks up the front walk, heart pounding, more than a bit nervous, but also challenged by the prospect of striking a deal," or "The new recruits next underwent a series of important balance tests in what was called the 'horror chamber.'"

You might have noticed that in the third-person examples, the present tense ("walks up") is used in one sentence, the past tense ("underwent") in the other. The past tense is appropriate for events already completed, whereas the present tense is used for habitual or ongoing actions. ("A dominant male goose usually flies at the head of the V-wedge during migration.") The present tense is also effective when you want to lend a sense of dramatic immediacy to a process, even if the steps were performed in the past. ("The surgeon gently separates the facial skin and muscle from the underlying bony skull.")

6. Explain the process, one step at a time.   Prewriting helped you identify key stages and sort out the directional and informational aspects of the process. Now you're ready to organize your raw material into an easy-to-follow sequence. At times your purpose will be to explain a process with a *fairly fixed chronological sequence*: how to make pizza, how to pot a plant, how to change a tire. In such cases, you should include all necessary steps, in the correct chronological order. However, if a strict chronological ordering of steps means that a particularly important part of the sequence gets buried in the middle, the sequence probably should be juggled so that the crucial step receives the attention it deserves.

Other times your goal will be to describe a process having *no commonly accepted sequence*. For example, in an essay explaining how to discipline a child or how to pull yourself out of a blue mood, you will have to come up with your own definition of the key steps and then arrange those steps in some logical order. You may also use process analyses to *reject* or *reformulate* a traditional sequence. In this case, you would propose a more logical series of steps: "Our system for electing congressional representatives is inefficient and undemocratic; it should be reformed in the following ways."

Whether the essay describes a generally agreed-on process or one that is not commonly accepted, you must provide all the details needed to explain the process. You readers should be able to understand, even visualize, the process. There should be no fuzzy patches or confusing cuts from one step to another. Don't, however, go into obsessive detail about minor stages or steps. If you dwell for several hundred words on how to butter the pan, your readers will never stay with you long enough to learn how to make the omelet.

It's not unusual, especially in less defined sequences, for some steps in a process to occur simultaneously and overlap. When this happens, you should present the steps in the most logical order, being sure to tell your readers that several steps are not perfectly distinct and may merge. For example, in an essay explaining how a species becomes extinct, you would have to indicate that overpopulation of hardy strains and destruction of endangered breeds are often simultaneous events. You would also need to clarify that the depletion of food sources both precedes and follows the demise of a species.

7. Provide readers with the help they need to follow the sequence.   As you move through the steps of a process analysis, don't forget to *warn readers about difficulties* they might encounter. For example, when writing a paper on the artistry involved in butterflying a shrimp, you might say something like this:

> Next, make a shallow cut with your sharpened knife along the convex curve of the shrimp's intestinal tract. The tract, usually a faint black line along the outside curve of the shrimp, is faintly visible beneath the translucent flesh. But some shrimp have a thick orange, blue, or gray line instead of a thin black one. In all cases, be careful not to slice too deeply, or you will end up with two shrimp halves instead of one butterflied shrimp.

You have told readers what to look for, citing the exceptions, and have warned them against making too deep a cut. Anticipating spots where communication might break down is a key part of writing an effective process analysis.

Transitional words and phrases are also critical in helping readers understand the order of the steps being described. Time signals like *first, next, now, while, after, before,* and *finally* provide readers with a clear sense of the sequence. Entire sentences can also be used to link parts of the process, reminding your audience of what has already been discussed and indicating what will now be explained: "Once the panel of experts finishes its evaluation of the exam questions, randomly selected items are field-tested in schools throughout the country."

8. Maintain an appropriate tone.   When writing a process analysis essay, be sure your tone is consistent with your purpose, your attitude toward your subject, and the effect you want to have on the reader. When explaining how fraternities and sororities recruit new members, do you want to use an objective, nonjudgmental tone, or do you want to project an angry, even accusatory tone? Once you settle on the essay's tone, maintain it throughout. If you're writing a light piece on the way computers are taking over our lives, you wouldn't include a grim step-by-step analysis of the way confidential computerized medical records may become public.

9. Open and close the process analysis effectively.   A paper developed primarily through process analysis should have a strong beginning. The introduction should state the process to be described and imply whether the essay has an informational or directional intent.

If you suspect readers are indifferent to your subject, use the introduction to motivate them, telling them how important the subject is:

> Do you enjoy the salad bars found in many restaurants? If you do, you probably have noticed that the vegetables are always crisp and fresh--no matter how many hours they have been exposed to the air. What are the restaurants doing to make the vegetables look so inviting? There's a simple answer. Many restaurants dip and spray the vegetables with potent chemicals to make them appetizing.

If you think your audience may be intimidated by your subject (perhaps because it's complex or relatively obscure), the introduction is the perfect spot to reassure them that the process being described is not beyond their grasp:

> Studies show that many people willingly accept a defective product just so they won't have to deal with the uncomfortable process of making a complaint. But once a few easy-to-learn basics are mastered, anyone can register a complaint that gets results.

Most process analysis essays don't end as soon as the last step in the sequence is explained. Instead, they usually include some brief final comments that round out the piece and bring it to a satisfying close. This final section of the essay may summarize the main steps in the process — not by repeating the steps verbatim but by rephrasing and condensing them in several concise sentences. The conclusion can also be an effective spot to underscore the significance of the process, recalling what may have been said in the introduction about the subject's importance. Or the essay can end by echoing the note of reassurance that may have been included at the start.

Despite the glut of "how-to" books on the market, effective process writing is not as easy to do as it might appear. Explaining how to do something is often as difficult as responding to the proverbial "How do I get there from here?" And explaining how something happened means re-creating often complex events so that logic and clarity take precedence over cloudiness and confusion. If, after reading your piece, the reader thinks or says, "I understand. I see what you mean," you can be confident that your process analysis has been successful. That's no small accomplishment.

STUDENT ESSAY

The following student essay was written by Robert Barry in response to this assignment:

> Stephen Leacock's "How to Live to Be 200" pokes fun at our obsessive concern with physical fitness. By observing people, identify another example of an obsessive behavior that borders on the addictive. Then write a light-spirited essay explaining the various stages in the addiction. Since your essay should be humorous in tone, be sure to describe an addiction that doesn't have serious consequences.

While reading Robert's paper, try to determine how effectively it applies the principles of process analysis. The annotations on Robert's paper and the commentary following it will help you look at the essay more closely.

Becoming a Videoholic
by Robert Barry

Introduction

In the last several years, videocassette recorders (VCRs) have become popular additions in many American homes. A recent newspaper article notes that one in three households has a VCR, with sales continuing to climb every day. VCRs seem to be the most popular technological breakthrough since television itself. No consumer warning labels are attached to these rapidly multiplying VCRs,

Start of two-sentence thesis

but they should be. VCRs can be dangerous. Barely aware of what is happening, a person can turn into a compulsive videotaper. The descent from innocent hobby to full-blown addiction takes place in several stages.

Topic sentence

First stage in process (VCR addiction)

In the first innocent stage, the unsuspecting person buys a VCR for occasional use. I was at this stage when I asked my parents if they would buy me a VCR as a combined birthday and high school graduation gift. With the VCR, I could tape reruns of Star Trek and Miami Vice, shows I would otherwise miss on nights I was at work. The VCR was perfect. I hooked it up to the old TV in my bedroom, recorded the intergalactic adventures of Captain Kirk and the high-voltage escapades of Sonny Crockett, then watched the tapes the next day. Occasionally, I taped a movie which my friends and I watched over the weekend. I had just one cassette, but that was all I needed since I watched every show I recorded and simply taped over the

Beginning of analogy to alcoholism

preceding show when I recorded another. In these early days, my VCR was the equivalent of light social drinking.

Topic sentence

Second stage in process

In the second phase on the road to videoholism, an individual uses the VCR more frequently and begins to stockpile tapes rather than watch them. My troubles began in July when my family went to the shore for a week's vacation. I programmed the VCR to tape all five episodes of

1

2

3

Star Trek while I was at the beach perfecting my tan. Since I used the VCR's long-play mode, I could get all five Star Treks on one cassette. But that ended up creating a problem. Even I, an avid Trekkie, didn't want to watch five shows in one sitting. I viewed two shows, but the three unwatched shows tied up my tape, making it impossible to record other shows. How did I resolve this dilemma? Very easily. I went out and bought several more cassettes. Once I had these additional tapes, I was free to record as many Star Treks as I wanted, plus I could tape reruns of classics like The Honeymooners and Mission: Impossible. Very quickly, I accumulated six Star Treks, four Honeymooners, and three Mission: Impossibles. Then a friend-- who shall go nameless--told me that only eighty-two episodes of Star Trek were ever made. Excited by the thought that I could acquire as impressive a collection of tapes as a Hollywood executive, I continued recording Star Trek, even taping shows while I watched them. Clearly, my once innocent

Continuation of analogy — hobby was getting out of control. I was now using the VCR on a regular basis--the equivalent of several stiff drinks a day.

Topic sentence — In the third stage of videoholism, the amount   4
of taping increases significantly, leading to an even
Third stage in process — more irrational stockpiling of cassettes. The catalyst that propelled me into this third stage was my parents' decision to get cable TV. Selfless guy that I am, I volunteered to move my VCR and hook it up to the TV in the living room, where the cable outlet was located. Now I could tape all the most recent

Continuation of analogy — movies and cable specials. With that delightful possibility in mind, I went out and bought two six-packs of blank tapes. Then, in addition to my regulars, I began to record a couple of other shows every day. I taped Rocky III, Magnum Force, a James Bond movie, an HBO comedy special with Eddie Murphy, and an MTV concert featuring Mick Jagger. Where did I get time to watch all these tapes? I didn't. Taping at this point was more satisfying than watching. Reason and common sense were abandoned. Getting things on tape had become an obsession, and I was taping all the time.

Topic sentence ──────▸ In the fourth stage, videoholism creeps into   5

Fourth stage in process

other parts of the addict's life, influencing behavior in strange ways. Secrecy becomes commonplace. One day, my mother came into my room and saw my bookcase filled with tapes--rather than with the paperbacks that used to be there. "Robert," she

Continuation of analogy

exclaimed, "isn't this getting a bit out of hand?" I assured her it was just a hobby, but I started hiding my tapes, putting them in a suitcase stored in my closet. I also taped at night, slipping downstairs to turn on the VCR after my parents had gone to bed and getting down first thing in the morning to turn off the VCR and remove the cassette before my parents noticed. Also, denial is not unusual during this stage of VCR addiction. At the dinner table, when my younger sister commented, "Robert tapes all the time," I laughingly told everyone-- including myself--that the taping was no big deal. I was getting bored with it and was going to stop any day, I assured my family. Obsessive behavior also characterizes the fourth stage of videoholism. Each week, I pulled out the TV magazine from the Sunday paper and went through it carefully, circling in red all the shows I wanted to tape. Another sign of addiction was my compulsive organization of all the tapes I had stockpiled. Working more diligently than I ever had for any term paper, I typed up labels and attached them to each cassette. I also created an elaborate list that showed my tapes broken down into categories such as Westerns, horror movies, and comedies.

Topic sentence ──────▸ In the final stage of an addiction, the individ-   6
ual either succumbs completely to the addiction or

Continuation of analogy

is able to break away from the habit. I broke my addiction, and I broke it cold turkey. This total withdrawal occurred when I went off to college. There was no point in taking my VCR to school because TVs were not allowed in the freshman dorms. Even though there were many things to

Final stage in process

occupy my time during the school week, cold sweats overcame me whenever I thought about everything on TV I was not taping. I even considered calling home and asking members of my family to tape things for me, but I knew they would think I was crazy. At the beginning of the semester, I also had to resist the overwhelming desire to travel the three hours home every weekend so I could get my fix. But after a while, the urgent need to tape subsided. Now, months later, as I write this, I feel detached and sober.

Conclusion

I have no illusions, though. I know that once a   7 videoholic, always a videoholic. Soon I will return home for the holidays, which, as everyone knows, can be a time for excess eating--and taping. But I

Final references to analogy

will cope with the pressure. I will take each day one at a time. I will ask my little sister to hide my blank tapes. And if I feel myself succumbing to the temptations of taping, I will pick up the telephone and dial the videoholics' hotline: 1-800-VCR-TAPE. I will win the battle.

COMMENTARY

Purpose, thesis, and tone.   Robert's essay is an example of *informational process analysis*; his purpose is to describe — rather than teach — the process of becoming a "videoholic." The title, with its coined term *videoholic*, tips us off that the essay is going to be entertaining. And the introductory paragraph clearly establishes the essay's playful, mock-serious tone. The tone established, Robert briefly defines the term *videoholic* as a "compulsive videotaper" and then moves to the essay's *thesis*: "Barely aware of what is happening, a person can turn into a compulsive videotaper. The descent from innocent hobby to full-blown addiction takes place in several stages."

Throughout the essay, Robert sustains the introduction's humor by mocking his own motivations and poking fun at his quirks: "Selfless guy that I am, I volunteered to move my VCR" (paragraph 4), and "Working more diligently than I ever had for any term paper, I typed up labels" (5). Robert probably uses a bit of *dramatic license* when reporting some of his obsessive behavior, and we, as readers, understand that he's exaggerating for comic effect. Most likely he didn't break out in a cold sweat at the thought of the TV shows he was unable to tape, and he probably didn't hide his tapes in a suitcase. Nevertheless, this tinkering with the truth is legitimate because it allows Robert to create material that fits the essay's lightly satiric tone.

Organization and topic sentences.   To meet the requirements of the assignment, Robert needed to provide a *step-by-step* explanation of a process. And because he invented the term *videoholism*, Robert also needed to invent the stages in the progression of his addiction. During his prewriting, Robert discovered five stages in his videoholism: Presented *chronologically*, these stages provide the organizing focus for his paper. Specifically, each supporting paragraph is devoted to one stage, with the *topic sentence* for each paragraph indicating the stage's distinctive characteristics.

Transitions.   Although Robert's essay is playful, it is nonetheless a process analysis and so must have an easy-to-follow structure. Keeping this in mind, Robert wisely includes *transitions* to signal what happened at each stage of his videoholism: "*Once* I had these additional tapes, I was free to record" (paragraph 3); "*Then,* in addition to my regulars, I began to record" (4); "*One day,* my mother came into my room" (5); and "*But after a while,* the urgent need to tape subsided" (6). In addition to such transitions, crisp questions are also used to move from idea to idea within a paragraph: "How did I resolve this dilemma? Very easily. I . . . bought several more cassettes" (3), and "Where did I get time to watch all these tapes? I didn't" (4).

Other patterns of development.   Even though Robert's essay is a process analysis, it contains elements of other patterns of development. For example, his paper is unified by an *analogy* — a sustained *comparison* between Robert's video addiction and the obviously more serious addiction to alcohol. Handled incorrectly, the analogy could have been offensive, but Robert makes the comparison work to his advantage. The analogy is stated specifically in several spots: "In these early days, my VCR was the equivalent of light social drinking" (2); "I was now using the VCR on a regular basis — the equivalent of several stiff drinks a day" (3). Another place where Robert touches wittily on the analogy occurs in the middle of the fourth paragraph: "I went out and bought two six-packs of blank tapes." To illustrate his progression toward videoholism, Robert depicts the *effects* of his addiction. Finally, he generates numerous lively details or *examples* to illustrate the different stages in his addiction.

Two unnecessary sentences.   Perhaps you noticed that Robert runs into a minor problem at the end of the fourth paragraph. Starting with the sentence "Reason and common sense were abandoned," he begins to ramble and repeat himself. The paragraph's last two sentences fail to add anything substantial. Take a moment to read paragraph 4 aloud, omitting the last two sentences. Note how much sharper the new conclusion is: "Where did I get time to watch all these tapes? I didn't. Taping at this point was more satisfying than watching." This new ending says all that needs to be said.

Revising the first draft.   When it was time to revise, Robert — in spite of his apprehension — showed his paper to his roommate and asked him to read it out loud. Robert knew this strategy would provide a more objective point of view on his work. His roommate, at first an unwilling recruit, nonetheless laughed as he read the essay aloud. That was just the response Robert wanted. But when his roommate got to the conclusion, Robert heard that the closing paragraph was flat and anticlimactic. Here is Robert's original conclusion.

Original Version of the Conclusion

I have no illusions, though, that I am over my videoholism. Soon I will be returning home for the holidays, which can be a time for excess taping. All I can do is ask my little sister to hide my blank tapes. After that, I will hope for the best.

Robert and his roommate brainstormed ways to make the conclusion livelier and more in spirit with the rest of the essay. They decided that the best approach would be to continue the playful, mock-serious tone that characterized earlier parts of the essay. Robert thus made three major changes in the conclusion. First, he tightened the first sentence of the paragraph ("I have no illusions, though, that I am over my videoholism"), making it crisper and more dramatic: "I have no illusions, though." Second, he added a few sentences to sustain the light, self-deprecating tone he had used earlier: "I know that once a videoholic, always a videoholic"; "But I will cope with the pressure"; "I will win the battle." Third, and perhaps most important, he returned to the alcoholism analogy: "I will take each day one at a time. . . . And if I feel myself succumbing to the temptations of taping, I will pick up the telephone and dial the videoholics' hotline. . . ."

These weren't the only changes Robert made while reworking his paper, but they give you some sense of how sensitive he was to the effect he wanted to achieve. Certainly, the recasting of the conclusion was critical to the overall success of this amusing essay.

Process analysis is at the heart of each of the following selections. In "How to Live to Be 200," Stephen Leacock gives some light-hearted instructions for those who believe exercise is the key to immortality. Sue Hubbell's "The Beekeeper," part narration and part description, centers on the surprising technique that beekeepers use to develop resistance to bee venom. Jessica Mitford's "The American Way of Death" looks at a process most of us will never perform but will, instead, have done *to* us. "How to Say Nothing in 500 Words," by Paul Roberts, shows students a way to write essays that will make their professors want to leave teaching. Last, Diane Cole's "Don't Just Stand There" offers guidance for responding effectively to offensive remarks, especially when they're cloaked in the guise of humor.

Stephen Leacock

Stephen Leacock (1869–1944) was born in Great Britain but spent most of his life in Canada. Educated at the University of Toronto, Leacock became a professor of economics at McGill University. In later life, he wrote humorous essays that brought him great popularity. Leacock's work is collected in such books as *Literary Lapses* (1910) and *Winnowed Wisdom* (1926). The following essay is from *Literary Lapses*.

How to Live to Be 200

Are you tired of being urged to exercise by talk show hosts and sleek TV celebrities? Are you annoyed by friends who brag about how often they work out or how many miles they run? Do you enjoy a good fast-food meal packed with preservatives, salt, and calories? If so, you have an ally in Stephen Leacock, who many years ago chided the Health Maniacs of his day. Health fanaticism, you see, is not new; there were health nuts even in the early 1900s. But, as Leacock points out, they didn't live long enough to enjoy the current health craze.

1   Twenty years ago I knew a man called Jiggins, who had the Health Habit.

2   He used to take a cold plunge every morning. He said it opened his pores. After it he took a hot sponge. He said it closed the pores. He got so that he could open and shut his pores at will.

3   Jiggins used to stand and breathe at an open window for half an hour before dressing. He said it expanded his lungs. He might, of course, have had it done in a shoe-store with a boot-stretcher, but after all it cost him nothing this way, and what is half an hour?

4   After he had got his undershirt on, Jiggins used to hitch himself up like a dog in harness and do Sandow exercises. He did them forwards, backwards, and hind-side up.

He could have got a job as a dog anywhere. He spent all his   5
time at this kind of thing. In his spare time at the office, he used
to lie on his stomach on the floor and see if he could lift himself
up with his knuckles. If he could, then he tried some other way
until he found one that he couldn't do. Then he would spend the
rest of his lunch hour on his stomach, perfectly happy.

In the evenings in his room he used to lift iron bars, cannon-   6
balls, heave dumb-bells, and haul himself up to the ceiling with
his teeth. You could hear the thumps half a mile.

He liked it.   7

He spent half the night slinging himself around his room. He   8
said it made his brain clear. When he got his brain perfectly clear,
he went to bed and slept. As soon as he woke, he began clearing it
again.

Jiggins is dead. He was, of course, a pioneer, but the fact that   9
he dumb-belled himself to death at an early age does not prevent a
whole generation of young men from following in his path.

They are ridden by the Health Mania.   10

They make themselves a nuisance.   11

They get up at impossible hours. They go out in silly little   12
suits and run Marathon heats before breakfast. They chase around
barefoot to get the dew on their feet. They hunt for ozone. They
bother about pepsin. They won't eat meat because it has too
much nitrogen. They won't eat fruit because it hasn't any. They
prefer albumen and starch and nitrogen to huckleberry pie and
doughnuts. They won't drink water out of a tap. They won't eat
sardines out of a can. They won't use oysters out of a pail. They
won't drink milk out of a glass. They are afraid of alcohol in any
shape. Yes, sir, afraid. "Cowards."

And after all their fuss they presently incur some simple   13
old-fashioned illness and die like anybody else.

Now people of this sort have no chance to attain any great   14
age. They are on the wrong track.

Listen. Do you want to live to be really old, to enjoy a grand,   15
green, exuberant, boastful old age and to make yourself a nuisance to your whole neighbourhood with your reminiscences?

Then cut out all this nonsense. Cut it out. Get up in the   16
morning at a sensible hour. The time to get up is when you have
to, not before. If your office opens at eleven, get up at ten-thirty.
Take your chance on ozone. There isn't any such thing anyway.

Or, if there is, you can buy a thermos bottle full for five cents, and put it on a shelf in your cupboard. If your work begins at seven in the morning, get up at ten minutes to, but don't be liar enough to say that you like it. It isn't exhilarating, and you know it.

Also, drop all that cold-bath nonsense. You never did it when   17
you were a boy. Don't be a fool now. If you must take a bath (you don't really need to), take it warm. The pleasure of getting out of a cold bed and creeping into a hot bath beats a cold plunge to death. In any case, stop gassing about your tub and your "shower," as if you were the only man who ever washed.

So much for that point.   18

Next, take the question of germs and bacilli. Don't be scared   19
of them. That's all. That's the whole thing, and if you once get on to that you never need to worry again.

If you see a bacilli, walk right up to it, and look it in the eye.   20
If one flies into your room, strike at it with your hat or with a towel. Hit it as hard as you can between the neck and the thorax. It will soon get sick of that.

But as a matter of fact, a bacilli is perfectly quiet and harm-   21
less if you are not afraid of it. Speak to it. Call out to it to "lie down." It will understand. I had a bacilli once, called Fido, that would come and lie at my feet while I was working. I never knew a more affectionate companion, and when it was run over by an automobile, I buried it in the garden with genuine sorrow.

(I admit this is an exaggeration. I don't really remember its   22
name; it may have been Robert.)

Understand that it is only a fad of modern medicine to say   23
that cholera and typhoid and diphtheria are caused by bacilli and germs; nonsense. Cholera is caused by a frightful pain in the stomach, and diptheria is caused by trying to cure a sore throat.

Now take the question of food.   24

Eat what you want. Eat lots of it. Yes, eat too much of it. Eat   25
till you can just stagger across the room with it and prop it up against a sofa cushion. Eat everything that you like until you can't eat any more. The only test is, can you pay for it? If you can't pay for it, don't eat it. And listen — don't worry as to whether your food contains starch, or albumen, or gluten, or nitrogen. If you are damn fool enough to want these things, go and buy them and eat all you want of them. Go to a laundry and get a bag of starch, and eat your fill of it. Eat it, and take a good long drink of glue

after it, and a spoonful of Portland cement. That will gluten you, good and solid.

If you like nitrogen, go and get a druggist to give you a canful of it at the soda counter, and let you sip it with a straw. Only don't think that you can mix all these things up with your food. There isn't any nitrogen or phosphorus or albumen in ordinary things to eat. In any decent household all that sort of stuff is washed out in the kitchen sink before the food is put on the table.   26

And just one word about fresh air and exercise. Don't bother with either of them. Get your room full of good air, then shut up the windows and keep it. It will keep for years. Anyway, don't keep using your lungs all the time. Let them rest. As for exercise, if you have to take it, take it and put up with it. But as long as you have the price of a hack and can hire other people to play baseball for you and run races and do gymnastics when you sit in the shade and smoke and watch them — great heavens, what more do you want?   27

Questions for Close Reading

1. What is the selection's thesis? Locate the sentence(s) in which Leacock states his main idea. If he doesn't state the thesis explicitly, express it in your own words.
2. What is the "Health Habit"? What does it include?
3. Why does Leacock call people who try to eat right "cowards"?
4. Instead of good health, what goals does the author imply should guide a person's daily behavior?
5. Refer to your dictionary as needed to define the following words used in the selection: *ozone* (paragraph 12), *pepsin* (12), and *cholera* (23).

Questions About the Writer's Craft

1. **The pattern.** What two processes does Leacock explain in this essay? How are the processes related?
2. Leacock uses the *imperative voice* ("Cut it out") from paragraph 15 on. What effect does the imperative have on the essay's tone?
3. Leacock uses exaggeration in his essay's title. Where else does he use exaggeration? Why do you suppose he uses this technique?
4. How would you characterize Leacock's sentence style? Why do you think Leacock frames his sentences in this way?

Questions for Further Thought

1. What kind of person does Leacock reveal himself to be? How seriously do you take his objections to health consciousness? Do you think he goes overboard?
2. Leacock describes a health maniac as an obsessed person. How do people become obsessed? Are obsessions always bad?
3. We're presently in the midst of a health and fitness boom. To what extent has this trend affected our culture in general and your life in particular?
4. Which is more important, to enjoy life's pleasures or to sacrifice some of them to keep physically fit? Are these two goals necessarily incompatible?

Writing Assignments Using Process Analysis as a Pattern of Development

∞ 1. Write a humorous essay showing how to conquer an addiction to some food, activity, or object that's not normally considered addictive. Since your paper will be light in tone, choose a topic that can be discussed in a playful manner. You might find it helpful to look at the student essay on page 351.
2. Imagine you're Jiggins and that Leacock has just "passed on" as a result of his Unhealthy Habit. Write an essay similar to Leacock's, deploring the daily habits of people like Leacock. Describe as specifically as you can how such people live, generating lively details to support your point. Then explain the steps these people should follow if they want to be healthy and live to be two hundred years old.

Writing Assignments Using Other Patterns of Development

3. Write an essay classifying one group's attitudes toward food. You might focus on junk-food addicts, food snobs, health-food fanatics, "chocoholics," finicky eaters, compulsive eaters, or dieters. Use specific facts and examples to convey how these people shop, cook, eat, and talk or think about food. Be sure to center your analysis on a single main point. Your tone may be serious or playful like Leacock's.
4. Leacock presents Jiggins, the health nut, as motivated by a concern for his health. In your experience, do people often have other, perhaps less legitimate motives for going to the gym or running? Write an essay about the "real" reasons people try to keep fit. Illustrate these reasons with specific examples of people you know.

Sue Hubbell

Sue Hubbell keeps bees on her ninety-acre farm in Missouri. Born and raised in Kalamazoo, Michigan, she holds a journalism degree from the University of Southern California and a library science degree from Drexel University in Philadelphia. Hubbell's free-lance writing has appeared in such publications as *Time, Sports Illustrated, Country Journal,* and *Harper's.* Her latest works are entitled *A Country Year: Living the Question* (1986) and *A Book of Bees* (1988). The following selection first appeared as a "Hers" column in the *New York Times* in 1984.

The Beekeeper

One of nature's miracles is the ability of bees to transform the nectar of flowers into honey. In the following essay, Sue Hubbell describes the removal of honey from the hives so it can be processed. Accomplishing this task means confronting thousands of angry bees. So Hubbell and her co-workers follow a series of unusual steps to protect themselves against the inevitable stings that await them. The process described by Hubbell implies something important about humans' tolerance of stressful situations.

For the past week I've been spending my afternoons out in the honey house getting things ready for the harvest. I'm making sure the screens are all tight because once I get started clouds of bees will surround the place and try to get in, lured by the scent of honey. I've been checking the machinery, repairing what isn't running properly, and I've been scrubbing everything down so that the health inspector will be proud. 1

My honey house contains a shiny array of stainless-steel tanks, a power uncapper for slicing honeycomb open, an extractor for spinning the honey out of the comb and a pump to move it — machinery that whirs, whomps, hums and looks very special. My neighbors call it the honey factory, and I'm not above insin- 2 uating slyly that what I'm really running back here in the woods is a still.

The bees have been working since early spring, gathering   3
nectar, first from wild plum, peach, and cherry blossoms, later from blackberries, sweet clover, water willow and other wild-flowers as they bloomed. As they have gathered it, their enzymes have changed the complex plant sugars in the nectar to the simple ones of honey. In the hive young bees have formed into work crews to fan the droplets of nectar with their wings, evaporating its water until it is thick and heavy. Summertime heat has helped them, and now the honey is ripe and finished. The bees have capped over each cell of honeycomb with snowy white wax from their bodies, so the honey is ready for my harvest.

The honey that I take from the bees is the extra that they will   4
not need for the winter; they store it above their hives in wooden boxes called supers. When I take it from them I stand behind the hives with a gasoline-powered machine called a bee blower and blow the bees out of the supers while the strong young men that I hire to help me carry the supers, weighing 60 pounds each, and stack them on pallets in the truck. There may be 30 to 50 supers in every one of my bee yards, and we have about half an hour to get them off the hives and stacked before the bees realize what we are up to and begin getting cross about it.

The time to harvest honey is summer's end, when it is hot.   5
The temper of the bees requires that we wear protective clothing: a full set of coveralls, a zippered bee veil and leather gloves. Even a very strong young man works up a sweat wrapped in a bee suit in the heat, hustling 60-pound supers while being harassed by angry bees. It is a hard job, harder even than haying, but jobs are scarce here and I've always been able to hire help.

This year David, the son of friends of mine, is working for   6
me. He is big and strong and used to labor, but he was nervous about bees. After we had made the job arrangement I set about desensitizing him to bee stings. I put a piece of ice on his arm to numb it and then, holding a bee carefully by its head, I put it on the numbed spot and let it sting him. A bee stinger is barbed and stays in the flesh, pulling loose from the body of the bee as it struggles to free itself. The bulbous poison sac at the top of the

stinger continues to pulsate after the bee has left, pumping the venom and forcing the stinger deeper into the flesh.

That first day I wanted David to have only a partial dose of venom, so after a minute I scraped the stinger out. A few people are seriously sensitive to bee venom; each sting they receive can cause a more severe reaction than the one before — reactions ranging from hives, breathing difficulties, accelerated heart beat and choking to anaphylactic shock and death. I didn't think David would be allergic in that way, but I wanted to make sure. 7

We sat down and had a cup of coffee and I watched him. The spot where the stinger went in grew red and began to swell. That was a normal reaction, and so was the itching that he felt later on. 8

The next day I coaxed a bee into stinging him again, repeating the procedure, but I left the stinger in place for 10 minutes, until the venom sac was empty. Again the spot was red, swollen and itchy but had disappeared in 24 hours. By that time David was ready to catch a bee himself and administer his own sting. He also decided that the ice cube was a bother and gave it up. I told him to keep to one sting a day until he had no redness or swelling and then to increase to two stings. He was ready for them the next day. The greater amount of venom caused redness and swelling for a few days, but soon his body could tolerate it without reaction and he increased the number of stings once again. 9

Today he told me he was up to six stings. His arms look as though they have track marks on them, but the fresh stings are having little effect. I'll keep him at it until he can tolerate 10 a day with no reaction and then I'll not worry about taking him out to the bee yard. 10

I know what will happen to him there. For the first few days his movements will be nervous and quick and he will be stung without mercy. After that he will relax and the bees, in turn, will calm down. 11

The reason I am hiring David this year is that a young man I have used in the past has moved away. We worked well together and he liked bees though even he was stung royally at first. I admired his courage the first day we were out together, for he stood holding a super from which I was blowing bees while his arm was fast turning into a pin cushion from stings. 12

When we carried the stacked supers to the honey house's   13
loading dock, he would scorn the hot bee veil as he wheeled the
supers on the handtruck despite the cross bees flying around the
dock. One time, as I opened the door for him to bring in the load,
I noticed that his face was contorted in what I took to be the
effort of getting the handtruck down the ramp. We quickly
wheeled the load of supers up to the scale, where we weigh
each load. He was going too fast, so that when he stopped at the
scale he fell backward and 350 pounds of supers dropped
on him. Pinned down, he loyally balanced himself on one fist
so that he didn't harm the honey pump against which he had
fallen. The reason for his knotted face and his speed was obvious
for the first time: He was being stung on the forehead by three
bees.

Good boss that I am, I did not choose that moment to go to   14
the cabin and make myself a cup of coffee; I picked the supers off
his chest, scraped off the stingers and helped him to his feet. It
became one of our shared legends of working together. This year
I miss him.

Now it is David, still shy about working for a friend of his   15
parents, still a little nervous about bees. He is 19 and eager to
please. But he is going to be fine. In a month we will have
finished and he will be easy and relaxed, and he and I will have
our own set of shared legends.

Questions for Close Reading

1. What is the selection's thesis? Locate the sentence(s) in which Hubbell states her main idea. If she doesn't state the thesis explicitly, express it in your own words.
2. Why does the author hire David to harvest the honey? What qualities does David have that make him a good choice?
3. What is desensitization? What role does it play in the honey harvesting process?
4. What are the supers, and what role do they play in the harvesting process? How do the bees use them? How do the people use them?
5. Refer to your dictionary as needed to define the following words used in the selection: *enzymes* (paragraph 3), *desensitize* (6), *bulbous* (6), *pulsate* (6), and *anaphylactic* (7).

Questions About the Writer's Craft

1. **The pattern.** How many steps are there in the process of making and gathering honey? Does Hubbell provide sufficient detail for you to understand this process?
2. What technical terms of the honey-making trade does the author take time to define? Where in the essay does she provide her definitions? What technical terms does she leave undefined? Why?
3. Where does Hubbell break out of the chronological sequence and present some additional information? Why do you think she includes this material in the essay? What does it add?
4. What is the author's attitude toward the essay's subject? Is the job of harvesting just another job, just in the day's work, or is it something more? Find places where this attitude is revealed.

Questions for Further Thought

1. Hubbell says that she has little trouble finding helpers because "jobs are scarce around here." Would you have to be desperate for a job to become a beekeeper's assistant? What other satisfactions might this job offer?
2. Is Hubbell a good boss? How would you describe her treatment of her employees?
3. Would you deliberately allow yourself to be stung by bees so you could work on a bee farm? Can you think of other jobs that require desensitization to pain? What are some of them? What kinds of pain are involved?
4. Is becoming "hardened" to physical or mental pain a good thing? A necessary thing? Explain.

Writing Assignments Using Process Analysis as a Pattern of Development

∞ 1. Write an essay about a personal experience that desensitized you to physical pain or to emotional distress. Describe the process of becoming used to the pain and growing able to perform without being physically harmed or unduly upset. Part of the essay should discuss the way the difficulties encountered helped you discover new things about yourself. Before writing the paper, you might want to read Richard Rodriguez's "Workers" (page 431) to see how one writer depicts his response to challenging work.
2. Write an essay describing a process that you know well, but that most people do not. You may have learned the process in school, on a job,

from a relative or friend, or on your own. As Hubbell does, explain the steps clearly enough that a wide audience of people could understand the sequence. Make sure you define any special terms. Possible subjects could be making bread from scratch, moving a piano, carving a decoy, refinishing furniture. The essay should make clear the pleasure derived from mastering the process.

Writing Assignments Using Other Patterns of Development

3. Hubbell clearly finds pleasure and satisfaction in her work. Write an essay exploring the three most important satisfactions you hope for in your future career. Be specific about what you want and why you want it. As part of the paper, explain how you became interested in this kind of work.

4. Hubbell's essay concludes with a "shared legend" — a story of a crisis in which the author and her employee helped each other, survived, and became closer. Write an essay about an experience that became the basis for a shared legend between you and someone else. Explore what it was about the event that made it legendary, showing how your bond with the other person changed or deepened as a result of the experience.

Jessica Mitford

Dubbed "Queen of the Muckrakers" by *Time*, English-born Jessica Mitford (1917–) came to the United States in 1939 at the age of twenty-one. Mitford worked as a bartender and salesperson before becoming an investigator for the Office of Price Administration in Washington. She didn't begin her writing career until the age of thirty-eight. Her books include two autobiographies, *Daughters and Rebels* (1960) and *A Fine Old Conflict* (1976); a critique of the American penal system, *Kind and Usual Punishment* (1974); and a collection of essays, *Poison Penmanship* (1979). The following selection is from the book that earned Mitford a national reputation as an investigative writer, *The American Way of Death* (1963). A scathing attack on the American funeral industry, this book shocked readers and enraged morticians.

The American Way of Death

If you were in charge of the funeral arrangements for a loved one, would you ask to have that person's lips sewed, eyes glued, blood drained, and face painted? If you answered "No," you probably don't know much about the world of mortuary science. In this world, the appearance of death is to be avoided, and the goal is to make people look as if they are asleep. In the following selection, Jessica Mitford parts the "formaldehyde curtain" to reveal our funeral practices. Such practices, she implies, reflect our deep-seated fear of death.

Embalming is indeed a most extraordinary procedure, and one must wonder at the docility of Americans who each year pay hundreds of millions of dollars for its perpetuation, blissfully ignorant of what it is all about, what is done, how it is done. Not one in ten thousand has any idea of what actually takes place.

Books on the subject are extremely hard to come by. They are not to be found in most libraries or bookshops.

In an era when huge television audiences watch surgical 2 operations in the comfort of their living rooms, when, thanks to the animated cartoon, the geography of the digestive system has become familiar territory even to the nursery school set, in a land where the satisfaction of curiosity about almost all matters is a national pastime, the secrecy surrounding embalming can, surely, hardly be attributed to the inherent gruesomeness of the subject. Custom in this regard has within this century suffered a complete reversal. In the early days of American embalming, when it was performed in the home of the deceased, it was almost mandatory for some relative to stay by the embalmer's side and witness the procedure. Today, family members who might wish to be in attendance would certainly be dissuaded by the funeral director. All others, except apprentices, are excluded by law from the preparation room.

A close look at what does actually take place may explain in 3 large measure the undertakes's intractable reticence concerning a procedure that has become his major *raison d'être*. Is it possible he fears that public information about embalming might lead patrons to wonder if they really want this service? If the funeral men are loath to discuss the subject outside the trade, the reader may, understandably, be equally loath to go on reading at this point. For those who have the stomach for it, let us part the formaldehyde curtain. . . .

The body is first laid out in the undertaker's morgue — or 4 rather, Mr. Jones is reposing in the preparation room — to be readied to bid the world farewell.

The preparation room in any of the better funeral establish- 5 ments has the tiled and sterile look of a surgery, and indeed the embalmer-restorative artist who does his chores there is beginning to adopt the term "dermasurgeon" (appropriately corrupted by some mortician-writers as "demisurgeon") to describe his calling. His equipment, consisting of scalpels, scissors, augers, forceps, clamps, needles, pumps, tubes, bowls and basins, is crudely imitative of the surgeon's, as is his technique, acquired in a nine- or twelve-month post-high-school course in an embalming school. He is supplied by an advanced chemical industry with a bewildering array of fluids, sprays, pastes, oils, powders, creams, to fix or soften tissue, shrink or distend it as needed, dry it here, restore the moisture there. There are cosmetics, waxes and paints to fill and cover features, even plaster of Paris to replace entire limbs. There are ingenious aids to prop and stabilize the cadaver: a Vari-Pose Head Rest, the Edwards Arm and Hand Positioner, the Repose Block (to support the shoulders during the embalming), and the Throop Foot Positioner, which resembles an old-fashioned stocks.

Mr. John H. Eckles, president of the Eckles College of Mortuary Science, thus describes the first part of the embalming procedure: "In the hands of a skilled practitioner, this work may be done in a comparatively short time and without mutilating the body other than by slight incision—so slight that it scarcely would cause serious inconvenience if made upon a living person. It is necessary to remove the blood, and doing this not only helps in the disinfecting, but removes the principal cause of disfigurements due to discoloration."   6

Another textbook discusses the all-important time element: "The earlier this is done, the better, for every hour that elapses between death and embalming will add to the problems and complications encountered. . . ." Just how soon should one get going on the embalming? The author tells us, "On the basis of such scanty information made available to this profession through its rudimentary and haphazard system of technical research, we must conclude that the best results are to be obtained if the subject is embalmed before life is completely extinct—that is, before cellular death has occurred. In the average case, this would mean within an hour after somatic death." For those who feel that there is something a little rudimentary, not to say haphazard, about this advice, a comforting thought is offered by another writer. Speaking of fears entertained in early days of premature burial, he points out, "One of the effects of embalming by chemical injection, however, has been to dispel fears of live burial." How true; once the blood is removed, chances of live burial are indeed remote.   7

To return to Mr. Jones, the blood is drained out through the veins and replaced by embalming fluid pumped in through the arteries. As noted in *The Principles and Practices of Embalming*, "every operator has a favorite injection and drainage point—a fact which becomes a handicap only if he fails or refuses to forsake   8 his favorites when conditions demand it." Typical favorites are the carotid artery, femoral artery, jugular vein, subclavian vein. There are various choices of embalming fluid. If Flextone is used, it will produce a "mild, flexible rigidity. The skin retains a velvety softness, the tissues are rubbery and pliable. Ideal for women and children." It may be blended with B. and G. Products Company's Lyf-Lyk tint, which is guaranteed to reproduce "nature's own skin texture . . . the velvety appearance of living tissue." Suntone comes in three separate tints: Suntan; Special Cosmetic Tint, a pink shade "especially indicated for young female subjects"; and Regular Cosmetic Tint, moderately pink.

About three to six gallons of a dyed and perfumed solution   9
of formaldehyde, glycerin, borax, phenol, alcohol, and water is soon circulating through Mr. Jones, whose mouth has been sewn together with a "needle directed upward between the upper lip and gum and brought out through the left nostril," with the corners raised slightly "for a more pleasant expression." If he should be bucktoothed, his teeth are cleaned with Bon Ami and coated with colorless nail polish. His eyes, meanwhile, are closed with flesh-tinted eye caps and eye cement.

The next step is to have at Mr. Jones with a thing called a   10
trocar. This is a long, hollow needle attached to a tube. It is jabbed into the abdomen, poked around the entrails and chest cavity, the contents of which are pumped out and replaced with "cavity fluid." This done, and the hole in the abdomen sewn up, Mr. Jones's face is heavily creamed (to protect the skin from burns which may be caused by leakage of the chemicals), and he is covered with a sheet and left unmolested for a while. But not for long—there is more, much more, in store for him. He has been embalmed, but not yet restored, and the best time to start the restorative work is eight to ten hours after embalming, when the tissues have become firm and dry.

The object of all this attention to the corpse, it must be   11
remembered, is to make it presentable for viewing in an attitude of healthy repose. "Our customs require the presentation of our dead in the semblance of normality . . . unmarred by the ravages of illness, disease or mutilation," says Mr. J. Sheridan Mayer in his *Restorative Art*. This is rather a large order since few people die in the full bloom of health, unravaged by illness and unmarked by some disfigurement. The funeral industry is equal to

the challenge: "In some cases the gruesome appearance of a mutilated or disease-ridden subject may be quite discouraging. The task of restoration may seem impossible and shake the confidence of the embalmer. This is the time for intestinal fortitude and determination. Once the formative work is begun and affected tissues are cleaned or removed, all doubts of success vanish. It is surprising and gratifying to discover the results which may be obtained."

The embalmer, having allowed an appropriate interval to   12
elapse, returns to the attack, but now he brings into play the skill and equipment of sculptor and cosmetician. Is a hand missing? Casting one in plaster of Paris is a simple matter. "For replacement purposes, only a cast of the back of the hand is necessary; this is within the ability of the average operator and is quite adequate." If a lip or two, a nose or an ear should be missing, the embalmer has at hand a variety of restorative waxes with which to model replacements. Pores and skin texture are simulated by stippling with a little brush, and over this cosmetics are laid on. Head off? Decapitation cases are rather routinely handled. Ragged edges are trimmed, and head joined to torso with a series of splints, wires and sutures. It is a good idea to have a little something at the neck — a scarf or high collar — when time for viewing comes. Swollen mouth? Cut out tissue as needed from inside the lips. If too much is removed, the surface contour can easily be restored by padding with cotton. Swollen necks and cheeks are reduced by removing tissue through vertical incisions made down each side of the neck. "When the deceased is casketed, the pillow will hide the suture incisions . . . as an extra precaution against leakage, the suture may be painted with liquid sealer."

The opposite condition is more likely to present itself — that   13
of emaciation. His hypodermic syringe now loaded with massage cream, the embalmer seeks out and fills the hollowed and sunken areas by injection. In this procedure the backs of the hands and fingers and the under-chin area should not be neglected.

Positioning the lips is a problem that recurrently challenges   14
the ingenuity of the embalmer. Closed too tightly they tend to give a stern, even disapproving expression. Ideally, embalmers feel, the lips should give the impression of being ever so slightly parted, the upper lip protruding slightly for a more youthful

appearance. This takes some engineering, however, as the lips tend to drift apart. Lip drift can sometimes be remedied by pushing one or two straight pins through the inner margin of the lower lip and then inserting them between the two front upper teeth. If Mr. Jones happens to have no teeth, the pins can just as easily be anchored in his Armstrong Face Former and Denture Replacer. Another method to maintain lip closure is to dislocate the lower jaw, which is then held in its new position by a wire run through holes which have been drilled through the upper and lower jaws at the midline. As the French are fond of saying, *il faut souffrir pour être belle.*[1]

If Mr. Jones has died of jaundice, the embalming fluid will very likely turn him green. Does this deter the embalmer? Not if he has intestinal fortitude. Masking pastes and cosmetics are heavily laid on, burial garments and casket interiors are color-correlated with particular care, and Jones is displayed beneath rose-colored lights. Friends will say, "How *well* he looks." Death by carbon monoxide, on the other hand, can be rather a good thing from the embalmer's viewpoint: "One advantage is the fact that this type of discoloration is an exaggerated form of a natural pink coloration." This is nice because the healthy glow is already present and needs but little attention.   15

The patching and filling completed, Mr. Jones is now shaved, washed and dressed. Cream-based cosmetic, available in pink, flesh, suntan, brunette, and blond, is applied to his hands and face, his hair is shampooed and combed (and, in the case of Mrs. Jones, set), his hands manicured. For the horny-handed son of toil special care must be taken; cream should be applied to remove ingrained grime, and the nails cleaned. "If he were not in the habit of having them manicured in life, trimming and shaping is advised for better appearance — never questioned by kin."   16

Jones is now ready for casketing (this is the present participle of the verb "to casket"). In this operation his right shoulder should be depressed slightly "to turn the body a bit to the right and soften the appearance of lying flat on the back." Positioning the hands is a matter of importance, and special rubber positioning blocks may be used. The hands should be cupped slightly for a   17

[1]One has to suffer to be beautiful.

more lifelike, relaxed appearance. Proper placement of the body requires a delicate sense of balance. It should lie as high as possible in the casket, yet not so high that the lid, when lowered, will hit the nose. On the other hand, we are cautioned, placing the body too low "creates the impression that the body is in a box."

Jones is next wheeled into the appointed slumber room   18
where a few last touches may be added — his favorite pipe placed in his hand or, if he was a great reader, a book propped into position. (In the case of little Master Jones a Teddy bear may be clutched.) Here he will hold open house for a few days, visiting hours 10 A.M. to 9 P.M.

Questions for Close Reading

1. What is the selection's thesis? Locate the sentence(s) in which Mitford states her main idea. If she doesn't state the thesis explicitly, express it in your own words.
2. Why, according to Mitford, do Americans know so little about the embalming process?
3. Mitford quotes from a textbook on embalming practices (paragraph 11). What does the passage reveal about the goals of mortuary science?
4. In what ways is the body made to look even better than it did when alive?
5. Refer to your dictionary as needed to define the following words used in the selection: *docility* (paragraph 1), *intractable* (3), *raison d'être* (3), *augers* (5), *distend* (5), *stippling* (12), and *jaundice* (15).

Questions About the Writer's Craft

1. **The pattern.** What are the main stages of the mortician's craft? What happens in each step? What words and phrases does Mitford use to indicate that she's moving from one step to the next?
2. Why does Mitford refer to the body being embalmed as Mr. Jones? What effect does this naming have on the reader?
3. Mitford interweaves her description of the embalming and restoring process with many quotations from mortuary science texts. Why do you suppose she does this? What do you notice about the writing style of the authors of these texts?
4. What is Mitford's tone in this essay? Do you feel she is being objective in her description of the funeral industry? Explain.

Questions for Further Thought

1. Now that you know more about it, does embalming strike you as a worthwhile process? Do you feel it is appropriate? Explain.
2. One embalmers' manual states that cleaning and trimming the nails of a working man is "never questioned by kin." Are kin prevented from questioning embalmers' techniques? Do you think the funeral industry as a whole takes advantage of grief and disorientation?
3. How does Mitford's description of the preparation-for-burial process illustrate that funerals are for the living, not for the dead? What kinds of final rites would show more respect for the dead — and for the process of dying?
4. Once, Mitford says, relatives prepared a body for burial, and death was thus blended into ordinary life. Today, the process of burial is given over to specialists. Do you think this change has harmed the survivors? Have any other natural aspects of life been turned over to "specialists" and thus been separated from daily life?

Writing Assignments Using Process Analysis as a Pattern of Development

1. Many important events in our lives are marked by celebrations or rituals. Often, the basic outlines of these rituals are established by tradition, but we can always personalize these traditions in one way or another. Select an important event that you will celebrate in the future and explain how you would like to experience the event. Your choice could include any of the following: your marriage, the birth of a child, your graduation, your parent's retirement, or some other notable occurrence.
2. Write a paper telling your survivors how you wish to be treated after death. Explain how they should conduct your funeral, whether they should embalm you, where they should put your remains, and, most important, what you would like said in your eulogy. Be as specific as possible as you outline the steps to be taken.

Writing Assignments Using Other Patterns of Development

3. Write an essay describing a funeral or viewing that you attended. Focus on what seems to you the most important scene. Your thesis should express a dominant feeling about the scene: depression, grief, discomfort, fear, relief, or some other emotion. Alternatively, write an essay describing any other ceremony or ritual you have experienced

(for example, a wedding, bar/bat mitzvah, or graduation). Your dominant feeling may be positive or negative.

4. Write an essay showing that Americans often pretend that death doesn't exist or isn't really happening. Give examples drawn from your own life, your family's life, or public events. You might consider the following: the expressions we use with children ("Grandpa's gone away"; "Kitty is sleeping"); the euphemistic language we have for death ("passed away"; "no longer with us"); our obsession with looking young and keeping fit; our beliefs about "eternal life"; people's resistance to making a will.

Paul Roberts

Paul Roberts (1917–1967) was a scholar of linguistics and a respected teacher whose textbooks helped scores of high school and college students become better writers. Roberts's works include *English Syntax* (1954) and *Patterns of English* (1956). The following selection is from his best-known book, *Understanding English* (1958).

How to Say Nothing in 500 Words

Student essays are written on the bus, in the cafeteria, during television shows, and after midnight. Not surprisingly, many are uninspired last-ditch attempts to fulfill an assignment. Paul Roberts, who spent many bleary-eyed hours reading such papers, has great fun presenting a typical freshman essay for analysis. He then provides students with lively and helpful advice on ways to write essays that are worth something.

Nothing About Something

It's Friday afternoon, and you have almost survived another 1 week of classes. You are just looking forward dreamily to the weekend when the English instructor says: "For Monday you will turn in a five-hundred word composition on college football."

Well, that puts a good big hole in the weekend. You don't 2 have any strong views on college football one way or the other. You get rather excited during the season and go to all the home games and find it rather more fun than not. On the other hand, the class has been reading Robert Hutchins in the anthology and perhaps Shaw's "Eighty-Yard Run," and from the class discussion you have got the idea that the instructor thinks college football is for the birds. You are no fool, you. You can figure out what side to take.

After dinner you get out the portable typewriter that you got 3 for high school graduation. You might as well get it over with and enjoy Saturday and Sunday. Five hundred words is about two double-spaced pages with normal margins. You put in a sheet of paper, think up a title, and you're off:

Why College Football Should Be Abolished

College football should be abolished because it's bad for the school and also bad for the players. The players are so busy practicing that they don't have any time for their studies.   4

This, you feel, is a mighty good start. The only trouble is that it's only thirty-two words. You still have four hundred and sixty-eight to go, and you've pretty well exhausted the subject. It comes to you that you do your best thinking in the morning, so you put away the typewriter and go to the movies. But the next morning you have to do your washing and some math problems, and in the afternoon you go to the game. The English instructor turns up too, and you wonder if you've taken the right side after all. Saturday night you have a date, and Sunday morning you have to go to church. (You shouldn't let English assignments interfere with your religion.) What with one thing and another, it's ten o'clock Sunday night before you get out the typewriter again. You make a pot of coffee and start to fill out your views on college football. Put a little meat on the bones.   5

Why College Football Should Be Abolished

In my opinion, it seems to me that college football should be abolished. The reason why I think this to be true is because I feel that football is bad for the colleges in nearly every respect. As Robert Hutchins says in his article in our anthology in which he discusses college football, it would be better if the colleges had race horses and had races with one another, because then the horses would not have to attend classes. I firmly agree with Mr. Hutchins on this point, and I am sure that many other students would agree too.   6

One reason why it seems to me that college football is bad is that it has become too commercial. In the olden   7 times when people played football just for the fun of it, maybe college football was all right, but they do not play football just for the fun of it now as they used to in the old days. Nowadays college football is what you might call a big business. Maybe this is not true at all schools, and I don't think it is especially true here at State, but certainly this is the case at most colleges and universities in America nowadays, as Mr. Hutchins points out in his very interesting article. Actually the coaches and alumni go around to the high schools and offer the high school stars large salaries to come to their colleges and play football for them. There was one case where a high school star was offered a convertible if he would play football for a certain college.

Another reason for abolishing college football is   8
that it is bad for the players. They do not have time to get a college education, because they are so busy playing football. A football player has to practice every afternoon from three to six, and then he is so tired that he can't concentrate on his studies. He just feels like dropping off to sleep after dinner, and then the next day he goes to his classes without having studied and maybe he fails the test.

(Good ripe stuff so far, but you're still a hundred and fifty-one words from home. One more push.)

Also I think college football is bad for the colleges   9
and the universities because not very many students get to participate in it. Out of a college of ten thousand students only seventy-five or a hundred play football, if that many. Football is what you might call a spectator sport. That means that most people go to watch it but do not play it themselves.

(Four hundred and fifteen. Well, you still have the conclusion, and when you retype it, you can make the margins a little wider.)

These are the reasons why I agree with Mr. Hut-   10
chins that college football should be abolished in American colleges and universities.

On Monday you turn it in, moderately hopeful, and on   11
Friday it comes back marked "weak in content" and sporting a
big "D."

This essay is exaggerated a little, not much. The English   12
instructor will recognize it as reasonably typical of what an assignment on college football will bring in. He knows that nearly
half of the class will contrive in five hundred words to say that
college football is too commercial and bad for the players. Most
of the other half will inform him that college football builds
character and prepares one for life and brings prestige to the
school. As he reads paper after paper all saying the same thing in
almost the same words, all bloodless, five hundred words dripping out of nothing, he wonders how he allowed himself to get
trapped into teaching English when he might have had a happy
and interesting life as an electrician or a confidence man.

Well, you may ask, what can you do about it? The subject is   13
one on which you have few convictions and little information.
Can you be expected to make a dull subject interesting? As a
matter of fact, this is precisely what you are expected to do. This is
the writer's essential task. All subjects, except sex, are dull until
somebody makes them interesting. The writer's job is to find the
argument, the approach, the angle, the wording that will take the
reader with him. This is seldom easy, and it is particularly hard in
subjects that have been much discussed: College Football, Fraternities, Popular Music, Is Chivalry Dead?, and the like. You will
feel that there is nothing you can do with such subjects except
repeat the old bromides. But there are some things you can do
which will make your papers, if not throbbingly alive, at least less
insufferably tedious than they might otherwise be.

Avoid the Obvious Content

Say the assignment is college football. Say that you've de-   14
cided to be against it. Begin by putting down the arguments that
come to your mind: it is too commercial, it takes the students'
minds off their studies, it is hard on the players, it makes the
university a kind of circus instead of an intellectual center, for
most schools it is financially ruinous. Can you think of any more
arguments just off hand? All right. Now when you write your
paper, *make sure that you don't use any of the material on this list*. If
these are the points that leap to your mind, they will leap to

everyone else's too, and whether you get a "C" or a "D" may depend on whether the instructor reads your paper early when he is fresh and tolerant or late, when the sentence "In my opinion, college football has become too commercial," inexorably repeated, has brought him to the brink of lunacy.

Be against college football for some reason or reasons of   15
your own. If they are keen and perceptive ones, that's splendid. But even if they are trivial or foolish or indefensible, you are still ahead so long as they are not everybody else's reasons too. Be against it because the colleges don't spend enough money on it to make it worth while, because it is bad for the characters of the spectators, because the players are forced to attend classes, because the football stars hog all the beautiful women, because it competes with baseball and is therefore un-American and possibly Communist inspired. There are lots of more or less unused reasons for being against college football.

Sometimes it is a good idea to sum up and dispose of the trite   16
and conventional points before going on to your own. This has the advantage of indicating to the reader that you are going to be neither trite nor conventional. Something like this:

> We are often told that college football should be   17
> abolished because it has become too commercial or because it is bad for the players. These arguments are no doubt very cogent, but they don't really go to the heart of the matter.

Then you go to the heart of the matter.

Take the Less Usual Side

One rather simple way of getting interest into your paper is   18
to take the side of the argument that most of the citizens will want to avoid. If the assignment is an essay on dogs, you can, if you choose, explain that dogs are faithful and lovable companions, intelligent, useful as guardians of the house and protectors of children, indispensable in police work—in short, when all is said and done, man's best friends. Or you can suggest that those big brown eyes conceal, more often than not, a vacuity of mind and an inconstancy of purpose; that the dogs you have known most intimately have been mangy, ill-tempered brutes, incapable

of instruction; and that only your nobility of mind and fear of arrest prevent you from kicking the flea-ridden animals when you pass them on the street.

Naturally, personal convictions will sometimes dictate your 19 approach. If the assigned subject is "Is Methodism Rewarding to the Individual?" and you are a pious Methodist, you have really no choice. But few assigned subjects, if any, will fall in this category. Most of them will lie in broad areas of discussion with much to be said on both sides. They are intellectual exercises and it is legitimate to argue now one way and now another, as debaters do in similar circumstances. Always take the side that looks to you hardest, least defensible. It will almost always turn out to be easier to write interestingly on that side.

This general advice applies where you have a choice of sub- 20 jects. If you are to choose among "The Value of Fraternities" and "My Favorite High School Teacher" and "What I Think About Beetles," by all means plump for the beetles. By the time the instructor gets to your paper, he will be up to his ears in tedious tales about the French teacher at Bloombury High and assertions about how fraternities build character and prepare one for life. Your views on beetles, whatever they are, are bound to be a refreshing change.

Don't worry too much about figuring out what the instruc- 21 tor thinks about the subject so that you can cuddle up with him. Chances are his views are no stronger than yours. If he does have convictions and you oppose them, his problem is to keep from grading you higher than you deserve in order to show he is not biased. This doesn't mean that you should always cantankerously dissent from what the instructor says; that gets tiresome too. And if the subject assigned is "My Pet Peeve," do not begin, "My pet peeve is the English instructor who assigns papers on 'my pet peeve.'" This was still funny during the War of 1812, but it has sort of lost its edge since then. It is in general good manners to avoid personalities.

Slip out of Abstraction

If you will study the essay on college football . . . you will 22 perceive that one reason for its appalling dullness is that it never gets down to particulars. It is just a series of not very glittering generalities: "football is bad for the colleges," "it has become too commercial," "football is a big business," "it is bad for the players," and so on. Such round phrases thudding against the reader's brain are unlikely to convince him, though they may well render him unconscious.

If you want the reader to believe that college football is bad   23
for the players, you have to do more than say so. You have to display the evil. Take your roommate, Alfred Simkins, the second-string center. Picture poor old Alfy coming home from football practice every evening, bruised and aching, agonizingly tired, scarcely able to shovel the mashed potatoes into his mouth. Let us see him staggering up to the room, getting out his econ textbook, peering desperately at it with his good eye, falling asleep and failing the test in the morning. Let us share his unbearable tension as Saturday draws near. Will he fail, be demoted, lose his monthly allowance, be forced to return to the coal mines? And if he succeeds, what will be his reward? Perhaps a slight ripple of applause when the third-string center replaces him, a moment of elation in the locker room if the team wins, of despair if it loses. What will he look back on when he graduates from college? Toil and torn ligaments. And what will be his future? He is not good enough for pro football, and he is too obscure and weak in econ to succeed in stocks and bonds. College football is tearing the heart from Alfy Simkins and, when it finishes with him, will callously toss aside the shattered hulk.

This is no doubt a weak enough argument for the abolition   24
of college football, but it is a sight better than saying, in three or four variations, that college football (in your opinion) is bad for the players.

Look at the work of any professional writer and notice how   25
constantly he is moving from the generality, the abstract statement, to the concrete example, the facts and figures, the illustration. If he is writing on juvenile delinquency, he does not just tell you that juveniles are (it seems to him) delinquent and that (in his opinion) something should be done about it. He shows you juveniles being delinquent, tearing up movie theatres in Buffalo, stabbing high school principals in Dallas, smoking marijuana in Palo Alto. And more than likely he is moving toward some specific remedy, not just a general wringing of the hands.

It is no doubt possible to be *too* concrete, too illustrative or   26 anecdotal, but few inexperienced writers err this way. For most the soundest advice is to be seeking always for the picture, to be always turning general remarks into seeable examples. Don't say, "Sororities teach girls the social graces." Say "Sorority life teaches a girl how to carry on a conversation while pouring tea, without sloshing the tea into the saucer." Don't say, "I like certain kinds of popular music very much." Say, "Whenever I hear Gerber Spinklittle play 'Mississippi Man' on the trombone, my socks creep up my ankles."

Get Rid of Obvious Padding

The student toiling away at his weekly English theme is too often tormented by a figure: five hundred words. How, he asks himself, is he to achieve this staggering total? Obviously by never using one word when he can somehow work in ten.   27

He is therefore seldom content with a plain statement like "Fast driving is dangerous." This has only four words in it. He takes thought, and the sentence becomes: 28

> In my opinion, fast driving is dangerous.

Better, but he can do better still:

> In my opinion, fast driving would seem to be rather dangerous.

If he is really adept, it may come out:

> In my humble opinion, though I do not claim to be an expert on this complicated subject, fast driving, in most circumstances, would seem to be rather dangerous in many respects, or at least so it would seem to me.

Thus four words have been turned into forty, and not an iota of content has been added.

Now this is a way to go about reaching five hundred words, and if you are content with a "D" grade, it is as good a way as any. But if you aim higher, you must work differently. Instead of stuffing your sentences with straw, you must try steadily to get rid   29 of the padding, to make your sentences lean and tough. If you are really working at it, your first draft will greatly exceed the required total, and then you will work it down, thus:

>It is thought in some quarters that fraternities do not contribute as much as might be expected to campus life.
>Some people think that fraternities contribute little to campus life.

>The average doctor who practices in small towns or in the country must toil night and day to heal the sick.
>Most country doctors work long hours.

>When I was a little girl, I suffered from shyness and embarrassment in the presence of others.
>I was a shy little girl.

>It is absolutely necessary for the person employed as a marine fireman to give the matter of steam pressure his undivided attention at all times.
>The fireman has to keep his eye on the steam gauge.

You may ask how you can arrive at five hundred words at this rate. Simply. You dig up more real content. Instead of taking a couple of obvious points off the surface of the topic and then circling warily around them for six paragraphs, you work in and explore, figure out the details. You illustrate. You say that fast driving is dangerous, and then you prove it. How long does it take to stop a car at forty and at eighty? How far can you see at night? What happens when a tire blows? What happens in a head-on collision at fifty miles an hour? Pretty soon your paper will be full of broken glass and blood and headless torsos, and reaching five hundred words will not really be a problem.

Call a Fool a Fool

Some of the padding in freshman themes is to be blamed not on anxiety about the word minimum but on excessive timidity. The student writes, "In my opinion, the principal of my high school acted in ways that I believe every unbiased person would have to call foolish." This isn't exactly what he means. What he means is, "My high school principal was a fool." If he was a fool, call him a fool. Hedging the thing about with "in-my-opinion's" and "it-seems-to-me's" and "as-I-see-it's" and "at-least-from-my-point-of-view's" gains you nothing. Delete these phrases whenever they creep into your paper.

The student's tendency to hedge stems from a modesty that 32 in other circumstances would be commendable. He is, he realizes, young and inexperienced, and he half suspects that he is dopey and fuzzy-minded beyond the average. Probably only too true. But it doesn't help to announce your incompetence six times in every paragraph. Decide what you want to say and say it as vigorously as possible, without apology and in plain words.

Linguistic diffidence can take various forms. One is what we 33 call *euphemism*. This is the tendency to call a spade "a certain garden implement" or women's underwear "unmentionables." It is stronger in some eras than others and in some people than others but it always operates more or less in subjects that are touchy or taboo: death, sex, madness, and so on. Thus we shrink from saying "He died last night" but say instead "passed away," "left us," "joined his Maker," "went to his reward." Or we try to take off the tension with a lighter cliché: "kicked the bucket," "cashed in his chips," "handed in his dinner pail." We have found all sorts of ways to avoid saying *mad*: "mentally ill," "touched," "not quite right upstairs," "feeble-minded," "innocent," "simple," "off his trolley," "not in his right mind." Even such a now plain word as *insane* began as a euphemism with the meaning "not healthy."

Modern science, particularly psychology, contributes many 34 polysyllables in which we can wrap our thoughts and blunt their force. To many writers there is no such thing as a bad schoolboy. Schoolboys are maladjusted or unoriented or misunderstood or in need of guidance or lacking in continued success toward satisfactory integration of the personality as a social unit, but they are never bad. Psychology no doubt makes us better men or women, more sympathetic and tolerant, but it doesn't make writing any easier. Had Shakespeare been confronted with psychology, "To be or not to be" might have come out, "To continue as a social unit or not to do so. That is the personality problem. Whether 'tis a better sign of integration at the conscious level to display a psychic tolerance toward the maladjustments and repressions induced by one's lack of orientation in one's environment or—" But Hamlet would never have finished the soliloquy.

Writing in the modern world, you cannot altogether avoid 35 modern jargon. Nor, in an effort to get away from euphemism, should you salt your paper with four-letter words. But you can do much if you will mount guard against those roundabout phrases, those echoing polysyllables that tend to slip into your writing to rob it of its crispness and force.

Beware of the Pat Expression

Other things being equal, avoid phrases like "other things 36 being equal." Those sentences that come to you whole, or in two or three doughy lumps, are sure to be bad sentences. They are no creation of yours but pieces of common thought floating in the community soup.

Pat expressions are hard, often impossible, to avoid, because 37 they come too easily to be noticed and seem too necessary to be dispensed with. No writer avoids them altogether, but good writers avoid them more often than poor writers.

By "pat expressions" we mean such tags as "to all practical 38 intents and purposes," "the pure and simple truth," "from where I sit," "the time of his life," "to the ends of the earth," "in the twinkling of an eye," "as sure as you're born," "over my dead body," "under cover of darkness," "took the easy way out," "when all is said and done," "told him time and time again," "parted the best of friends," "stand up and be counted," "gave him the best years of her life," "worked her fingers to the bone." Like other clichés, these expressions were once forceful. Now we should use them only when we can't possibly think of anything else.

Some pat expressions stand like a wall between the writer and 39 thought. Such a one is "the American way of life." Many student writers feel that when they have said that something accords with the American way of life or does not they have exhausted the subject. Actually, they have stopped at the highest level of abstraction. The American way of life is the complicated set of bonds between a hundred and eighty million ways. All of us know this when we think about it, but the tag phrase too often keeps us from thinking about it.

So with many another phrase dear to the politician: "this   40 great land of ours," "the man in the street," "our national heritage." These may prove our patriotism or give a clue to our political beliefs, but otherwise they add nothing to the paper except words.

Colorful Words

The writer builds with words, and no builder uses a raw   41 material more slippery and elusive and treacherous. A writer's work is a constant struggle to get the right word in the right place, to find that particular word that will convey his meaning exactly, that will persuade the reader or soothe him or startle or amuse him. He never succeeds altogether — sometimes he feels that he scarcely succeeds at all — but such successes as he has are what make the thing worth doing.

There is no book of rules for this game. One progresses   42 through everlasting experiment on the basis of ever-widening experience. There are few useful generalizations that one can make about words as words, but there are perhaps a few.

Some words are what we call "colorful." By this we mean   43 that they are calculated to produce a picture or induce an emotion. They are dressy instead of plain, specific instead of general, loud instead of soft. Thus, in place of "Her heart beat," we may write "Her heart *pounded, throbbed, fluttered, danced.*" Instead of "He sat in his chair," we may say, "He *lounged, sprawled, coiled.*" Instead of "It was hot," we may say, "It was *blistering, sultry, muggy, suffocating, steamy, wilting.*"

However, it should not be supposed that the fancy word is   44 always better. Often it is as well to write "Her heart beat" or "It was hot" if that is all it did or all it was. Ages differ in how they like their prose. The nineteenth century liked it rich and smoky. The twentieth has usually preferred it lean and cool. The twentieth-century writer, like all writers, is forever seeking the exact word, but he is wary of sounding feverish. He tends to pitch it low, to understate it, to throw it away. He knows that if he gets too colorful, the audience is likely to giggle.

See how this strikes you: "As the rich, golden glow of the   45 sunset died away along the eternal western hills, Angela's limpid blue eyes looked softly and trustingly into Montague's flashing brown ones, and her heart pounded like a drum in time with the joyous song surging in her soul." Some people like that sort of thing, but most modern readers would say, "Good grief," and turn on the television.

Colored Words

Some words we would call not so much colorful as colored —that is, loaded with associations, good or bad. All words — except perhaps structure words — have associations of some sort. We have said that the meaning of a word is the sum of the contexts in which it occurs. When we hear a word, we hear with it an echo of all the situations in which we have heard it before.   46

In some words, these echoes are obvious and discussable. The word *mother,* for example, has, for most people, agreeable associations. When you hear *mother* you probably think of home, safety, love, food, and various other pleasant things. If one writes, "She was like a mother to me," he gets an effect which he would not get in "She was like an aunt to me." The advertiser makes use of the associations of *mother* by working it in when he talks about his product. The politician works it in when he talks about himself.   47

So also with such words as *home, liberty, fireside, contentment, patriot, tenderness, sacrifice, childlike, manly, bluff, limpid.* All of these words are loaded with favorable associations that would be rather hard to indicate in a straightforward definition. There is more than a literal difference between "They sat around the fireside" and "They sat around the stove." They might have been equally warm and happy around the stove, but *fireside* suggests leisure, grace, quiet tradition, congenial company, and *stove* does not.   48

Conversely, some words have bad associations. *Mother* suggests pleasant things, but *mother-in-law* does not. Many mothers-in-law are heroically lovable and some mothers drink gin all day and beat their children insensible, but these facts of life are beside the point. The thing is that *mother* sounds good and *mother-in-law* does not.   49

Or consider the word *intellectual.* This would seem to be a 50
complimentary term, but in point of fact it is not, for it has
picked up associations of impracticality and ineffectuality and
general dopiness. So also with such words as *liberal, reactionary,
Communist, socialist, capitalist, radical, schoolteacher, truck driver,
undertaker, operator, salesman, huckster, speculator.* These convey
meanings on the literal level, but beyond that — sometimes, in
some places — they convey contempt on the part of the speaker.

The question of whether to use loaded words or not depends 51
on what is being written. The scientist, the scholar, try to avoid
them; for the poet, the advertising writer, the public speaker, they
are standard equipment. But every writer should take care that
they do not substitute for thought. If you write, "Anyone who
thinks that is nothing but a Socialist (or Communist or capitalist)," you have said nothing except that you don't like people who
think that, and such remarks are effective only with the most
naïve readers. It is always a bad mistake to think your readers
more naïve than they really are.

Colorless Words

But probably most student writers come to grief not with 52
words that are colorful or those that are colored but with those
that have no color at all. A pet example is *nice*, a word we would
find it hard to dispense with in casual conversation but which is
no longer capable of adding much to a description. Colorless
words are those of such general meaning that in a particular
sentence they mean nothing. Slang adjectives, like *cool* ("That's
real cool") tend to explode all over the language. They are applied to everything, lose their original force, and quickly die.

Beware also of nouns of very general meaning, like *circum-* 53
*stances, cases, instances, aspects, factors, relationships, attitudes,
eventualities,* etc. In most circumstances you will find that those
cases of writing which contain too many instances of words like
these will in this and other aspects have factors leading to unsatis-
factory relationships with the reader resulting in unfavorable attitudes on his part and perhaps other eventualities, like a grade of
"D." Notice also what "etc." means. It means "I'd like to make
this list longer, but I can't think of any more examples."

Questions for Close Reading

1. What is the selection's thesis? Locate the sentence(s) in which Roberts states his main idea. If he doesn't state the thesis explicitly, express it in your own words.
2. According to Roberts, what do students assume they have to do to get a good grade on an English composition?
3. How do "colorful words," "colored words," and "colorless words" differ? Which are preferred in essay writing?
4. What are Roberts's most important pieces of advice for the student writer?
5. Refer to the dictionary as needed to define the following words used in the selection: *bromides* (paragraph 13), *insufferably* (13), *inexorably* (14), *dissent* (21), *abolition* (24), *adept* (28), *euphemism* (33), and *insensible* (49).

Questions About the Writer's Craft

1. **The pattern.** What two processes does Roberts analyze in this essay? Is each process informational, directional, or a combination of the two?
2. Why do you think Roberts uses the second person "you" throughout the essay? How does this choice of point of view affect your response to the essay?
3. What is Roberts's tone in the essay? Find some typical examples of his tone. How does Roberts achieve this tone? Considering the author's intended audience, is this tone a good choice? Explain.
4. Does Roberts "practice what he preaches" about writing? Review the section headings of the essay and find examples of each piece of advice in the essay.

Questions for Further Thought

1. Roberts writes that making "a dull subject interesting . . . is precisely what you are expected to do" in college English. Do you agree that most writing subjects are dull? If so, do you think assignments could be made more interesting? And how could instructors get students to write honestly, instead of writing what they think the instructor wants to read?
2. Is Roberts's suggestion to write about the least obvious topic always appropriate? Would you follow this advice yourself? Explain why or why not.
3. In paragraph 14, Roberts says the difference between a "C" or a "D" may depend on when the teacher grades the paper. Do you think

instructors' grades are usually fair, objective, and appropriate? Or do they often seem arbitrary and subjective?

4. Do you think most students are preoccupied with word-counting and guessing the instructor's opinion on a topic? Are you? Why do some students handle writing assignments this way? What could professors do to encourage students to focus more on the challenge of writing?

Writing Assignments Using Process Analysis as a Pattern of Development

1. Write a humorous essay showing how to avoid doing schoolwork, household chores, or anything else most people tend to put off. You may use the second person as Roberts does. Or you may use the first person and describe your typical method of avoidance.

2. Borrowing some of Roberts's lively techniques, make a routine, predictable process interesting to read about. You might choose an activity such as how to register to vote, apply for a driver's license, sign up for college courses, take care of laundry, play a simple game, study for an exam, or some other familiar process.

Writing Assignments Using Other Patterns of Development

3. Should a composition course be required of all first-year college students? Write an essay arguing the value—or lack of value—of such a course. Follow Roberts's advice for writing a lively composition: avoid obvious padding, choose unusual points, avoid abstractions, go to the heart of the matter, use colorful words.

4. Write a paper detailing your experiences as a student in English classes—from elementary school up to now. Using several examples, describe how successfully or unsuccessfully English has been taught, and recommend any specific reforms or changes you feel are needed.

Diane Cole

Born in Baltimore in 1952, Diane Cole is a former contributing editor of *Psychology Today*. Her articles about psychological and career issues have appeared in numerous publications, including the *Wall Street Journal, Newsweek, Ms.*, and *Mademoiselle*. Cole has also written several books, among them *Hunting the Head Hunters: A Woman's Guide* (1988) and the forthcoming *After Great Pain: Coping With Loss and Change*. The following selection, which first appeared in a special supplement of the *New York Times* in 1989, was underwritten by the Anti-Defamation League of B'nai B'rith as part of its ongoing campaign against prejudice.

Don't Just Stand There

At one time or another, many of us have been offended by a sexist, racial, or ethnic remark—yet have said nothing. Paralyzed by the fear of being thought overly sensitive, thin-skinned, or a poor sport, we may let such insults go unchallenged. Diane Cole provides tips on how to respond calmly and constructively to such bigotry.

It was my office farewell party, and colleagues at the job I 1
was about to leave were wishing me well. My mood was one of
ebullience tinged with regret, and it was in this spirit that I spoke
to the office neighbor to whom I had waved hello every morning
for the past two years. He smiled broadly as he launched into a
long, rambling story, pausing only after he delivered the punch
line. It was a very long pause because, although he laughed, I did
not: This joke was unmistakably anti-Semitic.

I froze. Everyone in the office knew I was Jewish; what could 2
he have possibly meant? Shaken and hurt, not knowing what else
to do, I turned in stunned silence to the next well-wisher. Later,
still angry, I wondered, what else should I—could I—have
done?

Prejudice can make its presence felt in any setting, but hear-   3
ing its nasty voice in this way can be particularly unnerving. We
do not know what to do and often we feel another form of
paralysis as well: We think, "Nothing I say or do will change this
person's attitude, so why bother?"

But left unchecked, racial slurs and offensive ethnic jokes   4
"can poison the atmosphere," says Michael McQuillan, adviser
for racial/ethnic affairs for the Brooklyn borough president's
office. "Hearing these remarks conditions us to accept them; and
if we accept these, we can become accepting of other acts."

Speaking up may not magically change a biased attitude, but   5
it can change a person's behavior by putting a strong message
across. And the more messages there are, the more likely a person
is to change that behavior, says Arnold Kahn, professor of psychology at James Madison University, Harrisonburg, Virginia,
who makes this analogy: "You can't keep people from smoking in
their house, but you can ask them not to smoke in *your* house."

At the same time, "Even if the other party ignores or dis-   6
counts what you say, people always reflect on how others perceive
them. Speaking up always counts," says LeNorman Strong, director of campus life at George Washington University, Washington, D.C.

Finally, learning to respond effectively also helps people feel   7
better about themselves, asserts Cherie Brown, executive director
of the National Coalition Building Institute, a Boston-based
training organization. "We've found that, when people felt they
could at least in this small way make a difference, that made them
more eager to take on other activities on a larger scale," she says.
Although there is no "cookbook approach" to confronting such
remarks — every situation is different, experts stress — these are
some effective strategies.

> *When the "joke" turns on who you are — as a member*   8
> *of an ethnic or religious group, a person of color, a woman, a*
> *gay or lesbian, an elderly person, or someone with a physical*
> *handicap — shocked paralysis is often the first response.*
> *Then, wounded and vulnerable, on some level you want to*
> *strike back.*

Lashing out or responding in kind is seldom the most effec-   9 tive response, however. "That can give you momentary satisfaction, but you also feel as if you've lowered yourself to that other person's level," Mr. McQuillan explains. Such a response may further label you in the speaker's mind as thin-skinned, someone not to be taken seriously. Or it may up the ante, making the speaker, and then you, reach for new insults — or physical blows.

"If you don't laugh at the joke, or fight, or respond in kind   10
to the slur," says Mr. McQuillan, "that will take the person by surprise, and that can give you more control over the situation." Therefore, in situations like the one in which I found myself — a private conversation in which I knew the person making the remark — he suggests voicing your anger calmly but pointedly: "I don't know if you realize what that sounded like to me. If that's what you meant, it really hurt me."

State how *you* feel, rather than making an abstract statement   11
like, "Not everyone who hears that joke might find it funny." Counsels Mr. Strong: "Personalize the sense of 'this is how I feel when you say this.' That makes it very concrete" — and harder to dismiss.

Make sure you heard the words and their intent correctly by   12
repeating or rephrasing the statement: "This is what I heard you say. Is that what you meant?" It's important to give the other person the benefit of the doubt because, in fact, he may *not* have realized that the comment was offensive and, if you had not spoken up, would have had no idea of its impact on you.

For instance, Professor Kahn relates that he used to include   13
in his exams multiple-choice questions that occasionally contained "incorrect funny answers." After one exam, a student came up to him in private and said, "I don't think you intended this, but I found a number of those jokes offensive to me as a woman." She explained why. "What she said made immediate sense to me," he says. "I apologized at the next class, and I never did it again."

But what if the speaker dismisses your objection, saying,   14
"Oh, you're just being sensitive. Can't you take a joke?" In that case, you might say, "I'm not so sure about that, let's talk about that a little more." The key, Mr. Strong says, is to continue the dialogue, hear the other person's concerns, and point out your own. "There are times when you're just going to have to admit

defeat and end it," he adds, "but I have to feel that I did the best I could."

When the offending remark is made in the presence of others — at a staff meeting, for example — it can be even more distressing than an insult made privately. 15

"You have two options," says William Newlin, director of field services for the Community Relations division of the New York City Commission on Human Rights. "You can respond immediately at the meeting, or you can delay your response until afterward in private. But a response has to come." 16

Some remarks or actions may be so outrageous that they cannot go unnoted at the moment, regardless of the speaker or the setting. But in general, psychologists say, shaming a person in public may have the opposite effect of the one you want: The speaker will deny his offense all the more strongly in order to save face. Further, few people enjoy being put on the spot, and if the remark really was not intended to be offensive, publicly embarrassing the person who made it may cause an unnecessary rift or further misunderstanding. Finally, most people just don't react as well or thoughtfully under a public spotlight as they would in private. 17

Keeping that in mind, an excellent alternative is to take the offender aside afterward: "Could we talk for a minute in private?" Then use the strategies suggested above for calmly stating how you feel, giving the speaker the benefit of the doubt, and proceeding from there. 18

At a large meeting or public talk, you might consider passing the speaker a note, says David Wertheimer, executive director of the New York City Gay and Lesbian Anti-Violence Project: You could write, "You may not realize it, but your remarks were offensive because. . . ." 19

"Think of your role as that of an educator," suggests James M. Jones, Ph.D., executive director for public interest at the American Psychological Association. "You have to be controlled." 20

Regardless of the setting or situation, speaking up always raises the risk of rocking the boat. If the person who made the offending remark is your boss, there may be an even bigger risk to consider: How will this affect my job? Several things can help 21 minimize the risk, however. First, know what other resources you may have at work, suggests Caryl Stern, director of the A World of Difference – New York City campaign: Does your personnel office handle discrimination complaints? Are other grievance procedures in place?

You won't necessarily need to use any of these procedures, 22 Ms. Stern stresses. In fact, she advises, "It's usually better to try a one-on-one approach first." But simply knowing a formal system exists can make you feel secure enough to set up that meeting.

You can also raise the issue with other colleagues who heard 23 the remark: Did they feel the same way you did? The more support you have, the less alone you will feel. Your point will also carry more validity and be more difficult to shrug off. Finally, give your boss credit — and the benefit of the doubt: "I know you've worked hard for the company's affirmative action programs, so I'm sure you didn't realize what those remarks sounded like to me as well as the others at the meeting last week. . . ."

If, even after this discussion, the problem persists, go back 24 for another meeting, Ms. Stern advises. And if that, too, fails, you'll know what other options are available to you.

> *It's a spirited dinner party, and everyone's having a* 25
> *good time, until one guest starts reciting a racist joke. Every-*
> *one at the table is white, including you. The others are still*
> *laughing, as you wonder what to say or do.*

No one likes being seen as a party-pooper, but before decid- 26 ing that you'd prefer not to take on this role, you might remember that the person who told the offensive joke has already ruined your good time.

If it's a group that you feel comfortable in — a family gather- 27 ing, for instance — you will feel freer to speak up. Still, shaming the person by shouting "You're wrong!" or "That's not funny!" probably won't get your point across as effectively as other strategies. "If you interrupt people to condemn them, it just makes it harder," says Cherie Brown. She suggests trying instead to get at the resentments that lie beneath the joke by asking open-ended questions: "Grandpa, I know you always treat everyone with such respect. Why do people in our family talk that way about black people?" The key, Ms. Brown says, "is to listen to them first, so they will be more likely to listen to you."

If you don't know your fellow guests well, before speaking   28
up you could turn discreetly to your neighbors (or excuse yourself to help the host or hostess in the kitchen) to get a reading on how they felt, and whether or not you'll find support for speaking up. The less alone you feel, the more comfortable you'll be speaking up: "I know you probably didn't mean anything by that joke, Jim, but it really offended me. . . ." It's important to say that *you* were offended — not state how the group that is the butt of the joke would feel. "Otherwise," LeNorman Strong says, "you risk coming off as a goody two-shoes."

If you yourself are the host, you can exercise more control;   29
you are, after all, the one who sets the rules and the tone of behavior in your home. Once, when Professor Kahn's party guests began singing offensive, racist songs, for instance, he kicked them all out, saying, "You don't sing songs like that in my house!" And, he adds, "they never did again."

> *At school one day, a friend comes over and says, "Who*   30
> *do you think you are, hanging out with Joe? If you can be*
> *friends with those people, I'm through with you!"*

Peer pressure can weigh heavily on kids. They feel vulnerable   31
and, because they are kids, they aren't as able to control the urge to fight. "But if you learn to handle these situations as kids, you'll be better able to handle them as an adult," William Newlin points out.

Begin by redefining to yourself what a friend is and examin-   32
ing what friendship means, advises Amy Lee, a human relations specialist at Panel of Americans, an intergroup-relations training and educational organization. If that person from a different group fits your requirement for a friend, ask, "Why shouldn't I be friends with Joe? We have a lot in common." Try to get more information about whatever stereotypes or resentments lie beneath your friend's statement. Ms. Lee suggests: "What makes you think they're so different from us? Where did you get that information?" She explains: "People are learning these stereotypes from somewhere, and they cannot be blamed for that. So

examine where these ideas came from." Then talk about how your own experience rebuts them.

Kids, like adults, should also be aware of other resources to back them up: Does the school offer special programs for fighting prejudice? How supportive will the principal, the teachers, or other students be? If the school atmosphere is volatile, experts warn, make sure that taking a stand at that moment won't put you in physical danger. If that is the case, it's better to look for other alternatives.   33

These can include programs or organizations that bring kids from different backgrounds together. "When kids work together across race lines, that is how you break down the barriers and see that the stereotypes are not true," says Laurie Meadoff, president of CityKids Foundation, a nonprofit group whose programs attempt to do just that. Such programs can also provide what Cherie Brown calls a "safe place" to express the anger and pain that slurs and other offenses cause, whether the bigotry is directed against you or others.   34

In learning to speak up, everyone will develop a different style and a slightly different message to get across, experts agree. But it would be hard to do better than these two messages suggested by teenagers at CityKids: "Everyone on the face of the earth has the same intestines," said one. Another added, "Cross over the bridge. There's a lot of love on the streets."   35

Questions for Close Reading

1. What is the selection's thesis? Locate the sentence(s) in which Cole states her main idea. If she doesn't state the thesis explicitly, express it in your own words.
2. Why does Cole believe it is better to speak up against prejudice rather than to keep silent or ignore it?
3. Although Cole acknowledges that there is no "cookbook approach" for dealing with offensive comments, she nevertheless presents some general steps that can be followed. What are these general steps? The author also describes more specific steps that can be taken in particular situations. What are the situations and the steps to be taken?
4. According to Cole's sources, what types of comments and responses are *not* useful in dealing with prejudicial jokes and remarks?
5. Refer to your dictionary as needed to define the following words used in the selection: *ebullience* (paragraph 1), *anti-Semitic* (1), *slurs* (4),

discounts (6), *lashing* (9), *ante* (9), *abstract* (11), *personalize* (11), *rift* (17), *grievance* (21), and *volatile* (33).

Questions About the Writer's Craft

1. **The pattern.** Does Cole's process analysis have a primarily informative or persuasive purpose? How do you know? Where does the author suggest her purpose? How does her use of the second person "you" reinforce that purpose?
2. **Other patterns.** What examples does Cole provide to illustrate the process she's explaining? Why do you think she provides so many examples?
3. Cole uses quotations extensively in the essay. Why do you suppose she quotes so many people? What effect do you think Cole hopes the quotations will have on her readers?
4. What purpose do the essay's three italicized sections serve? Why might Cole have chosen italics for these sections? Which one of the three sections seems to address a different audience than the other two? Taking into account why this essay was written and where it was published (see the preview), do you think Cole is justified in shifting her essay's focus in this way? Why or why not? Is the shift effective? Explain.

Questions for Further Thought

1. Have you ever been a victim of or heard someone tell a joke based on a racial, sexist, ethnic, or other kind of stereotype? If so, how did you react? Would your reaction have been any different if you had read Cole's essay? Why or why not?
2. What reactions do you think you might encounter if you *did* speak out against insulting jokes and comments? Would these reactions affect your behavior? How?
3. With how much success have you attempted to change other people's objectionable attitudes, comments, and behaviors? Have you found people to be open to change or not? What do you consider the most effective approach for inducing people to change?
4. In paragraphs 30–31, Cole states that children, influenced by peer pressure, often find it difficult to be friends with anyone who is considered different. How influenced by peer pressure were you as a child, especially in your choice of friends? To what extent does the opinion of others still weigh upon your choice of friends?

Writing Assignments Using Process Analysis as a Pattern of Development

1. Cole describes a process for handling offensive *comments*, but there are many times when we wonder whether to protest someone's objectionable *behavior*. Write an essay explaining a process for dealing with one such behavior. You might describe a process for confronting a friend who forgets to repay loans, a teacher who grades unfairly, or a boss who treats employees rudely. Like Cole, tell readers what they should do if a step in the process doesn't yield the hoped-for results.

2. In paragraph 27, Cole describes a family gathering during which a grandchild confronts a grandfather as one adult to another. However, dealing with an older relative in such a forthright manner can be difficult, especially when a grown-up child isn't perceived as a mature individual by "regular" adults. Consider how hard or easy it has been for you (or another person) to get adult-type treatment from parents and other older relatives. Then write an essay describing the process by which a grown child can confront such relatives and request that they change their treatment of the "child" to reflect the person's status as an adult. Use examples from your own family and from friends' families when explaining how to deal — and not deal — with such relatives.

Writing Assignments Using Other Patterns of Development

3. Cole writes about one type of behavior that most of us find obnoxious — people making offensive remarks. But, as we all know, there are many types of obnoxious or annoying people. Focusing on a specific setting (a library, a highway, a store, a classroom) write a light-spirited essay in which you categorize the kinds of obnoxious people you typically encounter there. Be sure to provide vivid descriptions of the people and the behavior that makes them obnoxious.

∞ 4. When confronted by offensive language and behavior, people should — Cole argues — take a stand. Write an essay constructing your personal definition of *assertiveness*. Illustrate your definition by providing specific examples of what assertiveness is and what it isn't. Before planning your paper, you might want to read Barbara Ehrenreich's "What I've Learned From Men" (page 261), another essay that recommends taking a stand and speaking out.

Additional Writing Topics
PROCESS ANALYSIS

General Assignments

Develop one of the following topics through process analysis. Explain the process one step at a time, organizing the steps chronologically. If there's no agreed-upon sequence, design your own series of steps. Use transitions to ease the audience through the steps in the process. You may use any tone you wish, from serious to light.

Directional: How to Do Something

1. How to improve a course you have taken
2. How to drive defensively
3. How to get away with _____
4. How to succeed at a job interview
5. How to relax
6. How to show appreciation to others
7. How to get through school despite personal problems
8. How to be a responsible pet owner
9. How to conduct a garage or yard sale
10. How to look fashionable on a limited budget
11. How to protect a home from burglars
12. How to meet more people
13. How to improve the place where you work
14. How to gain or lose weight
15. How to complain effectively

Informational: How Something Happens

1. How a student becomes burned out
2. How a library's card or computerized catalog organizes books
3. How a dead thing decays (or some other natural process)
4. How the college registration process works
5. How *homo sapiens* chooses a mate
6. How a VCR (or some other machine) works
7. How a bad habit develops
8. How people fall into debt

Assignments with a Specific Purpose and Audience

1. An author of books for elementary school children, you want to show children how to do something—take care of a pet, get along with siblings, keep a room clean. Explain the process in terms a child would understand yet not find condescending.

2. As a driver's education instructor in a high school, you decide to prepare a handout dealing with one of the following: making a three-point turn, parallel parking, handling a skid, or any other driving maneuver. Explain the process one step at a time. Remember, your audience consists of teens who are just learning how to drive.

3. Write an article for *Consumer Reports* on how to shop for a certain product. Give specific steps explaining how to save money, buy a quality product, and the like.

4. Write a process analysis showing how to save a life by CPR, rescue breathing, the Heimlich maneuver, or some other method. Your audience will be average, everyday people who are taking a first-aid class.

5. Your closest friend plans to move into his or her own apartment but doesn't know the first thing about how to choose one. Explain the process of selecting an apartment—where to look, what to investigate, what questions to ask before signing a lease.

6. You write an "advice to the lovelorn" column for the campus newspaper. A correspondent writes saying that he or she wants to break up with a steady boyfriend/girlfriend but doesn't know how to do it without hurting the person. Give the writer guidance on how to end a meaningful relationship with a minimal amount of pain.

8

COMPARISON-CONTRAST

WHAT IS COMPARISON-CONTRAST?

We frequently try to make sense of the world by finding similarities and differences in our experiences. Seeing how things are alike (comparing) and seeing how they are different (contrasting) helps us impose meaning on experiences that otherwise might remain fragmented and disconnected. Barely aware of the fact that we're comparing and contrasting, we may think to ourselves, "I woke up in a great mood this morning, but now I feel uneasy and anxious. I wonder why I feel so different." This inner questioning, which often occurs in a flash, is just one example of the way we use comparison and contrast to understand ourselves and our world.

Comparing and contrasting also helps us make choices. We compare and contrast everything — from two brands of soap we might buy to two colleges we might attend. We listen to a favorite radio station, watch a preferred nightly news show, select a particular dessert from a menu — all because we have done some degree of comparing and contrasting. We often weigh these alternatives in an unstudied, casual manner, as when we flip from one radio station to another. But when we have to make important decisions, we tend to think rigorously about how things are alike or different: Should I live in a dorm or rent an apartment? Should I accept the higher-paying job or the lower-paying one that offers more challenges? Such a deliberate approach to comparison-contrast may also provide us with needed insight into complex contemporary issues: Is television's coverage of political campaigns more or less objective than it used to be? What are the merits of the various positions on abortion?

HOW COMPARISON-CONTRAST FITS YOUR PURPOSE AND AUDIENCE

When is it appropriate in writing to use the comparison-contrast method of development? Often an assignment's wording signals clearly that comparison-contrast is called for:

> Compare the way male and female relationships are depicted in *Cosmopolitan, Ms., Playboy,* and *Esquire.* Which publication has the most limited view of men and women? Which has the broadest perspective?

> Many social commentators have observed that both college students and their parents feel that colleges should equip young people with immediately marketable skills. Indicate whether you think this is an accurate assessment by comparing your own beliefs about the purpose of a college degree with those of your parents.

> Football, basketball, and baseball differ in the ways they appeal to fans. Contrast the unique drawing power of each sport and arrive at some conclusions about the nature of each sport's following.

> The issue of prayer in public school continues to receive attention. Take a position on the controversy by contrasting the views of those who believe prayer should be

allowed in public schools with those who believe it should be prohibited.

Other assignments will, in less obvious ways, lend themselves to comparison-contrast. For instance, although the words *compare* and *contrast* don't appear in the following assignments, essay responses to the assignments could be organized according to the comparison-contrast format:

> The emergence of the two-career family is one of the major phenomena of our culture. Discuss the advantages and disadvantages of having both parents work, showing how you feel about such two-career households.

> Some people believe that the 1950s, often called the golden age of television, produced several never-to-be-equaled comedy classics. Do you agree that such shows as *I Love Lucy* and *The Honeymooners* are superior to the situation comedies aired on television today?

> There has been considerable criticism recently of the news coverage by the city's two leading newspapers, the *Herald* and the *Beacon*. Indicate whether you think the criticism is valid by discussing the similarities and differences in the two papers' news coverage.

Note: The last assignment shows that a comparison-contrast essay may cover similarities *and* differences, not just one or the other.

As you have seen, comparison-contrast can be the key strategy for achieving an essay's purpose. But comparison-contrast can also be a supplemental method used to help make a point in an essay organized chiefly around another pattern of development. A serious, informative essay intended for laypeople might *define* clinical depression by contrasting that state of mind with ordinary run-of-the-mill blues. Writing humorously about the exhausting *effects* of trying to get in shape, you might dramatize your plight for readers by contrasting the leisurely way you used to spend your day with your current rigidly compulsive exercise regimen. Or, in an urgent *argumentation-persuasion* essay on the need for stricter controls over drug abuse in the workplace, you might provide readers with background by comparing several companies' approaches to the problem.

SUGGESTIONS FOR USING COMPARISON-CONTRAST IN AN ESSAY

The following suggestions will be helpful whether you use comparison-contrast as a dominant or supportive pattern of development.

1. Be sure your subjects are at least somewhat alike.   Unless you plan to develop an *analogy* (see below), the subjects you choose to compare or contrast should share some obvious characteristics or qualities. It makes sense to compare different parts of the country, two comedians, or several college teachers. But a reasonable paper wouldn't result from, let's say, a comparison of a television game show with a soap opera. Your subjects must belong to the same general group so that your comparison-contrast stays within good logical bounds and doesn't veer off into pointlessness.

2. Stay focused on your purpose.   When writing, remember that comparison-contrast isn't an end in itself. That is, your objective isn't to turn an essay into a mechanical list of "how *A* differs from *B*" or "how *A* is like *B*." Like the other patterns of development discussed in this book, comparison-contrast is a strategy for making a point or meeting a larger purpose.

Consider the assignment on page 407 about the two newspapers. Your purpose here might be simply to *inform*, to present information as objectively as possible: "This is what the *Herald*'s news coverage is like. This is what the *Beacon*'s news coverage is like."

More frequently, though, you'll use comparison-contrast to *evaluate* your subjects' pros and cons, your goal being to reach a conclusion or make a judgment: "Both the *Herald* and the *Beacon* spend too much time reporting local news," or "The *Herald*'s analysis of the recent hostage crisis was more insightful than the *Beacon*'s." Comparison-contrast can also be used to *persuade* readers to take action: "People interested in thorough coverage of international events should read the *Herald* rather than the *Beacon*." Persuasive essays may also propose a change, contrasting what now exists with a more ideal situation: "For the *Beacon* to compete with the *Herald*, it must assign more reporters to international stories."

Yet another purpose you might have in writing a comparison-contrast essay is to *clear up misconceptions* by revealing previously hidden similarities or differences. For example, perhaps your town's two newspapers are thought to be sharply different. However, a comparison-contrast analysis might reveal that—although one paper specializes in sensationalized stories while the other adopts a more muted approach—both resort to biased, emotionally charged analyses of local politics. Or the essay might illustrate that the tabloid's treatment of the local arts scene is surprisingly more comprehensive than that of its competitor.

Comparing and contrasting also make it possible to *draw an analogy* between two seemingly unrelated subjects. An analogy is an imaginative comparison that delves beneath the surface differences of subjects in order to expose their significant and often unsuspected similarities or differences. Your purpose may be to show that singles bars and zoos share a number of striking similarities. Or you may want to illustrate that wolves and humans raise their young in much the same way, but that wolves go about the process in a more civilized manner. The analogical approach can make a complex subject easier to understand—as when the national deficit is compared to a household budget gone awry. Analogies are often dramatic and instructive, challenging you and your audience to consider subjects in a new light. But analogies don't speak for themselves. You must make clear to the reader how the analogy demonstrates your purpose.

3. Formulate a strong thesis. An essay developed primarily through comparison-contrast should be focused by a solid thesis. Besides revealing your attitude, the thesis will often do the following:

- Name the subjects being compared and contrasted.
- Indicate whether the essay focuses on the subjects' similarities, differences, or both.
- State the essay's main point of comparison or contrast.

Not all comparison-contrast essays need thesis statements as structured as those that follow. Even so, these examples can serve as models of clarity. Note that the first thesis statement signals similarities, the second differences, and the last both similarities and differences:

Middle-aged parents are often in a good position to empathize with adolescent children because the emotional upheavals experienced by the two age groups are much the same.

The priorities of most retired people are more conducive to health and happiness than the priorities of most young professionals.

College students in their thirties and forties face many of the same pressures as younger students, but they are better equipped to withstand these pressures.

4. Select the points to be discussed.   Once you have identified the essay's subjects, purpose, and thesis, you need to decide which aspects of the subjects to compare or contrast. College professors, for instance, could be compared and contrasted on the basis of their testing methods, ability to motivate students, confidence in front of a classroom, personalities, level of enthusiasm, and so forth.

Brainstorming, freewriting, and mapping are valuable for gathering possible points to cover. Whichever prewriting technique you use, try to produce more raw material than you'll need, so that you have the luxury of narrowing the material down to the most significant points.

When selecting points to cover, be sure to consider your audience. Ask yourself: "Will my readers be familiar with this item? Will I need it to get my message across? Will my audience find this item interesting or convincing?" What your readers know, what they don't know, and what you can project about their reactions should influence your choices. And, of course, you need to select points that support your thesis. If your essay explains the differences between healthy, sensible diets and dangerous crash diets, it wouldn't be appropriate to talk about aerobic exercise. Similarly, imagine you want to write an essay making the point that, despite their differences, hard rock of the 1960s and punk rock of the 1970s both reflected young people's disillusionment with society. It wouldn't make much sense to contrast the long uncombed hairstyle of the 1960s with the short spikey cuts of the 1970s. But contrasting song lyrics (protest versus nihilistic messages) would help support your thesis and lead to interesting insights.

5. Organize the points to be discussed.   After deciding which points to include, you should use a systematic, logical plan for presenting those ideas. If the points aren't organized, your essay will be little more than a confusing jumble of ideas. There are two common ways to organize an essay developed wholly or in part by comparison-contrast: the one-side-at-a-time method and the point-by-point method. Although both strategies may be used in a paper, one method usually predominates.

In the *one-side-at-a-time method* of organization, you discuss everything relevant about one subject before moving to another subject. For example, responding to the earlier assignment that asked you to analyze the news coverage in two local papers, you might first talk about the *Herald*'s coverage of international, national, and local news; then you would discuss the *Beacon*'s coverage of the same categories. Note that the areas discussed should be the same for both newspapers. It wouldn't be logical to review the *Herald*'s coverage of international, national, and local news and then to detail the *Beacon*'s magazine supplements, modern living section, and comics page. Moreover, the areas compared and contrasted should be presented in the same order.

This is how you would organize the essay using the one-side-at-a-time method:

Everything about *A*	*Herald*'s news coverage:
	• International
	• National
	• Local
Everything about *B*	*Beacon*'s news coverage:
	• International
	• National
	• Local

In the *point-by-point method* of organization, you alternate from one aspect of the first subject to the same aspect of your other subject(s). For example, to use this method when comparing or contrasting the *Herald* and the *Beacon*, you would first discuss the *Herald*'s international coverage, then the *Beacon*'s international coverage; next the *Herald*'s national coverage, then the *Beacon*'s; and finally, the *Herald*'s local coverage, then the *Beacon*'s.

Using the point-by-point method, this is how the essay would be organized:

First aspect of *A* and *B*	*Beacon*: International coverage
	Herald: International coverage
Second aspect of *A* and *B*	*Beacon*: National coverage
	Herald: National coverage
Third aspect of *A* and *B*	*Beacon*: Local coverage
	Herald: Local coverage

Deciding which of these two methods of organization to use is largely a personal choice, though there are several factors to consider. The one-side-at-a-time method tends to convey a more unified feeling because it highlights broad similarities and differences. It is, therefore, an effective approach for subjects that are fairly uncomplicated. This strategy also works well when essays are brief; the reader won't find it difficult to remember what has been said about subject *A* when reading about subject *B*.

Because the point-by-point method permits more extensive coverage of similarities and differences, it is often a wise choice when subjects are complex. This pattern is also useful for lengthy essays since readers would probably find it difficult to remember, let's say, ten pages of information about subject *A* while reading the next ten pages about subject *B*. The point-by-point approach, however, may cause readers to lose sight of the broader picture, so remember to keep them focused on your central point.

6. Supply the reader with clear transitions.   Although a well-organized comparison-contrast format is important, it doesn't guarantee that readers will be able to follow your line of thought easily. *Transitions* — especially those signaling similarities or differences — are needed to show readers where they have been and where they are going. Such cues are essential in all writing, but they're especially crucial in a paper using comparison-contrast. By indicating clearly when subjects are being compared or contrasted, the transitions help weave the discussion into a coherent whole.

The transitions (in boldface) in the following examples could be used to *signal similarities* in an essay discussing the news coverage in the *Herald* and the *Beacon*:

- The *Beacon* **also** allots only a small portion of the front page to global news.
- **In the same way,** the *Herald* tries to include at least three local stories on the first page.
- **Likewise,** the *Beacon* emphasizes the importance of up-to-date reporting of town meetings.
- The *Herald* is **similarly** committed to extensive coverage of high school and college sports.

The transitions (in boldface) in these examples could be used to *signal differences*:

- **By way of contrast,** the *Herald*'s editorial page deals with national matters on the average of three times a week.
- **On the other hand,** the *Beacon* does not share the *Herald*'s enthusiasm for interviews with national figures.
- The *Beacon,* **however,** does not encourage its reporters to tackle national stories the way the *Herald* does.
- **But** the *Herald*'s coverage of the Washington scene is much more comprehensive than its competitor's.

When using comparison-contrast, try not to pay obsessive attention to the mechanics of organizing your essay. Although the paper should have a logical structure, you don't want the essay to deteriorate into a rote listing of how things are alike or different. Nor do you want to become a slave to format, forcing points into an artificial or uncomfortable fit, rather like Cinderella's stepsisters hacking off their toes in order to squeeze into the glass slipper. Remember, comparison-contrast is a means to an end; that end is to open up a subject for exploration and provide new ways of thinking about a subject.

STUDENT ESSAY

The following student essay was written by Carol Siskin in response to this assignment:

> In "That Lean and Hungry Look," Suzanne Britt contrasts two personality types, extolling the one normally considered less praiseworthy. In an essay of your own, contrast two personality types, life-styles, or stages of life, showing that the one most people consider inferior is actually superior.

While reading Carol's paper, try to determine how well it applies the principles of comparison-contrast. The annotations on Carol's paper and the commentary following it will help you look at the essay more closely.

The Virtues of Growing Older
by Carol Siskin

The first of a two-paragraph introduction → Our society worships youth. Advertisements convince us to buy Grecian Formula and Oil of Olay so we can hide the gray in our hair and smooth the lines on our face. Television shows feature attractive young stars with firm bodies, perfect complexions, and thick manes of hair. Middle-aged folks work out in gyms and jog down the street, trying to delay the effects of age.   1

The second introductory paragraph

Thesis

Topic sentence about appearance: First half

→ Wouldn't any person over thirty gladly sign with the devil just to be young again? Isn't aging an experience to be dreaded? Perhaps it is un-American to say so, but I believe the answer is "No." Being young is often pleasant, but being older has distinct advantages.   2

Start of what it's like being young

→ When young, you are apt to be obsessed with your appearance. When my brother Dave and I were teens, we worked feverishly to perfect the   3 bodies we had. Dave lifted weights, took mega-doses of vitamins, and drank a half-dozen milk shakes a day in order to turn his wiry adolescent frame into some muscular ideal. And as a teenager, I dieted constantly. No matter what I weighed, though, I was never satisfied with the way I looked. My legs were too heavy, my shoulders too broad, my waist too big. When Dave and I were young, we begged and pleaded for the "right" clothes. If our parents didn't get them for us, we felt our world would fall apart. How could we go to school wearing loose-fitting blazers when everyone else would be wearing smartly tailored leather jackets? We would be considered freaks. I often wonder how my parents, and parents in general, manage to tolerate their children during the adolescent years. Now, however, Dave and I are beyond such adolescent agonies. My rounded figure seems fine, and I don't deny myself a slice of pecan pie if I feel in the mood. Dave still works out, but he has actually become fond of his tall lanky frame. The two of us enjoy wearing fashionable clothes, but we are no longer slaves to style. And women, I'm embarrassed to admit, even more than men, have always seemed to be at the mercy of fashion. Now my clothes--and my brother's--are attractive yet easy to wear. We no longer feel anxious about what others will think. As long as we feel good about how we look, we are happy.

Being older is preferable to being younger in another way. Obviously, I still have important choices to make about my life, but I have already made many of the critical decisions that confront those just starting out. I chose the man I wanted to marry. I decided to have children. I elected to return to college to complete my education. But when you are young, major decisions await you at every turn. "What college should I attend? What career should I pursue? Should I get married? Should I have children?" These are just a few of the issues facing young people. It's no wonder that, despite their carefree facade, they are often confused, uncertain, and troubled by all the unknowns in their future.

Topic sentence:
Second half

Start of what it's like being older

Topic sentence about life choices: First half

Start of what it's like being older

Topic sentence: Second half

Start of what it's like being younger

4

Topic sentence about self-concept

Start of what it's like being young

Start of what it's like being older

Conclusion

But the greatest benefit of being forty is 5 knowing who I am. The most unsettling aspect of youth is the uncertainty you feel about your values, goals, and dreams. Being young means wondering what is worth working for. Being young means feeling happy with yourself one day and wishing you were never born the next. It means trying on new selves by taking up with different crowds. It means resenting your parents and their way of life one minute and then feeling you will never be as good or as accomplished as they are. By way of contrast, forty is sanity. I have a surer self-identity now. I don't laugh at jokes I don't think are funny. I can make a speech in front of a town meeting or complain in a store because I am no longer terrified that people will laugh at me; I am no longer anxious that everyone must like me. I no longer blame my parents for my every personality quirk or keep a running score of everything they did wrong raising me. Life has taught me that I, not they, am responsible for who I am. We are all human beings--neither saints nor devils.

Most Americans blindly accept the idea that 6 newer is automatically better. But a human life contradicts this premise. There is a great deal of happiness to be found as we grow older. My own parents, now in their sixties, recently told me that they are happier now than they have ever been. They would not want to be my age. Did this surprise me? At first, yes. Then it gladdened me. Their contentment holds out great promise for me as I move into the next--perhaps even better--phase of my life.

COMMENTARY

Purpose and thesis. In her essay, Carol disproves the widespread belief that being young is preferable to being old. The *comparison-contrast* pattern allows her to analyze the drawbacks of one and the merits of the other, thus providing the essay with an *evaluative purpose*. Using the title to indicate her point of view, Carol places the *thesis* at the end of her two-paragraph introduction: "Being young is often pleasant, but being older has distinct advantages." Note that the thesis accomplishes several things. It names the two subjects to be discussed and clarifies Carol's point of view about her subjects. The thesis also implies that the essay will focus on the contrasts between these two periods of life.

Points of support and overall organization.   To support her assertion that older is better, Carol supplies examples from her own life and organizes the examples around three main points: attitudes about appearance, decisions about life choices, and questions of self-concept. Using the *point-by-point method* to organize the overall essay, she explores each of these key ideas in a separate paragraph. Each paragraph is further focused by one or two sentences that serve as a topic sentence.

Sequence of points, organizational cues, and paragraph development.   Let's look more closely at the way Carol presents her three central points in the essay. She obviously considers appearance the least important of a person's worries, life choices more important, and self-concept the most critical. So she uses *emphatic order* to sequence the supporting paragraphs, with the phrase "But the greatest benefit" signaling the special significance of the last issue. Carol is also careful to use *transitions* to help readers follow her line of thinking: "*Now, however,* Dave and I are beyond such adolescent agonies" (3); "*But* when you are young, major decisions await you at every turn" (4); and "*By way of contrast,* forty is sanity" (5).

Although Carol has worked hard to write a well-organized paper—and has on the whole been successful—she doesn't feel compelled to make the paper fit a rigid format. As you've seen, the essay as a whole uses the point-by-point method, but each supporting paragraph uses the *one-side-at-a-time method*—that is, everything about one age group is discussed before there is a shift to the other age group. Notice too that the third and fifth paragraphs start with young people and then move to adults, whereas the fourth paragraph reverses the sequence by starting with older people.

Other patterns of development.   Carol obviously uses the comparison-contrast format to organize her ideas, but other patterns of development also come into play. To illustrate her points, she makes extensive use of *exemplification*, and her discussion also contains elements typical of *causal analysis*. Throughout the essay, for instance, she traces the effect of being a certain age on her brother, herself, and her parents.

A problem with unity.   As you read the third paragraph, you might have noted that Carol's essay runs into a problem. Two sentences in the paragraph disrupt the *unity* of Carol's discussion: "I often wonder how my parents, and parents in general, manage to tolerate their children during the adolescent years," and "women, I'm embarrassed to admit . . . have always seemed to be at the mercy of fashion." These sentences should be deleted because they don't develop the idea that adolescents are overly concerned with appearance.

Conclusion.   Carol's final paragraph brings the essay to a pleasing and interesting close. The conclusion recalls the point made in the introduction: Americans overvalue youth. Carol also uses the conclusion to broaden the scope of her discussion. Rather than continuing to focus on herself, she briefly mentions her parents and the pleasure they take in life. By bringing her parents into the essay, Carol is able to make a gently philosophical observation about the promise that awaits her as she grows older. The implication is that a similarly positive future awaits us, too.

Revising the first draft.   To help guide her revision, Carol asked her husband to read her first draft aloud. As he did, Carol took notes on what she sensed were the paper's strengths and weaknesses. She then jotted down her observations, as well as her husband's, on the draft. Keeping these comments in mind, Carol made a number of changes in her paper. You'll get a good sense of how she proceeded if you compare the original introduction reprinted here with the final version in the full essay.

Original Version of the Introduction

America is a land filled with people who worship youth. We admire dynamic young achievers; our middle-aged citizens work out in gyms; all of us wear tight tops and colorful sneakers--clothes that look fine on the young but ridiculous on aging bodies. Television shows revolve around perfect-looking young stars, while commercials entice us with products that will keep us young.

Wouldn't every older person want to be young again? Isn't aging to be avoided? It may be slightly unpatriotic to say so, but I believe the answer is "No." Being young may be pleasant at times, but I would rather be my forty-year-old self. I no longer have to agonize about my physical appearance, I have already made many of my crucial life decisions, and I am much less confused about who I am.

After hearing her original two-paragraph introduction read aloud, Carol was dissatisfied with what she had written. Although she wasn't quite sure how to proceed, she knew that the paragraphs were flat and that they failed to open the essay on a strong note. She decided to start by whittling down the opening sentence, making it crisper and more powerful: "Our society worships youth." That done, she eliminated two bland statements ("We admire dynamic young achievers," and "all of us wear tight tops and colorful sneakers") and made several vague references more concrete and interesting. For example, "Commercials entice us with products that will keep us young" became "Grecian Formula and Oil of Olay . . . hide the gray in our hair and smooth the lines on our face"; "perfect-looking young stars" became "attractive young stars with firm bodies, perfect complexions, and thick manes of hair." With the addition of these specifics, the first paragraph became more vigorous and interesting.

Carol next made some subtle changes in the two questions that opened the second paragraph of the original introduction. She replaced "Wouldn't every older person want to be young again?" and "Isn't aging to be avoided?" with two more emphatic questions: "Wouldn't any person over thirty gladly sign with the devil just to be young again?" and "Isn't aging an experience to be dreaded?" Carol also made some changes at the end of the original second paragraph. Because the paper is relatively short and the subject matter easy to understand, she decided to omit her somewhat awkward *plan of development* ("I no longer have to agonize about my physical appearance, I have already made many of my crucial life decisions, and I am much less confused about who I am"). This deletion made it possible to end the introduction with a strong statement of the essay's thesis.

Once these revisions were made, Carol was confident that her essay got off to a stronger start. Feeling reassured, she moved ahead and made changes in other sections of her paper. Such work enabled her to prepare a solid piece of writing that offers food for thought.

The selections in this chapter use comparison and contrast to explore a wide range of subjects. Ecologist Rachel Carson shows us two pictures in her "Fable for Tomorrow": one of a beautiful, environmentally healthy village, the other of the same village devastated by the irresponsible use of pesticides. With no pretense of objectivity, Suzanne Britt, in "That Lean and Hungry Look," contrasts fat and thin people and finds the latter an altogether inferior species. Richard Rodriguez's "Workers" is a highly personal account of different work situations. In "Sex, Lies, and Conversation," Deborah Tannen contrasts men's and women's different communication styles and explores the reasons behind those differences. Finally, Barry Lopez begins "My Horse" with thoughts on the relationship between a Native American and his horse, then draws comparisons between that partnership and his own with a battered Dodge van.

Rachel Carson

Once accused of being a fearmonger, biologist Rachel Carson (1907–64) is now recognized as one of the country's first environmentalists. She was the author of three popular books about the marine world: *The Sea Around Us* (1951), *Under the Sea Wind* (1952), and *The Edge of the Sea* (1955). But it was the publication of *Silent Spring* (1962), Carson's alarming study of the use of pesticides and herbicides, that brought her special attention and established her reputation as a passionate advocate for a clean environment. The following selection is taken from *Silent Spring*.

A Fable for Tomorrow

Fairy tales and fables often tell of people suffering under a wicked witch's curse. The evil spell robs life of its beauty and condemns people to a bleak existence until a clever hero or heroine finds a way to remove the curse and bring the story to a happy ending. But ecologist Rachel Carson's fable is different: the curse is one that we have brought upon ourselves and that we alone have the power to remove.

There was once a town in the heart of America where all life   1
seemed to live in harmony with its surroundings. The town lay in the midst of a checkerboard of prosperous farms, with fields of grain and hillsides of orchards where, in spring, white clouds of bloom drifted above the green fields. In autumn, oak and maple and birch set up a blaze of color that flamed and flickered across a backdrop of pines. Then foxes barked in the hills and deer silently crossed the fields, half hidden in the mists of the fall mornings.

Along the roads, laurel, viburnum and alder, great ferns and   2
wildflowers delighted the traveler's eye through much of the year. Even in winter the roadsides were places of beauty, where countless birds came to feed on the berries and on the seed heads of the dried weeds rising above the snow. The countryside was, in fact,

famous for the abundance and variety of its bird life, and when the flood of migrants was pouring through in spring and fall people traveled from great distances to observe them. Others came to fish the streams, which flowed clear and cold out of the hills and contained shady pools where trout lay. So it had been from the days many years ago when the first settlers raised their houses, sank their wells, and built their barns.

Then a strange blight crept over the area and everything   3
began to change. Some evil spell had settled on the community: mysterious maladies swept the flocks of chickens; the cattle and sheep sickened and died. Everywhere was a shadow of death. The farmers spoke of much illness among their families. In the town the doctors had become more and more puzzled by new kinds of sickness appearing among their patients. There had been several sudden and unexplained deaths, not only among adults but even among children, who would be stricken suddenly while at play and die within a few hours.

There was a strange stillness. The birds, for example — where   4
had they gone? Many people spoke of them, puzzled and disturbed. The feeding stations in the backyards were deserted. The few birds seen anywhere were moribund; they trembled violently and could not fly. It was a spring without voices. On the mornings that had once throbbed with the dawn chorus of robins, catbirds, doves, jays, wrens, and scores of other bird voices there was now no sound; only silence lay over the fields and woods and marsh.

On the farms the hens brooded, but no chicks hatched. The   5
farmers complained that they were unable to raise any pigs — the litters were small and the young survived only a few days. The apple trees were coming into bloom but no bees droned among the blossoms, so there was no pollination and there would be no fruit.

The roadsides, once so attractive, were now lined with   6
browned and withered vegetation as though swept by fire. These, too, were silent, deserted by all living things. Even the streams were now lifeless. Anglers no longer visited them, for all the fish had died.

In the gutters under the eaves and between the shingles of   7
the roofs, a white granular powder still showed a few patches;

some weeks before it had fallen like snow upon the roofs and the lawns, the fields and streams.

No witchcraft, no enemy action had silenced the rebirth of 8 new life in this stricken world. The people had done it themselves.

This town does not actually exist, but it might easily have a 9 thousand counterparts in America or elsewhere in the world. I know of no community that has experienced all the misfortunes I describe. Yet every one of these disasters has actually happened somewhere, and many real communities have already suffered a substantial number of them. A grim specter has crept upon us almost unnoticed, and this imagined tragedy may easily become a stark reality we all shall know.

Questions for Close Reading

1. What is the selection's thesis? Locate the sentence(s) in which Carson states her main idea. If she doesn't state the thesis explicitly, express it in your own words.
2. What are some of the delights of Carson's beautiful, healthy countryside?
3. When Carson writes of "a strange blight," an "evil spell" (3), whose point of view is she adopting?
4. What are the effects of the blight?
5. Refer to your dictionary as needed to define the following words used in the selection: *viburnum* (paragraph 2), *alder* (2), *moribund* (4), and *specter* (9).

Questions About the Writer's Craft

1. **The pattern.** To develop her essay, Carson uses the one-side-at-a-time method of comparison-contrast. What does this method enable her to do that the point-by-point approach would not?
2. **Other patterns.** Throughout the essay, Carson appeals to the reader's senses of sight and hearing. Which paragraphs are developed primarily through visual or auditory description? How do the sensory images in these paragraphs reinforce Carson's thesis?
3. Carson's diction (word choice) and sentence rhythm often resemble those of the Bible. For example, we read, "So it had been from the days many years ago" (2), "a strange blight crept over the area" (3), and "Everywhere was a shadow of death" (3). Why do you suppose Carson chose to echo the Bible in this way?

4. How does Carson's approach to her subject change in the last paragraph? What is the effect of this change?

Questions for Further Thought

1. What threat to the environment concerns you the most? Seepage from landfills? Disposal of nuclear wastes? Acid rain? Depletion of the ozone layer? What can the average person do to deal with this threat?

2. Environmentalists are sometimes referred to as "tree huggers." What attitude is suggested by this term? How do you feel about the term? About the attitude?

3. Do you think the concerns of environmentalists can be excessive and counterproductive? Explain.

4. Carson is concerned about the destruction of America's rural environment. Someone raised in a major city, however, may give little thought to flowing brooks, colorful orchards, and bird-songs. Why should someone accustomed to an urban environment care about what happens to forests, farmlands, or lakes?

Writing Assignments Using Comparison-Contrast as a Pattern of Development

1. Carson imagines a fictional town before and after a blight. Consider a place once special to you that has been changed for the worse by some external force. Perhaps the culprit was noise pollution, urban development, a tornado, or the like. Write an essay contrasting the place before and after the change. Reach some conclusion about the future of this formerly treasured place.

2. In her essay, Carson provides descriptive details unique to particular seasons. For example, she writes that "in autumn, oak and maple and birch set up a blaze of color that flamed and flickered across a backdrop of pines" (1). Choosing a place you know well, contrast its sights, sounds, and smells during one season with those you've noticed during another time of year. Use rich sensory details to convey the differences between the two seasons.

Writing Assignments Using Other Patterns of Development

3. Carson cites "white granular powder" (7) as the cause of the blight. Write an essay about a time you noticed a visible environmental problem — say, smog blurring a city skyline, soot coating a window, or medical syringes discarded on the beach. Use vivid narrative details to capture the effect of the experience on you.

∞ 4. Carson graphically shows the effects of herbicides and pesticides on the environment. Focus on some other less global environmental problem: graffiti on a public building; vandalized trees and shrubs; beer cans thrown in a neighborhood park, for example. Discuss the effects of this situation on the physical environment and on people's attitudes and actions. Conclude with suggestions about possible ways to remedy the problem. Gordon Parks's "Flavio's Home" (page 96) will help you appreciate the interaction between the environment and human behavior.

Suzanne Britt

Free-lance writer and textbook author Suzanne Britt studied at Salem College and Washington University. Her work has been published in the *Baltimore Sun, Newsday,* the *Boston Globe*, and the *New York Times*. A regular columnist for *North Carolina Gardens and Homes* and for a newsletter devoted to the works of Charles Dickens, Britt contributes to Duke University's *Books and Religion,* a publication featuring religious and social commentary. Britt's first book, *Skinny People Are Dull and Crunchy Like Carrots* (1982), is an expansion of the following essay, which was first published in *Newsweek*'s "My Turn" column. Her second book, *Show and Tell*, was published in 1982.

That Lean and Hungry Look[1]

When was the last time you saw a popular magazine that didn't advertise on its cover a new diet or exercise program? How many health clubs have sprung up in your town in recent years? Everywhere we look, we're bombarded by anti-fat propaganda. Essayist Suzanne Britt is fed up with it all. Here's her case for the idea that fat people have nothing to lose but skinnies have a lot to gain.

Caesar was right. Thin people need watching. I've been   1
watching them for most of my adult life, and I don't like what I
see. When these narrow fellows spring at me, I quiver to my toes.
Thin people come in all personalities, most of them menacing.
You've got your "together" thin person, your mechanical thin

---

[1]Britt's title is a reference to a line from Shakespeare's *Julius Caesar*. In the play, Caesar says he distrusts Cassius because Cassius has "a lean and hungry look; . . . such men are dangerous." Later in the play, Cassius helps assassinate Caesar, proving Caesar's fears were justified.

person, your condescending thin person, your tsk-tsk thin person, your efficiency-expert thin person. All of them are dangerous.

In the first place, thin people aren't fun. They don't know how to goof off, at least in the best, fat sense of the word. They've always got to be adoing. Give them a coffee break, and they'll jog around the block. Supply them with a quiet evening at home, and they'll fix the screen door and lick S&H green stamps. They say things like "there aren't enough hours in the day." Fat people never say that. Fat people think the day is too damn long already.

Thin people make me tired. They've got speedy little metabolisms that cause them to bustle briskly. They're forever rubbing their bony hands together and eyeing new problems to "tackle." I like to surround myself with sluggish, inert, easygoing fat people, the kind who believe that if you clean it up today, it'll just get dirty again tomorrow.

Some people say the business about the jolly fat person is a myth, that all of us chubbies are neurotic, sick, sad people. I disagree. Fat people may not be chortling all day long, but they're a hell of a lot *nicer* than the wizened and shriveled. Thin people turn surly, mean, and hard at a young age because they never learn the value of a hot-fudge sundae for easing tension. Thin people don't like gooey soft things because they themselves are neither gooey nor soft. They are crunchy and dull, like carrots. They go straight to the heart of the matter while fat people let things stay all blurry and hazy and vague, the way things actually are. Thin people want to face the truth. Fat people know there is no truth. One of my thin friends is always staring at complex, unsolvable problems and saying, "The key thing is. . . ." Fat people never say that. They know there isn't any such thing as the key thing about anything.

Thin people believe in logic. Fat people see all sides. The sides fat people see are rounded blobs, usually gray, always nebulous and truly not worth worrying about. But the thin person persists. "If you consume more calories than you burn," says one of my thin friends, "you will gain weight. It's that simple." Fat people always grin when they hear statements like that. They know better.

Fat people realize that life is illogical and unfair. They know very well that God is not in his heaven and all is not right with the world. If God is up there, fat people could have two doughnuts and a big orange drink anytime they wanted it.

Thin people have a long list of logical things they are always 7 spouting off to me. They hold up one finger at a time as they reel off these things, so I won't lose track. They speak slowly as if to a young child. The list is long and full of holes. It contains tidbits like "get a grip on yourself," "cigarettes kill," "cholesterol clogs," "fit as a fiddle," "ducks in a row," "organize," and "sound fiscal management." Phrases like that.

They think these 2,000-point plans lead to happiness. Fat 8 people know happiness is elusive at best and even if they could get the kind thin people talk about, they wouldn't want it. Wisely, fat people see that such programs are too dull, too hard, too off the mark. They are never better than a whole cheesecake.

Fat people know all about the mystery of life. They are the 9 ones acquainted with the night, with luck, with fate, with playing it by ear. One thin person I know once suggested that we arrange all the parts of a jigsaw puzzle into groups according to size, shape, and color. He figured this would cut the time needed to complete the puzzle by at least 50 percent. I said I wouldn't do it. One, I like to muddle through. Two, what good would it do to finish early? Three, the jigsaw puzzle isn't the important thing. The important thing is the fun of four people (one thin person included) sitting around a card table, working a jigsaw puzzle. My thin friend had no use for my list. Instead of joining us, he went outside and mulched the boxwoods. The three remaining fat people finished the puzzle and made chocolate, double-fudged brownies to celebrate.

The main problem with thin people is they oppress. Their 10 good intentions, bony torsos, tight ships, neat corners, cerebral machinations, and pat solutions loom like dark clouds over the loose, comfortable, spread-out, soft world of the fat. Long after fat people have removed their coats and shoes and put their feet up on the coffee table, thin people are still sitting on the edge of the sofa, looking neat as a pin, discussing rutabagas. Fat people are heavily into fits of laughter, slapping their thighs and whooping it up, while thin people are still politely waiting for the punch line.

Thin people are downers. They like math and morality and 11

reasoned evaluation of the limitations of human beings. They have their skinny little acts together. They expound, prognose, probe, and prick.

Fat people are convivial. They will like you even if you're   12
irregular and have acne. They will come up with a good reason why you never wrote the great American novel. They will cry in your beer with you. They will put your name in the pot. They will let you off the hook. Fat people will gab, giggle, guffaw, gallumph, gyrate, and gossip. They are generous, giving, and gallant. They are gluttonous and goodly and great. What you want when you're down is soft and jiggly, not muscled and stable. Fat people know this. Fat people have plenty of room. Fat people will take you in.

Questions for Close Reading

1. What is the selection's thesis? Locate the sentence(s) in which Britt states her main idea. If she doesn't state the thesis explicitly, express it in your own words.
2. Into what personality types does Britt categorize thin people? What do these personality types have in common?
3. Britt writes that thin people use their free time for such activities as jogging, fixing a screen door, and pasting in green stamps. How are these activities similar?
4. Why does Britt approve of fat people's tendency to "let things stay all blurry and hazy and vague"?
5. Refer to your dictionary as needed to define the following words used in the selection: *wizened* (paragraph 4), *nebulous* (5), *fiscal* (7), *mulch* (9), *machinations* (10), *expound* (11), and *convivial* (12).

Questions About the Writer's Craft

1. **The pattern.** Which comparison-contrast format does Britt use to develop her essay? Why might she have chosen this format?
2. How does Britt's choice of words and sentence structure establish an informal, light-hearted tone?
3. Why is Britt's carrot simile especially apt?
4. Where in the last paragraph does Britt use *alliteration* (the repetition of initial consonant sounds)? What might have been her reason for using this technique?

Questions for Further Thought

1. Britt pokes fun at thin people who "always got to be adoing." Which do you value most—goal-oriented activity or the ability to relax and have a good time? Why?
2. Britt admires fat people's ability to recognize the limits of logic. How might this ability enrich life? How might it create problems?
3. Britt mocks those who are uncompromisingly principled. How might a person's overly scrupulous principles make life difficult for that individual and others?
4. According to Britt, people in need of reassurance prefer a "soft and jiggly" person to a "muscled and stable" one. Which kind of person comforts you more—someone who seems vulnerable or someone who seems more immune to distress? Why?

Writing Assignments Using Comparison-Contrast as a Pattern of Development

1. Write an essay contrasting two people who represent markedly dissimilar types. Perhaps one person is messy, the other neat. Or maybe one is worldly-wise while the other is unsophisticated. Or one might be punctual while the other is always late. Use the one-side-at-a-time or the point-by-point method to highlight the differences between the two people. Adopting a light, waggish tone, argue—as Britt does— that one type is superior to the other.
2. Britt scoffs at thin people who "believe in logic." Take two decisions you made recently—one fairly logical, the other more emotional. Contrast how you went about making the decisions, the outcomes of the decisions, and so on. Reach some conclusion about the value of logic and emotion in your life.

Writing Assignments Using Other Patterns of Development

3. Britt enjoys the pleasures of good food and company. In an essay, recall a gathering where the food and company were especially satisfying. Through sensory details, convey the aroma, taste, and appearance of the food, as well as the social atmosphere.
4. Britt takes issue with the notion that thin is better than plump. What other prejudicial assumptions do you see at work in contemporary society? Select one and write an essay persuading readers that this idea is unfounded. Your tone may be serious or playful like Britt's.

Richard Rodriguez

In *Hunger of Memory* (1981), from which the following selection is taken, Richard Rodriguez describes his experiences growing up in America as a first-generation Mexican-American. Born in 1944 in San Francisco, Rodriguez spoke only Spanish for the first six years of his life. After winning a scholarship to a private high school, Rodriguez attended Stanford, Columbia, and the University of California at Berkeley where he earned a Ph.D. in English literature. Rodriguez now writes for a variety of publications (*The American Scholar* and *Harper's*, to name just two), and serves as an editor at Pacific News Service in San Francisco. His most recent book, *Mexico's Children* (1992), examines the experience of Mexicans living in the United States.

Workers

As a college student, you probably think about what you'll do after graduation. Perhaps you imagine finding work that offers respect and a sense of accomplishment. Richard Rodriguez discovered a very different world during a summer spent as a laborer, a world in which work meant survival and the boss was god. For such workers, there were no alternatives, no exits, no chances for fulfillment.

It was at Stanford, one day near the end of my senior year, 1 that a friend told me about a summer construction job he knew was available. I was quickly alert. Desire uncoiled within me. My friend said that he knew I had been looking for summer employment. He knew I needed some money. Almost apologetically he explained: It was something I probably wouldn't be interested in, but a friend of his, a contractor, needed someone for the summer to do menial jobs. There would be lots of shoveling and raking and sweeping. Nothing too hard. But nothing more interesting either. Still, the pay would be good. Did I want it? Or did I know someone who did?

I did. Yes, I said, surprised to hear myself say it.   2

In the weeks following, friends cautioned that I had no idea   3
how hard physical labor really is. ("You only *think* you know what it is like to shovel for eight hours straight.") Their objections seemed to me challenges. They resolved the issue. I became happy with my plan. I decided, however, not to tell my parents. I wouldn't tell my mother because I could guess her worried reaction. I would tell my father only after the summer was over, when I could announce that, after all, I did know what "real work" is like.

The day I met the contractor (a Princeton graduate, it turned   4
out), he asked me whether I had done any physical labor before. "In high school, during the summer," I lied. And although he seemed to regard me with skepticism, he decided to give me a try. Several days later, expectant, I arrived at my first construction site. I would take off my shirt to the sun. And at last grasp desired sensation. No longer afraid. At last become like a *bracero*. "We need those tree stumps out of here by tomorrow," the contractor said. I started to work.

I labored with excitement that first morning — and all the   5
days after. The work was harder than I could have expected. But it was never as tedious as my friends had warned me it would be. There was too much physical pleasure in the labor. Especially early in the day, I would be most alert to the sensations of movement and straining. Beginning around seven each morning (when the air was still damp but the scent of weeds and dry earth anticipated the heat of the sun), I would feel my body resist the first thrusts of the shovel. My arms, tightened by sleep, would gradually loosen; after only several minutes, sweat would gather in beads on my forehead and then — a short while later — I would feel my chest silky with sweat in the breeze. I would return to my work. A nervous spark of pain would fly up my arm and settle to burn like an ember in the thick of my shoulder. An hour, two passed. Three. My whole body would assume regular movements; my shoveling would be described by identical, even movements. Even later in the day, my enthusiasm for primitive sensation would survive the heat and the dust and the insects pricking my back. I would strain wildly for sensation as the day came to a

close. At three-thirty, quitting time, I would stand upright and slowly let my head fall back, luxuriating in the feeling of tightness relieved.

Some of the men working nearby would watch me and laugh. 6 Two or three of the older men took the trouble to teach me the right way to use a pick, the correct way to shovel. "You're doing it wrong, too fucking hard," one man scolded. Then proceeded to show me — what persons who work with their bodies all their lives quickly learn — the most economical way to use one's body in labor.

"Don't make your back do so much work," he instructed. I 7 stood impatiently listening, half listening, vaguely watching, then noticed his work-thickened fingers clutching the shovel. I was annoyed. I wanted to tell him that I enjoyed shoveling the wrong way. And I didn't want to learn the right way. I wasn't afraid of back pain. I liked the way my body felt sore at the end of the day.

I was about to, but, as it turned out, I didn't say a thing. 8 Rather it was at that moment I realized that I was fooling myself if I expected a few weeks of labor to gain me admission to the world of the laborer. I would not learn in three months what my father had meant by "real work." I was not bound to this job; I could imagine its rapid conclusion. For me the sensations were to be feared. Fatigue took a different toll on their bodies — and minds.

It was, I know, a simple insight. But it was with this realiza- 9 tion that I took my first step that summer toward realizing something even more important about the "worker." In the company of carpenters, electricians, plumbers, and painters at lunch, I would often sit quietly, observant. I was not shy in such company. I felt easy, pleased by the knowledge that I was casually accepted, my presence taken for granted by men (exotics) who worked with their hands. Some days the younger men would talk and talk about sex, and they would howl at women who drove by in cars. Other days the talk at lunchtime was subdued; men gathered in separate groups. It depended on who was around. There were rough, good-natured workers. Others were quiet. The more I remember that summer, the more I realize that there was no single *type* of worker. I am embarrassed to say I had not expected such diversity. I certainly had not expected to meet, for example, a plumber who was an abstract painter in his off hours and admired the work of Mark Rothko. Nor did I expect to meet so many workers with college diplomas. (They were the ones who were not surprised that I intended to enter graduate school in the fall.) I suppose what I really want to say here is painfully obvious, but I must say it nevertheless: The men of that summer were middle-class Americans. They certainly didn't constitute an oppressed society. Carefully completing their work sheets; talking about the fortunes of local football teams; planning Las Vegas vacations; comparing the gas mileage of various makes of campers — they were not *los pobres* my mother had spoken about.

On two occasions, the contractor hired a group of Mexican aliens. They were employed to cut down some trees and haul off debris. In all, there were six men of varying age. The youngest in his late twenties; the oldest (his father?) perhaps sixty years old. They came and they left in a single old truck. Anonymous men. They were never introduced to the other men at the site. Immediately upon their arrival, they would follow the contractor's directions, start working — rarely resting — seemingly driven by a fatalistic sense that work which had to be done was best done as quickly as possible.

I watched them sometimes. Perhaps they watched me. The only time I saw them pay me much notice was one day at lunchtime when I was laughing with the other men. The Mexicans sat apart when they ate, just as they worked by themselves. Quiet. I rarely heard them say much to each other. All I could hear were their voices calling out sharply to one another, giving directions. Otherwise, when they stood briefly resting, they talked among themselves in voices too hard to overhear.

The contractor knew enough Spanish, and the Mexicans — or at least the oldest of them, their spokesman — seemed to know enough English to communicate. But because I was around, the contractor decided one day to make me his translator. (He assumed I could speak Spanish.) I did what I was told. Shyly I went over to tell the Mexicans that the *patrón* wanted them to do something else before they left for the day. As I started to speak, I was afraid with my old fear that I would be unable to pronounce the Spanish words. But it was a simple instruction I had to convey. I could say it in phrases.

The dark sweating faces turned toward me as I spoke. They stopped their work to hear me. Each nodded in response. I stood there. I wanted to say something more. But what could I say in Spanish, even if I could have pronounced the words right? Perhaps I just wanted to engage them in small talk, to be assured of their confidence, our familiarity. I thought for a moment to ask them where in Mexico they were from. Something like that. And maybe I wanted to tell them (a lie, if need be) that my parents were from the same part of Mexico.

I stood there. 14

Their faces watched me. The eyes of the man directly in front 15 of me moved slowly over my shoulder, and I turned to follow his glance toward *el patrón* some distance away. For a moment I felt swept up by that glance into the Mexicans' company. But then I heard one of them returning to work. And then the others went back to work. I left them without saying anything more.

When they had finished, the contractor went over to pay 16 them in cash. (He later told me that he paid them collectively — "for the job," though he wouldn't tell me their wages. He said something quickly about the good rate of exchange "in their own country.") I can still hear the loudly confident voice he used with the Mexicans. It was the sound of the *gringo* I had heard as a very young boy. And I can still hear the quiet, indistinct sounds of the Mexican, the oldest, who replied. At hearing that voice I was sad for the Mexicans. Depressed by their vulnerability. Angry at myself. The adventure of the summer seemed suddenly ludicrous. I would not shorten the distance I felt from *los pobres* with a few weeks of physical labor. I would not become like them. They were different from me.

After that summer, a great deal — and not very much really 17 — changed in my life. The curse of physical shame was broken by the sun; I was no longer ashamed of my body. No longer would I deny myself the pleasing sensations of my maleness. During those years when middle-class black Americans began to assert with pride, "Black is beautiful," I was able to regard my complexion without shame. I am today darker than I ever was as a boy. I have taken up the middle-class sport of long-distance running. Nearly every day now I run ten or fifteen miles, barely clothed, my skin exposed to the California winter rain and wind or the summer sun of late afternoon. The torso, the soccer player's calves and thighs, the arms of the twenty-year-old I never was, I possess now in my thirties. I study the youthful parody shape in the mirror: the stomach lipped tight by muscle; the shoulders rounded by chin-ups; the arms veined strong. This man. A man. I meet him. He laughs to see me, what I have become.

The dandy. I wear double-breasted Italian suits and custom-made English shoes. I resemble no one so much as my father — the man pictured in those honeymoon photos. At that point in life when he abandoned the dandy's posture, I assume it. At the point when my parents would not consider going on vacation, I register at the Hotel Carlyle in New York and the Plaza Athenée in Paris. I am as taken by the symbols of leisure and wealth as they were. For my parents, however, those symbols became taunts, reminders of all they could not achieve in one lifetime. For me those same symbols are reassuring reminders of public success. I tempt vulgarity to be reassured. I am filled with the gaudy delight, the monstrous grace of the nouveau riche. 18

In recent years I have had occasion to lecture in ghetto high schools. There I see students of remarkable style and physical grace. (One can see more dandies in such schools than one ever will find in middle-class high schools.) There is not the look of casual assurance I saw students at Stanford display. Ghetto girls mimic high-fashion models. Their dresses are of bold, forceful color; their figures elegant, long; the stance theatrical. Boys wear shirts that grip at their overdeveloped muscular bodies. (Against a powerless future, they engage images of strength.) Bad nutrition does not yet tell. Great disappointment, fatal to youth, awaits them still. For the moment, movements in school hallways are dancelike, a procession of postures in a sexual masque. Watching them, I feel a kind of envy. I wonder how different my adolescence would have been had I been free. . . . But no, it is my parents I see — their optimism during those years when they were entertained by Italian grand opera. 19

The registration clerk in London wonders if I have just been to Switzerland. And the man who carries my luggage in New York guesses the Caribbean. My complexion becomes a mark of my leisure. Yet no one would regard my complexion the same way if I entered such hotels through the service entrance. That is only to say that my complexion assumes its significance from the context of my life. My skin, in itself, means nothing. I stress the point because I know there are people who would label me "dis- 20 advantaged" because of my color. They make the same mistake I made as a boy, when I thought a disadvantaged life was circumscribed by particular occupations. That summer I worked in the sun may have made me physically indistinguishable from the Mexicans working nearby. (My skin was actually darker because, unlike them, I worked without wearing a shirt. By late August my hands were probably as tough as theirs.) But I was not one of *los pobres*. What made me different from them was an attitude of *mind*, my imagination of myself.

I do not blame my mother for warning me away from the sun   21
when I was young. In a world where her brother had become an old man in his twenties because he was dark, my complexion was something to worry about. "Don't run in the sun," she warns me today. I run. In the end, my father was right — though perhaps he did not know how right or why — to say that I would never know what real work is. I will never know what he felt at his last factory job. If tomorrow I worked at some kind of factory, it would go differently for me. My long education would favor me. I could act as a public person — able to defend my interests, to unionize, to petition, to speak up — to challenge and demand. (I will never know what real work is.) I will never know what the Mexicans knew, gathering their shovels and ladders and saws.

Their silence stays with me now. The wages those Mexicans   22
received for their labor were only a measure of their disadvantaged condition. Their silence is more telling. They lack a public identity. They remain profoundly alien. Persons apart. People lacking a union obviously, people without grounds. They depend upon the relative good will or fairness of their employers each day. For such people, lacking a better alternative, it is not such an unreasonable risk.

Their silence stays with me. I have taken these many words to   23
describe its impact. Only: the quiet. Something uncanny about it. Its compliance. Vulnerability. Pathos. As I heard their truck rumbling away, I shuddered, my face mirrored with sweat. I had finally come face to face with *los pobres*.

Questions for Close Reading

1. What is the selection's thesis? Locate the sentence(s) in which Rodriguez states his main idea. If he doesn't state the thesis explicitly, express it in your own words.

2. What does Rodriguez find appealing about the construction job when his friend first offers it to him?
3. Once on the job, how long does it take Rodriguez to realize he will never be a "laborer"? Why does he feel this way?
4. According to Rodriguez, what makes him different from *los pobres*? Is poverty the only thing that makes them distinctive?
5. Refer to your dictionary as needed to define the following words used in the selection: *menial* (paragraph 1), *skepticism* (4), *luxuriating* (5), *diversity* (9), *ludicrous* (16), *nouveau riche* (18), and *pathos* (23).

Questions About the Writer's Craft

1. **The pattern.** One way Rodriguez develops his essay is by comparing and contrasting himself to the two groups of workers. Which group is he more like? What specifics does Rodriguez provide to show his similarity to this group and his dissimilarity to the other?
2. **Other patterns.** Rodriguez uses narration to develop his comparison-contrast of the two groups of workers. How many narrative segments appear in the essay? Why do you think Rodriguez puts the story about the Mexican workers last?
3. **Other patterns.** Rodriguez uses especially vivid language to describe the sun, his sweat, and the sensation of digging. Locate some examples of these descriptions. Which ones particularly stand out? Why?
4. Why does Rodriguez include some Spanish words in his essay? How is the use of these words related to the essay's overall theme?

Questions for Further Thought

1. Why does Rodriguez decide not to tell his parents about his summer job? What do you think his mother's fears would have been? How would your parents and friends react if you worked in construction (or in some other physically demanding job) after graduating from college?
2. Rodriguez discovers that "there is no single *type* of worker" on the construction job. What kind of preconceptions do you think he had about construction workers? What stereotypes do you, your family, and your friends have about other kinds of workers (teachers, lawyers, secretaries, bosses, and so forth)?
3. What does Rodriguez hope to gain from this job that he could not, presumably, learn at Stanford or in graduate school? Have you ever felt a similar need to learn outside the classroom?
4. How does Rodriguez characterize "real work" at the start of his summer? How would you say his definition of real work changes by

the end of the job? Do you agree with his belief that a college-educated person can never know the meaning of real work?

Writing Assignments Using Comparison-Contrast as a Pattern of Development

1. Write an essay comparing and/or contrasting a part-time or summer job you've had with your (or someone else's) full-time or "real" job. Use examples, description, anecdotes, and illustrations to clarify the points of comparison or contrast.
2. Compare and/or contrast the job you hope to have after graduation with a job you now have or have had in the past. Your analysis should reach conclusions about your interests, skills, and values.

Writing Assignments Using Other Patterns of Development

∞ 3. In an essay, define what you mean by the term *real work*. Support your definition by citing experiences you have had and/or have heard about. Sue Hubbell's "The Beekeeper" (page 363) should prompt some interesting thoughts about work.
4. Phil Donahue once did a show on people who had "terrible jobs." The guests included a garbage man, toll collector, car repossessor, IRS auditor, and diaper-service truck driver. Write an essay explaining what would be terrible work for you. It might be one or more of the jobs held by Donahue guests or some other type of job. Provide abundant reasons why you would never want to do such work and reach some conclusions about your priorities.

Deborah Tannen

The recipient of grants from the National Endowment for the Humanities, the Rockefeller Foundation, and the National Science Foundation, Deborah Tannen (1945–) is a linguistics professor at Georgetown University and has been a Distinguished McGraw Lecturer at Princeton University. She has shared her scholarly research with the general public through appearances on the *Today* show and CNN, through pieces in the *New York Times* and the *Washington Post*, and in popular books, including *That's Not What I Meant: How Conversational Style Makes or Breaks Relationships* (1987) and, most recently, her best-selling *You Just Don't Understand: Women and Men in Conversation* (1990). The following selection, adapted from *You Just Don't Understand*, appeared in the *New York Times* in June 1990.

Sex, Lies, and Conversation

"She says I never talk to her, but I don't know what she wants to talk about!" "When I talk to him, it's like talking to a brick wall!" Men and women blame each other for the communication problems they invariably encounter. But linguist Deborah Tannen explains that neither sex deliberately chooses to sabotage communication. Males and females simply approach communication with divergent, often conflicting skills and expectations.

I was addressing a small gathering in a suburban Virginia   1
living room — a women's group that had invited men to join them. Throughout the evening, one man had been particularly talkative, frequently offering ideas and anecdotes, while his wife sat silently beside him on the couch. Toward the end of the evening, I commented that women frequently complain that their husbands don't talk to them. This man quickly concurred. He gestured toward his wife and said, "She's the talker in our

family." The room burst into laughter; the man looked puzzled and hurt. "It's true," he explained. "When I come home from work I have nothing to say. If she didn't keep the conversation going, we'd spend the whole evening in silence."

This episode crystallizes the irony that although American 2 men tend to talk more than women in public situations, they often talk less at home. And this pattern is wreaking havoc with marriage.

The pattern was observed by political scientist Andrew 3 Hacker in the late '70s. Sociologist Catherine Kohler Riessman reports in her new book *Divorce Talk* that most of the women she interviewed — but only a few of the men — gave lack of communication as the reason for their divorces. Given the current divorce rate of nearly 50 percent, that amounts to millions of cases in the United States every year — a virtual epidemic of failed conversation.

In my own research, complaints from women about their 4 husbands most often focused not on tangible inequities such as having given up the chance for a career to accompany a husband to his, or doing far more than their share of daily life-support work like cleaning, cooking, social arrangements and errands. Instead, they focused on communication: "He doesn't listen to me," "He doesn't talk to me." I found, as Hacker observed years before, that most wives want their husbands to be, first and foremost, conversational partners, but few husbands share this expectation of their wives.

In short, the image that best represents the current crisis is 5 the stereotypical cartoon scene of a man sitting at the breakfast table with a newspaper held up in front of his face, while a woman glares at the back of it, wanting to talk.

Linguistic Battle of the Sexes

How can women and men have such different impressions of 6 communication in marriage? Why the widespread imbalance in their interests and expectations?

In the April [1990] issue of *American Psychologist*, Stanford 7 University's Eleanor Maccoby reports the results of her own and others' research showing that children's development is most influenced by the social structure of peer interactions. Boys and girls tend to play with children of their own gender, and their sex-separate groups have different organizational structures and interactive norms.

I believe these systematic differences in childhood socializa-   8
tion make talk between women and men like cross-cultural communication, heir to all the attraction and pitfalls of that enticing but difficult enterprise. My research on men's and women's conversations uncovered patterns similar to those described for children's groups.

For women, as for girls, intimacy is the fabric of relation-   9
ships, and talk is the thread from which it is woven. Little girls create and maintain friendships by exchanging secrets; similarly, women regard conversation as the cornerstone of friendship. So a woman expects her husband to be a new and improved version of a best friend. What is important is not the individual subjects that are discussed but the sense of closeness, of a life shared, that emerges when people tell their thoughts, feelings, and impressions.

Bonds between boys can be as intense as girls', but they are   10
based less on talking, more on doing things together. Since they don't assume talk is the cement that binds a relationship, men don't know what kind of talk women want, and they don't miss it when it isn't there.

Boys' groups are larger, more inclusive, and more hierarchi-   11
cal, so boys must struggle to avoid the subordinate position in the group. This may play a role in women's complaints that men don't listen to them. Some men really don't like to listen, because being the listener makes them feel one down, like a child listening to adults or an employee to a boss.

But often when women tell men, "You aren't listening," and   12
the men protest, "I am," the men are right. The impression of not listening results from misalignment in the mechanics of conversation. The misalignment begins as soon as a man and a woman take physical positions. This became clear when I studied videotapes made by psychologist Paul Dorval of children and adults talking to their same-sex best friends. I found that at every age, the girls and women faced each other directly, their eyes anchored on each other's faces. At every age, the boys and men sat at angles to each other and looked elsewhere in the room, periodically glancing at each other. They were obviously attuned to each

other, often mirroring each other's movements. But the tendency of men to face away can give women the impression they aren't listening even when they are. A young woman in college was frustrated: Whenever she told her boyfriend she wanted to talk to him, he would lie down on the floor, close his eyes, and put his arm over his face. This signaled to her, "He's taking a nap." But he insisted he was listening extra hard. Normally, he looks around the room, so he is easily distracted. Lying down and covering his eyes helped him concentrate on what she was saying.

Analogous to the physical alignment that women and men take in conversation is their topical alignment. The girls in my study tended to talk at length about one topic, but the boys tended to jump from topic to topic. The second-grade girls exchanged stories about people they knew. The second-grade boys teased, told jokes, noticed things in the room and talked about finding games to play. The sixth-grade girls talked about problems with a mutual friend. The sixth grade boys talked about fifty-five different topics, none of which extended over more than a few turns.   13

Listening to Body Language

Switching topics is another habit that gives women the impression men aren't listening, especially if they switch to a topic about themselves. But the evidence of the tenth-grade boys in my study indicates otherwise. The tenth-grade boys sprawled across their chairs with bodies parallel and eyes straight ahead, rarely looking at each other. They looked as if they were riding in a car, staring out the windshield. But they were talking about their feelings. One boy was upset because a girl had told him he had a drinking problem, and the other was feeling alienated from all his friends.   14

Now, when a girl told a friend about a problem, the friend responded by asking probing questions and expressing agreement and understanding. But the boys dismissed each other's problems. Todd assured Richard that his drinking was "no big problem" because "sometimes you're funny when you're off your butt." And when Todd said he felt left out, Richard responded, "Why should you? You know more people than me."   15

Women perceive such responses as belittling and unsuppor-   16
tive. But the boys seemed satisfied with them. Whereas women
reassure each other by implying, "You shouldn't feel bad because
I've had similar experiences," men do so by implying, "You
shouldn't feel bad because your problems aren't so bad."

There are even simpler reasons for women's impression that   17
men don't listen. Linguist Lynette Hirschman found that women
make more listener-noise, such as "mhm," "uhuh," and "yeah,"
to show "I'm with you." Men, she found, more often give silent
attention. Women who expect a stream of listener noise interpret
silent attention as no attention at all.

Women's conversational habits are as frustrating to men as   18
men's are to women. Men who expect silent attention interpret a
stream of listener noise as overreaction or impatience. Also, when
women talk to each other in a close, comfortable setting, they
often overlap, finish each other's sentences and anticipate what
the other is about to say. This practice, which I call "participatory
listenership," is often perceived by men as interruption, intru-
sion, and lack of attention.

A parallel difference caused a man to complain about his   19
wife, "She just wants to talk about her own point of view. If I
show her another view, she gets mad at me." When most women
talk to each other, they assume a conversationalist's job is to
express agreement and support. But many men see their conversational duty as pointing out the other side of an argument. This
is heard as disloyalty by women, and refusal to offer the requisite
support. It is not that women don't want to see other points of
view, but that they prefer them phrased as suggestions and inqui-
ries rather than as direct challenges.

In his book *Fighting for Life*, Walter Ong points out that   20
men use "agonistic" or warlike, oppositional formats to do almost anything; thus discussion becomes debate and conversation
becomes a competitive sport. In contrast, women see conversation as a ritual means of establishing rapport. If Jane tells a
problem and June says she has a similar one, they walk away
feeling closer to each other. But this attempt at establishing
rapport can backfire when used with men. Men take too literally
women's ritual "troubles talk," just as women mistake men's
ritual challenges for real attack.

The Sounds of Silence

These differences begin to clarify why women and men have   21
such different expectations about communication in marriage.
For women, talk creates intimacy. Marriage is an orgy of closeness: you can tell your feelings and thoughts, and still be loved.
Their greatest fear is being pushed away. But men live in a hierarchical world, where talk maintains independence and status. They
are on guard to protect themselves from being put down and
pushed around.

This explains the paradox of the talkative man who said of his   22
silent wife, "She's the talker." In the public setting of a guest
lecture, he felt challenged to show his intelligence and display his
understanding of the lecture. But at home, where he has nothing
to prove and no one to defend against, he is free to remain silent.
For his wife, being home means she is free from the worry that
something she says might offend someone, or spark disagreement, or appear to be showing off; at home she is free to talk.

The communication problems that endanger marriage can't   23
be fixed by mechanical engineering. They require a new concep-
tual framework about the role of talk in human relationships.
Many of the psychological explanations that have become second
nature may not be helpful, because they tend to blame either
women (for not being assertive enough) or men (for not being in
touch with their feelings). A sociolinguistic approach by which
male-female conversation is seen as cross-cultural communication allows us to understand the problem and forge solutions
without blaming either party.

Once the problem is understood, improvement comes natu-   24
rally, as it did to the young woman and her boyfriend who
seemed to go to sleep when she wanted to talk. Previously, she
had accused him of not listening, and he had refused to change
his behavior, since that would be admitting fault. But then she
learned about and explained to him the differences in women's
and men's habitual ways of aligning themselves in conversation.
The next time she told him she wanted to talk, he began, as usual,
by lying down and covering his eyes. When the familiar negative
reaction bubbled up, she reassured herself that he really was
listening. But then he sat up and looked at her. Thrilled, she asked

why. He said, "You like me to look at you when we talk, so I'll try to do it." Once he saw their differences as cross-cultural rather than right and wrong, he independently altered his behavior.

Women who feel abandoned and deprived when their hus-   25
bands won't listen to or report daily news may be happy to discover their husbands trying to adapt once they understand the place of small talk in women's relationships. But if their husbands don't adapt, the women may still be comforted that for men, this is not a failure of intimacy. Accepting the difference, the wives may look to their friends or family for that kind of talk. And husbands who can't provide it shouldn't feel their wives have made unreasonable demands. Some couples will still decide to divorce, but at least their decisions will be based on realistic expectations.

In these times of resurgent ethnic conflicts, the world desper-   26
ately needs cross-cultural understanding. Like charity, successful cross-cultural communication should begin at home.

Questions for Close Reading

1. What is the selection's thesis? Locate the sentence(s) in which Tannen states her main idea. If she doesn't state the thesis explicitly, express it in your own words.
2. In paragraphs 8, 23, and 26, Tannen refers to "cross-cultural communication" and "cross-cultural understanding." What does she mean by the term *cross-cultural*? Why is this term central to an understanding of the selection?
3. According to Tannen, what aspects of communication are "misaligned" when males and females talk?
4. What evidence does Tannen provide to show that understanding males' and females' differing communication styles can improve the way the sexes relate to each other?
5. Refer to your dictionary as needed to define the following words used in the selection: *irony* (paragraph 2), *epidemic* (3), *inequities* (4), *socialization* (8), *hierarchical* (11), *misalignment* (12), *analogous* (13), *belittling* (16), *requisite* (19), *agonistic* (20), *sociolinguistic* (23), and *resurgent* (26).

Questions About the Writer's Craft

1. **The pattern.** Which comparison-contrast method of organization (one-side-at-a-time or point-by-point) does Tannen use in the selection? Why might she have chosen this method?

2. **Other patterns.** Tannen provides many brief examples to contrast male and female communication behaviors. Where in the selection does she introduce extended examples about two specific couples? Why do you think she returns to each of these examples later in the selection?

3. Look closely at paragraph 6. Besides its brevity, what else is distinctive about the paragraph? What purpose does the paragraph serve?

4. Do you think Tannen is addressing her ideas to an audience of men, of women, or of both sexes? How can you tell? What techniques does she use to establish her credibility with this audience?

Questions for Further Thought

1. From your own experience, do you think Tannen's characterization of male and female communication styles is accurate? Do you know males or females who don't fit her descriptions? How can you account for these people's communication patterns?

2. Think about arguments between the sexes that you have witnessed or participated in. To what extent did gender differences in communication style contribute to the argument? Would familiarity with the concepts that Tannen discusses help minimize or resolve such arguments? Why or why not?

3. Tannen states that "most wives want their husbands to be, first and foremost, conversational partners, but few husbands share this expectation of their wives." Do you agree that men and women have such different emotional needs and expectations? Explain.

4. Think about your childhood experiences playing with other children. Were your playgroups predominantly same-sex? If children were encouraged to play more often in mixed groups, would male-female communication improve later in life? Why or why not?

Writing Assignments Using Comparison-Contrast as a Pattern of Development

1. Tannen analyzes differences in male and female communication behaviors. Pick another area where you perceive significant gender differences. You might, for example, consider the way males and females act at parties, shop for clothes, watch television, or furnish their rooms. Focusing on a single area, write an essay comparing and contrasting what you observe about male and female attitudes and behavior. Your essay may be serious or lighthearted. In either case, reach some conclusions — as Tannen does — about the causes of the differences you perceive.

∞ 2. Tannen points out that males and females often position their bodies differently when communicating. Spend some time on your college campus observing the body language of males and females as they walk, chat with friends, study at the library, congregate in the student center, raise their hands in class, listen to classroom discussion, and the like. See if you can detect any differences in the way that males and females use their bodies. Then write an essay comparing and contrasting the body language of college men and women. Barbara Ehrenreich's "What I've Learned From Men" (page 261) and Peter Farb's "In Other Words" (page 491) will provide additional perspectives on the nonverbal aspects of communication.

Writing Assignments Using Other Patterns of Development

∞ 3. Tannen attributes the rising divorce rate to a failure in communication between the sexes. In "The Faltering Family" (page 479), George Gallup suggests other possible causes for divorce. Write an essay discussing the forces that you see operating to undermine couples, either married or dating. You'll probably want to refer in your essay to Tannen's and Gallup's ideas, but don't feel constrained by what they write. You may decide that a completely different set of causes is at work in breaking couples up.

4. In paragraphs 15–16, Tannen states that males and females react in very different ways when a friend confides a problem. Using Tannen's analysis as a point of departure, get together with others and discuss more fully possible ways to respond in such a situation. After reviewing the material gathered, write an essay explaining the specific steps you think someone should take when a friend wants to talk about a problem. Indicate whether you feel the steps should be modified depending on the sex of the people involved.

Barry Lopez

Although Barry Lopez (1945–) is a native New Yorker, he grew up in California and has spent the last two decades living in rural Oregon. Lopez experienced the lure of Oregon when he studied at the University of Oregon (1969–70), after receiving from Notre Dame a B.A. in 1966 and an M.A. in 1968. From his rustic outpost in Oregon, Lopez, a contributing editor to *Harper's* and *North American Review*, has been inspired to write reflective essays on the bond among humans, animals, and the land. Lopez's books include *Desert Notes: Reflections in the Eye of a Raven* (1976), *Of Wolves and Men* (1979), *Arctic Dreams: Imagination and Desire in a Northern Landscape* (1986), and *Giving Birth to Thunder* (1990). In addition to receiving the American Book Award for *Arctic Dreams*, Lopez has been honored with an award in literature from the American Academy and Institute of Arts and Letters. The following selection first appeared in the *North American Review* in 1975.

My Horse

Native American warriors forged a bond with their horses — not a sentimental bond based on the animals' grace and beauty, but a tough attachment rooted in the warriors' dependence on their animals for mobility and status. Barry Lopez explains that a good deal could be learned about a warrior from his horse. Similarly, we can learn a good deal about Lopez from his "horse" — a battered truck that has a heart in harmony with its owner's.

It is curious that Indian warriors on the northern plains in the nineteenth century, who were almost entirely dependent on the horse for mobility and status, never gave their horses names. If you borrowed a man's horse and went off raiding for other horses, however, or if you lost your mount in battle and then jumped on mine and counted coup on an enemy — well, those horses would have to be shared with the man whose horse you borrowed, and that coup would be mine, not yours. Because even if I gave him no name, he was my horse.

If you were a Crow warrior and I a young Teton Sioux out   2
after a warrior's identity and we came over a small hill somewhere in the Montana prairie and surprised each other, I could tell a lot about you by looking at your horse.

Your horse might have feathers tied in his mane, or in his tail,   3
or a medicine bag tied around his neck. If I knew enough about the Crow, and had looked at you closely, I might make some sense of the decoration, even guess who you were if you were well-known. If you had painted your horse I could tell even more, because we both decorated our horses with signs that meant the same things. Your white handprints high on his flanks would tell me you had killed an enemy in a hand-to-hand fight. Small horizontal lines stacked on your horse's foreleg, or across his nose, would tell me how many times you had counted coup. Horse hoof marks on your horse's rump, or three-sided boxes, would tell me how many times you had stolen horses. If there was a bright red square on your horse's neck I would know you were leading a war party and that there were probably others out there in the coulees behind you.

You might be painted all over as blue as the sky and covered   4
with white dots, with your horse painted the same way. Maybe hailstorms were your power — or if I chased you a hailstorm might come down and hide you. There might be lightning bolts on the horse's legs and flanks, and I would wonder if you had lightning power, or a slow horse. There might be white circles around your horse's eyes to help him see better.

Or you might be like Crazy Horse, with no decoration, no   5
marks on your horse to tell me anything, only a small lightning bolt on your cheek, a piece of turquoise tied behind your ear.

You might have scalps dangling from your rein.   6

I could tell something about you by your horse. All this   7
would come to me in a few seconds. I might decide this was my moment and shout my war cry — *Hoka hey*! Or I might decide you were like the grizzly bear: I would raise my weapon to you in salute and go my way, to see you again when I was older.

I do not own a horse. I am attached to a truck, however, and   8

I have come to think of it in a similar way. It has no name; it never occurred to me to give it a name. It has little decoration; neither of us is partial to decoration. I have a piece of turquoise in the truck because I had heard once that some of the southwestern tribes tied a small piece of turquoise in a horse's hock to keep him from stumbling. I like the idea. I also hang sage in the truck when I go on a long trip. But inside, the truck doesn't look much different from others that look just like it on the outside. I like it that way. Because I like my privacy.

For two years in Wyoming I worked on a ranch wrangling 9 horses. The horse I rode when I had to have a good horse was a quarter horse and his name was Coke High. The name came with him. At first I thought he'd been named for the soft drink. I'd known stranger names given to horses by whites. Years later I wondered if some deviate Wyoming cowboy wise to cocaine had not named him. Now I think he was probably named after a rancher, an historical figure of the region. I never asked the people who owned him for fear of spoiling the spirit of my inquiry.

We were running over a hundred horses on this ranch. They 10 all had names. After a few weeks I knew all the horses and the names too. You had to. No one knew how to talk about the animals or put them in order or tell the wranglers what to do unless they were using the names — Princess, Big Red, Shoshone, Clay.

My truck is named Dodge. The name came with it. I don't 11 know if it was named after the town or the verb or the man who invented it. I like it for a name. Perfectly anonymous, like Rex for a dog, or Old Paint. You can't tell anything with a name like that.

The truck is a van. I call it a truck because it's not a car and 12 because "van" is a suburban sort of consumer word, like "oxford loafer," and I don't like the sound of it. On the outside it looks like any other Dodge Sportsman 300. It's a dirty tan color. There are a few body dents, but it's never been in a wreck. I tore the antenna off against a tree on a pinched mountain road. A boy in Midland, Texas, rocked one of my rear view mirrors off. A logging truck in Oregon squeeze-fired a piece of debris off the road and shattered my windshield. The oil pan and gas tank are pug-faced from high-centering on bad roads. (I remember a horse I rode for a while named Targhee whose hocks were scarred from tangles in barbed wire when he was a colt and who spooked a lot in high grass, but these were not like "dents." They were more like bad tires.)

I like to travel. I go mostly in the winter and mostly on two-lane roads. I've driven the truck from Key West to Vancouver, British Columbia, and from Yuma to Long Island over the past four years. I used to ride Coke High only about five miles every morning when we were rounding up horses. Hard miles of twisting and turning. About six hundred miles a year. Then I'd turn him out and ride another horse for the rest of the day. That's what was nice about having a remuda. You could do all you had to do and not take it all out on your best horse. Three car family. 13

My truck came with a lot of seats in it and I've never really known what to do with them. Sometimes I put the seats in and go somewhere with a lot of people, but most of the time I leave them out. I like riding around with that empty cavern of space behind my head. I know it's something with a history to it, that there's truth in it, because I always rode a horse the same way—with empty saddle bags. In case I found something. The possibility of finding something is half the reason for being on the road. 14

The value of anything comes to me in its use. If I am not using something it is of no value to me and I give it away. I wasn't always that way. I used to keep everything I owned—just in case. I feel good about the truck because it gets used. A lot. To haul hay and firewood and lumber and rocks and garbage and animals. Other people have used it to haul furniture and freezers and dirt and recycled newspapers. And to move from one house to another. When I lend it for things like that I don't look to get anything back but some gas (if we're going to be friends). But if you go way out in the country to a dump and pick up the things you can still find out there (once a load of cedar shingles we sold for $175 to an architect) I expect you to leave some of those things around my place when you come back—if I need them. 15

When I think back, maybe the nicest thing I ever put in that truck was timber wolves. It was a long night's drive from Oregon up into British Columbia. We were all very quiet about it; it was like moving clouds across the desert. 16

Sometimes something won't fit in the truck and I think 17

about improving it — building a different door system, for example. I am forever going to add better gauges on the dash and a pair of driving lamps and a sunroof, but I never get around to doing any of it. I remember I wanted to improve Coke High once too, especially the way he bolted like a greyhound through patches of cottonwood on a river flat. But all I could do with him was to try to rein him out of it. Or hug his back.

Sometimes, road-stoned in a blur of country like southwestern Wyoming or North Dakota, I talk to the truck. It's like wandering on the high plains under a summer sun, on plains where, George Catlin wrote, you were "out of sight of land." I say what I am thinking out loud, or point at things along the road. It's a crazy, sun-stroked sort of activity, a sure sign it's time to pull over, to go for a walk, to make a fire and have some tea, to lie in the shade of the truck. 18

I've always wanted to pat the truck. It's basic to the relationship. But it never works. 19

I remember when I was on the ranch, just at sunrise, after I'd saddled Coke High, I'd be huddled down in my jacket smoking a cigarette and looking down into the valley, along the river where the other horses had spent the night. I'd turn to Coke and run my hand down his neck and slap-pat him on the shoulder to say I was coming up. It made a bond, an agreement we started the day with. 20

I've thought about that a lot with the truck, because we've gone out together at sunrise on so many mornings. I've even fumbled around trying to do it. But metal won't give. 21

The truck's personality is mostly an expression of two ideas: "with-you" and "alone." When Coke High was "with-you" he and I were the same animal. We could have cut a rooster out of a flock of chickens, we were so in tune. It's the same with the truck: rolling through Kentucky on a hilly two-lane road, three in the morning under a full moon and no traffic. Picture it. You roll like water. 22

There are other times when you are with each other but there's no connection at all. Coke got that way when he was bored and we'd fight each other about which way to go around a tree. When the truck gets like that — "alone" — it's because it feels its Detroit fat-ass design dragging at its heart and making a fool out of it. 23

I can think back over more than a hundred nights I've slept   24
in the truck, sat in it with a lamp burning, bundled up in a parka,
reading a book. It was always comfortable. A good place to wait
out a storm. Like sleeping inside a buffalo.

The truck will go past 100,000 miles soon. I'll rebuild the   25
engine and put a different transmission in it. I can tell from
magazine advertisements that I'll never get another one like it.
Because every year they take more of the heart out of them. One
thing that makes a farmer or a rancher go sour is a truck that isn't
worth a shit. The reason you see so many old pickups in ranch
country is because these are the only ones with any heart. You can
count on them. The weekend rancher runs around in a new
pickup with too much engine and not enough transmission and
with the wrong sort of tires because he can afford anything, even
the worst. A lot of them have names for their pickups too.

My truck has broken down, in out of the way places at the   26
worst of times. I've walked away and screamed the foulness out of
my system and gotten the tools out. I had to fix a water pump in a
blizzard in the Panamint Mountains in California once. It took
all day with the Coleman stove burning under the engine block to
keep my hands from freezing. We drifted into Beatty, Nevada,
that night with it jury-rigged together with — I swear — baling
wire, and we were melting snow as we went and pouring it in to
compensate for the leaks.

There is a dent next to the door on the driver's side I put   27
there one sweltering night in Miami. I had gone to the airport to
meet my wife, whom I hadn't seen in a month. My hands were so
swollen with poison ivy blisters I had to drive with my wrists. I
had shut the door and was locking it when the window fell off its
runners and slid down inside the door. I couldn't leave the truck
unlocked because I had too much inside I didn't want to lose. So
I just kicked the truck a blow in the side and went to work on the
window. I hate to admit kicking the truck. It's like kicking a dog,
which I've never done.

Coke High and I had an accident once. We hit a badger hole   28
at a full gallop. I landed on my back and blacked out. When I
came to, Coke High was about a hundred yards away. He stayed a
hundred yards away for six miles, all the way back to the ranch.

I want to tell you about carrying those wolves, because it was   29
a fine thing. There were ten of them. We had four in the truck

with us in crates and six in a trailer. It was a five hundred mile trip. We went at night for the cool air and because there wouldn't be as much traffic. I could feel from the way the truck rolled along that its heart was in the trip. It liked the wolves inside it, the sweet odor that came from the crates. I could feel that same tireless wolf-lope developing in its wheels; it was like you might never have to stop for gas, ever again.

The truck gets very self-focused when it works like this; its heart is strong and it's good to be around it. It's good to be *with* it. You get the same feeling when you pull someone out of a ditch. Coke High and I pulled a Volkswagen out of the mud once, but Coke didn't like doing it very much. Speed, not strength, was his center. When the guy who owned the car thanked us and tried to pat Coke, the horse snorted and swung away, trying to preserve his distance, which is something a horse spends a lot of time on.   30

So does the truck.   31

Being distant lets the truck get its heart up. The truck has   32
been cold and alone in Montana at 38 below zero. It's climbed horrible, eroded roads in Idaho. It's been burdened beyond over-loading, and made it anyway. I've asked it to do these things because they build heart, and without heart all you have is a machine. You have nothing. I don't think people in Detroit know anything at all about heart. That's why everything they build dies so young.

One time in Arizona the truck and I came through one of the   33
worst storms I've ever been in, an outrageous, angry blizzard. But we went down the road, right through it. You couldn't explain our getting through by the sort of tires I had on the truck, or the fact that I had chains on, or was a good driver, or had a lot of weight over my drive wheels or a good engine, because it was more than this. It was a contest between the truck and the blizzard—and the truck wouldn't quit. I could have gone to sleep and the truck would have just torn a road down Interstate 40 on its own. It scared the hell out of me; but it gave me heart, too.

We came off the Mogollon Rim that night and out of the   34
storm and headed south for Phoenix. I pulled off the road to sleep for a few hours, but before I did I got out of the truck. It was raining. Warm rain. I tied a short piece of red avalanche cord into the grill. I left it there for a long time, like an eagle feather on a

horse's tail. It flapped and spun in the wind. I could hear it ticking against the grill when I drove.

When I have to leave that truck I will just raise up my left 35 arm — *Hoka hey!* — and walk away.

Questions for Close Reading

1. What is the selection's thesis? Locate the sentence(s) in which Lopez states his main idea. If he doesn't state the thesis explicitly, express it in your own words.
2. What similarities are there between the way Lopez treats his truck and the way Native Americans treated their horses?
3. What does Lopez mean when he refers to the truck's "heart" in paragraphs 29, 30, and 32–34? How, as he writes in paragraph 30, can a truck be "self-focused"?
4. What do we learn about Lopez from reading the essay? What does he directly tell us about himself? What qualities about him can we infer?
5. Refer to your dictionary as needed to define the following words used in the selection: *coup* (paragraph 1), *coulees* (3), *deviate* (9), *remuda* (13), *jury-rigged* (26), and *baling wire* (26).

Questions About the Writer's Craft

1. **The pattern.** Which does Lopez emphasize more in his essay, comparison or contrast? Why do you think he stresses what he does? When comparing and contrasting, where does Lopez use the one-side-at-a-time method? Where does he use the point-by-point method? Why might he have chosen to use each method where he does?
2. **Other patterns.** Where does Lopez incorporate brief narrative accounts into the essay? How do these narratives help him convey important information about himself and his truck?
3. Locate places in the essay where Lopez uses sentence fragments. Why do you think he makes such liberal use of nonstandard sentence structure? What effect do these fragments have on the essay's tone?
4. In the essay's final paragraph, Lopez evokes the Native American imagery that he presented in paragraph 7. What specific similarities do you see in these two paragraphs? Why might Lopez have chosen to end the essay as he does?

Questions for Further Thought

1. Do you identify with Lopez's personal, almost intimate relationship with his truck? For example, do you have an inanimate possession to

which you've given a name? Have you ever talked to an inanimate object, as Lopez says he has to his truck, or "patted" an object with affection? Why is this object so special to you?

2. In paragraphs 3–6, Lopez describes the symbols and objects that Native Americans used to identify themselves and their horses. What symbols and objects do people use today on their clothing, on their cars or trucks, in their homes, or elsewhere to create an image or identity? How do you feel about such "advertisements" of personal characteristics?

3. Native American culture has obviously influenced Lopez and given him a perspective from which to view his life. Are there cultures, ethnic groups, religions, or subcultures that you don't belong to by birth or heritage but that have helped you think about your life? If there are, explain how these groups or subcultures have influenced your thinking.

4. Lopez writes that his truck conveys two distinct personalities: "with-you" and "alone." What do you think causes an inanimate object to have such contrasting temperaments? Is it simply a matter of mechanical functioning or is something else involved? What might that be?

Writing Assignments Using Comparison-Contrast as a Pattern of Development

1. Lopez shows the parallels between an animate being, a horse, and an inanimate object, his truck. Think about possessions that are important to you, and select one that you relate to as if it were alive. Then write an essay evoking the similarities and differences between this possession and the animate being it resembles. You may emphasize similarities, as Lopez does, or you may give equal attention to similarities and differences. Your essay may have a serious or light-spirited tone.

2. Horses, commonly used in the past, have been largely replaced by cars, trucks, and other means of transportation. Think about other modern conveniences that are routinely used nowadays but that weren't available in an earlier generation. Focusing on one such innovation, write an essay comparing and contrasting life before and after the introduction of this technological development. For example, you might compare and contrast the play of the "Nintendo" generation with the games that children played before such diversions were invented, or you might compare and contrast cooking before and after the microwave. Depending on your subject, you may need to research your paper by talking with those older than you: parents, grandparents, siblings, and the like.

Writing Assignments Using Other Patterns of Development

3. Lopez feels that Detroit's latest crop of trucks has no "heart." What other items do you think have lost "heart"? Write an essay illustrating the extent to which Americans' pursuit of the new and improved may actually compromise quality. Provide numerous compelling examples to illustrate your point.

∞ **4.** Lopez reveals that possessions are valuable to him only when they serve some purpose. What criteria do you feel people should use when deciding what they should own and how much they should own? Focus on a specific group of people (for example, college students, just-married young couples, a family of four), and write a paper in which you cite specific examples of the types of possessions that you feel are and aren't legitimate. The following essays offer a number of perspectives on the role of possessions in everyday life: Gordon Parks's "Flavio's Home" (page 96), Jeanne Wakatsuki Houston and James D. Houston's "Manzanar" (page 132), Anne Morrow Lindbergh's "Channelled Whelk" (page 219), and Janet Mendell Goldstein's "The Quick Fix Society" (page 332).

Additional Writing Topics
COMPARISON-CONTRAST

General Assignments

Using comparison-contrast, write an essay on any of the following topics. Your thesis should indicate whether the two subjects are being compared, contrasted, or both. Organize the paper by arranging the details in a one-side-at-a-time or point-by-point pattern. Remember to use organizational cues to help the audience follow your analysis.

1. Two-career family versus one-career family
2. Two approaches for dealing with problems
3. Children's pastimes today and yesterday
4. Two rooms where you spend a good deal of time
5. Neighborhood stores versus shopping malls
6. Two characters in a novel or other literary work
7. Living at home versus living in an apartment or dorm
8. Two attitudes toward money
9. A sports team then and now
10. Watching a movie on television versus viewing it in a theater
11. Two attitudes about a controversial subject
12. Two approaches to parenting
13. Walking or biking versus driving a car
14. Marriage versus living together
15. The atmosphere in two classes
16. Two approaches to studying
17. The place where you live and the place where you would like to live
18. Two comedians
19. The coverage of an event on television versus the coverage in a newspaper
20. Significant trend versus passing fad
21. Two horror or adventure movies
22. Typewriter versus word processor
23. Two candidates for an office
24. Your attitude before and after getting to know someone
25. Two friends with different life-styles

Assignments with a Specific Purpose and Audience

1. You would like to change your campus living arrangements. Perhaps you want to move from a dormitory to an off-campus apartment or

from home to a dorm. Before you do, though, you'll have to convince your parents (who are paying most of your college costs) that the move will be beneficial. Write out what you would say to your parents. Contrast your current situation with your proposed one, explaining why the new arrangement would be better.

2. As a store manager, you decide to write a memo to all sales personnel explaining how to keep customers happy. Compare and/or contrast the needs and shopping habits of several different consumer groups (by age, spending ability, or sex), and show how to make each comfortable in your store.

3. As a member of the College Orientation Committee, you volunteer to write a guide on "Passing Exams" for first-year college students. You decide to contrast the right and wrong ways to prepare for and take exams. Although your purpose is basically serious, leaven the section on how *not* to approach exams with some humor.

4. You work as a volunteer for a mental health hot line. Many people call simply because they feel "stressed out." Prepare a brochure for these people, recommending a "Type B" approach to stressful situations. Focus the brochure on the contrast between "Type A" and "Type B" personalities: the former is nervous, hard-driving, competitive; the latter is relaxed and noncompetitive. Give specific examples of how each "type" tends to act in stressful situations.

5. As president of your student senate, you're concerned about the way your school is dealing with a particular situation (for example, advisement, parking, financial assistance). Write a letter to your college president contrasting the way your school handles the situation with another school's approach. In your conclusion, point out the advantages of adopting the other college's strategy.

6. Your old high school has invited you back to make a speech before an audience of seniors. The topic will be "how to choose the college that is right for you." Write your speech in the form of a comparison-contrast analysis. Focus on the choices available (two-year versus four-year schools, large versus small, local versus faraway, and so on), showing the advantages and/or disadvantages of each.

9

CAUSE-EFFECT

WHAT IS CAUSE-EFFECT?

Superstition has it that curiosity killed the cat. Maybe so. Yet our science, technology, storytelling, and fascination with the past and future all spring from our determination to know "Why" and "What if." Seeking explanations, young children barrage adults with endless questions: "Why do trees grow tall?" "What would happen if the sun didn't shine?" But children aren't the only ones who wonder in this way. All of us think in terms of cause and effect, sometimes consciously, sometimes unconsciously: "Why did they give me such an odd look?" we wonder, or "How would I do at another college?" we speculate. This exploration of reasons and results is also at the heart of most professions: "What led to our involvement in Vietnam?" historians question; "What will happen if we administer this experimental drug?" scientists ask.

Cause-effect writing, often called *causal analysis*, is rooted in this elemental need to make connections. Because the drive to

461

understand reasons and results is so fundamental, causal analysis is a common kind of writing. An article analyzing the unexpected outcome of an election, a report linking poor nutrition to low academic achievement, an editorial analyzing the impact of a proposed tax cut—all are examples of cause-effect writing.

Done well, cause-effect pieces can uncover the subtle and often surprising connections between events or phenomena. By rooting out causes and projecting effects, causal analysis enables us to make sense of our experiences, revealing a universe that is somewhat less arbitrary and chaotic.

HOW CAUSE-EFFECT FITS YOUR PURPOSE AND AUDIENCE

Many assignments and exam questions in college involve writing essays that analyze causes, effects, or both. Sometimes, as in the following examples, you'll be asked to write an essay developed primarily through the cause-effect pattern:

> Although divorces have leveled off in the last few years, the number of marriages ending in divorce is still greater than it was a generation ago. What do you think are the causes of this phenomenon?

> Political commentators were surprised that so few people voted in the last election. Discuss the probable causes of this weak voter turnout.

> Americans never seem to tire of gossip about the rich and famous. What effect has this fascination with celebrities had on American culture?

> The federal government is expected to pass legislation that will significantly reduce the funding of student loans. Analyze the possible effects of such a cutback.

Other assignments and exam questions may not explicitly ask you to address causes and effects, but they may use words that suggest causal analysis would be appropriate. Consider these examples, paying special attention to the words in boldface:

In contrast to the socially involved youth of the 1960s, many young people today tend to remove themselves from political issues. What do you think are the **sources** of the political apathy found among 18- to 25-year-olds? (*cause*)

A number of experts forecast that drug abuse will be the most significant factor affecting American productivity in the coming decade. Evaluate the validity of this observation by discussing the **impact** of drugs in the workplace. (*effect*)

According to school officials, a predictable percentage of entering students drop out of college at some point during their first year. What **motivates** students to drop out? What **happens** to them once they leave? (*cause and effect*)

In addition to serving as the primary strategy for achieving an essay's purpose, causal analysis can also be a supplemental method used to help make a point in an essay developed chiefly through another pattern of development. Assume, for example, that you want to write an essay *defining* the term *the homeless*. To help readers see that unfavorable circumstances can result in nearly anyone becoming homeless, you might discuss some of the unavoidable, everyday factors causing people to live on streets and in subway stations. Similarly, in a *persuasive* proposal urging your college administration to institute an honors program, you would probably spend some time analyzing the positive effect of such a program on students and faculty.

SUGGESTIONS FOR USING CAUSE-EFFECT IN AN ESSAY

The following suggestions will be helpful whether you use causal analysis as a dominant or supportive pattern of development.

1. **Stay focused on the purpose of your analysis.** When writing a causal analysis, don't lose sight of your overall purpose. Consider, for example, an essay on the causes of widespread child

abuse. If you're concerned primarily with explaining the problem of child abuse to your readers, you might take a purely *informative* approach:

> Although parental stress is the immediate cause of child abuse, the more compelling reason for such behavior lies in the way parents were themselves mistreated in their own families.

Or you might want to *persuade* the audience about some point or idea concerning child abuse:

> The tragic consequences of child abuse provide strong support for more aggressive handling of such cases by social workers and judges.

Then again, you could choose a *speculative* approach, your main purpose being to suggest possibilities:

> Psychologists disagree about the potential effect on youngsters of all the media attention to child abuse. Will children exposed to this media coverage grow up assertive, self-confident, and able to protect themselves? Or will they become fearful and distrustful?

These examples illustrate that an essay's causal analysis may have more than one purpose. For instance, although the last example points to a paper with a primarily speculative purpose, the essay would probably start by informing readers of experts' conflicting views. The paper would also have a persuasive slant if it ended by urging readers to complain to the media about their sensationalized treatment of the child-abuse issue.

2. Adapt content and tone to your purpose and readers.   Your purpose and audience determine what supporting material and what tone will be most effective in a cause-effect essay. Assume you want to direct your essay on child abuse to general readers who know little about the subject. To *inform* readers, you might use facts and expert opinion to provide an objective discussion of the causes of child abuse. Your analysis might show the following: (1) adults who were themselves mistreated as children tend to abuse their own offspring; (2) marital stress contributes to the mistreatment of children; and (3) certain personality disorders increase the likelihood of child abuse. Sensitive to what your readers would and wouldn't understand, you would stay away from technical, highly formal language. Rather than writing "Pathological preabuse symptomatology predicts adult transference of high aggressivity," you would say "Psychologists can often predict, on the basis of family histories, who will abuse children."

Now imagine that your purpose is to *convince* future social workers that the failure of social service agencies to act authoritatively in child-abuse cases often has tragic consequences. Hoping to encourage more responsible behavior in the prospective social workers, you would adopt a more emotional approach in the essay, perhaps citing wrenching case histories that dramatize what happens when child abuse isn't taken seriously.

3. Think rigorously about causes and effects. To write a meaningful causal analysis, you should do some careful thinking about the often complex relationship between causes and effects. Children tend to oversimplify causes and effects ("Mommy and Daddy are getting divorced because I was bad the other day") and adults' arguments can be characterized by hasty, often slipshod thinking ("All these immigrants willing to work cheaply have made us lose our jobs"). But imprecise thinking has no place in essay writing. You should be willing to dig for causes, to think creatively about effects. You should examine your subject in depth, looking beyond the obvious and superficial.

Brainstorming, freewriting, and mapping will help you explore causes and effects thoroughly. No matter which prewriting technique you use, generate as many explanations as possible by asking yourself questions like these:

> *Causes:* What happened? What are the possible reasons? Which are most likely? Who was involved? Why?
>
> *Effects:* What happened? Who was involved? What were the observable results? What are some possible future consequences? Which consequences are negative? Which are positive?

If you remain open and look beyond the obvious, you'll discover that a cause may have many effects. Imagine you're writing a paper on the effects of cigarette smoking. Prewriting would probably generate a number of consequences that could be discussed, some less obvious but perhaps more interesting than others: increased risk of lung cancer and heart disease, legal battles regarding the rights of smokers and nonsmokers, lower birth weights in babies of mothers who smoke, and developmental problems experienced by such underweight infants.

In the same way, prewriting will help you see that an effect may have multiple causes. An essay analyzing the reasons for world hunger could discuss many causes, again some less evident but perhaps more thought-provoking than others: climatic changes, inefficient use of land, cultural predispositions for large families, and poor management of international relief funds.

Your analysis may also uncover a *causal chain* in which one cause (or effect) brings about another, which, in turn, brings about another, and so on. Here's an example of a causal chain: Prohibition went into effect; bootleggers and organized crime stepped in to supply public demand for alcoholic beverages; ordinary citizens began breaking the law by buying illegal alcohol and patronizing speakeasies; disrespect for legal authority became widespread and acceptable. As you can see, a causal chain often leads to interesting points. In this case, the subject of Prohibition leads not just to the obvious (illegal consumption of alcohol) but also to the more complex issue of society's decreasing respect for legal authority.

Don't grapple with so complex a chain, however, that you become hopelessly entangled. If your subject involves multiple causes and effects, limit what you'll discuss. Identify which causes and effects are *primary* and which are *secondary*. How extensively you cover secondary factors will depend on your purpose and audience. In an essay intended to inform a general audience about the harmful effects of pesticides, you would most likely focus on everyday dangers — polluted drinking water, residues in food, and the like. You probably wouldn't include a discussion of more long-range consequences (evolution of resistant insects, disruption of the soil's acid-alkaline balance).

Similarly, decide whether to focus on *immediate*, more obvious causes and effects, or on less obvious, more *remote* ones. Or perhaps you need to focus on both. In an essay about a faculty strike at your college, should you attribute the strike simply to the faculty's failure to receive a salary increase? Or should you also examine other factors: the union's failure to accept a salary package that satisfied most professors; the administration's inability to coordinate its negotiating efforts? It may be more difficult to explore more remote causes and effects, but it can also lead to more original and revealing essays. Thoughtful analyses take these less obvious considerations into account.

When developing a causal analysis, be careful to avoid the *post hoc fallacy*. Named after the Latin phrase *post hoc, ergo propter hoc*, meaning "after this, therefore because of this," this kind of faulty thinking occurs when you assume that simply because one event *followed* another, the first event *caused* the second. For example, if the Republicans win a majority of seats in Congress and, several months later, the economy collapses, can you conclude that the Republicans caused the collapse? A quick assumption of "Yes" fails the test of logic, for the timing of events could be coincidental and not indicative of any cause-effect relationship. The collapse may have been triggered by uncontrolled inflation that began well before the congressional elections. (For more information on the *post hoc* fallacy, see page 590.)

Also, be careful not to mistake *correlation* for *causation*. Two events correlate when they occur at about the same time. Such co-occurrence, however, doesn't guarantee a cause-effect relationship. For instance, while the number of ice cream cones eaten and the instances of heat prostration both increase during the summer months, this doesn't mean that eating ice cream causes heat prostration! A third factor — in this case, summer heat — is the actual cause. When writing causal analyses, then, use with caution words that imply a causal link (such as *therefore* and *because*). Words that express simply time of occurrence (like *following* and *previously*) are safer and more objective.

Finally, keep in mind that a rigorous causal analysis involves more than loose generalizations about causes and effects. Creating plausible connections may require library research, interviewing, or both. Often you'll need to provide facts, statistics, details, personal observations, or other corroborative material if readers are going to accept the reasoning behind your analysis.

4. Write a thesis that focuses the paper on causes, effects, or both. The thesis in an essay developed through causal analysis often indicates whether the essay will deal mostly with causes, effects, or both. Here, for example, are three thesis statements for causal analyses dealing with the public school system. You'll see that each thesis signals that essay's particular emphasis:

> Our school system has been weakened by an overemphasis on trendy electives. (*causes*)

> An ineffectual school system has led to crippling teachers' strikes and widespread disrespect for the teaching profession. (*effects*)

> Bureaucratic inefficiency has created a school system unresponsive to children's emotional, physical, and intellectual needs. (*causes and effects*)

Note that the thesis statement — in addition to signaling whether the paper will discuss causes or effects or both — may also point to the essay's plan of development. Consider the last thesis statement; it makes clear that the paper will discuss children's emotional needs first, their physical needs second, and their intellectual needs last.

The thesis statement in a causal analysis doesn't have to specify whether the essay will discuss causes, effects, or both. Nor does the thesis have to be worded in such a way that the essay's plan of development is apparent. But when first writing cause-effect essays, you may find that a highly focused thesis will keep your analysis on track.

5. Choose an organizational pattern.   There are two basic ways to organize the points in a cause-effect essay: you may use a chronological or an emphatic sequence. If you select a *chronological order*, you discuss causes and effects in the order in which they occur or will occur. Suppose you're writing an essay on the causes for the popularity of imported cars. These causes might be discussed in chronological sequence: American plant workers became frustrated and dissatisfied on the job; some workers got careless while others deliberately sabotaged the production of sound cars; a growing number of defective cars hit the market; consumers grew dissatisfied with American cars and switched to imports.

Chronology might also be used to organize a discussion about effects. Imagine you want to write an essay about the need to guard against disrupting delicate balances in the country's wildlife. You might start the essay by discussing what happened when the starling, a non-native bird, was introduced into the American environment. Because the starling had few natural predators, the starling population soared out of control; the starlings took over food sources and habitats of native species; the bluebird, a native species, declined and is now threatened with extinction.

Although a chronological pattern can be an effective way to organize material, a strict time sequence can present a problem if your primary cause or effect ends up buried in the middle of the sequence. In such a case, you might use *emphatic order*, reserving the most significant cause or effect for the end. For example, time order could be used to present the reasons behind a candidate's unexpected victory: Less than a month after the candidate's earlier defeat, a full-scale fund-raising campaign for the next election was started; the candidate spoke to many crucial power groups early in the campaign; the candidate did exceptionally well in the pre-election debates; good weather and large voter turnout on election day favored the candidate. However, if you believe that the candidate's appearance before influential groups was the key factor in the victory, it would be more effective to emphasize that point by saving it for the end. This is what is meant by emphatic order — saving the most important point for last.

Emphatic order is an especially effective way to sequence cause-effect points when readers hold what, in your opinion, are mistaken or narrow views about a subject. To encourage readers to look more closely at the issues, you present what you consider the erroneous or obvious views first, show why they are unsound or limited, then present what you feel to be the actual causes and effects. Such a sequence nudges the audience into giving further thought to the causes and effects you have discovered. Here are informal outlines for two causal analyses using this approach.

Subject: The causes of the riot at a rock concert

1. Some commentators blame the excessively hot weather.
2. Others cite drug use among the concertgoers.
3. Still others blame the liquor sold at the concessions.

4. But the real cause of the disaster was poor planning by the concert promoters.

Subject: The effects of campus crime

1. Immediate problems
   a. Students feel insecure and fearful.
   b. Many night-time campus activities have been curtailed.
2. More significant long-term problems
   a. Unfavorable publicity about campus crime will affect future student enrollments.
   b. Hiring faculty will become more difficult.

When using emphatic order in a causal analysis, you might want to word the thesis in such a way that it signals which point your essay will stress. Look at the following thesis statements:

Although many immigrants arrive in this country without marketable skills, their most pressing problem is learning how to make their way in a society whose language they don't know.

The space program has led to dramatic advances in computer technology and medical science. Even more important, though, the program has helped change many people's attitudes toward the planet we live on.

These thesis statements reflect an awareness of the complex nature of cause-effect relationships. While not dismissing secondary issues, the statements establish which points the writer considers most noteworthy. The second thesis, for instance, indicates that the paper will touch on the technological and medical advances made possible by the space program but will emphasize the way the program has changed people's attitudes toward the earth.

6. Use language that hints at the complexity of cause-effect relationships. Because it's difficult — if not impossible — to identify causes and effects with certainty, you should avoid such absolutes as "It must be obvious" and "There is no doubt." Instead, try phrases like "Most likely" or "It's probable that." Using such language is not indecisive; rather, it reflects your understanding of the often tangled nature of causes and effects. Be careful, though, of going to the other extreme and being reluctant to take a stand on the issues. If you've thought carefully about causes and effects, you have a right to state your analysis with conviction. Don't undercut the hard work you've done by writing as if your ideas were unworthy of your reader's attention.

Cause-effect writing is gratifying for both writer and audience. As a writer, you experience the pleasure of stretching your mind, confident that your exploration of causes and effects has gone beyond the obvious. Readers feel a comparable satisfaction, knowing that they have a clearer understanding of an event or a phenomenon. Causal analysis also has the potential for generating vigorous discussion and honest disagreement about a variety of issues — from reasons for international terrorism to consequences of reducing support for school lunch programs. Cause-effect writing is certainly one of the most critical ways we have for thinking about matters that concern us.

STUDENT ESSAY

The following student essay was written by Carl Novack in response to this assignment:

> In "The Faltering Family," George Gallup, Jr., points to a number of factors that have caused the decline of the American family. Think of another institution, process, or practice that has changed recently and discuss several factors you believe are responsible for the change.

While reading Carl's paper, try to determine how well it applies the principles of causal analysis. The annotations on Carl's paper and the commentary following it will help you look at the essay more closely.

Americans and Food

by Carl Novack

Introduction

An offbeat but timely cartoon recently appeared in the local newspaper. The single panel showed a gravel-pit operation with piles of raw

1

earth and large cranes. Next to one of the cranes stood the owner of the gravel pit--a grizzled, tough-looking character, hammer in hand, pointing proudly to the new sign he had just tacked up. The sign read, "Fred's Fill Dirt and Croissants." The cartoon illustrates an interesting phenomenon: the changing food habits of Americans. Our meals used to consist of something like home-cooked pot roast, mashed potatoes laced with butter and salt, a thick slice of apple pie topped with a healthy scoop of vanilla ice cream--plain, heavy meals, cooked from scratch, and eaten leisurely at home.

Thesis ⟶ But America has changed, and as it has, so have what we Americans eat and how we eat it.

We used to have simple, unsophisticated   2
tastes and looked with suspicion at anything more exotic than hamburger. Admittedly, we did adopt some foods from the various immigrant groups who flocked to our shores. We learned to eat Chinese

Topic sentence:
Background food, pizza, and bagels. But in the last few years,
paragraph the international character of our diet has grown tremendously. We can walk into any mall in Middle America and buy pita bread, quiche, and tacos. Such foods are often changed on their journey from exotic imports to ordinary "American" meals (no Pakistani, for example, eats frozen-on-a-stick boysenberry-flavored yogurt), but the imports are still

Topic sentence: a long way from hamburger on a bun.
Three causes
answer the ⟶ Why have we become more worldly in our   3
question tastes? For one thing, television blankets the country with information about new food products and
First cause trends. Viewers in rural Montana know that the latest craving in Washington, D.C., is Cajun cooking or that something called tofu is now available

Second cause in the local supermarket. Another reason for the growing international flavor of our food is that many young Americans have traveled abroad and gotten hooked on new tastes and flavors. Backpacking students and young professionals vacationing in Europe come home with cravings for
Third cause authentic French bread or German beer. Finally, continuing waves of immigrants settle in the cities where many of us live, causing significant changes in what we eat. Vietnamese, Haitians, and Thais,

for instance, bring their native foods and cooking styles with them and eventually open small markets or restaurants. In time, the new food will become Americanized enough to take its place in our national diet.

Topic sentence: Another cause ——→ Our growing concern with health has also affected the way we eat. For the last few years, the media have warned us about the dangers of our traditional diet, high in salt and fat, low in fiber. The media also began to educate us about the dangers of processed foods pumped full of chemical additives. **Start of a causal chain** —— As a result, consumers began to demand healthier foods, and manufacturers started to change some of their products. Many foods, such as lunch meat, canned vegetables, and soups, were made available in low-fat, low-sodium versions. Whole-grain cereals and higher-fiber breads also began to appear on the grocery shelves. Moreover, the food industry started to produce all-natural products--everything from potato chips to ice cream--without additives and preservatives. Not surprisingly, the restaurant industry responded to this switch to healthier foods, luring customers with salad bars, broiled fish, and steamed vegetables.

4

Topic sentence: Another cause ——→ Our food habits are being affected, too, by the rapid increase in the number of women working outside the home. Sociologists and other experts believe that two important factors triggered this phenomenon: the women's movement and a changing economic climate. Women were assured that it was acceptable, even rewarding, to work outside the home; many women also discovered that they had to work just to keep up with the cost of living. As the traditional role of homemaker changed, so did the way families ate. With Mom working, there wasn't time for her to prepare the traditional three square meals a day. Instead, families began looking for alternatives to provide quick meals. **Start of a causal chain** —— What was the result? For one thing, there was a boom in fast-food restaurants. The suburban or downtown strip that once contained a lone McDonald's now features Wendy's, Roy Rogers, Taco Bell, Burger King, and Pizza Hut. Families

5

also began to depend on frozen foods as another time-saving alternative. Once again, though, demand changed the kind of frozen food available. Frozen foods no longer consist of foil trays divided into greasy fried chicken, watery corn niblets, and lumpy mashed potatoes. Supermarkets now stock a range of supposedly gourmet frozen dinners--from fettucini in cream sauce to braised beef en brochette.

Conclusion

It may not be possible to pick up a ton of fill   6
dirt and a half-dozen croissants at the same place, but America's food habits are definitely changing. If it is true that "you are what you eat," then America's identity is evolving along with its diet.

COMMENTARY

Title and introduction.   Asked to prepare a paper analyzing the reasons behind a change in our lives, Carl decided to write about a shift he had noticed in Americans' eating habits. The title of the essay, "Americans and Food," identifies Carl's subject but could be livelier and more interesting.

Despite his rather uninspired title, Carl starts his *causal analysis* in an engaging way—with the vivid description of a cartoon. He then connects the cartoon to his subject with the following sentence: "The cartoon illustrates an interesting phenomenon: the changing food habits of Americans." To back up his belief that there has been a revolution in our eating habits, Carl uses the first paragraph to summarize the kind of meal that people used to eat. He then moves into his *thesis*: "But America has changed, and as it has, so have what Americans eat and how we eat it." The thesis implies that Carl's paper will focus on both causes and effects.

Purpose.   Carl's *purpose* was to write an *informative* causal analysis. But before he could present the causes of the change in eating habits, he needed to show that such a change had, in fact, taken place. He therefore uses the second paragraph to document one aspect of this change—the internationalization of our eating habits.

Topic sentences.   At the start of the third paragraph, Carl uses a question — "Why have we become more worldly in our tastes?" — to signal that his discussion of causes is about to begin. This question also serves as the paragraph's *topic sentence,* indicating that the paragraph will focus on reasons for the increasingly international flavor of our food. The next two paragraphs, also focused by topic sentences, identify two other major reasons for the change in eating habits: "Our growing concern with health has also affected the way we eat" (paragraph 4), and "Our food habits are being affected, too, by the rapid increase in the number of women working outside the home" (5).

Other patterns of development.   Carl draws on two patterns — comparison-contrast and exemplification — to develop his causal analysis. At the heart of the essay is a basic *contrast* between the way we used to eat and the way we eat now. And throughout his essay, Carl provides convincing *examples* to demonstrate the validity of his points. Consider for a moment the third paragraph. Here Carl asserts that one reason for our new eating habits is our growing exposure to international foods. He then presents concrete evidence to show that we have indeed become more familiar with international cuisine: Television exposes rural Montana to Cajun cooking; students traveling abroad take a liking to French bread; urban dwellers enjoy the exotic fare served by numerous immigrant groups. The fourth and fifth paragraphs use similarly specific evidence (for example, "low-fat, low-sodium versions" of "lunchmeat, canned vegetables, and soups") to illustrate the soundness of key ideas.

Causal chains.   Let's look more closely at the evidence in the essay. Not satisfied with obvious explanations, Carl thought through his ideas carefully and even brainstormed with friends to arrive at as comprehensive an analysis as possible. Not surprisingly, much of the evidence Carl uncovered took the form of *causal chains*. In the fourth paragraph, Carl writes, "The media also began to educate us about the dangers of processed foods pumped full of chemical additives. As a result, consumers began to demand healthier foods, and manufacturers started to change some of their products." And the next paragraph shows how the changing role of American women caused families to look for alternative ways of eating. This shift, in turn, caused the restaurant and food industries to respond with a wide range of food alternatives.

Making the paper easy to follow.   Although Carl's analysis digs beneath the surface and reveals complex cause-effect relationships, he wisely limits his pursuit of causal chains to *primary causes and effects*. He doesn't let the complexities distract him from his main purpose: to show why and how the American diet is changing. Carl is also careful to provide his essay with abundant *connecting devices*, making it easy for readers to see the links between points. Consider the use of *transitions* (signaled by italics) in the following sentences: "*Another* reason for the growing international flavor of our food is that many young Americans have traveled abroad" (3); "*As a result*, consumers began to demand healthier foods" (4); and "*As* the traditional role of homemaker changed, so did the way families ate" (5).

A problem with the essay's close.   When reading the essay, you probably noticed that Carl's conclusion is a bit weak. Although his reference to the cartoon works well, the rest of the paragraph limps to a tired close. Ending an otherwise vigorous essay with such a slight conclusion undercuts the effectiveness of the whole paper. Carl spent so much energy developing the body of his essay that he ran out of the stamina needed to conclude the piece more forcefully. Careful budgeting of his time would have allowed him to prepare a stronger concluding paragraph.

Revising the first draft.   When Carl was ready to revise, he showed the first draft of his essay to several classmates. Listening carefully to what they said, he jotted down their most helpful comments and eventually transferred them, numbered in order of importance, to his draft. Comparing Carl's original version of his fourth paragraph (shown here) with his final version in the essay will show you how he went about revising.

Original Version of the Fourth Paragraph
   A growing concern with health has also affected the way we eat, especially because the media has sent us warnings the last few years about the dangers of salt, sugar, food additives, high-fat and

low-fiber diets. We have started to worry that our traditional meals may have been shortening our lives. As a result, consumers demanded healthier foods and manufacturers started taking some of the salt and sugar out of canned foods. "All-natural" became an effective selling point, leading to many preservative-free products. Restaurants, too, adapted their menus, luring customers with light meals. Because we now know about the link between overweight and a variety of health problems, including heart attacks, we are counting calories. In turn, food companies made fortunes on diet beer and diet cola. Sometimes, though, we seem a bit confused about the health issue; we drink soda that is sugar-free but loaded with chemical sweeteners. Still, we believe we are lengthening our lives through changing our diets.

On the advice of his classmates, Carl decided to omit all references to the way our concern with weight has affected our eating habits. It's true, of course, that calorie-counting has changed how we eat. But as soon as Carl started to discuss this point, he got involved in a causal chain that undercut the paragraph's unity. He ended up describing the paradoxical situation in which we find ourselves. In an attempt to eat healthy, we stay away from sugar and use instead artificial sweeteners that probably aren't very good for us. This is an interesting issue, but it detracts from the point Carl wants to make: that our concern with health has affected our eating habits in a *positive* way.

Carl's editing team also pointed out that the paragraph's first sentence contained too much material to be an effective topic sentence. Carl corrected the problem by breaking the overlong sentence into two short ones: "Our growing concern with health has also affected the way we eat. For the last few years, the media have warned us about the dangers of our traditional diet, high in salt and fat, low in fiber." The first of these sentences serves as a crisp topic sentence that focuses the rest of the paragraph.

Finally, Carl agreed with his classmates that the fourth paragraph lacked convincing specifics. When revising, he changed "manufacturers started taking some of the salt and sugar out of canned foods" to the more specific "Many foods, such as lunch meats, canned vegetables, and soups, were made available in low-fat, low-sodium versions." Similarly, generalizations about "light meals" and "all-natural products" gained life through the addition of concrete examples: restaurants lured "customers with salad bars, broiled fish, and steamed vegetables," and the food industry produced "everything from potato chips to ice cream — without additives and preservatives."

Carl did an equally good job revising other sections of his paper. With the exception of the weak spots already discussed, he made the changes needed to craft a well-reasoned essay, one that demonstrates his ability to analyze a complex phenomenon.

The selections in this chapter analyze a range of cause-effect relationships. In "The Faltering Family," George Gallup, Jr., studies why the American family is changing and makes some disturbing projections about future changes. Peter Farb's "In Other Words" describes a rather surprising cause of some children's poor school performance. With poignancy, Alice Walker traces, in "Beauty: When the Other Dancer Is the Self," the impact on her life of a disfiguring eye injury. Lewis Thomas examines why "The Lie Detector" works as it does and comes away encouraged by what he learns about human nature. Finally, Jonathan Kozol asks the question "Are the Homeless Crazy?" and arrives at an answer that doesn't leave much room for optimism.

George Gallup, Jr.

Born in Illinois in 1930, George Gallup, Jr., is president of the Gallup Poll, the well-known research firm that measures public opinion. Gallup resides in Princeton, New Jersey, where he graduated from the University, and has served as executive director of the Princeton Religion Research Center. He has published articles about religion, politics, and other current issues. His books include *America's Search for Faith* (1980), with David Poling; *My Kid on Drugs?* (1981), with Art Linkletter; and *Adventures in Immortality* (1982) and *Forecast 2000* (1985), both with William Proctor. The following essay is from *Forecast 2000*.

The Faltering Family

For better or worse, the American family—one of the nation's fundamental cornerstones—has changed in response to a variety of cultural forces. Based on the results of several national opinion polls, the following selection presents George Gallup's conclusions about the future of the family. According to Gallup, if current trends continue, the traditional family will fade into a mere memory.

In a recent Sunday school class in a United Methodist 1
Church in the Northeast, a group of eight- to ten-year-olds were in a deep discussion with their two teachers. When asked to choose which of ten stated possibilities they most feared happening, their response was unanimous. All the children most dreaded a divorce between their parents.

Later, as the teachers, a man and a woman in their late 2
thirties, reflected on the lesson, they both agreed they'd been shocked at the response. When they were the same age as their students, they said, the possibility of their parents' being divorced never entered their heads. Yet in just one generation, children seemed to feel much less security in their family ties.

Nor is the experience of these two Sunday school teachers an   3
isolated one. Psychiatrists revealed in one recent newspaper investigation that the fears of children definitely do change in
different periods; and in recent times, divorce has become one of
the most frequently mentioned anxieties. In one case, for example, a four-year-old insisted that his father rather than his mother
walk him to nursery school each day. The reason? He said many
of his friends had "no daddy living at home, and I'm scared that
will happen to me" (*New York Times*, May 2, 1983).

In line with such reports, our opinion leaders expressed great   4
concern about the present and future status of the American
family. In the poll 33 percent of the responses listed decline in
family structure, divorce, and other family-oriented concerns as
one of the five major problems facing the nation today. And 26
percent of the responses included such family difficulties as one
of the five major problems for the United States in the year 2000.

Historical and sociological trends add strong support to   5
these expressions of concern. For example, today about one marriage in every two ends in divorce. Moreover, the situation seems
to be getting worse, rather than better. In 1962, the number of
divorces was 2.2 per 1,000 people, according to the National
Center for Health Statistics. By 1982, the figure had jumped to
5.1 divorces per 1,000 people—a rate that had more than doubled in two decades.

One common concern expressed about the rise in divorces   6
and decline in stability of the family is that the family unit has
traditionally been a key factor in transmitting stable cultural and
moral values from generation to generation. Various studies have
shown that educational and religious institutions often can have
only a limited impact on children without strong family support.

Even grandparents are contributing to the divorce statistics.   7
One recent study revealed that about 100,000 people over the age
of fifty-five get divorced in the United States each year. These
divorces are usually initiated by men who face retirement, and the
relationships being ended are those that have endured for thirty
years or more (*New York Times Magazine*, December 19, 1982).

What are the pressures that have emerged in the past twenty   8
years that cause long-standing family bonds to be broken?

Many now agree that the sexual revolution of the 1960s   9
worked a profound change on our society's family values and

personal relationships. Certainly, the seeds of upheaval were present before that critical decade. But a major change that occurred in the mid-sixties was an explicit widespread rejection of the common values about sexual and family relationships that most Americans in the past had held up as an ideal.

We're just beginning to sort through all the changes in social   10
standards that have occurred. Here are some of the major pressures that have contributed to those changes:

Pressure One: Alternative Lifestyles

Twenty years ago, the typical American family was depicted   11
as a man and woman who were married to each other and who produced children (usually two) and lived happily ever after. This was the pattern that young people expected to follow in order to become "full" or "normal" members of society. Of course, some people have always chosen a different route — remaining single, taking many partners, or living with a member of their own sex. But they were always considered somewhat odd, and outside the social order of the traditional family.

In the last two decades, this picture has changed dramati-   12
cally. In addition to the proliferation of single people through divorce, we also have these developments:

- Gay men and women have petitioned the courts for the   13
  right to marry each other and to adopt children. These demands are being given serious consideration, and there may even be a trend of sorts in this direction. For example, the National Association of Social Workers is increasingly supporting full adoption rights for gay people (*New York Times*, January 10, 1983).
- Many heterosexual single adults have been permitted to   14
  adopt children and set up single-parent families. So being unattached no longer excludes people from the joys of parenthood.
- Some women have deliberately chosen to bear children out   15
  of wedlock and raise them alone. In the past, many of these children would have been given up for adoption, but no longer.

  A most unusual case involved an unmarried psycholo-   16

gist, Dr. Afton Blake, who recently gave birth after being artificially inseminated with sperm from a sperm bank to which Nobel Prize winners had contributed (*New York Times*, September 6, 1983).

- In a recent Gallup Youth Poll, 64 percent of the teenagers 17 questioned said that they hoped their lives would be different from those of their parents. This included having more money, pursuing a different kind of profession, living in a different area, having more free time — and staying single longer.

    Most surveys show increasing numbers of unmarried 18 couples living together. Also, there are periodic reports of experiments in communal living, "open marriages," and other such arrangements. Although the more radical approaches to relationships tend to come and go and never seem to attract large numbers of people, the practice of living together without getting married seems to be something that's here to stay. The law is beginning to respond to these arrangements with awards for "palimony" — compensation for long-term unmarried partners in a relationship. But the legal and social status of unmarried people who live together is still quite uncertain — especially as far as any children of the union are concerned.

- Increasing numbers of married couples are choosing to 19 remain childless. Planned Parenthood has even established workshops for couples to assist them in making this decision (*Los Angeles Herald-Examiner*, November 27, 1979).

So clearly, a situation has arisen during the last twenty years 20 in which traditional values are no longer as important. Also, a wide variety of alternatives to the traditional family have arisen. Individuals may feel that old-fashioned marriage is just one of many options.

Pressure Two: Sexual Morality

Attitudes toward sexual morality have changed as dramati- 21 cally in the last two decades as have the alternatives to traditional marriage. Hear what a widely used college textbook, published in 1953, said about premarital sex:

The arguments against premarital coitus outweigh 22
those in its favor. Except for the matter of temporary
physical pleasure, all arguments about gains tend to be
highly theoretical, while the risks and unpleasant consequences tend to be in equal degree highly practical. . . .

The promiscuity of young men is certainly poor 23
preparation for marital fidelity and successful family life.
For girls it is certainly no better and sometimes leads
still further to the physical and psychological shock of
abortion or the more prolonged suffering of bearing an
illegitimate child and giving it up to others. From the
viewpoint of ethical and religious leaders, the spread of
disease through unrestrained sex activities is far more
than a health problem. They see it as undermining the
dependable standards of character and the spiritual
values that raise life to the level of the "good society."

(This comes from *Marriage and the Family* by Professor Ray E.
Baber of Pomona College, California, which was part of the
McGraw-Hill Series in Sociology and Anthropology and required
reading for some college courses.)

Clearly, attitudes have changed a great deal in just three 24
decades. Teenagers have accepted the idea of premarital sex as the
norm. In one recent national poll, 52 percent of girls and 66
percent of boys favored having sexual relations in their teens.
Ironically, however, 46 percent of the teenagers thought that
virginity in their future marital partner was fairly important.
Youngsters, in other words, display some confusion about what
they want to do sexually, and what they expect from a future
mate.

But of course, only part of the problem of defining sexual 25
standards lies with young people and premarital sex. The strong
emphasis on achieving an active and rewarding sex life has probably played some role in encouraging many husbands and wives
into rejecting monogamy. Here's some of the evidence that's
been accumulating:

- Half of the men in a recent nationwide study admitted 26
  cheating on their wives (*Pensacola Journal*, May 30, 1978).
- Psychiatrists today say they see more patients who are 27

thinking about having an extramarital affair and who wonder if it would harm their marriage (*New York Post*, November 18, 1976).

- A psychiatrist at the Albert Einstein College of Medicine   28 says, "In my practice I have been particularly struck by how many women have been able to use an affair to raise their consciousness and their confidence."

So the desire for unrestrained sex now tends to take a place   29 among other more traditional priorities, and this can be expected to continue to exert strong pressure on marriage relationships.

Pressure Three: The Economy

The number of married women working outside the home   30 has been increasing steadily, and most of these women are working out of economic necessity. As a result, neither spouse may have time to concentrate on the nurturing of the children or of the marriage relationship.

One mother we interviewed in New Jersey told us about her   31 feelings when she was forced to work full time in a library after her husband lost his job.

"It's the idea that I have no choice that really bothers me,"   32 she said. "I have to work, or we won't eat or have a roof over our heads. I didn't mind working part-time just to have extra money. I suppose that it's selfish, but I hate having to work every day and then to come home, fix dinner, and have to start doing housework. Both my husband and I were raised in traditional families, where the father went to work and the mother stayed home and took care of the house and children. [My husband] would never think of cooking or doing housework. I've raised my boys the same way, and now I'm paying for it. Sometimes, I almost hate my husband, even though I know it's not his fault."

Unfortunately, such pressures probably won't ease in the   33 future. Even if the economy improves and the number of unemployed workers decreases, few women are likely to give up their jobs. Economists agree that working-class women who have become breadwinners during a recession can be expected to remain in the work force. One reason is that many unemployed men aren't going to get their old jobs back, even when the economy improves.

"To the extent that [the men] may have to take lower-paying   34
service jobs, their families will need a second income," says Michelle Brandman, associate economist at Chase Econometrics. "The trend to two-paycheck families as a means of maintaining family income is going to continue" (*Wall Street Journal*, December 8, 1982).

In addition to the pressures of unemployment, the cost of   35
having, rearing, and educating children is steadily going up. Researchers have found that middle-class families with two children *think* they're spending only about 15 percent of their income on their children. Usually, though, they *actually* spend about 40 percent of their money on them. To put the cost in dollars and cents, if you had a baby in 1977, the estimated cost of raising that child to the age of eighteen will be $85,000, and that figure has of course been on the rise for babies born since then (*New York Daily News*, July 24, 1977).

Another important factor that promises to keep both spouses   36
working full time in the future is the attitude of today's teenagers toward these issues. They're not so much concerned about global issues like overpopulation as they are about the high cost of living. Both boys and girls place a lot of emphasis on having enough money so that they can go out and do things. Consequently, most teenage girls surveyed say they expect to pursue careers, even after they get married.

So it would seem that by the year 2000 we can expect to see   37
more working mothers in the United States. The woman who doesn't hold down any sort of outside job but stays at home to care for her children represents a small percentage of wives today. By the end of the century, with a few exceptions here and there, she may well have become a part of America's quaint past.

As women have joined the work force in response to eco-   38
nomic needs, one result has been increased emotional strains on the marriage and family relationships. But there's another set of pressures that has encouraged women to pursue careers. That's the power of feminist philosophy to permeate attitudes in grassroots America during the past couple of decades.

Pressure Four: Grassroots
Feminist Philosophy

Many women may not agree with the most radical expres-   39
sions of feminist philosophy that have arisen in the past decade or
so. But most younger women — and indeed, a majority of women
in the United States — tend to agree with most of the objectives
that even the radical feminist groups have been trying to achieve.
The basic feminist philosophy has filtered down to the grass
roots, and young boys and girls are growing up with feminist
assumptions that may have been foreign to their parents and
grandparents.

For example, child care and housework are no longer re-   40
garded strictly as "women's work" by the young people we've
polled. Also, according to the Gallup Youth Poll, most teenage
girls want to go to college and pursue a career. Moreover, they
expect to marry later in life and to continue working after they're
married. Another poll, conducted by the *New York Times* and
CBS News, revealed that only 2 percent of the youngest age
group interviewed — that is, those eighteen to twenty-nine years
old — preferred "traditional marriage." By this, they meant a
marriage in which the husband is exclusively a provider and the
wife is exclusively a homemaker and mother.

If these young people continue to hold views similar to these   41
into later life, it's likely that the changes that are occurring today
in the traditional family structure will continue. For one thing,
more day-care centers for children will have to be established.
Consequently, the rearing of children will no longer be regarded
as solely the responsibility of the family, but will become a community or institutional responsibility.

But while such developments may lessen the strain on   42
mothers and fathers, they may also weaken the bonds that hold
families together. Among other things, it may become psychologically easier to get a divorce if a person is not getting along with a
spouse, because the divorcing spouses will believe it's less likely
that the lives of the children will be disrupted.

So the concept of broadening the rights of women vis-à-vis   43
their husbands and families has certainly encouraged women to
enter the working world in greater numbers. They're also more

inclined to seek a personal identity that isn't tied up so much in their homelife.

These grassroots feminist forces have brought greater bene-   44
fits to many, but at the same time they've often worked against traditional family ties, and we remain uncertain about what is going to replace them. Feminists may argue that the traditional family caused its own demise — or else why would supposedly content wives and daughters have worked so hard to transform it? Whatever its theories, though, feminism is still a factor that, in its present form, appears to exert a destabilizing influence on many traditional familial relationships among husbands, wives, and children.

As things stand now, our family lives are in a state of flux and   45
will probably continue to be out of balance until the year 2000. The pressures we've discussed will continue to have an impact on our family lives in future years. But at the same time, counter-forces, which tend to drive families back together again, are also at work.

One of these factors is a traditionalist strain in the large   46
majority of American women. The vast majority of women in this country — 74 percent — continue to view marriage with children as the most interesting and satisfying life for them personally, according to a Gallup Poll for the White House Conference on Families released in June, 1980.

Another force supporting family life is the attitude of Ameri-   47
can teenagers toward divorce. According to a recent Gallup Youth Poll, 55 percent feel that divorces are too easy to get today. Also, they're concerned about the high rate of divorce, and they want to have enduring marriages themselves. But at the same time — in a response that reflects the confusion of many adult Americans on this subject — 67 percent of the teens in this same poll say it's right to get a divorce if a couple doesn't get along together. In other words, they place little importance on trying to improve or salvage a relationship that has run into serious trouble.

There's a similar ambivalence in the experts we polled. As   48
we've seen, 33 percent of them consider family problems as a top concern today, and 26 percent think these problems will be a big

difficulty in the year 2000. But ironically, less than 3 percent suggest that strengthening family relationships is an important consideration in planning for the future! It's obvious, then, that we're confused and ambivalent in our feelings about marriage and the family. Most people know instinctively, without having to read a poll or a book, that happiness and satisfaction in life are rooted largely in the quality of our personal relationships. Furthermore, the most important of those relationships usually begin at home. So one of the greatest challenges we face before the year 2000, both as a nation and as individuals, is how to make our all-important family ties strong and healthy. It's only upon such a firm personal foundation that we can hope to venture forth and grapple effectively with more public problems.

Questions for Close Reading

1. What is the selection's thesis? Locate the sentence(s) in which Gallup states his main idea. If he doesn't state the thesis explicitly, express it in your own words.
2. According to Gallup, what are the major pressures that have caused the change in American attitudes toward marriage and family?
3. What new styles of pairing up and parenting have entered the American mainstream and now compete with traditional marriage?
4. Why are more and more women choosing to work outside the home? Why does the author believe that this is a permanent life-style change for American women?
5. Refer to your dictionary as needed to define the following words in the selection: *explicit* (paragraph 9), *proliferation* (12), *inseminated* (16), *salvage* (47), and *ambivalence* (48).

Questions About the Writer's Craft

1. **The pattern.** In this selection, Gallup tries to account for changes in the American ideals of marriage and family. Why do you think he uses the term *pressures* rather than *causes*?
2. What techniques does Gallup use to introduce the selection? What feeling toward marriage and family does this introduction create in you? How is the introduction related to the data presented in the selection?
3. Examine the supporting evidence for each "pressure." For which ones does Gallup provide facts or statistics? What kinds of evidence does he provide for the other pressures?

4. How does Gallup create a sense of objectivity? Which word choices suggest his personal opinions about the transformation in American family values?

Questions for Further Thought

1. Gallup believes that changing gender roles have helped undermine the traditional family structure. Do you think his assessment is fair? Why or why not?

2. Gallup's statement that "one marriage in two ends in divorce" suggests that 50 percent of the country's marriages dissolve. But the statistics mean that, in a given year, the number of divorces is equal to half the number of new marriages — *not* to the total number of marriages in the country. Can you find other places where Gallup's statistics are open to misinterpretation (for example, look closely at paragraph 4)? How do these instances affect your view of Gallup's causal analysis?

3. Does the media's depiction of family life reflect changes in American culture or does the depiction help bring about those changes? Explain.

4. How widespread are the alternative life-styles in the lives of people you know and go to school with?

Writing Assignments Using Cause-Effect as a Pattern of Development

1. Writing in 1985, Gallup places much of the blame for the family's decline on women. He ignores, however, a number of personal and social factors that add stress to family life: Substance abuse, mental illness, homelessness, and industry's failure to provide day-care services to employees with young children are just some of the factors that come to mind. Select *one* of these factors, or another that seems important to you, and write an essay analyzing its effect on the family.

2. Write an essay explaining how people are affected when those close to them choose an alternative life-style. For example, think of someone you know who has chosen divorce, single parenthood, a gay life-style, cohabitation, or some other nontraditional way of life. Decide what positive and/or negative effects resulted from this choice, and discuss these effects in your essay. You may wish to evaluate the choice on the basis of how it turned out, but avoid generalizing from one case to universal rules of behavior.

Writing Assignments Using Other Patterns of Development

3. When a family breaks apart, many lives are disrupted. Parents, children, grandparents, other relatives, friends, even neighbors must cope with disorder and confusion. Choose one of these groups and write an essay illustrating the kinds of turmoil that the group may face. Develop the paper by drawing on your own and/or other people's experience. Include some brief recommendations about how the group might cope with the situation.

4. To what extent, and in what light, do alternative life-styles (extramarital affairs, divorce, single parenthood, and so on) appear in the plots of television sitcoms and dramas? To get some idea, watch TV for a week and take notes. Write up your findings in the form of a letter to *TV Guide*, either criticizing or praising the TV networks for the way they present one or two such life-styles. Support your argument with specific references to the shows you viewed.

Peter Farb

Peter Farb (1929–80) was born in New York and attended Vanderbilt University. Farb served as a consultant to the Smithsonian Institution and as a visiting lecturer at Yale University. A deep interest in language and human cultures led Farb to write *Face of North America* (1963), *Man's Rise to Civilization as Shown by the Indians of North America* (1968), and *Word Play: What Happens When People Talk* (1973). The following selection is from *Word Play*.

In Other Words

How can Clever Hans, a horse that solved mathematical problems, provide insight into a serious problem in public education? Surprisingly, there is a strong connection. In this essay, Peter Farb uses the story of Clever Hans to show how subtly a teacher's body language can affect children's performance in the classroom.

Early in this century, a horse named Hans amazed the people 1
of Berlin by his extraordinary ability to perform rapid calculations in mathematics. After a problem was written on a blackboard placed in front of him, he promptly counted out the answer by tapping the low numbers with his right forefoot and multiples of ten with his left. Trickery was ruled out because Hans's owner, unlike owners of other performing animals, did not profit financially—and Hans even performed his feats whether or not the owner was present. The psychologist O. Pfungst witnessed one of these performances and became convinced that there had to be a more logical explanation than the uncanny intelligence of a horse.

Because Hans performed only in the presence of an audience 2
that could see the blackboard and therefore knew the correct answer, Pfungst reasoned that the secret lay in observation of the

audience rather than of the horse. He finally discovered that as soon as the problem was written on the blackboard, the audience bent forward very slightly in anticipation to watch Hans's fore-feet. As slight as that movement was, Hans perceived it and took it as his signal to begin tapping. As his taps approached the correct number, the audience became tense with excitement and made almost imperceptible movements of the head — which sig-naled Hans to stop counting. The audience, simply by expecting Hans to stop when the correct number was reached, had actually told the animal when to stop. Pfungst clearly demonstrated that Hans's intelligence was nothing but a mechanical response to his audience, which unwittingly communicated the answer by its body language.

The "Clever Hans Phenomenon," as it has come to be 3 known, raises an interesting question. If a mere horse can detect unintentional and extraordinarily subtle body signals, might they not also be detected by human beings? Professional gamblers and con men have long been known for their skill in observing the body-language cues of their victims, but only recently has it been shown scientifically that all speakers constantly detect and inter-pret such cues also, even though they do not realize it.

An examination of television word games several years ago 4 revealed that contestants inadvertently gave their partners body-language signals that led to correct answers. In one such game, contestants had to elicit certain words from their partners, but they were permitted to give only brief verbal clues as to what the words might be. It turned out that sometimes the contestants also gave body signals that were much more informative than the verbal clues. In one case, a contestant was supposed to answer *sad* in response to his partner's verbal clue of *happy* — that is, the correct answer was a word opposite to the verbal clue. The partner giving the *happy* clue unconsciously used his body to indicate to his fellow contestant that an opposite word was needed. He did that by shifting his body and head very slightly to one side as he said *happy*, then to the other side in expectation of an opposite word.

Contestants on a television program are usually unsophisti- 5 cated about psychology and linguistics, but trained psychological experimenters also unintentionally flash body signals which are sometimes detected by the test subjects — and which may distort the results of experiments. Hidden cameras have revealed that the sex of the experimenter, for example, can influence the responses of subjects. Even though the films showed that both male and female experimenters carried out the experiments in the same way and asked the same questions, the experimenters were very much aware of their own sex in relation to the sex of the subjects. Male experimenters spent 16 percent more time carrying out experiments with female subjects than they did with male subjects; similarly, female experimenters took 13 percent longer to go through experiments with male subjects than they did with female subjects. The cameras also revealed that chivalry is not dead in the psychological experiment; male experimenters smiled about six times as often with female subjects as they did with male subjects.

The important question, of course, is whether or not such nonverbal communication influences the results of experiments. The answer is that it often does. Psychologists who have watched films made without the knowledge of either the experimenters or the subjects could predict almost immediately which experimenters would obtain results from their subjects that were in the direction of the experimenters' own biases. Those experimenters who seemed more dominant, personal, and relaxed during the first moments of conversation with their subjects usually obtained the results that they secretly hoped the experiments would yield. And they somehow communicated their secret hopes in a completely visual way, regardless of what they said or their paralanguage when they spoke. That was made clear when these films were shown to two groups, one of which saw the films without hearing the sound track while the other heard only the sound track without seeing the films. The group that heard only the voices could not accurately predict the experimenters' biases — but those who saw the films without hearing the words immediately sensed whether or not the experimenters were communicating their biases. 6

A person who signals his expectations about a certain kind of behavior is not aware that he is doing so — and usually he is indignant when told that his experiment was biased — but the subjects themselves confirm his bias by their performances. Such bias in experiments has been shown to represent self-fulfilling prophecies. In other words, the experimenters' expectations 7 about the results of the experiment actually result in those expectations coming true. That was demonstrated when each of twelve experimenters was given five rats bred from an identical strain of laboratory animals. Half of the experimenters were told that their rats could be expected to perform brilliantly because they had been bred especially for high intelligence and quickness in running through a maze. The others were told that their rats could be expected to perform very poorly because they had been bred for low intelligence. All the experimenters were then asked to teach their rats to run a maze.

Almost as soon as the rats were put into the maze it became clear that those for which the experimenters had high expectations would prove to be the better performers. And the rats which were expected to perform badly did in fact perform very badly, even though they were bred from the identical strain as the excellent performers. Some of these poor performers did not even budge from their starting positions in the maze. The misleading prophecy about the behavior of the two groups of rats was fulfilled — simply because the two groups of experimenters unconsciously communicated their expectations to the animals. Those experimenters who anticipated high performance were friendlier to their animals than those who expected low performance; they handled their animals more, and they did so more gently. Clearly, the predictions of the experimenters were communicated to the rats in subtle and unintended ways — and the rats behaved accordingly.   8

Since animals such as laboratory rats and Clever Hans can detect body-language cues, it is not surprising that human beings are just as perceptive in detecting visual signals about expectations for performance. It is a psychological truth that we are likely to speak to a person whom we expect to be unpleasant in such a way that we force him to act unpleasantly. But it has only recently become apparent that poor children — often black or Spanish-speaking — perform badly in school because that is what their teachers expect of them, and because the teachers manage to convey that expectation by both verbal and nonverbal channels. True to the teachers' prediction, the black and brown children probably will do poorly — not necessarily because children from minority groups are capable only of poor performance, but be-   9 cause poor performance has been expected of them. The first grade may be the place where teachers anticipate poor performances by children of certain racial, economic, and cultural backgrounds — and where the teachers actually teach these children how to fail.

Evidence of the way the "Clever Hans Phenomenon" works in many schools comes from a careful series of experiments by psychologist Robert Rosenthal and his co-workers at Harvard University. They received permission from a school south of San Francisco to give a series of tests to the children in the lower grades. The teachers were blatantly lied to. They were told that the test was a newly developed tool that could predict which children would be "spurters" and achieve high performance in the coming year. Actually, the experimenters administered a new kind of IQ test that the teachers were unlikely to have seen previously. After IQ scores were obtained, the experimenters selected the names of 20 percent of the children completely at random. Some of the selected children scored very high on the IQ test and others scored low, some were from middle-class families and others from lower-class. Then the teachers were lied to again. The experimenters said that the tests singled out this 20 percent as the children who could be expected to make unusual intellectual gains in the coming year. The teachers were also cautioned not to discuss the test results with the pupils or their parents. Since the names of these children had been selected completely at random, any difference between them and the 80 percent not designated as "spurters" was completely in the minds of the teachers.

All the children were given IQ tests again during that school year and once more the following year. The 20 percent who had been called to the attention of their teachers did indeed turn in the high performances expected of them — in some cases dramatic increases of 25 points in IQ. The teachers' comments about these children also were revealing. The teachers considered them more happy, curious, and interesting than the other 80 percent — and they predicted that they would be successes in life, a prophecy they had already started to fulfill. The experiment plainly showed that children who are expected to gain intellectually do gain and that their behavior improves as well.

The results of the experiment are clear—but the explanation   12
for the results is not. It might be imagined that the teachers
simply devoted more time to the children singled out for high
expectations, but the study showed that was not so. Instead, the
influence of the teachers upon these children apparently was
much more subtle. What the teachers said to them, how and
when it was said, the facial expressions, gestures, posture, perhaps
even touch that accompanied their speech—some or all of these
things must have communicated that the teachers expected improved performance from them. And when these children responded correctly, the teachers were quicker to praise them and
also more lavish in their praise. Whatever the exact mechanism
was, the effect upon the children who had been singled out was
dramatic. They changed their ideas about themselves, their behavior, their motivation, and their learning capacities.

The lesson of the California experiment is that pupil per-   13
formance does not depend so much upon a school's audio-visual
equipment or new textbooks or enriching trips to museums as it
does upon teachers whose body language communicates high
expectations for the pupils—even if the teacher thinks she
"knows" that a black, a Puerto Rican, a Mexican-American, or
any other disadvantaged child is fated to do poorly in school.
Apparently, remedial instruction in our schools is misdirected. It
is needed more by the middle-class teachers than by the disadvantaged children.

Questions for Close Reading

1. What is the selection's thesis? Locate the sentence(s) in which Farb
   states his main idea. If he doesn't state the thesis explicitly, express it
   in your own words.
2. Does Farb consider the "Clever Hans Phenomenon" a truly inexplic-
   able phenomenon, or does he give reasons for it? What kinds of
   people and animals are likely to detect and interpret body language
   clues?
3. The author refers to an experiment that used rats in a maze. Who was
   really the subject of that experiment, the rats or someone else?
4. What did the Harvard experiment in the San Francisco schools prove?
   In this experiment, who were the "rats"?
5. Refer to your dictionary as needed to define the following words used
   in the selection: *unwittingly* (paragraph 2), *linguistics* (5), and *blatantly* (10).

Questions About the Writer's Craft

1. **The pattern.** Scientific experiments are set up to limit the possible causes of an effect. In describing the "Clever Hans Phenomenon," Farb reveals that naive viewers thought the cause of the phenomenon was one thing (Hans doing math in his head), while the psychologist Pfungst determined the cause to be something else (Hans reacting to body movements of the audience). Locate other places where Farb uses the same pattern: an effect with two possible causes — one simple, one subtle.

2. **Other patterns.** Farb's essay begins with a detailed example of a clever horse years ago and follows with a recent example of game-show contestants. Why do you think the writer places these examples before the discussion of modern scientific experiments? Why do you suppose he saves for last the research on schoolchildren?

3. A qualifier is a word that moderates or "tones down" the certainty of a statement. *Often, usually, almost,* and *sometimes* are common qualifiers. Their absence and the use of terms like *always* and *never* produce "unqualified" statements. Look for qualifiers in the selection — especially in places where Farb interprets research for us. Does he qualify his statements more or less as the essay goes on?

4. Is Farb serious in his closing remarks about who really needs remedial work? Why does he make his final point this way?

Questions for Further Thought

1. What are the "other words" Farb refers to in the title? How are they different from the words we use when we speak aloud?

2. Are you aware of the subtle (and sometimes not-so-subtle) differences in the ways teachers perceive and thus treat students? Discuss these differences by providing specific examples from your own experience.

3. In at least two of the research projects that Farb discusses, the scientists lied to their subjects. In the grade school experiment, a direct result of the lie was that teachers favored some students, and, presumably, looked on others with disfavor. Do you think it was ethical for researchers to set up an experiment on the basis of lies? Explain.

4. In our dealings with each other, are we sufficiently careful of our body language? What could we do to make our nonverbal communication more productive?

Writing Assignments Using Cause-Effect as a Pattern of Development

∞ 1. As Farb shows, none of us can escape fully other people's expectations. Such expectations may motivate or discourage us. Analyze the extent to which you or someone you know well has been influenced by others' expectations. Langston Hughes's "Salvation" (page 186), Santha Rama Rau's "By Any Other Name" (page 191), Alice Walker's "Beauty: When the Other Dancer Is the Self" (page 499), William Raspberry's "The Handicap of Definition" (page 563), and Virginia Woolf's "Professions for Women" (page 721) should get you thinking about the extent to which our inner worlds may be shaped by others.

2. As Farb implies, many game shows test the contestants' ability to guess or "mind-read" other people's responses. Sometimes in our own lives we have the feeling that people have read our minds, or that we have read theirs. Brainstorm a list of such experiences you have had. Then pick one or two and write an essay in which you examine the experience(s). Analyze the factors that contributed to the effect of "mind-reading." These could include detecting someone's body language cues, knowing another person's habits or opinions, being familiar with his or her schedule, or sharing a common or similar past experience.

Writing Assignments Using Other Patterns of Development

∞ 3. Imagine that you're the principal of a public school attended by disadvantaged students. After determining whether the school is at the elementary, middle-grades, or senior-high level, write a letter to your faculty briefly explaining the gist of the Rosenthal experiment. Then make three recommendations to your staff about techniques they can use to encourage high achievement in students. When making your proposals, keep in mind that teachers may have deep-seated biases of which they're not aware. Choose your tone and words carefully; you want to avoid offending the faculty or implying that they're not trying to do their best. Before planning the essay, you might want to read William Raspberry's "The Handicap of Definition" (page 563) and Alice Walker's "Beauty: When the Other Dancer Is the Self" (page 499). Raspberry's essay provides insight into the way labels can inhibit growth, while Walker's essay dramatizes the powerful effect a teacher can have on a child.

∞ 4. Read William Raspberry's "The Handicap of Definition" (page 563). Then, citing both the Rosenthal study and Raspberry's essay in your introduction, write an essay about a person — one you know personally or have heard about — who surpassed the restricted expectations held by other people. Support your thesis with dramatic evidence showing how the person overcame the obstacles imposed by others.

Alice Walker

The eighth child of Georgia sharecroppers, Alice Walker (1944–   ) has built a reputation as a sensitive chronicler of the black experience in America. After studying at Spelman College in Atlanta, Walker graduated from Sarah Lawrence College in New York. Soon after that, she worked in the civil rights movement helping to register black voters and teaching in Mississippi's Head Start program. The recipient of numerous writing fellowships and the founder of her own publishing company, Walker has written extensively: a biography, *Langston Hughes, American Poet* (1973); poetry, *Revolutionary Petunias and Other Poems* (1973); short stories, collected in *In Love & Trouble* (1973) and *You Can't Keep a Good Woman Down* (1981); essays, gathered in *Living by the Word* (1988); and novels, including *Meridian* (1976), *The Color Purple* (1982), and *The Temple of My Familiar* (1989). *The Color Purple* won both the Pulitzer Prize and the American Book Award and was made into a feature film. The following selection comes from Walker's 1983 collection of essays, *In Search of Our Mothers' Gardens*.

Beauty: When the Other Dancer Is the Self

A disfiguring injury can seriously affect anyone's self-esteem. Alice Walker sustained such an injury as a child. In this essay, she describes what happened to her and provides glimpses of her Southern childhood and the people who changed her life for better or worse. Walker's experience is a commentary on the role of good looks in a young girl's life and on the importance of good sense in gaining self-acceptance and esteem as an adult.

It is a bright summer day in 1947. My father, a fat, funny   1
man with beautiful eyes and a subversive wit, is trying to decide

which of his eight children he will take with him to the county fair. My mother, of course, will not go. She is knocked out from getting most of us ready: I hold my neck stiff against the pressure of her knuckles as she hastily completes the braiding and then beribboning of my hair.

My father is the driver for the rich old white lady up the road. 2
Her name is Miss Mey. She owns all the land for miles around, as well as the house in which we live. All I remember about her is that she once offered to pay my mother thirty-five cents for cleaning her house, raking up piles of her magnolia leaves, and washing her family's clothes, and that my mother — she of no money, eight children, and a chronic earache — refused it. But I do not think of this in 1947. I am two and a half years old. I want to go everywhere my daddy goes. I am excited at the prospect of riding in a car. Someone has told me fairs are fun. That there is room in the car for only three of us doesn't faze me at all. Whirling happily in my starchy frock, showing off my biscuit-polished patent-leather shoes and lavender socks, tossing my head in a way that makes my ribbons bounce, I stand, hands on hips, before my father. "Take me, Daddy," I say with assurance; "I'm the prettiest!"

Later, it does not surprise me to find myself in Miss Mey's 3
shiny black car, sharing the back seat with the other lucky ones. Does not surprise me that I thoroughly enjoy the fair. At home that night I tell the unlucky ones all I can remember about the merry-go-round, the man who eats live chickens, and the teddy bears, until they say: that's enough baby Alice. Shut up now, and go to sleep.

It is Easter Sunday, 1950. I am dressed in a green, flocked, 4
scalloped-hem dress (handmade by my adoring sister, Ruth) that has its own smooth satin petticoat and tiny hot-pink roses tucked into each scallop. My shoes, new T-strap patent leather, again highly biscuit-polished. I am six years old and have learned one of the longest Easter speeches to be heard that day, totally unlike the speech I said when I was two: "Easter lilies / pure and white / blossom in / the morning light." When I rise to give my speech I do so on a great wave of love and pride and expectation. People in the church stop rustling their new crinolines. They seem to

hold their breath. I can tell they admire my dress, but it is my spirit, bordering on sassiness (womanishness), they secretly applaud.

"That girl's a little *mess*," they whisper to each other, pleased.   5

Naturally I say my speech without stammer or pause, unlike   6
those who stutter, stammer, or, worst of all, forget. This is before the word "beautiful" exists in people's vocabulary, but "Oh, isn't she the *cutest* thing?" frequently floats my way. "And got so much sense!" they gratefully add . . . for which thoughtful addition I thank them to this day.

It was great fun being cute. But then, one day, it ended.   7

I am eight years old and a tomboy. I have a cowboy hat,   8
cowboy boots, checkered shirt and pants, all red. My playmates are my brothers, two and four years older than I. Their colors are black and green, the only difference in the way we are dressed. On Saturday nights we all go to the picture show, even my mother; Westerns are her favorite kind of movie. Back home, "on the ranch," we pretend we are Tom Mix, Hopalong Cassidy, Lash LaRue (we've even named one of our dogs Lash LaRue); we chase each other for hours rustling cattle, being outlaws, delivering damsels from distress. Then my parents decide to buy my brothers guns. These are not "real" guns. They shoot "BBs," copper pellets my brothers say will kill birds. Because I am a girl, I do not get a gun. Instantly I am relegated to the position of Indian. Now there appears a great distance between us. They shoot and shoot at everything with their new guns. I try to keep up with my bow and arrows.

One day while I am standing on top of our makeshift   9
"garage" — pieces of tin nailed across some poles — holding my bow and arrow and looking out toward the fields, I feel an incredible blow in my right eye. I look down just in time to see my brother lower his gun.

Both brothers rush to my side. My eye stings, and I cover it   10
with my hand. "If you tell," they say, "we will get a whipping. You don't want that to happen, do you?" I do not. "Here is a piece of wire," says the older brother, picking it up from the roof; "say you stepped on one end of it and the other flew up and hit you." The pain is beginning to start. "Yes," I say. "Yes, I will say that is what happened." If I do not say this is what happened, I

know my brothers will find ways to make me wish I had. But now I will say anything that gets me to my mother.

Confronted by our parents we stick to the lie agreed upon. They place me on a bench on the porch and I close my left eye while they examine the right. There is a tree growing from underneath the porch that climbs past the railing to the roof. It is the last thing my right eye sees. I watch as its trunk, its branches, and then its leaves are blotted out by the rising blood.   11

I am in shock. First there is intense fever, which my father tries to break using lily leaves bound around my head. Then there are chills: my mother tries to get me to eat soup. Eventually, I do not know how, my parents learn what has happened. A week after the "accident" they take me to see a doctor. "Why did you wait so long to come?" he asks, looking into my eye and shaking his head. "Eyes are sympathetic," he says. "If one is blind, the other will likely become blind too."   12

This comment of the doctor's terrifies me. But it is really how I look that bothers me most. Where the BB pellet struck there is a glob of whitish scar tissue, a hideous cataract, on my eye. Now when I stare at people — a favorite pastime, up to now — they will stare back. Not at the "cute" little girl, but at her scar. For six years I do not stare at anyone, because I do not raise my head.   13

Years later, in the throes of a mid-life crisis, I ask my mother and sister whether I changed after the "accident." "No," they say, puzzled. "What do you mean?"   14

What do I mean?   15

I am eight, and, for the first time, doing poorly in school, where I have been something of a whiz since I was four. We have just moved to the place where the "accident" occurred. We do not know any of the people around us because this is a different county. The only time I see the friends I knew is when we go back to our old church. The new school is the former state penitentiary. It is a large stone building, cold and drafty, crammed to overflowing with boisterous, ill-disciplined children. On the third floor there is a huge circular imprint of some partition that has been torn out.   16

"What used to be here?" I ask a sullen girl next to me on our way past it to lunch.   17

"The electric chair," says she. 18

At night I have nightmares about the electric chair; and 19
about all the people reputedly "fried" in it. I am afraid of the
school, where all the students seem to be budding criminals.

"What's the matter with your eye?" they ask, critically. 20

When I don't answer (I cannot decide whether it was an 21
"accident" or not), they shove me, insist on a fight.

My brother, the one who created the story about the wire, 22
comes to my rescue. But then brags so much about "protecting"
me, I become sick.

After months of torture at the school, my parents decide to 23
send me back to our old community, to my old school. I live with
my grandparents and the teacher they board. But there is no room
for Phoebe, my cat. By the time my grandparents decide there *is*
room, and I ask for my cat, she cannot be found. Miss Yarbor-
ough, the boarding teacher, takes me under her wing, and begins
to teach me to play the piano. But soon she marries an African —
a "prince," she says — and is whisked away to his continent.

At my old school there is at least one teacher who loves me. 24
She is the teacher who "knew me before I was born" and bought
my first baby clothes. It is she who makes life bearable. It is her
presence that finally helps me turn on the one child at the school
who continually calls me "one-eyed bitch." One day I simply
grab him by his coat and beat him until I am satisfied. It is my
teacher who tells me my mother is ill.

My mother is lying in bed in the middle of the day, some- 25
thing I have never seen. She is in too much pain to speak. She has
an abscess in her ear. I stand looking down on her, knowing that
if she dies, I cannot live. She is being treated with warm oils and
hot bricks held against her cheeks. Finally a doctor comes. But I
must go back to my grandparents' house. The weeks pass but I am
hardly aware of it. All I know is that my mother might die, my
father is not so jolly, my brothers still have their guns, and I am
the one sent away from home.

"You did not change," they say. 26

Did I imagine the anguish of never looking up? 27

I am twelve. When relatives come to visit I hide in my room. 28
My cousin Brenda, just my age, whose father works in the post

office and whose mother is a nurse, comes to find me. "Hello," she says. And then she asks, looking at my recent school picture, which I did not want taken, and on which the "glob," as I think of it, is clearly visible, "You still can't see out of that eye?"

"No," I say, and flop back on the bed over my book.   29

That night, as I do almost every night, I abuse my eye. I rant   30
and rave at it, in front of the mirror. I plead with it to clear up before morning. I tell it I hate and despise it. I do not pray for sight. I pray for beauty.

"You did not change," they say.   31

I am fourteen and baby-sitting for my brother Bill, who lives   32
in Boston. He is my favorite brother and there is a strong bond between us. Understanding my feelings of shame and ugliness he and his wife take me to a local hospital, where the "glob" is removed by a doctor named O. Henry. There is still a small bluish crater where the scar tissue was, but the ugly white stuff is gone. Almost immediately I become a different person from the girl who does not raise her head. Or so I think. Now that I've raised my head I win the boyfriend of my dreams. Now that I've raised my head I have plenty of friends. Now that I've raised my head classwork comes from my lips as faultlessly as Easter speeches did, and I leave high school as valedictorian, most popular student, and *queen*, hardly believing my luck. Ironically, the girl who was voted most beautiful in our class (and was) was later shot twice through the chest by a male companion, using a "real" gun, while she was pregnant. But that's another story in itself. Or is it?

"You did not change," they say.   33

It is now thirty years since the "accident." A beautiful jour-   34
nalist comes to visit and to interview me. She is going to write a cover story for her magazine that focuses on my latest book. "Decide how you want to look on the cover," she says. "Glamorous, or whatever."

Never mind "glamorous," it is the "whatever" that I hear.   35
Suddenly all I can think of is whether I will get enough sleep the night before the photography session: if I don't, my eye will be tired and wander, as blind eyes will.

At night in bed with my lover I think up reasons why I   36
should not appear on the cover of a magazine. "My meanest

critics will say I've sold out," I say. "My family will now realize I write scandalous books."

"But what's the real reason you don't want to do this?" he   37
asks.

"Because in all probability," I say in a rush, "my eye won't be   38
straight."

"It will be straight enough," he says. Then, "Besides, I   39
thought you'd made your peace with that."

And I suddenly remember that I have.   40

I remember: 41

I am talking to my brother Jimmy, asking if he remembers   42
anything unusual about the day I was shot. He does not know I
consider that day the last time my father, with his sweet home
remedy of cool lily leaves, chose me, and that I suffered and raged
inside because of this. "Well," he says, "all I remember is standing by the side of the highway with Daddy, trying to flag down a
car. A white man stopped, but when Daddy said he needed somebody to take his little girl to the doctor, he drove off."

I remember: 43

I am in the desert for the first time. I fall totally in love with   44
it. I am so overwhelmed by its beauty, I confront for the first
time, consciously, the meaning of the doctor's words years ago:
"Eyes are sympathetic. If one is blind, the other will likely become blind too." I realize I have dashed about the world madly,
looking at this, looking at that, storing up images against the
fading of the light. *But I might have missed seeing the desert!* The
shock of that possibility—and gratitude for over twenty-five
years of sight—sends me literally to my knees. Poem after poem
comes—which is perhaps how poets pray.

On Sight   45

> *I am so thankful I have seen*
> *The Desert*
> *And the creatures in the desert*
> *And the desert Itself.*
>
> *The desert has its own moon*
> *Which I have seen*
> *With my own eye.*
> *There is no flag on it.*

Trees of the desert have arms
All of which are always up
That is because the moon is up
The sun is up
Also the sky
The stars
Clouds
None with flags.

If there were flags, I doubt
the trees would point.
Would you?

But mostly, I remember this: 46

I am twenty-seven, and my baby daughter is almost three.   47
Since her birth I have worried about her discovery that her
mother's eyes are different from other people's. Will she be embarrassed? I think. What will she say? Every day she watches a
television program called "Big Blue Marble." It begins with a
picture of the earth as it appears from the moon. It is bluish, a
little battered-looking, but full of light, with whitish clouds swirling around it. Every time I see it I weep with love, as if it is a
picture of Grandma's house. One day when I am putting Rebecca
down for her nap, she suddenly focuses on my eye. Something
inside me cringes, gets ready to try to protect myself. All children
are cruel about physical differences, I know from experience, and
that they don't always mean to be is another matter. I assume
Rebecca will be the same.

But no-o-o-o. She studies my face intently as we stand, her   48
inside and me outside the crib. She even holds my face maternally
between her dimpled little hands. Then, looking every bit as
serious and lawyerlike as her father, she says, as if it may just
possibly have slipped my attention: "Mommy, there's a *world* in
your eye." (As in, "Don't be alarmed, or do anything crazy.")
And then, gently, but with great interest: "Mommy, where did
you *get* that world in your eye?"

For the most part, the pain left then. (So what, if my brothers   49
grew up to buy even more powerful pellet guns for their sons and
to carry real guns themselves. So what, if a young "Morehouse
man" once nearly fell off the steps of Trevor Arnett Library
because he thought my eyes were blue.) Crying and laughing I ran

to the bathroom, while Rebecca mumbled and sang herself off to sleep. Yes indeed, I realized, looking into the mirror. There *was* a world in my eye. And I saw that it was possible to love it: that in fact, for all it had taught me of shame and anger and inner vision, I *did* love it. Even to see it drifting out of orbit in boredom, or rolling up out of fatigue, not to mention floating back at attention in excitement (bearing witness, a friend has called it), deeply suitable to my personality, and even characteristic of me.

That night I dream I am dancing to Stevie Wonder's song   50 "Always" (the name of the song is really "As," but I hear it as "Always"). As I dance, whirling and joyous, happier than I've ever been in my life, another bright-faced dancer joins me. We dance and kiss each other and hold each other through the night. The other dancer has obviously come through all right, as I have done. She is beautiful, whole and free. And she is also me.

Questions for Close Reading

1. What is the selection's thesis? Locate the sentence(s) in which Walker states her main idea. If she doesn't state the thesis explicitly, express it in your own words.
2. How does Walker's injury affect her ability to express herself and relate to others?
3. What is the connection between the loss of young Alice's cat and her teacher's marriage (paragraph 23)?
4. How do you interpret the essay's title—"Beauty: When the Other Dancer Is the Self"? How does the title reinforce Walker's thesis?
5. Refer to your dictionary as needed to define the following words used in the selection: *subversive* (paragraph 1), *chronic* (2), *flocked* (4), *crinoline* (4), *cataract* (13), and *abscess* (25).

Questions About the Writer's Craft

1. **The pattern.** Walker's essay is structured around a causal chain that shows the interaction between the external and the internal. Explain how Walker develops this chain throughout the essay.
2. **Other patterns.** Although Walker narrates incidents occurring from infancy to midlife, she writes in the present tense. Why do you think she does this?
3. How does Walker signal the ages at which she experiences a crisis or some other major event? What technique does she use?

4. The refrain "You did not change" occurs in differing contexts throughout Walker's essay. What is the effect of this repetition?

Questions for Further Thought

1. Walker believes that her father's attitude toward her changed after her injury. Has someone's attitude toward you ever changed dramatically? What precipitated the change? What were its consequences?
2. Walker says that she lied about the cause of her injury partly to protect herself from her brothers' possible retaliation. If a person is bullied and intimidated, what is the best course of action — to comply with those more powerful, to go against their wishes secretly, or to defy them openly and face the consequences? Why?
3. Walker recalls being "relegated to the position of Indian." Think of a time when you were excluded from participation in some activity because of your age, sex, race, or economic status. How did you feel about being excluded?
4. Walker tells us that although she was the valedictorian and the "most popular student" in her high school class, another student was voted most beautiful. If you could be academically outstanding, extremely well liked, or strikingly good looking, which one would you choose? Why?

Writing Assignments Using Cause-Effect as a Pattern of Development

1. An event initially viewed as handicapping can prove, as Walker shows, to be a blessing. Write a paper showing the effect on your life of an experience that at first seemed negative but turned out for the best.
2. Walker expects her daughter to react with revulsion to her eye injury. To her surprise, her daughter's reaction is tender and gentle. Think of a time you expected someone to treat you with kindness, but instead you were treated harshly, or, conversely, you expected severity but were met with generosity. In an essay, trace the causes of your faulty expectation as well as the possible reasons for the other person's unexpected behavior. Draw some conclusions about human nature.

Writing Assignments Using Other Patterns of Development

3. Walker writes of an experience in which joyful, exuberant play turned —in an instant— to terror. Write about a time in your own or in someone else's life when there was a sudden reversal of events—a positive experience that became negative or vice versa. Use vivid images, varied sentence structure, and dialogue to capture what happened. Did the event leave a lasting impression? If so, end by writing briefly about this effect.

∞ 4. Walker mentions two elementary school teachers who responded to her in a loving, supportive way. Write a letter to beginning grade school teachers outlining the steps they should (and should not) take to make their students' school experience a positive one. Peter Farb's "In Other Words" (page 491) will help you appreciate the powerful influence that teachers can exert on children.

Lewis Thomas

Lewis Thomas (1913–) has earned a reputation as an outstanding scientist and physician. A graduate of Princeton University and Harvard Medical School, Thomas has held both the deanship of Yale University's medical school and the presidency of Sloan-Kettering Memorial Cancer Center. But more remarkable than Thomas's professional accomplishments is his gift for communicating the wonder of medicine and biology to the average reader. His essays, many of which first appeared in the *New England Journal of Medicine*, are less about medicine than they are about what he calls the "mystery of being." Thomas has published many books: the memoir, *The Youngest Science* (1983); and four essay collections, *Lives of a Cell* (1974), which won a National Book Award; *The Medusa and the Snail* (1979); *Late Night Thoughts on Listening to Mahler's Ninth Symphony* (1984); and *Etcetera, Etcetera* (1990). The following selection is from *Late Night Thoughts*.

The Lie Detector

The evidence against the innate goodness of the human race seems overwhelming at times. But writer-physician Lewis Thomas, expressing himself in typically plain-spoken but elegant prose, takes comfort in what a lie detector reveals about human impulses and instincts.

Every once in a while the reasons for discouragement about 1 the human prospect pile up so high that it becomes difficult to see the way ahead, and it is then a great blessing to have one conspicuous and irrefutable good thing to think about ourselves, something solid enough to step onto and look beyond the pile.

Language is often useful for this, and music. A particular 2 painting, if you have the right receptors, can lift the spirits and hold them high enough to see a whole future for the race. The sound of laughter in the distance in the dark can be a marvelous encouragement. But these are chancy stimuli, ready to work only if you happen to be ready to receive them, which takes a bit of luck.

I have been reading magazine stories about the technology of   3
lie detection lately, and it occurs to me that this may be the thing I've been looking for, an encouragement propped up by genuine, hard scientific data. It is promising enough that I've decided to take as given what the articles say, uncritically, and to look no further. For a while, anyway.

Lying Is a Strain

As I understand it, a human being cannot tell a lie, even a   4
small one, without setting off a kind of smoke alarm somewhere deep in a dark lobule of the brain, resulting in the sudden discharge of nerve impulses, or the sudden outpouring of neurohormones of some sort, or both. The outcome, recorded by the lie-detector gadgetry, is a highly reproducible cascade of changes in the electrical conductivity of the skin, the heart rate, and the manner of breathing, similar to the responses to various kinds of stress.

Lying, then, is stressful, even when we do it for protection,   5
or relief, or escape, or profit, or just for the pure pleasure of lying and getting away with it. It is a strain, distressing enough to cause the emission of signals to and from the central nervous system warning that something has gone wrong. It is, in a pure physiological sense, an unnatural act.

Now I regard this as a piece of extraordinarily good news,   6
meaning, unless I have it all balled up, that we are a moral species by compulsion, at least in the limited sense that we are biologically designed to be truthful to each other. Lying doesn't hurt, mind you, and perhaps you could tell lies all day and night for years on end without being damaged, but maybe not — maybe the lie detector informs us that repeated, inveterate untruthfulness will gradually undermine the peripheral vascular system, the sweat glands, the adrenals, and who knows what else. Perhaps we should be looking into the possibility of lying as an etiologic agent for some of the common human ailments still beyond explaining, recurrent head colds, for instance, or that most

human of all unaccountable disorders, a sudden pain in the lower mid-back.

Truth: Genetically Required?

It makes a sort of shrewd biological sense, and might there- 7
fore represent a biological trait built into our genes, a feature of
humanity as characteristic for us as feathers for birds or scales for
fish, enabling us to live, at our best, the kinds of lives we are
designed to live. This is, I suppose, the "sociobiological" view to
take, with the obvious alternative being that we are brought up
this way as children in response to the rules of our culture. But if
the latter is the case, you would expect to encounter, every once
in a while, societies in which the rule does not hold, and I have
never heard of a culture in which lying was done by everyone as a
matter of course, all life through, nor can I imagine such a group
functioning successfully. Biologically speaking, there is good reason for us to restrain ourselves from lying outright to each other
whenever possible. We are indeed a social species, more interde-
pendent than the celebrated social insects; we can no more live a
solitary life than can a bee; we are obliged, as a species, to rely on
each other. Trust is a fundamental requirement for our kind of
existence, and without it all our linkages would begin to snap
loose.

The restraint is a mild one, so gentle as to be almost imper- 8
ceptible. But it is there; we know about it from what we call guilt,
and now we have a neat machine to record it as well.

It seems a trivial thing to have this information, but perhaps 9
it tells us to look again, and look deeper. If we had better instruments, designed for profounder probes, we might see needles
flipping, lines on charts recording quantitative degrees of mean-
ness of spirit, or a lack of love. I do not wish for such instruments,
I hope they will never be constructed; they would somehow
belittle the issues involved. It is enough, quite enough, to know
that we cannot even tell a plain untruth, betray a trust, without
scaring some part of our own brains. I'd rather guess at the rest.

Questions for Close Reading

1. What is the selection's thesis? Locate the sentence(s) in which
Thomas states his main idea. If he doesn't state the thesis explicitly,
express it in your own words.

2. For what reasons does Thomas call lying an "unnatural act"? How does he feel about its being "unnatural"?

3. Thomas writes that receptivity to language, music, art, and laughter "takes a bit of luck" (paragraph 2). What do you think he means by this statement?

4. To his "sociobiological" view of truth telling, Thomas contrasts another viewpoint. What is this other interpretation? Does he give this other interpretation equal evidence? Why or why not?

5. Refer to your dictionary as needed to define the following words used in the selection: *irrefutable* (paragraph 1), *receptors* (2), *stimuli* (2), *lobule* (4), *neurohormones* (4), *inveterate* (6), and *etiologic* (6).

Questions About the Writer's Craft

1. **The pattern.** At the heart of Thomas's essay is a causal chain consisting of a series of interwoven causes and effects. What is this causal chain?

2. Thomas mixes technical terms from neuroscience with a rather informal style, involving contractions, the first-person ("I") point of view, colloquial expressions ("unless I have it all balled up"), and sentence fragments. Why might he have chosen to blend two such contrasting styles?

3. When presenting his viewpoint, Thomas uses a number of qualifiers: "it occurs to me" (3), "as I understand it" (4), "unless I have it all balled up" (6), and "I suppose" (7). What is the effect of these qualifiers? Do they contribute to or detract from his credibility?

4. Thomas's next-to-last paragraph is shorter than any other in the essay. What function does this brief paragraph serve?

Questions for Further Thought

1. Thomas opens his essay by saying that "reasons for discouragement about the human prospect" sometimes "pile up." But he doesn't go on to specify these reasons. What might these reasons be? What do you find most discouraging about our future?

2. Thomas doesn't differentiate between "white" lies and intentionally hurtful ones. For you, what situations might justify lying?

3. Thomas writes that he requires scientific evidence to support an optimistic outlook. Which is more important to you — concrete evidence or faith? Explain.

4. In nature, opossums "play dead," birds feign broken wings, and chimpanzees direct competitors away from a food source by falsely indicating that the food is located elsewhere. In what ways might humans' ability to deceive also serve an important function? Explain.

Writing Assignments Using Cause-Effect as a Pattern of Development

∞ 1. Reasons for lying, Thomas writes, include profit, protection, pleasure, and kindness. Write an essay tracing the reasons for a lie that you or someone else (a parent, friend, or public figure) once told. Also analyze the effect of the lie. Langston Hughes's "Salvation" (page 186) may provide some insight into the psychology of lying. End the paper with some conclusions about when lying is and is not acceptable.

2. Thomas welcomes the use of the lie detector but has qualms about the development of similar technologies. Focus on one technological breakthrough (word processors, videotape recorders, telephone answering machines) and discuss its negative and positive effects. Although your analysis may be serious or playful, it should have a basically persuasive intent.

Writing Assignments Using Other Patterns of Development

3. Thomas claims, "Trust is a fundamental requirement for our . . . existence." In an essay, define the word *trust*. Consider dramatic examples, brief anecdotes, a comparison of two people when developing the definition. Your essay should illustrate Thomas's point that without trust "all our linkages would . . . snap loose."

∞ 4. According to Thomas, "We are a moral species by compulsion." Write an essay in which you argue for or against this contention. Remembering to consider the opposing opinion, develop your argument by citing several examples of human behavior. Before writing the paper, you might want to read Mark Twain's "The Damned Human Race" (page 619), an essay that presents a point of view very different from Thomas's.

Jonathan Kozol

Jonathan Kozol was born in 1936 and graduated from Harvard University in 1958. He has taught not only in prestigious universities such as Yale but also in several public schools nationwide. Kozol established his reputation as a passionate voice for educational reform with the 1967 publication of *Death at an Early Age: The Destruction of the Hearts and Minds of Negro Children in the Boston Public Schools*, for which he won a National Book Award. His later books, which continue to explore the devastating human cost of poverty, include *On Being a Teacher* (1981), *Illiterate America* (1985), *Rachel and Her Children: Homeless Families in America* (1986), and *Savage Inequalities: Children in America's Schools* (1991). The following selection first appeared in *Harper's* in September 1988.

Are the Homeless Crazy?

When faced with something we fear, we tend to push it away, to assume that it's foreign and strangely alien. That way we keep the situation at arm's length, where it can more easily be dismissed as beyond our comprehension. According to Jonathan Kozol, such a defense mechanism is at work when we assume that most homeless people are mentally ill. The truth about the homeless, though, is both simpler *and* more complex.

It is commonly believed by many journalists and politicians that the homeless of America are, in large part, former patients of large mental hospitals who were deinstitutionalized in the 1970s —the consequence, it is sometimes said, of misguided liberal opinion that favored the treatment of such persons in community-based centers. It is argued that this policy, and the subsequent failure of society to build such centers or to provide them in sufficient number, is the primary cause of homelessness in the United States.

Those who work among the homeless do not find that explanation satisfactory. While conceding that a certain number of the homeless are or have been mentally unwell, they believe that, in the case of most unsheltered people, the primary reason is economic rather than clinical. The cause of homelessness, they say with disarming logic, is the lack of homes and of income with which to rent or acquire them. 2

They point to the loss of traditional jobs in industry (two million every year since 1980) and to the fact that half of those who are laid off end up in work that pays a poverty-level wage. They point out that since 1968 the number of children living in poverty has grown by three million, while welfare benefits to families with children have declined by 35 percent. 3

And they note, too, that these developments have occurred during a time in which the shortage of low-income housing has intensified as the gentrification[1] of our major cities has accelerated. Half a million units of low-income housing are lost each year to condominium conversion as well as to arson, demolition, or abandonment. Between 1978 and 1980, median rents climbed 30 percent for people in the lowest income sector, driving many of these families into the streets. Since 1980, rents have risen at even faster rates. 4

Hard numbers, in this instance, would appear to be of greater help than psychiatric labels in telling us why so many people become homeless. Eight million American families now use half or more of their income to pay their rent or mortgage. At the same time, federal support for low-income housing dropped from $30 billion (1980) to $7.5 billion (1988). Under Presidents Ford and Carter, 500,000 subsidized private housing units were constructed. By President Reagan's second term, the number had dropped to 25,000. 5

In our rush to explain the homeless as a psychiatric problem even the words of medical practitioners who care for homeless people have been curiously ignored. A study published by the Massachusetts Medical Society, for instance, has noted that, with 6

[1]Gentrification occurs when members of the middle and upper-middle classes buy, improve, and move into low-income dwellings, thus strengthening the economic base of a neighborhood but also dislodging the less-well-off residents who previously lived there.

the exceptions of alcohol and drug use, the most frequent illnesses among a sample of the homeless population were trauma (31 percent), upper-respiratory disorders (28 percent), limb disorders (19 percent), mental illness (16 percent), skin diseases (15 percent), hypertension (14 percent), and neurological illnesses (12 percent). Why, we may ask, of all these calamities, does mental illness command so much political and press attention? The answer may be that the label of mental illness places the destitute outside the sphere of ordinary life. It personalizes an anguish that is public in its genesis; it individualizes a misery that is both general in cause and general in application.

There is another reason to assign labels to the destitute and   7
single out mental illness from among their many afflictions. All these other problems — tuberculosis, asthma, scabies, diarrhea, bleeding gums, impacted teeth, etc. — bear no stigma, and mental illness does. It conveys a stigma in the United States. It conveys a stigma in the [former] Soviet Union as well. In both nations the label is used, whether as a matter of deliberate policy or not, to isolate and treat as special cases those who, by deed or word or by sheer presence, represent a threat to national complacence. The two situations are obviously not identical, but they are enough alike to give Americans reason for concern.

The notion that the homeless are largely psychotics who   8
belong in institutions, rather than victims of displacement at the hands of enterprising realtors, spares us from the need to offer realistic solutions to the deep and widening extremes of wealth and poverty in the United States. It also enables us to tell ourselves that the despair of homeless people bears no intimate connection to the privileged existence we enjoy — when, for example, we rent or purchase one of those restored town houses that once provided shelter for people now huddled in the street.

What is to be made, then, of the supposition that the home-   9
less are primarily the former residents of mental hospitals, persons who were carelessly released during the 1970s? Many of them are, to be sure. Among the older men and women in the streets and shelters, as many as one-third (some believe as many as one-half) may be chronically disturbed, and a number of these people were deinstitutionalized during the 1970s. But to operate on that assumption in a city such as New York — where nearly half the homeless are small children whose average age is six —

makes no sense. Their parents, with an average age of twenty-seven, are not likely to have been hospitalized in the 1970s, either.

A frequently cited set of figures tells us that in 1955 the 10 average daily census of non-federal psychiatric institutions was 677,000, and that by 1984 the number had dropped to 151,000. But these people didn't go directly from a hospital room to the street. The bulk of those who had been psychiatric patients and were released from hospitals during the 1960s and early 1970s had been living in low-income housing, many in skid-row hotels or boardinghouses. Such housing — commonly known as SRO (single-room occupancy) units — was drastically diminished by the gentrification of our cities that began in the early '70s. Almost 50 percent of SRO housing was replaced by luxury apartments or office buildings between 1970 and 1980, and the remaining units have been disappearing even more rapidly.

Even for those persons who are ill and were deinstitutiona- 11 lized during the decades before 1980, the precipitating cause of homelessness in 1987 is not illness but loss of housing. SRO housing offered low-cost sanctuaries for the homeless, providing a degree of safety and mutual support for those who lived within them. They were a demeaning version of the community health centers that society had promised; they were the de facto "halfway houses" of the 1970s. For these people too — at most half of the homeless single persons in America — the cause of homelessness is lack of housing.

Even in those cases where mental instability is apparent, 12 homelessness itself is often the precipitating factor. For example, many pregnant women without homes are denied prenatal care because they constantly travel from one shelter to another. Many are anemic. Many are denied essential dietary supplements by recent federal cuts. As a consequence, some of their children do not live to see their second year of life. Do these mothers some-times show signs of stress? Do they appear disorganized, de-pressed, disordered? Frequently. They are immobilized by pain, traumatized by fear. So it is no surprise that when researchers enter the scene to ask them how they "feel," the resulting reports tell us that the homeless are emotionally unwell. The reports do not tell us that we have *made* these people ill. They do not tell us that illness is a natural response to intolerable conditions. Nor do they tell us of the strength and the resilience that so many of these people retain despite the miseries they must endure.

A writer in the *New York Times* describes a homeless woman   13
standing on a traffic island in Manhattan. "She was evicted from her small room in the hotel just across the street," and she is determined to get revenge. Until she does, "nothing will move her from that spot. . . . Her argumentativeness and her angry fixation on revenge, along with the apparent absence of hallucinations, mark her as a paranoid." Most physicians, I imagine, would be more reserved in passing judgment with so little evidence, but this reporter makes his diagnosis without hesitation. "The paranoids of the street," he says, "are among the most difficult to help."

Perhaps so. But does it depend on who is offering the help? Is   14
anyone offering to help this woman get back her home? Is it crazy to seek vengeance for being thrown into the street? The absence of anger, some psychiatrists believe, might indicate much greater illness.

"No one will be turned away," says the mayor of New York   15
City, as hundreds of young mothers with their infants are turned from the doors of shelters season after season. That may sound to some like a denial of reality. "Now you're hearing all kinds of horror stories," says the president of the United States as he denies that anyone is cold or hungry or unhoused. On another occasion he says that the unsheltered "are homeless, you might say, by choice." That sounds every bit as self-deceiving.

The woman standing on the traffic island screaming for   16
revenge until her room has been restored to her sounds relatively healthy by comparison. If three million homeless people did the same, and all at the same time, we might finally be forced to listen.

Questions for Close Reading

1. What is the selection's thesis? Locate the sentence(s) in which Kozol states his main idea. If he doesn't state the thesis explicitly, express it in your own words.
2. What, in Kozol's opinion, is the connection between recent real estate policies and homelessness? What effect have the last few presidential administrations had on homelessness?
3. What changes in the U.S. economy have affected the homeless?

4. According to Kozol, why might the public prefer to hear that the homeless are mentally ill rather than learn about the real causes of homelessness?

5. Refer to your dictionary as needed to define the following words used in the selection: *deinstitutionalized* (paragraph 1), *disarming* (2), *condominium* (4), *subsidized* (5), *hypertension* (6), *psychotics* (8), *displacement* (8), *precipitating* (11), *sanctuaries* (11), *fixation* (13), and *paranoid* (13).

Questions About the Writer's Craft

1. **The pattern.** What seems to be Kozol's purpose for pointing out the basic cause of homelessness? Is his purpose mainly informative, speculative, or persuasive? How do you know? Where in the essay does Kozol imply his purpose?

2. **Other patterns.** Locate places where Kozol uses the argumentation technique of refutation to oppose those who believe that homelessness results from mental illness. What do these refutation passages suggest about the probable views of Kozol's audience?

3. Identify places in paragraph 12 where Kozol uses parallel structure and questions to express his points. Why do you think he chooses to use these two techniques? What effect do they have on his essay's tone?

4. Why do you suppose Kozol returns at the essay's end to the image (introduced in paragraph 13) of the homeless woman who won't leave the traffic island? How does the repetition of this image serve Kozol's purpose?

Questions for Further Thought

1. In paragraph 9, Kozol indicates that almost half of the homeless in Manhattan are young children "whose average age is six." The children's parents, in turn, are typically about twenty-seven years old. Does this information surprise you? Who do you usually picture when you think of the homeless? Do you view the situation differently now that you've read Kozol's analysis? Explain.

2. Do you agree, as Kozol asserts in paragraph 8, that most of us live with the belief that "the despair of homeless people bears no intimate connection to the privileged existence we enjoy?" Do you think that everyday people — you, your instructor, your friends and family — can be considered partially responsible for the problem of homelessness? If so, in what ways?

3. Do you know personally or have you heard or read about anyone who

is helping the homeless? If so, who are they? Why did they get involved? What effects have their efforts had?

4. Who do you think should solve the problem of the homeless? Should it be the mayors and presidents that Kozol cites in paragraphs 5 and 14? Or the social workers and advocates that he refers to in paragraph 2? Should individuals and private citizens take action? Or can the homeless help themselves, as Kozol suggests in his conclusion? Determine who should be involved, and explain what these people should do.

Writing Assignments Using Cause-Effect as a Pattern of Development

1. Do you think it's a good idea to give money, blankets, clothes, or food to people sleeping on the street? Discuss with others the possible effects of such direct assistance, and consider other measures that might be as (or more) effective. Then write a paper analyzing the effects of various means of helping the homeless. At the end, state your opinion about which approach or combination of approaches is most productive.

2. Homelessness isn't the only serious problem facing the country. Focus on another situation that strikes you as critical — perhaps drug addiction among pregnant women, sexual harassment, or the availability of semiautomatic weapons. Brainstorm with others to determine why the problem resists resolutions, despite its obvious importance. Then write an essay discussing the causes for society's failure to take action on the situation. In your conclusion, describe steps that should be taken to remedy the problem. You may need to conduct some library research to develop your ideas.

Writing Assignments Using Other Patterns of Development

3. According to Kozol, labeling the homeless "mentally ill" obscures not only the basic cause of homelessness but also the true nature of the homeless individual. In an essay, narrate a time that you initially misjudged someone because of a label you attached to the person. Convey the individual's genuine character as well as your progressive discovery of the person behind the label. To get a better sense of the way prejudicial attitudes can distort the way we perceive others, you may want to read some of the following essays: Maya Angelou's "Grandmother's Victory" (page 158), Santha Rama Rau's "By Any Other Name" (page 191), Peter Farb's "In Other Words" (page 491),

William Raspberry's "The Handicap of Definition" (page 563), and
Migdia Chinea-Varela's "My Life as a 'Twofer'" (page 613).

∞ 4. Kozol criticizes former President Ronald Reagan and former New
York City Mayor Ed Koch for their callous stance toward the homeless. Examine the position of a campus, local, state, or national
candidate or official on some important issue of your choice. Write
an essay arguing that this person should or shouldn't hold a position
of power. H. L. Mencken's "The Politician" (page 551) may provide
some helpful background for your essay.

Additional Writing Topics
CAUSE-EFFECT

General Assignments

Write an essay that analyzes the causes and/or effects of any of the following topics. Determine your purpose before beginning to write: Will the essay be informative, persuasive, or speculative? As you prewrite, think rigorously about causes and effects; try to identify causal chains. Provide solid evidence for the thesis and use either chronological or emphatic order to organize your supporting points.

1. Sleep deprivation
2. Having the parents you have
3. Lack of communication in a relationship
4. Overexercising or not exercising
5. A particular TV or rock star's popularity
6. Skill or ineptitude in sports
7. A major life decision
8. Stiffer legal penalties for drunken driving
9. Changing attitudes toward protecting the environment
10. A particular national crisis
11. The mass movement of women into the work force
12. Choosing to attend this college
13. "Back to basics" movement in schools
14. Headaches
15. An act of violence
16. A natural event: leaves turning, birds migrating, animals hibernating, an eclipse occurring
17. Pesticide use
18. Use of computers in the classroom
19. Banning disposable cans and bottles
20. A bad habit
21. A fear of _____
22. Legalizing drugs
23. Abolishing the F grade
24. Joining a particular organization
25. Owning a pet

Assignments with a Specific Purpose and Audience

1. A debate about the prominence of athletics at colleges and universities is going to be broadcast on the local cable station. For this debate,

prepare a speech pointing out either the harmful or beneficial effects of "big-time" college athletic programs.

2. Why do students "flunk out" of college? Write an article for the campus newspaper outlining the main causes of failure. Your goal is to steer students away from dangerous habits and situations that lead to poor grades or dropping out.

3. Write a letter to the editor of your favorite newspaper, analyzing the causes of the country's current "trash crisis." Be sure to mention the nationwide love affair with disposable items and the general disregard of the idea of thrift.

4. Employed by your college's work-study office, you've been asked to write a brief pamphlet: "Things to Keep in Mind If You Plan to Work While Attending College." The pamphlet will be given to your fellow students, and it will focus on the effects—both negative and positive—of combining a part-time job with college studies.

5. Why do you think teenage suicide is on the rise? Write a fact sheet for parents of teenagers and for high school guidance counselors, describing the factors that could make a young person desperate enough to attempt suicide. At the end, suggest what parents and counselors can do to help confused, unhappy, young people.

6. Some communities have conducted campaigns encouraging residents to give up television for a fixed period of time. You feel your community should participate in such an experiment. Write a letter to your mayor encouraging a public relations effort in favor of "Turn off the TV Month." Cite specifically the positive effects such a program would have on parents, children, and the community in general.

10

DEFINITION

WHAT IS DEFINITION?

In Lewis Carroll's wise and whimsical tale, *Through the Looking Glass*, Humpty Dumpty proclaims, "When *I* use a word . . . , it means just what I choose it to mean — neither more nor less." If the world were filled with characters like Humpty Dumpty, all of them bending words to their own purposes and accepting no challenges to their personal definitions, communication would be an exercise in frustration. You would say a word, and it would mean one thing to you but perhaps something completely different to a close friend. Without a common understanding, the two of you would talk at cross-purposes, missing each other's meanings as you blundered through a conversation.

For language to communicate, words must have accepted *definitions*. Dictionaries, the sourcebooks for accepted definitions, are compilations of current word-meanings, enabling speakers of a language to understand one another. But as you might suspect, things are not as simple as they first appear. We all know that a word like *discipline* has a standard dictionary definition. We also know, though, that parents argue every day over the meaning of "discipline" and that controversies about the meaning of "discipline" rage within school systems year after year. Moreover, many of the wrenching moral debates of our time also boil down to questions of definition. Much of the controversy over abortion, for instance, centers on what is meant by "life" and when it "begins."

Words can, in short, be slippery. Each of us has unique experiences, attitudes, and values that influence the way we use words and the way we interpret the words of others. Lewis Carroll may have been exaggerating, but Humpty Dumpty's attitude exists — in a very real way — in all of us.

In addition to the idiosyncratic interpretations that may attach to words, some words may shift in meaning over time. The word *pedagogue*, for instance, used to mean "a teacher or leader of children." Over the last several years, though, *pedagogue* has come to mean "a dogmatic, pedantic teacher." And, of course, we invent other words (*modem, byte*) as the need arises.

Writing a definition, then, is no simple task. Primarily, the writer tries to answer basic questions: "What does _____ mean?" and "What is the special or true nature of _____?" The word to be defined may be an object, a concept, a type of person, a place, or a phenomenon. Potential subjects might be the "user-friendly" computer, animal rights, a model teacher, cabin fever. As you will see, there are various strategies for expanding definitions far beyond the single-word synonyms or brief phrases that dictionaries provide.

HOW DEFINITION FITS YOUR PURPOSE AND AUDIENCE

Many times, short-answer exam questions call for definitions. Consider the following examples:

> Define the term *mob psychology*.
> What is the difference between a metaphor and a simile?
> How would you explain what a religious cult is?

In such cases, a good response might involve a definition of several sentences or several paragraphs.

Other times, definition may be used in an essay organized mainly around another pattern of development. In this situation, all that's needed is a brief formal definition or a short definition given in your own words. For instance, a *process analysis* showing readers how computers have revolutionized the typical business office might start with a textbook definition of the term *artificial intelligence*. In an *argumentation-persuasion* paper urging students to support recent efforts to abolish fraternities and sororities, you could refer to the definitions of *blackballing* and *hazing* found in the university handbook. Or your personal definition of *hero* could be the starting point for a *causal analysis* that explains to readers why there are few real heroes in today's world.

But the most complex use of definition, and the one we are primarily concerned with in this chapter, involves exploring a subject through an *extended definition*. Extended definition allows you to apply a personal interpretation to a word, to make a case for a revisionist view of a commonly accepted meaning, to analyze words representing complex or controversial issues. "Pornography," "gun control," "secular humanism," and "right-to-life" would be excellent subjects for extended definition — each is multifaceted, often misunderstood, and fraught with emotional meaning. "Junk food," "anger," "leadership," "anxiety" could make interesting subjects, especially if the extended definition helped readers develop a new understanding of the word. You might, for example, define "anxiety," not as a negative state to be avoided but as a positive force that propels us to take action.

An extended definition could perhaps run several paragraphs or a few pages. Keep in mind, however, that an extended definition may require a chapter or even an entire book to develop. If this seems unlikely, remember that theologians, philosophers, and pop psychologists have devoted entire texts to such concepts as "evil" and "love."

SUGGESTIONS FOR USING DEFINITION IN AN ESSAY

The following suggestions will be helpful whether you use definition as a dominant or supportive pattern of development.

1. Stay focused on the essay's purpose, audience, and tone. Since your purpose for writing an extended definition shapes the entire paper, you need to keep that objective in mind when developing your definition. Suppose you decide to write an essay defining *jazz*. The essay could be purely *informative* and discuss the origins of jazz, its characteristic tonal patterns, and some of the great jazz musicians of the past. Or the essay could move beyond pure information and take on a *persuasive* edge. It might, for example, argue that jazz is the only contemporary form of music worth considering seriously.

Just as your purpose in writing will vary, so will your tone. A strictly informative definition will generally assume a detached, objective tone ("Apathy is an emotional state characterized by listlessness and indifference"). By way of contrast, a definition essay with a persuasive slant might be urgent in tone ("To combat student apathy, we must design programs that engage students in campus life"), or it might take a satiric approach ("An apathetic stance is a wise choice for any thinking student").

As you write, keep thinking about your audience as well. Not only do your readers determine what terms need to be defined (and in how much detail), but they also keep you focused on the essay's purpose and tone. For instance, you probably wouldn't write a serious, informative piece for the college newspaper about the "mystery meat" served in the campus cafeteria. Instead, you would adopt a light tone as you defined the culinary horror and might even make a persuasive pitch about improving the food prepared on campus.

2. Formulate an effective definition. A definition essay sometimes begins with a brief *formal definition* — the dictionary's, a textbook's, or the writer's — and then expands that initial definition with supporting details. Formal definitions are traditionally worded as three-part statements that consist of the following: the *term*, the *class* to which the term belongs, and the *characteristics* that distinguish the term from other members of its class.

Term	Class	Characteristics
The peregrine falcon,	an endangered bird,	is the world's fastest flyer.

Term	Class	Characteristics
A bodice-ripper	is a paperback book,	usually read by women, that deals with highly charged romance in exotic places and faraway times.
Back to basics	is a trend in education	that emphasizes skill mastery through rote learning.

A definition that meets these guidelines will clarify what your subject *is* and what it *is not*. These guidelines also establish the boundaries of your definition, removing unlike items from consideration in your (and your reader's) mind. For example, defining "back to basics" as a trend that emphasizes rote learning signals a certain boundary; it lets readers know that other educational trends, such as those that emphasize children's social or emotional development, will not be part of the essay's definition.

If you decide to include a formal definition, avoid tired openers like "the dictionary says" or "according to Webster." Such weak starts are just plain boring and often herald an unimaginative essay. You should also keep in mind that a strict dictionary definition may actually confuse readers. Suppose you're writing a paper on the way all of us absorb ideas and values from the media. Likening this automatic response to the process of osmosis, you decide to open the paper with a dictionary definition. If you write, "Osmosis is the tendency of a solvent to disperse through a semipermeable membrane into a more concentrated medium," readers are apt to be baffled, even hostile. Remember: The purpose of a definition is to clarify meaning, not obscure it.

You should also stay clear of ungrammatical "is when" definitions: "Blind ambition is when you want to get ahead, no matter how much other people are hurt." Instead, write "Blind ambition is wanting to get ahead, no matter how much other people are hurt." A final pitfall to avoid in writing formal definitions is *circularity*, saying the same thing twice and therefore defining nothing: "A campus tribunal is a tribunal composed of various members of the university community." Circular definitions like this often repeat the term being defined (*tribunal*) or use words having the same meaning (*campus; university community*). In this case, we learn nothing about what a campus tribunal is; the writer says only that "*X* is *X*."

3. Develop the extended definition.   You can choose from a variety of patterns when formulating an extended definition. Description, narration, process, and comparison-contrast can be used — alone or in combination. Imagine that you're planning to write an extended definition of "robotics." You might develop the term by providing *examples* of the ways robots are currently being used in scientific research; by *comparing* and *contrasting* human and robot capabilities; or by *classifying* robots, starting with the most basic and moving to the most advanced or futuristic models.

Which patterns of development to use will often become apparent during the prewriting stage. Here is a list of prewriting questions as well as the pattern of development implied by each question.

Question	Pattern of Development
How does *X* look, taste, smell, feel, and sound?	Description
What does *X* do? When? Where?	Narration
What are some typical instances of *X*?	Illustration
What are *X*'s component parts? What different forms can *X* take?	Division-classification
How does *X* work?	Process analysis
What is *X* like or unlike?	Comparison-contrast
What leads to *X*? What are *X*'s consequences?	Cause-effect

Those questions yielding the most material often suggest the effective pattern(s) for developing an extended definition.

4. Organize the material that develops the definition. If you use a single pattern to develop the extended definition, apply the principles of organization suited to that pattern, as described in the appropriate chapter of this book. Assume that you're defining "fad" by means of *process analysis*. You might organize your paragraphs according to the steps in the process: a fad's slow start as something avant-garde or eccentric; its wildfire acceptance by the general public; the fad's demise as it becomes familiar or tiresome. If you want to define "character" by means of a single *narration*, you would probably organize paragraphs chronologically.

In a definition essay using several methods of development, you should devote separate paragraphs to each pattern. A definition of "relaxation," for instance, might start with a paragraph that *narrates* a particularly relaxing day; then it might move to a paragraph that describes several *examples* of people who find it difficult to unwind; finally, it might end with a paragraph that explains a *process* for relaxing the mind and body.

5. Write an effective introduction. It may be helpful to provide—near the start of a definition essay—a brief formal definition of the term you're going to develop in the rest of the paper. Beyond this basic element, the introduction may include a number of other features. You may explain the *origin* of the term being defined: "Acid rock is a term first coined in the 1960s to describe music that was written or listened to under the influence of the drug LSD." Similarly, you may explain the *etymology*, or linguistic origin, of the key word that focuses the paper. "The term *vigilantism* is derived from the Latin word meaning 'to watch and be awake.'"

You may also use the introduction to clarify what the subject is *not*. Such *definition by negation* can be an effective strategy at the beginning of a paper, especially if readers don't share your view of the subject. In such a case, you might write something like this: "The gorilla, far from being the vicious killer of jungle movies and popular imagination, is a sedentary, gentle creature living in a closely knit family group." Such a statement provides the special focus of your essay and signals some of the misconceptions or fallacies soon to be discussed.

In addition, you may include in the introduction a *stipulative definition*, one that puts special restrictions on a term: "Strictly defined, a mall refers to a one- or two-story enclosed building containing a variety of retail shops and at least two large anchor stores. Highway-strip shopping centers or downtown centers cannot be considered true malls." When a term has multiple meanings, or when its meaning has become fuzzy through misuse, a stipulative definition sets the record straight right at the start, so that readers know exactly what is, and is not, being defined.

Finally, the introduction may end with a *plan of development* that indicates how the definition essay will unfold. A student who returned to school after having raised a family decided to write a paper defining the midlife crisis that led to her enrollment in college. After providing a brief formal definition of midlife crisis, the student rounded off her introduction with this sentence: "Such a midlife crisis starts with vague misgivings, turns into depression, and ends with a significant change in life-style."

———————————

Semanticists, those who study the nature of language, have noted that meaning lies in people, not in words. Because words are symbols—and therefore open to multiple interpretations— dictionaries can only be starting points, never ultimate authorities. The complex nature of language makes the formulation of definitions an important part of writing. Extended definitions are one way we can sort out for ourselves the confusing nature of a word or term. We see the importance of definition every day. The courts define "right to privacy"; the campus handbook explains what "plagiarism" is; international negotiators try to forge an agreement on the meaning of "arms parity." Because definition essays can be developed so many ways, they make demands quite different from most other assignments. Definition essays are, in short, a challenge worth mastering.

STUDENT ESSAY

The following student essay was written by Laura Chen in response to this assignment:

In "Entropy," K. C. Cole takes a scientific term from physics and gives it a broader definition and a wider application. Choose another specialized term and define it in such a way that you reveal something significant about contemporary life.

While reading Laura's paper, try to determine how well it applies the principles of definition. The annotations on Laura's paper and the commentary following it will help you look at the essay more closely.

Physics in Everyday Life
by Laura Chen

Introduction — A boulder sits on a mountainside for a thousand years. The boulder will remain there forever unless an outside force intervenes. Suppose a force does affect the boulder--an earthquake, for instance. Once the boulder begins to thunder down the mountain, it will remain in motion and head in one direction only--downhill--until another force interrupts its progress. If the boulder tumbles into a gorge, it will finally come to rest as gravity anchors it to the earth once more. In both cases, the boulder is exhibiting the physical principle of inertia: the tendency of matter to remain at rest or, if moving, to keep moving in one direction unless affected by an outside force. Inertia, an important factor in the world of physics, also plays a crucial role in the human world. Inertia affects our individual lives as well as the direction taken by society as a whole.

Formal definition · **Thesis** · **Plan of development**

Inertia often influences our value systems and personal growth. Inertia is at work, for example, when people cling to certain behaviors and views. Like the boulder firmly fixed to the mountain, most people are set in their ways. Without thinking, they vote Republican or Democratic because they have always voted that way. They regard with suspicion a couple having no children, simply because everyone else in the neighborhood has a large family. It is only when an outside force--a jolt of some sort-- occurs that people change their views. A white

Topic sentence · **Start of a series of causes and effects**

1

2

American couple may think little about racial discrimination, for instance, until they adopt an Asian child and must comfort her when classmates tease her because she looks different. Parents may consider promiscuous any unmarried teenage girl who has a baby until their seventeen-year-old honors student confesses that she is pregnant. Personal jolts like these force people to think, perhaps for the first time, about issues that now affect them directly.

Topic sentence ——————▶ To illustrate how inertia governs our lives, it is 3 helpful to compare the world of television with real life. On TV, inertia does not exist. Television shows

Start of a series —————— and commercials show people making all kinds of of contrasts drastic changes. They switch brands of coffee or try a new hair color with no hesitation. In one car commercial, an ambitious young accountant abandons her career with a flourish and is seen driving off into the sunset as she heads for a small cabin by the sea to write poetry. In a soap opera, a character may progress from homemaker to hooker to nun in a single year. But in real life, inertia rules. People tend to stay where they are, to keep their jobs, to be loyal to products. A second major difference between television and real life is that, on television, everyone takes prompt and dramatic action to solve problems. The construction worker with a thudding headache is pain-free at the end of the sixty-second commercial; the police catch the murderer within an hour; the family learns to cope with their son's life-threatening drug addiction by the time the made-for-TV movie ends at eleven. But in the real world, inertia persists, so that few problems are solved neatly or quickly. Illnesses drag on, few crimes are solved, and family conflicts last for years.

Topic sentence ——————▶ Inertia is, most importantly, a force at work in 4 the life of our nation. Again, inertia is two-sided. It keeps us from moving and, once we move, it keeps us pointed in one direction. We find ourselves mired in a certain path, accepting the inferior, even

Start of a series —————— the dangerous. We settle for toys that break, winter of examples coats with no warmth, and rivers clogged with pollution. Inertia also compels our nation to keep moving in one direction--despite the uncomfortable suspicion that it is the wrong direction. We are not sure if manipulating genes is a good idea, yet we continue to fund scientific projects in genetic engineering. More than fifty years ago, we were shaken when we saw the devastation caused by an atomic bomb. But we went on to develop weapons hundreds of times more destructive. Although warned that excessive television viewing may be harmful, we continue to watch hours of television each day.

Conclusion   We have learned to defy gravity, one of the   5
basic laws of physics; we fly high above the earth, even float in outer space. But most of us have not learned to defy inertia. Those special individuals who are able to act when everyone else seems paralyzed are rare. But the fact that such people do exist means that inertia is not all-powerful. If we use our reasoning ability and our creativity, we can conquer inertia, just as we have conquered gravity.

COMMENTARY

Introduction.   As the title of her essay suggests, Laura has taken a scientific term (*inertia*) from a specialized field and drawn on the term to help explain some everyday phenomena. Using the *simple-to-complex* approach to structure the introduction, she opens with a vivid *descriptive* example of inertia. This description is then followed by a *formal definition* of inertia: "the tendency of matter to remain at rest or, if moving, to keep moving in one direction unless affected by an outside force." Laura wisely begins the paper with the easy-to-understand description rather than with the more-difficult-to-grasp scientific definition. Had the order been reversed, the essay would not have gotten off to nearly as effective a start. She then ends her introductory paragraph with a *thesis*, "Inertia, an important factor in the world of physics, also plays a crucial role in the human world," and with a *plan of development*, "Inertia affects our individual lives as well as the direction taken by society as a whole."

Organization.   To support her definition of inertia and her belief that it can rule our lives, Laura generates a number of compelling examples. She organizes these examples by grouping them into three major points, each point signaled by a *topic sentence* that opens each of the essay's three supporting paragraphs (2–4).

A definite organizational strategy determines the sequence of Laura's three central points. The essay moves from the way inertia affects the individual to the way it affects the nation. The phrase "most importantly" at the start of the fourth paragraph indicates that Laura has arranged her points emphatically, believing that inertia's impact on society is most critical.

A weak example.   When reading the fourth paragraph, you might have noticed that Laura's examples aren't sequenced as effectively as they could be. To show that we, as a nation, tend to keep moving in the same direction, Laura discusses our ongoing uneasiness about genetic engineering, nuclear arms, and excessive television viewing. The point about nuclear weapons is most significant, yet it gets lost because it's sandwiched in the middle. The paragraph would be stronger if it ended with the point about nuclear arms. Moreover, the example about excessive television viewing doesn't belong in this paragraph since, at best, it has limited bearing on the issue being discussed.

Other patterns of development.   In addition to using numerous *examples* to illustrate her points, Laura draws on several other patterns of development to show that inertia can be a powerful force. In the second and fourth paragraphs, she uses *causal analysis* to explain how inertia can paralyze people and nations. The second paragraph indicates that only "an outside force — a jolt of some sort —" can motivate inert people to change. To support this view, Laura provides two examples of parents who experience such jolts. Similarly, in the fourth paragraph, she contends that inertia causes the persistence of specific national problems: shoddy consumer goods and environmental pollution.

Another pattern, *comparison-contrast*, is used in the third paragraph to highlight the differences between television and real life: on television, people zoom into action, but in everyday life, people tend to stay put and muddle through. The essay also contains a distinct element of *argumentation-persuasion*, since Laura clearly wants readers to accept her definition of inertia and her view that it often governs human behavior.

Conclusion. Laura's *conclusion* rounds off the essay nicely and brings it to a satisfying close. Laura refers to another law of physics, one with which we are all familiar — gravity. By creating an *analogy* between gravity and inertia, she suggests that our ability to defy gravity should encourage us to defy inertia. The analogy enlarges the scope of the essay; it allows Laura to reach out to her readers by challenging them to action. Such a challenge is, of course, appropriate in a definition essay having a persuasive bent.

Revising the first draft. When it was time to rework her essay, Laura began by reading her paper aloud. She noted in the margin of her draft the problems she detected, numbering them in order of importance. After reviewing her notes, she started to revise in earnest, paying special attention to her third paragraph. The first draft of that paragraph is reprinted here:

Original Version of the Third Paragraph

The ordinary actions of daily life are, in part, determined by inertia. To understand this, it is helpful to compare the world of television with real life, for, in the TV-land of ads and entertainment, inertia does not exist. For example, on television, people are often shown making all kinds of drastic changes. They switch brands of coffee or try a new hair color with no hesitation. In one car commercial, a young accountant leaves her career and sets off for a cabin by the sea to write poetry. In a soap opera, a character may progress from homemaker to hooker to nun in a single year. In contrast, inertia rules in real life. People tend to stay where they are, to keep their jobs, to be loyal to products (wives get annoyed if a husband brings home the wrong brand or color of bathroom tissue from the market). Middle-aged people wear the hairstyles or makeup that suited them in high school. A second major difference between television and real life is that, on TV, everyone takes prompt and dramatic action to solve problems. A woman finds the solution to dull clothes at the end of a commercial; the police catch the murderer within an hour; the family learns to cope with a son's disturbing life-style by the time the movie is over. In contrast, the law of real-life inertia means that few problems are solved neatly or quickly. Things, once started, tend to stay as they are. Few crimes are actually solved. Medical problems are not easily diagnosed. Messy wars in foreign countries seem endless. National problems are identified, but Congress does not pass legislation to solve them.

After rereading what she had written, Laura realized that her third paragraph rambled. To give it more focus, she removed the last two sentences ("Messy wars in foreign countries seem endless" and "National problems are identified, but Congress does not pass legislation. . . .") because they referred to national affairs but were located in a section focusing on the individual. Further, she eliminated two flat, unconvincing examples: wives who get annoyed when their husbands bring home the wrong brand of bathroom tissue and middle-aged people whose hairstyles and makeup are outdated. Condensing the two disjointed sentences that originally opened the paragraph also helped tighten this section of the essay. Note how much crisper the revised sentences are: "To illustrate how inertia rules our lives, it is helpful to compare the world of television with real life. On TV, inertia does not exist."

Laura also worked to make the details and the language in the paragraph more specific and vigorous. The vague sentence "A woman finds the solution to dull clothes at the end of the commercial" is replaced by the more dramatic "The construction worker with a thudding headache is pain-free at the end of the sixty-second commercial." Similarly, Laura changed a "son's disturbing life-style" to a "son's life-threatening drug addiction"; "by the time the movie is over" became "by the time the made-for-TV movie ends at eleven"; and "a young accountant leaves her career and sets off for a cabin by the sea to write poetry" was changed to "an ambitious young accountant abandons her career with a flourish and is seen driving off into the sunset as she heads for a small cabin by the sea to write poetry."

Once these changes were made, Laura decided to round off the paragraph with a powerful summary statement highlighting how real life differs from television: "Illnesses drag on, few crimes are solved, and family conflicts last for years."

These third-paragraph revisions are similar to those that Laura made elsewhere in her first draft. Her astute changes enabled her to turn an already effective paper into an especially thoughtful analysis of human behavior.

As the selections in this chapter show, definition essays generally use a variety of patterns to develop the concept at the heart of the essay. K. C. Cole uses facts, examples, and anecdotes in the essay "Entropy" to show how a specialized concept applies to everyday life. In "Why I Want a Wife," Judy Brady generates examples to clarify her definition of a traditional wife. H. L. Mencken employs examples, description, and brief narratives as he defines the essence of "The Politician." Marie Winn draws a compelling analogy to clarify her definition of "TV Addiction." Finally, in "The Handicap of Definition," William Raspberry presents his understanding of the way that African-Americans define their "blackness."

K. C. Cole

K. C. Cole's writings about science, especially physics, have made a great deal of specialized knowledge available to the general public. A graduate of Barnard College, Cole has contributed numerous articles to such publications as the *New York Times*, the *Washington Post*, and *Newsday*, and writes a regular column for *Discover* magazine. Her work with the Exploratorium, a San Francisco science museum, led her to write several books on the exhibits there. In 1985, Cole published a collection of essays, *Sympathetic Vibrations: Reflections on Physics as a Way of Life*. The book *What Only a Mother Can Tell You About Having a Baby* appeared in 1986. The following selection was first published as a "Hers" column in the *New York Times* in 1982.

Entropy

Complex scientific principles often seem exotic and intelligible only to those with specialized knowledge. But the natural laws at work in the universe control all creatures, not just a select few. In her essay, K. C. Cole takes a specialized concept from physics and shows how it is a factor in everyone's daily life.

It was about two months ago when I realized that entropy 1 was getting the better of me. On the same day my car broke down (again), my refrigerator conked out and I learned that I needed root-canal work in my right rear tooth. The windows in the bedroom were still leaking every time it rained and my son's baby sitter was still failing to show up every time I really needed her. My hair was turning gray and my typewriter was wearing out. The house needed paint and I needed glasses. My son's sneakers were developing holes and I was developing a deep sense of futility.

After all, what was the point of spending half of Saturday at 2 the Laundromat if the clothes were dirty all over again the following Friday?

Disorder, alas, is the natural order of things in the universe. 3
There is even a precise measure of the amount of disorder, called
entropy. Unlike almost every other physical property (motion,
gravity, energy), entropy does not work both ways. It can only
increase. Once it's created it can never be destroyed. The road to
disorder is a one-way street.

Because of its unnerving irreversibility, entropy has been 4
called the arrow of time. We all understand this instinctively.
Children's rooms, left on their own, tend to get messy, not neat.
Wood rots, metal rusts, people wrinkle and flowers wither. Even
mountains wear down; even the nuclei of atoms decay. In the city
we see entropy in the rundown subways and worn-out sidewalks
and torn-down buildings, in the increasing disorder of our lives.
We know, without asking, what is old. If we were suddenly to see
the paint jump back on an old building, we would know that
something was wrong. If we saw an egg unscramble itself and
jump back into its shell, we would laugh in the same way we
laugh at a movie run backward.

Entropy is no laughing matter, however, because with every 5
increase in entropy energy is wasted and opportunity is lost.
Water flowing down a mountainside can be made to do some
useful work on its way. But once all the water is at the same level
it can work no more. That is entropy. When my refrigerator was
working, it kept all the cold air ordered in one part of the kitchen
and warmer air in another. Once it broke down the warm and
cold mixed into a lukewarm mess that allowed my butter to melt,
my milk to rot and my frozen vegetables to decay.

Of course the energy is not really lost, but it has defused and 6
dissipated into a chaotic caldron of randomness that can do us no
possible good. Entropy is chaos. It is loss of purpose.

People are often upset by the entropy they seem to see in the 7
haphazardness of their own lives. Buffeted about like so many
molecules in my tepid kitchen, they feel that they have lost their
sense of direction, that they are wasting youth and opportunity at
every turn. It is easy to see entropy in marriages, when the
partners are too preoccupied to patch small things up, almost
guaranteeing that they will fall apart. There is much entropy in
the state of our country, in the relationships between nations —
lost opportunities to stop the avalanche of disorders that seems
ready to swallow us all.

Entropy is not inevitable everywhere, however. Crystals and   8
snowflakes and galaxies are islands of incredibly ordered beauty
in the midst of random events. If it was not for exceptions to
entropy, the sky would be black and we would be able to see
where the stars spend their days; it is only because air molecules in
the atmosphere cluster in ordered groups that the sky is blue.

The most profound exception to entropy is the creation of   9
life. A seed soaks up some soil and some carbon and some sunshine and some water and arranges it into a rose. A seed in the
womb takes some oxygen and pizza and milk and transforms it
into a baby.

The catch is that it takes a lot of energy to produce a baby. It   10
also takes energy to make a tree. The road to disorder is all
downhill but the road to creation takes work. Though combating
entropy is possible, it also has its price. That's why it seems so
hard to get ourselves together, so easy to let ourselves fall apart.

Worse, creating order in one corner of the universe always   11
creates more disorder somewhere else. We create ordered energy
from oil and coal at the price of the entropy of smog.

I recently took up playing the flute again after an absence of   12
several months. As the uneven vibrations screeched through the
house, my son covered his ears and said, "Mom, what's wrong
with your flute?" Nothing was wrong with my flute, of course. It
was my ability to play it that had atrophied, or entropied, as the
case may be. The only way to stop that process was to practice
every day, and sure enough my tone improved, though only at the
price of constant work. Like anything else, abilities deteriorate
when we stop applying our energies to them.

That's why entropy is depressing. It seems as if just breaking   13
even is an uphill fight. There's a good reason that this should be
so. The mechanics of entropy are a matter of chance. Take any
ice-cold air molecule milling around my kitchen. The chances are
that it will wander in the direction of my refrigerator at any point
are exactly 50-50. The chances that it will wander away from my
refrigerator are also 50-50. But take billions of warm and cold
molecules mixed together, and the chances that all the cold ones
will wander toward the refrigerator and all the warm ones will
wander away from it are virtually nil.

Entropy wins not because order is impossible but because   14
there are always so many more paths toward disorder than toward

order. There are so many more different ways to do a sloppy job than a good one, so many more ways to make a mess than to clean it up. The obstacles and accidents in our lives almost guarantee that constant collisions will bounce us on to random paths, get us off the track. Disorder is the path of least resistance, the easy but not the inevitable road.

Like so many others, I am distressed by the entropy I see   15
around me today. I am afraid of the randomness of international events, of the lack of common purpose in the world; I am terrified that it will lead into the ultimate entropy of nuclear war. I am upset that I could not in the city where I live send my child to a public school; that people are unemployed and inflation is out of control; that tensions between sexes and races seem to be increasing again; that relationships everywhere seem to be falling apart.

Social institutions — like atoms and stars — decay if energy is   16
not added to keep them ordered. Friendships and families and economies all fall apart unless we constantly make an effort to keep them working and well oiled. And far too few people, it seems to me, are willing to contribute consistently to those efforts.

Of course, the more complex things are, the harder it is. If   17
there were only a dozen or so air molecules in my kitchen, it would be likely — if I waited a year or so — that at some point the six coldest ones would congregate inside the freezer. But the more factors in the equation — the more players in the game — the less likely it is that their paths will coincide in an orderly way. The more pieces in the puzzle, the harder it is to put back together once order is disturbed. "Irreversibility," said a physicist, "is the price we pay for complexity."

Questions for Close Reading

1. What is the selection's thesis? Locate the sentence(s) in which Cole states her main idea. If she doesn't state the thesis explicitly, express it in your own words.
2. How does entropy differ from the other properties of the physical world? Is the image "the arrow of time" helpful in establishing this difference?
3. Why is the creation of life an exception to entropy? What is the relationship between entropy and energy?

4. Why does Cole say that entropy "is no laughing matter"? What is so depressing about the entropy she describes?
5. Refer to your dictionary as needed to define the following words used in the selection: *futility* (paragraph 1), *dissipated* (6), *buffeted* (7), *tepid* (7), and *atrophied* (12).

Questions About the Writer's Craft

1. **The pattern.** What is Cole's underlying purpose in defining the scientific term *entropy*? What gives the essay its persuasive edge?
2. What tone does Cole adopt to make reading about a scientific concept more interesting? Identify places in the essay where her tone is especially prominent.
3. Cole uses such words as *futility, loss*, and *depressing*. How do these words affect you? Why do you suppose she chose such terms? Find similar words in the essay.
4. Many of Cole's sentences follow a two-part pattern: "The road to disorder is all downhill but the road to creation takes work" (paragraph 10). Find other examples of this pattern in the essay. Why do you think Cole uses it so often?

Questions for Further Thought

1. Besides the examples provided by Cole, what instances of entropy do you see around you?
2. Is entropy in nature the same as entropy in society? In a marriage? In a city? In international relations? Do you accept Cole's application of the term *entropy* to these various areas of life? Why or why not?
3. Entropy means that paint peels, "people wrinkle, flowers wither." How does our society respond to these phenomena?
4. Cole writes that it's "so hard to get ourselves together, so easy to let ourselves fall apart." If so, why do we bother? Overall, would you say the author is optimistic or pessimistic about humans getting themselves together?

Writing Assignments Using Definition as a Pattern of Development

1. Define *order* or *disorder* by applying the term to a system that you know well—for example, your school, dorm, family, or workplace. Develop your definition through any combination of writing patterns: by supplying examples, by showing contrasts, by analyzing the process underlying the system.

2. Choose, as Cole does, a technical term that you think will be unfamiliar to most readers. In a humorous or serious paper, define the term as it is used technically; then show how the term can shed light on some aspect of your life. For example, the concept in astronomy of a *supernova* could be used to explain your sudden emergence as a new star on the athletic field, in your schoolwork, or on the social scene. Here are a few suggested terms:

symbiosis	volatility	resonance
velocity	erosion	catalyst
neutralization	equilibrium	malleability

Writing Assignments Using Other Patterns of Development

3. Can one person make much difference in the amount of entropy — disorder and chaos — in the world? Share your view in an essay. Use examples of people who have tried to overcome the tendency of things to "fall apart." Make clear whether you think these people succeeded or failed in their attempts.
4. Cole claims that we humans are "buffeted about like so many molecules." Write an essay arguing either that people do or do not control their own fates. Support your point with a series of specific examples.

Judy Brady

Judy Brady was born in 1937 in San Francisco and was educated at the University of Iowa where she received her B.F.A.
in 1962. She became a free-lance writer during the 1960s and
has written articles on such issues as abortion, education, and
the labor and women's movements for a variety of publications. The provocative essay reprinted here first appeared in
Ms. magazine in 1971 and has become a classic of feminist
satire.

Why I Want a Wife

According to the dictionary, a wife is a "woman married to a
man." But, as many women know, a wife is much more: cook,
housekeeper, nutritionist, chauffeur, friend, sex partner, valet,
nurse, social secretary, ego-builder, and more. Rather than
complain about all the responsibilities she and other women
assume, Judy Brady explains why she herself would like to have
a wife.

I belong to that classification of people known as wives. I am   1
A Wife. And, not altogether incidentally, I am a mother.

Not too long ago a male friend of mine appeared on the   2
scene from the Midwest fresh from a recent divorce. He had one
child, who is, of course, with his ex-wife. He is obviously looking
for another wife. As I thought about him while I was ironing one
evening, it suddenly occurred to me that I, too, would like to
have a wife. Why do I want a wife?

I would like to go back to school so that I can become   3
economically independent, support myself, and, if need be, support those dependent upon me. I want a wife who will work and
send me to school. And while I am going to school I want a wife
to take care of my children. I want a wife to keep track of the
children's doctor and dentist appointments. And to keep track of

mine, too. I want a wife to make sure my children eat properly and are kept clean. I want a wife who will wash the children's clothes and keep them mended. I want a wife who is a good nurturant attendant to my children, arranges for their schooling, makes sure that they have an adequate social life with their peers, takes them to the park, the zoo, etc. I want a wife who takes care of the children when they are sick, a wife who arranges to be around when the children need special care, because, of course, I cannot miss classes at school. My wife must arrange to lose time at work and not lose the job. It may mean a small cut in my wife's income from time to time, but I guess I can tolerate that. Needless to say, my wife will arrange and pay for the care of the children while my wife is working.

I want a wife who will take care of *my* physical needs. I want a   4
wife who will keep my house clean. A wife who will pick up after my children, a wife who will pick up after me. I want a wife who will keep my clothes clean, ironed, mended, replaced when need be, and who will see to it that my personal things are kept in their proper place so that I can find what I need the minute I need it. I want a wife who cooks the meals, a wife who is a *good* cook. I want a wife who will plan the menus, do the necessary grocery shopping, prepare the meals, serve them pleasantly, and then do the cleaning up while I do my studying. I want a wife who will care for me when I am sick and sympathize with my pain and loss of time from school. I want a wife to go along when our family takes a vacation so that someone can continue to care for me and my children when I need a rest and a change of scene.

I want a wife who will not bother me with rambling com-   5
plaints about a wife's duties. But I want a wife who will listen to me when I feel the need to explain a rather difficult point I have come across in my course of studies. And I want a wife who will type my papers for me when I have written them.

I want a wife who will take care of the details of my social   6
life. When my wife and I are invited out by my friends, I want a wife who will take care of the babysitting arrangements. When I meet people at school that I like and want to entertain, I want a wife who will have the house clean, will prepare a special meal, serve it to me and my friends, and not interrupt when I talk about the things that interest me and my friends. I want a wife who will have arranged that the children are fed and ready for bed before

my guests arrive so that the children do not bother us. I want a wife who takes care of the needs of my guests so that they feel comfortable, who makes sure that they have an ashtray, that they are passed the hors d'oeuvres, that they are offered a second helping of the food, that their wine glasses are replenished when necessary, that their coffee is served to them as they like it. And I want a wife who knows that sometimes I need a night out by myself.

I want a wife who is sensitive to my sexual needs, a wife who   7
makes love passionately and eagerly when I feel like it, a wife who makes sure that I am satisfied. And, of course, I want a wife who will not demand sexual attention when I am not in the mood for it. I want a wife who assumes the complete responsibility for birth control, because I do not want more children. I want a wife who will remain sexually faithful to me so that I do not have to clutter up my intellectual life with jealousies. And I want a wife who understands that *my* sexual needs may entail more than strict adherence to monogamy. I must, after all, be able to relate to people as fully as possible.

If, by chance, I find another person more suitable as a wife   8
than the wife I already have, I want the liberty to replace my present wife with another one. Naturally, I will expect a fresh, new life; my wife will take the children and be solely responsible for them so that I am left free.

When I am through with school and have acquired a job, I   9
want my wife to quit working and remain at home so that my wife can more fully and completely take care of a wife's duties.

My God, who *wouldn't* want a wife?   10

Questions for Close Reading

1. What is the selection's thesis? Locate the sentence(s) in which Brady states her main idea. If she doesn't state the thesis explicitly, express it in your own words.
2. What event sparked Brady to think about why she would like to have a wife? How is this event related to her thesis?
3. What are the duties of a wife, according to Brady?
4. How are a wife's duties different from her spouse's? Which roles apply to the wife and not to her spouse?
5. Refer to your dictionary as needed to define the following words used in the selection: *nurturant* (paragraph 3), *replenished* (6), *entail* (7), and *adherence* (7).

Questions About the Writer's Craft

1. **The pattern.** How does Brady develop her definition of *wife*? Does she ever provide a direct summary statement of what a wife is? Explain.
2. What is Brady's tone in this essay? How does this tone help readers understand her definition of what it is to be a "wife"?
3. Why do you suppose the author repeats "I want a wife" over and over? How does this repetition add to the essay's effectiveness?
4. Are the reasons why Brady wants a wife listed in any particular order? Why do you think she saves for last sexual needs and the right to divorce?

Questions for Further Thought

1. This essay was first published in 1971, when the women's movement was still new. Have times changed? Or is Brady's message still relevant today?
2. Brady concludes, "My God, who *wouldn't* want a wife?" Would you? Why or why not?
3. Brady casts herself in the role of a certain kind of spouse. What's your opinion of this spouse? How do you think most husbands would react to this essay?
4. Do you know any married women who are the kind of "wife" that Brady describes? Are these people happy? Do you see any positive aspects to such a relationship?

Writing Assignments Using Definition as a Pattern of Development

1. Adopting either a positive or negative viewpoint, write an essay defining a husband. Use either "I want a husband" or "I don't want a husband" as your theme. Build your definition around numerous examples of the ways husbands behave.
2. Define what you mean by the phrase "a good marriage" — that is, the kind of marriage you would like to have. Develop your definition in an essay that explains what a couple should do to make a good marriage a reality.

Writing Assignments Using Other Patterns of Development

3. Write an essay defending the life-style of a traditional homemaker. Remembering to take the opposing viewpoint into account, try to persuade your audience that it is a worthy and fulfilling life-style. To

support your point, provide plentiful reasons and examples of the life-style's benefits and advantages.

∞ 4. Brady claims that men and women experience marriage differently. Pick one other area that you think reflects sharp differences between the sexes. Possibilities include the following:

Friendships
Dating protocol
Academic achievement
Clothing worn
Language used

Using the comparison-contrast format to analyze the area selected, discuss what you observe about male and female attitudes and behavior. Part of your paper should deal with the extent to which societal expectations define these characteristic patterns. Alleen Pace Nilsen's "Sexism and Language" (page 228), Barbara Ehrenreich's "What I've Learned From Men" (page 261), and Deborah Tannen's "Sex, Lies, and Conversation" (page 440) will provide insight into the complexities of male-female interaction and behavior.

H. L. Mencken

With a cool eye and biting wit, H. L. Mencken (1880–1956) examined the mores and foibles of American culture. A prolific writer, Mencken founded the journal *American Mercury*, edited the *Baltimore Sun*, and published dozens of books, including studies of American English and several volumes of autobiography. Known for his ability to puncture pretensions and skewer foolishness, Mencken invented the term *booboisie* to describe the middle class and insisted that no one ever went broke underestimating the intelligence of the American people. The essay reprinted here was published in *A Mencken Chrestomathy* (1949).

The Politician

Politicians are not, for the most part, highly respected. We seem to enjoy electing our public officials so that we can later claim, "They're all crooks." In the following selection, H. L. Mencken denounces the politicians of his day for being dealers in "hokum" and "hooey." Before deciding that Mencken exaggerates, think for a while about the many political scandals that Mencken didn't live long enough to witness.

After damning politicians up hill and down dale for many 1 years, as rogues and vagabonds, frauds and scoundrels, I sometimes suspect that, like everyone else, I often expect too much of them. Though faith and confidence are surely more or less foreign to my nature, I not infrequently find myself looking to them to be able, diligent, candid, and even honest. Plainly enough, that is too large an order, as anyone must realize who reflects upon the manner in which they reach public office. They seldom if ever get there by merit alone, at least in democratic states. Sometimes, to be sure, it happens, but only by a kind of miracle. They are chosen normally for quite different reasons, the chief of which is simply their power to impress and enchant the intellectually underprivileged. It is a talent like any other, and when it is exercised by a radio crooner, a movie actor or a bishop, it even takes on a certain austere and sorry respectability. But it is obviously not identical with a capacity for the intricate problems of statecraft.

Those problems demand for their solution — when they are   2 soluble at all, which is not often — a high degree of technical proficiency, and with it there should go an adamantine kind of integrity, for the temptations of a public official are almost as cruel as those of a glamor girl or a dipsomaniac. But we train a man for facing them, not by locking him up in a monastery and stuffing him with wisdom and virtue, but by turning him loose on the stump. If he is a smart and enterprising fellow, which he usually is, he quickly discovers there that hooey pleases the boobs a great deal more than sense. Indeed, he finds that sense really disquiets and alarms them — that it makes them, at best, intolerably uncomfortable, just as a tight collar makes them uncomfortable, or a speck of dust in the eye, or the thought of Hell. The truth, to the overwhelming majority of mankind, is indistinguishable from a headache. After trying a few shots of it on his customers, the larval statesman concludes sadly that it must hurt them, and after that he taps a more humane keg, and in a little while the whole audience is singing "Glory, glory, hallelujah," and when the returns come in the candidate is on his way to the White House.

I hope no one will mistake this brief account of the political   3 process under democracy for exaggeration. It is almost literally true. I do not mean to argue, remember, that all politicians are villains in the sense that a burglar, a child-stealer, or a Darwinian are villains. Far from it. Many of them, in their private characters, are very charming persons, and I have known plenty that I'd trust with my diamonds, my daughter or my liberty, if I had any such things. I happen to be acquainted to some extent with nearly all the gentlemen, both Democrats and Republicans, who are currently itching for the Presidency, including the present incumbent, and I testify freely that they are all pleasant fellows, with qualities above rather than below the common. The worst of them is a great deal better company than most generals in the army, or writers of murder mysteries, or astrophysicists, and the best is a really superior and wholly delightful man – full of sound knowledge, competent and prudent, frank and enterprising, and quite as honest as any American can be without being clapped into a madhouse. Don't ask me what his name is, for I am not in politics. I can only tell you that he has been in public life a long while, and has not been caught yet.

But will this prodigy, or any of his rivals, ever unload any 4 appreciable amount of sagacity on the stump? Will any of them venture to tell the plain truth, the whole truth and nothing but the truth about the situation of the country, foreign or domestic? Will any of them refrain from promises that he knows he can't fulfill — that no human being *could* fulfill? Will any of them utter a word, however obvious, that will alarm and alienate any of the huge packs of morons who now cluster at the public trough, wallowing in the pap that grows thinner and thinner, hoping against hope? Answer: maybe for a few weeks at the start. Maybe before the campaign really begins. Maybe behind the door. But not after the issue is fairly joined, and the struggle is on in earnest. From that moment they will all resort to demagogy, and by the middle of June of election year the only choice among them will be a choice between amateurs of that science and professionals.

They will all promise every man, woman and child in the 5 country whatever he, she or it wants. They'll all be roving the land looking for chances to make the rich poor, to remedy the irremediable, to succor the unsuccorable, to unscramble the unscrambleable, to dephlogisticate the undephlogisticable. They will all be curing warts by saying words over them, and paying off the national debt with money that no one will have to earn. When one of them demonstrates that twice two is five, another will prove that it is six, six and a half, ten, twenty, n. In brief, they will divest themselves of their character as sensible, candid and truthful men, and become simply candidates for office, bent only on collaring votes. They will all know by then, even supposing that some of them don't know it now, that votes are collared under democracy, not by talking sense but by talking nonsense, and they will apply themselves to the job with a hearty yo-heave-ho. Most of them, before the uproar is over, will actually convince themselves. The winner will be whoever promises the most with the least probability of delivering anything.

Some years ago I accompanied a candidate for the Presidency 6 on his campaign-tour. He was, like all such rascals, an amusing fellow, and I came to like him very much. His speeches, at the start, were full of fire. He was going to save the country from all the stupendous frauds and false pretenses of his rival. Every time that rival offered to rescue another million of poor fish from the neglects and oversights of God he howled his derision from the back platform of his train. I noticed at once that these blasts of common sense got very little applause, and after a while the candidate began to notice it too. Worse, he began to get word from his spies on the train of his rival that the rival was wowing them, panicking them, laying them in the aisles. They threw flowers, hot dogs and five-cent cigars at him. In places where the times were especially hard they tried to unhook the locomotive from his train, so that he'd have to stay with them awhile longer, and promise them some more. There were no Gallup polls in those innocent days, but the local politicians had ways of their own for finding out how the cat was jumping, and they began to join my candidate's train in the middle of the night, and wake him up to tell him that all was lost, including honor. This had some effect upon him — in truth, an effect almost as powerful as that of sitting in the electric chair. He lost his intelligent manner, and became something you could hardly distinguish from an idealist. Instead of mocking he began to promise, and in a little while he was promising everything that his rival was promising, and a good deal more.

One night out in the Bible country, after the hullabaloo of the day was over, I went into his private car along with another newspaper reporter, and we sat down to gabble with him. This other reporter, a faithful member of the candidate's own party, began to upbraid him, at first very gently, for letting off so much hokum. What did he mean by making promises that no human being on this earth, and not many of the angels in Heaven, could ever hope to carry out? In particular, what was his idea in trying to work off all those preposterous bile-beans and snake-oils on the poor farmers, a class of men who had been fooled and rooked by every fresh wave of politicians since Apostolic times? Did he really believe that the Utopia he had begun so fervently to preach would ever come to pass? Did he honestly think that farmers, as a body, would ever see all their rosy dreams come true, or that the share-croppers in their lower ranks would ever be more than a hop, skip and jump from starvation? The candidate thought awhile, took a long swallow of the coffin-varnish he carried with him, and then replied that the answer in every case was no. He was well aware, he said, that the plight of the farmers was intrinsically hopeless, and would probably continue so, despite doles from the treasury, for centuries to come. He had no notion that anything could be done about it by merely human means, and certainly not by political means: it would take a new Moses, and a whole series of miracles. "But you forget, Mr. Blank," he concluded sadly, "that our agreement in the premisses must remain purely personal. You are not a candidate for President of the United States. *I am.*" As we left him his interlocutor, a gentleman grown gray in Washington and long ago lost to every decency, pointed the moral of the episode. "In politics," he said, "man must learn to rise above principle." Then he drove it in with another: "When the water reaches the upper deck," he said, "follow the rats."

Questions for Close Reading

1. What is the selection's thesis? Locate the sentence(s) in which Mencken states his main idea. If he doesn't state the thesis explicitly, express it in your own words.
2. Mencken writes his essay as a political "insider." From this perspective, what are the characteristics of the politician? What changes does a politician undergo once he or she begins campaigning?
3. Who is at fault for the deplorable political situation Mencken describes — the politicians themselves or the voters who elected them? Find evidence in the essay to support your answer.
4. Mencken is neither a politician nor a typical voter — he is a journalist. Why does Mencken say that he avoids "naming names"? How did journalists of Mencken's time view their responsibilities as reporters?
5. Refer to your dictionary as needed to define the following words used in the selection: *candid* (paragraph 1), *austere* (1), *adamantine* (2), *dipsomaniac* (2), *larval* (2), *sagacity* (4), *demagogy* (4), *succor* (5), and *interlocutor* (7).

Questions About the Writer's Craft

1. **The pattern.** Mencken uses a variety of patterns to convince readers to accept his definition of a politician. Identify places where exemplification, process analysis, or other patterns of development appear in the essay. What hard evidence (facts, statistics, and so on) does Mencken use to support his ideas?

2. Note what Mencken says about himself at the start of the essay and in occasional self-references. How does he create a sense of himself as a credible commentator on presidential politics? Does he consider himself to be addressing "packs of morons" or another type of audience? Explain.
3. Mencken's humor is derived largely from the satiric technique known as *invective*, or insult. For instance, Mencken calls voters "boobs" and says they are more receptive to "hooey" than to sense. Find other examples of invective in the essay.
4. Another technique that Mencken uses to achieve satiric effect is to juxtapose ideas or items that aren't normally related. In paragraph 2, he groups three things that make people uncomfortable: "a tight collar . . . or a speck of dust in the eye, or the thought of Hell." Find other such juxtapositions in the essay. In each case, what effect does the juxtaposition have on the point Mencken is making at the time?

Questions for Further Thought

1. This essay was written nearly fifty years ago. Is it still valid now? Have our political process and our politicians changed? What similarities exist between the politicians Mencken describes and politicians today?
2. Satirists, by definition, exaggerate the vices of their targets and ignore their virtues, if any. Do you think Mencken is being unfair to those who run for office or unfair to the American public? Which good qualities of both does he deliberately omit?
3. How do Americans decide whom to vote for? Do we look at the candidates' records, experience, or stands on various issues? Or are we largely swayed by physical appearance, public speaking skills, wit, and personality? How effective are advertising campaigns in determining voters' choices?
4. What constitutes the ideal training for a future politician? Mencken suggests (facetiously) "locking him up in a monastery and stuffing him with wisdom and virtue." Should a political candidate be scholarly, worldly wise, or some combination of the two?

Writing Assignments Using Definition as a Pattern of Development

1. Choose your favorite target: any group of people you feel is worthy of criticism. Write a satiric essay in which you define this group by decrying its members' faults. Use Mencken's techniques (insults, juxtapositions, disparaging comparisons, bold slang, and a peppering of

fancy words). Here are some possible groups to consider: a teenage "type" (jock, preppie, campus queen, and so on); the boss; the doctor, lawyer, or other professional person; the teacher; the rock star or fan; the professional _____ (name a sport) player.

∞ 2. After studying Mencken's essay and considering other examples of satire — on television, in the movies, in humor magazines and comic strips — decide how you would define *satire*. Before developing your definition, you might read one or more of these satirical essays: James Thurber's "University Days" (page 238), Stephen Leacock's "How to Live to Be 200" (page 258), Judy Brady's "Why I Want a Wife" (page 546), and Jonathan Swift's "A Modest Proposal" (page 628). Then write an extended definition explaining what satire is, how it operates, and what it accomplishes. Use specific examples to support your ideas.

Writing Assignments Using Other Patterns of Development

∞ 3. Do you think that TV lessens or exacerbates the tendency of politicians to deliver "hokum"? Write an essay arguing either that television helps root out do-nothing or dishonest politicians or that it makes style the determining factor in political success. Reading what Neil Postman has to say about television in "Future Shlock" (page 247) may give you a better sense of one side of the argument.

∞ 4. Write an essay explaining why you voted (or would have voted) for _____ in the most recent presidential election. What factors led to your choice? Be honest: Were you swayed by personality, looks, the choices of friends and family, the candidate's record on public issues? How much of your choice was based on solid information? How much on image or slogans? Neil Postman's "Future Shlock" (page 247) and Ann McClintock's "Propaganda Techniques in Today's Advertising" (page 323) may suggest ideas worth pursuing.

Marie Winn

Born in Czechoslovakia and brought by her family to New York, Marie Winn was educated at Radcliffe College. The author or editor of ten children's books, Winn developed a special interest in the effect of television on children. She has contributed numerous articles to such publications as the *New York Times* and *Village Voice*. Winn's provocative and influential study, *The Plug-In Drug: Television, Children and Family*, was originally published in 1977 and revised in 1985. The selection that follows is from that book. Other books by Winn include *Children Without Childhood* (1983) and *Unplugging the Plug-In Drug* (1987).

TV Addiction

You arrive home from work or school. Do you automatically flick on the TV—or is it already on, even though no one is watching? Television has become an overwhelming presence in our lives. In the following selection, Marie Winn suggests that television can be as addictive as alcohol and drugs. She warns that TV addiction, like other addictions, can cause people to lose their families, leave their jobs, and distort their perspective on life.

The word "addiction" is often used loosely and wryly in conversation. People will refer to themselves as "mystery book addicts" or "cookie addicts." E. B. White writes of his annual surge of interest in gardening: "We are hooked and are making an attempt to kick the habit." Yet nobody really believes that reading mysteries or ordering seeds by catalogue is serious enough to be compared with addictions to heroin or alcohol. The word "addiction" is here used jokingly to denote a tendency to overindulge in some pleasurable activity.

People often refer to being "hooked on TV." Does this, too,

fall into the lighthearted category of cookie eating and other pleasures that people pursue with unusual intensity, or is there a kind of television viewing that falls into the more serious category of destructive addiction?

When we think about addiction to drugs or alcohol, we 3 frequently focus on negative aspects, ignoring the pleasures that accompany drinking or drug-taking. And yet the essence of any serious addiction is a pursuit of pleasure, a search for a "high" that normal life does not supply. It is only the inability to function without the addictive substance that is dismaying, the dependence of the organism upon a certain experience and an increasing inability to function normally without it. Thus a person will take two or three drinks at the end of the day not merely for the pleasure drinking provides, but also because he "doesn't feel normal" without them.

An addict does not merely pursue a pleasurable experience 4 and need to experience it in order to function normally. He needs to *repeat* it again and again. Something about that particular experience makes life without it less than complete. Other potentially pleasurable experiences are no longer possible, for under the spell of the addictive experience, his life is peculiarly distorted. The addict craves an experience and yet he is never really satisfied. The organism may be temporarily sated, but soon it begins to crave again.

Finally a serious addiction is distinguished from a harmless 5 pursuit of pleasure by its distinctly destructive elements. A heroin addict, for instance, leads a damaged life: his increasing need for heroin in increasing doses prevents him from working, from maintaining relationships, from developing in human ways. Similarly an alcoholic's life is narrowed and dehumanized by his dependence on alcohol.

Let us consider television viewing in the light of the conditions that define serious addictions. 6

Not unlike drugs or alcohol, the television experience allows 7 the participant to blot out the real world and enter into a pleasurable and passive mental state. The worries and anxieties of reality are as effectively deferred by becoming absorbed in a television program as by going on a "trip" induced by drugs or alcohol. And just as alcoholics are only inchoately aware of their addiction, feeling that they control their drinking more than they really do ("I can cut it out any time I want — I just like to have three or four drinks before dinner"), people similarly overestimate their control over television watching. Even as they put off other activities to spend hour after hour watching television, they feel they could easily resume living in a different, less passive style. But somehow or other while the television set is present in their homes, the click doesn't sound. With television pleasures available, those other experiences seem less attractive, more difficult somehow.

A heavy viewer (a college English instructor) observes: "I   8
find television almost irresistible. When the set is on, I cannot ignore it. I can't turn it off. I feel sapped, will-less, enervated. As I reach out to turn off the set, the strength goes out of my arms. So I sit there for hours and hours."

The self-confessed television addict often feels he "ought" to   9
do other things — but the fact that he doesn't read and doesn't plant his garden or sew or crochet or play games or have conversations means that those activities are no longer as desirable as television viewing. In a way a heavy viewer's life is as imbalanced by his television "habit" as a drug addict's or an alcoholic's. He is living in a holding pattern, as it were, passing up the activities that lead to growth or development or a sense of accomplishment. This is one reason people talk about their television viewing so ruefully, so apologetically. They are aware that it is an unproductive experience, that almost any other endeavor is more worthwhile by any human measure.

Finally it is the adverse effect of television viewing on the   10
lives of so many people that defines it as a serious addiction. The television habit distorts the sense of time. It renders other experiences vague and curiously unreal while taking on a greater reality for itself. It weakens relationships by reducing and sometimes eliminating normal opportunities for talking, for communicating.

And yet television does not satisfy, else why would the viewer   11
continue to watch hour after hour, day after day? "The measure of health," writes Lawrence Kubie, "is flexibility . . . and especially the freedom to cease when sated." But the television viewer can never be sated with his television experiences — they do not provide the true nourishment that satiation requires — and thus he finds that he cannot stop watching.

Questions for Close Reading

1. What is the selection's thesis? Locate the sentence(s) in which Winn states her main idea. If she doesn't state the thesis explicitly, express it in your own words.
2. Why, according to Winn, is a gardening addiction or a mystery book addiction a humorous kind of habit? What does she call "the essence of any serious addiction"?
3. In paragraph 7, the author says that television allows the viewer "to enter into a pleasurable . . . mental state," and later that "television does not satisfy." How does Winn prepare you earlier in the essay for this seeming contradiction?
4. Since television does "not provide the true nourishment that satiation requires," what activities does Winn suggest as truly nourishing alternatives?
5. Refer to your dictionary as needed to define the following words used in the selection: *wryly* (paragraph 1), *inchoately* (7), *ruefully* (9), *adverse* (10), and *satiation* (11).

Questions About the Writer's Craft

1. **The pattern.** At the beginning of the essay, Winn uses definition by negation to clarify her interpretation of the term *television addiction.* What kinds of things does Winn say are *not* the equivalents of TV addiction? Why does she use this strategy of definition by negation?
2. How does Winn organize the two extended definitions of addiction and TV addiction? How does this organizational pattern help Winn persuade readers to accept her point that TV is addicting?
3. What does the quotation from the TV addict add to Winn's argument? Why do you think Winn chooses a quotation from this person?
4. How does the lengthy discussion of addiction (paragraphs 3–5) help Winn to convince readers that television is indeed addicting?

Questions for Further Thought

1. Do you agree with Winn that excess television viewing is as addictive as drug and alcohol abuse? Is using the medical idea of addiction a productive way for our society to go about understanding and solving the problem of "too much TV"?
2. Consider the characteristics of addiction as presented in paragraphs 3–5. Do you think all types of people are likely to become addicted to something? Are there any types of people who might be totally immune?
3. Do you or people you know watch too much television? Or do you

find yourself addicted to some other electronic medium — or another nondrug activity? Is your addiction humorous or serious?

4. Reformed alcoholics and drug abusers are taught to avoid places where they might feel tempted. Few families would be willing to get rid of their televisions. What methods could parents or individuals use to prevent or lessen TV addiction?

Writing Assignments Using Definition as a Pattern of Development

1. In her introduction, Winn describes how people often use a very serious term — *addiction* — when referring to a light or harmless experience. Think of another term that you feel is serious, but that people use lightly and apply loosely. Your choice could be *friendship, love, hate,* or another word. Begin with an example that shows how the word is misused, and then provide an extended definition clarifying the proper use of the term.

2. TV addiction is only one of many forms of addiction. Others, such as addictions to gambling, baseball games, cars, bingo, chocolate, and the latest clothing styles, also exist. Write an essay on another addiction, using one of the addictions just listed or another of your own choice.

Writing Assignments Using Other Patterns of Development

∞ 3. Many kinds of television shows come in for criticism — "tabloid TV" talk shows, sitcoms, game shows, children's cartoons, news broadcasts, and so forth. Pick one kind of TV show and write an essay defending the genre. Or argue that this type of show has no merit. Your essay may be serious or playful. Neil Postman's view of television in "Future Shlock" (page 247) may spur you to imaginative thinking of your own.

4. You have probably heard from older relatives (or may yourself know) what life was like before TV. Write an essay for your future children or grandchildren describing what life was like before one or several of these new technologies: VCRs, cable TV, computers, microwave ovens, cash cards, and the like. Persuade your descendants that life was better *or* worse before these items were invented.

William Raspberry

Journalist William Raspberry was born in Okolona, Mississippi. From his mother, an English teacher and amateur poet,
Raspberry learned to care "about the rhythm and grace of
words." His father, a shop teacher, taught him "that neither
end tables nor arguments are worthwhile unless they stand
solidly on all four legs." Raspberry graduated from Indiana
Central College and later joined the staff of the Indianapolis
Recorder as a reporter and editor. Following a two-year stint in
the army, he was hired by the *Washington Post*, where his
nationally syndicated column has originated since 1971. His
coverage of the Watts race riots in 1965 won him the Capital
Press Club Journalist of the Year award. Raspberry's views have
been shaped by accidents of time and history: being born into
a family of teachers, growing up as an African-American in
segregated Mississippi, and coming of age in the era of the civil
rights and women's movements. Raspberry's carefully reasoned arguments defy politics and place him in neither the
liberal nor the conservative camp. He believes instead that
both opportunity *and* self-motivation are essential if minorities are to move into mainstream American life. *Looking Backward at Us*, a collection of Raspberry's columns, was published
in 1991. The following selection appeared in Raspberry's
Washington Post column in 1982.

The Handicap of Definition

If youngsters are repeatedly told that they—indeed, the ethnic
group to which they belong—are good at some things but not
at others, eventually they'll internalize such assertions. Developing this point further, William Raspberry discusses the effect
of such ingrained assumptions, asserting that ill-founded beliefs about what it means to be black have taken a tragic toll on
his fellow African-Americans. Urging a reexamination of such
limiting preconceptions, Raspberry advocates a more encom-
passing definition of black identity.

I know all about bad schools, mean politicians, economic 1
deprivation and racism. Still, it occurs to me that one of the
heaviest burdens black Americans — and black children in
particular — have to bear is the handicap of definition: the question of what it means to be black.

Let me explain quickly what I mean. If a basketball fan says 2
that the Boston Celtics' Larry Bird plays "black," the fan intends
it — and Bird probably accepts it — as a compliment. Tell pop
singer Tom Jones he moves "black" and he might grin in appreciation. Say to Teena Marie or the Average White Band that they
sound "black" and they'll thank you.

But name one pursuit, aside from athletics, entertainment or 3
sexual performance, in which a white practitioner will feel com-
plimented to be told he does it "black." Tell a white broadcaster
he talks "black" and he'll sign up for diction lessons. Tell a white
reporter he writes "black" and he'll take a writing course. Tell a
white lawyer he reasons "black" and he might sue you for slander.

What we have here is a tragically limited definition of black- 4
ness, and it isn't only white people who buy it.

Think of all the ways black children can put one another 5
down with charges of "whiteness." For many of these children,
hard study and hard work are "white." Trying to please a teacher
might be criticized as acting "white." Speaking correct English is
"white." Scrimping today in the interest of tomorrow's goals is
"white." Educational toys and games are "white."

An incredible array of habits and attitudes that are conducive 6
to success in business, in academia, in the nonentertainment
professions are likely to be thought of as somehow "white." Even
economic success, unless it involves such "black" undertakings as
numbers banking, is defined as "white."

And the results are devastating. I wouldn't deny that blacks 7
often are better entertainers and athletes. My point is the harm
that comes from too narrow a definition of what is black.

One reason black youngsters tend to do better at basketball, 8
for instance, is that they assume they can learn to do it well, and
so they practice constantly to prove themselves right.

Wouldn't it be wonderful if we could infect black children 9
with the notion that excellence in math is "black" rather than
white, or possibly Chinese? Wouldn't it be of enormous value if
we could create the myth that morality, strong families, determi-

nation, courage and love of learning are traits brought by slaves from Mother Africa and therefore quintessentially black?

There is no doubt in my mind that most black youngsters 10 could develop their mathematical reasoning, their elocution and their attitudes the way they develop their jump shots and their dance steps: by the combination of sustained, enthusiastic practice and the unquestioned belief that they can do it.

In one sense, what I am talking about is the importance of 11 developing positive ethnic traditions. Maybe Jews have an innate talent for communication; maybe the Chinese are born with a gift for mathematical reasoning; maybe blacks are naturally blessed with athletic grace. I doubt it. What is at work, I suspect, is assumption, inculcated early in their lives, that this is a thing our people do well.

Unfortunately, many of the things about which blacks make 12 this assumption are things that do not contribute to their career success — except for that handful of the truly gifted who can make it as entertainers and athletes. And many of the things we concede to whites are the things that are essential to economic security.

So it is with a number of assumptions black youngsters make 13 about what it is to be a "man": physical aggressiveness, sexual prowess, the refusal to submit to authority. The prisons are full of people who, by this perverted definition, are unmistakably men.

But the real problem is not so much that the things defined 14 as "black" are negative. The problem is that the definition is much too narrow.

Somehow, we have to make our children understand that 15 they are intelligent, competent people, capable of doing whatever they put their minds to and making it in the American mainstream, not just in a black subculture.

What we seem to be doing, instead, is raising up yet another 16 generation of young blacks who will be failures — by definition.

Questions for Close Reading

1. What is the selection's thesis? Locate the sentence(s) in which Raspberry states his main idea. If he doesn't state the thesis explicitly, express it in your own words.
2. In paragraph 14, Raspberry emphasizes that the word *black* presents a problem not because it's negative but because it has become "much

too narrow." According to Raspberry, what limitations have become associated with the term *black*? What negative consequences does he see resulting from these limitations?

3. In paragraph 11, Raspberry talks about "positive ethnic traditions." What does he mean by this term? What examples does he provide?

4. In Raspberry's opinion, what needs to be done to ensure the future success of African-American children?

5. Refer to your dictionary as needed to define the following words used in the selection: *diction* (paragraph 3), *scrimping* (5), *array* (6), *quintessentially* (9), *elocution* (10), *inculcated* (11), and *concede* (12).

Questions About the Writer's Craft

1. **The pattern.** Raspberry is primarily concerned with showing how limited the definition of *black* has come to be in our society. In the course of the essay, though, he also defines three other terms. Locate these terms and their definitions. How do the definitions and the effects of the definitions help Raspberry make his point about the narrowness of the term *black*?

2. **Other patterns.** In his opening paragraph, Raspberry uses the argumentation technique of refutation. What does he refute? What does he achieve by using this strategy at the very beginning of the essay?

3. A black journalist, Raspberry writes a nationally syndicated column that originates in the *Washington Post*, a major newspaper serving the nation's capital and the nation as a whole. Consider these facts when examining Raspberry's use of the pronouns *I*, *we*, and *our* in the essay. What do these pronouns seem to imply about Raspberry's intended audience? What is the effect of these pronouns?

4. Raspberry has chosen a relatively abstract topic to write about — the meaning of the term *black*. What techniques does he use to draw in readers and keep them engaged? Consider his overall tone, choice of examples, and use of balanced sentence structure.

Questions for Further Thought

1. Raspberry focuses on the limitations inherent in several terms. Can you think of other terms used to define a specific group of people? Do such terms ever have positive effects? If they do, in what circumstances?

2. Among your family and friends, do you detect any prejudice for or against the values Raspberry characterizes as "white" — for example, "hard study and hard work," "trying to please" a teacher, using "correct English," "scrimping," or buying "educational toys or games"? What does your response suggest about your family's or your friends' underlying assumptions?

3. Raspberry states that it isn't inherited talent that determines what a person accomplishes, but the person's belief that he or she can indeed achieve. Do you agree? In which situations might inherited or innate talent be critical? In which situations might a person's self-confidence outweigh the genetic factor?

4. In paragraph 15, Raspberry explains that black children should be given a self-image that encourages them to succeed "in the American mainstream, not just in a black subculture." Do you agree that involvement in a subculture isn't as important as participation in the "American mainstream"? Do you have any criticisms of the "American mainstream" that make you less than enthusiastic about encouraging those outside it to join in?

Writing Assignments Using Definition as a Pattern of Development

∞ 1. Raspberry points out how restrictive the definitions of *black* and *white* can be. Do you think that the definitions of *male* and *female* can be equally restrictive? Focusing on the term *male* or *female*, write an essay showing how the term was defined as you were growing up. Considering the messages conveyed by your family, the educational system, and society at large, indicate whether you came to perceive the term as limiting or liberating. Before planning your paper, you may want to read one or more of the following essays, all of which deal with the way gender roles influence behavior: Anne Morrow Lindbergh's "Channelled Whelk" (page 219), Alleen Pace Nilsen's "Sexism and Language" (page 228), Barbara Ehrenreich's "What I've Learned From Men" (page 261), Deborah Tannen's "Sex, Lies, and Conversation" (page 440), and Judy Brady's "Why I Want a Wife" (page 546).

2. In paragraph 15, Raspberry seems to define *success* as "making it in the American mainstream," but not everyone would agree that this is what constitutes success. Write an essay in which you offer your personal definition of *success*. One way to proceed might be to contrast what you consider success with what you consider failure. Or you might narrate the success story of a person you respect highly. No matter how you proceed, be sure to provide telling specifics that support your definition.

Writing Assignments Using Other Patterns of Development

∞ 3. Like most people, you've probably had a "defining" term applied to you at one time or another. Perhaps you've been called "shy" or "stubborn" or "the class clown" or "the athlete in the family."

Focusing on one such label that's been applied to you, write an essay showing the effect of this term on your life. Be sure to explain why you got the label and how you felt about it. The following essays will give you additional perspectives on the way that labels and names affect people's lives and self-image: Santha Rama Rau's "By Any Other Name" (page 191), Peter Farb's "In Other Words" (page 491), Alice Walker's "Beauty: When the Other Dancer Is the Self" (page 499), Migdia Chinea-Varela's "My Life as a 'Twofer'" (page 613), and Joan Didion's "On Self-Respect" (page 711).

4. In his conclusion, Raspberry makes a plea for providing the younger generation with a more positive, more expansive definition of *black*. Consider the beliefs and principles that today's older generation seems to impart to the younger generation. Write an essay showing which aspects of this value system seem helpful and valid and which do not. Also explain what additional values and convictions the older generation should be passing on. How should parents, teachers, and others convey these precepts?

Additional Writing Topics
DEFINITION

General Assignments

Use definition to develop any of the following topics. Once you fix on a limited subject, decide if the essay has an informative or persuasive purpose. The paper might begin with the etymology of the term, a stipulative definition, or a definition by negation. You may want to use a number of writing patterns—such as description, comparison, narration, process analysis—to develop the definition. Remember, too, that the paper doesn't have to be scholarly and serious. There is no reason it can't be a lighthearted discussion of the meaning of a term.

1. Fads
2. A family fight
3. Helplessness
4. An epiphany
5. A workaholic
6. A Pollyanna
7. A con artist
8. A stingy person
9. A team player
10. A Yiddish term like *mensch, klutz, chutzpah*, or *dreck*, or a term from some other ethnic group
11. Idiomatic expressions
12. Fast food
13. A perfect day
14. Hypocrisy
15. Inner peace
16. Obsession
17. Generosity
18. Exploitation
19. Depression
20. A double bind

Assignments with a Specific Purpose and Audience

1. *Newsweek* magazine runs a popular column called "My Turn," consisting of readers' opinions on subjects of general interest. Write a piece for this column defining *today's college students*. Use the piece to dispel some negative stereotypes (for example, that college students are apathetic, ill-informed, self-centered, and materialistic).
2. You're an attorney arguing a case of sexual harassment—a charge your client has leveled against her boss, a business executive. To win the case, you must present to the jury a clear definition of exactly what *sexual harassment* is and isn't. Write such a definition for your opening remarks in court.

3. You have been asked to write part of a pamphlet for students who come to the college health clinic. For this pamphlet, define *one* of the following conditions and its symptoms: *depression, stress, burnout, test anxiety, addiction* (to alcohol, drugs, or TV), *workaholism*. Part of the pamphlet should describe ways to cope with the condition described.

4. A new position has opened in your company. Write a job description to be sent to employment agencies who will screen candidates. Your description should define the job's purpose, state the duties involved, and outline essential qualifications.

5. Part of your job as peer counselor in your college's counseling center involves helping people communicate more effectively. To assist students, write a definition of some term that you think represents an essential component of a strong interpersonal relationship. You might, for example, define *respect, sharing, equality*, or *trust*. Part of the definition should employ definition by negation, a discussion of what the term is *not*.

6. Having waited on tables for several years at a resort hotel, you've been asked by the hotel manager to give some pointers to this year's new dining hall staff. Prepare a talk in which you define *courtesy*, the quality you consider most essential to the job. Use specific examples to illustrate your definition.

11

ARGUMENTATION-
PERSUASION

WHAT IS
ARGUMENTATION-PERSUASION?

"You can't possibly believe what you're saying."
"Look, I know what I'm talking about, and that's that."

Does this heated exchange sound familiar? Probably. When we hear the word *argument*, most of us think of a verbal battle propelled by stubbornness and irrational thought, with one person pitted against the other.

Argumentation in writing, though, is a different matter. Using clear thinking and logic, the writer tries to convince readers of the soundness of a particular opinion on a controversial issue. If, while trying to convince, the writer uses emotional language and dramatic appeals to readers' concerns, beliefs, and values, then the piece is called *persuasion*. Besides encouraging acceptance of an opinion, persuasion often encourages readers (or another group) to commit themselves to a course of action.

Assume you're writing an essay protesting the federal government's policy of offering aid to those suffering from hunger in other countries while many Americans go hungry. If your purpose is to document, coolly and objectively, the presence of hunger in the United States, you would prepare an argumentation essay. Such an essay would be filled with statistics, report findings, and expert opinion to demonstrate how widespread hunger is nationwide. If, however, your purpose is to shake up readers, even motivate them to write letters to their congressional representatives and push for a change in policy, you would write a persuasive essay. In this case, your essay might contain emotional accounts of undernourished children, ill-fed pregnant women, and nearly starving elderly people.

Because people respond rationally *and* emotionally to situations, argumentation and persuasion are usually *combined*. Suppose you decide to write an article for the campus newspaper advocating a pre-Labor Day start for the school year. Your audience includes the college administration, students, and faculty. The article might begin by *arguing* that several schools starting the academic year earlier were able to close for the month of January and thus reduce heating and other maintenance expenses. Such an argument, supported by documented facts and figures, would help convince the administration. Realizing that you also have to gain student and faculty support for your idea, you might argue further that the proposed change would mean that students and faculty could leave for winter break with the semester behind them — papers written, exams taken, grades calculated and recorded. To make this part of your argument especially compelling, you could adopt a *persuasive* strategy by using emotional appeals and positively charged language: "Think how pleasant it would be to sleep late, spend time with family and friends, toast the New Year — without having to worry about work awaiting you back on campus."

When argumentation and persuasion blend in this way, emotion *supports* rather than *replaces* logic and sound reasoning. Although some writers resort to emotional appeals to the exclusion of rational thought, when you prepare argumentation-persuasion essays, you should advance your position through a balanced appeal to reason and emotion.

HOW ARGUMENTATION-PERSUASION FITS YOUR PURPOSE AND AUDIENCE

You probably realize that argumentation, persuasion, or a combination of the two is everywhere: an editorial urging the overhaul of an ill-managed literacy program; a commercial for a new shampoo; a scientific report advocating increased funding for AIDS research. Your own writing involves argumentation-persuasion as well. When you prepare a *causal analysis, descriptive piece, narrative*, or *definition essay*, you advance a specific point of view: MTV has a negative influence on teens' view of sex; Cape Cod in winter is imbued with a special kind of magic; a disillusioning experience can teach people much about themselves; *character* can be defined as the willingness to take unpopular positions on difficult issues. Indeed, an essay organized around any of the patterns of development described in this book may have a persuasive intent. You might, for example, encourage readers to try out a *process* you've explained, or to see one of the two movies you've *compared*.

Argumentation-persuasion, however, involves more than presenting a point of view and providing evidence. Unlike other forms of writing, it assumes controversy and addresses opposing viewpoints. Consider the following assignments, all of which require the writer to take a position on a controversial issue:

In parts of the country, communities established for older citizens or childless couples have refused to rent to families with children. How do you feel about this situation? What do you think are the rights of the parties involved?

Citing the fact that the highest percentage of automobile accidents involve young men, insurance companies consistently charge their highest rates to young males. Is this policy fair? Why or why not?

Some colleges and universities have instituted a "no pass, no play" policy for athletes. Explain why this policy is or is not a good idea.

It's impossible to predict with absolute certainty what will make readers accept the view you advance or take the action you propose. But the ancient Greeks, who formulated our basic concepts of logic, isolated three factors crucial to the effectiveness of argumentation-persuasion: *logos, pathos*, and *ethos*.

Your main concern in an argumentation-persuasion essay should be with the *logos*, or soundness, of your argument: the facts, statistics, examples, and authoritative statements you gather to support your viewpoint. This supporting evidence must be unified, specific, sufficient, accurate, and representative (see pages 41–44). Imagine, for instance, you want to convince people that a popular charity misappropriates the money it receives from the public. Your readers, inclined to believe in the good works of the charity, will probably dismiss your argument unless you can substantiate your claim with valid, well-documented evidence that enhances the *logos* of your position.

Sensitivity to the *pathos*, or the emotional power of language, is another key consideration for writers of argumentation-persuasion essays. *Pathos* appeals to readers' needs, values, and attitudes, encouraging them to commit themselves to a viewpoint or course of action. The *pathos* of a piece derives partly from the writer's language. *Connotative* language — words with strong emotional overtones — can move readers to accept a point of view and may even spur them to act.

Advertising and propaganda generally rely on *pathos* to the exclusion of logic, using emotion to influence and manipulate. Consider the following pitches for a man's cologne and a woman's perfume. The language — and the attitudes to which it appeals — is different in each case:

Brawn: Experience the power. Bold. Yet subtle. Clean. Masculine. The scent for the man who's in charge.

Black Lace is for you — the woman who dresses for success but who dares to be provocative, slightly naughty. Black Lace. Perfect with pearls by day and with diamonds by night.

The appeal to men plays on the impact that words like *Brawn, bold, power*, and *in charge* may have for some males. Similarly, the charged words *Black Lace, provocative, naughty*, and *diamonds* are intended to appeal to business women who — in the advertiser's mind, at least — are looking for ways to reconcile sensuality and professionalism. (For more on slanted language, read Ann McClintock's "Propaganda Techniques in Today's Advertising," page 323.)

Like an advertising copywriter, you must select language that reinforces your message. In a paper supporting an expanded immigration policy, you might use evocative phrases like "land of liberty," "a nation of immigrants," and "America's open-door policy." However, if you were arguing for strict immigration quotas, you might use language like "save jobs for unemployed Americans," "flood of unskilled labor," and "illegal aliens." Remember, though, such emotionally charged language should support, not supplant, clear thinking.

Finally, whenever you write an argumentation-persuasion essay, you should establish your *ethos*, or credibility and integrity. You cannot expect readers to accept or act on your viewpoint unless you convince them that you know what you're talking about and that you're worth listening to. Be sure, then, to tell readers about any experiences you've had that make you knowledgeable about the issue being discussed. You will also come across as knowledgeable and trustworthy if you present a logical, reasoned argument that takes opposing views into account. And make sure that your appeals to emotion aren't excessive. Overwrought emotionalism undercuts credibility. Remember, too, that *ethos* isn't constant. A writer may have credibility on one subject but not on another: An army general might be a reliable source for information on military preparedness but not for information on federal funding of day care.

Writing an effective argumentation-persuasion essay involves an interplay of *logos, pathos*, and *ethos*. The exact balance among these factors is determined by your audience and purpose (that is, whether you want the audience simply to agree with your view or whether you also want them to take action). More than any other kind of writing, argumentation-persuasion requires that you *analyze your readers* and tailor your approach to them. You need to determine how much they know about the issue, how they feel about you and your position, what their values and attitudes are, what motivates them.

In general, most readers will fall into one of three broad categories: supportive, wavering, or hostile. Each type of audience requires a different blend of *logos, pathos*, and *ethos* in an argumentation-persuasion essay.

1. A supportive audience.   If your audience agrees with your position and trusts your credibility, you don't need a highly reasoned argument dense with facts, examples, and statistics. Although you may want to solidify support by providing additional information (*logos*), you can rely primarily on *pathos* — a strong emotional appeal — to reinforce readers' commitment to your shared viewpoint. Assume that you belong to a local fishing club and have volunteered to write an article encouraging members to support threatened fishing rights in state parks. You might begin by stating that fishing strengthens the fish population by thinning out overcrowded streams. Since your audience would certainly be familiar with this idea, you wouldn't need to devote much discussion to it. Instead, you would attempt to move them emotionally. You might evoke the camaraderie in the sport, the pleasure of a perfect cast, the beauty of the outdoors, and perhaps conclude with "If you want these enjoyments to continue, please make a generous contribution to our fund."

2. A wavering audience.   At times, readers may be interested in what you have to say but may not be committed fully to your viewpoint. Or perhaps they're not as informed about the subject as they should be. In either case, you don't want to risk alienating them with a heavy-handed emotional appeal. Concentrate instead on *ethos* and *logos*, bolstering your image as a reliable source and providing the evidence needed to advance your position. If you want to convince an audience of high school seniors to take a year off to work between high school and college, you might establish your credibility by recounting the year you spent working and by showing the positive effects it had on your life (*ethos*). In addition, you could cite studies indicating that delayed entry into college is related to higher grade point averages. A year's savings, you would explain, allow students to study when they might otherwise need to hold down a job to earn money for tuition (*logos*).

3. A hostile audience. An apathetic, skeptical, or hostile audience is obviously most difficult to convince. With such an audience, you should avoid emotional appeals because they might seem irrational, sentimental, or even comical. Instead, weigh the essay heavily in favor of logical reasoning and hard-to-dispute facts (*logos*). Assume your college administration is working to ban liquor from the student pub. You plan to submit to the campus newspaper an open letter supporting this generally unpopular effort. To sway other students, you cite the positive experiences of schools that have gone dry. Many colleges, you explain, have found their tavern revenues actually increase because all students—not just those of drinking age—can now support the pub. With the greater revenues, some schools have upgraded the food served in the pubs and have hired disc jockeys or musical groups to provide entertainment. Many schools have also seen a sharp reduction in alcohol-related vandalism. By arguing soundly and citing the facts, you encourage readers to reconsider their position. (For more help in analyzing your audience, see pages 20–21.)

SUGGESTIONS FOR USING ARGUMENTATION-PERSUASION IN AN ESSAY

1. At the beginning of the paper, identify the controversy surrounding the issue and state your position in the thesis. Your introduction should clarify the controversy about the issue. In addition, it should provide as much background information as your readers are likely to need.

The thesis of an argumentation-persuasion paper is often called the *assertion* or *proposition*. Occasionally, the proposition appears at the paper's end, but it is usually stated at the beginning. If you state the thesis right away, your audience knows where you stand and is better able to evaluate the evidence presented.

Remember: Argumentation-persuasion assumes conflicting viewpoints. Be sure your proposition focuses on a controversial issue and indicates your view. Avoid a proposition that is merely factual; what is demonstrably true allows little room for debate.

To see the difference between a factual statement and an effective thesis, examine the two statements that follow:

Fact: In the past decade, the nation's small farmers have suffered financial hardships.

Thesis: Inefficient management, rather than competition from agricultural conglomerates, is responsible for the financial plight of the nation's small farmers.

The first statement is certainly true. It would be difficult to find anyone who believes that these are easy times for small farmers. Because the statement invites little opposition, it can't serve as the focus of an argumentation-persuasion essay. The second statement, though, takes a controversial stance on a complex issue. Such a proposition is a valid starting point for a paper intended to argue and persuade.

Remember also to keep the proposition narrow and specific, so you can focus your thoughts in a purposeful way. Consider the following statements:

Broad thesis: The welfare system has been abused over the years.

Narrow thesis: No one except the disabled and mothers of preschool-aged children should be eligible to receive welfare payments.

If you tried to write a paper based on the first statement, you would face an unmanageable task — showing all the ways that welfare has been abused. Your readers would also be confused about what to expect in the paper: Will it discuss unscrupulous bureaucrats, fraudulent bookkeeping, dishonest recipients? In contrast, the revised thesis is limited and specific. It signals that the paper will propose restricting welfare payments to two groups. Such a proposal will surely have opponents and is thus appropriate for argumentation-persuasion.

The thesis in an argumentation-persuasion essay can simply state your opinion about an issue, or it can go a step further and call for some action:

Opinion: The lack of affordable day-care centers discriminates against lower-income families.

Call for action: The federal government should support the creation of more day-care centers in low-income neighborhoods.

In either case, your stand on the issue must be clear to your readers.

2. Provide strong support for the thesis.   Finding convincing evidence is a crucial step in preparing an argumentation-persuasion essay. Much support will be generated during the prewriting stage. As in any effective paper, the evidence must be *unified, adequate, specific, accurate,* and *representative* (see pages 41–44). It might consist of personal experiences or observations. Or it could be gathered from outside sources — statistics; facts; examples; or expert authority taken from books, articles, reports, interviews, and documentaries. A paper arguing that elderly Americans are better off than they used to be might incorporate the following kinds of evidence:

- *Personal observation or experience:* A description of the writer's grandparents who are living comfortably on Social Security and pensions.
- *Statistics from a report:* A statement that the per capita after-tax income of older Americans is $335 greater than the national average.
- *Fact from a newspaper article:* The point that the majority of elderly Americans do not live in nursing homes or on the streets; rather, they have their own houses or apartments.
- *Examples from interviews:* Accounts of several elderly couples living comfortably in well-managed retirement villages in Florida.
- *Expert authority cited in a documentary:* A statement by Dr. Marie Sanchez, a specialist in geriatrics: "An over-sixty-five American today is likely to be healthier, and have a longer life expectancy, than a fifty-year-old living only a decade ago."

As you seek outside evidence, you may — perhaps to your dismay — come across information that undercuts your argument. Resist the temptation to ignore such material; instead, use the evidence to arrive at a more balanced, perhaps somewhat qualified viewpoint. Conversely, don't blindly accept points made by sources agreeing with you. Retain a healthy skepticism, analyzing the material as rigorously as if it were advanced by the opposing side.

Also, keep in mind that outside sources aren't infallible. They may have biases that cause them to skew evidence. So be sure to evaluate your sources. If you're writing an essay supporting a woman's right to abortion, the National Abortion Rights Action League (NARAL) can supply abundant statistics, case studies, and reports. But realize that NARAL won't give you the complete picture; it will probably present evidence that supports its "pro-choice" position only. To counteract such bias, you should review what those with differing opinions have to say. You should, for example, examine material published by such "pro-life" organizations as the National Right-to-Life Committee — keeping in mind, of course, that this material is also bound to present support for its viewpoint only. Remember, too, that there are more than two sides to a complex issue. To get as broad a perspective as possible, you should also track down sources that have no axe to grind — that is, sources that make a deliberate effort to examine all sides of the issue. For example, published proceedings from a debate on abortion or an in-depth article that aims to synthesize various views on abortion would broaden your understanding of this controversial subject.

Whatever sources you use, be sure to *document* (give credit to) that material. Otherwise, readers may dismiss your evidence as nothing more than your subjective opinion, or they may conclude that you have *plagiarized* — tried to pass off someone else's ideas as your own. (Documentation isn't necessary when material is commonly known or is a matter of historical or scientific record.) In brief informal papers, documentation may consist of simple citations like "Psychologist Aaron Beck believes depression is the result of distorted thoughts" or "*Newsweek* (May 1, 1989) reports that most college-admissions procedures are chaotic." In longer, more formal papers, documentation is more detailed (see Chapter 13). One additional point: Because documentation lends a note of objectivity to writing, it may not be appropriate in a paper that cites sources to use the first-person point of view ("I, like many college students, agree with the government report that . . ."). To be on the safe side, check with your instructor to see if you should use the third-person point of view ("Many college students agree with the government report that . . .") instead.

3. Seek to create goodwill.   To avoid alienating readers with views different from your own, stay away from condescending expressions like "Anyone can see that . . ." or "It's obvious that . . ." Also, guard against personalizing the debate and being confrontational: "*My opponents* find the law ineffective" sounds adversarial, whereas "*Those opposed* to the law find it ineffective" or "*Opponents* of the law find it ineffective" is more evenhanded. The last two statements also focus — as they should —on the issue, not on the people involved in the debate.

Goodwill can also be established by finding a *common ground* —some points on which all sides can agree, despite their differences. Assume a township council has voted to raise property taxes. The additional revenues will be used to preserve, as parkland, a wooded area that would otherwise be sold to developers. Before introducing its tax-hike proposal, the council would do well to remind homeowners of everyone's shared goals: maintaining the town's beauty and preventing the community's overdevelopment. This reminder of the common values shared by the town council and homeowners will probably make residents more receptive to the tax hike.

4. Organize the supporting evidence.   The support for an argumentation-persuasion paper can be organized in a variety of ways. Any of the patterns of development described in this book (description, narration, definition, causal analysis, and so on) may be used — singly or in combination — to develop the essay's proposition. Imagine you're writing a paper arguing that car racing should be banned from television. Your essay might contain a *description* of a horrifying accident that was televised in graphic detail; you might devote part of the paper to a *causal analysis* showing that the broadcast of such races encourages teens to drive carelessly; you could include a *process analysis* to explain how young drivers "soup up" their cars in a dangerous attempt to imitate the racers seen on television. If your essay includes several patterns, you may need a separate paragraph for each.

When presenting evidence, arrange it so you create the strongest possible effect. In general, you should end with your most compelling point, leaving readers with dramatic evidence that underscores your proposition's validity.

5. Acknowledge and perhaps refute differing viewpoints.   If your essay has a clear thesis and strong logical support, you've taken important steps toward winning readers over. However, because argumentation-persuasion focuses on controversial issues, you should also consider contrary points of view. A good argument seeks out conflicting viewpoints, acknowledges them, perhaps even admits they have some merit. Such a strategy strengthens your argument in several ways. It helps you anticipate objections, alerts you to flaws in your own position, and makes you more aware of the other sides' weaknesses. Further, by acknowledging dissenting views, you come across as reasonable and thorough—qualities that may disarm readers and leave them more receptive to your argument.

You can use a number of techniques to deal with dissenting positions. Here are three particularly effective strategies.

First, you can use a two-part proposition consisting of a subordinate clause followed by a main clause. The first part of the proposition (the subordinate clause) *acknowledges opposing opinions*; the second part (the main clause) *states your opinion* and implies that your view stands on more solid ground. With such an approach you may (but you don't have to) discuss opposing opinions. The following thesis statement illustrates this strategy (the opposing viewpoint is underlined once; the writer's position is underlined twice):

Although some instructors think that standardized finals restrict academic freedom, such exams are preferable to those prepared by individual professors.

Second, you can take one or two paragraphs to *summarize* arguments raised by *opposing viewpoints* and grant (when appropriate) the validity of some of those points. Then you go on to present evidence for your position.

Third, you can *refute* all or part of the *dissenting views* by pointing out their flaws. Refutation means pointing out problems with dissenting views and thereby highlighting your position's superiority. You may focus on the opposing sides' inaccurate or inadequate evidence, or you may point to their faulty logic. (Some common types of illogical thinking are discussed on pages 585, 587–88, and 590–92.)

Let's consider how you could refute a competing position in an essay that supports sex education in public schools. You might start by acknowledging the opposing viewpoint's key argument: "Sex education should be the prerogative of parents." After granting the validity of this view in an ideal world, you might show that many parents don't provide such education. You could present statistics on the number of parents who avoid discussing sex with their children because the subject makes them uncomfortable; you could cite studies revealing that children in single-parent homes are apt to receive even less parental guidance about sex; and you could give examples of young people whose parents provided sketchy, even misleading information.

There are various ways to develop a paper's refutation section. The best method to use depends on the paper's length and the complexity of the issue. Two possible sequences are outlined here:

First Strategy	Second Strategy
• State your proposition.	• State your proposition.
• Cite opposing viewpoints and the evidence for those views.	• Cite opposing viewpoints and the evidence for those views.
• Refute opposing viewpoints by presenting counterarguments.	• Refute opposing viewpoints by presenting counterarguments.
	• Present additional evidence for your proposition.

In the first strategy, you simply refute all or part of the opposing positions' arguments. The second strategy takes the first one a step further by presenting *additional evidence* to support your proposition. In such a case, the additional evidence *must be different* from the points made in the refutation. The additional evidence may appear at the essay's end (as in the preceding outline), or it may be given near the beginning (after the proposition); it may also be divided between the beginning and end.

No matter which strategy you select, you may refute opposing views *in toto* or one point at a time. (For more on comparing and contrasting the sides of an issue, see pages 411–12.) Throughout the essay, be sure to provide clear signals so that readers can distinguish your arguments from the other sides': "Despite the claims of those opposed to the plan, many think that . . ." and "Those not in agreement think that. . . ."

6. Use induction or deduction to think logically about your argument. The line of reasoning used to develop an argument is the surest indicator of how rigorously you have thought through your position. There are two basic ways to think about a subject: *inductively* and *deductively*. Though the following discussion treats induction and deduction as separate processes, the two often overlap and complement each other.

Inductive reasoning involves examination of specific cases, facts, or examples. Based on these specifics, you then draw a conclusion or make a generalization. This is the kind of thinking scientists use when they examine evidence (the results of experiments, for example) and then draw a *conclusion*: "Smoking increases the risk of cancer." All of us use inductive reasoning in everyday life. We might think the following: "My head is aching" (evidence); "My nose is stuffy" (evidence); "I'm coming down with a cold" (conclusion). Based on the conclusion, we might go a step further and take some action: "I'll take an aspirin."

With inductive reasoning, the conclusion reached can serve as the proposition for an argumentation essay. (Of course, the essay will most likely include elements of persuasion since strict argumentation — with no appeal to emotions — is uncommon.) If the paper advances a course of action, the proposition often mentions the action, signaling an essay with a distinctly persuasive purpose.

Let's suppose that you're writing a paper about a crime wave in the small town where you live. You might use inductive thinking to structure the essay's argument:

Several people were mugged last month while shopping in the center of town. (*evidence*)

Several homes and apartments were burglarized in the past few weeks. (*evidence*)

Several cars were stolen from people's driveways over the weekend. (*evidence*)

The police force hasn't adequately protected town residents. (*conclusion, or proposition, for an argumentation essay with probable elements of persuasion*)

The police force should take steps to upgrade its protection of town residents. (*conclusion, or proposition, for an argumentation essay with a clearly persuasive intent*)

This inductive sequence highlights a possible structure for the essay. After providing a clear statement of your proposition, you might detail recent muggings, burglaries, and car thefts. Then you could move to the opposing viewpoint: a description of the steps the police say they have taken to protect town residents. At that point, you would refute the police's claim, citing additional evidence that shows the measures taken have not been sufficient. Finally, if you wanted your essay to have a decidedly persuasive purpose, you could end by recommending specific action the police should take to improve its protection of the community.

As in all essays, your evidence should be *specific, unified, sufficient*, and *representative* (see pages 41–44). These last two characteristics are critical when you think inductively; they guarantee that your conclusion would be equally valid even if other evidence were presented. Insufficient or atypical evidence often leads to *hasty generalizations* that mar the essay's logic. For example, you might think the following: "Some elderly people are very wealthy and do not need Social Security checks" (evidence), and "Some Social Security recipients illegally collect several checks" (evidence). If you then conclude, "Social Security is a waste of taxpayers' money," your conclusion is invalid and hasty because it's based on only a few atypical examples. Millions of Social

586 **Argumentation-Persuasion**

Security recipients aren't wealthy and don't abuse the system. If you've failed to consider the full range of evidence, any action you propose ("The Social Security system should be disbanded") will probably be considered suspect by thoughtful readers. It's possible, of course, that Social Security should be disbanded, but the evidence leading to such a conclusion must be sufficient and representative.

When reasoning inductively, you should also be careful that the evidence you collect is *recent* and *accurate*. No valid conclusion can result from dated or erroneous evidence. To ensure that your evidence is sound, you also need to evaluate the reliability of your sources. When a person who is legally drunk claims to have seen a flying saucer, the evidence is shaky, to say the least. But if two respected scientists, both with 20-20 vision, saw the saucer, their evidence is worth considering.

Finally, it's important to realize that there's always an element of uncertainty in inductive reasoning. The conclusion can never be more than an *inference*, involving what logicians call an *inductive leap*. There could be other explanations for the evidence cited and thus other positions to take and actions to advocate. For example, given a small town's crime wave, you might conclude not that the police force has been remiss but that residents are careless about protecting themselves and their property. In turn, you might call for a different kind of action—perhaps that the police conduct public workshops in self-defense and home security. In an inductive argument, your task is to weigh the evidence, consider alternative explanations, then choose the conclusion and course of action that seem most valid.

Unlike inductive reasoning, which starts with a specific case and moves toward a generalization or conclusion, *deductive reasoning* begins with a generalization that is then applied to a specific case. This movement from general to specific involves a three-step form of reasoning called a *syllogism*. The first part of a syllogism is called the *major premise*, a general statement about an entire group. The second part is the *minor premise*, a statement about an individual within that group. The syllogism ends with a *conclusion* about that individual.

Just as you use inductive thinking in everyday life, you use deductive thinking—often without being aware of it—to sort out your experiences. When trying to decide which car to buy, you might think as follows:

Major premise:	In an accident, large cars are safer than small cars.
Minor premise:	The Turbo Titan is a large car.
Conclusion:	In an accident, the Turbo Titan will be safer than a small car.

Based on your conclusion, you might decide to take a specific action, buying the Turbo Titan rather than the smaller car you had first considered.

To create a valid syllogism and thus arrive at a sound conclusion, you need to avoid two major pitfalls of deductive reasoning. First, be sure not to start with a *sweeping* or *hasty generalization* as your *major premise*. Second, don't accept as truth a *faulty conclusion*. Let's look at each problem.

Sweeping major premise.   Perhaps you're concerned about a trash-to-steam incinerator scheduled to open near your home. Your thinking about the situation might follow these lines:

Major premise:	Trash-to-steam incinerators have had serious problems and pose significant threats to the well-being of people living near the plants.
Minor premise:	The proposed incinerator in my neighborhood will be a trash-to-steam plant.
Conclusion:	The proposed trash-to-steam incinerator in my neighborhood will have serious problems and pose significant threats to the well-being of people living near the plant.

Having arrived at this conclusion, you might decide to join organized protests against the opening of the incinerator. But your thinking is somewhat illogical. Your *major premise* is a *sweeping* one because it indiscriminately groups all trash-to-steam plants into a single category. It's unlikely that you're familiar with the operations of all trash-to-steam incinerators in this country and abroad; it's probably not true that *all* such plants have had serious difficulties that endangered the public. For your argument to reach a valid conclusion, the major premise must be based on repeated observations or verifiable facts. You would have a better argument, and thus reach a more valid conclusion, if you restricted or qualified the major premise, applying it to some, not all, of the group:

Major premise:	A number of trash-to-steam incinerators have had serious problems and posed significant threats to the well-being of people living near the plants.
Minor premise:	The proposed incinerator in my neighborhood will be a trash-to-steam plant.
Conclusion:	It's possible that the proposed trash-to-steam incinerator in my neighborhood will run into serious problems and pose significant threats to the well-being of people living near the plant.

This new conclusion, the result of more careful reasoning, would probably encourage you to learn more about trash-to-steam incinerators in general and about the proposed plant in particular. If further research still left you feeling uncomfortable about the plant, you would probably decide to join the protest. On the other hand, your research might convince you that the plant has incorporated into its design a number of safeguards that have been successful at other plants. This added information could reassure you that your original fears were unfounded. In either case, the revised deductive process would lead to a more informed conclusion and course of action.

Faulty conclusion. Your syllogism — and thus your reasoning — would also be invalid if your *conclusion reverses the "if . . . then" relationship implied in the major premise.* Assume you plan to write a letter to the college newspaper urging the resignation of the student government president. Perhaps you pursue a line of reasoning that goes like this:

Major premise:	Students who plagiarize papers must appear before the Faculty Committee on Academic Policies and Procedures.

Minor premise:	Yesterday, Jennifer Kramer, president of the student government, appeared before the Faculty Committee on Academic Policies and Procedures.
Conclusion:	Jennifer must have plagiarized a paper.
Action:	Jennifer should resign her position as president of the student government.

Such a chain of reasoning is illogical and unfair. Here's why. *If* students plagiarize their papers, *then* they must appear before the committee. However, the converse isn't necessarily true — that *if* students appear before the committee, *then* they must have plagiarized. In other words, not *all* students appearing before the committee have been called up on plagiarism charges. For example, Jennifer could have been speaking on behalf of another student; she could have been protesting some action taken by the committee; she could have been seeking the committee's help on an article she plans to write about academic honesty. The conclusion doesn't allow for these other possible explanations.

Now that you're aware of potential problems associated with deductive reasoning, let's look at the way you can use a syllogism to structure an argumentation-persuasion essay. Suppose you decide to write a paper advocating support for a projected space mission. You know that controversy surrounds the space program, especially since seven astronauts died in a 1986 launch. Confident that the tragedy has led to more rigorous controls, you want to argue that the benefits of an upcoming mission outweigh its risks. A deductive pattern could be used to develop your argument. In fact, outlining your thinking as a syllogism might help you formulate a proposition, organize your evidence, deal with opposing viewpoints, and — if appropriate — propose a course of action:

Major premise:	Space programs in the past have led to important developments in technology, especially in medical science.
Minor premise:	The Cosmos Mission is the newest space program.

Proposition *(essay might be* *persuasive):*	The Cosmos Mission will most likely lead to important developments in technology, especially in medical science.
Proposition *(essay clearly is* *persuasive):*	Congress should continue its funding of the Cosmos Mission.

Having outlined the deductive pattern of your thinking, you might begin by stating your proposition and then discuss some new procedures developed to protect the astronauts and the rocket system's structural integrity. With that background established, you could detail the opposing claim that little of value has been produced by the space program so far. You could then move to your refutation, citing significant medical advances derived from former space missions. Finally, the paper might conclude on a persuasive note, with a plea to Congress to continue funding the latest space mission.

7. Recognize logical fallacies.   When writing an argumentation-persuasion essay, you need to recognize *logical fallacies* both in your own argument and in points raised by opposing sides. Work to eliminate such gaps in logic from your own writing and, when they appear in opposing arguments, try to expose them in your refutation. Logicians have identified many logical fallacies —including the sweeping or hasty generalization and the faulty conclusion discussed on pages 585 – 89. Other logical fallacies are described in Ann McClintock's "Propaganda Techniques in Today's Advertising" (page 323) and in the paragraphs that follow.

The *post hoc fallacy* (short for a Latin phrase meaning "after this, therefore because of this") occurs when you conclude that a cause-effect relationship exists simply because one event preceded another. Let's say you note the growing number of immigrants settling in a nearby city, observe the city's economic decline, and conclude that the immigrants' arrival caused the decline. Such a chain of thinking is faulty because it assumes a cause-effect relationship based purely on co-occurrence. Perhaps the immigrants' arrival was a factor in the economic slump, but there could also be other reasons: the lack of financial incentives to attract business to the city, restrictions on the size of the city's manufacturing facilities, citywide labor disputes that make companies leery of settling in the area. Your argument should also consider these possibilities. (For more on the *post hoc* fallacy, see page 467.)

The *non sequitur fallacy* (Latin for "it does not follow") is an even more blatant muddying of cause-effect relationships. In this case, a conclusion is drawn that has no logical connection to the evidence cited: "Millions of Americans own cars, so there is no need to fund public transportation." The faulty conclusion disregards the millions of Americans who don't own cars; it also ignores pollution and road congestion, both of which could be reduced if people had access to safe, reliable public transportation.

An *ad hominem argument* (from the Latin meaning "to the man") occurs when someone attacks a person rather than a point of view. Suppose your college plans to sponsor a physicians' symposium on the abortion controversy. You decide to write a letter to the school paper opposing the symposium. Taking swipes at two of the invited doctors who disapprove of abortion, you mention that one was recently involved in a messy divorce and that the other is alleged to have a drinking problem. By hurling personal invective, you avoid discussing the issue. Mudslinging is a poor substitute for reasoned argument.

Appeals to questionable or *faulty authority* also weaken an argument. Most of us have developed a healthy suspicion of phrases like *sources close to, an unidentified spokesperson states, experts claim*, and *studies show*. If these people and reports are so reliable, they should be clearly identified.

Begging the question involves failure to establish proof for a debatable point. The writer expects readers to accept as given a premise that's actually controversial. For instance, you would have trouble convincing readers that prayer should be banned from public schools if you based your argument on the premise that school prayer violates the U.S. Constitution. If the Constitution does, either explicitly or implicitly, prohibit prayer in public education, your essay must demonstrate that fact. You can't build a strong argument if you pretend there's no controversy surrounding your premise.

A *false analogy* wrongly implies that because two things share *some* characteristics, they are therefore *alike in all respects*. You might, for example, compare nicotine and marijuana. Both, you could mention, involve health risks and have addictive properties. If, however, you go on to conclude, "Driving while smoking a cigarette isn't illegal, so driving while smoking marijuana shouldn't be illegal either," you're employing a false analogy. You've overlooked a major difference between tobacco and marijuana: Marijuana impairs perception and coordination—important aspects of driving—while there's no evidence that tobacco does the same.

The *either/or fallacy* occurs when you assume that a particular viewpoint or course of action can have only one of two diametrically opposed outcomes—either totally this or totally that. Say you argue as follows: "Unless colleges continue to offer scholarships based solely on financial need, no one who is underprivileged will be able to attend college." Such a statement ignores the fact that bright, underprivileged students could receive scholarships based on their potential or their demonstrated academic excellence.

Finally, a *red herring argument* is an intentional digression from the issue—a ploy to deflect attention from the matter being discussed. Imagine that you're arguing that condoms shouldn't be dispensed to high school students. You would introduce a red herring if you began to rail against parents who fail to provide their children with any information about sex. Most people would agree that parents *should* provide such information. However, the issue being discussed is not parents' irresponsibility but the pros and cons of schools distributing condoms to students.

Few of today's critical problems—the battle against AIDS, unemployment, terrorism, care for the homeless—lend themselves to quick solutions. Overwhelmed by endless facts and speculations, many of us look to experts to help us arrive at meaningful positions on these complex issues. We may read one article and conclude, "Yes, this position makes sense," only to read another article that advances an opposing but equally compelling viewpoint. Perhaps the key to finding answers is to rely on ourselves—not on the experts—to sort out information and ideas. Writing an argumentation-persuasion essay helps us discover how we feel and what we think. Weighing fact against fact, stipulation against stipulation, we use reason to draw conclusions based on clear thinking. Argumentation-persuasion also gives us a chance to share such a well-reasoned point of view with others, perhaps even convincing readers of our position's soundness. Indeed, as average people with limited political clout or recognized expertise, we may find that argumentation-persuasion provides us with considerable power.

STUDENT ESSAY

The following student essay was written by Mark Simmons in response to this assignment:

> In "My Pistol-Packing Kids," Jean Marzollo invites controversy by attacking the popular notion that aggressive toys and games encourage hostile behavior. Select another controversial issue, one that you feel strongly about. Conduct library research to gather evidence in support of your position, and brainstorm with others to identify some points that might be raised by those who oppose your view. Then, using logic and formal, documented evidence, convince readers that your viewpoint is valid.

Your instructor may not ask you to include research in your essay. But, if you're asked—as Mark was—to research your paper and to provide *formal documentation*, you'll want to pay special attention to the way Mark credits his sources. You'll also find it helpful to refer to Chapter 13, "A Concise Guide to Documentation" (page 727). If your instructor wants you to research your paper but will accept *informal documentation*, the material on page 580 should come in handy.

Whether or not you include research in your paper, the annotations on Mark's essay and the comments following it will help you determine how well it applies the principles of argumentation-persuasion.

Compulsory National Service
by Mark Simmons

Introduction

Our high school history class spent several weeks studying the events of the 1960s. The most interesting thing about that decade was the spirit of service and social commitment among young people. In the '60s, young people thought about issues beyond themselves; they joined the Peace Corps and participated in freedom marches against segregation. They accepted President Kennedy's urging to "Ask not what your country can do for you; ask what you can do for your country." Most young people today, despite their obvious concern with careers and getting ahead, would also like an opportunity to make a worthwhile contribution to society. By instituting a program of compulsory national service, our country could tap this desire in young people. Such a system would yield significant benefits.

Start of two-sentence thesis

Definition paragraph

What exactly is meant by compulsory national service? Traditionally, it has tended to mean that everyone between the ages of seventeen and twenty-five would serve the country for two years. Young people could choose between two major options: military service or a public-service corps. They could serve their time at any point within the eight-year span. The unemployed or the uncertain could join immediately after high school; college-bound students could complete their education before joining the national service. Recently, though, Senator Sam Nunn and Representative Dave McCurdy have given a new twist to the definition of compulsory national service. They have proposed a plan that would require all high school graduates applying for federal aid for college tuition to serve either in the military or in a Citizens Corps. Anyone in the Citizens Corps would be required to work full-time at public-service duties for one or two years. During that time, participants would receive $100 a week and, at the end of the time, they would be given a voucher worth $10,000 for each year of civilian service. The voucher could

Beginning of summary of a source's ideas

1

2

Parenthetic citation — page number *and* author are given since the author is not cited earlier in the sentence	then be applied toward college credit, employment training, or downpayment on a house (Sudo 9).
	The traditional plan for compulsory national service and the one proposed by Nunn and McCurdy are just two of many variations that have been discussed over the years. While this country debates the concept, some nations such as France have gone ahead and accepted it enthusiastically.
Common knowledge isn't documented	The idea could also be workable in this country. Unfortunately, opponents have prevented the idea from taking hold. They contend, first of all, that the
Topic sentence	program would cost too much; they argue that a great deal of money would have to be spent admin-
Beginning of summary of three points made by the opposing viewpoint	istering the program. In addition, young people would have to receive wages for their work, and some of them would need housing--both expensive items. Another argument against compulsory national service is that it would demoralize young people; the plan would prevent the young from moving ahead with their careers and would make them feel as though they were engaged in work that had no personal reward. A final argument is that compulsory service would lay the groundwork for a military state. The picture is painted of an army of young robots totally at the mercy of the government, like the Hitler Youth of the Second World War.
Topic sentence: refutation of first point	Despite opponents' claims that compulsory national service would involve exorbitant costs, the program would not have to be that expensive to run. To date, no definite figures have been es- tablished on the program's cost (Shapiro 32), but the program might use as a model the California Conservation Corps, which has achieved great benefits at reasonable expense (Moore 25). Also, the sums required for wages and housing could be reduced considerably through payments made by the towns, cities, and states using the corps' ser- vices. And the economic benefits of the program could be significant. As public-policy experts Rich-
Attribution giving authors' full names and area of expertise	ard Danzig and Peter Szanton argue, the service corps could perform a wide variety of tasks. It could repair highways, public buildings, and inner-city

3

4

neighborhoods. The corps could organize recycling projects; it could staff public health clinics, day-care centers, legal aid centers, and homes for the handicapped (296). The corps could also monitor pollution, clean up litter, provide day-care services, work with the homeless, and help care for the country's growing elderly population (Boldt 7). All these projects would help solve many of the problems that plague our nation, and they would probably cost less than if they were handled by traditional government bureaucracies or by private industry (Moore 25).

Also, rather than undermining the spirit of   5
young people, as opponents contend, the program would likely boost their morale. Many young people feel enormous pressure and uncertainty. They are not sure what they want to do, or they have trouble finding a way to begin their careers. Compulsory national service could give young people a much-needed breathing space. As Edward Lewis, president of St. Mary's College, says, "Many students are not ready for college at seventeen or eighteen and they need an extra year to mature. This kind of program responds to that need" (qtd. in Fowler 3). And Joseph Duffey, chancellor of the University of Massachusetts, feels that such a program also provides important "opportunities for knowledge and training" (29). The executive director of the Coalition for National Service argues that a public-service stint enriches participants' lives in yet another way. When young people return to the academic world, the director contends, they find that their real-world experience adds "breadth to their grasp of . . . subject matter by exposing them to topics not covered in lectures . . ." (Eberly, National Service 86). Equally important, compulsory national service could provide an emotional boost for the young; all of them would experience the pride that comes from working hard, reaching goals, acquiring skills, and handling responsibilities (Levine 4). A positive mind-set would also result from the sense of community that would be created by serving in the national ser-

---

Marginal notes (left column):

Just the page number is provided here because the authors' names are cited in the preceding attribution

Topic sentence: refutation of second point

Full-sentence quotation is preceded by a comma and begins with a capital letter

Where secondary source was quoted

Quotation is blended into the sentence (no comma and the quotation begins with a lowercased word)

Quotation with middle and final ellipses

Author and partial title are provided because the Works Cited page lists two works by this author

Only the authors' last names are given because their full names appear earlier, in an attribution →

vice. All young people--rich or poor, educated or not, regardless of sex or social class--would come together during this time. Each young person, as Danzig and Szanton state, would have the satisfaction of knowing that he or she has made a "worthwhile contribution, both as an individual and as part of a group" (205).

Topic sentence: refutation of third point →

Finally, in contrast to what opponents claim, compulsory national service would not signal the start of a dictatorship. Although the service would be required, young people would have complete freedom to choose any two years between the ages of seventeen and twenty-five. They would also have complete freedom to choose the branch of the military or public-service corps that suits them best. And the corps would not need to be outfitted in military uniforms or to live in barrack-like camps. It could be set up like a regular job, with young people living at home as much as possible, following a nine-to-five schedule, enjoying all the personal freedoms that would ordinarily be theirs. Also, a dictatorship would no more likely emerge from a program of compulsory national service than it has from our present military system. We would still have a series of checks and balances to prohibit the taking of power by one group or individual. We should also keep in mind that our system is different from that of Fascist regimes; our long tradition of personal liberty makes improbable the seizing of absolute power by one person or faction. A related but even more important point to remember is that freedom does not mean people are guaranteed the right to pursue only their individual needs. That is mistaking selfishness for freedom. And, as everyone knows, selfishness leads only to misery. The national service would not take away freedom. On the contrary, serving in the corps would help young people grasp this larger concept of freedom, a concept that is badly needed to counteract the deadly "look out for number one" attitude that is spreading like a poison across the nation.

Conclusion:

Perhaps there will never be a time like the   7

6

echoes material
in the
introduction

Attribution
ending with a
colon leading
to a long
quotation

Long
quotation is
indented ten
spaces

For an
indented
quotation, the
period is
placed <u>before</u>
the parenthetic
citation

Partial title is
provided here
because two
works by this
author are
listed in Works
Cited

Newspaper
article

Book with two
authors

Section from a
weekly
publication

Book with one
author

Second source
by preceding
author

1960s when so many young people were concerned
with remaking the world. Still, a good many of
today's young people want meaningful work. They
want to feel that what they do makes a difference.
A program of compulsory national service would
tap this willingness in young people, helping them
realize the best in themselves. Such a program
would also help us resolve some of the country's
social problems. Eberly expresses with eloquence
his belief in the power of such a program:

> The promise of national service can be
> manifested in many ways: in cleaner air
> and fewer forest fires; in well-cared for
> infants and old folks; in a better-educated
> citizenry and better-satisfied work force;
> perhaps in a more peaceful world. Na-
> tional service has a lot of promise. It's a
> promise well worth keeping. ("What Pres-
> ident Bush Should Do" 651)

It is apparent that compulsory national service is
an idea whose time has come.

Works Cited

Boldt, David R. "National Service: A Call to All
Youth." <u>Philadelphia Inquirer</u> 21 Apr. 1991, late
ed.: E7.

Danzig, Richard, and Peter Szanton. <u>National Service:
What Would It Mean?</u> Lexington, MA: Lexington, 1986.

Duffey, Joseph. "Reconstituting America Through
National Service." <u>Vital Speeches of the Day</u> 5
Oct. 1989: 26-29.

Eberly, Donald. <u>National Service: A Promise to Keep</u>.
Rochester, NY: Alden, 1988.

---. "What President Bush Should Do About National
Service." <u>Vital Speeches of the Day</u> 15 Aug. 1989:
651-53.

Fowler, Margaret. "New Interest in National Youth
Corps." <u>New York Times</u> 16 May 1989, nat'l. ed.,
sec. 2: 3.

Article from a bimonthly magazine → Levine, Arthur. "Toward a National Service Program." Change Sept.-Oct. 1989: 4.

Article from a weekly magazine → Moore, Thomas. "For Whom the Corps Toils." U.S. News & World Report 13 Feb. 1989: 24-25.

Shapiro, Walter. "The Gap Between Will and Market." Time 6 Feb. 1989: 32.

Sudo, Phil. "Mandatory National Service?" Scholastic Update 23 Feb. 1990: 9.

COMMENTARY

Blend of argumentation and persuasion.   In his essay, Mark tackles a controversial issue. He takes the position that compulsory national service would benefit both the country as a whole and its young people in particular. Mark's essay is a good example of the way argumentation and persuasion often mix: Although the paper presents Mark's position in a logical, well-reasoned manner (argumentation), it also appeals to readers' personal values and suggests a course of action (persuasion).

Audience analysis.   When planning the essay, Mark realized that his audience — his composition class — would consist largely of two kinds of readers. Some, not sure of their views, would be inclined to agree with him if he presented his case well. Others would probably be reluctant to accept his view. Because of this mixed audience, Mark knew he couldn't depend on *pathos* (an appeal to emotion) to convince readers. Rather, his argument had to rely mainly on *logos* (reason) and *ethos* (credibility). So Mark organized his essay around a series of logical arguments — many of them backed by expert opinion — and he evoked his own authority by drawing on his knowledge of history and his "inside" knowledge of young people.

Introduction and thesis.   Mark introduces his subject by discussing an earlier decade when large numbers of young people worked for social change. Mark's references to the Peace Corps, freedom marches, and President Kennedy reinforce his image as a knowledgeable source and establish a context for his position. These historical references also lead into the two-sentence thesis at the end of the introduction: "By instituting a system of compulsory national service, our country could tap this desire in young people. Such a system would yield significant benefits."

Background paragraph and use of outside sources.   The second paragraph provides a working *definition* of compulsory national service by presenting two common interpretations of the concept. Such background information guarantees that Mark's readers will share his understanding of the essay's central concept.

The second paragraph also illustrates Mark's first use of outside sources. Because the assignment called for research in support of an argument, Mark went to the library and identified sources that helped him defend his position. If Mark's instructor had required extensive investigation of an issue, Mark would have been obligated both to dig more deeply into his subject and to use more scholarly and specialized sources. But given the instructor's requirements, Mark proceeded just as he should have: He searched out expert opinion that supported his viewpoint; he presented that evidence clearly; he documented his sources carefully.

Acknowledging the opposing viewpoint.   Having explained the meaning of compulsory national service, Mark is now in a good position to launch his argument. Even though he wasn't required to research the opposing viewpoint, Mark wisely decided to get together with some friends to brainstorm some issues that might be raised by the dissenting view. He acknowledges this position in the *topic sentence* of the essay's third paragraph: "Unfortunately, opponents have prevented the idea from taking hold." Next he summarizes the main points the dissenting opinion might advance: compulsory national service would be expensive, demoralizing to young people, and dangerously authoritarian. Mark uses the rest of the essay to counter these criticisms.

Refutation.   The next three paragraphs (4–6) *refute* the opposing stance and present Mark's evidence for his position. Mark structures the essay so that readers can follow his *counterargument* with ease. Each paragraph argues against one opposing point and begins with a *topic sentence* that serves as Mark's response to the dissenting view. Note the way the italicized portion of each topic sentence recalls a dissenting point cited earlier: "Despite opponents' claims that *compulsory national service would involve exorbitant costs*, the program would not have to be that expensive to run" (paragraph 4); "Also, rather than *undermining the spirit of young people*, as opponents contend, the program would likely boost their morale" (5); "Finally, in contrast to what opponents claim, *compulsory national service would not signal the start of a dictatorship*" (6). Mark also guides the reader through the various points in the refutation by using *transitions* within paragraphs: "*And* the economic benefits . . . could be significant" (4); "*Moreover*, participating in compulsory national service could provide an emotional boost . . ." (5); "*Also*, a dictatorship would no more likely emerge . . ." (6).

Throughout the three-paragraph refutation, Mark uses outside sources to lend power to his argument. If the assignment had called for in-depth research, he would have cited facts, statistics, and case studies to develop this section of his essay. Given the nature of the assignment, though, Mark's reliance on expert opinion is perfectly acceptable.

Mark successfully incorporates material from these outside sources into his refutation. He doesn't, for example, string one quotation numbingly after another; instead he usually develops his refutation by *summarizing* expert opinion and saves *direct quotations* for points that deserve emphasis. Moreover, whenever Mark quotes or summarizes a source, he provides clear signals to indicate that the material is indeed borrowed. (If you'd like some suggestions for citing outside sources in an essay of your own, see pages 580 and 728–32.)

Some problems with the refutation. Overall, Mark's three-paragraph refutation is strong, but it would have been even more effective if the paragraphs had been resequenced. As it now stands, the last paragraph in the refutation (6) seems anticlimactic. Unlike the preceding two paragraphs, which are developed through fairly extensive reference to outside sources, paragraph 6 depends entirely on Mark's personal feelings and interpretations for its support. Of course, Mark was under no obligation to provide research in all sections of the paper. Even so, the refutation would have been more persuasive if Mark had placed the final paragraph in the refutation in a less emphatic position. He could, for example, have put it first or second in the sequence, saving for last either of the other two more convincing paragraphs.

You may also have felt that there's another problem with the third paragraph in the refutation. Here, Mark seems to lose control of his counterargument. Beginning with "And, as everyone knows . . . ," Mark falls into the *logical fallacy* called *begging the question*. He shouldn't assume that everyone agrees that a selfish life inevitably brings misery. He also indulges in charged emotionalism when he refers — somewhat melodramatically — to the "deadly 'look out for number one' attitude that is spreading like a poison across the nation."

Inductive reasoning.   In part, Mark arrived at his position *inductively*, through a series of *inferences* or *inductive leaps*. He started with some personal *observations* about the nation and its young people. Then, to support those observations, he added his friends' insights as well as information gathered through research. Combined, all this material led him to the general *conclusion* that compulsory national service would be both workable and beneficial.

Other patterns of development.   To develop his argument, Mark draws on several patterns of development. The second paragraph relies on *definition* to clarify what is meant by compulsory national service. The introduction and conclusion *compare* and *contrast* young people of the 1960s with those of today. And, to support his position, Mark uses a kind of *causal analysis*; he both speculates on the likely consequences of compulsory national service and cites expert opinion to illustrate the validity of some of those speculations.

Conclusion.   Despite some problems in the final section of his refutation, Mark comes up with an effective close for the essay. He starts by echoing the point made in the introduction about the 1960s and restates his thesis. Then he includes a dramatic quotation from a knowledgeable source; the quotation lends credibility to the crisp assertion and suggested course of action at the very end of the essay.

Revising the first draft.   Given the complex nature of his argument, Mark found that he had to revise his essay several times.

One way to illustrate some of the changes he made is to compare his final introduction with the original draft reprinted here:

Original Version of the Introduction

"There's no free lunch." "You can't get something for nothing." "You have to earn your way." In America, these sayings are not really true. In America, we gladly take but give back little. In America, we receive economic opportunity, legal protection, the right to vote, and, most of all, a personal freedom unequaled throughout the world. How do we repay our country for such gifts? In most cases, we don't. This unfair relationship must be changed. The best way to make a start is to institute a system of national compulsory service for young people. This system would be of real benefit to the country and its citizens.

When Mark met with a classmate for a feedback session, he found that his partner had a number of helpful suggestions for revising various sections of the essay. But Mark's partner focused most of her comments on the essay's introduction because she felt it needed special attention. Following his classmate's suggestion, Mark deleted the original introduction's references to Americans in general. He made this change because he wanted readers to know—from the very start of the essay—that the paper would focus not on all Americans but on American youth. To reinforce this emphasis, he also added the point about the social commitment characteristic of young people in the 1960s. Besides providing a logical lead-in to the thesis, this reference to an earlier period gave the discussion an important historical perspective and lent a note of authority to Mark's argument. Mark was also pleased to see that adding this new material helped unify and smooth out the paragraph.

These are just a few of the many changes Mark made while reworking his essay. Because he budgeted his time carefully, he was able to revise thoroughly. With the exception of some weak spots in the refutation, Mark's essay is well-reasoned and convincing.

The selections ahead demonstrate that argumentation-persuasion can stimulate thinking on numerous issues. Jean Marzollo, in "My Pistol-Packing Kids," contends that the violence in children's play doesn't lead to overall aggression. In "My Life as a 'Twofer,'" Migdia Chinea-Varela presents her case for refusing an affirmative-action career opportunity. Mark Twain's "The Damned Human Race" makes some compelling points about flaws in human nature. With scathing irony, Jonathan Swift advocates, in "A Modest Proposal," a solution to the agony of Ireland's poor. In "Free Speech on Campus," Nat Hentoff uses the power of the pen to assail campus liberals and leftists, arguing that their brand of censorship is as dangerous as any other. Camille Paglia, in "Rape: A Bigger Danger Than Feminists Know," argues that it's women who are responsible for preventing rape. Susan Jacoby rebuts Paglia, arguing that "Common Decency" is something women should be able to expect from men. Edward I. Koch, in "Death and Justice," and David Bruck, in "The Death Penalty," take opposing stands on capital punishment. Finally, Louis Nizer, in "Low-Cost Drugs for Addicts?" and Beth Johnson Ruth, in "Our Drug Problem," tackle different sides of the controversy surrounding the legalization of drugs.

Jean Marzollo

A Connecticut native, Jean Marzollo received her B.A. in English from the University of Connecticut and her M.A. from Harvard University. Before becoming a free-lance writer, Marzollo taught high school and directed educational programs for disadvantaged children. Her articles have appeared in many popular magazines, including *Redbook, Parents, Mademoiselle*, and *Working Mother*. The author of several books for children and teenagers, she has recently started a novel for adults. Her most recent book is *Your Maternity Leave: How to Leave Work, Have a Baby, Go Back to Work Without Getting Lost, Trapped, or Sandbagged Along the Way* (1991). The following selection was first published in *Parents* magazine (1977).

My Pistol-Packing Kids

Marbles, hopscotch, and hide-and-seek are all old, familiar childhood games. But the most favorite of all may be "Bang, bang, you're dead." All children seem to enjoy games of make-believe violence, played with sticks, pointed fingers, or toy weapons that shoot plastic darts, "laser" beams, or rubber projectiles. Parents debate whether such games are healthy or damaging to young minds. Drawing primarily on her observations of her own children, Jean Marzollo maintains that such shoot-'em-up games have valuable hidden dimensions that parents may not at first appreciate.

One day as I was loading the dishwasher, I glanced over at   1
my two boys, Danny and David, ages seven and five, respectively, and thought how sweet and quiet they are. I wonder what they are drawing so intently; I think I'll go see. I went over to the kitchen table and found, rather to my dismay, two lurid pictures of outer space battles. Blood and destruction was everywhere.

These frail little babes I held in my arms, what made them   2
grow up and want to create things like this? Repeatedly? Given

clay, they make monsters and destroy them limb by limb with
home-made clay bombs. Given yarn, they devise tarantula traps
behind the couch. Given board and blocks they rig ramps to crash
their cars into each other at high speed.

Outdoors, straight sticks are knives and bent ones are guns.   3
Danny and David stick them into their belts and swagger around
on the grass like John Wayne and Burt Reynolds.

Oh, sure, they also like to roll out cookie dough, play the   4
piano, build sand castles, and pet cats, but nothing, I have noticed, quite catches their fancy as does violence.

With their friends they are superheroes or spacemen, and, as   5
I watch them run around shooting each other, I sometimes feel
guilty that it was I who took them to (and enjoyed) the movies
Superman, Star Wars, and *The Empire Strikes Back*. Adding to this
guilt is the fact that my husband and I let them watch Saturday
morning cartoons so we can sleep late.

On a slow, regular basis their innocent little minds have been   6
contaminated with kiddie media culture. It's excessively violent,
which is why Danny and David, at the ripe old ages of five and
seven, like it so much. They are at the ages when they know what
they see on television is not real. Instead of worrying about reality
as they did when they were three or four, they now spend their
energy memorizing the exact order in which their favorite cartoons appear.

What About the Kids of Parents
Who Say "No"?

Good and stalwart friends of ours, wishing to protect their   7
children's minds from nefarious influences, do not buy TVs, do
not permit guns, and do not take their children to ungentle
movies. But when their children come to visit, they dive into the
box in the entryway that contains two squirt guns, a plastic laser
gun, an orange pistol that shoots rubber darts (all of which have
been lost), and a homemade wooden machine gun. Although
these kids have never watched morning TV, they know exactly
how to play with toy weapons, and they do so with the passion of
converts.

Secretly, wickedly, I feel better. Why? Because I'm haunted   8
by the idea that our actions, or the lack of them, may be bringing

out in our children a natural tendency toward aggressive violence that should be suppressed. In a time of assassinations, political terrorism, nuclear buildup, and much publicized violence in people's daily lives, we desire more consciously than ever peace and safety in the world. It is out of this concern that we worry about the place and legitimacy of toy guns in the lives of our children.

What if, we wonder, all parents kept all children from toy 9 weapons and the media that glorifies them; wouldn't the world be better off? We could take the TV and the laser guns to the dump. But what about the sticks, yarns, and crayons? Should we take them, too?

We could also lay down the law: no more torpedoes in the 10 bathtub. Play only with rubber ducks. No more bows and arrows may be made out of construction toys. Make houses instead. No more clay bombs. Make bowls. Our laws would require rigid surveillance and strict discipline, but the means (our dictatorship) would be justified by the end (their innocence). Childhood, after all, should be a time of kittens, mittens, gingerbread, and yo-yo's.

Think positive. Be happy. Play nice, our laws would say. 11

But our children don't want to play nice. They want to have 12 fun. And they have so much fun *pretending* to wipe each other out.

Kids Want Both Sides

It seems kids want to learn about *both* sides of childhood, not 13 just the mittens and kittens side, full of discovery and nurturing, but also the ghosts and ghouls side, full of dread and helplessness. Watching our children and their friends at play, it is clear to me that the mock violence in their play has a great deal to do with their need to *do* something about the underside of their lives. In order to fight back the witches, giants, and werewolves that menace them in the night, they run around in the daytime with toy pistols, toy knives, and toy swords. When I stop to think about their play in these terms, I find I can accept it.

I'm not talking about condoning real violence, nor am I 14 suggesting we avoid the responsibilities to teach morals and ethics to our children. As a matter of course, we teach them that no matter how mad they are at someone else, they must not hit, bite, pull hair, and pinch. We teach them to protest verbally, to negotiate a deal if they can, or simply to say, "I'm not going to play with you anymore if you do that." We teach them basically not to hurt others to get their own way. And just as we teach our children safety precautions about cars, roads, matches, broken glass, and electrical outlets, we caution them about real knives and guns. We tell them how very dangerous these things are, how they must be used correctly, and that the use of guns is prohibited for young children.

"Your Thing, Not Mine"

Guns are a particularly sensitive topic for parents, and many   15
of us feel uncomfortable when our children lust for plastic ones. Although I do not prohibit my children from playing with them, I try to make it clear that such activity is their thing, not mine. I say, "Don't point that rifle at me because it reminds me of a real gun and I don't like real guns." I also insist that gunplay take place outside.

Some friends of mine won't buy toy guns but permit their   16
children to do so with their own money. Others will not allow any toy guns in their homes but do not interfere if their children play guns with sticks or their fingers. Still other parents own real guns, go hunting, and bring home carcasses on the top of the car. Their children, we hope, learn the ethic of the hunter: one must be a good shot, one must kill only for food.

But the use of real guns is not really the point here. Danny   17
and David do not use real guns nor would they want to. *They are using toys and they are only pretending.* While I admit that it can be unsettling to see how truly inspired they can be at their games, I am impressed by their powers of invention and the fact that what they are doing is not only fun, but refined, effective, and safe.

It is refined in the sense that the children organize them-   18
selves to take the different parts involved. They also know how to act out all the parts and how to cooperate with each other to enhance the overall drama. They have a remarkable ability to improvise scenes and an almost professional attitude about giving and taking directions. Listening to them play with their little men dolls, it is almost as if I were listening to puppeteers or movie directors.

"All right," says Danny. "You land our guy behind the   19
mountain, and I'll find him and blast him out of the water."

"Okay, here goes." (Realistic landing sounds.) "Let's set up   20
camp here. Oh no! They found us. Watch out!" (Explosion
sounds. Swimming sounds.) "Look, here's an underwater cave!
Let's go in!" (Aside) "Let's pretend the cave is really a giant
shark."

"Yeah, and I'll kill it and save you."   21

"Okay. Oh no! It's a giant shark! Look at those teeth!"   22

Their Own Play Therapy

It seems to me that fantasy play is effective in the sense that it   23
allows children to blow off a lot of steam. Let's face it, on some
level every child lives with tyrants (us) on whom he or she is
absolutely dependent. We may be benevolent tyrants, but we are
tyrants nonetheless, and the whole thrust of our children's growing up is to liberate themselves from us.

By playing out fantasies, children release frustrations and   24
experience illusory control over things, such as big people's
power and the threat of death, over which, in fact, they have no
control at all. Day after day, they take turns acting out scene after
scene in which they as good guys heroically defend themselves
against horrible bad guys. Every child I have watched can play
both roles.

In a way children are their own play therapists, helping each   25
other cope with pent-up rage. They seem to know how long each
session should last. The game is over when the kids are bored, or
tired, or someone thinks of something else to do and everyone
agrees; in short, when enough steam has been blown off.

As far as I can see, violent fantasies are safe precisely because   26
they're not real. They are thrilling for the same reason. Children
don't want to get hurt. From my observation, the kids who enjoy
playing with toy guns in the yard are those who have already
learned to be cautious around cars, ovens, and climbing equipment. *They don't want to get hurt and they know how not to.* Just
because they crash toy cars now does not mean they will drive real
ones over cliffs when they are twenty. And just because they love
to shoot each other with imaginary guns now does not mean they
will abuse guns when they grow up.

It takes more than toy guns to make a killer. Conversely,   27
many peace-loving grown-ups I know tell me they played war
with a vengeance when they were little.

No Winners, No Losers?

Another important point: Have you ever noticed that in   28
mock violent play no one ever wins or loses? You get shot, you
fall down, you get up, you shoot someone else. A five-year-old
can play as skillfully as an eight-year-old. The weakest child is on a
par with the strongest. The game is safe emotionally as well as
physically.

Paradoxically, games that involve less violent imagination   29
but more real jeopardy are harder for children to play, and one
has to be mature enough to handle them. To play baseball, for
example, you have to be able to strike out without bursting into
tears. In Monopoly you have to be able to land on Park Place
when someone else owns it and lose all your money. In a class
play you have to be able to keep going even though some kid in
the back row whistles.

I don't want to see my kids strike out or forget their lines,   30
but I know they may, that they have to, and that they will put up
with such discomfort in order to participate in the next stage of
life. On their own, I suspect, they will realize eventually that
fantasy violence is for little kids. What's for big kids? Real violence? No, at least not for kids who have learned about love and
respect for others.

Graduating into Life

For older kids there is a stage of activity that moves closer to   31
real life. Sports, science projects, model making, music lessons,
dancing, arts and crafts — all these activities help children sharpen their skills, develop their imagination, and explore their interests. The toy guns, toy dolls, and toy cars will be given away or
collect dust on a shelf in the basement. Real tools and real equipment will have replaced them.

Eventually, Danny and David will move on to real life with   32
its possibilities for real jeopardy, real success, real independence,
and satisfaction. By then I hope they will have gained whatever
skills and strength of character they need to play this last, and

hardest, and most rewarding game of all. I trust that part of their maturity will be based upon the ability they gained at an early age to distinguish between fantasy and reality.

Questions for Close Reading

1. What is the selection's thesis? Locate the sentence(s) in which Marzollo states her main idea. If she doesn't state the thesis explicitly, express it in your own words.
2. Why, according to Marzollo, do kids want to play at violence?
3. Marzollo suggests children progress through different stages of maturity. What are these? In which stages do children focus on reality and in which on fantasy?
4. What does Marzollo mean by saying that play with toy guns is "refined"? How is it "effective" and safe?
5. Refer to your dictionary as needed to define the following words used in the selection: *stalwart* (paragraph 7), *legitimacy* (8), *condoning* (14), *improvise* (18), and *vengeance* (27).

Questions About the Writer's Craft

1. **The pattern.** Why do you think Marzollo chooses the first-person point of view to develop her argument? How do you suppose Marzollo hopes the first-person approach will affect her readers?
2. **Other patterns.** What contrast makes the introduction dramatic? How does this contrast underlie the theme of the essay?
3. Examine the places where Marzollo uses direct quotations rather than reporting conversation indirectly. What is gained by using exact words at these points?
4. Marzollo asks rhetorical questions at several points in the essay. How do these questions help focus her argument? How do these questions function as transitional devices?

Questions for Further Thought

1. What kinds of games involving pretended violence, destruction, and death did you play as a child? What was your parents' reaction?
2. From your experience, do you think all children (both male and female, from various ethnic groups and economic backgrounds) play games of pretended violence? Would you say such play is normal?
3. It has been said that play is "the child's work," meaning that through play children try on new behaviors and skills and test their abilities. Would Marzollo agree? What things specifically can children learn through play?
4. What might be some of the reasons that adults like violent action

movies (such as the Rambo and Dirty Harry series)? Do you see any connection between children's fantasy play and the popularity of these films? Are these films beneficial, harmless, or dangerous for people to view?

Writing Assignments Using Argumentation-Persuasion as a Pattern of Development

1. In paragraphs 15 and 16, Marzollo mentions four different parental attitudes toward guns. Write an essay that makes a case for parents' adopting one of these attitudes. After citing possible counterarguments, support your proposition with a balanced appeal to reason and emotion. Draw on your own experiences as a child, babysitter, neighbor, parent, and so on.

2. One of Marzollo's points is that physical play and fantasy have important healing roles in children's lives. Write an essay defending the role of physical activity and/or fantasy in adults' lives as a way to release pent-up rage about things that can't be controlled. Make your proposition as specific as possible, supporting it with examples from your own life and with references to films, TV programs, and books. At some point in the essay, you should acknowledge briefly the opposing view: that escaping from reality can have negative repercussions.

Writing Assignments Using Other Patterns of Development

3. Write an essay about the games (physical, fantasy, or other) that helped you grow up. These may have been games that taught you about yourself, others, feelings, or life in general. Describe the games that absorbed you and explain their benefits.

4. Marzollo contends that childhood play with weapons isn't a cause of violence among adults. What, then, do you think are the roots of such violence? Prepare an essay exploring the causes of *one* kind of violence that you find particularly distressing. If you decide to write about street crime, date rape, or racial assault, you'll find it helpful to read, respectively, Louis Nizer's "Low-Cost Drugs for Addicts?" (page 682) and Beth Johnson Ruth's "Our Drug Problem" (page 687); Camille Paglia's "Rape: A Bigger Danger Than Feminists Know" (page 650) and Susan Jacoby's "Common Decency" (page 658); and Maya Angelou's "Grandmother's Victory" (page 158). No matter which area you focus on, you'll probably need to conduct some library research to deepen your understanding of the issue.

Migdia Chinea-Varela

Migdia Chinea-Varela was born in Cuba but left that country in 1962 when her family became part of a mass exodus of Cubans opposed to the policies of the Castro regime. She grew up in south Florida as part of the exile community there. A graduate of the University of California in Los Angeles, Chinea-Varela works in Hollywood, where for eight years she was the only Latin woman writing for the film and television industry. She has written for Columbia Pictures and for many television programs, including *Punky Brewster*, *What's Happening Now!*, *One Day at a Time*, and *Diff'rent Strokes*. Chinea-Varela's work on NBC's *Facts of Life* won her an Emmy nomination. A frequent panelist on radio and television shows nationwide, she was the recipient of the City of Los Angeles Human Relations Award and the Nosotros Golden Eagle Writing Award. Many of her dramatic projects involve the fate of Cuba and the experiences of Cuban exiles. The selection here first appeared in *Newsweek* in 1988.

My Life as a "Twofer"

Suppose you've worked hard for years to establish yourself in your profession and are then offered a job—not on the basis of your accomplishments but because of your gender or ethnic identity. Would accepting such a position devalue the quality of your work? In the following essay, Migdia Chinea-Varela explains how it feels to be treated not as an individual but as someone who can fill a quota.

This Christmas I'll be celebrating my tenth anniversary as a   1
card-carrying member of the film industry's Writers Guild. Ten brain-numbing years and a debilitating employment lull during the five-month-long writers' strike have taken their toll. Last week I'd awakened in what can only be described as profound financial melancholia and was taking inventory of my career alternatives

when the phone rang. The caller was a friend at the Writers Guild of America, West. Great news, he said. Several production companies were starting "access" programs for minorities, women, the elderly and the disabled. They'd requested a sampler of scripts ASAP[1] from which to fish out two, maybe *three* writers for freelance assignments. It could even lead to staff jobs, he said.

My imagination flashes to a TV scene in which I grab the   2
lifeline and submit my best script. I subsequently get chosen for a plum writing assignment that quickly turns into a staff position, where I do such a bang-up job that I become the show's producer and an Emmy award winner as well. In real life, however, I thank the guild rep for his good-faith efforts and tell him that my answer is no. Though I helped found and then chaired the Latino writer's committee, I don't want to send in my scripts.

Why? Why would anyone pass up such a sweet deal? Every-   3
one knows how tough the film and television industry is. Yet contacts are everything, the insiders say. It helps if you have an agent with hot connections who believes in you and is willing to put in the time required to promote your career. It helps if you attended the "right" film school. It's a matter of timing. It's difficult for everyone. Yes, but consider this — if you're a member of a minority group, the equation should be multiplied by ten; and if you're a minority woman, then add thirty more points.

So what's my problem? Why not take advantage of every   4
opportunity that comes my way? The answer is: I've been in this situation before and I don't like the way it makes me feel. There's something almost insulting about these well-meaning affirmative-action searches. In the past I'd always rationalized my participation partly because I needed the break and even more because I needed the money. And as fate would have it, whenever a film- or TV-production company saw fit to round up minorities for a head count, I always came out on top. But the truth is that I've never felt good about it.

I've asked myself the obvious questions. Am I being picked   5
for my writing ability, or to fulfill a quota? Have I been selected because I'm a "twofer" — a female Hispanic, or because they were enthralled with my deftly drawn characters and strong, original story line? My writing career, it appears, has taken a particu-

---

[1]Shorthand for "as soon as possible."

larly tortuous course. I've gone from being a dedicated writer to being a dedicated *minority* writer, which seems limiting for someone who was first inspired by Woody Allen.

Truth is, that even with the aid of special programs, job   6
assignments for writers who fit the "minority" category are inexplicably few and far between. The sad employment statistics reveal that ethnic minorities comprise less than 3 percent of our guild. Those who work do so less frequently and for a lot less money, yet the publicity harvested by the special programs creates the illusion of equal opportunity where very little exists. I don't want to seem overly gloomy. Nevertheless, my work's almost always seen on shows that have a minority star like *The Facts of Life*, *What's Happening Now!* and *Punky Brewster*.

Except for *The Cosby Show*, minorities are not being taken   7
seriously enough to write about their real lives outside of the ghetto. Though few of us will admit to it — for fear of speaking out or being tagged as ungrateful — we're reminded of our status in not-so-subtle ways. I remember the time I was waiting for a story meeting where I wanted to pitch several ideas. As I chatted with the production secretary, an aspiring writer herself, I could hear laughter coming from inside the conference room. Finally, the executive in charge stepped outside, followed by five young men. Judging by the look of satisfaction on their faces, it had probably been a profitable session. The executive greeted me effusively by saying, as he turned to the rest of the group, "Meet M-I-G-D-I-A V-A-R-R-R-R-E-L-A. She's one of our minority writers." This comment drew a tight smile from my lips, as one and all present reacted with extravagant expressions of support. Somehow I knew right then and there that my project would be down for the count. KO'd with kindness.

Killer sharks: More recently, I was spilling my guts to a   8
friend with a recognizable name whose uncle was a famous writer. After sharing my woes and commiserating as fellow writers often do, we parted with that old cliché: "We're in the same boat." Suddenly it dawned on me that hell *no*, we're not even close. We're no doubt on the same ocean, but hardly in the same boat. From where I sit, my friend's being attended to on a luxury liner while I'm all alone paddling a canoe, surrounded by killer sharks and in the midst of a typhoon.

I'd like to think that after ten years of paying my dues as a   9 professional writer that I've earned the right to walk through the front door. After so many years, it's depressing to feel that I have to tag myself a minority as an incentive to those who may hire me. Why can't I get a job on my own merits? Am I destined to spend the rest of my writing career hooked up to these kinds of life-support systems?

I'm painfully aware that affirmative action, what little there   10
is of it, may be the only way minorities are given a chance to compete. However, for me, it has become a stigma of sorts. In my view, there can be no affirmative action without segregation — nor any end to the segregation if our names must be kept on separate lists. I'd like to propose instead a simple scenario: a fair job market where employment is commensurate with ability regardless of gender, racial or ethnic background. I make a pitch, they like my story, I get the job. Why not?

Questions for Close Reading

1. What is the selection's thesis? Locate the sentence(s) in which Chinea-Varela states her main idea. If she doesn't state the thesis explicitly, express it in your own words.
2. According to Chinea-Varela, what is the status of minorities in the entertainment industry? What evidence does she provide to illustrate this status?
3. Chinea-Varela at one time chaired the committee to promote opportunities for Latino writers in Hollywood. Why, then, does she decline to submit scripts to the "access programs for minorities"? What problems does she have with "affirmative-action searches"?
4. What, according to Chinea-Varela, would be the ideal way for hiring to be conducted in the entertainment industry?
5. Refer to your dictionary as needed to define the following words used in the selection: *debilitating* (paragraph 1), *melancholia* (1), *rationalized* (4), *tortuous* (5), *inexplicably* (6), *effusively* (7), and *commensurate* (10).

Questions About the Writer's Craft

1. **The pattern.** Where in the essay does Chinea-Varela present the opposing viewpoint? How does she deal with these views?
2. **Other patterns.** Chinea-Varela uses dialogue, both indirect and direct, in several places in the essay. Why do you think she uses this narrative technique when making her argument?

3. Find places in the essay where Chinea-Varela uses questions. What purpose do these questions serve?

4. How would you characterize Chinea-Varela's word choice? How does her word choice affect the essay's tone?

Questions for Further Thought

1. Chinea-Varela describes a time when she turned down a job opportunity because of the way it made her feel. Would you have rejected this chance, had you been in her position? Why or why not?

2. Have you ever been embarrassed, as Chinea-Varela was, by someone calling attention to something about you that was "special" or different? Or have you seen someone else being treated in such a way? If so, how did you — or the person involved — handle the situation?

3. Chinea-Varela wants "a fair job market where employment is commensurate with ability." Do you believe such a fair job market exists for anyone nowadays — minority or not? Explain.

4. Chinea-Varela comments, "There's something almost insulting about these well-meaning affirmative-action searches." In what ways can affirmative-action policies insult people? How might opportunities for minorities be expanded *without* insulting anyone?

Writing Assignments Using Argumentation-Persuasion as a Pattern of Development

1. As a minority, Chinea-Varela has mixed feelings about affirmative action. Do you think that employers should give preferential treatment to minorities when hiring? Or do you oppose such policies? To assure that your position is more than a reflexive, emotional reaction, conduct some library research on the origins of affirmative-action hiring policies, the effect of such policies, and so on. Then write an essay arguing either for or against affirmative action in hiring. You may also want to ask friends, family members, and instructors if affirmative-action policies have in any way affected their job-seeking experiences. Take their experiences (and any of your own) into account as you develop your argument.

2. Chinea-Varela mentions several television shows that feature minorities. Since the time her essay was written, a number of other shows with minority stars have been televised. Watch several of the most popular of these shows, taking careful notes on the way that minorities are depicted. Then write a paper arguing that television reinforces *or* helps dismantle harmful stereotypes about minorities. Support your position with specific examples from the shows, citing characters

and incidents that prove your point. To strengthen your argument further, acknowledge opposing positions at some point in the essay.

Writing Assignments Using Other Patterns of Development

3. At the beginning of her essay, Chinea-Varela imagines what a fair job market might be like. Choose a situation that you think is inherently unfair and imagine what it might be like if it were drastically improved. For example, you might imagine your job suddenly free of tyrannical supervisors and impossible workloads, or you might imagine a more just way for awarding scholarships at your college. Write an essay comparing and contrasting life before and after such an improvement. End with a brief explanation of the steps that should be taken to bring about the improvement.

4. Like Chinea-Varela, most of us have said "no" at some point in our lives, thereby disappointing someone else—perhaps even ourselves. Write an essay narrating a time when you said "no" to someone or something. Tell what events led up to your decision and explain the consequences it had for you and for others.

Mark Twain

Mark Twain is a central figure in American literature. Published in 1884, *The Adventures of Huckleberry Finn*, Twain's finest work, recounts a journey down the Mississippi by two memorable figures, a white boy and a black slave. Twain was born Samuel Langhorne Clemens in 1835 and was raised in Hannibal, Missouri. During his early years, he worked as a riverboat pilot, newspaper reporter, printer, and gold prospector. Although his popular image is as the author of such comic works as *The Adventures of Tom Sawyer* (1876), *Life on the Mississippi* (1883), and *The Prince and the Pauper* (1882), Twain had a darker side that may have resulted from the bitter experiences of his life: financial failure and the deaths of his wife and daughter. His last writings are savage, satiric, and pessimistic. The following selection is taken from *Letters From the Earth*, one of Twain's later works.

The Damned Human Race

Does today's newspaper contain a headline about people fighting somewhere in the world? Most likely. In this selection, Mark Twain concludes that the combative and cruel nature of human beings makes them the lowest of creatures, not the highest. He concludes his scathing indictment by supplying a startling reason for humans' warlike nature.

I have been studying the traits and dispositions of the "lower animals" (so-called), and contrasting them with the traits and dispositions of man. I find the result humiliating to me. For it obliges me to renounce my allegiance to the Darwinian theory of the Ascent of Man from the Lower Animals; since it now seems plain to me that the theory ought to be vacated in favor of a new and truer one, this new and truer one to be named the *Descent* of Man from the Higher Animals.

In proceeding toward this unpleasant conclusion I have not 2 guessed or speculated or conjectured, but have used what is commonly called the scientific method. That is to say, I have subjected every postulate that presented itself to the crucial test of actual experiment, and have adopted it or rejected it according to the result. Thus I verified and established each step of my course in its turn before advancing to the next. These experiments were made in the London Zoological Gardens, and covered many months of painstaking and fatiguing work.

Before particularizing any of the experiments, I wish to state   3
one or two things which seem to more properly belong in this place than further along. This in the interest of clearness. The massed experiments established to my satisfaction certain generalizations, to wit:

1. That the human race is of one distinct species. It exhibits slight variations — in color, stature, mental caliber, and so on — due to climate, environment, and so forth; but it is a species by itself, and not to be confounded with any other.
2. That the quadrupeds are a distinct family, also. This family exhibits variations — in color, size, food preferences and so on; but it is a family by itself.
3. That the other families — the birds, the fishes, the insects, the reptiles, etc. — are more or less distinct, also. They are in the procession. They are links in the chain which stretches down from the higher animals to man at the bottom.

Some of my experiments were quite curious. In the course of   4
my reading I had come across a case where, many years ago, some hunters on our Great Plains organized a buffalo hunt for the entertainment of an English earl — that, and to provide some fresh meat for his larder. They had charming sport. They killed seventy-two of those great animals; and ate part of one of them and left the seventy-one to rot. In order to determine the difference between an anaconda and an earl — if any — I caused seven young calves to be turned into the anaconda's cage. The grateful reptile immediately crushed one of them and swallowed it, then lay back satisfied. It showed no further interest in the calves, and no disposition to harm them. I tried this experiment with other

anacondas; always with the same result. The fact stood proven that the difference between an earl and an anaconda is that the earl is cruel and the anaconda isn't; and that the earl wantonly destroys what he has no use for, but the anaconda doesn't. This seemed to suggest that the anaconda was not descended from the earl. It also seemed to suggest that the earl was descended from the anaconda, and had lost a good deal in the transition.

I was aware that many men who have accumulated more 5 millions of money than they can ever use have shown a rabid hunger for more, and have not scrupled to cheat the ignorant and the helpless out of their poor servings in order to partially appease that appetite. I furnished a hundred different kinds of wild and tame animals the opportunity to accumulate vast stores of food, but none of them would do it. The squirrels and bees and certain birds made accumulations, but stopped when they had gathered a winter's supply, and could not be persuaded to add to it either honestly or by chicane. In order to bolster up a tottering reputation the ant pretended to store up supplies, but I was not deceived. I know the ant. These experiments convinced me that there is this difference between man and the higher animals: he is avaricious and miserly, they are not.

In the course of my experiments I convinced myself that 6 among the animals man is the only one that harbors insults and injuries, broods over them, waits till a chance offers, then takes revenge. The passion of revenge is unknown to the higher animals.

Roosters keep harems, but it is by consent of their concu- 7 bines; therefore no wrong is done. Men keep harems, but it is by brute force, privileged by atrocious laws which the other sex were allowed no hand in making. In this matter man occupies a far lower place than the rooster.

Cats are loose in their morals, but not consciously so. Man, 8 in his descent from the cat, has brought the cat's looseness with him but has left the unconsciousness behind — the saving grace which excuses the cat. The cat is innocent, man is not.

Indecency, vulgarity, obscenity — these are strictly confined 9 to man; he invented them. Among the higher animals there is no trace of them. They hide nothing; they are not ashamed. Man, with his soiled mind, covers himself. He will not even enter a drawing room with his breast and back naked, so alive are he and his mates to indecent suggestion. Man is "The Animal that Laughs." But so does the monkey, as Mr. Darwin pointed out; and so does the Australian bird that is called the laughing jackass. No — Man is the Animal that Blushes. He is the only one that does it — or has occasion to.

At the head of this article we see how "three monks were burnt to death" a few days ago, and a prior "put to death with atrocious cruelty." Do we inquire into the details? No; or we should find out that the prior was subjected to unprintable mutilations. Man — when he is a North American Indian — gouges out his prisoner's eyes; when he is King John, with a nephew to render untroublesome, he uses a red-hot iron; when he is a religious zealot dealing with heretics in the Middle Ages, he skins his captive alive and scatters salt on his back; in the first Richard's time he shuts up a multitude of Jew families in a tower and sets fire to it; in Columbus's time he captures a family of Spanish Jews and — but *that* is not printable; in our day in England a man is fined ten shillings for beating his mother nearly to death with a chair, and another man is fined forty shillings for having four pheasant eggs in his possession without being able to satisfactorily explain how he got them. Of all the animals, man is the only one that is cruel. He is the only one that inflicts pain for the pleasure of doing it. It is a trait that is not known to the higher animals. The cat plays with the frightened mouse; but she has this excuse, that she does not know that the mouse is suffering. The cat is moderate — unhumanly moderate: she only scares the mouse, she does not hurt it; she doesn't dig out its eyes, or tear off its skin, or drive splinters under its nails — man-fashion; when she is done playing with it she makes a sudden meal of it and puts it out of its trouble. Man is the Cruel Animal. He is alone in that distinction. 10

The higher animals engage in individual fights, but never in organized masses. Man is the only animal that deals in that atrocity of atrocities, War. He is the only one that gathers his brethren about him and goes forth in cold blood and with calm pulse to exterminate his kind. He is the only animal that for sordid wages will march out, as the Hessians did in our Revolution, and as the boyish Prince Napoleon did in the Zulu war, and help to slaughter strangers of his own species who have done him no harm and with whom he has no quarrel. 11

Man is the only animal that robs his helpless fellow of his 12
country—takes possession of it and drives him out of it or
destroys him. Man has done this in all the ages. There is not an
acre of ground on the globe that is in possession of its rightful
owner, or that has not been taken away from owner after owner,
cycle after cycle, by force and bloodshed.

Man is the only Slave. And he is the only animal who en- 13
slaves. He has always been a slave in one form or another, and has
always held other slaves in bondage under him in one way or
another. In our day he is always some man's slave for wages, and
does that man's work; and this slave has other slaves under him
for minor wages, and they do *his* work. The higher animals are the
only ones who exclusively do their own work and provide their
own living.

Man is the only Patriot. He sets himself apart in his own 14
country, under his own flag, and sneers at the other nations, and
keeps multitudinous uniformed assassins on hand at heavy expense to grab slices of other people's countries, and keep *them*
from grabbing slices of *his*. And in the intervals between campaigns he washes the blood off his hands and works for "the
universal brotherhood of man"—with his mouth.

Man is the Religious Animal. He is the only Religious Ani- 15
mal. He is the only animal that has the True Religion—several of
them. He is the only animal that loves his neighbor as himself,
and cuts his throat if his theology isn't straight. He has made a
graveyard of the globe in trying his honest best to smooth his
brother's path to happiness and heaven. He was at it in the time
of the Caesars, he was at it in Mahomet's time, he was at it in the
time of the Inquisition, he was at it in France a couple of centuries, he was at it in England in Mary's day, he has been at it ever
since he first saw the light, he is at it today in Crete—as per the
telegrams quoted above—he will be at it somewhere else tomorrow. The higher animals have no religion. And we are told that
they are going to be left out, in the Hereafter. I wonder why? It
seems questionable taste.

Man is the Reasoning Animal. Such is the claim. I think it is 16
open to dispute. Indeed, my experiments have proven to me that
he is the Unreasoning Animal. Note his history, as sketched
above. It seems plain to me that whatever he is he is *not* a
reasoning animal. His record is the fantastic record of a maniac. I

consider that the strongest count against his intelligence is the fact that with that record back of him he blandly sets himself up as the head animal of the lot: whereas by his own standards he is the bottom one.

In truth, man is incurably foolish. Simple things which the   17
other animals easily learn, he is incapable of learning. Among my experiments was this. In an hour I taught a cat and a dog to be friends. I put them in a cage. In another hour I taught them to be friends with a rabbit. In the course of two days I was able to add a fox, a goose, a squirrel and some doves. Finally a monkey. They lived together in peace; even affectionately.

Next, in another cage I confined an Irish Catholic from   18
Tipperary, and as soon as he seemed tame I added a Scotch Presbyterian from Aberdeen. Next a Turk from Constantinople; a Greek Christian from Crete; an Armenian; a Methodist from the wilds of Arkansas; a Buddhist from China; a Brahman from Benares. Finally, a Salvation Army Colonel from Wapping. Then I stayed away two whole days. When I came back to note results, the cage of Higher Animals was all right, but in the other there was but a chaos of gory odds and ends of turbans and fezzes and plaids and bones and flesh — not a specimen left alive. These Reasoning Animals had disagreed on a theological detail and carried the matter to a Higher Court.

One is obliged to concede that in true loftiness of character,   19
Man cannot claim to approach even the meanest of the Higher Animals. It is plain that he is constitutionally incapable of approaching that altitude; that he is constitutionally afflicted with a Defect which must make such approach forever impossible, for it is manifest that this defect is permanent in him, indestructible, ineradicable.

I find this Defect to be *the Moral Sense*. He is the only animal   20
that has it. It is the secret of his degradation. It is the quality *which enables him to do wrong*. It has no other office. It is incapable of performing any other function. It could never have been intended to perform any other. Without it, man could do no wrong. He would rise at once to the level of the Higher Animals.

Since the Moral Sense has but the one office, the one   21
capacity — to enable man to do wrong — it is plainly without value to him. It is as valueless to him as is disease. In fact, it manifestly *is* a disease. *Rabies* is bad, but it is not so bad as this

disease. Rabies enables a man to do a thing which he could not do when in a healthy state: kill his neighbor with a poisonous bite. No one is the better man for having rabies: The Moral Sense enables a man to do wrong. It enables him to do wrong in a thousand ways. Rabies is an innocent disease, compared to the Moral Sense. No one, then, can be the better man for having the Moral Sense. What, now, do we find the Primal Curse to have been? Plainly what it was in the beginning: the infliction upon man of the Moral Sense; the ability to distinguish good from evil; and with it, necessarily, the ability to *do* evil; for there can be no evil act without the presence of consciousness of it in the doer of it.

And so I find that we have descended and degenerated, from some far ancestor—some microscopic atom wandering at its pleasure between the mighty horizons of a drop of water perchance—insect by insect, animal by animal, reptile by reptile, down the long highway of smirchless innocence, till we have reached the bottom stage of development—namable as the Human Being. Below us—nothing.   22

Questions for Close Reading

1. What is the selection's thesis? Locate the sentence(s) in which Twain states his main idea. If he doesn't state the thesis explicitly, express it in your own words.
2. Because of their intelligence, humans are usually called the highest animal. What, according to Twain, are the specific traits that make humans the lowest animal?
3. How does the story of the earl who hunted down seventy-two buffalo show that an anaconda is superior to an earl?
4. What does Twain mean when he points out that humankind is the only animal that "has occasion to" blush? What are some of the occasions for blushing that he highlights in the essay?
5. Refer to your dictionary as needed to define the following words used in the selection: *confounded* (paragraph 3), *anaconda* (4), *wantonly* (4), *chicane* (5), *heretics* (10), *constitutionally* (19), *ineradicable* (19), and *smirchless* (22).

Questions About the Writer's Craft

1. **The pattern.** Most writers don't tell the reader outright the reasoning process they used to arrive at their essay's proposition. But Twain

claims that he reached his conclusion about human beings inductively—through the use of the "scientific method." Why does Twain make this claim?

2. Where in the essay does Twain try to shock the audience? Why do you think he adopts this technique?

3. **Other patterns.** In some paragraphs, Twain provides numerous examples of political and religious atrocities. Why do you suppose he supplies so many examples?

4. Black humor is defined as "the use of the morbid and the absurd for comic purposes." What elements of the morbid and the absurd do you find in Twain's essay? Would you say "The Damned Human Race" is an example of black humor? Explain.

Questions for Further Thought

1. Twain wrote this essay in the early 1900s. Is what he says about humans true today? If Twain were writing today, what events and situations would he include in this essay as proof of humanity's lowness?

2. Is Twain's indictment excessive? Has he gone overboard, or do we humans deserve his indictment? Explain.

3. If a person behaved like the cat with a mouse described in paragraph 10, would that person be evil—or innocent like the cat? Is it behavior that is the problem for Twain, or is it something else?

4. Twain's essay hinges on an idea most of us take for granted—that the human species tops a hierarchy of creatures. We are, we assume, the end result of a complex evolutionary process. What would happen if we became aware that we weren't the cleverest, most powerful creature in the universe? Which of our beliefs, habits, and actions might change as a result?

Writing Assignments Using Argumentation-Persuasion as a Pattern of Development

∞ 1. In an essay, argue that human beings are worthy of being considered the "highest animal." The paper should acknowledge and then refute Twain's charges that people are miserly, vengeful, foolish, and so on. To support your proposition, use specific examples of how human beings can be kind, caring, generous, and peace-loving. You might find it helpful to read Lewis Thomas's "The Lie Detector" (page 510), an essay focusing on the more positive aspects of human nature.

∞ 2. Write an essay agreeing with Twain that it is our everyday meannesses, unkindnesses, and cruelties that make us the "lowest animal."

Use compelling examples to support your argument, including description and dialogue whenever appropriate. You might focus on one of the following topics:

Violence toward children
Abuse of animals
Hurtful sarcasm
Insults of a racial, sexist, or religious nature
Indifference to the unfortunate

Somewhere in the essay, you should acknowledge the view that humans are capable of considerable kindness and compassion. To gain some insight into this more optimistic perspective, you might want to read Lewis Thomas's "The Lie Detector" (page 510).

Writing Assignments Using Other Patterns of Development

∞ 3. What failings of human decency do you see around you every day in your town, on your campus, or at your job? Write an essay showing that inhumanity resides not just in atrocities but also in ordinary acts of indifference. Before planning the paper, you might want to see what Jonathan Kozol, in "Are the Homeless Crazy?" (page 515), has to say about people's often uncaring attitude—in this case, toward the homeless. In your essay, you may use Twain's kind of bitter sarcasm, or you may adopt a more objective, less vitriolic tone.

4. How could humans become less cruel? Write an essay outlining a new process for raising children or "re-civilizing" adults—a process that, if instituted, would improve human morality.

Jonathan Swift

The foremost satirist in the English language, Jonathan Swift (1667–1745) is most famous as the author of *Gulliver's Travels* (1726), an often scorching indictment of human conduct. Born in Ireland, Swift moved to London at a young age and in 1694 was ordained an Anglican priest. In 1714 he was appointed the dean of St. Patrick's Cathedral in Dublin, a minor post the ambitious Swift accepted with reluctance. For most of his life, Swift was an outspoken public figure, writing satiric poems, plays, and essays aimed at political and religious targets. His works include *A Tale of a Tub* and *The Battle of the Books*, both published in 1704. More than two decades later, outraged by the British government's treatment of the Irish people, Swift wrote "A Modest Proposal," the classic essay reprinted here.

A Modest Proposal

In 1729, Ireland was in tragic condition. Poverty was widespread, a devastating famine was in its third year, and people were starving. Moreover, the British government, which ruled Ireland, imposed high taxes on the already impoverished populace. Enraged by these injustices, Swift wrote a powerful satire attacking the English and wealthy Irish for ignoring the existence of the suffering masses. Speaking not as himself but in the guise of an impartial observer, Swift suggested an outrageous solution to Ireland's problems, a solution in keeping with the inhumanity he saw rampant in Ireland.

It is a melancholy object to those who walk through this great town[1] or travel in the country, when they see the streets, the roads, and cabin doors, crowded with beggars of the female sex, followed by three, four, or six children, all in rags and importun- 1

[1]Dublin.

ing every passenger for an alms. These mothers, instead of being able to work for their honest livelihood, are forced to employ all their time in strolling to beg sustenance for their helpless infants, who, as they grow up, either turn thieves for want of work, or leave their dear native country to fight for the Pretender in Spain, or sell themselves to the Barbadoes.[2]

2   I think it is agreed by all parties that this prodigious number of children in the arms, or on the backs, or at the heels of their mothers, and frequently of their fathers, is in the present deplorable state of the kingdom a very great additional grievance; and therefore whoever could find out a fair, cheap, and easy method of making these children sound, useful members of the commonwealth would deserve so well of the public as to have his statue set up for a preserver of the nation.

3   But my intention is very far from being confined to provide only for the children of professed beggars; it is of a much greater extent, and shall take in the whole number of infants at a certain age who are born of parents in effect as little able to support them as those who demand our charity in the streets.

4   As to my own part, having turned my thoughts for many years upon this important subject, and maturely weighed the several schemes of other projectors, I have always found them grossly mistaken in their computation. It is true, a child just dropped from its dam may be supported by her milk for a solar year, with little other nourishment; at most not above the value of two shillings, which the mother may certainly get, or the value in scraps, by her lawful occupation of begging; and it is exactly at one year old that I propose to provide for them in such a manner as instead of being a charge upon their parents or the parish, or wanting food and raiment for the rest of their lives, they shall on the contrary contribute to the feeding, and partly to the clothing, of many thousands.

5   There is likewise another great advantage in my scheme, that it will prevent those involuntary abortions, and that horrid practice of women murdering their bastard children, alas, too frequent among us, sacrificing the poor innocent babes, I doubt, more to avoid the expense than the shame, which would move tears and pity in the most savage and inhuman breast.

---

[2]Many poor Irish were leaving the country to try to find a living elsewhere.

The number of souls in this kingdom being usually reckoned   6
one million and a half, of these I calculate there may be about two
hundred thousand couples whose wives are breeders, from which
number I subtract thirty thousand couples who are able to maintain their own children, although I apprehend there cannot be so
many under the present distress of the kingdom; but this being
granted, there will remain an hundred and seventy thousand
breeders. I again subtract fifty thousand for those women who
miscarry, or whose children die by accident or disease within the
year. There only remain an hundred and twenty thousand children of poor parents annually born. The question therefore is,
how this number shall be reared and provided for, which, as I
have already said, under the present situation of affairs, is utterly
impossible by all the methods hitherto proposed. For we can
neither employ them in handicraft nor agriculture; we neither
build houses (I mean in the country) nor cultivate land. They can
very seldom pick up livelihood by stealing till they arrive at six
years old, except where they are of towardly parts;[3] although I
confess they learn the rudiments much earlier, during which time
they can however be looked upon only as probationers, as I have
been informed by a principal gentleman in the county of Cavan,
who protested to me that he never knew above one or two instances under the age of six, even in a part of the kingdom so
renowned for the quickest proficiency in that art.

I am assured by our merchants that a boy or a girl before   7
twelve years old is no salable commodity; and even when they
come to this age, they will not yield above three pounds, or three
pounds and half a crown at most on the Exchange; which cannot
turn to account either to the parents or the kingdom, the charge
of nutriment and rags having been at least four times that value.

I shall now therefore humbly propose my own thoughts,   8
which I hope will not be liable to the least objection.

I have been assured by a very knowing American of my   9
acquaintance in London, that a young healthy child well nursed is
at a year old a most delicious, nourishing, and wholesome food,
whether stewed, roasted, baked, or boiled; and I make no doubt
that it will equally serve in fricassee or a ragout.

I do therefore humbly offer it to public consideration that of   10

---

[3]Prematurely developed.

the hundred and twenty thousand children, already computed, twenty thousand may be reserved for breed, whereof only one fourth part to be males, which is more than we allow to sheep, black cattle, or swine; and my reason is that these children are seldom the fruits of marriage, a circumstance not much regarded by our savages, therefore one male will be sufficient to serve four females. That the remaining hundred thousand may at a year old be offered in sale to the persons of quality and fortune through the kingdom, always advising the mother to let them suck plentifully in the last month, so as to render them plump and fat for a good table. A child will make two dishes at an entertainment for friends; and when the family dines alone, the fore or hind quarter will make a reasonable dish, and seasoned with a little pepper or salt will be very good boiled on the fourth day, especially in winter.

I have reckoned upon a medium that a child just born will 11 weigh twelve pounds, and in a solar year if tolerably nursed increaseth to twenty-eight pounds.

I grant this food will be somewhat dear, and therefore very 12 proper for landlords, who, as they have already devoured most of the parents, seem to have the best title to the children.

Infant's flesh will be in season throughout the year, but more 13 plentiful in March, and a little before and after. For we are told by a grave author, an eminent French physician,[4] that fish being a prolific diet, there are more children born in Roman Catholic countries about nine months after Lent, than at any other season; therefore, reckoning a year after Lent, the markets will be more glutted than usual, because the number of popish infants is at least three to one in this kingdom; and therefore it will have one other collateral advantage, by lessening the number of Papists among us.

I have already computed the charge of nursing a beggar's 14 child (in which list I reckon all cottagers, laborers, and four fifths of the farmers) to be about two shillings per annum, rags included; and I believe no gentleman would repine to give ten shillings for the carcass of a good fat child, which, as I have said, will make four dishes of excellent nutritive meat, when he hath only some particular friend or his own family to dine with him.

---

[4]François Rabelais, a sixteenth-century comic writer.

Thus the squire will learn to be a good landlord, and grow popular among the tenants; the mother will have eight shillings net profit, and be fit for work till she produces another child.

Those who are more thrifty (as I must confess the times   15
require) may flay the carcass; the skin of which artifically[5] dressed will make admirable gloves for ladies, and summer boots for fine gentlemen.

As to our city of Dublin, shambles[6] may be appointed for this   16
purpose in the most convenient parts of it, and butchers we may be assured will not be wanting; although I rather recommend buying the children alive, and dressing them hot from the knife as we do roasting pigs.

A very worthy person, a true lover of his country, and whose   17
virtues I highly esteem, was lately pleased in discoursing on this matter to offer a refinement upon my scheme. He said that many gentlemen of his kingdom, having of late destroyed their deer, he conceived that the want of venison might be well supplied by the bodies of young lads and maidens, not exceeding fourteen years of age nor under twelve, so great a number of both sexes in every county being now ready to starve for want of work and service; and these to be disposed of by their parents, if alive, or otherwise by their nearest relations. But with due deference to so excellent a friend and so deserving a patriot, I cannot be altogether in his sentiments; for as to the males, my American acquaintance assured me from frequent experience that their flesh was generally tough and lean, like that of our schoolboys, by continual exercise, and their taste disagreeable; and to fatten them would not answer the charge. Then as to the females, it would, I think with humble submission, be a loss to the public, because they soon would become breeders themselves; and besides, it is not improbable that some scrupulous people might be apt to censure such a practice (although indeed very unjustly) as a little bordering upon cruelty; which, I confess, hath always been with me the strongest objection against any project, how well soever intended.

But in order to justify my friend, he confessed that this   18
expedient was put into his head by the famous Psalmanazar,[7] a

---

[5]Skillfully.

[6]Slaughterhouses.

[7]A Frenchman, Georges Psalmanazar, who fooled London society into thinking he was from the exotic land of Formosa.

native of the island Formosa, who came from thence to London above twenty years ago, and in conversation told my friend that in his country when any young person happened to be put to death, the executioner sold the carcass to the persons of quality as a prime dainty; and that in his time the body of a plump girl of fifteen, who was crucified for an attempt to poison the emperor, was sold to his Imperial Majesty's prime minister of state, and other great mandarins of the court, in joints from the gibbet, at four hundred crowns. Neither indeed can I deny that if the same use were made of several plump young girls in this town, who without one single groat to their fortunes cannot stir abroad without a chair,[8] and appear at the playhouse and assemblies in foreign fineries which they never will pay for, the kingdom would not be the worse.

Some persons of a desponding spirit are in great concern   19 about that vast number of poor people who are aged, diseased, or maimed, and I have been desired to employ my thoughts what course may be taken to ease the nation of so grievous an encumbrance. But I am not in the least pain upon that matter, because it is very well known that they are every day dying and rotting by cold and famine, and filth and vermin, as fast as can be reasonably expected. And as to the younger laborers, they are now in almost as hopeful a condition. They cannot get work, and consequently pine away for want of nourishment to a degree that if any time they are accidentally hired to common labor, they have not strength to perform it; and thus the country and themselves are happily delivered from the evils to come.

I have too long digressed, and therefore shall return to my   20 subject. I think the advantages by the proposal which I have made are obvious and many, as well as of the highest importance.

For first, as I have already observed, it would greatly lessen   21 the number of Papists, with whom we are yearly overrun, being the principal breeders of the nation as well as our most dangerous enemies; and who stay at home on purpose to deliver the kingdom to the Pretender, hoping to take their advantage by the absence of so many good Protestants, who have chosen rather to

---

[8]A groat was a coin worth several pennies; a chair was a sedan chair in which a person was carried by servants.

leave their country than to stay at home and pay tithes against their conscience to an Episcopal curate.

Secondly, the poorer tenants will have something valuable of   22
their own, which by law may be made liable to distress,[9] and help
to pay their landlord's rent, their corn and cattle being already
seized and money a thing unknown.

Thirdly, whereas the maintenance of an hundred thousand   23
children, from two years old and upwards, cannot be computed
at less than ten shillings a piece per annum, the nation's stock will
be thereby increased fifty thousand pounds per annum, besides
the profit of a new dish introduced to the tables of all gentlemen
of fortune in the kingdom who have any refinement in taste. And
the money will circulate among ourselves, the goods being entirely of our own growth and manufacture.

Fourthly, the constant breeders, besides the gain of eight   24
shillings sterling per annum by the sale of their children, will be
rid of the charge for maintaining them after the first year.

Fifthly, this food would likewise bring great custom to tav-   25
erns, where the vintners will certainly be so prudent as to procure
the best receipts for dressing it to perfection, and consequently
have their houses frequented by all the fine gentlemen, who justly
value themselves upon their knowledge in good eating; and a
skillful cook, who understands how to oblige his guests, will
contrive to make it as expensive as they please.

Sixthly, this would be a great inducement to marriage, which   26
all wise nations have either encouraged by rewards or enforced by
laws and penalties. It would increase the care and tenderness of
mothers toward their children, when they were sure of a settlement for life to the poor babes, provided in some sort by the
public, to their annual profit instead of expense. We should see
an honest emulation among the married women, which of them
could bring the fattest child to the market. Men would become as
fond of their wives during the time of pregnancy as they are now
of their mares in foal, their cows in calf, or sows when they are
ready to farrow; nor offer to beat or kick them (as is too frequent
a practice) for fear of a miscarriage.

Many other advantages might be enumerated. For instance,   27
the addition of some thousand carcasses in our exportation of

[9]Seizure for the payment of debts.

barreled beef, the propagation of swine's flesh, and improvements in the art of making good bacon, so much wanted among us by the great destruction of pigs, too frequent at our tables, which are no way comparable in taste or magnificence to a well-grown, fat, yearling child, which roasted whole will make a considerable figure at a lord mayor's feast or any other public entertainment. But this and many others I omit, being studious of brevity.

Supposing that one thousand families in this city would be constant customers for infants' flesh, besides others who might have it at merry meetings, particularly weddings and christenings, I compute that Dublin would take off annually about twenty thousand carcasses, and the rest of the kingdom (where probably they will be sold somewhat cheaper) the remaining eighty thousand.   28

I can think of no one objection that will possibly be raised against this proposal, unless it should be urged that the number of people will be thereby much lessened in the kingdom. This I freely own, and it was indeed one principal design in offering it to the world. I desire the reader will observe; that I calculate my remedy for this one individual kingdom of Ireland and for no other that ever was, is, or I think ever can be upon earth. Therefore, let no man talk to me of other expedients: of taxing our absentees at five shillings a pound: of using neither clothes nor household furniture except what is of our own growth and manufacture: of utterly rejecting the materials and instruments that promote foreign luxury: of curing the expensiveness of pride, vanity, idleness, and gaming in our women: of introducing a vein of parsimony, prudence, and temperance: of learning to love our country, in the want of which we differ even from Laplanders and the inhabitants of Topinamboo:[10] of quitting our animosities and factions, nor acting any longer like the Jews,[11] who were murdering one another at the very moment their city was taken: of being a little cautious not to sell our country and conscience for nothing: of teaching landlords to have at least one degree of mercy toward their tenants: lastly, of putting a spirit of honesty, industry, and skill into our shopkeepers; who, if a resolution could   29

---

[10]A place in the Brazilian jungle.

[11]Rival factions were at war within Jerusalem when the city was seized by the Romans in 70 A.D.

now be taken to buy only our native goods, would immediately unite to cheat and exact upon us in the price, the measure, and the goodness, nor could ever yet be brought to make one fair proposal of just dealing, though often and earnestly invited to it.

Therefore, I repeat, let no man talk to me of these and the like expedients, till he hath at least some glimpse of hope that there will ever be some hearty and sincere attempt to put them in practice. 30

But as to myself, having been wearied out for many years with offering vain, idle, visionary thoughts, and at length utterly despairing of success, I fortunately fell upon this proposal, which, as it is wholly new, so it hath something solid and real, of no expense and little trouble, full in our own power, and whereby we can incur no danger in disobliging England. For this kind of commodity will not bear exportation, the flesh being of too tender a consistence to admit a long continuance in salt, although perhaps I could name a country which would be glad to eat up our whole nation without it. 31

After all, I am not so violently bent upon my own opinion as to reject any offer proposed by wise men, which shall be found equally innocent, cheap, easy, and effectual. But before something of that kind shall be advanced in contradiction to my scheme, and offering a better, I desire the author or authors will be pleased maturely to consider two points. First, as things now stand, how they will be able to find food and raiment for an hundred thousand useless mouths and backs. And secondly, there being a round million of creatures in human figure throughout this kingdom, whose sole subsistence put into a common stock would leave them in debt two millions of pounds sterling, adding those who are beggars by profession to the bulk of farmers, cottagers, and laborers, with their wives and children who are beggars in effect; I desire those politicians who dislike my overture, and may perhaps be so bold to attempt an answer, that they will first ask the parents of these mortals whether they would not at this day think it a great happiness to have been sold for food at a year old in this manner I prescribe, and thereby have avoided such a perpetual scene of misfortunes as they have since gone through by the oppression of landlords, the impossibility of paying rent without money or trade, the want of common sustenance, with neither house nor clothes to cover them from the 32 inclemencies of the weather, and the most inevitable prospect of entailing the like or greater miseries upon their breed forever.

I profess, in the sincerity of my heart, that I have not the least 33 personal interest in endeavoring to promote this necessary work, having no other motive than the public good of my country, by advancing our trade, providing for infants, relieving the poor, and giving some pleasure to the rich. I have no children by which I can propose to get a single penny; the youngest being nine years old, and my wife past childbearing.

Questions for Close Reading

1. What is the selection's thesis? Locate the sentence(s) in which Swift states his main idea. If he doesn't state the thesis explicitly, express it in your own words.
2. Swift mentions several economic, social, and political realities in Ireland that prompted him to write this essay. Identify a few of them.
3. What twisted reasoning does the speaker use to argue that his proposal will improve relationships between husbands and wives and between parents and children?
4. What problems does the speaker contend the British government will solve if it permits the butchering and sale of infants from impoverished families?
5. Refer to your dictionary as needed to define the following words used in the selection: *importuning* (paragraph 1), *alms* (1), *prodigious* (2), *raiment* (4), *prolific* (13), *repine* (14), *discoursing* (17), *encumbrance* (19), and *vintners* (25).

Questions About the Writer's Craft

1. **The pattern.** *Satire* uses humor to criticize a situation and create awareness of the need for change; *irony*, often used in satire, occurs when a writer or speaker implies — rather than explicitly states — a discrepancy or incongruity. (*Verbal irony* involves a discrepancy between literal words and what's actually meant. In *situational irony*, the circumstances are themselves incongruous.) How do satire and irony help Swift accomplish what a more conventional approach to persuasion would not?
2. Swift uses language laden with emotion to convey a sarcastic, downright bitter tone. Locate several examples of emotionally charged language. How does this language support Swift's real purpose for writing "A Modest Proposal"?
3. In paragraph 20, the speaker apologizes for having "digressed" in the

last few paragraphs. Do paragraphs 17, 18, and 19 really represent a digression, or are they germane to the issue? Explain.

4. Writers of argumentation-persuasion essays often anticipate and then refute opposing opinions. In what paragraph does the speaker in "A Modest Proposal" refute the dissenting viewpoint? What is the real purpose of this refutation?

Questions for Further Thought

1. Are the causes of the poverty that Swift saw in eighteenth-century Ireland similar to some of the economic problems we experience in this country? Explain.

2. In paragraph 29, the speaker rejects several proposals that Swift actually believes would help alleviate poverty in Ireland. Which of these proposals might be used to address the problem of poverty in our nation?

3. Do the well-off, even the merely comfortable, have a responsibility to the poor? If so, what is the nature and extent of this responsibility?

4. Swift's epitaph reads, "He has gone where savage indignation can no longer lacerate his heart." About what do you feel "savage indignation"? What can you do about the situations that outrage you?

Writing Assignments Using Argumentation-Persuasion as a Pattern of Development

1. Select a subject that you feel strongly about—one that has an ethical or moral dimension to it. Then, like Swift, use an ironic approach to convince readers of your position. In other words, argue for one point of view while pretending to advance the other. For example, if you're concerned about some colleges' exemption of their star athletes from conventional academic requirements, you could write an essay arguing the "advantages" of letting student-athletes "coast" through college.

2. Read what Jonathan Kozol has to say in "Are the Homeless Crazy?" (page 515) about one segment of this country's poor—the homeless. Then write an essay advocating the steps that ordinary citizens can take to help alleviate the problem. As you draft your proposal, keep in mind what Kozol says about people's insensitivity and apathy. What persuasive strategies will you adopt to puncture this callous disregard?

**Writing Assignments Using Other
Patterns of Development**

∞ 3. At the beginning of "A Modest Proposal," Swift describes briefly the poverty he witnessed in his native land. How would *you* describe the face of poverty? Write an essay describing an impoverished, blighted area. What are its streets, houses, stores, and people like? Organizing the essay around a dominant impression, depict what you see, smell, hear, and feel. Gordon Parks's "Flavio's Home" (page 96) will help you see how you might approach such an essay.

4. Seeking to improve the Irish economy, Swift advocates boycotting foreign-made products. Do you believe the United States should impose restrictive tariffs and import limits on goods manufactured abroad? Write a paper in which you identify the positive and negative consequences of such protective measures. Gather information by brainstorming with others and, if necessary, go to the library to locate several articles on this issue.

Nat Hentoff

Nat Hentoff was born in Boston in 1925. His writings for the *Village Voice* and *New Yorker*, his columns for the *Washington Post*, and his more than twenty-five books of fiction and non-fiction have earned him the reputation as a respected voice of the political Left. Privacy, drug testing, racism, the draft, abortion, and educational reform have all come under Hentoff's keen observation. In 1987, Hentoff published his autobiography, *Boston Boy*, and 1989 saw the publication of his latest book, *The First Freedom: The Tumultuous History of Free Speech in America*. Despite his political stance as a leftist, Hentoff has criticized the zeal of the Left in suppressing speech it finds offensive. Such concerns led him to write the following essay, first published in the *Progressive* in May 1989.

Free Speech on Campus

Censorship, book-burning, imprisonment of political opponents—all are tools of ultra-Right, totalitarian governments bent on silencing the opposition. But what about attempts at colleges and universities to restrict racist, sexist, and otherwise bigoted speech? Should such efforts be condoned? "No," says Nat Hentoff. With characteristic fervor, Hentoff explains why he's concerned by the Left's adoption of rightist tactics to suppress campus views that aren't considered politically correct.

A flier distributed at the University of Michigan some   1
months ago proclaimed that blacks "don't belong in classrooms, they belong hanging from trees."

At other campuses around the country, manifestations of   2
racism are becoming commonplace. At Yale, a swastika and the words WHITE POWER! were painted on the building housing the University's Afro-American Cultural Center. At Temple Univer-

sity, a White Students Union has been formed with some 130 members.

Swastikas are not directed only at black students. The Nazi 3 symbol has been spray-painted on the Jewish Student Union at Memphis State University. And on a number of campuses, women have been singled out as targets of wounding and sometimes frightening speech. At the law school of the State University of New York at Buffalo, several women students have received anonymous letters characterized by one professor as venomously sexist.

These and many more such signs of the resurgence of bigotry 4 and knownothingism throughout the society—as well as on campus—have to do solely with speech, including symbolic speech. There have also been physical assaults on black students and on black, white, and Asian women students, but the way to deal with physical attacks is clear: call the police and file a criminal complaint. What is to be done, however, about speech alone —however disgusting, inflammatory, and rawly divisive that speech may be?

At more and more colleges, administrators—with the en- 5 thusiastic support of black students, women students, and liberal students—have been answering that question by preventing or punishing speech. In public universities, this is a clear violation of the First Amendment. In private colleges and universities, suppression of speech mocks the secular religion of academic freedom and free inquiry.

The Student Press Law Center in Washington, D.C.—a vital 6 source of legal support for student editors around the country— reports, for example, that at the University of Kansas, the student host and producer of a radio news program was forbidden by school officials from interviewing a leader of the Ku Klux Klan. So much for free inquiry on that campus.

In Madison, Wisconsin, the *Capital Times* ran a story in 7 January about Chancellor Sheila Kaplan of the University of Wisconsin branch at Parkside, who ordered her campus to be scoured of "some anonymously placed white supremacist hate literature." Sounding like the legendary Mayor Frank ("I am the law") Hague of Jersey City, who booted "bad speech" out of town, Chancellor Kaplan said, "This institution is not a lamppost standing on the street corner. It doesn't belong to everyone."

Who decides what speech can be heard or read by everyone?   8
Why, the Chancellor, of course. That's what George III[1] used to
say, too.

University of Wisconsin political science professor Carol   9
Tebben thinks otherwise. She believes university administrators
"are getting confused when they are acting as censors and trying
to protect students from bad ideas. I don't think students need to
be protected from bad ideas. I think they can determine for
themselves what ideas are bad."

After all, if students are to be "protected" from bad ideas,   10
how are they going to learn to identify and cope with them?
Sending such ideas underground simply makes them stronger and
more dangerous.

Professor Tebben's conviction that free speech means just   11
that has become a decidedly minority view on many campuses. At
the University of Buffalo Law School, the faculty unanimously
adopted a "Statement Regarding Intellectual Freedom, Tolerance, and Political Harassment." Its title implies support of intellectual freedom, but the statement warned students that once
they enter "this legal community," their right to free speech must
become tempered "by the responsibility to promote equality and
justice."

Accordingly, swift condemnation will befall anyone who en-   12
gages in "remarks directed at another's race, sex, religion, national origin, age, or sex preference." Also forbidden are "other
remarks based on prejudice and group stereotype."

This ukase is so broad that enforcement has to be alarmingly   13
subjective. Yet the University of Buffalo Law School provides no
due-process procedures for a student booked for making any of
these prohibited remarks. Conceivably, a student caught playing a
Lenny Bruce, Richard Pryor, or Sam Kinison[2] album in his room
could be tried for aggravated insensitivity by association.

When I looked into this wholesale cleansing of bad speech at   14
Buffalo, I found it had encountered scant opposition. One pro-

[1]King of England at the time of the American Revolution, George III reportedly lost his sanity in his later years.

[2]Lenny Bruce was a stand-up comic popular in the 1950s and early 1960s.
Bruce's caustic social commentary and his use of language that many considered
offensive established the precedent for the confrontational style of many recent
comedians, including Richard Pryor and Sam Kinison.

tester was David Gerald Jay, a graduate of the law school and a cooperating attorney for the New York Civil Liberties Union. Said the appalled graduate: "Content-based prohibitions constitute prior restraint and should not be tolerated."

You would think that the law professors and administration 15 at this public university might have known that. But hardly any professors dissented, and among the students only members of the conservative Federalist Society spoke up for free speech. The fifty-strong chapter of the National Lawyers Guild was on the other side. After all, it was more important to go on record as vigorously opposing racism and sexism than to expose oneself to charges of insensitivity to these malignancies.

The pressures to have the "right" attitude — as proved by 16 having the "right" language in and out of class — can be stifling. A student who opposes affirmative action, for instance, can be branded a racist.

At the University of California at Los Angeles, the student 17 newspaper ran an editorial cartoon satirizing affirmative action. (A student stops a rooster on campus and asks how the rooster got into UCLA. "Affirmative action," is the answer.) After outraged complaints from various minority groups, the editor was suspended for violating a publication policy against running "articles that perpetuate derogatory or cultural stereotypes." The art director was also suspended.

When the opinion editor of the student newspaper at Cali- 18 fornia State University at Northridge wrote an article asserting that the sanctions against the editor and art director at UCLA amounted to censorship, he was suspended too.

At New York University Law School, a student was so dis- 19 turbed by the pall of orthodoxy at that prestigious institution that he wrote to the school newspaper even though, as he said, he expected his letter to make him a pariah among his fellow students.

Barry Endick described the atmosphere at NYU created by "a 20 host of watchdog committees and a generally hostile classroom reception regarding any student comment right of center." This "can be arguably viewed as symptomatic of a prevailing spirit of academic and social intolerance of . . . any idea which is not 'politically correct.'"

He went on to say something that might well be posted on 21

campus bulletin boards around the country, though it would probably be torn down at many of them: "We ought to examine why students, so anxious to wield the Fourteenth Amendment, give short shrift to the First. Yes, Virginia, there are racist assholes. And you know what, the Constitution protects them, too."

Not when they engage in violence or vandalism. But when   22
they speak or write, racist assholes fall right into this Oliver Wendell Holmes[3] definition — highly unpopular among bigots, liberals, radicals, feminists, sexists, and college administrators: "If there is any principle of the Constitution that more imperatively calls for attachment than any other, it is the principle of free thought — not free only for those who agree with us, but freedom for the thought we hate."

The language sounds like a pietistic Sunday sermon, but if it   23
ever falls wholly into disuse, neither this publication nor any other journal of opinion — right or left — will survive.

Sometimes, college presidents and administrators sound as if   24
they fully understand what Holmes was saying. Last year, for example, when the *Daily Pennsylvanian*[4] — speaking for many at the University of Pennsylvania — urged that a speaking invitation to Louis Farrakhan[5] be withdrawn, University President Sheldon Hackney disagreed.

"Open expression," said Hackney, "is the fundamental prin-   25
ciple of a university." Yet consider what the same Sheldon Hackney did to the free-speech rights of a teacher at his own university. If any story distills the essence of the current decline of free speech on college campuses, it is the Ballad of Murray Dolfman.

For twenty-two years, Dolfman, a practicing lawyer in Phila-   26
delphia, had been a part-time lecturer in the Legal Studies Department of the University of Pennsylvania's Wharton School. For twenty-two years, no complaint had ever been made against him; indeed his student course evaluations had been outstanding. Each year students competed to get into his class.

On a November afternoon in 1984, Dolfman was lecturing   27

---

[3]Holmes was Associate Justice of the Supreme Court (1902–32).
[4]The student newspaper at the University of Pennsylvania.
[5]The leader of the Black Nation of Islam, Farrakhan holds controversial views that have been called anti-Semitic and racially inflammatory.

about personal-service contracts. His style somewhat resembles that of Professor Charles Kingsfield in *The Paper Chase*.[6] Dolfman insists that students he calls on be prepared — or suffer the consequences. He treats all students this way — regardless of race, creed, or sex.

This day, Dolfman was pointing out that no one can be forced to work against his or her will — even if a contract has been signed. A court may prevent the resister from working for someone else so long as the contract is in effect but, Dolfman said, there can "be nothing that smacks of involuntary servitude."   28

Where does this concept come from? Dolfman looked around the room. Finally, a cautious hand was raised: "The Constitution?"   29

"Where in the Constitution?" No hands. "The Thirteenth Amendment," said the teacher. So, what does *it* say? The students were looking everywhere but at Dolfman.   30

"We will lose our liberties," Dolfman often told his classes, "if we don't know what they are."   31

On this occasion, he told them that he and other Jews, as ex-slaves, spoke at Passover of the time when they were slaves under the Pharaohs so that they would remember every year what it was like not to be free.   32

"We have ex-slaves here," Dolfman continued, "who should know about the Thirteenth Amendment." He asked black students in the class if they could tell him what was in that amendment.   33

"I wanted them to really think about it," Dolfman told me recently, "and know its history. You're better equipped to fight racism if you know all about those post–Civil War amendments and civil rights laws."   34

The Thirteenth Amendment provides that "neither slavery nor involuntary servitude . . . shall exist within the United States."   35

The black students in his class did not know what was in that amendment, and Dolfman had them read it aloud. Later, they   36

[6]Charles Kingsfield was the demanding law professor in the television show *The Paper Chase*. The series, popular in the 1970s, chronicled the struggles of first-year law students at a prestigious university.

complained to university officials that they had been hurt and humiliated by having been referred to as ex-slaves. Moreover, they said, they had no reason to be grateful for a constitutional amendment which gave them rights which should never have been denied them — and gave them precious little else. They had not made these points in class, although Dolfman — unlike Professor Kingsfield — encourages rebuttal.

Informed of the complaint, Dolfman told the black students   37
he had intended no offense, and he apologized if they had been offended.

That would not do — either for the black students or for the   38
administration. Furthermore, there were mounting black-Jewish tensions on campus, and someone had to be sacrificed. Who better than a part-time Jewish teacher with no contract and no union? He was sentenced by — George Orwell[7] would have loved this — the Committee on Academic Freedom and Responsibility.

On his way to the stocks, Dolfman told President Sheldon   39
Hackney that if a part-time instructor "can be punished on this kind of charge, a tenured professor can eventually be booted out, then a dean, and then a president."

Hackney was unmoved. Dolfman was banished from the   40
campus for what came to be a year. But first he was forced to make a public apology to the entire university and then he was compelled to attend a "sensitivity and racial awareness" session. Sort of like a Vietnamese reeducation camp.

A few conservative professors objected to the stigmatization   41
of Murray Dolfman. I know of no student dissent. Indeed, those students most concerned with making the campus more "sensitive" to diversity exulted in Dolfman's humiliation. So did most liberals on the faculty.

If my children were still of college age and wanted to attend   42
the University of Pennsylvania, I would tell them this story. But where else could I encourage them to go?

---

[7]British essayist and novelist, George Orwell often wrote about the fragile line separating democratic and despotic institutions. (For more information on Orwell, see page 166.)

Questions for Close Reading

1. What is the selection's thesis? Locate the sentence(s) in which Hentoff states his main idea. If he doesn't state the thesis explicitly, express it in your own words.
2. What evidence does Hentoff present to support his statement that there's a "resurgence of bigotry and knownothingism throughout the society"?
3. According to Hentoff, how have officials on campuses at the University of Kansas, the University of Wisconsin, and the University of California at Los Angeles interfered with free inquiry and free speech? What reasons did university officials give for their actions?
4. Why, in Hentoff's opinion, should college campuses permit all types of speech? According to Hentoff, what problems arise when free speech is curtailed?
5. Refer to your dictionary as needed to define the following words used in the selection: *venomously* (paragraph 3), *knownothingism* (4), *ukase* (13), *dissented* (15), *malignancies* (15), *sanctions* (18), *pall* (19), *pariah* (19), *pietistic* (23), *distills* (25), *stocks* (39), and *stigmatization* (41).

Questions About the Writer's Craft

1. **The pattern.** Writing on a complex and controversial issue, Hentoff wisely confronts the opposing viewpoint — in this case, the position that the free speech of extremists should be suppressed. What strategies does Hentoff use to deal with this view?
2. **Other patterns.** Where in the selection does Hentoff use examples and a narrative account to support his argument? How do the examples and the narrative help him support his case?
3. What tone does Hentoff employ when describing those who believe that sometimes it is necessary to limit free speech? How do Hentoff's sentence structure and word choice help create this tone?
4. Examine the quotations in paragraphs 20–22. Why do you think Hentoff chooses to quote these two particular individuals — law student Barry Endick and Supreme Court Justice Oliver Wendell Holmes? What does he achieve by juxtaposing Endick's words with those of Holmes?

Questions for Further Thought

1. Hentoff states that violent action motivated by bigotry should be handled by calling the police and filing a criminal complaint. But he believes that offensive speech motivated by bigotry is a different issue

and doesn't call for suppression. Do you agree that these two situations should be handled differently? Do you think that the difference between a bigoted action and bigoted speech is always apparent? Explain.

2. How far should society go in protecting what law student Barry Endick calls "racist assholes" and in guarding the rights of extremists' free speech? Are there ideas and political positions that you would prefer to see suppressed? Which ones? How comfortable are you with ideas that are opposed to your own?

3. Is it necessary for students to be exposed to "bad ideas" during their education, as Hentoff indicates in paragraph 10? Do you find that there's intolerance of "bad" or out-of-favor ideas at your college? Does your school have any guidelines that limit the expression of such ideas? How do you feel about the guidelines?

4. Reread Hentoff's description of the incident that occurred in instructor Murray Dolfman's class at the University of Pennsylvania Law School (paragraphs 26–37). Do you feel, as Hentoff does, that Dolfman was incorrectly punished? Why or why not?

Writing Assignments Using Argumentation-Persuasion as a Pattern of Development

1. In paragraph 11, Hentoff cites the University of Buffalo Law School's caution about the importance of balancing free speech with "the responsibility to promote equality and justice." Consider the stereotyping, the economic deprivations, and the personal slurs that many members of minority groups continue to suffer. Then decide which you believe is more important: totally free speech or the protection of the rights, feelings, and status of groups that have been discriminated against. Write an essay in which you argue that on college campuses protecting "equality and justice" either is or isn't more important than protecting freedom of speech. Provide specific examples to defend your position, and don't forget to deal with opposing viewpoints.

2. Hentoff decries the punishment of student journalists who published a cartoon satirizing affirmative action. However, satire and comedy often rely for their bite on ethnic, political, and gender stereotypes. Carefully consider the comedy and satire currently in vogue. Does it provide harmless entertainment? Does it perpetuate negative stereotypes? Does it open up helpful discussion and debate? Prepare an essay in which you argue your position. Remembering to acknowledge opposing viewpoints, support your case with plentiful examples.

Writing Assignments Using Other
Patterns of Development

3. What procedures has your college or university established so that people on campus—faculty, staff, and/or students—can file grievances if they feel they have been discriminated against in some way? In an essay, describe this process and indicate whether you feel it's adequate. If it isn't, explain what steps need to be taken to improve the procedures.

∞ 4. Stereotyping isn't restricted to minorities. Most of us have felt unfairly stereotyped at some time or another, perhaps because of gender, physical or intellectual abilities, even a hobby or interest. Write an essay about a time you were treated unfairly or cruelly because of some personal characteristic. Be sure to show how the event affected you. The following essays will provide insight into the potentially corrosive effect of labels and stereotypes: Jeanne Wakatsuki Houston and James D. Houston's "Manzanar" (page 132), Santha Rama Rau's "By Any Other Name" (page 191), Peter Farb's "In Other Words" (page 491), Alice Walker's "Beauty: When the Other Dancer Is the Self" (page 499), Jonathan Kozol's "Are the Homeless Crazy?" (page 515), William Raspberry's "The Handicap of Definition" (page 563), and Migdia Chinea-Varela's "My Life as a 'Twofer'" (page 613).

Camille Paglia

Before 1991, Camille Paglia, Professor of Humanities at Philadelphia's University of the Arts, was known primarily for her electrifying performance in the classroom. Then came the publication of Paglia's *Sexual Personae: Art and Decadence from Nefertiti to Emily Dickinson*, a sweeping book that moves with dizzying speed from the days of cave art to the nineteenth century. *Sexual Personae* makes the case that man creates art as a defensive response to woman's terrifying cosmic power — specifically, her sexual and procreative force. At once illuminating and murky, insightful and simplistic, the book appeared at a time when people around the world were grappling with new ways for thinking about what it means to be male and female. Suddenly Paglia became an international celebrity. Paglia, who seeks out opportunities to express her controversial views, has been both revered and reviled for making statements like these: "Male aggression and lust are the energizing factors in culture" and "If I ever get into a dating situation where I was raped and overwhelmed, I would say, 'Oh well, I misread the signals.'" Born in 1947, Paglia earned her doctorate from Yale University, where her Ph.D. thesis was an early version of *Sexual Personae*. During the coming year, she expects to complete the second volume of *Sexual Personae*, which will examine the evolution of art and eroticism in movies, television, sports, and rock music. The following selection, written in Paglia's characteristically provocative style, first appeared in *Newsday* in 1988.

Rape: A Bigger Danger Than Feminists Know

Are there fundamental obstacles that prevent men and women from ever truly understanding one another? Will the sexes be forever at war? Is there "only one thing" men want from women, and is it women's responsibility to foil men's efforts to get it? In this essay, Camille Paglia advances answers to these and other questions.

Rape is an outrage that cannot be tolerated in civilized soci- 1
ety. Yet feminism, which has waged a crusade for rape to be taken
more seriously, has put young women in danger by hiding the
truth about sex from them.

In dramatizing the pervasiveness of rape, feminists have told 2
young women that before they have sex with a man, they must
give consent as explicit as a legal contract's. In this way, young
women have been convinced that they have been the victims of
rape. On elite campuses in the Northeast and on the West Coast,
they have held consciousness-raising sessions, petitioned administrations, demanded inquests. At Brown University, outraged,
panicky "victims" have scrawled the names of alleged attackers
on the walls of women's rest rooms. What marital rape was to the
'70s, "date rape" is to the '90s.

The incidence and seriousness of rape do not require this 3
kind of exaggeration. Real acquaintance rape is nothing new. It
has been a horrible problem for women for all of recorded history. Once, father and brothers protected women from rape.
Once, the penalty for rape was death. I come from a fierce Italian
tradition where, not so long ago in the motherland, a rapist
would end up knifed, castrated, and hung out to dry.

But the old clans and small rural communities have broken 4
down. In our cities, on our campuses far from home, young
women are vulnerable and defenseless. Feminism has not prepared them for this. Feminism keeps saying the sexes are the
same. It keeps telling women they can do anything, go anywhere,
say anything, wear anything. No, they can't. Women will always
be in sexual danger.

One of my male students recently slept overnight with a 5
friend in a passageway of the Great Pyramid in Egypt. He described the moon and sand, the ancient silence and eerie echoes. I
am a woman. I will never experience that. I am not stupid enough
to believe I could ever be safe there. There is a world of solitary
adventure I will never have. Women have always known these
somber truths. But feminism, with its pie-in-the-sky fantasies
about the perfect world, keeps young women from seeing life as it
is.

We must remedy social injustice whenever we can. But there 6
are some things we cannot change. There are sexual differences
that are based in biology. Academic feminism is lost in a fog of

social constructionism. It believes we are totally the product of our environment. This idea was invented by Rousseau.[1] He was wrong. Emboldened by dumb French language theory, academic feminists repeat the same hollow slogans over and over to each other. Their view of sex is naive and prudish. Leaving sex to the feminists is like letting your dog vacation at the taxidermist's.

The sexes are at war. Men must struggle for identity against   7
the overwhelming power of their mothers. Women have menstruation to tell them they are women. Men must do or risk something to be men. Men become masculine only when other men say they are. Having sex with a woman is one way a boy becomes a man.

College men are at their hormonal peak. They have just left   8
their mothers and are questing for their male identity. In groups, they are dangerous. A woman going to a fraternity party is walking into Testosterone Flats, full of prickly cacti and blazing guns. If she goes, she should be armed with resolute alertness. She should arrive with girlfriends and leave with them. A girl who lets herself get dead drunk at a fraternity party is a fool. A girl who goes upstairs alone with a brother at a fraternity party is an idiot. Feminists call this "blaming the victim." I call it common sense.

For a decade, feminists have drilled their disciples to say,   9
"Rape is a crime of violence but not of sex." This sugar-coated Shirley Temple nonsense has exposed young women to disaster. Misled by feminism, they do not expect rape from the nice boys from good homes who sit next to them in class.

Aggression and eroticism, in fact, are deeply intertwined.   10
Hunt, pursuit and capture are biologically programmed into male sexuality. Generation after generation, men must be educated, refined, and ethically persuaded away from their tendency toward anarchy and brutishness. Society is not the enemy, as feminism ignorantly claims. Society is woman's protection against rape. Feminism, with its solemn Carry Nation[2] repressiveness, does not see what is for men the eroticism or fun element in rape, especially the wild, infectious delirium of gang rape. Women who do not understand rape cannot defend themselves against it.

[1] A French political writer and philosopher (1712–78).
[2] A nineteenth-century reformer who advocated the abolition of alcohol.

The date-rape controversy shows feminism hitting the wall of   11
its own broken promises. The women of my '60s generation were
the first respectable girls in history to swear like sailors, get drunk,
stay out all night—in short, to act like men. We sought total
sexual freedom and equality. But as time passed, we woke up to
cold reality. The old double standard protected women. When
anything goes, it's women who lose.

Today's young women don't know what they want. They see   12
that feminism has not brought sexual happiness. The theatrics of
public rage over date rape are their way of restoring the old sexual
rules that were shattered by my generation. Yet nothing about the
sexes has really changed. The comic film *Where the Boys Are*
(1960), the ultimate expression of '50s man-chasing, still speaks
directly to our time. It shows smart, lively women skillfully anticipating and fending off the dozens of strategies with which horny
men try to get them into bed. The agonizing date-rape subplot
and climax are brilliantly done. The victim, Yvette Mimieux,
makes mistake after mistake, obvious to the other girls. She allows
herself to be lured away from her girlfriends and into isolation
with boys whose character and intentions she misreads. *Where the
Boys Are* tells the truth. It shows courtship as a dangerous game in
which the signals are not verbal but subliminal.

Neither militant feminism, which is obsessed with politically   13
correct language, nor academic feminism, which believes that
knowledge and experience are "constituted by" language, can
understand preverbal or nonverbal communication. Feminism,
focusing on sexual politics, cannot see that sex exists in and
through the body. Sexual desire and arousal cannot be fully translated into verbal terms. This is why men and women misunder-
stand each other.

Trying to remake the future, feminism cut itself off from   14
sexual history. It discarded and suppressed the sexual myths of
literature, art and religion. Those myths show us the turbulence,
the mysteries and passions of sex. In mythology we see men's
sexual anxiety, their fear of woman's dominance. Much sexual
violence is rooted in men's sense of psychological weakness
toward women. It takes many men to deal with one woman.
Woman's voracity is a persistent motif. Clara Bow,[3] it was ru-

---

[3]A movie star from the Roaring Twenties era.

mored, took on the USC[4] football team on weekends. Marilyn Monroe, singing "Diamonds Are a Girl's Best Friend," rules a conga line of men in tuxes. Half-clad Cher, in the video for "If I Could Turn Back Time," deranges a battleship of screaming sailors and straddles a pink-lit cannon. Feminism, coveting social power, is blind to woman's cosmic sexual power.

To understand rape, you must study the past. There never   15
was and never will be sexual harmony. Every woman must be prudent and cautious about where she goes and with whom. When she makes a mistake, she must accept the consequences and, through self-criticism, resolve never to make that mistake again. Running to mommy and daddy on the campus grievance committee is unworthy of strong women. Posting lists of guilty men in the toilet is cowardly, infantile stuff.

The Italian philosophy of life espouses high-energy confron-   16
tation. A male student makes a vulgar remark about your breasts? Don't slink off to whimper with the campus shrinking violets. Deal with it. On the spot. Say, "Shut up, you jerk! And crawl back to the barnyard where you belong!" In general, women who project this take-charge attitude toward life get harassed less often. I see too many dopey, immature, self-pitying women walking around like melting sticks of butter. It's the Yvette Mimieux syndrome: make me happy. And listen to me weep when I'm not.

The date-rape debate is already smothering in propaganda   17
churned out by the expensive Northeastern colleges and universities, with their overconcentration of boring, uptight academic feminists and spoiled, affluent students. Beware of the deep manipulativeness of rich students who were neglected by their parents. They love to turn the campus into hysterical psychodramas of sexual transgression, followed by assertions of parental authority and concern. And don't look for sexual enlightenment from academe, which spews out mountains of books but never looks at life directly.

As a fan of football and rock music, I see in the simple,   18
swaggering masculinity of the jock and in the noisy posturing of the heavy-metal guitarist certain fundamental, unchanging truths about sex. Masculinity is aggressive, unstable, combustible. It is also the most creative cultural force in history. Women must

[4]University of Southern California.

reorient themselves toward the elemental powers of sex, which can strengthen or destroy.

The only solution to date rape is female self-awareness and   19
self-control. A woman's number-one line of defense against rape is herself. When a real rape occurs, she should report it to the police. Complaining to college committees because the courts "take too long" is ridiculous. College administrations are not a branch of the judiciary. They are not equipped or trained for legal inquiry. Colleges must alert incoming students to the problems and dangers of adulthood. Then colleges must stand back and get out of the sex game.

Questions for Close Reading

1. What is the selection's thesis? Locate the sentence(s) in which Paglia states her main idea. If she doesn't state the thesis explicitly, express it in your own words.
2. In Paglia's opinion, why are women more "vulnerable and defenseless" now than in the past?
3. According to Paglia, what "truths about sex" has feminism hidden from young women?
4. What does Paglia believe is "the only solution to date rape?"
5. Refer to your dictionary as needed to define the following words used in the selection: *inquests* (paragraph 2), *testosterone* (8), *constituted* (13), *grievance* (15), and *judiciary* (19).

Questions About the Writer's Craft

1. **The pattern.** Examine the way Paglia develops her argument in paragraphs 6 and 8. Which of her assertions in these paragraphs can be assumed to be true without further proof? Why do you think Paglia includes these essentially incontestable statements? Conversely, which of her assertions in paragraphs 6 and 8 require further proof before their truth can be demonstrated? Does Paglia provide such support? Explain.
2. **Other patterns.** How does Paglia use the comparison-contrast pattern to develop her argument?
3. Paglia's style is frequently characterized by short sentences strung together with few transitions. Locate some examples of this style. Why might Paglia have chosen this style? What is its effect?
4. Where does Paglia use emotional, highly connotative language? Where does she employ strongly worded absolute statements? Do you

think that this use of *pathos* makes Paglia's argument more or less convincing? Explain.

Questions for Further Thought

1. Do young women today believe that "they can [safely] do anything, go anywhere, say anything, wear anything," as Paglia claims in paragraph 4? Or do the young women you know behave more moderately and cautiously? Explain.
2. In paragraph 16, Paglia advocates that women adopt an assertive, even combative response to men who harass them. Do you agree that such an approach works? If not, how do you think women should handle harassment? What do you think constitutes harassment?
3. Assume a young woman who had been drinking heavily is raped at a party. Should she, as Paglia says in paragraph 15, "accept the consequences and . . . resolve never to make that mistake again"? Should she, as students at Brown University and elsewhere have done, write the name of the attacker on the walls of women's rest rooms? Should she report what happened to the campus grievance committee and file charges with the police? Or should she deal with the offense and offender in yet another way? How?
4. Do you think that men who commit date rape believe they have done wrong? Or do they believe they engaged in a permissible expression of their masculinity? Do men in general think that "no" means "yes"? Explain.

Writing Assignments Using Argumentation-Persuasion as a Pattern of Development

∞ 1. Read Susan Jacoby's "Common Decency" (page 658), an essay that takes exception to Paglia's view of date rape. Decide which writer presents her case more convincingly. Then write an essay arguing that the *other writer* has trouble making a strong case for her position. Consider the merits and flaws (including any logical fallacies) in the argument, plus such issues as the writer's credibility, strategies for dealing with the opposing view, and use of emotional appeals. Throughout, support your opinion with specific examples drawn from the selection. Keep in mind that you're critiquing the effectiveness of the writer's argument. It's not appropriate, then, simply to explain why you agree or disagree with the writer's position or merely to summarize what the writer says.

∞ 2. Paglia criticizes those who claim that the environment, or social climate, is primarily responsible for shaping gender differences. She believes that such differences "are based in biology." Write an essay arguing your own position about the role that environment and biology play in determining sex-role attitudes and behavior. Remembering to acknowledge opposing views, defend your own viewpoint with plentiful examples based on your experiences and observations. You may also need to conduct some library research to gather support for your position. The following essays will provide insights that you may want to draw upon in your paper: Alleen Pace Nilsen's "Sexism and Language" (page 228), Barbara Ehrenreich's "What I've Learned From Men" (page 261), Deborah Tannen's "Sex, Lies, and Conversation" (page 440), and Judy Brady's "Why I Want a Wife" (page 546).

Writing Assignments Using Other Patterns of Development

3. Paglia writes in paragraph 8 that "men become masculine only when other men say they are. Having sex with a woman is one way a boy becomes a man." Write an essay constructing your own definition of masculinity. Comment on the extent to which you feel being sexually active is an important criterion, but also include other hallmarks of masculinity.

4. Date rape seems to be on the rise. Brainstorm with others to identify what may be leading to its growing occurrence. Focusing on several related factors, write an essay showing how these factors contribute to the problem. Possible factors include the following: the way males and females are depicted in the media (advertisements, movies, television, rock videos); young people's use of alcohol; the emergence of co-ed college dorms. At the end of the essay, offer some recommendations about what can be done to create a safer climate for dating.

Susan Jacoby

In her first job as a newspaper reporter, Susan Jacoby (1947–) carefully avoided doing "women's stories," believing that such features weren't worthy of a serious journalist. However, Jacoby's opinion changed with the times, especially as women's issues began to gain increasing attention. Indeed, many of her essays—including those in the *New York Times* and *McCall's*—have dealt with women's concerns. A good number of Jacoby's essays have been collected in *The Possible She* (1979) and the forthcoming *Money, Manners, and Morals*. The following selection, published in the *New York Times* in April 1991, was written in response to the book *Sexual Personae* by Camille Paglia (see page 650).

Common Decency

In the last several years, debate has raged over the complex issues surrounding date rape. Some claim that saying "no" should be enough to protect a woman from sexual assault by a male acquaintance. Others contend that women are naive if they don't recognize that men are ruled by ungovernable sexual passions. This second point of view is one that Susan Jacoby finds depressing. Why? According to Jacoby, it assumes that the world is inhabited by hostile brutes rather than by civilized human beings.

She was deeply in love with a man who was treating her   1
badly. To assuage her wounded ego (and to prove to herself that she could get along nicely without him), she invited another man, an old boyfriend, to a dinner *à deux* in her apartment. They were on their way to the bedroom when, having realized that she wanted only the man who wasn't there, she changed her mind. Her ex-boyfriend was understandably angry. He left her apartment with a not-so-politely phrased request that she leave him out of any future plans.

And that is the end of the story — except for the fact that he   2
was eventually kind enough to accept her apology for what was
surely a classic case of "mixed signals."

I often recall this incident, in which I was the embarrassed   3
female participant, as the controversy over "date rape" —
intensified by the assault that William Kennedy Smith[1] has been
accused of — heats up across the nation. What seems clear to me
is that those who place acquaintance rape in a different category
from "stranger rape" — those who excuse friendly social rapists
on grounds that they are too dumb to understand when "no"
means no — are being even more insulting to men than to
women.

These apologists for date rape — and some of them are   4
women — are really saying that the average man cannot be
trusted to exercise any impulse control. Men are nasty and men
are brutes — and a woman must be constantly on her guard to
avoid giving a man any excuse to give way to his baser instincts.

If this view were accurate, few women would manage to get   5
through life without being raped, and few men would fail to
commit rape. For the reality is that all of us, men as well as
women, send and receive innumerable mixed signals in the course
of our sexual lives — and that is as true in marital beds at age fifty
as in the back seats of cars at age fifteen.

Most men somehow manage to decode these signals without   6
using superior physical strength to force themselves on their
partners. And most women manage to handle conflicting male
signals without, say, picking up carving knives to demonstrate
their displeasure at sexual rejection. This is called civilization.

Civilized is exactly what my old boyfriend was being when he   7
didn't use my muddleheaded emotional distress as an excuse to
rape me. But I don't owe him excessive gratitude for his decent
behavior — any more than he would have owed me special thanks
for not stabbing him through the heart if our situations had been
reversed. Most date rapes do not happen because a man honestly
mistakes a woman's "no" for a "yes" or a "maybe." They occur

---

[1]William Kennedy Smith, the nephew of John, Robert, and Edward Kennedy,
was acquitted of rape charges in 1991. The trial, broadcast on television, created a
national furor and generated heated debate on the issue of date rape.

because a minority of men — an ugly minority, to be sure — can't stand to take "no" for an answer.

This minority behavior — and a culture that excuses it on grounds that boys will be boys — is the target of the movement against date rape that has surfaced on many campuses during the past year.   8

It's not surprising that date rape is an issue of particular importance to college-age women. The campus concentration of large numbers of young people, in an unsupervised environment that encourages drinking and partying, tends to promote sexual aggression and discourage inhibition. Drunken young men who rape a woman at a party can always claim they didn't know what they were doing — and a great many people will blame the victim for having been there in the first place.   9

That is the line adopted by antifeminists like Camille Paglia,[2] author of the controversial *Sexual Personae: Art and Decadence From Nefertiti to Emily Dickinson*. Paglia, whose views strongly resemble those expounded twenty years ago by Norman Mailer[3] in *The Prisoner of Sex*, argues that feminists have deluded women by telling them they can go anywhere and do anything without fear of rape. Feminism, in this view, is both naïve and antisexual because it ignores the power of women to incite uncontrollable male passions.   10

Just to make sure there is no doubt about a woman's place, Paglia also links the male sexual aggression that leads to rape with the creative energy of art. "There is no female Mozart," she has declared, "because there is no female Jack the Ripper." According to this "logic," one might expect to discover the next generation of composers in fraternity houses and dorms that have been singled out as sites of brutal gang rapes.   11

This type of unsubtle analysis makes no distinction between sex as an expression of the will to power and sex as a source of pleasure. When domination is seen as an inevitable component of sex, the act of rape is defined not by a man's actions but by a woman's signals.   12

It is true, of course, that some women (especially the young) initially resist sex not out of real conviction but as part of the   13

[2]For information on Camille Paglia, see page 650.
[3]An American essayist and novelist.

elaborate persuasion and seduction rituals accompanying what was once called courtship. And it is true that many men (again, especially the young) take pride in the ability to coax a woman a step further than she intended to go.

But these mating rituals do not justify or even explain date 14 rape. Even the most callow youth is capable of understanding the difference between resistance and genuine fear; between a half-hearted "no, we shouldn't" and tears or screams; between a woman who is physically free to leave a room and one who is being physically restrained.

The immorality and absurdity of using mixed signals as an 15 excuse for rape is cast in high relief when the assault involves one woman and a group of men. In cases of gang rape in a social setting (usually during or after a party), the defendants and their lawyers frequently claim that group sex took place but no force was involved. These upright young men, so the defense invariably contends, were confused because the girl had voluntarily gone to a party with them. Why, she may have even displayed sexual interest in *one* of them. How could they have been expected to understand that she didn't wish to have sex with the whole group?

The very existence of the term "date rape" attests to a slow 16 change in women's consciousness that began with the feminist movement of the late 1960s. Implicit in this consciousness is the conviction that a woman has the right to say no at any point in the process leading to sexual intercourse — and that a man who fails to respect her wishes should incur serious legal and social consequences.

The other, equally important half of the equation is respect 17 for men. If mixed signals are the real cause of sexual assault, it behooves every woman to regard every man as a potential rapist.

In such a benighted universe, it would be impossible for a 18 woman (and, let us not forget, for a man) to engage in the tentative emotional and physical exploration that eventually pro-duces a mature erotic life. She would have to make up her mind right from the start in order to prevent a rampaging male from misreading her intentions.

Fortunately for everyone, neither the character of men nor 19 the general quality of relations between the sexes is that crude. By censuring the minority of men who use ordinary socializing as an excuse for rape, feminists insist on sex as a source of pure pleasure rather than as a means of social control. Real men want an eager sexual partner — not a woman who is quaking with fear or even one who is ambivalent. Real men don't rape.

Questions for Close Reading

1. What is the selection's thesis? Locate the sentence(s) in which Jacoby states her main idea. If she doesn't state the thesis explicitly, express it in your own words.
2. Why does Jacoby feel that she doesn't owe her old boyfriend a great deal of gratitude, even though she sent mixed signals about what type of relationship she wanted?
3. What does Jacoby mean in paragraph 6 by her comment, "This is called civilization"? How does this comment support her thesis?
4. Why does Jacoby think that it's insulting to men to accept Paglia's notion that men are ruled by uncontrollable passions?
5. Refer to your dictionary as needed to define the following words used in the selection: *apologists* (paragraph 4), *deluded* (10), *unsubtle* (12), *implicit* (16), *benighted* (18), *erotic* (18), *rampaging* (18), and *ambivalent* (19).

Questions About the Writer's Craft

1. **The pattern.** One way to refute an idea is to carry it to its logical extreme, thus revealing its inherent falsity or absurdity. This technique is called *reductio ad absurdum*. Examine paragraphs 4–5 and 15 and explain how Jacoby uses this technique to refute Paglia's position on date rape.
2. **Other patterns.** Locate places in the essay where Jacoby compares and contrasts male and female behavior or the behavior of rapists and nonrapists. How does her use of comparison-contrast help her build her argument?
3. What introduction technique (see pages 60–62) does Jacoby use to begin the essay? How does this type of introduction help her achieve her persuasive goal?
4. How would you characterize Jacoby's tone? Identify specific sentences and words that convey this tone. What effect might Jacoby have hoped this tone would have on readers?

Questions for Further Thought

1. Do you agree with Jacoby that the cause of date rape is the failure to "take 'no' for an answer"? How difficult or easy is it to take "no" for an answer in any circumstances? Explain.

2. Do you accept Jacoby's statement that courtship rituals "do not justify or even explain date rape"? Or do you agree with Camille Paglia (page 650) that dating is inherently a "dangerous game"? Explain.

3. The phrase, "Boys will be boys," used by Jacoby in paragraph 8, is often cited to explain certain types of male behavior. What kinds of actions typically fall in this category? Do you feel that date rape is one of them? Do you feel it's all right for boys or men to "be boys"? If not, how might they be persuaded to be "real men" — the kind who, according to Jacoby, "don't rape"?

4. In your relations, sexual or not, with the opposite sex, have you found there to be conflict and "the will to power," as Jacoby puts it in paragraph 12? Or have you experienced equality and mutual respect? Which do you feel is typical of your generation? Which do you feel might prevail in future generations?

Writing Assignments Using Argumentation-Persuasion as a Pattern of Development

∞ 1. Jacoby feels that Camille Paglia and others "excuse rapists." If you haven't already done so, read "Rape: A Bigger Danger Than Feminists Know" (page 650) to see what Paglia says about who bears primary responsibility for preventing rape. Then decide to what degree you feel men who commit date rape should be held accountable for their actions. Argue your position in an essay, making reference to both Jacoby's and Paglia's ideas to support your case. Also include reasons and evidence of your own.

2. Determine what your campus is doing about date rape. Does it have a formal policy defining date rape, a hearing process, ongoing workshops, discussions during orientation for incoming students? Write a paper describing what your college is doing to deal with date rape. Then argue either that more attention should be devoted to this issue or that your college has adopted fair and comprehensive measures to deal with the problem. If you feel the college should do more, indicate what additional steps should be taken.

Writing Assignments Using Other Patterns of Development

∞ 3. Jacoby acknowledges that males and females often send "mixed signals" and cause each other confusion. Select one time that you found "mixed signals" with a person of the opposite sex to be a problem. For example, you might have conflicted because of different ways of expressing anger or because of dissimilar styles in asking for support. Describe what happened and explain why you think such mixed signals occurred. Before writing the paper, you may want to read "Sex, Lies, and Conversation" (page 440) to see what Deborah Tannen has to say about some basic differences between men and women.

4. Interview some males and females to determine their definition of date rape. In an essay discuss any differences between the two sexes' perspectives. That done, present your own definition of date rape, explaining what it is and what it isn't.

Edward I. Koch

Born in 1924, Edward I. Koch was mayor of New York City from 1977 to 1989. With characteristic flamboyance, Koch calls himself "the sort of person who might give other people ulcers." Controversial and outspoken, Koch was elected mayor after campaigning on an anti-crime and anti-spending platform. Active in New York City politics throughout the 1960s, Koch also served in the U.S. House of Representatives from 1966 until the time he became mayor. Koch, trained as an attorney, has written two autobiographical books, *Mayor* (1984) and *Politics* (1985). He coauthored the book *His Eminence and Hizzoner* (1989) with the equally controversial John Cardinal O'Connor. The following essay, "Death and Justice," was published in the *New Republic* in 1985.

Death and Justice

Critics of capital punishment call the death penalty state-sanctioned murder. On the contrary, says Ed Koch, the death penalty "affirms the value of human life." To develop his position, Koch examines his opponents' arguments point by point, concluding that execution is the only adequate punishment for cold-blooded killing.

Last December [1984] a man named Robert Lee Willie, who 1
had been convicted of raping and murdering an 18-year-old woman, was executed in the Louisiana state prison. In a statement issued several minutes before his death, Mr. Willie said: "Killing people is wrong. . . . It makes no difference whether it's citizens, countries, or governments. Killing is wrong." Two weeks later in South Carolina, an admitted killer named Joseph Carl Shaw was put to death for murdering two teenagers. In an appeal to the governor for clemency, Mr. Shaw wrote: "Killing is wrong when I did it. Killing is wrong when you do it. I hope you have the courage and moral strength to stop the killing."

It is a curiosity of modern life that we find ourselves being   2
lectured on morality by cold-blooded killers. Mr. Willie previously had been convicted of aggravated rape, aggravated kidnapping, and the murders of a Louisiana deputy and a man from
Missouri. Mr. Shaw committed another murder a week before the
two for which he was executed, and admitted mutilating the body
of the 14-year-old girl he killed. I can't help wondering what
prompted these murderers to speak out against killing as they
entered the death-house door. Did their newfound reverence for
life stem from the realization that they were about to lose their
own?

Life is indeed precious, and I believe the death penalty helps   3
to affirm this fact. Had the death penalty been a real possibility in
the minds of these murderers, they might well have stayed their
hand. They might have shown moral awareness before their victims died, and not after. Consider the tragic death of Rosa Velez,
who happened to be home when a man named Luis Vera burglarized her apartment in Brooklyn. "Yeah, I shot her," Vera admitted. "She knew me, and I knew I wouldn't go to the chair."

During my 22 years in public service, I have heard the pros   4
and cons of capital punishment expressed with special intensity.
As a district leader, councilman, congressman, and mayor, I have
represented constituencies generally thought of as liberal. Because I support the death penalty for heinous crimes of murder, I
have sometimes been the subject of emotional and outraged attacks by voters who find my position reprehensible or worse. I
have listened to their ideas. I have weighed their objections carefully. I still support the death penalty. The reasons I maintained
my position can be best understood by examining the arguments
most frequently heard in opposition.

1. *The death penalty is "barbaric."* Sometimes opponents of   5
capital punishment horrify with tales of lingering death on the
gallows, of faulty electric chairs, or of agony in the gas chamber.
Partly in response to such protests, several states such as North
Carolina and Texas switched to execution by lethal injection. The
condemned person is put to death painlessly, without ropes,
voltage, bullets, or gas. Did this answer the objections of death
penalty opponents? Of course not. On June 22, 1984, the *New
York Times* published an editorial that sarcastically attacked the
new "hygienic" method of death by injection, and stated that

"execution can never be made humane through science." So it's not the method that really troubles opponents. It's the death itself they consider barbaric.

Admittedly, capital punishment is not a pleasant topic. How- 6 ever, one does not have to like the death penalty in order to support it any more than one must like radical surgery, radiation, or chemotherapy in order to find necessary these attempts at curing cancer. Ultimately we may learn how to cure cancer with a simple pill. Unfortunately, that day has not yet arrived. Today we are faced with the choice of letting the cancer spread or trying to cure it with the methods available, methods that one day will almost certainly be considered barbaric. But to give up and do nothing would be far more barbaric and would certainly delay the discovery of an eventual cure. The analogy between cancer and murder is imperfect, because murder is not the "disease" we are trying to cure. The disease is injustice. We may not like the death penalty, but it must be available to punish crimes of cold-blooded murder, cases in which any other form of punishment would be inadequate and, therefore, unjust. If we create a society in which injustice is not tolerated, incidents of murder — the most flagrant form of justice — will diminish.

2. *No other major democracy uses the death penalty.* No other 7 major democracy — in fact, few other countries of any description — are plagued by a murder rate such as that in the United States. Fewer and fewer Americans can remember the days when unlocked doors were the norm and murder was a rare and terrible offense. In America the murder rate climbed 122 percent between 1963 and 1980. During that same period, the murder rate in New York City increased by almost 400 percent, and the statistics are even worse in many other cities. A study at M.I.T. showed that based on 1970 homicide rates a person who lived in a large American city ran a greater risk of being murdered than an American soldier in World War II ran of being killed in combat. It is not surprising that the laws of each country differ according to differing conditions and traditions. If other countries had our murder problem, the cry for capital punishment would be just as loud as it is here. And I daresay that any other major democracy where 75 percent of the people supported the death penalty would soon enact it into law.

3. *An innocent person might be executed by mistake.* Consider 8

the work of Adam Bedau, one of the most implacable foes of capital punishment in this country. According to Mr. Bedau, it is "false sentimentality to argue that the death penalty should be abolished because of the abstract possibility that an innocent person might be executed." He cites a study of the 7,000 executions in this country from 1893 to 1971, and concludes that the record fails to show that such cases occur. The main point, however, is this. If government functioned only when the possibility of error didn't exist, government wouldn't function at all. Human life deserves special protection, and one of the best ways to guarantee that protection is to assure that convicted murderers do not kill again. Only the death penalty can accomplish this end. In a recent case in New Jersey, a man named Richard Biegenwald was freed from prison after serving 18 years for murder; since his release he has been convicted of committing four murders. A prisoner named Lemuel Smith, while serving four life sentences for murder (plus two life sentences for kidnapping and robbery) in New York's Green Haven Prison, lured a woman corrections officer into the chaplain's office and strangled her. He then mutilated and dismembered her body. An additional life sentence for Smith is meaningless. Because New York has no death penalty statute, Smith has effectively been given a license to kill.

But the problem of multiple murder is not confined to the   9
nation's penitentiaries. In 1981, 91 police officers were killed in the line of duty in this country. Seven percent of those arrested in the cases that have been solved had a previous arrest for murder. In New York City in 1976 and 1977, 85 persons arrested for homicide had a previous arrest for murder. Six of these individuals had two previous arrests for murder, and one had four previous murder arrests. During those two years the New York police were arresting for murder persons with a previous arrest for murder on the average of one every 8.5 days. This is not surprising when we learn that in 1975, for example, the median time served in Massachusetts for homicide was less than two and a half years. In 1976 a study sponsored by the Twentieth Century Fund found that the average time served in the United States for first-degree murder is ten years. The median time served may be considerably lower.

4. Capital punishment cheapens the value of human life. On   10
the contrary, it can be easily demonstrated that the death penalty

strengthens the value of human life. If the penalty for rape were lowered, clearly it would signal a lessened regard for the victims' suffering, humiliation, and personal integrity. It would cheapen their horrible experience, and expose them to an increased danger of recurrence. When we lower the penalty for murder, it signals a lessened regard for the value of the victim's life. Some critics of capital punishment, such as columnist Jimmy Breslin, have suggested that a life sentence is actually a harsher penalty for murder than death. This is sophistic nonsense. A few killers may decide not to appeal a death sentence, but the overwhelming majority make every effort to stay alive. It is by exacting the highest penalty for the taking of human life that we affirm the highest value of human life.

5. *The death penalty is applied in a discriminatory manner.* 11
This factor no longer seems to be the problem it once was. The appeals process for a condemned prisoner is lengthy and painstaking. Every effort is made to see that the verdict and sentence were fairly arrived at. However, assertions of discrimination are not an argument for ending the death penalty but for extending it. It is not justice to exclude everyone from the penalty of the law if a few are found to be so favored. Justice requires that the law be applied equally to all.

6. *Thou shalt not kill.* The Bible is our greatest source of 12
moral inspiration. Opponents of the death penalty frequently cite the sixth of the Ten Commandments in an attempt to prove that capital punishment is divinely proscribed. In the original Hebrew, however, the Sixth Commandment reads, "Thou Shalt Not Commit Murder," and the Torah specifies capital punishment for a variety of offenses. The biblical viewpoint has been upheld by philosophers throughout history. The greatest thinkers of the nineteenth century — Kant, Locke, Hobbes, Rousseau, Montesquieu, and Mill — agreed that natural law properly authorizes the sovereign to take life in order to vindicate justice. Only Jeremy Bentham was ambivalent. Washington, Jefferson, and Franklin endorsed it. Abraham Lincoln authorized executions for deserters in wartime. Alexis de Tocqueville, who expressed profound respect for American institutions, believed that the death penalty was indispensable to the support of social order. The United States Constitution, widely admired as one of the seminal achievements in the history of humanity, condemns cruel and

inhuman punishment, but does not condemn capital punishment.

7. *The death penalty is state-sanctioned murder.* This is the   13
defense with which Messrs. Willie and Shaw hoped to soften the
resolve of those who sentenced them to death. By saying in effect,
"You're no better than I am," the murderer seeks to bring his
accusers down to his own level. It is also a popular argument
among opponents of capital punishment, but a transparently
false one. Simply put, the state has rights that the private individual does not. In a democracy, those rights are given to the state by
the electorate. The execution of a lawfully condemned killer is no
more an act of murder than is legal imprisonment an act of
kidnapping. If an individual forces a neighbor to pay him money
under threat of punishment, it's called extortion. If the state does
it, it's called taxation. Rights and responsibilities surrendered by
the individual are what give the state its power to govern. This
contract is the foundation of civilization itself.

Everyone wants his or her rights, and will defend them jeal-   14
ously. Not everyone, however, wants responsibilities, especially
the painful responsibilities that come with law enforcement.
Twenty-one years ago a woman named Kitty Genovese was assaulted and murdered on a street in New York. Dozens of neighbors heard her cries for help but did nothing to assist her. They
didn't even call the police. In such a climate the criminal understandably grows bolder. In the presence of moral cowardice, he
lectures us on our supposed failings and tries to equate his crimes
with our quest for justice.

The death of anyone — even a convicted killer — diminishes   15
us all. But we are diminished even more by a justice system that
fails to function. It is an illusion to let ourselves believe that
doing away with capital punishment removes the murderer's deed
from our conscience. The rights of society are paramount. When
we protect guilty lives, we give up innocent lives in exchange.
When opponents of capital punishment say to the state: "I will
not let you kill in my name," they are also saying to murderers:
"You can kill in your *own* name as long as I have an excuse for not
getting involved."

It is hard to imagine anything worse than being murdered   16
while neighbors do nothing. But something worse exists. When

those same neighbors shrink back from justly punishing the murderer, the victim dies twice.

Questions for Close Reading

1. What is the selection's thesis? Locate the sentence(s) in which Koch states his main idea. If he doesn't state the thesis explicitly, express it in your own words.
2. According to Koch, what is it about the death penalty that its opponents find objectionable? Are such objections, in Koch's opinion, justified? Why or why not?
3. What arguments does Koch use to try to convince readers that the death penalty doesn't run counter to traditional religious and philosophical thought?
4. In Koch's view, how does the death penalty affirm the fact that "life is . . . precious"? Why, according to Koch, would punishing murderers with anything less than the death penalty be unjust?
5. Refer to your dictionary as needed to define the following words used in the selection: *reverence* (paragraph 2), *constituencies* (4), *heinous* (4), *reprehensible* (4), *lethal* (5), *implacable* (8), and *sophistic* (10).

Questions About the Writer's Craft

1. **The pattern.** Where does Koch try to establish his *ethos*? What does this attempt to establish his credibility say about Koch's perception of his audience's point of view?
2. Where does Koch draw on hard evidence to develop his argument? What is the effect of this evidence?
3. What instances do you find in Koch's essay of emotional appeals and connotative language? How do you think Koch intends readers to react to such appeals and emotionally charged language?
4. Why might Koch have decided to conclude his essay with the Kitty Genovese anecdote? How does this anecdote contribute to his arguments in support of capital punishment?

Questions for Further Thought

1. If you were opposed to capital punishment before reading "Death and Justice," has Koch's essay prompted you to reexamine your views? Which of Koch's arguments do you find most convincing? Which are least convincing? Why?
2. According to Koch, if "the death penalty [had] been a real possibility," the three convicted murderers he quotes early in the essay

"might well have stayed their hand." Do you agree? Can you think of situations in which fear of the death penalty might *not* deter a potential killer?

3. Consider the religious and philosophical principles that Koch uses to defend capital punishment (paragraph 12). In what ways are or aren't those principles consistent with your own?

4. Koch calls the failure of Kitty Genovese's neighbors to help a case of moral cowardice. Do you agree that this is an age of moral cowardice, or can you dispute such a negative assessment by citing examples of significant moral courage?

Writing Assignments Using Argumentation-Persuasion as a Pattern of Development

∞ 1. Koch bases his refutation of the standard arguments against capital punishment on a number of principles to which he is strongly committed. Some of these are stated clearly in the text:

> "If we create a society in which injustice is not tolerated, the incidence of murder—the most flagrant form of injustice—will diminish" (paragraph 6).
>
> "It is 'false sentimentality to argue that the death penalty should be abolished because of the abstract possibility that an innocent person might be executed'" (8).
>
> "The death penalty strengthens the value of human life" (10).

Drawing upon what you've read in "Death and Justice" and on what you know about the issue of capital punishment, write an essay that supports or refutes one of these principles or any other that Koch makes in his essay. Part of your paper should acknowledge and, if possible, refute the opposing viewpoint. To become more familiar with that viewpoint, read David Bruck's "The Death Penalty" (page 674).

2. Using the same organizational strategy as Koch, write an essay that argues for or against a particular stand on another controversial issue. Begin by stating and defending your position. Then, identify and refute several of the standard opposing arguments. Possible topics include the banning of college fraternities and sororities, allowing prayer in public schools, and implementing new graduation requirements at a college.

Writing Assignments Using Other Patterns of Development

∞ 3. Read David Bruck's "The Death Penalty" (page 674), an essay written in response to Koch's. Then write a strictly informative paper comparing and contrasting Koch's and Bruck's views. Don't ally yourself with either side, but do focus on those points you consider most important to an objective discussion of the capital punishment issue.

4. Have you or anyone you know well ever witnessed or been a victim of violence? If so, write a narrative about the incident. Use taut sentences, descriptive detail, and climactic time order to convey the fear, helplessness, and anger that you or the person you're writing about felt. End with a statement about the event's impact on your life or on the other person's.

David Bruck

In 1980, attorney David Bruck (1949–) left his job as a public defender so that he could specialize in the defense of death-row inmates. He has since represented numerous death-row clients in South Carolina and Florida. A frequent lecturer and consultant on the death penalty, Bruck has had his analyses of legal issues published in the *Washington Post* and the *New York Times*. He has also discussed capital punishment on a variety of television programs, including the *MacNeil/Lehrer Newshour* and *Nightline*. Written in response to Ed Koch's argument in favor of the death penalty (see page 665), the following article first appeared in the *New Republic* in May 1985.

The Death Penalty

Few topics evoke such heated emotional response as capital punishment. Advocates call the death penalty the only fitting punishment for murderers; opponents consider the execution of a killer as immoral as the original crime. Vigorously opposed to capital punishment, David Bruck believes that the lust for vengeance blinds supporters of the death penalty to many injustices.

Mayor Ed Koch contends that the death penalty "affirms   1
life." By failing to execute murderers, he says, we "signal a lessened regard for the value of the victim's life." Koch suggests that people who oppose the death penalty are like Kitty Genovese's neighbors, who heard her cries for help but did nothing while an attacker stabbed her to death.

This is the standard "moral" defense of death as punish-   2
ment: even if executions don't deter violent crime any more effectively than imprisonment, they are still required as the only means we have of doing justice in response to the worst of crimes.

Until recently, this "moral" argument had to be considered   3 in the abstract, since no one was being executed in the United States. But the death penalty is back now, at least in the southern states, where every one of the more than 30 executions carried out over the last two years has taken place. Those of us who live in those states are getting to see the difference between the death penalty in theory, and what happens when you actually try to use it.

South Carolina resumed executing prisoners in January with   4
the electrocution of Joseph Carl Shaw. Shaw was condemned to death for helping to murder two teenagers while he was serving as a military policeman at Fort Jackson, South Carolina. His crime, propelled by mental illness and PCP, was one of terrible brutality. It is Shaw's last words ("Killing was wrong when I did it. It is wrong when you do it. . . .") that so outraged Mayor Koch: he finds it "a curiosity of modern life that we are being lectured on morality by cold-blooded killers." And so it is.

But it was not "modern life" that brought this curiosity into   5
being. It was capital punishment. The electric chair was J. C. Shaw's platform. (The mayor mistakenly writes that Shaw's statement came in the form of a plea to the governor for clemency: actually Shaw made it only seconds before his death, as he waited, shaved and strapped into the chair, for the switch to be thrown.) It was the chair that provided Shaw with celebrity and an opportunity to lecture us on right and wrong. What made this weird moral reversal even worse is that J. C. Shaw faced his own death with undeniable dignity and courage. And while Shaw died, the TV crews recorded another "curiosity" of the death penalty — the crowd gathered outside the death-house to cheer on the executioner. Whoops of elation greeted the announcement of Shaw's death. Waiting at the penitentiary gates for the appearance of the hearse bearing Shaw's remains, one demonstrator started yelling, "Where's the beef?"

For those who had to see the execution of J. C. Shaw, it   6
wasn't easy to keep in mind that the purpose of the whole spectacle was to affirm life. It will be harder still when Florida executes a cop-killer named Alvin Ford. Ford has lost his mind during his years of death-row confinement, and now spends his days trembling, rocking back and forth, and muttering unintelligible prayers. This has led to litigation over whether Ford meets a centuries-old legal standard for mental competency. Since the

Middle Ages, the Anglo-American legal system has generally prohibited the execution of anyone who is too mentally ill to understand what is about to be done to him and why. If Florida wins its case, it will have earned the right to electrocute Ford in his present condition. If it loses, he will not be executed until the state has first nursed him back to some semblance of mental health.[1]

We can at least be thankful that this demoralizing spectacle 7 involves a prisoner who is actually guilty of murder. But this may not always be so. The ordeal of Lenell Jeter—the young black engineer who recently served more than a year of a life sentence for a Texas armed robbery that he didn't commit—should remind us that the system is quite capable of making the very worst sort of mistake. That Jeter was eventually cleared is a fluke. If the robbery had occurred at 7 P.M. rather than 3 P.M., he'd have had no alibi, and would still be in prison today. And if someone had been killed in that robbery, Jeter probably would have been sentenced to death. We'd have seen the usual execution-day interviews with state officials and the victim's relatives, all complaining that Jeter's appeals took too long. And Jeter's last words from the gurney would have taken their place among the growing literature of death-house oration that so irritates the mayor.

Koch quotes Hugo Adam Bedau, a prominent abolitionist, 8 to the effect that the record fails to establish that innocent defendants have been executed in the past. But this doesn't mean, as Koch implies, that it hasn't happened. All Bedau was saying was that doubts concerning executed prisoners' guilt are almost never resolved. Bedau is at work now on an effort to determine how many wrongful death sentences may have been imposed: his list of murder convictions since 1900 in which the state eventually *admitted* error is some 400 cases long. Of course, very few of these cases involved actual executions: the mistakes that Bedau documents were uncovered precisely because the prisoner was alive and able to fight for his vindication. The cases where someone is executed are the very cases in which we're least likely to learn that we got the wrong man.

[1]On June 26, 1986, the Supreme Court prohibited the execution of convicted murderers who are so insane they do not understand they will be executed. However, if Ford regains his sanity, Florida may execute him.

I don't claim that executions of entirely innocent people will   9
occur very often. But they will occur. And other sorts of mistakes
already have. Roosevelt Green was executed in Georgia two days
before J. C. Shaw. Green and an accomplice kidnapped a young
woman. Green swore that his companion shot her to death after
Green had left, and that he knew nothing about the murder.
Green's claim was supported by a statement that his accomplice
made to a witness after the crime. The jury never resolved whether
Green was telling the truth, and when he tried to take a polygraph
examination a few days before his scheduled execution, the state
of Georgia refused to allow the examiner into the prison. As the
pressure for symbolic retribution mounts, the courts, like the
public, are losing patience with such details. Green was electrocuted on January 9, while members of the Ku Klux Klan rallied
outside the prison.

Then there is another sort of arbitrariness that happens all   10
the time. Last October, Louisiana executed a man named Ernest
Knighton. Knighton had killed a gas station owner during a
robbery. Like any murder, this was a terrible crime. But it was not
premeditated, and is the sort of crime that very rarely results in a
death sentence. Why was Knighton electrocuted when almost
everyone else who committed the same offense was not? Was it
because he was black? Was it because his victim and all 12 members of the jury that sentenced him were white? Was it because
Knighton's court-appointed lawyer presented no evidence on his
behalf at his sentencing hearing? Or maybe there's no reason
except bad luck. One thing is clear: Ernest Knighton was picked
out to die the way a fisherman takes a cricket out of a bait jar. No
one cares which cricket gets impaled on the hook.

Not every prisoner executed recently was chosen that ran-   11
domly. But many were. And having selected these men so casually, so blindly, the death penalty system asks us to accept that
the purpose of killing each of them is to affirm the sanctity of
human life.

The death penalty states are also learning that the death   12
penalty is easier to advocate than it is to administer. In Florida,
where executions have become almost routine, the governor reports that nearly a third of his time is spent reviewing the clemency requests of condemned prisoners. The Florida Supreme
Court is hopelessly backlogged with death cases. Some have taken

refute Koch.
example

five years to decide, and the rest of the Court's work waits in line behind the death appeals. Florida's death row currently holds more than 230 prisoners. State officials are reportedly considering building a special "death prison" devoted entirely to the isolation and electrocution of the condemned. The state is also considering the creation of a special public defender unit that will do nothing else but handle death penalty appeals. The death penalty, in short, is spawning death agencies.

And what is Florida getting for all of this? The state went through almost all of 1983 without executing anyone: its rate of intentional homicide declined by 17 percent. Last year Florida executed eight people—the most of any state, and the sixth highest total for any year since Florida started electrocuting people back in 1924. Elsewhere in the U.S. last year, the homicide rate continued to decline. But in Florida, it actually rose by 5.1 percent.   13

But these are just the tiresome facts. The electric chair has been a centerpiece of each of Koch's recent political campaigns, and he knows better than anyone how little the facts have to do with the public's support for capital punishment. What really fuels the death penalty is the justifiable frustration and rage of people who see that the government is not coping with violent crime. So what if the death penalty doesn't work? At least it gives us the satisfaction of knowing that we got one or two of the sons of bitches.   14

Perhaps we want retribution on the flesh and bone of a handful of convicted murderers so badly that we're willing to close our eyes to all of the demoralization and danger that come with it. A lot of politicians think so, and they may be right. But if they are, then let's at least look honestly at what we're doing. This lottery of death both comes from and encourages an attitude toward human life that is not reverent, but reckless.   15

And that is why the mayor is dead wrong when he confuses such fury with justice. He suggests that we trivialize murder unless we kill murderers. By that logic, we also trivialize rape unless we sodomize rapists. The sin of Kitty Genovese's neighbors wasn't that they failed to stab her attacker to death. Justice does demand that murderers be punished. And common sense demands that society be protected from them. But neither justice   16 nor self-preservation demands that we kill men whom we have already imprisoned.

The electric chair in which J. C. Shaw died earlier this year   17 was built in 1912 at the suggestion of South Carolina's governor at the time, Cole Blease. Governor Blease's other criminal justice initiative was an impassioned crusade in favor of lynch law. Any lesser response, the governor insisted, trivialized the loathsome crimes of interracial rape and murder. In 1912 a lot of people agreed with Governor Blease that a proper regard for justice required both lynching and the electric chair. Eventually we are going to learn that justice requires neither.

Questions for Close Reading

1. What is the selection's thesis? Locate the sentence(s) in which Bruck states his main idea. If he doesn't state the thesis explicitly, express it in your own words.
2. Bruck refers to Ed Koch's (see page 665) belief that being lectured on morality by convicted killers is a "curiosity of modern life." Bruck then goes on to mention things he finds even more curious about the death penalty. What are they?
3. What does Bruck's essay reveal about the J. C. Shaw case that Koch's essay does not? How do these new facts support Bruck's thesis?
4. In paragraph 12, Bruck writes that states now executing prisoners are "learning that the death penalty is easier to advocate than . . . to administer." What does he mean? What evidence does he give to support this point?
5. Refer to your dictionary as needed to define the following words used in the selection: *semblance* (paragraph 6), *retribution* (9), *impaled* (10), *clemency* (12), *spawning* (12), *tiresome* (14), and *trivialize* (16).

Questions About the Writer's Craft

1. **The pattern.** Where in the essay does Bruck use appeals to reason to support his argument? Where does he use appeals to emotion? Which does he emphasize? What does this emphasis say about the way Bruck perceives his readers?
2. Like many writers of argumentation-persuasion essays, Bruck spends time refuting opposing opinions, in this case those of former New York City Mayor Ed Koch. Which of Koch's points provide the organizational framework for Bruck's argument? Why might Bruck have selected these points and not others?

3. In paragraph 10, Bruck uses a series of *rhetorical questions* — questions he doesn't expect his readers to answer. What is the effect of these questions?

4. In the essay's conclusion, Bruck explains that the electric chair in which J. C. Shaw died had been built at the suggestion of Governor Cole Blease, a man who also fervently supported lynch law. Why do you think Bruck introduces this new fact at the very end of the essay? What purpose does it serve?

Questions for Further Thought

1. If you were in favor of the death penalty before reading this essay, in what way have your views been altered? Which of Bruck's arguments do you find most convincing? Which did you find least convincing?

2. Bruck reports the crowd's bloodthirsty reaction at J. C. Shaw's execution. What other examples can you think of to illustrate this human tendency to gawk at the plight of others? Why do humans react this way?

3. Bruck implies that, because J. C. Shaw's crime was "propelled by mental illness and PCP," Shaw should not have been put to death. Do you believe that we should stay the executioner's hand in special cases? Explain.

4. According to Bruck, the claim that "we trivialize murder unless we kill murderers" is as wrong-headed as the idea that "we trivialize rape unless we sodomize rapists." Do you agree, or do you feel that in some instances the penalty for a crime should be as severe as the crime itself? Explain.

Writing Assignments Using Argumentation-Persuasion as a Pattern of Development

∞ 1. Bruck bases his argument against the death penalty on several important key points, the following among them:

The death penalty negates the sanctity of human life.

The death penalty offers no more practical deterrent to violent crime than imprisonment.

The death penalty is pronounced disproportionately against minorities.

The death penalty may result in the execution of innocent people.

Write an essay either defending or challenging *one* of these points. No matter which position you take, one section of your paper should recognize and, if possible, rebut opposing viewpoints. If you haven't already done so, be sure to read Ed Koch's "Death and Justice" (page 665) before planning your paper.

2. Develop an argument in which you try to persuade readers that life imprisonment is a just way of punishing convicted murderers and that there is no need to impose the death penalty. Try to anticipate and refute objections others might have to your position.

Writing Assignments Using Other Patterns of Development

3. Bruck believes that many people support the death penalty out of frustration with the criminal justice system rather than out of commitment to a particular ideology. Write an essay analyzing the consequences of this disillusionment with the criminal justice system. What other effects does it have on our beliefs and on the way we lead our lives?

4. Think of a law, regulation, procedure, or policy that has, like the death penalty, run into difficulty being implemented. Possible subjects include banning alcohol from campus parties, legalizing gambling, and building low-income housing in middle-income neighborhoods. Write an essay explaining the steps that should be taken to make things run more efficiently. Before presenting your step-by-step discussion, describe problems with the current law or policy.

Louis Nizer

One of this country's best-known attorneys, Louis Nizer (1902–) has shared his legal expertise and courtroom experiences in such best-sellers as *My Life in Court* (1961), *The Jury Returns* (1966), and *Reflections Without Mirrors* (1978). Portions of his books have been adapted for the theater, cinema, and television. Respected for his lucid prose style, Nizer has written for such diverse publications as the *New York Times, Reader's Digest, McCall's*, and numerous scholarly legal journals. In addition to being a skilled attorney, author, and lecturer, Nizer is an accomplished painter and composer. The following essay was first published in the *New York Times* in 1986.

Low-Cost Drugs for Addicts?

Drug addiction and drug-related crimes cost the nation millions of dollars and thousands of lives each year. Louis Nizer argues that many of the ills associated with drug use exist only because narcotics are illegal. Legalizing drugs, he contends, would sharply reduce what many believe is the number one problem facing our nation today.

1 We are losing the war against drug addiction. Our strategy is wrong. I propose a different approach.

2 The Government should create clinics, manned by psychiatrists, that would provide drugs for nominal charges or even free to addicts under controlled regulations. It would cost the Government only 20 cents for a heroin shot, for which the addicts must now pay the mob more than $100, and there are similar price discrepancies in cocaine, crack and other such substances.

3 Such a service, which would also include the staff support of psychiatrists and doctors, would cost a fraction of what the na-

tion now spends to maintain the land, sea and air apparatus necessary to interdict illegal imports of drugs. There would also be a savings of hundreds of millions of dollars from the elimination of the prosecutorial procedures that stifle our courts and overcrowd our prisons.

We see in our newspapers the triumphant announcements by Government agents that they have intercepted huge caches of cocaine, the street prices of which are in the tens of millions of dollars. Should we be gratified? Will this achievement reduce the number of addicts by one? All it will do is increase the cost to the addict of his illegal supply.

Many addicts who are caught committing a crime admit that they have mugged or stolen as many as six or seven times a day to accumulate the $100 needed for a fix. Since many of them need two or three fixes a day, particularly for crack, one can understand the terror in our streets and homes. It is estimated that there are in New York City alone 200,000 addicts, and this is typical of cities across the nation. Even if we were to assume that only a modest percentage of a city's addicts engage in criminal conduct to obtain the money for the habit, requiring multiple muggings and thefts each day, we could nevertheless account for many of the tens of thousands of crimes each day in New York City alone.

Not long ago, a Justice Department division issued a report stating that more than half the perpetrators of murder and other serious crimes were under the influence of drugs. This symbolizes the new domestic terror in our nation. This is why our citizens are unsafe in broad daylight on the most traveled thoroughfares. This is why typewriters and television sets are stolen from offices and homes and sold for a pittance. This is why parks are closed to the public and why murders are committed. This is why homes need multiple locks, and burglary systems, and why store windows, even in the most fashionable areas, require iron gates.

The benefits of the new strategy to control this terrorism would be immediate and profound.

First, the mob would lose the main source of its income. It could not compete against a free supply for which previously it exacted tribute estimated to be hundreds of millions of dollars, perhaps billions, from hopeless victims.

Second, pushers would be put out of business. There would be no purpose in creating addicts who would be driven by desperate compulsion to steal and kill for the money necessary to maintain their habit. Children would not be enticed. The mob's macabre public-relations program is to tempt children with free drugs in order to create customers for the future. The wave of street crimes in broad daylight would diminish to a trickle. Homes and stores would not have to be fortresses. Our recreational areas could again be used. Neighborhoods would not be scandalized by sordid street centers where addicts gather to obtain their supply from slimy merchants.

Third, police and other law-enforcement authorities, domestic or foreign, would be freed to deal with traditional nondrug crimes.   10

There are several objections that might be raised against such a salutary solution.   11

First, it could be argued that by providing free drugs to the addict we would consign him to permanent addiction. The answer is that medical and psychiatric help at the source would be more effective in controlling the addict's descent than the extremely limited remedies available to the victim today. I am not arguing that the new strategy will cure everything. But I do not see many addicts being freed from their bonds under the present system.   12

In addition, as between the addict's predicament and the safety of our innocent citizens, which deserves our primary concern? Drug-induced crime has become so common that almost every citizen knows someone in his immediate family or among his friends who has been mugged. It is these citizens who should be our chief concern.   13

Another possible objection is that addicts will cheat the system by obtaining more than the allowable free shot. Without discounting the resourcefulness of the bedeviled addict, it should be possible to have Government cards issued that would be punched so as to limit the free supply in accord with medical authorization.   14

Yet all objections become trivial when matched against the crisis itself. What we are witnessing is the demoralization of a great society: the ruination of its school children, athletes and executives, the corrosion of the workforce in general.   15

Many thoughtful sociologists consider the rapidly spreading drug use the greatest problem that our nation faces — greater and   16 more real and urgent than nuclear bombs or economic reversal. In China, a similar crisis drove the authorities to apply capital punishment to those who trafficked in opium — an extreme solution that arose from the deepest reaches of frustration.

Free drugs will win the war against the domestic terrorism 17 caused by illicit drugs. As a strategy, it is at once resourceful, sensible and simple. We are getting nowhere in our efforts to hold back the ocean of supply. The answer is to dry up demand.

Questions for Close Reading

1. What is the selection's thesis? Locate the sentence(s) in which Nizer states his main idea. If he doesn't state the thesis explicitly, express it in your own words.
2. Nizer believes his plan would yield numerous benefits. What are they?
3. Nizer acknowledges some possible objections to his plan. What are they? How does he refute these arguments?
4. How much concern does Nizer have for those addicted to drugs? How do you know?
5. Refer to your dictionary as needed to define the following words used in the selection: *nominal* (paragraph 2), *interdict* (3), *cache* (4), *macabre* (9), *salutary* (11), *consign* (12), and *illicit* (17).

Questions About the Writer's Craft

1. **The pattern.** Which of the two possible strategies for organizing a refutation (see page 583) does Nizer use in this essay?
2. Nizer's essay starts with a brief introductory paragraph consisting of three crisp, almost clipped sentences. What is the effect of this unusually brief introduction?
3. What words with militaristic connotations does Nizer use in his essay? What might have been Nizer's reason for using such language?
4. To what audience does Nizer seem to be addressing his proposal? How do you know?

Questions for Further Thought

1. Besides those Nizer mentions, what additional objections might people have to legalizing drugs? How valid are these objections?
2. Nizer holds drug users accountable for their acts. Do you think that courts should take into account the environmental and psychological factors that may have precipitated a crime? Explain.
3. Can any of Nizer's ideas be used to argue that other "vices" should be legalized? Consider, for example, gambling or prostitution.

4. Nizer suggests that organized crime is most responsible for the country's drug problem. Can you identify other players in this tragedy?

Writing Assignments Using Argumentation-Persuasion as a Pattern of Development

∞ **1.** Nizer argues that legalizing drugs would not necessarily increase the number of addicts and that it would definitely reduce crime. Write an essay supporting or challenging *one* of these conclusions. No matter which side you take, assume that some readers are opposed to your point of view. Acknowledge and try to dismantle as many of their objections as you can. Beth Johnson Ruth's "Our Drug Problem" (page 687) will familiarize you with some of the counterarguments to Nizer's position.

2. Propose measures that *one* of the following groups might take to educate people about the effects of drug addiction: parent groups; public schools; colleges or universities; the local, state, or federal government. Put your proposal in the form of a letter to the appropriate person (a high school principal, college president, and so on). Try to anticipate and rebut possible objections to your proposal.

Writing Assignments Using Other Patterns of Development

3. According to psychologists, many individuals have an "addictive personality." Referring to people you know well, write an essay defining this term. However, instead of focusing on addiction to a substance, illustrate the "addictive personality" by writing about the excessive need for approval, danger, competition, and the like.

4. Assume that the Dean of Students has asked you to write an open letter to be published in next year's orientation brochure for first-year students. Your assignment is to warn incoming students about the long-term effects of drug abuse, or too much partying, or excessive procrastination — anything that might affect their well-being and success in college. Develop your letter by drawing on your own and other people's experiences. You might, in addition, use a source like the *Readers' Guide to Periodical Literature* to track down helpful articles, so that you can include relevant facts, statistics, or expert opinion in your letter.

Beth Johnson Ruth

A journalist and free-lance writer, Beth Johnson Ruth received
an advanced degree in literacy education from Syracuse University. Ruth's crisp, no-nonsense prose style has served her
well in the public relations writing she has done for a college
news bureau and a community mental health center. Formerly
on the faculties of Goshen College and New England College,
Ruth has also written for a number of publications, among
them the *Starke County Ledger* and the *New Hampshire Business
Review*. Revised for this text, the following selection is taken
from a collection of Ruth's essays dealing with the impact of
drugs on society.

Our Drug Problem

Nearly everyone agrees that drug abuse is an overwhelming
national problem. But a solution to that problem finds far less
consensus. Some advocate such drastic measures as the automatic execution of drug dealers. Others favor the legalization
of narcotics, believing that the illicit nature of the drug trade is
largely responsible for our predicament. Beth Johnson Ruth
argues in this selection that the removal of legal restraints
would be the beginning of a drug-induced nightmare from
which America might never awaken.

Imagine, if you will, the final reel of a trashy "B" movie   1
based on the Biblical story of Sodom and Gomorrah. You remember the tale of two cities so given over to evil practices,
immorality, and mindless self-indulgence that God finally destroyed them by raining down fire and brimstone.

What sort of activity do you suppose a filmmaker would   2
choose in order to portray, in an updated fashion, the wickedness
of Sodom and Gomorrah? The perfect choice, in my mind, would
be unrestricted drug use. Think of the potential for destructive
behavior: self-annihilation through drug overdose; sexual excesses

with no concern for consequences; reckless acts leading to crippling or fatal accidents; obsession with narcotics to the point of ignoring family needs . . . the possibilities go on and on. Unlimited access to drugs would provide the perfect metaphor for the legendary evil that was Sodom and Gomorrah.

Incredibly, in America today, supposedly responsible and intelligent people are recommending the legalization of narcotics. The war on drugs has been lost, they say; it's time to stop pouring enormous resources into a futile battle. Let's change strategies, they argue, and try attacking the problem by removing all legal restrictions on drug use.   3

Has a more ludicrous proposal ever been seriously introduced for public discussion? Are we honestly being asked to consider raising our children in a society that says, "Yes, we know that these substances will ruin your and your family's lives and will kill you sooner or later. We'd really rather you didn't use drugs, but it's just too difficult to try to enforce the law"?   4

Apparently we are. Conservative columnist William F. Buckley, Jr., Nobel Prize-winning economist Milton Friedman, Mayor Kurt Schmoke of Baltimore, and U.S. Reps. Fortney Stark of California and Steny Hoyer of Maryland have been among the respected—and presumably not drug-addled—folks who have suggested that legalization of drugs is an idea whose time may have come.   5

Let's look at their arguments one by one. But be forewarned; dismantling them will not take too much time or effort.   6

"Legalizing drugs would mean the end of drug-related crime." Presumably it's true that if narcotics were legalized, druglords, pushers, and drug gangs would no longer reap enormous profits. It does not follow, however, that the addicted would be any less driven to desperate measures to obtain a fix. To feed their habit, many would obtain money by resorting to robbery and prostitution. Indeed, as the number of addicts continued to grow, so would the number of drug-related crimes.   7

"The government could tax drug sales and regulate the purity of narcotics if they were sold legally." The advocates of legalization point out that two other addictive substances—alcohol and tobacco—are legal and subject to government regulation. True. But with what results? Alcohol and tobacco combined are responsible for about 500,000 deaths each year. In   8

1988, the reported death toll related to illegal drugs was 6,756. Would we consider it progress to have more people dying from injecting, inhaling, and consuming purer forms of poison?

"The war on drugs is simply too expensive and too ineffec-   9
tive. The country can't afford to continue spending money at this rate." No doubt about it, the price tag attached to fighting drug abuse is phenomenal. It's estimated that federal, state, and local governments spend about $8 billion a year on drug enforcement. Add to that the uncounted billions spent on feeding and housing those imprisoned for drug-related crimes (more than a third of all federal prisoners fall into this category), and you end up with some breathtaking sums.

True, the war on drugs is not being won. The courts are   10
overflowing with cases waiting to be tried. Huge seizures of narcotics stop only a small fraction of the drugs coming into the country. Countless dragnets snare only the small-time pusher, not the drug kingpin. Clearly, as it is being waged now, the national fight against drug abuse is futile.

The only thing more costly than continuing the current war   11
on drugs would be the legalization of narcotics; such a measure would claim innumerable human lives. "People say only 10 percent of those who drink are problem drinkers, so they assume that only 10 percent of the people who take drugs will become addicts," observes Mitchell Rosenthal, president of Phoenix House, a New York City-based drug rehabilitation program. "But there is no reason to believe that if we made [drugs like] crack available . . . that only 10 percent would be addicted; the number would probably be more like 75 percent."

Currently, drug abuse costs American industry over $70 bil-   12
lion per year through lost productivity. Imagine how that figure would soar if legal restraints were removed. If people didn't have to drive into a seedy neighborhood . . . if they didn't risk arrest and disgrace . . . if they could justify their actions as legal . . . how many could resist trying drugs "just once"? And how many addicts started out by experimenting with drugs "just once"? Every one of them, that's how many. Moreover, what would be the fate of addicts if narcotics were available legally? In the words of one cocaine addict, "I'd be dead. . . . I'd just sit down with a big pile of the stuff and snort it until I dropped."

One more number to consider: Today, the health costs of   13 treating drug abuse are estimated at $60 billion per year. Care to guess what that figure might become if drugs were made legal?

Aren't these facts enough to dissuade anyone from believing   14 that the legalization of narcotics has anything to recommend it? Why, then, would anyone recommend legalization? The answer has to do with racism, elitism, and sheer indifference to the suffering of others. "These people are going to kill themselves anyway," many middle-class Americans reason. "I'm not going to have my tax dollars used to try to save them. Besides, what does it matter if drugs wipe out a generation — as long as it's a generation of black and Hispanic kids?"

If you doubt that this kind of thinking is pervasive, consider   15 the public indifference to the last decade's gutting of education and job-training programs. Such programs address the major causes of drug abuse: poverty and despair. When the number of families living beneath the poverty level increased more than sixfold between 1979 and 1988, did more fortunate Americans protest? Who objected when federal funds for low-income housing dropped from $32 billion to $9 billion between 1981 and 1988? There was little public protest when federal aid for public education decreased by nearly $6 billion in the 1980s. Nor did the average American complain when funding of job-training programs dropped by $40 billion from 1981 to 1988. And the minimum wage, despite a recent increase, has fallen to its lowest level in terms of buying power since 1955. Is it any wonder that poor teenagers choose the lucrative jobs offered by druglords over the chance to flip hamburgers at a fast-food restaurant? Given the harshness of their lives, it's not surprising that the underprivileged have turned to drugs in such massive numbers.

The nation's devastating drug problem illustrates that our   16 country is reaping what it has sowed: a harvest of poverty, violence, and despair. That the problem has grown to this extent is immoral in itself; to encourage it further through the legalization of narcotics would be not only impractical but also unethical. Unless this once-great country acts quickly to address the drug problem in the only way that can work — through providing real education, more affordable housing, and greater employment opportunities — it will truly deserve comparison with cities that suffered the fate of fire and brimstone.

Questions for Close Reading

1. What is the selection's thesis? Locate the sentence(s) in which Ruth states her main idea. If she doesn't state the thesis explicitly, express it in your own words.
2. According to Ruth, for what reasons do "supposedly responsible and intelligent people" advocate the legalization of narcotics?
3. How does the number of deaths from illegal drug abuse compare with the number of deaths from the abuse of alcohol and tobacco? In what ways does this information strengthen Ruth's argument?
4. Ruth admits that, as it is currently being fought, the war on drugs is ineffectual and costly. Why, then, is she against legalizing narcotics? What does she advocate instead?
5. Refer to your dictionary as needed to define the following words used in the selection: *ludicrous* (paragraph 4), *addled* (5), *forewarned* (6), *dismantling* (6), *dissuade* (14), and *elitism* (14).

Questions About the Writer's Craft

1. **The pattern.** Ruth often employs provocative, even inflammatory language, as when she refers to the idea of legalizing narcotics as "ludicrous." Find additional examples of such language. What assumptions about her audience might have motivated Ruth to adopt this style?
2. Ruth also draws on facts, statistics, illustrations, and expert testimony to support her argument. Identify examples in the essay of each kind of evidence. What is the effect of this evidence?
3. Ruth creates an interesting *analogy* when she compares the consequences of legalizing narcotics to the fate of Sodom and Gomorrah. What purpose does this analogy serve? Where else does the author use *figurative language*?
4. Although Ruth works to refute the arguments of her opponents, she also concedes points to the opposing view. In paragraph 9, for example, she admits, "No doubt about it, the price tag attached to fighting drug abuse is phenomenal." Why does she make such concessions?

Questions for Further Thought

1. In paragraph 12, Ruth argues that narcotics abuse would soar if there were no risk attached to buying drugs. Is this a fair conclusion? Do you know people who would begin using or would increase their consumption of drugs if legal restraints were removed?
2. Ruth claims that the real causes of most drug abuse are poverty and

despair. What, then, accounts for the abuse of illegal substances like cocaine and marijuana among the middle class and the rich?

3. Some people believe that drug addicts are criminals and should, if convicted, suffer stiff prison sentences. Others consider drug abuse a disease that can be corrected only through careful, compassionate medical attention. What's your opinion? Explain.

4. For Ruth, "real education, more affordable housing, and greater employment opportunities" are the only genuine solutions for the drug problem. What specific measures do you think should be taken to help stem the tide of drug abuse in this country?

Writing Assignments Using Argumentation-Persuasion as a Pattern of Development

∞ 1. Ruth contends that a "sickening current of . . . racism and elitism and sheer indifference to the suffering of others" is behind the proposal to legalize drugs. Write an essay in which you defend or challenge Ruth's charge. Remember to mention and, when possible, refute opposing arguments. Louis Nizer's "Low-Cost Drugs for Addicts?" (page 682) will familiarize you with a viewpoint sharply different from Ruth's.

2. Assume that your college's Office of Student Life has just hired you as a peer counselor whose job it is to reach out to students in distress. Your first task is to write a letter to students with drug and/or alcohol problems, persuading them to seek help through the college's professional and peer counseling services. The letter will be posted on campus bulletin boards and will appear in the student newspaper. As you write the letter, keep in mind that people in difficulty often resist offers of help. What persuasive strategies can you use to overcome this resistance?

Writing Assignments Using Other Patterns of Development

3. In an essay, examine the possible effects of mandatory drug testing on a specific group of people (for example, public school students, college athletes, airline employees). Be sure your paper expresses a clear attitude toward such a program. Brainstorm with others and conduct library research to gather material for your essay.

4. Assume that you're a student member of your college's Disciplinary Action Committee. On this week's agenda is the case of a student who has been caught selling drugs on campus. Write a brief report detailing the step-by-step procedure you think your college should follow with this and similar cases.

Additional Writing Topics

ARGUMENTATION-PERSUASION

General Assignments

Using argumentation-persuasion, develop one of the topics below in an essay. After choosing a topic, think about your purpose and audience. Remember that the paper's thesis should state the issue under discussion as well as your position on the issue. As you work on developing evidence, you might want to do some outside research. Keep in mind that effective argumentation-persuasion usually means that some time should be spent acknowledging and perhaps refuting opposing points of view. Be careful not to sabotage your argument by basing your case on a logical fallacy.

1. Mercy killing
2. Hiring quotas
3. Giving birth-control devices to teenagers
4. Prayer in the schools
5. Living off campus
6. The drinking age
7. Spouses sharing housework equally
8. Smoking in public places
9. Big-time sports in college
10. Music videos
11. Working mothers with young children
12. Acid rain
13. Drugs on campus
14. Political campaigns
15. Requiring college students to pass a comprehensive exam in their majors before graduating
16. Fifty-five-mile-per-hour speed limit
17. Putting elderly parents in nursing homes
18. An optional pass/fail system for courses
19. The homeless
20. Nonconformity in a neighborhood: allowing a lawn to go wild, keeping many pets, painting a house an odd color, or some other atypical behavior

Assignments with a Specific Purpose and Audience

1. A college has rejected your or your child's application on the basis of low SAT scores. Write to the college admissions director, arguing

that SAT scores are not a fair indicator of your or your child's abilities and potential.

2. As a staff writer for the college opinion magazine, you've been asked to nominate the "Outstanding Man or Woman on Campus," to be featured on the magazine's cover. Write a letter to your supervising editor in support of your nominee.

3. You and your parents don't agree on some aspect of your romantic life (you want to live with your boyfriend/girlfriend and they don't approve; you want to get married and they want you to wait; they simply don't like your partner). Write your parents a letter explaining why your preference is reasonable. Try hard to win them over to your side and remember not to be antagonistic.

4. As a high school teacher, you support some additional restriction on students. The restriction might be "no radios in school," "no T-shirts," "no food in class," "no smoking on school grounds." Write an article for the school newspaper, justifying this new rule to the student body.

5. Someone you know is convinced that the music you listen to is trashy or boring. Write a letter to the person arguing that your music has value. Support your contention with specific references to lyrics, musical structure, and performers' talent.

6. Assume you're a member of a racial, ethnic, or social minority. You might, for example, be a Native American, an elderly person, a female executive. On a recent television show or in a TV commercial, you saw something that depicts your group in an offensive way. Write a letter (to the network or the advertiser) expressing your feelings and explaining why you feel the material should be taken off the air.

12

FOR FURTHER READING

Throughout this book, you've studied the patterns of development—narration, process analysis, definition, and so on—in depth. You've seen how the patterns are used as strategies for generating, developing, and organizing ideas for essays. You've also learned that, in practice, most types of writing combine two or more patterns. The two sections that follow provide additional information about these important points. The rest of the chapter then gives you an opportunity to look more closely at the way several writers use the patterns of development in their work.

THE PATTERNS IN ACTION:
DURING THE WRITING PROCESS

The patterns of development come into play throughout the composing process. In the prewriting stage, awareness of the patterns encourages you to think about your subject in fresh, new ways. Assume, for example, that you've been asked to write an essay about the way children are disciplined in school. However, you draw a blank as soon as you try to limit this general subject. To break the logjam, you could apply one or more patterns of development to your subject. *Comparison-contrast* might prompt you to write an essay investigating the differences between your parents' and your own feelings about school discipline. *Division-classification* might lead you to another paper—one that categorizes the kinds of discipline used in school. And *cause-effect* might point to still another essay—one that explores the way students react to being suspended.

Further along in the writing process—after you've identified your limited subject and your thesis—the patterns of development can help you generate your paper's evidence. Imagine that your thesis is "Teachers shouldn't discipline students publicly just to make an example of them." You're not sure, though, how to develop this thesis. Calling upon the patterns might spark some promising possibilities. *Narration* might encourage you to recount the disastrous time you were singled out and punished for the misdeeds of an entire class. Using *definition*, you might explain what is meant by an *autocratic* disciplinary style. *Argumentation-persuasion* might prompt you to advocate a new plan for disciplining students fairly and effectively.

The patterns of development also help you organize your ideas by pointing the way to an appropriate framework for a paper. Suppose you plan to write an essay for the campus newspaper about the disturbingly high incidence of shoplifting among college students; your purpose is to warn young people away from this tempting, supposedly victimless crime. You believe that many readers will be deterred from shoplifting if you tell them about the harrowing *process* set in motion once a shoplifter is detected. With this step-by-step explanation in mind, you can now map out the essay's content: what happens when a shoplifter is detained by a salesperson, questioned by store security personnel, led to a police car, booked at the police station, and tried in a courtroom.

THE PATTERNS IN ACTION: IN AN ESSAY

Although this book devotes a separate chapter to each of the nine patterns of development, all chapters emphasize the same important point: Most writing consists of several patterns, with the dominant pattern providing the piece's organizational framework. To reinforce this point, each chapter contains a section, "How [the Pattern] Fits Your Purpose and Audience," that shows how a writer's purpose often leads to a blending of patterns. You might also have noticed that one of the "Questions About the Writer's Craft" following each professional selection often asks you to analyze the piece's combination of patterns. Further, the "Writing Assignments Using Other Patterns of Development" encourage you to discover for yourself which mix of patterns would work best in a given piece of writing. In short, all through *The Macmillan Reader* we emphasize that the patterns of development are far from being mechanical formulas. On the contrary: They are practical strategies that open up options in every stage of the composing process.

In this section of the book, you'll have a chance to focus on the way writers combine patterns in their essays. The following six selections are by three writers whose styles and subjects differ sharply. (Before reading the selections, you'll probably find it helpful to glance back at pages 28–29 so you can review the broad purpose of each pattern of development.) As you read each selection, ask yourself these questions:

- What is the writer's *purpose* and *thesis*?
- What *pattern of development dominates* the essay? How does this pattern help the writer support the essay's thesis and fulfill the essay's purpose?
- What *other patterns appear* in the essay? How do these patterns help the writer support the essay's thesis and fulfill the essay's purpose?

Your responses to these questions will reward you with a richer understanding of the way writers work and with a deeper appreciation of three skilled prose stylists.

Martin Luther King, Jr.

A quarter of a century after his assassination, Martin Luther King, Jr. (1929–68), is still recognized as the towering figure in the struggle for civil rights in America. Born in Atlanta, Georgia, King earned doctorates from Boston University and Chicago Theological Seminary and served as pastor of a Baptist congregation in Montgomery, Alabama. Advocating a philosophy of nonviolent resistance to racial injustice, he led bus boycotts, marches, and sit-ins that brought about passage of the 1964 Civil Rights Act and the Voting Rights Act of 1965. Dr. King was awarded the Nobel Peace Prize in 1964. The first of the following two selections by King is taken from *Where Do We Go From Here: Community or Chaos?* (1967); the second comes from *Stride Toward Freedom* (1958).

Where Do We Go From Here: Community or Chaos?

Political leaders present convincing arguments for military aggression. They advocate supplying weapons to countries that are fighting communism; they urge the stockpiling of deadly warheads as a defense strategy; they argue for the funding of nuclear missiles euphemistically called "peace-keepers." But to Dr. King the belief that war can lead to peace is absurd. In this essay, he maintains that only nonviolent methods can bring stability and peace to a troubled world.

A final problem that mankind must solve in order to survive 1
in the world house that we have inherited is finding an alternative
to war and human destruction. Recent events have vividly reminded us that nations are not reducing but rather increasing
their arsenals of weapons of mass destruction. The best brains in
the highly developed nations of the world are devoted to military

technology. The proliferation of nuclear weapons has not been halted, in spite of the limited-test-ban treaty.

In this day of man's highest technical achievement, in this 2
day of dazzling discovery, of novel opportunities, loftier dignities and fuller freedoms for all, there is no excuse for the kind of blind craving for power and resources that provoked the wars of previous generations. There is no need to fight for food and land. Science has provided us with adequate means of survival and transportation, which make it possible to enjoy the fullness of this great earth. The question now is, do we have the morality and courage required to live together as brothers and not be afraid?

One of the most persistent ambiguities we face is that every- 3
body talks about peace as a goal, but among the wielders of power peace is practically nobody's business. Many men cry "Peace! Peace!" but they refuse to do the things that make for peace.

The large power blocs talk passionately of pursuing peace 4
while expanding defense budgets that already bulge, enlarging already awesome armies and devising ever more devastating weapons. Call the roll of those who sing the glad tidings of peace and one's ears will be surprised by the responding sounds. The heads of all the nations issue clarion calls for peace, yet they come to the peace table accompanied by bands of brigands each bearing unsheathed swords.

The stages of history are replete with the chants and choruses 5
of the conquerors of old who came killing in pursuit of peace. Alexander, Genghis Khan, Julius Caesar, Charlemagne and Napoleon were akin in seeking a peaceful world order, a world fashioned after their selfish conceptions of an ideal existence. Each sought a world at peace which would personify his egotistic dreams. Even within the life span of most of us, another megalomaniac strode across the world stage. He sent his blitzkrieg-bent legions blazing across Europe, bringing havoc and holocaust in his wake. There is grave irony in the fact that Hitler could come forth, following nakedly aggressive expansionist theories, and do it all in the name of peace.

So when in this day I see the leaders of nations again talking 6
peace while preparing for war, I take fearful pause. When I see our country today intervening in what is basically a civil war, mutilating hundreds of thousands of Vietnamese children with napalm, burning villages and rice fields at random, painting the valleys of

that small Asian country red with human blood, leaving broken bodies in countless ditches and sending home half-men, mutilated mentally and physically; when I see the unwillingness of our government to create the atmosphere for a negotiated settlement of this awful conflict by halting bombings in the North and agreeing unequivocally to talk with the Vietcong—and all this in the name of pursuing the goal of peace—I tremble for our world.[1] I do so not only from dire recall of the nightmares wreaked in the wars of yesterday, but also from dreadful realization of today's possible nuclear destructiveness and tomorrow's even more calamitous prospects.

Before it is too late, we must narrow the gaping chasm   7
between our proclamations of peace and our lowly deeds which precipitate and perpetuate war. We are called upon to look up from the quagmire of military programs and defense commitments and read the warnings on history's signposts.

One day we must come to see that peace is not merely a   8
distant goal that we seek but a means by which we arrive at that goal. We must pursue peaceful ends through peaceful means. How much longer must we play at deadly war games before we heed the plaintive pleas of the unnumbered dead and maimed of past wars?

President John F. Kennedy said on one occasion, "Mankind   9
must put an end to war or war will put an end to mankind." Wisdom born of experience should tell us that war is obsolete. There may have been a time when war served as a negative good by preventing the spread and growth of an evil force, but the destructive power of modern weapons eliminates even the possibility that war may serve any good at all. If we assume that life is worth living and that man has a right to survive, then we must find an alternative to war. In a day when vehicles hurtle through outer space and guided ballistic missiles carve highways of death through the stratosphere, no nation can claim victory in war. A so-called limited war will leave little more than a calamitous legacy of human suffering, political turmoil and spiritual disillusionment. A world war will leave only smoldering ashes as mute

---

[1]Only after more than 58,000 Americans had been killed did the United States withdraw from Vietnam. The war then continued until the North Vietnamese, aided by the Vietcong, took over all of Vietnam.

testimony of a human race whose folly led inexorably to ultimate death. If modern man continues to flirt unhesitatingly with war, he will transform his earthly habitat into an inferno such as even the mind of Dante[2] could not imagine.

Therefore I suggest that the philosophy and strategy of non- 10
violence become immediately a subject for study and for serious experimentation in every field of human conflict, by no means excluding the relations between nations. It is, after all, nation-states which make war, which have produced the weapons that threaten the survival of mankind and which are both genocidal and suicidal in character.

We have ancient habits to deal with, vast structures of power, 11
indescribably complicated problems to solve. But unless we abdi-cate our humanity altogether and succumb to fear and impotence in the presence of the weapons we have ourselves created, it is as possible and as urgent to put an end to war and violence between nations as it is to put an end to poverty and racial injustice.

The United Nations is a gesture in the direction of nonvio- 12
lence on a world scale. There, at least, states that oppose one another have sought to do so with words instead of with weapons. But true nonviolence is more than the absence of vio-lence. It is the persistent and determined application of peaceable power to offenses against the community—in this case the world community. As the United Nations moves ahead with the giant tasks confronting it, I would hope that it would earnestly exam-ine the uses of nonviolent direct action.

I do not minimize the complexity of the problems that need 13
to be faced in achieving disarmament and peace. But I am con-vinced that we shall not have the will, the courage and the insight to deal with such matters unless in this field we are prepared to undergo a mental and spiritual re-evaluation, a change of focus which will enable us to see that the things that seem most real and powerful are indeed now unreal and have come under sentence of death. We need to make a supreme effort to generate the readi-ness, indeed the eagerness, to enter into the new world which is now possible, "the city which hath foundation, whose Building and Maker is God."

[2]In *The Divine Comedy* (1321), Italian poet Dante depicts the burning tor-ments of hell endured by a lost soul before it can attain salvation.

It is not enough to say, "We must not wage war." It is   14
necessary to love peace and sacrifice for it. We must concentrate
not merely on the eradication of war but on the affirmation of
peace. A fascinating story about Ulysses and the Sirens[3] is preserved for us in Greek literature. The Sirens had the ability to sing
so sweetly that sailors could not resist steering toward their island. Many ships were lured upon the rocks, and men forgot
home, duty and honor as they flung themselves into the sea to be
embraced by arms that drew them down to death. Ulysses, determined not to succumb to the Sirens, first decided to tie himself
tightly to the mast of his boat and his crew stuffed their ears with
wax. But finally he and his crew learned a better way to save
themselves: They took on board the beautiful singer Orpheus,
whose melodies were sweeter than the music of the Sirens. When
Orpheus sang, who would bother to listen to the Sirens?

So we must see that peace represents a sweeter music, a   15
cosmic melody that is far superior to the discords of war. Somehow we must transform the dynamics of the world power struggle
from the nuclear arms race, which no one can win, to a creative
contest to harness man's genius for the purpose of making peace
and prosperity a reality for all the nations of the world. In short,
we must shift the arms race into a "peace race." If we have the
will and determination to mount such a peace offensive, we will
unlock hitherto tightly sealed doors of hope and bring new light
into the dark chambers of pessimism.

[3]Ulysses and the Sirens, as well as Orpheus (mentioned later in the paragraph), are all figures in Greek mythology.

Martin Luther King, Jr.

Three Kinds of Resistance to Oppression

The architect of the modern American civil rights movement analyzes two common reactions to the experience of being oppressed. He then offers a third response, explaining that it provides the only path to a lasting and honorable freedom.

Oppressed people deal with their oppression in three characteristic ways. One way is acquiescence: the oppressed resign themselves to their doom. They tacitly adjust themselves to oppression, and thereby become conditioned to it. In every movement toward freedom some of the oppressed prefer to remain oppressed. Almost 2,800 years ago Moses set out to lead the children of Israel from the slavery of Egypt to the freedom of the promised land. He soon discovered that slaves do not always welcome their deliverers. They become accustomed to being slaves. They would rather bear those ills they have, as Shakespeare pointed out, than flee to others that they know not of. They prefer the "fleshpots of Egypt" to the ordeals of emancipation. 1

There is such a thing as the freedom of exhaustion. Some people are so worn down by the yoke of oppression that they give up. A few years ago in the slum areas of Atlanta, a Negro guitarist used to sing almost daily: "Been down so long that down don't bother me." This is the type of negative freedom and resignation that often engulfs the life of the oppressed. 2

But this is not the way out. To accept passively an unjust system is to cooperate with that system; thereby the oppressed become as evil as the oppressor. Noncooperation with evil is as much a moral obligation as is cooperation with good. The oppressed must never allow the conscience of the oppressor to slumber. Religion reminds every man that he is his brother's 3 keeper. To accept injustice or segregation passively is to say to the oppressor that his actions are morally right. It is a way of allowing his conscience to fall asleep. At this moment the oppressed fails to be his brother's keeper. So acquiescence — while often the easier way — is not the moral way. It is the way of the coward. The Negro cannot win the respect of his oppressor by acquiescing; he merely increases the oppressor's arrogance and contempt. Acquiescence is interpreted as proof of the Negro's inferiority. The Negro cannot win the respect of the white people of the South or the peoples of the world if he is willing to sell the future of his children for his personal and immediate comfort and safety.

A second way that oppressed people sometimes deal with   4 oppression is to resort to physical violence and corroding hatred. Violence often brings about momentary results. Nations have frequently won their independence in battle. But in spite of temporary victories, violence never brings permanent peace. It solves no social problem; it merely creates new and more complicated ones.

Violence as a way of achieving racial justice is both impracti-   5 cal and immoral. It is impractical because it is a descending spiral ending in destruction for all. The old law of an eye for an eye leaves everybody blind. It is immoral because it seeks to humiliate the opponent rather than win his understanding; it seeks to annihilate rather than to convert. Violence is immoral because it thrives on hatred rather than love. It destroys community and makes brotherhood impossible. It leaves society in monologue rather than dialogue. Violence ends by defeating itself. It creates bitterness in the survivors and brutality in the destroyers. A voice echoes through time saying to every potential Peter, "Put up your sword." History is cluttered with the wreckage of nations that failed to follow this command.

If the American Negro and other victims of oppression suc-   6 cumb to the temptation of using violence in the struggle for freedom, future generations will be the recipients of a desolate night of bitterness, and our chief legacy to them will be an endless reign of meaningless chaos. Violence is not the way.

The third way open to oppressed people in their quest for   7 freedom is the way of nonviolent resistance. Like the synthesis in Hegelian philosophy, the principle of nonviolent resistance seeks to reconcile the truths of two opposites — acquiescence and violence — while avoiding the extremes and immoralities of both. The nonviolent resister agrees with the person who acquiesces that one should not be physically aggressive toward his opponent; but he balances the equation by agreeing with the person of violence that evil must be resisted. He avoids the nonresistance of the former and the violent resistance of the latter. With nonviolent resistance, no individual or group need submit to any wrong, nor need anyone resort to violence in order to right a wrong.

It seems to me that this is the method that must guide the 8 actions of the Negro in the present crisis in race relations. Through nonviolent resistance the Negro will be able to rise to the noble height of opposing the unjust system while loving the perpetrators of the system. The Negro must work passionately and unrelentingly for full stature as a citizen, but he must not use inferior methods to gain it. He must never come to terms with falsehood, malice, hate, or destruction.

Nonviolent resistance makes it possible for the Negro to 9 remain in the South and struggle for his rights. The Negro's problem will not be solved by running away. He cannot listen to the glib suggestion of those who would urge him to migrate en masse to other sections of the country. By grasping his great opportunity in the South he can make a lasting contribution to the moral strength of the nation and set a sublime example of courage for generations yet unborn.

By nonviolent resistance, the Negro can also enlist all men of 10 good will in his struggle for equality. The problem is not a purely racial one, with Negroes set against whites. In the end, it is not a struggle between people at all, but a tension between justice and injustice. Nonviolent resistance is not aimed against oppressors but against oppression. Under its banner, consciences, not racial groups, are enlisted.

Joan Didion

Known for her taut prose style and sharp social commentary, Joan Didion (1934–) graduated from the University of California at Berkeley. Her essays have appeared in the *Saturday Evening Post*, the *American Scholar*, and the *National Review*, as well as in two collections: *Slouching Towards Bethlehem* (1969) and *The White Album* (1979). *Salvador* (1983) is a book-length essay about a 1982 visit to Central America. The coauthor of several screenplays, Didion has also written novels, including *River Run* (1963), *Play It as It Lays* (1971), *A Book of Common Prayer* (1977), and *Democracy* (1984). The two selections that follow are from *The White Album*.

In Bed

Perhaps you're skeptical of people who take to bed with a bad headache, or maybe you use the term *migraine* to describe your own occasional discomfort. If so, reading this essay will probably put you in your place. A chronic migraine sufferer since childhood, Joan Didion frequently falls victim to bouts of debilitating pain. Brace yourself for some excruciating details; you'll never use the word *migraine* loosely again.

Three, four, sometimes five times a month, I spend the day in bed with a migraine headache, insensible to the world around me. Almost every day of every month, between these attacks, I feel the sudden irrational irritation and flush of blood into the cerebral arteries which tell me that migraine is on its way, and I take certain drugs to avert its arrival. If I did not take the drugs, I would be able to function perhaps one day in four. The physiological error called migraine is, in brief, central to the given of my life. When I was fifteen, sixteen, even twenty-five, I used to think that I could rid myself of this error by simply denying it, character over chemistry. "Do you have headaches *sometimes? frequently? never?*" the application forms would demand. "Check one."

Wary of the trap, wanting whatever it was that the successful circumnavigation of that particular form could bring (a job, a scholarship, the respect of mankind and the grace of God), I would check one. *"Sometimes,"* I would lie. That in fact I spent one or two days a week almost unconscious with pain seemed a shameful secret, evidence not merely of some chemical inferiority but of all my bad attitudes, unpleasant tempers, wrongthink.

For I had no brain tumor, no eyestrain, no high blood pres- 2
sure, nothing wrong with me at all: I simply had migraine headaches, and migraine headaches were, as everyone who did not have them knew, imaginary. I fought migraine then, ignored the warnings it sent, went to school and later to work in spite of it, sat through lectures in Middle English and presentations to advertisers with involuntary tears running down the right side of my face, threw up in washrooms, stumbled home by instinct, emptied ice trays onto my bed and tried to freeze the pain in my right temple, wished only for a neurosurgeon who would do a lobotomy on house call, and cursed my imagination.

It was a long time before I began thinking mechanistically 3
enough to accept migraine for what it was: something with which I would be living, the way some people live with diabetes. Migraine is something more than the fancy of a neurotic imagination. It is an essentially hereditary complex of symptoms, the most frequently noted but by no means the most unpleasant of which is a vascular headache of blinding severity, suffered by a surprising number of women, a fair number of men (Thomas Jefferson had migraine, and so did Ulysses S. Grant, the day he accepted Lee's surrender), and by some unfortunate children as young as two years old. (I had my first when I was eight. It came on during a fire drill at the Columbia School in Colorado Springs, Colorado. I was taken first home and then to the infirmary at Peterson Field, where my father was stationed. The Air Corps doctor prescribed an enema.) Almost anything can trigger a specific attack of migraine: stress, allergy, fatigue, an abrupt change in barometric pressure, a contretemps over a parking ticket. A flashing light. A fire drill. One inherits, of course, only the predisposition. In other words I spent yesterday in bed with a headache not merely because of my bad attitudes, unpleasant tempers, and wrongthink, but because both my grandmothers

had migraine, my father has migraine, and my mother has migraine.

No one knows precisely what it is that is inherited. The   4
chemistry of migraine, however, seems to have some connection
with the nerve hormone named serotonin, which is naturally
present in the brain. The amount of serotonin in the blood falls
sharply at the onset of migraine, and one migraine drug, methysergide, or Sansert, seems to have some effect on serotonin.
Methysergide is a derivative of lysergic acid (in fact Sandoz Phar-
maceuticals first synthesized LSD-25 while looking for a migraine
cure), and its use is hemmed about with so many contraindica-
tions and side effects that most doctors prescribe it only in the
most incapacitating cases. Methysergide, when it is prescribed, is
taken daily, as a preventive; another preventive which works for
some people is old-fashioned ergotamine tartrate, which helps to
constrict the swelling blood vessels during the "aura," the period
which in most cases precedes the actual headache.

Once an attack is under way, however, no drug touches it.   5
Migraine gives some people mild hallucinations, temporarily
blinds others, shows up not only as a headache but as a gastroin-
testinal disturbance, a painful sensitivity to all sensory stimuli, an
abrupt overpowering fatigue, a strokelike aphasia, and a crippling
inability to make even the most routine connections. When I am
in a migraine aura (for some people the aura lasts fifteen minutes,
for others several hours), I will drive through red lights, lose the
house keys, spill whatever I am holding, lose the ability to focus
my eyes or frame coherent sentences, and generally give the appearance of being on drugs, or drunk. The actual headache, when
it comes, brings with it chills, sweating, nausea, a debility that
seems to stretch the very limits of endurance. That no one dies of
migraine seems, to someone deep into an attack, an ambiguous
blessing.

My husband also has migraine, which is unfortunate for him   6
but fortunate for me: perhaps nothing so tends to prolong an
attack as the accusing eye of someone who has never had a
headache. "Why not take a couple of aspirin," the unafflicted will
say from the doorway, or "I'd have a headache, too, spending a
beautiful day like this inside with all the shades drawn." All of us
who have migraine suffer not only from the attacks themselves

but from this common conviction that we are perversely refusing to cure ourselves by taking a couple of aspirin, that we are making ourselves sick, that we "bring it on ourselves." And in the most immediate sense, the sense of why we have a headache this Tuesday and not last Thursday, of course we often do. There certainly is what doctors call a "migraine personality," and that personality tends to be ambitious, inward, intolerant of error, rather rigidly organized, perfectionist. "You don't look like a migraine personality," a doctor once said to me. "Your hair's messy. But I suppose you're a compulsive housekeeper." Actually my house is kept even more negligently than my hair, but the doctor was right nonetheless: perfectionism can also take the form of spending most of a week writing and rewriting and not writing a single paragraph.

But not all perfectionists have migraine, and not all migrainous people have migraine personalities. We do not escape heredity. I have tried in most of the available ways to escape my own migrainous heredity (at one point I learned to give myself two daily injections of histamine with a hypodermic needle, even though the needle so frightened me that I had to close my eyes when I did it), but I still have migraine. And I have learned now to live with it, learned when to expect it, how to outwit it, even how to regard it, when it does come, as more friend than lodger. We have reached a certain understanding, my migraine and I. It never comes when I am in real trouble. Tell me that my house is burned down, my husband has left me, that there is gunfighting in the streets and panic in the banks, and I will not respond by getting a headache. It comes instead when I am fighting not an open but a guerrilla war with my own life, during weeks of small household confusions, lost laundry, unhappy help, canceled appointments, on days when the telephone rings too much and I get no work done and the wind is coming up. On days like that my friend comes uninvited. 7

And once it comes, now that I am wise in its ways, I no longer fight it. I lie down and let it happen. At first every small apprehension is magnified, every anxiety a pounding terror. Then the pain comes, and I concentrate only on that. Right there is the usefulness of migraine, there in that imposed yoga, the concentration on the pain. For when the pain recedes, ten or twelve 8 hours later, everything goes with it, all the hidden resentments, all the vain anxieties. The migraine has acted as a circuit breaker, and the fuses have emerged intact. There is a pleasant convalescent euphoria. I open the windows and feel the air, eat gratefully, sleep well. I notice the particular nature of a flower in a glass on the stair landing. I count my blessings.

Joan Didion

On Self-Respect

What determines how we feel about ourselves? Is it our ability to land the right job, achieve the right look, be accepted by the right people? For Joan Didion, self-respect is none of these things. It's what happens in the still hours of the morning when we lie alone in bed with no one but ourselves for company. Then, during those moments of self-reckoning, we discover whether we have the "toughness and . . . moral nerve" that's at the heart of self-respect.

Once, in a dry season, I wrote in large letters across two   1
pages of a notebook that innocence ends when one is stripped of
the delusion that one likes oneself. Although now, some years
later, I marvel that a mind on the outs with itself should have
nonetheless made painstaking record of its every tremor, I recall
with embarrassing clarity the flavor of those particular ashes. It
was a matter of misplaced self-respect.

I had not been elected to Phi Beta Kappa.[1] This failure could   2
scarcely have been more predictable or less ambiguous (I simply
did not have the grades), but I was unnerved by it; I had somehow
thought myself a kind of academic Raskolnikov,[2] curiously exempt from the cause-effect relationships which hampered others.
Although even the humorless nineteen-year-old that I was must
have recognized that the situation lacked real tragic stature, the
day that I did not make Phi Beta Kappa nonetheless marked the
end of something, and innocence may well be the word for it. I
lost the conviction that lights would always turn green for me,

[1]An honorary society of college students with records of high academic
achievement.
[2]In Dostoyevsky's *Crime and Punishment* (1866), Raskolnikov deliberately
sets out to commit murder to show that he is exempt from conventional moral
codes. However, he is subsequently plagued by guilt and remorse.

the pleasant certainty that those rather passive virtues which had won me approval as a child automatically guaranteed me not only Phi Beta Kappa keys but happiness, honor, and the love of a good man; lost a certain touching faith in the totem power of good manners, clean hair, and proven competence on the Stanford-Binet scale.[3] To such doubtful amulets had my self-respect been pinned, and I faced myself that day with the nonplused apprehension of someone who has come across a vampire and has no crucifix at hand.

Although to be driven back upon oneself is an uneasy affair at best, rather like trying to cross a border with borrowed credentials, it seems to me now the one condition necessary to the beginnings of real self-respect. Most of our platitudes notwithstanding, self-deception remains the most difficult deception. The tricks that work on others count for nothing in that very well-lit back alley where one keeps assignations with oneself: no winning smiles will do here, no prettily drawn lists of good intentions. One shuffles flashily but in vain through one's marked cards — the kindness done for the wrong reason, the apparent triumph which involved no real effort, the seemingly heroic act into which one had been shamed. The dismal fact is that self-respect has nothing to do with the approval of others — who are, after all, deceived easily enough; has nothing to do with reputation, which, as Rhett Butler told Scarlett O'Hara, is something people with courage can do without.   3

To do without self-respect, on the other hand, is to be an unwilling audience of one to an interminable documentary that details one's failings, both real and imagined, with fresh footage spliced in for every screening. *There's the glass you broke in anger, there's the hurt on X's face; watch now, this next scene, the night Y came back from Houston, see how you muff this one.* To live without self-respect is to lie awake some night, beyond the reach of warm milk, phenobarbital, and the sleeping hand on the coverlet, counting up the sins of commission and omission, the trusts betrayed, the promises subtly broken, the gifts irrevocably wasted through sloth or cowardice or carelessness. However long we postpone it, we eventually lie down alone in that notoriously uncomfortable bed, the one we make ourselves. Whether or not   4

---

[3] A test designed to measure intelligence.

we sleep in it depends, of course, on whether or not we respect ourselves.

To protest that some fairly improbable people, some people   5
who *could not possibly respect themselves*, seem to sleep easily enough is to miss the point entirely, as surely as those people miss it who think that self-respect has necessarily to do with not having safety pins in one's underwear. There is a common superstition that "self-respect" is a kind of charm against snakes, something that keeps those who have it locked in some unblighted Eden, out of strange beds, ambivalent conversations, and trouble in general. It does not at all. It has nothing to do with the face of things, but concerns instead a separate peace, a private reconciliation. Although the careless, suicidal Julian English in *Appointment in Samarra*[4] and the careless, incurably dishonest Jordan Baker in *The Great Gatsby*[5] seem equally improbable candidates for self-respect, Jordan Baker had it, Julian English did not. With that genius for accommodation more often seen in women than in men, Jordan took her own measure, made her own peace, avoided threats to that peace: "I hate careless people," she told Nick Carraway.[6] "It takes two to make an accident."

Like Jordan Baker, people with self-respect have the courage   6
of their mistakes. They know the price of things. If they choose to commit adultery, they do not then go running, in an excess of bad conscience, to receive absolution from the wronged parties; nor do they complain unduly of the unfairness, the undeserved embarrassment, of being named corespondent. In brief, people with self-respect exhibit a certain toughness, a kind of moral nerve; they display what was once called *character*, a quality which, although approved in the abstract, sometimes loses ground to other, more instantly negotiable virtues. The measure of its slipping prestige is that one tends to think of it only in connection with homely children and United States senators who have been defeated, preferably in the primary, for reelection. Nonetheless, character — the willingness to accept responsibility for one's own life — is the source from which self-respect springs.

Self-respect is something that our grandparents, whether or   7

[4]A novel by American writer John O'Hara.
[5]A novel by American writer F. Scott Fitzgerald.
[6]A character in *The Great Gatsby*.

not they had it, knew all about. They had instilled in them, young, a certain discipline, the sense that one lives by doing things one does not particularly want to do, by putting fears and doubts to one side, by weighing immediate comforts against the possibility of larger, even intangible, comforts. It seemed to the nineteenth century admirable, but not remarkable, that Chinese Gordon put on a clean white suit and held Khartoum against the Mahdi; it did not seem unjust that the way to free land in California involved death and difficulty and dirt. In a diary kept during the winter of 1846, an emigrating twelve-year-old named Narcissa Cornwall noted coolly: "Father was busy reading and did not notice that the house was being filled with strange Indians until Mother spoke about it." Even lacking any clue as to what Mother said, one can scarcely fail to be impressed by the entire incident: the father reading, the Indians filing in, the mother choosing the words that would not alarm, the child duly recording the event and noting further that those particular Indians were not, "fortunately for us," hostile. Indians were simply part of the *donnée*.[7]

In one guise or another, Indians always are. Again, it is a 8 question of recognizing that anything worth having has its price. People who respect themselves are willing to accept the risk that the Indians will be hostile, that the venture will go bankrupt, that the liaison may not turn out to be one in which *every day is a holiday because you're married to me*. They are willing to invest something of themselves; they may not play at all, but when they do play, they know the odds.

That kind of self-respect is a discipline, a habit of mind that 9 can never be faked but can be developed, trained, coaxed forth. It was once suggested to me that, as an antidote to crying, I put my head in a paper bag. As it happens, there is a sound physiological reason, something to do with oxygen, for doing exactly that, but the psychological effect alone is incalculable: it is difficult in the extreme to continue fancying oneself Cathy in *Wuthering Heights*[8] with one's head in a Food Fair bag. There is a similar case

[7]From the French, meaning "given" — that is, the raid was an accepted fact and life went on despite it.

[8]A reference to Catherine Earnshaw in Emily Bronte's *Wuthering Heights* (1848). In the novel, Cathy and the wild Heathcliff love each other with a passionate — and tragic — intensity.

for all the small disciplines, unimportant in themselves; imagine maintaining any kind of swoon, commiserative or carnal, in a cold shower.

But those small disciplines are available only insofar as they represent larger ones. To say that Waterloo[9] was won on the playing fields of Eton[10] is not to say that Napoleon might have been saved by a crash program in cricket; to give formal dinners in the rain forest would be pointless did not the candlelight flickering on the liana call forth deeper, stronger disciplines, values instilled long before. It is a kind of ritual, helping us to remember who and what we are. In order to remember it, one must have known it.   10

To have that sense of one's intrinsic worth which constitutes self-respect is potentially to have everything: the ability to discriminate, to love and to remain indifferent. To lack it is to be locked within oneself, paradoxically incapable of either love or indifference. If we do not respect ourselves, we are on the one hand forced to despise those who have so few resources as to consort with us, so little perception as to remain blind to our fatal weaknesses. On the other, we are peculiarly in thrall to everyone we see, curiously determined to live out—since our self-image is untenable—their false notions of us. We flatter ourselves by thinking this compulsion to please others an attractive trait: a gist for imaginative empathy, evidence of our willingness to give. Of *course* I will play Francesca[11] to your Paolo, Helen Keller[12] to anyone's Annie Sullivan: no expectation is too misplaced, no role too ludicrous. At the mercy of those we cannot but hold in contempt, we play roles doomed to failure before they are begun, each defeat generating fresh despair at the urgency of divining and meeting the next demand made upon us.   11

It is the phenomenon sometimes called "alienation from self." In its advanced stages, we no longer answer the telephone, because someone might want something; that we could say *no* without drowning in self-reproach is an idea alien to this game.   12

---

[9]The scene of Napoleon's final defeat.

[10]A private preparatory school for British boys.

[11]A thirteenth-century Italian woman seduced into an affair by her brother-in-law, Paolo.

[12]An American writer and lecturer, blind and deaf from infancy, who was taught to speak and read by her teacher, Annie Sullivan.

Every encounter demands too much, tears the nerves, drains the will, and the specter of something as small as an unanswered letter arouses such disproportionate guilt that answering it becomes out of the question. To assign unanswered letters their proper weight, to free us from the expectations of others, to give us back to ourselves — there lies the great, the singular power of self-respect. Without it, one eventually discovers the final turn of the screw: one runs away to find oneself, and finds no one at home.

Virginia Woolf

Virginia Woolf is considered one of the most innovative writers of the twentieth century. Born in 1882 in London, Woolf was educated at home by her father, a well-known biographer, critic, and scholar. Along with her sister, Woolf became a key member of the Bloomsbury Group, a circle of writers and artists committed to the highest standards in art and literature. Woolf married a fellow Bloomsbury member, author and publisher Leonard Woolf. Together, they established Hogarth Press, which went on to publish Woolf's ground-breaking writings, including the novels *Mrs. Dalloway* (1923) and *To the Lighthouse* (1927), as well as the collection of essays *A Room of One's Own* (1920). Woolf's experimentation with point of view and her use of stream of consciousness earned her a place as a pivotal figure in English literature. Although Woolf's work met with critical acclaim and her collaboration with her husband was productive, Woolf was troubled all her life by severe depression. She committed suicide in 1941. The first of the following two selections by Woolf, "The Death of the Moth," appeared in the volume *The Death of the Moth and Other Essays* (1948); the second, "Professions for Women," was delivered as a speech to the Women's Service League in 1931.

The Death of the Moth

A moth dying on the windowsill is hardly an unusual sight and generally won't excite much emotion. But Virginia Woolf, with characteristic depth of perception, sees the moth as an emblem of the eternal battle between life and death.

Moths that fly by day are not properly to be called moths; 1 they do not excite that pleasant sense of dark autumn nights and ivy-blossom which the commonest yellow-underwing asleep in the shadow of the curtain never fails to rouse in us. They are hybrid creatures, neither gay like butterflies nor sombre like their own species. Nevertheless the present specimen, with his narrow hay-coloured wings, fringed with a tassel of the same colour, seemed to be content with life. It was a pleasant morning, mid-September, mild, benignant, yet with a keener breath than that of the summer months. The plough was already scoring the field opposite the window, and where the share had been, the earth was pressed flat and gleamed with moisture. Such vigour came rolling in from the fields and the down beyond that it was difficult to keep the eyes strictly turned upon the book. The rooks too were keeping one of their annual festivities; soaring round the tree tops until it looked as if a vast net with thousands of black knots in it had been cast up into the air; which, after a few moments, sank slowly down upon the trees until every twig seemed to have a knot at the end of it. Then, suddenly, the net would be thrown into the air again in a wider circle this time, with the utmost clamour and vociferation, as though to be thrown into the air and settle slowly down upon the tree tops were a tremendously exciting experience.

The same energy which inspired the rooks, the ploughmen, 2 the horses, and even, it seemed, the lean bare-backed downs, sent the moth fluttering from side to side of his square of the window-pane. One could not help watching him. One was, indeed, conscious of a queer feeling of pity for him. The possibilities of pleasure seemed that morning so enormous and so various that to have only a moth's part in life, and a day moth's at that, appeared a hard fate, and his zest in enjoying his meagre opportunities to the full, pathetic. He flew vigorously to one corner of his compartment, and, after waiting there a second, flew across to the other. What remained for him but to fly to a third corner and then to a fourth? That was all he could do, in spite of the size of the downs, the width of the sky, the far-off smoke of houses, and the romantic voice, now and then, of a steamer out at sea. What he could do he did. Watching him, it seemed as if a fibre, very thin but pure, of the enormous energy of the world had been thrust into his frail and diminutive body. As often as he crossed the pane, I could fancy that a thread of vital light became visible. He was little or nothing but life.

Yet, because he was so small, and so simple a form of the 3 energy that was rolling in at the open window and driving its way through so many narrow and intricate corridors in my own brain and in those of other human beings, there was something marvellous as well as pathetic about him. It was as if someone had taken a tiny bead of pure life and decking it as lightly as possible with down and feathers, had set it dancing and zigzagging to show us the true nature of life. Thus displayed one could not get over the strangeness of it. One is apt to forget all about life, seeing it humped and bossed and garnished and cumbered so that it has to move with the greatest circumspection and dignity. Again, the thought of all that life might have been had he been born in any other shape caused one to view his simple activities with a kind of pity.

After a time, tired by his dancing apparently, he settled on the window ledge in the sun, and, the queer spectacle being at an end, I forgot about him. Then, looking up, my eye was caught by him. He was trying to resume his dancing, but seemed either so stiff or so awkward that he could only flutter to the bottom of the window-pane; and when he tried to fly across it he failed. Being intent on other matters I watched these futile attempts for a time without thinking, unconsciously waiting for him to resume his flight, as one waits for a machine, that has stopped momentarily, to start again without considering the reason of its failure. After perhaps a seventh attempt he slipped from the wooden ledge and fell, fluttering his wings, on to his back on the window sill. The helplessness of his attitude roused me. It flashed upon me that he was in difficulties; he could no longer raise himself; his legs struggled vainly. But, as I stretched out a pencil, meaning to help him to right himself, it came over me that the failure and awkwardness were the approach of death. I laid the pencil down again.

The legs agitated themselves once more. I looked as if for the enemy against which he struggled. I looked out of doors. What had happened there? Presumably it was midday, and work in the fields had stopped. Stillness and quiet had replaced the previous animation. The birds had taken themselves off to feed in the brooks. The horses stood still. Yet the power was there all the same, massed outside, indifferent, impersonal, not attending to anything in particular. Somehow it was opposed to the little hay-coloured moth. It was useless to try to do anything. One could only watch the extraordinary efforts made by those tiny legs against an oncoming doom which could, had it chosen, have submerged an entire city, not merely a city, but masses of human beings; nothing, I knew had any chance against death. Nevertheless after a pause of exhaustion the legs fluttered again. It was superb, this last protest, and so frantic that he succeeded at last in righting himself. One's sympathies, of course, were all on the side of life. Also, when there was nobody to care or to know, this gigantic effort on the part of an insignificant little moth, against a power of such magnitude, to retain what no one else valued or desired to keep, moved one strangely. Again, somehow, one saw life, a pure bead. I lifted the pencil again, useless though I knew it to be. But even as I did so, the unmistakable tokens of death showed themselves. The body relaxed, and instantly grew stiff. The struggle was over. The insignificant little creature now knew death. As I looked at the dead moth, this minute wayside triumph of so great a force over so mean an antagonist filled me with wonder. Just as life had been strange a few minutes before, so death was now as strange. The moth having righted himself now lay most decently and uncomplainingly composed. O yes, he seemed to say, death is stronger than I am.

Virginia Woolf

Professions for Women

In the following speech given to the Women's Service League in 1931, Virginia Woolf uses her experience as a writer to describe the obstacles standing between women and accomplishment in their chosen fields. Those barriers, she points out, don't necessarily assume an outwardly malevolent form; often they appear in the guise of an angel.

When your secretary invited me to come here, she told me that your Society is concerned with the employment of women and she suggested that I might tell you something about my own professional experiences. It is true I am a woman; it is true I am employed; but what professional experiences have I had? It is difficult to say. My profession is literature; and in that profession there are fewer experiences for women than in any other, with the exception of the stage — fewer, I mean, that are peculiar to women. For the road was cut many years ago — by Fanny Burney, by Aphra Behn, by Harriet Martineau, by Jane Austen, by George Eliot[1] — many famous women, and many more unknown and forgotten, have been before me, making the path smooth, and regulating my steps. Thus, when I came to write, there were very few material obstacles in my way. Writing was a reputable and harmless occupation. The family peace was not broken by the scratching of a pen. No demand was made upon the family purse. For ten and sixpence one can buy paper enough to write all the plays of Shakespeare — if one has a mind that way. Pianos and models, Paris, Vienna and Berlin, masters and mistresses, are not needed by a writer. The cheapness of writing paper is, of course,

1

---

[1]Fanny Burney (1752–1840), Aphra Behn (1640–89), Harriet Martineau (1802–76), Jane Austen (1775–1817), and Marian Evans (1819–80), whose pen name was George Eliot, were all English women of letters.

the reason why women have succeeded as writers before they have succeeded in the other professions.

But to tell you my story — it is a simple one. You have only got to figure to yourselves a girl in a bedroom with a pen in her hand. She had only to move that pen from left to right — from ten o'clock to one. Then it occurred to her to do what is simple and cheap enough after all — to slip a few of those pages into an envelope, fix a penny stamp in the corner, and drop the envelope into the red box at the corner. It was thus that I became a journalist; and my effort was rewarded on the first day of the following month — a very glorious day it was for me — by a letter from an editor containing a cheque for one pound ten shillings and sixpence. But to show you how little I deserve to be called a professional woman, how little I know of the struggles and difficulties of such lives, I have to admit that instead of spending that sum upon bread and butter, rent, shoes and stockings, or butcher's bills, I went out and bought a cat — a beautiful cat, a Persian cat, which very soon involved me in bitter disputes with my neighbors.

What could be easier than to write articles and to buy Persian cats with the profits? But wait a moment. Articles have to be about something. Mine, I seem to remember, was about a novel by a famous man. And while I was writing this review, I discovered that if I were going to review books I should need to do battle with a certain phantom. And the phantom was a woman, and when I came to know her better I called her after the heroine of a famous poem, "The Angel in the House." It was she who used to come between me and my paper when I was writing reviews. It was she who bothered me and wasted my time and so tormented me that at last I killed her. You who come of a younger and happier generation may not have heard of her — you may not know what I mean by the Angel in the House. I will describe her as shortly as I can. She was intensely sympathetic. She was immensely charming. She was utterly unselfish. She excelled in the difficult arts of family life. She sacrificed herself daily. If there was chicken, she took the leg; if there was a draught she sat in it — in short she was so constituted that she never had a mind or a wish of her own, but preferred to sympathize always with the minds and wishes of others. Above all — I need not say it — she was pure. Her purity was supposed to be her chief beauty — her blushes, her great grace. In those days—the last of Queen Victoria—every house had its Angel. And when I came to write I encountered her with the very first words. The shadow of her wings fell on my page; I heard the rustling of her skirts in the room. Directly, that is to say, I took my pen in hand to review that novel by a famous man, she slipped behind me and whispered: "My dear, you are a young woman. You are writing about a book that has been written by a man. Be sympathetic; be tender; flatter; deceive; use all the arts and wiles of our sex. Never let anybody guess that you have a mind of your own. Above all, be pure." And she made as if to guide my pen. I now record the one act for which I take some credit to myself, though the credit rightly belongs to some excellent ancestors of mine who left me a certain sum of money—shall we say five hundred pounds a year?—so that it was not necessary for me to depend solely on charm for my living. I turned upon her and caught her by the throat. I did my best to kill her. My excuse, if I were to be had up in a court of law, would be that I acted in self-defence. Had I not killed her she would have killed me. She would have plucked the heart out of my writing. For, as I found, directly I put pen to paper, you cannot review even a novel without having a mind of your own, without expressing what you think to be the truth about human relations, morality, sex. And all these questions, according to the Angel in the House, cannot be dealt with freely and openly by women; they must charm, they must conciliate, they must—to put it bluntly—tell lies if they are to succeed. Thus, whenever I felt the shadow of her wing or the radiance of her halo upon my page, I took up the inkpot and flung it at her. She died hard. Her fictitious nature was of great assistance to her. It is far harder to kill a phantom than a reality. She was always creeping back when I thought I had despatched her. Though I flatter myself that I killed her in the end, the struggle was severe; it took much time that had better have been spent upon learning Greek grammar; or in roaming the world in search of adventures. But it was a real experience; it was an experience that was bound to befall all women writers at that time. Killing the Angel in the House was part of the occupation of a woman writer.

But to continue my story. The Angel was dead; what then remained? You may say that what remained was a simple and common object—a young woman in a bedroom with an inkpot.   4

In other words, now that she had rid herself of falsehood, that young woman had only to be herself. Ah, but what is "herself"? I mean, what is a woman? I assure you, I do not know. I do not believe that you know. I do not believe that anybody can know until she has expressed herself in all the arts and professions open to human skill. That indeed is one of the reasons why I have come here — out of respect for you, who are in process of showing us by your experiments what a woman is, who are in process of providing us, by your failures and successes, with that extremely important piece of information.

But to continue the story of my professional experiences. I made one pound ten and six by my first review; and I bought a Persian cat with the proceeds. Then I grew ambitious. A Persian cat is all very well, I said; but a Persian cat is not enough. I must have a motor car. And it was thus that I became a novelist — for it is a very strange thing that people will give you a motor car if you will tell them a story. It is a still stranger thing that there is nothing so delightful in the world as telling stories. It is far pleasanter than writing reviews of famous novels. And yet, if I am to obey your secretary and tell you my professional experiences as a novelist, I must tell you about a very strange experience that befell me as a novelist. And to understand it you must try first to imagine a novelist's state of mind. I hope I am not giving away professional secrets if I say that a novelist's chief desire is to be as unconscious as possible. He has to induce in himself a state of perpetual lethargy. He wants life to proceed with the utmost quiet and regularity. He wants to see the same faces, to read the same books, to do the same things day after day, month after month, while he is writing, so that nothing may break the illusion in which he is living — so that nothing may disturb or disquiet the mysterious nosings about, feelings round, darts, dashes and sudden discoveries of that very shy and illusive spirit, the imagination. I suspect that this state is the same both for men and women. Be that as it may, I want you to imagine me writing a novel in a state of trance. I want you to figure to yourself a girl sitting with a pen in her hand, which for minutes, and indeed for hours, she never dips into the inkpot. The image that comes to my mind when I think of this girl is the image of a fisherman lying sunk in dreams on the verge of a deep lake with a rod held out over the water. She was letting her imagination sweep un-

5

checked round every rock and cranny of the world that lies sub-merged in the depths of our unconscious being. Now came the experience, the experience that I believe to be far commoner with women writers than with men. The line raced through the girl's fingers. Her imagination had rushed away. It had sought the pools, the depths, the dark places where the largest fish slumber. And then there was a smash. There was an explosion. There was foam and confusion. The imagination had dashed itself against something hard. The girl was roused from her dream. She was indeed in a state of the most acute and difficult distress. To speak without figure she had thought of something, something about the body, about the passions which it was unfitting for her as a woman to say. Men, her reason told her, would be shocked. The consciousness of what men will say of a woman who speaks the truth about her passions had roused her from her artist's state of unconsciousness. She could write no more. The trance was over. Her imagination could work no longer. This I believe to be a very common experience with women writers — they are impeded by the extreme conventionality of the other sex. For though men sensibly allow themselves great freedom in these respects, I doubt that they realize or can control the extreme severity with which they condemn such freedom in women.

These then were two very genuine experiences of my own.   6
These were two of the adventures of my professional life. The first — killing the Angel in the House — I think I solved. She died. But the second, telling the truth about my own experiences as a body, I do not think I solved. I doubt that any woman has solved it yet. The obstacles against her are still immensely powerful — and yet they are very difficult to define. Outwardly, what is simpler than to write books? Outwardly, what obstacles are there for a woman rather than for a man? Inwardly, I think, the case is very different: she has still many ghosts to fight, many prejudices to overcome. Indeed it will be a long time still, I think, before a woman can sit down to write a book without finding a phantom to be slain, a rock to be dashed against. And if this is so in literature, the freest of all professions for women, how is it in the new professions which you are now for the first time entering?

Those are the questions that I should like, had I time, to ask   7
you. And indeed, if I have laid stress upon these professional experiences of mine, it is because I believe that they are, though in

different forms, yours also. Even when the path is nominally open — when there is nothing to prevent a woman from being a doctor, a lawyer, a civil servant — there are many phantoms and obstacles, as I believe, looming in her way. To discuss and define them is, I think, of great value and importance; for thus only can the labour be shared, the difficulties be solved. But besides this, it is necessary also to discuss the ends and the aims for which we are fighting, for which we are doing battle with these formidable obstacles. Those aims cannot be taken for granted; they must be perpetually questioned and examined. The whole position, as I see it — here in this hall surrounded by women practicing for the first time in history I know not how many different professions — is one of extraordinary interest and importance. You have won rooms of your own in the house hitherto exclusively owned by men. You are able, though not without great labor and effort, to pay the rent. You are earning your five hundred pounds a year. But this freedom is only a beginning; the room is your own, but it is still bare. It has to be furnished; it has to be decorated; it has to be shared. How are you going to furnish it, how are you going to decorate it? With whom are you going to share it, and upon what terms? These, I think, are questions of the utmost importance and interest. For the first time in history you are able to ask them; for the first time you are able to decide for yourselves what the answers should be. Willingly would I stay and discuss those questions and answers — but not tonight. My time is up; and I must cease.

13

A CONCISE GUIDE TO DOCUMENTATION

In Chapter 11, you learned the importance of *documention* — giving credit to the sources whose words and ideas you borrow in an essay (see page 580). That earlier discussion showed you how to document sources in informal papers. This chapter will show you how to use the documentation system of the Modern Language Association (MLA)[1] when citing sources in more formal papers.

The following discussion covers key features of the MLA system. For more detailed coverage, you may want to consult a recent composition handbook or the latest edition of the *MLA Handbook for Writers of Research Papers*. For a sample paper that

---

[1]MLA documentation is appropriate in papers written for humanities courses, such as your composition class. If you're writing a paper for a course in the social sciences (for example, psychology, economics, or sociology), your professor will probably expect you to use the citation format developed by the American Psychological Association (APA). For information about APA documentation, consult a composition handbook or the most recent edition of the *Publication Manual of the American Psychological Association*.

uses MLA documentation, turn to the student essay on pages 594–99.

WHAT TO DOCUMENT

You may inadvertently fall into the trap of *plagiarizing* — passing off someone else's ideas as your own — if you're not sure when you need to acknowledge outside sources in an essay. To avoid plagiarism, you must provide documentation in the following situations:

- When you include a *word-for-word quotation* from a source.
- When you *summarize or restate in your own words* ideas or information from a source, unless that material is *commonly known* or is a *matter of historical or scientific record*.
- When you *combine a summary and a quotation*.

An important note: On the whole, you should try to state borrowed material in your own words. A string of quotations signals that you haven't sufficiently evaluated and distilled your sources. Use quotations sparingly; draw upon them only when they dramatically illustrate key points you want to make. Also, keep in mind that quotations won't, by themselves, make your case for you. You need to interpret and comment on them, showing how they support your points.

HOW TO DOCUMENT

The MLA documentation system uses the *parenthetic reference*, a brief note in parentheses inserted into the text after borrowed material. The parenthetic reference doesn't provide full bibliographic information, but it presents enough so that readers can turn to the Works Cited list (see page 732) at the end of the paper for complete information. If the method of documentation you learned in high school involved footnotes or endnotes, you will be happy to know that parenthetic documentation — currently the preferred method — is much easier to use. While it is now accepted by most college professors, be sure to check with your professors to determine their documentation preferences.

Whenever you quote or summarize material from an outside

source, you must do two things: (1) *identify the author* and (2) *specify the page(s)* in your source on which the material appears. The author's name may be given *either* in a lead-in sentence (often called the *attribution*) *or* in the parentheses following the borrowed material. The page number *always* appears in parentheses. The examples that follow, using material from George Gallup's "The Faltering Family" (see page 479), illustrate the MLA documentation style. (If you like, turn to Gallup's piece and compare the documentation with the original.)

Using Parentheses Only

Nowadays, several alternative family life-styles are common, but a generation ago, most families consisted of "a man and a woman who were married to each other and who produced children (usually two) and lived happily ever after" (Gallup 481).

It's clear that "we're confused . . . in our feelings about marriage and the family" (Gallup 488).

In the early 1980s, most women believed that being married and having children would offer them the best prospect of a satisfying life (Gallup 487).

Using Parentheses and Attributions

Pollster George Gallup argues, "The basic feminist philosophy has filtered down to the grass roots . . ." (486).

Gallup believes that another factor contributing to change in the family has been the "power of feminist philosophy to permeate . . ." attitudes (485) and modify behavior.

Gallup states that most families find they need dual incomes to meet the escalating costs of raising children--expenses that are, in practice, almost three times greater than parents imagine (485).

Key Points to Remember

Take a moment to look again at the preceding examples and note the following points:

- The parenthetic reference is placed *immediately after* the borrowed material, at a natural pause in the sentence or at the end of the sentence.

- The parenthetic reference is placed *before* any *internal punctuation* (a comma or semicolon) as well as *before* any *terminal punctuation* (a period or question mark).
- When the author's name is provided in the attribution, the name is *not* repeated in the parentheses.
- The first time an author is referred to in an attribution, the author's *full name* is given; afterwards, only the *last name* is provided.
- Sometimes, to inform readers of an author's area of expertise, the person may be identified by profession ("*Pollster* George Gallup . . ."), title, or affiliation.
- When the author's name is provided in the parentheses, only the last name is given.
- The page number comes directly after the author's name. (If the source is only one page long, only the author's name is needed.)
- There is no punctuation between the author's name and the page number.
- There is no *p.* or *page* preceding the page number.
- Words may be deleted from a quotation as long as the author's original meaning isn't changed. In such a case, three spaced periods—called an *ellipsis* (. . .)—are inserted in place of the deleted words. An ellipsis is not needed, however, when material is omitted from the start of a quotation.

Three Other Important Points

Here are three additional situations you may encounter when documenting sources:

1. More than one source by the same author. When your paper includes references to more than one work by the same author, you must specify—either in the parentheses or in the attribution—the particular work being cited. You do this by providing the *title*, as well as the author's name and the page(s). As with the author's name, the title may be given in *either* the attribution *or* the parenthetic citation. Here are some examples:

In <u>The Language and Thought of the Child</u>, Jean Piaget states that "discussion forms the basis for a logical point of view" (240).

Piaget considers dialogue essential to the development of logical thinking (<u>Language and Thought</u> 240).

<u>The Child's Conception of the World</u> shows that young children think that the name of something can never change (Piaget 81).

Young children assume that everything has only one name and that no others are possible (Piaget, <u>Child's Conception</u> 81).

Notice that when a work is named in the attribution, the full title appears; when a title is given in the parenthetic citation, though, only the first few significant words appear.

2. Long quotations. A quotation extending beyond four typed lines starts on a new line and is indented ten spaces from the left margin throughout. Since this so-called *block format* already indicates a quotation, quotation marks are unnecessary. Double-space the block quotation, as you do the rest of your paper. Long quotations, which should be used sparingly, require a lead-in. A lead-in that *isn't* a full sentence is followed by a comma, while a lead-in that *is* a full sentence (as in the accompanying example) is followed by a colon:

Gallup cites changed sexual mores as one reason for the decline of marriage:

> Clearly, attitudes have changed a great deal in just three decades. Teenagers have accepted the idea of premarital sex as the norm. In one recent national poll, 52 percent of girls and 66 percent of boys favored having sexual relations in their teens. Ironically, however, 46 percent of the teenagers thought that virginity in their future marital partner was fairly important. (483)

Notice that the page number appears in parentheses, just as in a short quotation. But in a long quotation, the parenthetic citation is placed two spaces *after* the period that ends the quotation.

3. Quoting or summarizing a source within a source. If you quote or summarize a *secondhand source* (someone whose ideas come to you only through another source), you need to make this clear. The parenthetic documentation should indicate "as quoted in" with the abbreviation *qtd. in*:

According to Sherman, "Recycling has, in several communities, created unanticipated expenses" (qtd. in Pratt 3-4).

Sherman explains that recycling can be surprisingly costly (qtd. in Pratt 3-4).

Your Works Cited list would include the source you actually read (Pratt), rather than the source you refer to secondhand (Sherman).

LIST OF WORKS CITED

A documented paper ends with a list of Works Cited, which includes only those sources you actually acknowledge in the paper. Placed on its own page, the Works Cited list provides the reader with full bibliographic information about the sources cited in the parenthetic references (see page 729). By referring to the Works Cited list that appears at the end of the student essay on pages 598–99, you will notice the following:

- The list is organized alphabetically by authors' last names. Entries without an author are alphabetized by the first major word in the title (that is, not *A, An*, or *The*).
- Entries are not numbered.
- If an entry runs longer than one line, each additional line is indented five spaces. Entries are double-spaced with no extra space between entries. (*Note*: Because of space constraints, the Works Cited list on pages 598–99 has been single-spaced and placed directly after the essay's final paragraph rather than on a separate page.)

Sample Works Cited Entries

Listed here are sample Works Cited entries for the most commonly used kinds of sources. Refer to these samples when you prepare your own Works Cited list, taking special care to reproduce the punctuation and spacing exactly. If you don't spot an entry for the kind of source you need to document, consult the *MLA Handbook* for more comprehensive examples.

Book With One Author

Yesley, Marjorie G. <u>Political Campaigns: A Retrospective</u>. New York:
Vintage, 1979.

Several Works by the Same Author

Reedy, George E. <u>The Presidency in Flux</u>. New York: Columbia UP,
1973.

---. <u>The Twilight of the Presidency</u>. New York: World, 1970.

If you use more than one work by the same author, list each
book separately. Give the author's name in the first entry only;
begin the entries for other books by that author with three hy-
phens followed by a period. Arrange the works alphabetically by
title.

Book With Two or Three Authors

Beddoes, Richard, Stan Fischler, and Ira Gitler. <u>Hockey! The Story of
the World's Fastest Sport</u>. Toronto: Collier-Macmillan, 1969.

Book With Four or More Authors

Dansker, Isadora, et al. <u>Geological Formations in New England</u>.
Boston: Newtown, 1990.

For a work with four or more authors, give only the first
author's name followed by a comma and *et al.* (Latin for "and
others").

Revised Edition of a Book

Fiedler, Leslie A. <u>Love and Death in the American Novel</u>. 2nd ed.
New York: Dell, 1966.

Book With an Editor or Translator

Jonson, Ben. <u>Epicoene</u>. Ed. L. A. Beaurline. Lincoln: U of Nebraska,
1966.

An Anthology or Compilation of Several Authors

Ghiselin, Brewster, ed. <u>The Creative Process: A Symposium</u>. Berkeley:
U of California P, 1952.

Section of an Anthology or Compilation of Several Authors

Shapero, Harold. "The Musical Mind." The Creative Process: A
    Symposium. Ed. Brewster Ghiselin. Berkeley: U of California P,
    1952. 49-53.

Use *UP*, as in *Columbia UP* and *U of California P*, to abbreviate the names of university presses.

Section or Chapter in a Book by One Author

Canin, Ethan. "The Year of Getting to Know Us." Emperor of the Air.
    New York: Harper, 1988. 21-43.

Article From a Weekly or Biweekly Magazine

Strobe, Talbot. "Why Kohl Is Right." Time 15 May 1989: 26.

"Short Takes." Publishers Weekly 22 Aug. 1986: 20.

Article From a Monthly or Bimonthly Magazine

Steele, Shelby. "The Recoloring of Campus Life: Student Racism,
    Academic Pluralism, and the End of a Dream." Harper's Feb.
    1989: 47-55.

Article From a Daily Newspaper

Bartlett, Sarah. "Why Wall Street's So Topsy-Turvy." New York Times
    7 May 1989, natl. ed., sec. 3: 1, 8.

Article From a Scholarly Journal

Connors, Robert J. "Personal Writing Assignment." College
    Composition and Communication 38 (1987): 166-83.

Juneja, Renu. "The Trinidad Carnival: Ritual, Performance, Spectacle,
    and Symbol." Journal of Popular Culture 21.4 (1988): 87-90.

Some journals are paged continuously (the first example);
the first issue of each year starts with page one, and each subsequent issue picks up where the previous one left off. For such
journals, use numerals to indicate the volume number after the

title, and then indicate the year in parentheses. Note that neither *volume* nor *vol.* is used. The article's page(s) appear at the end, separated from the year by a colon.

For a journal that pages each issue separately (the second example), use numerals to indicate the *volume and issue numbers*; separate the two with a period but leave no space after the period.

Television or Radio Program

"Colonial Days." The United States and the Philippines: In Our
   Image. Narr. Stanley Karnow. Part 1 of 3. PBS. WHYY-TV.
   Philadelphia. 8 May 1989.

Movie, Videotape, Filmstrip, or Slide Program

Field of Dreams. Dir. Phil Alden Robinson. With Kevin Costner.
   Universal, 1989.

Personal Interview

Harrow, Morgan. Personal interview. 5 Aug. 1989.

Lecture

Bateman, Paul. "The Media and the Electoral Process." Lecture.
   Sociology 202, Kirkwood University. New Castle, 10 Oct. 1989.

GLOSSARY

Abstract and concrete language refers to two different qualities of words. Abstract words and phrases convey concepts, qualities, emotions, and ideas that we can think and talk about but not actually see or experience directly. Examples of abstract words are *conservatism, courage, avarice, joy,* and *hatred.* Words or phrases whose meanings are directly seen or experienced by the senses are concrete terms. Examples of phrases using concrete words are *split-level house, waddling penguin*, and *short pink waitress uniform.*

Adequate — see *Evidence.*

Ad hominem **argument** — see *Logical fallacies.*

Analogy refers to an imaginative comparison between two subjects that seem to have little in common. Often a complex idea or topic can be made understandable by comparing it to a more familiar subject, and such an analogy can be developed over several paragraphs or even an entire essay. For example, to explain how the economic difficulties of farmers weaken an entire nation, a writer might create an analogy between failing farms and a cancer that slowly destroys a person's life.

Argumentation-persuasion tries to encourage readers to accept a writer's point of view on some controversial issue. In *argumentation,* a writer uses objective reasoning, facts, and hard evidence to demonstrate the soundness of a position. In *persuasion*, the writer uses appeals to the readers' emotions and value systems, often in the hope of encouraging them to take a specific action. Argumentation and persuasion are frequently used together in an essay. For example, a writer might argue for the construction of a highway through town by pointing out that the road would bring new business, create new jobs, and lighten traffic. The writer also might try to persuade readers to vote for a highway appropriations bill by appealing to their emotions, claiming that the highway would allow people to get home faster, thus giving them more time for family life and leisure activities. A whole essay can be organized around argumentation-persuasion, or an essay developed chiefly through another pattern may contain elements of argumentation-persuasion.

Assertion refers to the *thesis* of an *argumentation-persuasion* essay. The assertion, or *proposition*, is a point of view or opinion on a controversial issue or topic. The assertion cannot be merely a statement of a fact. Such statements as "Women still experience discrimination in the job market," "General Rabb would make an ideal mayor for our town," and "This university should devote more funds to raising the quality of the food services" are examples of assertions that could serve as theses for argumentation-persuasion essays.

Audience refers to a writer's intended readers. In planning the content and tone of an essay, you should identify your audience and consider its needs. How similar are the members of your audience to you in knowledge and point of view? What will they need to know for you to achieve your *purpose*? What *tone* will make them open to receiving your message? For example, if you were to write a description of a trip to Disney World, you would have to explain a lot more to an eighty-year-old grandmother who had never seen a theme park than to a young parent who has probably visited several. If you wrote about the high cost of clothing for an economics professor, you would choose a serious, analytic tone and supply statistical evidence for your points. If you write about the same topic for the college newspaper, you might use a tone tinged with humor and provide helpful hints on finding bargain clothing.

Begging the question — see *Logical fallacies.*

Brainstorming is a technique used in the *prewriting* stage. It helps you discover the limited subject you can successfully write about and also generates raw material — ideas and details — to develop that subject. In brainstorming, you allow your mind to play freely with the subject. You try to capture fleeting thoughts about it, no matter how random, minor, or tangential, and jot them down rapidly before they disappear from your mind.

Causal analysis—see *Cause-effect.*

Causal chain refers to a series of causes and effects, in which the result or effect of a cause becomes itself the cause of a further effect, and so on. For example, a person's alarm clock failing to buzz might begin a causal chain by causing the person to oversleep. Oversleeping then causes the person to miss the bus, and missing the bus causes the person to arrive late to work. Arriving late causes the person to miss an important phone call, which causes the person to lose a chance at a lucrative contract.

Cause-effect, sometimes called *causal analysis,* involves analyzing the reasons for or results of an event, action, decision, or phenomenon. Writers develop an essay through an analysis of causes whenever they attempt to answer such questions as "Why has this happened?" or "Why does this exist?" When writers explore such questions as "What happens or would happen if a certain change occurs?" or "What will happen if a condition continues?" their essays involve a discussion of effects. Some cause-effect essays concentrate on the causes of a situation, some focus on the effects, and others present both causes and effects. Causal analysis can be an essay's central pattern, or it can be used to help support a point in an essay developed primarily through another pattern.

Characteristics—see *Formal definition.*

Chronological sequence—see *Narrative sequence* and *Organization.*

Circularity is an error in *formal definition* resulting from using variations of the to-be-defined word in the definition. For example, "A scientific hypothesis is a hypothesis made by a scientist about the results of an experiment" is circular because the unknown term is used to explain itself.

Class—see *Formal definition.*

Coherence refers to the clear connection among the various parts of an essay. As a writer, you can draw upon two key strategies to make writing coherent. You can use a clear *organizational format* (for example, a chronological, spatial, emphatic, or simple-to-complex sequence). You can also provide *appropriate signaling* or *connecting devices* (transitions, bridging sentences, repeated words, synonyms, and pronouns).

Comparison-contrast means explaining the similarities and/or differences between events, objects, people, ideas, and so on. The comparison-contrast format can be used to meet a purely factual purpose ("This is how *A* and *B* are alike or different"). But usually writers use comparison-contrast to make a judgment about the relative merits of the subjects under discussion. Sometimes a writer will concentrate solely on similarities *or* differences. For instance, when writing about married versus single life, you would probably devote most of your time to discussing the difference between these life-styles. Other times, comparison and contrast are found together. In an essay analyzing two approaches to U.S. foreign policy, you would probably discuss the similarities *and* the differences in the goals and methods characteristic of each approach. Comparison-contrast can be the dominant pattern in an essay, or it can help support a point in an essay developed chiefly through another pattern.

Conclusion refers to the one or more paragraphs that bring an essay to an end. Effective conclusions give the reader a sense of completeness and finality. Writers often use the conclusion as a place to reaffirm the *thesis* and to express a final thought about the subject. Methods of conclusion include summarizing main points, using a quotation, predicting an outcome, and recommending an action.

Conflict creates tension in the readers of a *narration*. It is produced by the opposition of characters or other forces in a story. Conflict can occur between individuals, between a person and society or nature, or within a person. Readers wonder how a conflict will be resolved and read on to find out.

Connecting devices signal the relationships among ideas in an essay. They help the reader follow the train of thought from sentence to sentence and from paragraph to paragraph. There are three types of connectives. *Transitions* are words that briefly indicate the coming flow of meaning. They can signal an additional or contrasting point, an enumeration of ideas, the use of an example, or other movement of ideas. *Linking sentences* summarize a point just made and then introduce a follow-up point. *Repeated words, synonyms*, and *pronouns* create a sense of flow by keeping important concepts in the mind of the reader.

Connotative and denotative language describe the ability of language to emphasize one or another aspect of a word's range of meaning. *Denotative language* stresses the dictionary meaning of words. *Connotative language* emphasizes the echoes of feeling that cluster around some words. For example, the terms *weep, bawl, break down*, and *sob* all denote the same thing: to cry. But they have different associations and call up different images. A writer employing the connotative resources of language would choose the term among these that suggested the appropriate image.

Controlling idea — see *Thesis*.

Deductive reasoning is a form of logical thinking in which general statements believed to be true are applied to specific situations or cases. The result of deduction is a conclusion or prediction about the specific situation. Deduction is often expressed in a three-step pattern called a *syllogism*. The first part of the syllogism is a general statement about a large class of items or situations, the *major prem-ise*. The second part is the *minor premise*, a more limited statement about a specific item or case. The third part is the *conclusion*, drawn from the major premise, about that specific case or item. Deductive reasoning is very common in everyday thinking. For example, you might use deduction when car shopping:

In an accident, large cars are safer than small cars. (*major premise*)

The Turbo Titan is a large car. (*minor premise*)

In an accident, the Turbo Titan will be safer than a small car. (*conclusion*)

Definition explains the meaning of a word or concept. The brief formal definitions found in the dictionary can be useful if you need to clarify or restrict the meaning of a term used in an essay. In such cases, the definition is short and to the point. But you may also use an *extended definition* in an essay, taking several paragraphs, even the entire piece, to develop the meaning of a term. You may use extended definition to convey a personal slant on a well-known term, to refute a commonly held interpretation of a word, or to dissect a complex or controversial issue. Definition can be the chief method of development in an essay, or it can help support a point in an essay organized around another pattern.

Definition by negation is a method of defining a term by first explaining what the term is *not*, and then going on to explain what it is. For example, you might begin a critical essay about television with a definition by negation: "Television, far from being a medium that dispenses only light, insubstantial fare, actually disseminates a dangerously distorted view of family life." Definition by negation can provide a stimulating introduction to an essay.

Denotative language — see *Connotative and denotative language*.

Description involves the use of vivid word pictures to express what the five senses have experienced. The subject of a descriptive essay can be a person, a place, an object, or an event. Description can be the dominant pattern in an essay, or it can be used as a supplemental method in an essay developed chiefly through another pattern.

There are two main types of description. In an *objective descrip-tion*, a writer provides details about a subject without conveying the emotions the subject arouses. For example, if you were involved in a traffic accident, your insurance agent might ask you to write an objective description of the events leading up to and during the crash. But in a *subjective description*, the writer's goal is to evoke in the reader the emotions felt during the experience. For example, in a cautionary letter to a friend who has a habit of driving dangerously, you might write a subjective description of your horrifying close call with death during a car accident.

Development—see *Evidence.*

Dialogue is the writer's way of directly presenting the exact words spoken by characters in a *narration.* By using dialogue, writers can convey people's individuality and also add drama and immediacy to an essay.

Directional process analysis—see *Process analysis.*

Division-classification refers to a logical method for analyzing a single subject or several related subjects. Though often used together in an essay, division and classification are separate processes. *Division* involves breaking a subject or idea into its component parts. For instance, the concept "an ideal vacation" could be divided according to its destination, accommodations, or cost. *Classification* involves organizing a number of related items into categories. For example, in an essay about the overwhelming flow of paper in our everyday lives, you might classify the typical kinds of mail most people receive: personal mail (letters, birthday cards, party invitations), business mail (bills, bank statements, charge-card receipts), and junk mail (flyers about bargain sales, solicitations to donate, contest announcements). Division-classification can be the dominant pattern in a paper, or it may be used to support a point in an essay organized chiefly around another pattern of development.

Dominant impression refers to the purpose of a descriptive essay. While some descriptive essays have a thesis, others do not; instead, they convey a dominant impression or main point. For example, one person writing a descriptive essay about New York City might use its architectural diversity as a focal point. Another person writing a description of Manhattan might concentrate on the overpowering sense of hustle and speed about everyone and everything in the city. Both writers would select only those details that supported their dominant impressions.

Dramatic license refers to the writer's privilege, when writing a narrative, to alter facts or details to strengthen the support of the *thesis* or *narrative point.* For example, a writer is free to flesh out the description of an event whose specific details may be partially forgotten or to modify or omit details of a narrative that do not contribute to the meaning the writer wishes to convey.

Either-or fallacy—see *Logical fallacies.*

Emphatic sequence—see *Organization.*

Ethos refers to a writer's reliability or credibility. Such an image of trustworthiness is particularly important to readers of an *argumentation-persuasion* essay or piece. Writers establish their *ethos* by using reason and logic, by being moderate in their appeals to emotions, by avoiding a hostile tone, and by demonstrating overall knowledgeability of the subject. The most effective argumentation-persuasion involves an interplay of *ethos, logos,* and *pathos.*

Etymology refers to the history of a word or term. All English words have their origins in other, often ancient, languages. Giving a brief etymology of a word can help a writer establish the context for developing an *extended definition* of the word. For example, the word *criminal* is derived from a Latin word meaning "accusation/accused." Today, our word *criminal* goes beyond the concept of "accused" to mean "guilty."

Evidence lends substance to a writer's main ideas and thus helps the reader to accept the writer's viewpoint. Evidence should meet several criteria. First of all, it should be *unified,* in the sense that all supporting ideas and details should relate directly to the key point the writer is making. Second, evidence should be *adequate*; there should be enough evidence to convince the reader to agree with the thesis. Third, evidence should be *specific*; that is, vivid and detailed rather than vague and general. Fourth, evidence must be *accurate* and not overstate or understate information. Fifth, evidence should be *representative,* relying on the typical rather than the atypical to make a point. The bulk of an essay is devoted to supplying evidence. Supporting the thesis with solid evidence is the third stage in the writing process.

Exemplification, at the heart of all effective writing, involves using concrete specifics to support generalizations. In exemplification, writers provide examples or instances that support or clarify broader statements. You might support the thesis statement, "I have a close-knit family," by using such examples as the following: "We have a regular Sunday dinner at my grandmother's house with at least ten family members present"; "My sisters and brothers visit my parents every week"; "I spend so much time on the phone talking with my sisters that sometimes I have trouble finding time for my new college friends." Exemplification may be an essay's central pattern, or it may supplement an essay developed mainly around another pattern.

Extended definition—see *Definition.*

Fallacies—see *Logical fallacies.*

False analogy—See *Logical fallacies.*

Figures of speech are imaginative comparisons between two things usually thought of as dissimilar. Some major figures of speech are *simile, metaphor,* and *personification. Similes* are comparisons that use the signal words *like* or *as*: "Superman was as powerful as a locomotive." *Metaphors,* which do not use signal words, directly equate unlike things: "The boss is a tiger when it comes to landing a contract." "The high-powered pistons of the boxer's arms pummeled his opponent." *Personification* attributes human characteristics to inanimate things or nonhuman beings: "The angry clouds unleashed their fury on the town"; "The turtle shyly poked his head out of his shell."

First draft refers to the writer's first try at producing a basic, unpolished version of the whole essay. It is often referred to as the "rough" draft, and nothing about it is final or unchangeable. The process of writing the first draft often brings up new ideas or details. Writers sometimes break off writing the draft to *brainstorm* or *freewrite* as new ideas occur to them and then return to the draft with new inspiration. You shouldn't worry about spelling, grammar, or style in the first-draft stage; instead, you should keep focused on casting your ideas into sentence and paragraph form. Writing the first draft is the fifth stage in the writing process.

Flashback — see *Narrative sequence.*

Flashforward — see *Narrative sequence.*

Formal definition involves stating a definition in a three-part pattern of about one sentence in length. In presenting a formal definition, a writer puts the *term* in a *class* and then lists the *characteristics* that separate the term from other members of its class. For example, a formal definition of a word processor might be, "A word processor (term) is an electronic machine (class) that is used to write, edit, store, and produce typewritten documents (characteristics)." Writers often use a formal definition to prepare a reader for an extended definition that follows.

Freewriting is most often used during the *prewriting* stage to help writers generate ideas about a limited topic. To use this method, write nonstop for five or ten minutes about everything your topic brings to mind. Disregard grammar, spelling, and organization as you keep your pen and mind moving. Freewriting is similar to *brainstorming*, except that the result is a rambling, detail-filled paragraph rather than a list. Freewriting can also be used to generate ideas during later stages of the writing process.

Gender-biased language gives the impression that one sex is more important, powerful, or valuable than the other. When writing, you should work to replace such sexist language with *gender-neutral* or *nonsexist* terms that convey no sexual prejudice. First of all, try to avoid *sexist vocabulary* that demeans or excludes one of the sexes: *stud, jock, chick, fox*, and so on. Also, just as adult males should be called *men*, adult females should be referred to as *women*, not *girls*. And men shouldn't be empowered with professional and honorary titles (*President* Bush) while professional women — such as prime ministers — are assigned only personal titles (*Mrs.* Thatcher). Here are some examples of the way you can avoid words that exclude women: Change "chairman" to *chairperson*, "layman" to *layperson*, "congressman" to *congressional representative*, "workmen" to *workers*, the "average guy" to the *average person*. Second, be aware of the fact that indefinite singular nouns—those representing a general group of people consisting of both genders—can lead to *sexist pronoun use*: for example, "On *his* first day of school, a young child often experiences separation anxiety." This sentence excludes female children from consideration, although the situation being described applies equally to them. Third, recognize that indefinite pronouns like *anyone*, *each*, and *everybody* may also pave the way to sexist pronoun use. Although such pronouns often refer to a number of individuals, they're considered singular. So, wanting to be grammatically correct, you may write a sentence like the following: "Everybody wants *his* favorite candidate to win." The sentence, however, is sexist because *everybody* is certainly not restricted to men. One way to avoid this type of sexist construction is to use both male and female pronouns: "Everybody wants *his or her* favorite candidate to win." Another approach is to use *s/he* in place of *he*. A third possibility is to use the gender-neutral pronouns *they, their*, or *themselves*: "Everybody wants *their* favorite candidate to win." Be warned, though. Some people object to using these plural pronouns with singular indefinite pronouns, even though the practice is common in everyday speech. Two alternative strategies enable you to eliminate the need for *any* gender-marked singular pronouns. First, you can change singular general nouns or indefinite pronouns to their plural equivalents and then use nonsexist plural pronouns. For example, you may change "A *workaholic* feels anxious when *he* isn't busy" to "*Workaholics* feel anxious when *they're* not busy" and "*Everyone* in the room expressed *his* opinion freely" to "*Those* in the room expressed *their* opinions freely." Second, you can recast the sentence to omit the singular pronoun: For instance, you may change "A *manager* usually spends part of each day settling squabbles among *his* staff" to "A manager usually spends part of each day settling *staff squabbles*" and "No *one* wants *his* taxes raised" to "No one wants *to pay more taxes*."

Hasty generalization—see *Logical fallacies*.

Inductive reasoning is a form of logical thinking in which specific cases and facts are examined to draw a wider-ranging conclusion. The result of inductive reasoning is a generalization that is applied to situations or cases similar to the ones examined. Induction is typical of scientific investigation and of everyday thinking. For example, on the basis of specific experiences, you may have concluded that when you feel chilly in a room where everyone else is comfortable, you are likely to develop a cold and fever in the next day or two. In an *argumentation-persuasion* essay, the conclusion reached by induction would be your *assertion* or *thesis.*

Inference is the term for a conclusion based on *inductive reasoning.* Because the reasoning behind specific cases may not be simple, there is usually an element of uncertainty in an inductive conclusion. Choosing the correct explanation for specific cases is a matter of carefully weighing and selecting alternative conclusions.

Informational process analysis—see *Process analysis.*

Introduction refers to the first paragraph or several paragraphs of an essay. The introduction serves three purposes. It informs readers of the general subject of the essay, it catches their attention, and it presents the controlling idea or thesis. The methods of introducing an essay include the use of an anecdote, a quotation or surprising statistic or fact, and questions. Or you may narrow your discussion down from a broad subject to a more limited one.

Irony occurs when a writer or speaker implies (rather than states directly) a discrepancy or incongruity of some kind. *Verbal irony,* which is often tongue-in-cheek, involves a discrepancy between the literal words and what's actually meant ("I know you must be unhappy about receiving the highest grade in the course"). If the ironic comment is designed to be hurtful or insulting, it qualifies as *sarcasm* ("Congratulations! You failed the final exam"). In *situational irony,* the circumstances are themselves incongruous. For example, situational irony abounds in the selection *Manzanar* (page 132) by Jeanne Wakatsuki Houston and James D. Houston. At Manzanar, Japanese-Americans played American football, sang American songs, and saluted the American flag—yet they were imprisoned by the U.S. government and were surrounded on all sides by barbed wire and armed guards.

Journal writing is a form of prewriting, in which writers make daily entries in a private journal, much as they would in a diary. Whether they focus on one topic or wander freely, journal writers jot down striking incidents, images, and ideas encountered in the course of a day. Such journal material can produce ideas for future essays.

Logical fallacies are easily committed mistakes in reasoning that writers must avoid, especially when writing *argumentation-persuasion* essays. There are many kinds of logical fallacies. Here are several:

Ad hominem argument occurs when someone attacks another person's point of view by criticizing that person, not the issue. Often called "mudslinging," *ad hominem* arguments try to invalidate a person's ideas by revealing unrelated, past or present, personal or ethical flaws. For example, to claim a person cannot govern the country well because it can be proven he or she has had an extramarital affair is to use an *ad hominem* argument.

Begging the question is a fallacy in which the writer assumes the truth of something that needs to be proven. Imagine a writer argues the following: "A law should be passed requiring dangerous pets like German shepherds and Doberman pinschers to be restrained by fences, leashes, and muzzles." Such an argument begs the question since it assumes readers will automatically accept the view that such dogs are indeed dangerous.

Either-or fallacies occur when it's argued that a complex situation can be resolved in only one of two possible ways. Here's an example: "If the administration doesn't grant striking professors more money, the college will never be able to attract outstanding teachers in years ahead." Such an argument oversimplifies matters. Excellent teachers might be attracted to a college for a variety of reasons, not just because of good salaries: the school's location, research facilities, reputation for scholarship, hardworking students, and so on.

False analogy erroneously suggests that because two things are alike in some regards, they are similar in all ways. In the process, significant differences between the two are disregarded. If you argue that a woman prosecuting a rapist is subjected to a second rape in court, you're guilty of a false analogy. As embarrassing, painful, and hurtful as the court proceedings may be, the woman is not physically assaulted, as she was when she was raped. Also, as difficult as her decision to seek justice might be, she's in court by choice and not against her will.

Hasty generalizations are unsound *inductive inferences* based on too few instances of a behavior, situation, or process. For example, it would be a hasty generalization to conclude that you're allergic to a food such as curry because you once ate it and became ill. There are several other possible explanations for your illness, and only repetitions of this experience or a lab test could prove conclusively that you're allergic to this spice.

Non sequiturs are faulty conclusions about cause and effect. Here's an example: "Throughout this country's history, most physicians have been male. Women apparently have little interest in becoming doctors." The faulty conclusion accords one factor—the possible vocational preferences of women—the status of sole cause. The conclusion fails to consider pressures on women to devote themselves to homemaking and to avoid an occupation sexually stereotyped as "masculine."

Post hoc thinking results when it's presumed that one event caused another just because it occurred first. For instance, if your car broke down the day after you lent it to your brother, you would be committing the *post hoc* fallacy if you blamed him, unless you knew he did something to your car's engine.

Questionable authority, revealed by such phrases as "studies show" and "experts claim," undercuts a writer's credibility. Readers become suspicious of such vague and unsubstantial appeals to authority. Writers should demonstrate the reliability of their sources by citing them specifically.

Red herring arguments are deliberate attempts to focus attention on a peripheral matter rather than examine the merits of the issue under discussion. Imagine that a local environmental group advocates stricter controls for employees at a nearby chemical plant. The group points out that plant employees are repeatedly exposed to high levels of toxic chemicals. If you respond, "Many of the employees are illegal aliens and shouldn't be allowed to take jobs from native-born townspeople," you're throwing in a red herring. By bringing in immigration policies, you sidetrack attention from the matter at hand: the toxic level to which plant employees — illegal aliens or not — are exposed.

Logos is a major factor in creating an effective argument. It refers to the soundness of *argumentation*, as created by the use of facts, statistics, information, and commentary by authoritative sources. The most effective arguments involve an interplay among *logos, pathos*, and *ethos*.

Major premise — see *Deductive reasoning*.

Minor premise — see *Deductive reasoning*.

MLA documentation is the system developed by the Modern Language Association for citing sources in a paper. When you quote or summarize source material, you must do two things within your paper's text: (1) identify the author and (2) specify the pages on which the material appears. You may provide the author's name in a lead-in sentence or within parentheses following the borrowed material; the page number always appears in parentheses, inserted in the text after the borrowed material. The material in the parentheses is called a *parenthetic reference*. A paper using MLA documentation ends with a *Works Cited* list, which includes only those sources actually acknowledged in the paper. Entries are organized alphabetically by authors' last names. Entries without an author are alphabetized by the first major word in the title.

Narration means recounting an event or a series of related events to make a point. Narration can be an essay's principal pattern of development, or it can be used to supplement a paper organized primarily around another pattern. For instance, to persuade readers to avoid drug use, a writer might use the narrative pattern by recounting the story of an abuser's addiction and recovery.

Narrative point refers to the meaning the writer intends to convey to a reader by telling a certain story. This narrative point might be a specific message, or it might be a feeling about the situation, people, or place of the story. This underlying meaning is achieved by presenting details that support it and eliminating any that are non-essential. For example, in an essay about friendship, a writer's point might be that friendships change when one of the friends acquires a significant partner of the opposite sex. The writer would focus on the details of how her close female friend had less time for her, changed their usual times of getting together, and confided in her less. The writer would omit judgments of the friend's choice of boyfriend and her friend's declining grades because these details, while real for the writer, would distract the reader from the essay's narrative point.

Narrative sequence refers to the order in which a writer recounts events. When you follow the order of the events as they happened, you're using *chronological sequence*. This sequence, in which you begin at the beginning and end with the last event, is the most basic and commonly used narrative sequence. If you interrupt this flow to present an event that happened before the beginning of the narrative sequence, you're employing a *flashback*. If you skip ahead to an event later than the one that comes next in your narrative, you're using the *flashforward* technique.

Non sequiturs — see *Logical fallacies*.

Objective description — see *Description*.

One-side-at-a-time method refers to one of the two techniques for organizing a *comparison-contrast* essay. In using this method, a writer discusses all the points about one of the compared and contrasted subjects before going on to the other. For example, in an essay titled "Single or Married?" a writer might first discuss single life in terms of amount of independence, freedom of career choice, and companionship. Then the writer would, within reason, discuss married life in terms of these same three subtopics. The issues the writer discusses in each half of the essay would be identical and presented in the same order. See also *Point-by-point method*.

Organization refers to the process of arranging evidence to support a thesis in the most effective way. When organizing, a writer decides what ideas come first, next, and last. In *chronological* sequence, details are arranged according to occurrence in time. In *spatial* sequence, details appear in the order in which they occur in space. In *emphatic* order, ideas are sequenced according to importance, with the most significant, outstanding, or convincing evidence being reserved for last. In *simple-to-complex* order, easy-to-grasp material is presented before more-difficult-to-comprehend information. Organizing is the fourth stage of the writing process.

Outlining involves making a formal plan before writing a *first draft*. Writing an outline helps you determine whether your supporting evidence is logical and adequate. As you write, you can use the outline to keep yourself on track. Many writers use the indentation system of Roman numerals, letters, and Arabic numbers to outline; sometimes writers use a less formal system.

Paradox refers to a statement that seems impossible, contrary to common sense, or self-contradictory, yet that can—after consideration —be seen to be plausible or true. For example, Oscar Wilde produced a paradox when he wrote "When the gods wish to punish us, they answer our prayers." The statement doesn't contradict itself because often, Wilde believes, that which we wish for turns out to be the very thing that will bring us the most pain.

Parenthetic reference—see *MLA documentation*.

Pathos refers to the emotional power of an *argumentation-persuasion* essay. By appealing to the needs, values, and attitudes of readers and by using *connotative language*, writers can increase the chances that readers will come to agree with the ideas in an essay. Although *pathos* is an important element of persuasion, such emotional appeals should reinforce rather than replace reason. The most effective argumentation-persuasion involves an interplay among *pathos, logos*, and *ethos*.

Plan of development refers to a technique whereby the writer supplies the reader with a brief map of the main points to be covered in an essay. If used, the plan of development occurs as part of the *thesis* or in a sentence following the thesis. In it, the main ideas are mentioned in the order they'll appear in the supporting paragraphs. Longer essays and term papers usually need a plan of development to maintain unity, but shorter papers may do without one.

Point-by-point method refers to one of the two techniques for organizing a *comparison-contrast* essay. A writer using this method moves from one aspect of one subject to the same aspect of another subject before going on to the second aspect of each subject. For example, in an essay titled "Single or Married?" a writer might first discuss the amount of independence a person has when single and when married. Then, the writer might go on to discuss how much freedom of career choice a person has when single and when married. Finally, the writer might discuss, in turn, the amount of companionship available in each of the two life-styles. See also *One-side-at-a-time method*.

Point of view refers to the perspective a writer chooses when writing about a subject. If you narrate events as you experience them, you're using the *first-person* point of view. You might say, for example, "*I* noticed jam on the child's collar and holes in her shirt." If you relate the events from a distance—as if you observed them but did not experience them personally—you're using the *third-person* point of view, for instance, "Jam splotched the child's collar, and her shirt had several holes in it." The point of view should be consistent throughout an essay.

Post hoc thinking—see *Logical fallacies*.

Prewriting is the first stage of the writing process. During prewriting, you jot down rough ideas about your subject without yet moving to writing a draft of your essay. Your goals at this stage are to (1) understand the boundaries of the assignment, (2) discover the limited subject you could write about, (3) generate raw material about the limited subject, and (4) organize the raw material into a very rough *scratch outline*. If you keep in mind that prewriting is "unofficial," it can be a low-pressure, even enjoyable activity.

Process analysis refers to writing that explains the steps involved in doing something or the sequence of stages in an event or behavior. There are two types of process analysis. In *directional process analysis*, readers are shown how to do something step by step. Cookbook recipes, tax form instructions, and how-to books are some typical uses of directional process analysis. In *informational process analysis*, the writer explains how something is done or occurs, without expecting the reader to attempt the process. "A Senator's Road to Political Power," "How a Bee Makes Honey," and "How a Convict Gets Paroled" would be titles of essays developed through informational process analysis. Process analysis can be the dominant mode in an essay, as in these examples, or it may help make a point in an essay developed chiefly through another pattern. For example, in a cause-effect essay that explores the impact of the two-career family, process analysis might be used to explain how parents arrange for day care.

Proofreading involves rereading a final draft carefully to catch any errors in spelling, grammar, punctuation, or typing that have slipped by. While such errors are minor, a significant number of them can seriously weaken the effectiveness of an essay. Proofreading is the last stage in the writing process.

Proposition—see *Assertion*.

Purpose is the reason a writer has for preparing a particular essay. Usually, writers frame their purposes in terms of the effect they wish to have on their *audience*. They may wish to explore the personal meaning of a subject or experience, explain an idea or process, provide information, influence opinion, or entertain. Many essays combine purposes, with one purpose predominating and providing the essay's focus.

Red herring argument — see *Logical fallacies*.

Refutation is an important strategy in *argumentation-persuasion*. In refutation, writers acknowledge that there are opposing views on the subject under discussion and then go on to do one of two things. Sometimes they may admit that the opposing views are somewhat valid but assert that their own position has more merit and devote their essay to demonstrating that merit. For example, a writer might assert, "Business majors often find interesting and lucrative jobs. However, in the long run, liberal arts graduates have many more advantages in the job market because the breadth of their background helps them think better, learn faster, and communicate more effectively." This writer would concentrate on proving the advantages that liberal arts graduates have. At other times, writers may choose to argue actively against an opposing position by dismantling that view point by point. Such refutation of opposing views can strengthen the writer's own arguments.

Repeated words, synonyms, and pronouns — see *Connecting devices*.

Revision means, literally, "reseeing" a *first draft* with a fresh eye, as if the writer had not actually prepared the draft. When revising, you move from more global issues (like clarifying meaning and organization) to more specific matters (like finetuning sentences and word choice). While revising, you make whatever changes are necessary to increase the essay's effectiveness. You might strengthen your thesis, resequence paragraph order, or add more transitions. Such changes often make the difference between mediocre and superior writing. Revision, itself a multi-stage process, is the last stage of the writing process.

Satire is a humorous form of social criticism usually aimed at society's institutions or human behavior. Often irreverent as well as witty, satire is serious in purpose: to point out evil, injustice, and absurdity and bring about change through an increase in awareness. Satire ranges widely in tone: it may be gentle or biting; it may sarcastically describe a real situation or use fictional characters and events to spoof reality. Satire often makes use of *irony*. Examples of essays using satire in this book include Stephen Leacock's "How to Live to Be 200" and Jonathan Swift's "A Modest Proposal."

Scratch outline refers to your first informal plan for an essay, devised at the end of the *prewriting* stage. In making a scratch outline, you select ideas and details from your raw material for inclusion in your essay and discard the rest. You also arrange these ideas in an order that makes sense and that will help you achieve your *purpose*. A scratch outline is tentative and flexible, and can be reshaped as needed.

Sensory description vividly evokes the sights, smells, taste, sounds, and physical feelings of a scene or event. For example, if a writer carefully chooses words and images, readers can see the vibrant reds and oranges of falling leaves, taste the sourness of an underripe grapefruit, hear the growling of motorcycles as a gang sweeps through a town, smell the spicy aroma of a grandmother's homemade tomato soup, and feel the pulsing pain of a jaw after Novocain wears off. Sensory description is particularly important in writing *description* or *narration*.

Sentence variety adds interest to the style of an essay or paragraph. In creating sentence variety, writers mix different kinds of sentences and sentence patterns. For example, you might vary the way your sentences open or intersperse short sentences with long ones, simple sentences with complex ones. Repetitive sentence patterns tend to make readers lose interest.

Spatial sequence — see *Organization.*

Specific — see *Evidence.*

Stipulative definition is a way of restricting a term for the purposes of discussion. Many words have multiple meanings that can get in the way of clarity when a writer is creating an *extended definition.* For example, you might stipulate the following definition of *foreign car*: "While many American automobiles use parts or even whole engines made by foreign car manufacturers, for the purposes of discussion, 'foreign car' refers only to those automobiles designed and manufactured wholly by a company based in another country. By this definition, a European vehicle made in Pennsylvania is *not* a foreign car."

Subjective description — see *Description.*

Support — see *Evidence.*

Syllogism — see *Deductive reasoning.*

Term — see *Formal definition.*

Thesis is the central idea in any essay, usually expressed in a one- or two-sentence *thesis statement.* Writers accomplish two things by providing a thesis statement in an essay; they indicate the essay's limited subject and express an attitude about that subject. Also called the *controlling idea*, the thesis statement consists of a particular slant, angle, or point of view about the limited subject. Stating the thesis is the second stage of the writing process.

Tone conveys your attitude toward yourself, your purpose, your topic, and your readers. As in speaking, tone in writing may be serious, playful, sarcastic, and so on. Generally, readers detect tone more by how you say something (that is, through your sentence structure and word choice) rather than by what you say.

Topic sentence is the term for the sentence(s) that convey the main idea of a paragraph. Such sentences are often, but not always, found at the start of a paragraph. They provide a statement of the subject to be discussed and an indication of the writer's attitude toward that subject. Writers usually concern themselves with topic sentences during the writing of the first draft, the fifth stage of the writing process.

Transitions—see *Connecting devices*.

Unified—see *Evidence*.

Works Cited—see *MLA documentation*.

Acknowledgements

Angelou, Maya, "Grandmother's Victory." From *I Know Why the Caged Bird Sings* by Maya Angelou. Copyright © 1969 by Maya Angelou. Reprinted by permission of Random House, Inc.

Baker, Russell, "In My Day." Reprinted from *Growing Up* by Russell Baker, © 1982. Used with permission of Congdon & Weed, Chicago.

Brady, Judy, "Why I Want a Wife." Reprinted by permission of the author.

Britt, Suzanne, "That Lean and Hungry Look." Reprinted by permission of the author.

Bruck, David, "The Death Penalty." Reprinted by permission of *The New Republic,* © 1985, The New Republic, Inc.

Carson, Rachel, "A Fable for Tomorrow." From *Silent Spring* by Rachel Carson. Copyright © 1962 by Rachel L. Carson, © renewed 1990 by Roger Christie. Reprinted by permission of Houghton Mifflin Company. All rights reserved.

Chinea-Varela, Migdia, "My Life as a 'Twofer.'" Reprinted by permission of the author.

Cole, Diane, "Don't Just Stand There." Copyright © 1989 by Diane Cole. Reprinted by permission of Riverside Literary Agency.

Cole, K. C., "Entropy." From *The New York Times,* March 18, 1982. Copyright © 1982 by The New York Times Company. Reprinted by permission.

Didion, Joan, "In Bed." From *The White Album* by Joan Didion. Copyright © 1979 by Joan Didion. Reprinted by permission of Farrar, Straus & Giroux, Inc. "On Self-Respect" from *Slouching Towards Bethlehem* by Joan Didion. Copyright © 1961, 1968 by Joan Didion. Reprinted by permission of Farrar, Straus & Giroux, Inc.

Dillard, Annie, "In the Jungle." From *Teaching a Stone to Talk* by Annie Dillard. Copyright © 1982 by Annie Dillard. Reprinted by permission of HarperCollins Publishers.

Ehrenreich, Barbara, "What I've Learned from Men." Reprinted by permission of the author.

Farb, Peter, "In Other Words." From *Word Play: What Happens When People Talk* by Peter Farb. Copyright © 1973 by Peter Farb. Reprinted by permission of Alfred A. Knopf, Inc.

Gallup, George Jr., "The Faltering Family." From *Forecast 2000* by George Gallup, Jr. with William Proctor. Copyright © 1984 by George Gallup, Jr. Reprinted by permission of William Morrow & Company, Inc.

Goldstein, Janet Mendell, "The Quick Fix Society." Reprinted by permission of the author.

Hentoff, Nat, "Free Speech on Campus." Reprinted by permission of the author.

Hilfiker, David, "Making Medical Mistakes." Copyright © 1984 by *Harper's Magazine*. All rights reserved. Reprinted from the May issue by special permission.

Houston, Jeanne Wakatsuki, and James D. Houston, "Manzanar." From *Farewell to Manzanar* by Jeanne Wakatsuki Houston and James D. Houston. Copyright © 1973 by James D. Houston. Reprinted by permission of Houghton Mifflin Company. All rights reserved.

Hubbell, Sue, "The Beekeeper." From the *New York Times,* August 2, 1984. Copyright © 1984 by The New York Times Company. Reprinted by permission.

Hughes, Langston, "Salvation." From *The Big Sea* by Langston Hughes. Copyright © 1940 by Langston Hughes. Renewal copyright © 1968 by Arna Bontemps and George Houston Bass. Reprinted by permission of Hill and Wang, a division of Farrar, Straus & Giroux, Inc.

Jacoby, Susan, "Common Decency." From the *New York Times*, May 19, 1991. Copyright © 1991 by The New York Times Company. Reprinted by permission.

King, Martin Luther Jr., "Where Do We Go From Here?" Pages 181–186 from *Where Do We Go from Here: Chaos or Community?* by Martin Luther King, Jr. Copyright © 1967 by Martin Luther King, Jr. Reprinted by permission of HarperCollins Publishers. Excerpt from "Three Types of Resistance to Oppression" from *Stride Toward Freedom* by Martin Luther King, Jr. Copyright © 1958 by Martin Luther King, Jr. Reprinted by permission of HarperCollins Publishers.

Koch, Edward, "Death and Justice." Reprinted by permission of *The New Republic,* © 1985, The New Republic, Inc.

Kozol, Jonathan, "Are the Homeless Crazy?" From *Rachel and Her Children: Homeless Families in America* by Jonathan Kozol. Copyright © 1988 by Jonathan Kozol. Reprinted by permission of Crown Publishers, Inc.

Lindbergh, Anne Morrow, "Channelled Whelk." From *Gift from the Sea* by Anne Morrow Lindbergh. Copyright © 1955 by Anne Morrow Lindbergh. Reprinted by permission of Pantheon Books, a division of Random House.

Lopez, Barry, "My Horse." Reprinted by permission of Sterling Lord Literistic, Inc. Copyright © 1975 by Barry Lopez.

Marzollo, Jean, "My Pistol-Packing Kids." From *Parents Magazine,* January 1983. Copyright © 1983 by Jean Marzollo. Reprinted by permission of Jean Marzollo.

McClintock, Ann, "Propaganda Techniques in Today's Advertising." Reprinted by permission of the author.

Mencken, H. L., "The Politician." From *A Mencken Chrestomathy* by H. L. Mencken. Copyright 1924 by Alfred A. Knopf, Inc. and renewed 1952 by H. L. Mencken. Reprinted by permission of Alfred A. Knopf, Inc.

Mitford, Jessica, "The American Way of Death." Reprinted by permission of Jessica Mitford. All rights reserved. Copyright © 1963, 1978 by Jessica Mitford.

Nilsen, Alleen Pace, "Sexism and Language." From "Sexism as Shown Through the English Vocabulary," from *Sexism and Language* by Alleen Pace Nilsen, Haig Bosmajian, H. Lee Gershuny, and Julia P. Stanley. Copyright 1977 by the National Council of Teachers of English. Reprinted with permission.

Nizer, Louis, "How About Low-Cost Drugs for Addicts?" From the *New York Times,* June 8, 1986. Copyright © 1986 by The New York Times Company. Reprinted by permission.

Orwell, George, "Shooting an Elephant." From *Shooting an Elephant and Other Essays* by George Orwell, copyright 1950 by Sonia Brownell Orwell and renewed 1978 by Sonia Pitt-Rivers, reprinted by permission of Harcourt Brace Jovanovich, Inc.

Paglia, Camille, "Rape: A Bigger Danger Than Feminists Know." Reprinted by permission of the author.

Parks, Gordon, "Flavio's Home." From *Voices in the Mirror* by Gordon Parks. Copyright © 1990 by Gordon Parks. Used by permission of Doubleday, a division of Bantam Doubleday Dell Publishing Group, Inc.

Postman, Neil, "Future Schlock." From *Conscientious Objections* by Neil Postman. Copyright © 1988 by Neil Postman. Used by permission of Alfred A. Knopf, Inc.

Raspberry, William, "The Handicap of Definition." © 1982, Washington Post Writers Group. Reprinted with permission.

Rau, Santhu Rama, "By Any Other Name." From *Gifts of Passage* by Santhu Rama Rau. Copyright 1951, 1952, 1954, © 1955, 1957, 1958, 1960, 1961 by Vasanthi Rama Rau Bowers. Reprinted by permission of HarperCollins Publishers.

Roberts, Paul, "How to Say Nothing in 500 Wrods." From *Understanding English* by Paul Roberts. Copyright © 1958 by Paul Roberts. Reprinted by permission of HarperCollins Publishers.

Rodriguez, Richard, "Workers." From *Hunger of Memory* by Richard Rodriguez. Copyright © 1982 by Richard Rodriguez. Reprinted by permission of David R. Godine, Publisher.

Ruth, Beth Johnson, "Our Drug Problem." Reprinted by permission of Trend Publications, 31 Price's Lane, Moylan, Pa 19065.

Tannen, Deborah, "Sex, Lies, and Conversation." From the *Washington Post*, June 24, 1990. Reprinted by permission of International Creative Management, Inc. Copyright © 1990 by Deborah Tannen.

Theroux, Phyllis, "The Worry Factor." Copyright © 1981 by Phyllis Theroux, from *Night Lights* by Phyllis Theroux. Used by permission of Viking Penguin, a division of Penguin Books USA Inc.

Thomas, Lewis, "The Lie Detector." Copyright © 1980 by Lewis Thomas, from *Late Night Thoughts on Listening to Mahler's Ninth* by Lewis Thomas. Used by permission of Viking Penguin, a division of Penguin Books USA Inc.

Thurber, James, "University Days." Copyright © 1933, 1961 James Thurber. From *My Life and Hard Times,* published by Harper & Row.

Twain, Mark, "The Damned Human Race." Page 223–229 from *Mark Twain: Letters from the Earth* edited by Bernard DeVoto. Copyright © 1962 by The Mark Twain Co. Reprinted by permission of HarperCollins Publishers.

Viorst, Judith, "Friends, Good Friends—And Such Good Friends." Copyright © 1977 by Judith Viorst. Originally appeared in *Redbook.*

Walker, Alice, "Beauty: When the Other Dancer Is the Self." From *In Search of Our Mothers' Gardens: Womanist Prose,* copyright © 1983 by Alice Walker, reprinted by permission of Harcourt Brace Jovanovich, Inc.

Watkins, T. H., "Little Deaths." Reprinted by permission of the author.

White, E. B., "Once More to the Lake." From *Essays of E. B. White* by E. B. White. Copyright 1941 by E. B. White. Reprinted by permission of HarperCollins Publishers.

Winn, Marie, "TV Addiction." From *The Plug-In Drug* by Marie Winn. Copyright © 1977, 1985 by Marie Winn Miller. Used by permission of Viking Penguin, a division of Penguin Books USA Inc.

Woolf, Virginia, "The Death of the Moth" and "Professions for Women." From *The Death of the Moth and Other Essays,* copyright 1942 by Harcourt Brace Jovanovich, Inc. and renewed 1970 by Marjorie T. Parsons, Executrix, reprinted by permission of the publisher.

Zinsser, William, "College Pressures." Copyright © 1979 by William K. Zinsser. Reprinted by permission of the author.

Index

(Continued)

To the Student
From the Authors

By now, you realize that almost all writing goes through a series of revisions. The same was true for this book. *The Macmillan Reader*, third edition has been reworked a number of times, with each revision taking into account student's and instructor's reactions to drafts of material.

Before we prepare the fourth edition of *The Macmillan Reader*, we'd like to know how you, the student, feel about the book. We hope you'll spend a few minutes completing this brief questionnaire. You can be sure that your responses will help shape subsequent editions. Please send your completed survey to the College English Editor, Macmillan Publishing Company, 866 Third Avenue, New York, NY 10022.

Thanks for your time.

College————————— City and state———————————

Course title————————— Instructor———————————

DESCRIPTION

	I really liked.	It was okay.	I didn't like.	I didn't read.
Parks, *Flavio's Home*	———	———	———	———
Baker, *In My Day*	———	———	———	———
Dillard, *In the Jungle*	———	———	———	———
White, *Once More to the Lake*	———	———	———	———
Houston and Houston, *Manzanar*	———	———	———	———

NARRATION	I really liked.	It was okay.	I didn't like.	I didn't read.
Angelou, *Grandmother's Victory*	——	——	——	——
Orwell, *Shooting an Elephant*	——	——	——	——
Watkins, *Little Deaths*	——	——	——	——
Hughes, *Salvation*	——	——	——	——
Rau, *By Any Other Name*	——	——	——	——

EXEMPLIFICATION

Lindbergh, *Channelled Whelk*	——	——	——	——
Nilsen, *Sexism and Language*	——	——	——	——
Thurber, *University Days*	——	——	——	——
Postman, *Future Shlock*	——	——	——	——
Ehrenreich, *What I've Learned From Men*	——	——	——	——

DIVISION-CLASSIFICATION

Viorst, *Friends, Good Friends — and Such Good Friends*	——	——	——	——
Zinsser, *College Pressures*	——	——	——	——
Hilfiker, *Making Medical Mistakes*	——	——	——	——
McClintock, *Propaganda Techniques in Today's Advertising*	——	——	——	——
Goldstein, *The Quick Fix Society*	——	——	——	——

PROCESS ANALYSIS

Leacock, *How to Live to Be 200*	——	——	——	——

	I really liked.	It was okay.	I didn't like.	I didn't read.
Hubbell, *The Beekeeper*	____	____	____	____
Mitford, *The American Way of Death*	____	____	____	____
Roberts, *How to Say Nothing in 500 Words*	____	____	____	____
Cole, *Don't Just Stand There*	____	____	____	____

COMPARISON-CONTRAST

Carson, *A Fable for Tomorrow*	____	____	____	____
Britt, *That Lean and Hungry Look*	____	____	____	____
Rodriquez, *Workers*	____	____	____	____
Tannen, *Sex, Lies, and Conversation*	____	____	____	____
Lopez, *My Horse*	____	____	____	____

CAUSE-EFFECT

Gallup, *The Faltering Family*	____	____	____	____
Farb, *In Other Words*	____	____	____	____
Walker, *Beauty: When the Other Dancer Is the Self*	____	____	____	____
Thomas, *The Lie Detector*	____	____	____	____
Kozol, *Are the Homeless Crazy?*	____	____	____	____

DEFINITION

Cole, *Entropy*	____	____	____	____
Brady, *Why I Want a Wife*	____	____	____	____
Mencken, *The Politician*	____	____	____	____

	I really liked.	It was okay.	I didn't like.	I didn't read.
Winn, *TV Addiction*	____	____	____	____
Raspberry, *The Handicap of Definition*	____	____	____	____

ARGUMENTATION-PERSUASION

Marzollo, *My Pistol-Packing Kids*	____	____	____	____
Chinea-Varela, *My Life as a "Twofer"*	____	____	____	____
Twain, *The Damned Human Race*	____	____	____	____
Swift, *A Modest Proposal*	____	____	____	____
Hentoff, *Free Speech on Campus*	____	____	____	____
Paglia, *Rape: A Bigger Danger Than Feminists Know*	____	____	____	____
Jacoby, *Common Decency*	____	____	____	____
Koch, *Death and Justice*	____	____	____	____
Bruck, *The Death Penalty*	____	____	____	____
Nizer, *Low-Cost Drugs for Addicts?*	____	____	____	____
Ruth, *Our Drug Problem*	____	____	____	____

FOR FURTHER READING

King, *Where Do We Go From Here: Community or Chaos?*	____	____	____	____
King, *Three Kinds of Resistance to Oppression*	____	____	____	____
Didion, *In Bed*	____	____	____	____
Didion, *On Self-Respect*	____	____	____	____

	I really liked.	It was okay.	I didn't like.	I didn't read.
Woolf, *The Death of the Moth*	——	——	——	——
Woolf, *Professions for Women*	——	——	——	——

Any general comments or suggestions?

Name _____ Date _____

Address _____

THANKS AGAIN!